CALENDAR OF
COUNCIL MINUTES
1668 - 1783

NEW YORK (COLONY)
COUNCIL

CALENDAR OF COUNCIL MINUTES 1668 - 1783

Compiled by
Berthold Fernow

Preface by
A.J.F. van Laer

Introduction by
Peter R. Christoph

HARBOR HILL BOOKS
Harrison, New York

1987

Library of Congress Cataloging-in-Publication Data

New York (State)   Council.
  Calendar of Council minutes, 1668-1783.

    At head of title: New York (Colony). Council
    "Reprinted from New York State Library Bulletin 58
  (History 6), Albany 1902"—T.p. verso.
    Includes index.
        1. New York (State)   Council—Archives—Catalogs.
  2. New York (State)—History—Colonial period, ca. 1600-1775—Sources—Bibliography—Catalogs.   3. New York (State)—History—Revolution, 1775-1783—
  Sources—Bibliography—Catalogs. 4. New York State Library—Catalogs. I. Fernow,
  Berthold, 1837-1908. II. Van Laer, Arnold J. F. (Arnold Johan Ferdinand), 1869-
  1955. III. Title.

  CD3406.5 1987   328.747'01   87-8463
  ISBN 0-916346-58-7

Reprinted from

New York State Library Bulletin 58
(History 6)

Albany 1902

Harbor Hill Books, P.O. Box 407, Harrison, N.Y., 10528

Introduction

Through much of its history, the Council of the Colony of New York was second only to the Governor in power and authority and in the personal prestige of its members. Sitting with the Governor, it served as the colony's highest appellate court. It was also the Governor's cabinet, and after 1691 it functioned additionally as a legislative body, concurrent with the General Assembly. In the absence of the Governor and Deputy Governor, the oldest member (in actual age, not years of service) became president of the Council and acting governor.

Members of the Council were commissioned by the Governor and served at his will, rather than for a fixed term. They were selected from the British and colonial gentry: military officers, career government officials, lawyers, and wealthy colonial merchants and landowners.

The Council minutes are a record of meetings of the Governor and Council. Matters under consideration had been presented in petitions, letters, reports of committees, and court files of cases on appeal which are in the administrative files, a separate record series. The result of Council discussions was the issuing of orders, warrants, letters, commissions, passes and licenses which were recorded in books of general entries.

Readers will note occasional gaps in the minutes, which do not necessarily indicate a suspension of meetings. Sometimes minutes were not taken, or at least not preserved. In large part the unrecorded meetings dealt with a single issue, usually with just the Governor, Secretary and perhaps one or two members of the Council present, the issue quickly resolved and an order given. In searching the administrative files and books of general entries, readers will therefore find orders issued on days for which there is no other record of a Council meeting, as well as stray notes and memoranda of meetings with Indians who dropped in on the Governor to exchange pleasantries.

Unfortunately, the Council minutes were among the records damaged in the State Capitol fire of March, 1911. Of twenty eight volumes the first fourteen (to 1772) survive in fair to good condition with some singed edges and partial loss of text, and the last fourteen (to 1776) range from good to poor. The administrative files after 1721 are similarly damaged and incomplete, while nothing remains of the general entries after 1688. Fortunately in the case of the Council minutes, copies were filed with the Board of Trade and its successors from 1686 to 1775 and may be found in the Public Record Office of Great Britain, among the Colonial Office Papers, Class 5.

Custody of the colony's records passed from the Secretary of the Colony of New York to the Secretary of the State of New York, and later to the New York State Library. Today the records reside in the State Archives: questions about the availability of particular documents should be directed to that office.

Abstracts of many of the colonial records and the complete text of some early volumes have been published. Of the Council minutes themselves, the only complete run of material ever printed appeared with supporting documents in the two volume *Minutes of the Executive Council of the Province of New York, Administration of Francis Lovelace, 1668-1673*, edited by Victor Hugo Paltsits (Albany, State of New York, 1910). The administrative files 1664-1778 are listed in the second volume of the *Calendar of Historical Manuscripts in the Office of the Secretary of State, Albany, N.Y.*, edited by E.B. O'Callaghan (Albany, Weed Parsons, 1866 [reprinted Ridgewood, N.J., Gregg Press, 1968]). One volume of the files has been published as *Administrative Papers of Governors Richard Nicolls and Francis Lovelace, 1664-1673*, edited by Peter R. Christoph (Baltimore, Genealogical Publishing Co., 1980). Six volumes of records for the administration of Sir Edmund Andros, 1674-1680, are in preparation by P.R. and Florence A. Christoph for publication by Heart of the Lakes, Interlaken, N.Y. Those general entries that survive were published in two volumes, the *Books of General Entries of the Colony of New York, 1664-1673*, and *Books of General Entries of the Colony of New York, 1674-1688*, edited by P.R. and F.A. Christoph (Baltimore, Genealogical Publishing Co., 1982).

The reissue of the *Calendar of Council Minutes* provides historians with a detailed and accurate record of New York colonial history from the vantage point of the highest level of government, and genealogists with information on thousands of persons. It is at once the most concise and most complete record in print of New York province, invaluable in view of the extensive damage to all the colonial manuscript record series.

May, 1987   Peter R. Christoph

Associate Librarian
Manuscripts and Special Collections
The New York State Library

University of the State of New York

New York State Library

MELVIL DEWEY Director

Bulletin 58   March 1902

HISTORY 6

CALENDAR OF COUNCIL MINUTES

1668–1783

ALBANY

UNIVERSITY OF THE STATE OF NEW YORK

1902

University of the State of New York

REGENTS

With years of election

1874 ANSON JUDD UPSON L.H.D. D.D. LL.D.

Chancellor, Glens Falls

1892 WILLIAM CROSWELL DOANE D.D. LL.D.

Vice-Chancellor, Albany

1873 MARTIN I. TOWNSEND M.A. LL.D.   –   –   – Troy

1877 CHAUNCEY M. DEPEW LL.D.   –   –   –   New York

1877 CHARLES E. FITCH LL.B. M.A. L.H.D.   –   – Rochester

1878 WHITELAW REID M.A. LL.D.   –   –   –   New York

1881 WILLIAM H. WATSON M.A. LL.D. M.D.   –   – Utica

1881 HENRY E. TURNER LL.D.   –   –   –   –   Lowville

1883 ST CLAIR McKELWAY M.A. L.H.D. LL.D. D.C.L. Brooklyn

1885 DANIEL BEACH Ph.D. LL.D.   –   –   –   Watkins

1888 CARROLL E. SMITH LL.D.   –   –   – Syracuse

1890 PLINY T. SEXTON LL.D.   –   –   –   Palmyra

1890 T. GUILFORD SMITH M.A. C.E. LL.D.   –   – Buffalo

1893 LEWIS A. STIMSON B.A. LL.D. M.D.   –   –   New York

1895 ALBERT VANDER VEER Ph.D. M.D.   –   –   – Albany

1895 CHARLES R. SKINNER M.A. LL.D.

Superintendent of Public Instruction, ex officio

1897 CHESTER S. LORD M.A. LL.D.   –   –   –   Brooklyn

1897 TIMOTHY L. WOODRUFF M.A. Lieutenant-Governor, ex officio

1899 JOHN T. McDONOUGH LL.B. LL.D. Secretary of State, ex officio

1900 THOMAS A. HENDRICK M.A. LL.D.   –   –   Rochester

1901 BENJAMIN B. ODELL JR LL.D. Governor, ex officio

1901 ROBERT C. PRUYN M.A. –   –   –   –   – Albany

1902 WILLIAM NOTTINGHAM M.A. Ph.D. –   –   – Syracuse

SECRETARY

Elected by Regents

1900 JAMES RUSSELL PARSONS JR M.A.

DIRECTORS OF DEPARTMENTS

1888 MELVIL DEWEY M.A. *State Library and Home Education*

1890 JAMES RUSSELL PARSONS JR M.A.

Administrative, College and High School Dep'ts

1890 FREDERICK J. H. MERRILL Ph.D. *State Museum*

New York State Library

Bulletin 58   April 1901

HISTORY 6

CALENDAR OF COUNCIL MINUTES 1668–1783

PREFACE

This calendar covering the executive minutes of the New York colonial council from 1668–1783, was prepared by Mr Berthold Fernow, keeper of historical records, shortly before his resignation Ap. 1, 1889, and was intended to form with other calendars an additional volume of the series of *Documents relative to the colonial history of the state of New York.*

Numbering of volumes. No minutes exist for the period directly following the surrender of New Netherland to the English, Aug. 29, 1664, the earliest being those of the council convened by Gov. Francis Lovelace, Sep. 2, 1668. Many of the executive acts of Gov. Richard Nicolls's administration are to be found in " General entries 1664–65 " and " Court of assize, 1665–72," which volumes were for that reason listed by John Van Ness Yates in his *Report of the secretary of state relative to the records, etc. in his office,* 1820, as 1 and 2 of a set of 33 volumes of colonial council minutes and general entries, while the first volume of regular council minutes 1668–78 was marked 3. This volume consists of two parts; the first ending July 11, 1673, and the second beginning Oct. 31, 1674. Minutes for the intervening period of Dutch control are found in " New York colonial mss ", 23: 1–270 and have been translated and printed as " Minutes of council of the administrations of commanders Evertsen and Benckes and of Anthony Colve, governor of New Netherland, 1673 and 1674 ", in *Documents relative to the colonial history of the state of New York*, 2: 569–730. Toward the end of the second part of the volume another interruption in the minutes occurs from Nov. 10, 1677–Aug. 17, 1678, including the period of Gov. Edmund Andros's visit to England and the temporary administration of Capt. Anthony Brockholls. Minutes for this period may be found in " New York colonial mss ", vol. 26–27.

A volume of " General entries 1671–74 " having been marked 4, the next volume of council minutes, covering the years 1683–88 is marked 5, leaving a gap from 1678 to 1683; part of the minutes for that period, up to November 1680, may be found in "New York colonial mss" vol. 29, while other executive acts are recorded in "General entries 1678–80," vol. 32, and "Entries 1682–83," vol. 33. A gap in the council minutes occurs again between vol. 5, breaking off with the last council under Gov. Thomas Dongan Aug. 2, 1688, and vol. 6 beginning with the first council under Gov. Henry Sloughter, Mar. 19, 1691. For the first year of this period, when New York was united with New England under Gov. Sir Edmund Andros, no regular proceedings are among the New York archives, but for the years 1689–91, covering the administration of Jacob Leisler, a full record of commissions, appointments, orders, accounts, etc. with numerous letters are found in vol. 36 of "New York colonial mss." After vol. 6 the minutes form one uninterrupted series till Mar. 11, 1776. A few pages of minutes of the councils of Gov. James Robertson and Lt.-gov. Andrew Elliott from Mar. 23, 1780–Nov. 19, 1783, held at New York city then in the hands of the British are also recorded.

Legislative minutes. Beginning with the first regular colonial legislature, convened in 1691 by Gov. Sloughter, the council became a legislative body, coordinate with the assembly. Its legislative minutes have been printed as the *Journal of the legislative council of the colony of New York begun the 9th day of Ap. 1691 and ended the 3d day of Ap. 1775,* 2 v. Alb. 1861, and for that reason are not entered in this calendar.

In vol. 6–8, executive and legislative minutes are kept separate, the latter at the end of each volume. Vol. 6 contains also the minutes of the council in its judicial capacity 1687–88, and vol. 7, proceedings of the court of oyer and terminer, 1679–85. In vol. 9–17, 1702–36, the two functions were mingled and the minutes printed as legislative have been marked by a pen or pencil line in the margin. Vol. 18, 20, 22, 24, 27, 28 and 30 contain only legislative minutes and were printed entire. as also some minutes of 1775–76, found in vol. 26.

Of the greater part of these minutes the state library has two and in some cases even three copies. The first and most complete set described above and used for the compilation of this calendar, consists of engrossed minutes except vol. 9–11, which are made up of blank books of rough copies. The second set, covering with some interruptions the years 1709–76, consists entirely of blank books from which a few minutes not found in the bound volumes of engrossed minutes have been inserted in the calendar. The third set containing the original drafts of the proceedings of 1754–75 are in the form of loose sheets.

A. J. F. van Laer

ARRANGEMENT AND ABBREVIATIONS

In left column dates are those of council sessions; names indicate other than regular place of meeting. In right column are given volume number of manuscript minutes and under it, opposite each entry, the exact page referred to. Page citations within entries, e. g. (p. 10), refer to other entries in this calendar for the same manuscript volume. Other citations are to documents bearing on the subject of the minute calendared.

In references volume and page numbers are separated by a colon, e. g. 22:99 means vol. 22, p. 99.

The abbreviations used are given below. Numbers following the full title are the location (or call) numbers in the state library.

Doc. rel. to col. hist. N. Y.

Documents relative to the colonial history of the state of New York. v. 12.   Alb. 1877.   974.7   qN421

Doc. hist. N. Y.

Documentary history of the state of New York. 4 v. O.   Alb. 1849–51.   974.7   N424
——— 4 v.   Q.   Alb. 1850–51.   974.7   qN423
The quarto edition is indicated by Q prefixed to the reference; Q 1:75.

Hough. *Pemaquid.*

Hough, F. B. Papers relating to Pemaquid and parts adjacent in the present state of Maine, known as Cornwall county when under the colony of New York. 136p.   Alb. 1856.   974.15   B772

Hough. *Nantucket.*

Hough, F. B. Papers relating to the island of Nantucket, Marthas Vineyard and other islands adjacent known as Dukes county while under the colony of New York. 162p.   Alb. 1856.   974.49   N151

Jour.

Journal of the legislative council of the colony of New York 1691–1775. 2 v.   Alb. 1861.   Mss room

Jour. assembly N. Y.

Journal of the votes and proceedings of the general assembly of the colony of New York, 1691–1765. 2 v.   N. Y. 1764–66.
                                                           V328.7471   fA

L. P.

Landpapers, 1642–1803. 63 v.

Original mss in the office of the secretary of state: for contents see *Calendar of N. Y. colonial manuscripts, indorsed land papers.* Alb. 1864.

N. Y. col. mss.

New York colonial mss. 103 v.   Mss room
Described in *N. Y. state library bulletin: history 3,* p.215–17.

COLONIAL GOVERNORS 1664-1783

In the following list of colonial governors dates represent, as nearly as could be ascertained from manuscript sources, the actual beginning of each administration, i. e. the first official act of a newly appointed governor. For a temporary administration the date of the governor's departure has been chosen in preference to that of the appointment or the oath of office in council of his lieutenant. Beginning with Sir Danvers Osborne, 10 Oct. 1753, all dates are given according to new style; for preceding dates, old style has been used in conformity with the records. Indiscriminate use of old style and new style dates in *Civil list of New York, New York legislative manual* and *Harper's book of facts* will account for most of the discrepancies.

The list of members of the council printed below, is taken from *Civil list of the colony and state of New York*, Alb. 1889, p. 363–64.

29 Aug. 1664	Richard Nicolls.	
23 May 1668[1]	Francis Lovelace.	
30 July 1673	Cornelis Evertse jr, and a council of war.	
9 Sep. 1673	Anthony Colve.	
31 Oct. 1674	Edmund Andros.	
16 Nov. 1677	Anthony Brockholls, commander-in-chief.	
8 Aug. 1678	Sir Edmund Andros, knt.	
7 Jan. 16⁹⁰⁄₈₁	Anthony Brockholls, commander-in-chief.	
27 Aug. 1683[2]	Thomas Dongan.	
11 Aug. 1688	Sir Edmund Andros.	
9 Oct. 1688	Francis Nicholson, lt.-gov.	

3 June 1689	Jacob Leisler.[3]	
19 Mar. 16⁹⁰⁄₉₁	Henry Sloughter.	
26 July 1691	Richard Ingoldesby,[4] commander-in-chief.	
30 Aug. 1692	Benjamin Fletcher.	
2 Ap. 1698	Richard Coote, earl of Bellomont.	
16 May 1699	John Nanfan, lt.-gov.	
24 July 1700	Richard Coote, earl of Bellomont.	
5 Mar. 17⁰⁰⁄₀₁ to 19 May 1701	{ Col. William Smith. Col. Abraham De Peyster. Col. Peter Schuyler.[5]	
19 May 1701	John Nanfan, lt.-gov.	
3 May 1702	Edward Hyde, viscount Cornbury.	

[1] Documents signed by Gov. Nicolls are found as late as 21 Aug. 1668, while a warrant on the treasurer, the earliest record signed by Lovelace as governor, is dated 23 May 1668. Instructions for Capⁿ John Backer for yᵉ well regulating of yᵉ Militia and other Affairs at Albany, "were given at Albany by both the Governors in August 1668", see "Orders, warrants, letters", 2:233.

[2] From 25 Oct. 1687–28 Mar. 1688, Gov. Dongan was absent at Albany and Major Brockholls in command at New York.

[3] Assumed the title of lt.-gov., Dec. 8, 1689, and was executed for high treason May 16, 1691.

[4] The council administered the government from July 23, when Gov. Sloughter died, to July 26.

[5] The earl of Bellomont died Mar. 5, 1701. During the absence of Lt.-Gov. Nanfan, and till May 19, 1701, the government was administered by the council, at which the oldest councilor presided during this period.

18 Dec.	1708	John Lord Lovelace.
6 May	1709	Peter Schuyler, pres.
9 May	1709	Richard Ingoldesby,[1] lt.-gov.
10 Ap.	1710	Gerardus Beekman, pres.
14 June	1710	Robert Hunter.
21 July	1719	Peter Schuyler, pres.
17 Sep.	1720	William Burnet.
15 Ap.	1728	John Montgomerie.
1 July	1731	Rip Van Dam, pres.
1 Aug.	1732	William Cosby.
10 Mar.	17 3⁄6	George Clarke, pres.
30 Oct.	1736	George Clarke, lt.-gov.
22 Sep.	1743	George Clinton.[2]
10 Oct.	1753	Sir Danvers Osborne,[3] bart.
12 Oct.	1753	James De Lancey, lt.-gov.
3 Sep.	1755	Sir Charles Hardy, knt.
3 June	1757	James De Lancey, lt.-gov.
4 Aug.	1760	Cadwallader Colden, pres.

8 Aug.	1761	Cadwallader Colden, lt.-gov.
26 Oct.	1761	Robert Monckton.
18 Nov.	1761	Cadwallader Colden, lt.-gov.
14 June	1762	Robert Monckton.
28 June	1763	Cadwallader Colden, lt.-gov.
13 Nov.	1765	Sir Henry Moore, bart.
12 Sep.	1769	Cadwallader Colden, lt.-gov.
19 Oct.	1770	John Murray, earl of Dunmore.
9 July	1771	William Tryon.
7 Ap.	1774	Cadwallader Colden, lt.-gov.
28 June	1775	William Tryon.
23 Mar.	1780	James Robertson.[4]
15 Ap.	1783	Andrew Elliott,[4] lt.-gov.
[13 June?]	1781	James Robertson.
15 Ap.	1783	Andrew Elliott, lt.-gov.

COUNCIL OF THE COLONY OF NEW YORK

Years	Councilors	Years	Councilors
1665	Thomas Topping	1675-88	Frederick Phillipse
1665-67	Robert Needham	1676-80	William Darvall
1665-72	Thomas Willett	1680-88	Stephen Van Cortlandt
1667-73	Thomas Delaval	1683	John Youngs
1667-80	Mathias Nicolls	1683-86	John Spragge
1668-69	Ralph Whitefield	1683-86	Lucas Santen
1669-73	Cornelius Van Ruyven	1683-88	Anthony Brockholls
1670-73	Cornelis Steenwyck	1684-85	Lewis Morris
1671-73	Thomas Lovelace	1684-85	John Palmer
1672-79	John Laurence	1685	Nicholas Bayard
1674-79	Anthony Brockholls	1685	James Graham
1674-81	William Dyre	1685-88	Jervas Baxter

[1] Commission revoked Sep. 17, 1709, communicated to the council Ap. 10, 1710.

[2] John West, 7th Lord De La Warr was appointed governor, June 1737, but resigned that commission in September following.

[3] Committed suicide, Oct. 12, 1753.

[4] Military governors during the revolutionary war, not recognized by the state of New York.

Years	Councilors	Years	Councilors
1686–88	John Youngs	1692–97	Caleb Heathcote
1687–88	Nicholas Bayard	1692–98	John Laurence
1687–88	James Graham	1692–98	Richard Townley[2]
1687–88	John Palmer	1692–98	John Youngs
1688	John Allen	1692–1720	Peter Schuyler
1688	Walter Clarke	1693–98	William Pinhorne
1688	Joseph Dudley	1698	Robert Livingston
1688	Robert Mason	1698–1702	Abraham de Peyster
1688	Walter Newberry	1698–1702	Samuel Staats
1688	Edward Randolph	1698–1702	Robert Walters
1688	Richard Smith	1699–1700	James Graham
1688	John Usher	1701	Robert Livingston
1688	John Walley	1701–2	Thomas Weaver
1688	John Winthrop	1701–2	William Atwood
1688	John Youngs	1702–3	John Bridges
1689	Richard Panton	1702–4	Sampson Shelton Brough-
1689	Theunis Roelofsen		ton
1689	Jan. Demarest	1702–6	William Laurence
1689	Daniel De Klercke	1702–8	Wolfgang William Ro-
1689	Johannis Vermillye		mer
1689	Samuel Edsall	1702–20	Caleb Heathcote
1689	Peter De La Noy	1702–23	Gerardus Beeckman
1690	Gerardus Beeckman	1702–35	Rip van Dam
1690	Peter De La Noy	1703–4	Matthew Ling
1690	Samuel Edsall	1703–9	Thomas Wenham
1690	Hendrick Jansen (van	1704–19	Kiliaen van Rensselaer
	Feurden)	1705–15	Roger Mompesson
1690	William Laurence	1705–21	Adolph Phillipse
1690	Jacob Milborne	1705–28	John Barbarie
1690	Samuel Staats	1708	Abraham De Peyster
1690	Johannis Vermillye	1708–9	William Peartree
1690	Thomas Williams	1708–11	David Provoost
1691	William Pinhorne[1]	1710–16	Samuel Staats
1691–92	Joseph Dudley	1710–22	Abraham De Peyster
1691–97	Thomas Willett	1710–31	Robert Walters
1691–98	Nicholas Bayard	1711–25	Thomas Byerly
1691–98	Chidley Brooke	1716–22	John Johnston
1691–98	Gabriel Monvielle	1716–36	George Clarke
1691–98	William Nicoll	1720–35	Francis Harison
1691–98	Frederick Phillipse	1721–29	Lewis Morris
1691–1700	Stephen van Cortlandt	1721–37	James Alexander
1691–1704	William Smith	1721–76	Cadwallader Colden
1692	Thomas Johnson		

[1] Suspended Sep. 1, 1692.
[2] Refused to sit, being a resident of East Jersey.

Years	Councilors	Years	Councilors
1723-32	William Provoost	1755-60	James De Lancey
1723-41	Abraham van Horne	1755-69	George Clarke jr
1725-50	Philip Livingston	1755-76	Daniel Horsemanden
1726-61	Archibald Kennedy	1758-68	William Walton
1729-53	James De Lancey	1758-76	John Watts
1730-48	Philip Courtland	1759-62	Josiah Martin
1733-44	Henry Lane	1760-76	Oliver De Lancey
1733-47	Daniel Horsemanden	1762-63	Benjamin Pratt
1738-54	George Clarke jr	1762-68	William Alexander
1744-58	Joseph Murray	1764-71	Joseph Reade
1745	Sir Peter Warren	1764-76	Charles Ward Apthorpe
1745-46	Jeremias van Rensselaer	1764-76	Roger Morris
1745-49	John Moore	1767-72	Henry Cruger
1745-58	John Rutherford	1767-76	William Smith jr
1746-47	Stephen Bayard	1769	James De Lancey
1748-56	Edward Holland	1769-76	Hugh Wallace
1750-56	James Alexander	1769-76	Henry White
1751-74	Sir William Johnson	1771-76	William Axtell
1752-63	John Chambers	1773-76	John Harris Cruger
1753-67	William Smith	1775-76	James Jauncey

CLERKS OF THE COUNCIL

1664-93	Secretary of the province	28 Sep. 1698	Barne Cosens
1693	David Jamison	24 Mar. 1706	Secretary of the province

COUNCIL MINUTES

1669   **v. 3**
Oct. 18   Orders concerning the insurrection in Delaware bay. The
          Long Fin sentenced to be whipped and branded in the face
          (see *Doc. rel. to col. hist. N. Y.* 12:469). Will the Indian
          sentenced to death for rape on a white woman.   13
p. m.   Order regulating customs duties on tobacco, sugar and other
          " grosse goods."   15
1670
Jan. 25   Order concerning the Long Fin. Wm. Douglas' case taken
          into consideration (see *Doc. rel. to col. hist. N. Y.* 12:472).   16
Ap. 1   Orders on petitions: of Abr'm Frost for a review of a judg-
          ment against him at the suits of Wm. Osborne and John
          Firman; in the case between Nicasius de Sille and his wife;
          of Nicholas Wright concerning his daughter and her hus-
          band Eleazer Leveridge. Staten Island business deferred.   17
     7   Hearing of Indians, who claim to be the lawful owners of
          Staten Island.   19
     9   Hearing continued.   22
    13   Hearing continued; the island to be surrendered " by Turfe
          & Twigg " to Thomas Lovelace and Mathias Nicolls, as
          the governor's deputies.   25
May 14   Deliberations on the relations between Martin's Vineyard
          and the province of New York, started by a letter from
          Mr Mayhew (see Hough. *Nantucket,* p. 20-21). Connecticut
          boundaries. Peace between the Maquaes and north Indians.
          Capt. John Baker dismissed the service (see *N. Y. col. mss,*
          22:78-91); Capt. Salisbury appointed in his place. Eleazer
          Leveridge granted a divorce from his reputed wife
          Rebeccah.   26
July 7   Order concerning the difference between John Archer of
          Fordham and the three farms, Betts, Tippett and Heddy
          (p. 10). Katharine Harrison, accused of witchcraft by
          Thos. Hunt sr and Edward Waters in behalf of the town
          of Westchester, appears with her attorney Capt. Ponton
          and admits that as a resident of Wethersfield she has been
          tried for witchcraft and found guilty by the jury at Hart-
          ford, but acquitted by the bench; order of the Hartford
          court concerning her, signed by John Allen, secretary.   28
Aug. 24   Case against Widow Katharine Harrison continued; con-
          stable Edward Waters and John Quimby for Westchester,
          Capt. Ponton, Thos. Hunt sr and jr, Roger Townsend
          and —— More for Widow Harrison; letters from Capt.
          Talcott and John Allen produced; Josiah Willard testifies;
          case referred to the court of assizes.   30
Oct. 22   The schout of Albany continued in his office. Former order
          concerning Maritien Damens and Jan Clute's exchange of
          land to stand. Order on a letter from Capt. Salisbury

1670   **v. 3**

about New England people trading at Albany. Father
Pierron to be watched. Town and fort at Albany. Peace
between the Maquaes and the Mahicanders. Bridge money.
Stealing of canoes. Enumeration of inhabitants of Albany
called for. Marriage of Eleazer Leveridge with Rebeccah
Wright declared null. Customs at the Whorekill abolished. **31**

Dec. 1   Order on a petition of Richard Smith about the boundaries
of Nesaquake lands in dispute with Huntington. Letter
about the peace between Maquaes and Machicanders to be
sent to Gov. Winthrop. Order on a petition of Johannes
de Decker concerning some negroes claimed by him and
salary due by the West India company. Philipp Pieters'
[Schuyler] title to land on Staten Island declared invalid,
Jacob Melyn, from whom he derives it, having sold it to
the West India company. Order about Domines Hook, in
dispute between Mr Sharpe, Mr van Brugh and Mr Bayard.
Inhabitants of Seatalcott (Brookhaven) allowed to purchase Indian lands within their patent. House in Pearl
street to be sold.   **34**

5   Case of the heirs of Anna Bogardus [Anneke Jans] against
Mr Sharpe about the sale of Domines Hook.   **37**

21   Hearing on the petition of Johannes de Decker. Mynheer
Stuyvesant and Resolved Waldron testifying.   **38**

29   Order concerning the claim of Johannes de Decker to land
on Staten Island. Indian deed of sale to people of Southampton and their election of a sachem to be confirmed and
constable's staves sent to them. No liquor to be sold to
the Indians at Southampton.   **40**

p. m.   Orders: on a petition of John Cooper about Indians assist-
ing as whalers and customs officers; on papers received
from the court of sessions for Flushing, Hemstead and
Jamaica.   **41**

1671

Jan. 11   Richard Smith of Huntington. Order on a petition of soldiers for land on Staten Island. Orders on Seatalcott business, Mr Lane appearing for the town; Mr Lane and Mr
Woodhull propose to purchase from the Indians and settle
two farms at the Wading Place.

Feb. 24   Wyckerscreek Indians are willing to sell their lands. Charles
Bridges and wife to be placed in possession of the estate
of John Cockram, mortgaged to them. Eleazer Leveridge
to satisfy his divorced wife, Rebeccah Wright, for her marriage portion. Capt. Seamans. Etienne Gaigneau.
Jacques Guyon. Orders on petitions: of Peter Stanten-
burgh, Jan Vigue et al. about land; of Jacobus and Cornelis Loper. Delaware business to be deferred until Capt.

1671   **v. 3**

Carr's arrival; a letter to be sent there by Peter Rambo.
Letters of administration upon the estate of Samuel Mayo
at Oysterbay granted to Anthony Wright. Gravesend to
have a confirmatory patent for land, formerly belonging
to Robert Pennoyer and given to the town. Mr Coe to
report on the business of Joseph Thurston. Order authorizing the haven master to make arrests on the river. Order on a petition of Capt. Wm. Lawrence for a patent
to land at Flushing (see *N. Y. col. mss*, 22:111).
Orders: concerning the estate of John Cockram, late of Newtown
alias Middleborough, vested in Charles Bridges and his
wife Sarah, subject to a payment to John Sharpe; for
payment to Capt. John Seamans for work done at Hempstead; on a petition of Capt. Silvester Salisbury about
a difference with Frederick Gysberts.   44

Mar. 8   Elias Doughty having bought the interest of Charles and
Sarah Bridges in the estate of John Cockram (p. 44), to
receive title for it. Order concerning the payment of
money borrowed for building the dominie's house at
Breuklyn, to Mr Heggeman, then schout. Title of Jan
Vigne and Peter Stoutenbergh to land near the Water Port
to remain good. Action on Huntington business deferred, also on West India company business. No wheat in
grain to be exported for a year. No strange sloops allowed to go to Albany. Consideration of the refusal of
Southampton and Southold to take out new patents post-
poned.   51

27   Reports of Jeremiah van Rensselaer and Capt. Phil. Pieters
Schuyler of Albany concerning fortifications, excise, ministers' and town officers' salaries considered and orders
thereon.   53

Ap. 15   Proceedings of the commissioners sent to the east end of
L. I. the mayor of New York, Mathias Nicoles and Isaac
Bedloo, approved and ordered to be recorded. Indian murders at Delaware; sale of liquor to Indians there; many
families desire to settle at Apoquining and Bombay Hook
among them Mr Jones, Mr Wharton and Mr Whale.   57

26   Answers to a petition of inhabitants of Staten Island presented by Thos. Carle and Nathan Whitmore. Gideon
Marlette called before the council. Election of commissaries at Kingston postponed. Capt. Chambers to be
justice of the peace for the three towns in Esopus. Courts
at Marbletown and Hurley.   58

27   Mr Stillwell and Nathaniel Brittaine to lay out lots upon the
hills on Staten Island; a highway toward the bridge and
the Greatkill to be made; new lots to be added to the
old town.   59

1671   v. 3

May 18   Esopus affairs: report of Mr Mayor and Capt. Lovelace on
them; the commissaries chosen by them confirmed. Delaware affairs: purchase of the Whorekill by the Dutch to
be recorded; loss of Jan de Capre's sloop. Albany affairs:
proceedings of Mr Mayor of New York and Capt. Lovelace about the excise confirmed. Mr Beeckman and Stoffel
Hoogelandt proposed to succeed Govert Loockermans as
a lieutenant at New York; Beeckman commissioned.
Proposition for raising a troop of horse in the city to be
considered. Officers for the troop of horse in the north
and west end of Long Island to be returned to the governor for nomination. Order on a petition concerning
the export of corn.   60

June 14   New Castle and Whorekill affairs: order concerning dis-
tilleries at New Castle; concerning settlements at the
Whorekill.   63

21   Patents issued by the officers in Delaware, confirmed. The
grant to Mr Mills to extend only to the north side of
Whorekill. Order on a report by Mr Payne and Mr Terry
concerning Matinicock Indians.   64

28   Nantuckett affairs; orders made about titles to land on the
island.   65

29   Tristram Coffin appointed chief magistrate at Nantuckett.   65

p. m.   Order on a petition of Willem Hendricks Baker and other
Lutherans of New York against their minister.   66

July 6   Order on a petition and proposals of Mr Mayhew concerning Martin's Vineyard (see Hough. *Nantucket*, p. 32).   67

7   Mr Mayhew with two assistants elected by the two towns
on Martin's Vineyard to hold court for cases up to £5; appeals to be made to their general court; Mayhew to be
governor over the Indians on the island (see Hough.
Nantucket, p. 33); allowed to make purchases of land from
the Indians for the duke of York (see *Book of Indian
purchases*).

8   Order on Mr Mayhew's and Mr Brenton's claims upon Elizabeth islands. Three assistants to be elected for a court
on Martin's Vineyard; Mr Mayhew as president to have
double vote. Mr Mayhew sr acknowledges he has sold
his claim upon Elizabeth islands, but his grandchild sus-
tains the claim as his father's right; Daniel Wilcocks claim
to be recorded; the whole adjudged to Mr Brenton.   69

12   Quit rent to be paid by Mr Mayhew fixed. The former order
against export of wheat continued. Order on petition
of Govert Loockerman's wife about Capt. Manning's purchase. Richard Smith vs Huntington.   70

1671   v. 3

13   Richard Gildersleeve and Capt. John Seamans appear on be-
      half of Hempstead, against a grant to Mr Terry and to
      claim Matinicock land.   71

Sep. 25   Gov. Phil. Carterett and Capt. James Carterett of New Jer-
          sey present. Mr Tom sends report by Peter Alricks of
          murders committed by Indians on Matinicock island in
          Delaware river. Meeting on the case adjourned to Eliza-
          bethtown.   71

Oct. 25   Order directing the mayor and aldermen to make an inves-
          tigation into the disturbances caused by George Spurre,
          Humphrey Davenport and others in seizing the ship Ex-
          pectation, Isaac Melyen, commander. Capt. Manning and
          Mr Dervall added to the bench.   74

30   Negotiations for the land claimed by the Wyckerscreek In-
      dians from Monussing to Harlem river and from John
      Richardson's cross to Wyckerscreek; price asked by the
      Indians.   75

Nov. 7   Governors Lovelace and Carterett, Messrs Steenwyck, Thos.
Elizabethtown Lovelace, Capt. Berry, Messrs de la Prairie, Pardon and
N. J.   Nicolls. The Indian murders on Matiniconck island and
          orders for preventing further mischief (see *Doc. rel. to col.
          hist. N. Y.* 12:484).   77

Dec. 5   Action on Capt. Salisbury's petition against Fred'k Gysbert
Fort James (p. 44) postponed. Orders on petitions: of Domine Sam-
          uel Drisius for his salary in arrears for two years; of Coen-
          raat ten Eyck and Boel Roeloffs about an orphan's estate
          for which they are trustees; of Francis de Bruyne against
          Gravesend; of inhabitants of Breuklyn for the lot formerly
          belonging to Charles Gabry and confiscated to the duke
          of York; of Newtown about their boundaries with Bos-
          wyck. Agreement made between Fred'k Lubberts and
          Michael Heynelle confirmed. Staten Island settlements.
          Proposals of the French minister to bring protestant fam-
          ilies from Europe approved. Order about fencing in town
          lots. A third militia company to be formed in New York
          city. One half of Capt. Wilkins' fine remitted. Report of
          Mr de la Vale concerning the peace made at Albany be-
          tween Maquaes and Mahicanders approved. Younker
          Vosch's estate to be secured.   87

1672

Jan. 11   Case of Messrs Badgard, Ripley and Darvall against a bond
          of Mr Walker given at Jamaica, W. I. for a junk sailing
          to Campeachy bay.   88

18   Order upon a report of Capt. Dudley Lovelace and Capt. Jac-
      ques Cortelyou on the differences between Mr Pell and Mr

1672   **v. 3**

Richbell concerning land on Stony or Gravelly or Chap-
men's brook; Elias Doughty, Mr Ponton and Francis
Yeates testify about it.   89

May 17   Order on a petition of Capt. Salisbury about rent due from
Fred'k Gysberts for a house in Stone street. Proposals
of Mr Paine (Penne) to be considered later. Title of Hendrick Jansen to land on Maspethkills, L. I. confirmed.
Boundaries between Newtown and Boswyck to be resurveyed. Schenectady tappers to continue their business until further orders. New Castle, Del. to be an incorporated
bailywick; English laws introduced there, etc. (see *Doc. rel.
to col. hist. N. Y.* 12:496). Whalefishing at Oysterbay.
Capt. Manning's petition about Capt. Blagg to be considered later. Action of the officers in Delaware in resisting the claims of Maryland on the Whorekill approved.   91

20   Complaint of Capt. Manning against Capt. Blagg for carrying off a soldier (Barth Salter) and for not showing respect to the duke's flag examined; Capt. Blagg not held;
Philipp Jones, Mr Wasslyn, Mr Dyor, John Harris, James
Westmore and others witnesses.   96

24   Orders made on receipt of a letter from Lord Arlington
brought from Boston by Mr Sharpe: care to be taken of
the shipping, a war in Europe being imminent; battery for
the protection of ships in the harbor to be erected. Capt.
Haselwood to take letters to England. Correspondence
with Major general Leverett to be recorded.   99

June 10   Trouble in New Jersey between Gov. Carterett and Capt.
James Carterett. Delaware affairs. Cornelys Wyncoop
and Joost Adriaensen to be new commissaries at Kingston. Hempstead to be allowed to call a minister. Orders
on petitions: from Mad Man's Neck; from Matinicock
about commonage; of Widow Nevius about a ferry; of
Daniel Denton concerning a difference with Daniel Whitehead; of Hendrick Rooseboom sexton at Albany praying
to be allowed to bury Lutherans.   101

24   Contested election for constable and overseers in Hempstead; Robert Jackson, Simon Seryon, I. Smith, Thos.
Hicks, James Pine contestants. Returns of voluntary
contributions for repairs to the fort from Hempstead and
Flushing. Thos. Hunt jr to be released under bond.
Gerrit Trevis, the tinker, likewise. Whalefishing. Indian
affairs. Thos. Lovelace, High sheriff John Manning, Allard Anthony, Capt. Rich'd Morris, Mr Gibbs and Thos.
Rombout to be comm'rs for receiving contributions for the
fort. New order against the exportation of corn to be

1672   v. 3

issued. Commissioners to view the boundaries between Gravesend and New Utrecht. Correspondence with Capt. Carterett to be recorded. Order in the Hempstead election case, Robert Jackson confirmed as constable, John Smith Rocksen and John Carrman as overseers.   104

July 1   Contributions for repairing New York fortifications. Order for the release of Daniel Browne a planter at the Whorekill imprisoned for abusive language against the duke under bonds. Taxes on liquor to be imposed at the Whorekill for the repair of damages done by pirates. The bakers allowed to ship grain to Milford for grinding. Order concerning Mr Paine's proposals. Ariantie Bleeke widow of Joannes Nevius, allowed to continue the ferry kept by her husband. Agreement between Newtown and Boswyck confirmed. Capt. Carterett reports Indian plots against the English.   108

6   Declaration of war against the states general to be published at the gate of the fort and at the state house. Council to be enlarged.   114

Sep. 6   Inquiry to be made in Rhode Island about the imprisonment of Mr Paine there. Orders: concerning Schenectady town court; Indian trading house; huts on the hill at Albany; on a petition of Richard Smith of Nesaquake for a rehearing of the case between him and Huntington. Reports of Mr Lovelace and Capt. Manning about Mr Richbell's differences with his neighbors. Report of Mr Gibbs and Mr Rider of proceedings at Fordham; approved. Action on Thos. Pettit's "business about a divorce" postponed. Country rates to continue as before. House in the fort at Albany to be repaired.   115

Nov. 19   John Jennings and Wm. Jane of Southampton against John Cooper for evil words against the government; Thos. Travally's deposition read and the case referred to the next court of sessions; Wm. Brawley of Southampton comes as witness. John Jennings to be customer at Southampton vice John Laughton; Edward Petty at Southold; Wm. Perkins at Easthampton. Capt. Howell's commission renewed for one year. Mr Jenning's business about his bargain referred to the sessions. Order on a petition of Isaac Melyn for leave to unload his ship Expectation for repairs; Mayor John Lawrence of New York, Capt. Isaac Bedloo, Alderman Johannes van Burgh and Jacob Leysler to be arbitrators.   119

22   Richard Smith vs Huntington; Thos. Benedict and Henry Whitney witnesses. New order on petition of Isaac Melyn (p. 119).   122

1673   **v. 3**

Jan. 27   Order on a report from Albany that John Steward a soldier there, has been murdered by two north Indians of Naractak castle; Capt. Silvester Salisbury, Capt. Jeremias van Rensselaer, the commissaries and the officers of the militia to sit as a court of oyer and terminer for the trial of the Indians. Order on a petition of Antonia van Curler, widow of Arent van Curler for leave to trade with the Indians at Schenectady. Order on a letter from Isaac Graveraat schout at Esopus about contributions for fort repairs and taxes. Capt. Chambers to be exempt from taxes. Capt. Pawling to be thanked for his vigilance concerning the Esopus Indians. Vessels coming from New York with the governor's license to be allowed free passage up Delaware river. Action on letters from Mr Wharton and Capt. Cantwell about Whorekill matters deferred until the return of Henryck the Loper. Wm. Douglas of Delaware to be sent by Wm. Shackerley to the Barbadoes to be sold. Orders on the petitions of Benj. Johnson and Thos. Faulx for discharge from prison. Consideration of the Quakers' paper suspended. Orders: on a petition of inhabitants of Manhattan island against Capt. Manning's patent for land by the Frenchman's; about hogs running in the city; on a petition of Sarah widow of Nicholas Davis for protection against her late husband's creditors.   125

     28   A packet from Whitehall received by the hands of George Moore arrived from England via Boston.   135

Ap. 14   Business of Peter Groenendyke and Mr Gardner of Nantuckett deferred. Order for the reducing of Whorekill. Quakers' paper about the fortifications considered. Military laws to be attended. Order on a petition of the bakers about the cure-masters. Kingdom's and Tys Barent's affairs referred back to the justices who tried them before. Order on Jan Jansen's petition deferred. Mr Nicholls' charges in Delaware to be paid. Surveys from Mr Wharton to be patented.   136

     18   Trial of Peter Smith alias Groenendyke for seducing two girls, Annetie daughter of Juriam Blanck sr and Maria de la Noy, under promise of marriage; Jurian Blanck sr and jr, daughter Catherine, Albert Bosch his son-in-law, and Peter de la Noy brother of Maria prosecuting.   139

     22   Trial of Peter Groenendyke continued; Annetie Romers, Reyneer Willems baker, Cornelissen the fisher, testify; Groenendyke to pay damages and a fine.   141

     29   Order prohibiting the exportation of wheat.   145

1673   **v. 3**

May 15   Letters received from the duke of York, Lord Berkeley and
Sir George Carterett about New Jersey. Col. Nicolls'
patent to Elizabethtown made void by the duke. Post
rider to Milford to continue until further orders. Beacons to be erected. Former orders about the reduction
of Whorekill to be carried out. Court of sessions adjourned. Justices of the east riding to nominate three
persons for the governor to make a selection for high
sheriff of Long Island. Case of Daniel Lane postponed
until the arrival of his wife. Order on a petition of Mary
Dobson about a payment to Mr Gabry. Order concerning a transaction in wheat between Asser Levy, Nicholas
de Meyer, van der Cooley and Capt. Chambers.   147

22   Orders: about a quarrel between Capt. Pawling and Mr
Graveraat; on a complaint of Capt. Chambers against Edward Whittaker and his wife about a reputed witch.   150

June 12   Proclamation to issue for the re-arrest of Daniel Lane; his
wife and daughter are released under bonds; Harry Newton the jailer to be examined. Order appointing a general day of fasting and prayer. Prohibition to export
wheat suspended. Order upon a complaint of the cus-
tomers and customhouse regulations. English laws introduced at the Esopus. A new alderman to be nominated
in place of Mr Darvale, and a new militia captain in place
of Isaac Bedloo.   151

24   Order fixing the value of wampum. Order on a petition of
the bakers about the surveyor or cure-master of bread and
flour (p. 136). Prohibition to export wheat to be enforced.   155

July 4   Order taking off the excise from small beer and fresh meats
and advancing the rate on liquor, wine and beer.   158

Volume 3   Part 2   1674-78

1674

Oct. 31   The fort surrendered to the governor. Mathias Nicolls
sworn of the council at the city hall and three constables
sworn in for the city.   1

Nov. 2   Order continuing in office all magistrates and other officials
at Albany, Esopus, the Delaware, etc. who held office before the coming of the Dutch in July 1673, excepting Peter
Alricks who had offered his services to the Dutch on the
Delaware.   1

4   Michael Siston appointed schout, Wm. Parker marshall and
Sergt. Thos. Sharpe clerk of the entries, at Albany; Richard Pretty to take an account of the great excise there.

1674   v. 8

Capt. Thos. Chambers to be as formerly justice of the
peace. George Hall to be schout at Esopus. Capt.
Edmund Cantwell reappointed schout or sherrif, Wm.
Tom secretary, on the Delaware river, both to take possession of the fort etc. at Newcastle and be receivers of
quit rents and other duties. Tristram Coffin sr, Matthew
Mayhew and Thos. Dogget before the council on behalf
of Martin's Vineyard and Nantuckett.   2

7   Answer given to Tristram Coffin etc. recorded elsewhere.   3

10   Mayor, aldermen and sheriff of New York appointed and
sworn.   3

16   Mayor and aldermen meet before the governor in the fort.
Flour to be examined before shipping and marked with
the town brand, meats likewise. Orders concerning
weights and measures, bakers' bread, fortifications, gate
at the Smith's valley.   3

21   The same, Capt. Anthony Brockholes and Wm. Dyre present. Order for the recovery of the provincial records in
the hands of Nicholas Bayard secretary under Gov. Colve.
Confiscations made by the Dutch to be void.   5

27   Justices for the west riding of Long Island commissioned
and sworn in.   6

Nov. 30   Justices for the north riding commissioned and sworn in.   6

Dec. 4   Consultation in the fort, the governor, Capt. Richard Griffith, Capt. Cassibelam Burton, Capt. Anthony Brockholes, Wm. Dyre, the mayor and aldermen present. Letter from the three eastern towns of Long Island signed
by John Mulford, John Howell and John Youngs declining
to acknowledge the authority of New York; and order
thereon.   6

1675

Jan. 8   Fishing company to be established with £10 shares. Market
day fixed for the city (see *N. Y. col. mss*, 24:67). John
Burroughs of Newtown summoned with the constable for
two letters reflecting on the government. Constable of
Huntington sent for to answer for not obeying orders.
Council to meet every Friday.   10

Jan. 15   John Jackson constable of Hempstead brings John Jennings before council according to warrant; Jennings is
charged by —— Scudder of Maspethkills with taking
away his brother's indentures as apprentice to Scudder;
sentenced to prison. Petition of Nath. Brittaine against
John Sharpe about a servant referred to the court of
sessions. The constable of Newtown (p. 10) discharged
upon recommendation of Richard Betts member of the

1675   **v. 3**

Gravesend sessions; John Burroughs to be whipped and
imprisoned; warrant to the sheriff for carrying out the sentence. Capt. Manning to be tried for surrendering Fort
James to the Dutch.   11

19 Trial of Isaac Platt constable of Huntington (p. 10); fined
20s. for the poor.   16

22 Order concerning vacant lots in the city (see *N. Y. col.
mss*, 24:56). Order on the petition of Nicholas Bayard
about Gov. Colve's power of attorney (see *N. Y. col. mss*,
24:34). Preparations for the trial of Capt. Manning (see
N. Y. col. mss, 24:36-53). Supervisor of drift whales on
Long Island to be appointed. Long Island sachems called
before the council. Order of the court of sessions about
the differences and separation of Wm. Hallet and his wife
Susannah confirmed.   17

29 Trial of Capt. Manning (p. 11, 17) commenced; he is committed to the sherrif. Appeal of Nicholas de Meyer from
a judgment of the mayor's court referred back to the
court.   20

Feb. 2 Articles against Capt. John Manning (p. 20); trial continued.   21

5 Trial continued; Capt. Manning sentenced to be dismissed
the service.   23

19 Prohibition to export corn continued. Trial of the case of
Daniel, Mattys and Jacobus de Haart, Cooke and West
attorneys, against Jacob Tennisse Key, Jan Hendricks
van Bommel and Jacques Cousseau, Allard Anthony and
Mr Sharpe attorneys, about the estate of their brother
Balthazar de Haart (see *N. Y. col. mss*, 24:58). Order on
a petition of Jan Jansen Verryn. On an appeal of Wm.
Dyre in re de Meyer (p. 20). In re Richard Smith vs
Huntington.   24

Mar. 5 The governor and council and the mayor with the aldermen. Order concerning the militia. No ballast to be
thrown into the harbor. Prohibition to export corn continued. Customs regulations; New York, Southampton
and Southold to be ports of entry.   26

18 Gov. Phil. Carterett of New Jersey present. Cornelius
Steenwyck, Johannes van Brugh, Johannes de Peyster,
Nicholas Bayard, Eguidius Luyck, Wm. Beekman, Jacob
Kip and Antonio de Mill to be committed and examined
on the charge of disturbing the government (see *N. Y. col.
mss*, 24:73). Magistrates to keep the fortifications in repair. Order about hogs running in the streets to be enforced.   27

1675   **v. 3**

24   Gov. Andros reports on his journey to Connecticut. Orders
concerning constables' watches and Indians on Long
Island. Magister Jacobus Fabricius and John Ogle to
be sent from Delaware to New York as prisoners for disturbing the peace. Delaware land matters. Court of admiralty to sit in the case of the ketch Susannah.   **44**

Aug. 5   Encouragement to immigrants from Europe. Staten Island
land matters. Tackpousha sachem of Mashpeage
against Hempstead represented by Rich'd Gildersleeve sr
and George Hewlett. Condemned ketch Susannah to be
sold at auction. Order on a petition of widow Elizabeth
Bedloo for letters of administration on her late husband's
estate. Letters of administration on Balth. de Haart's
estate granted to his brothers, Daniel, Matthias and
Jacobus (p. 24). Order in re widows Betts and Tippett vs
John Archer about land. New rate of assessment to be
made. Report on the accounts of widow Anna Elizabeth
Wessells and Peter Nys for the tappers' excise approved.   **45**

Sep. 10   Fred'k Philipps sworn of the council. Indian affairs.   **50**

14   Indian affairs. Wm. Laurence to be justice of the peace for
the north riding. Order on a complaint of Capt. Thos.
Townsend of Oysterbay that, as the quakers refuse to bear
arms, it is impossible to keep a strict watch as ordered.   **51**

15   Order to restore to the Indians of Long Island their arms,
except to those of Easthampton and Shelter island, who
have paid contributions to the Narragansetts. Proclamation to issue quieting the people's minds. Order for the
safety of Long Island towns. Magister Fabricius suspended from ministerial duties. Delaware land matters;
dikes, Capt. Carr's meadow. Blockhouse at Newcastle
to be removed and built on the backside of the town.   **52**

25   Complaint of Do. Nicholas van Rensselaer against Do. van
Nieuwenhuysen examined (see *Doc. hist. N. Y.* 3:872-74;
Q 3:526-27).   **54**

28   Cannons to be sent to Nantuckett and Martin's Vineyard for
protection against the Indians (see Hough. *Nantucket*
p. 88).   **57**

30   Do. van Nieuwenhuysen, Elders Jeronimus Ebbing, and Peter
Stoutenberg, Deacons Jacob Teunissen Kay, Reyneer
Willemsen, Gerrit van Tright and Isaac van Vleck before
the council in re van Rensselaer (p. 54) (see *Doc. hist. N. Y.*
3:875; Q 3:527).   **58**

Oct. 15   Order on a request and proposals from Schenectady presented by Sander Leenderts Glen and Ludovicus Cobey
about land purchased from the Indians, Indian trade,

1676   **v. 3**

24   The above are released under bonds. Order on a report of
      Mathias Nicolls and Samuel Leete who had been to Boston
      with an application to the governor.   84

26   Resolutions and orders on a letter from Gov. Coddington of
      Rhode Island, concerning the late Indian war and Indian
      affairs. Gov. Andros to go to Albany. Wickerscreek
      Indians allowed to plant near Spiting Devill on Manhattan
      island. Letter to be written to the governor of Rhode
      Island.   85

Ap. 4   Gov. Andros returned from Albany reports on his confer-
      ences with the Maquaes. Wickerscreek and Long Island
      Indians sent for to meet the governor. Letters received
      from Sir Wm. Berkeley, governor of Virginia, and from
      the council of Connecticut.   87

8   Regulations for the cutting of timber, and for the Albany
      excise. Prohibition to export grain continued; Thos.
      Thatcher to have liberty to export a small quantity of meal.
      Boats passing through Hell Gate to take out custom
      house permits. Order relating to the case of Mrs Cath-
      erine Lane (p. 63).   87

10   Samuel Willis and Wm. Pitkin with a letter from the council
      of Connecticut present. The letter and answer to it.   90

23   Verbal answers to letters from the council of Boston and from
      the council of Connecticut to be sent by Daniel Burre to
      the latter, and by Richard Patteshall to the former.   93

May 3   Gov. Carterett and Maior John Fenwick present. Considera-
      tion of Fenwyck's business suspended. John Palmer's
      proposition to take the mill on Staten Island agreed to.   94

5   Orders upon the report of Joseph Carpenter that many people
      in Rhode Island are homeless. Long Island towns to
      assist the sufferers.   94

17   Constable Symon Seryon, Overseers Robert Jackson, John
      Ellison and Rich'd Vallentine of Hempstead before the
      council on a charge of neglect of duty; discharged. Order
      concerning Hempstead lands. Mr Paterson's case.   95

23   Correspondence with the governor and council of Boston to
      be sent by the mayor of New York.   97

26   Orders concerning unfenced lots, decayed houses etc. in New
      York city.   98

28   Order upon news received from Rhode Island, Nantuckett
      and Martin's Vineyard. Long Island Indians to have their
      arms restored to them.   99

29   Order for restoring the arms to the Indians. Order relating
      to the Indians at Anne Hook's Neck. North Indians who
      submit to be protected against the Maquaes.   99

1676

30   Gov. Andros to go to Albany; the Maquaes and Sinnekes to be called to meet him. The French receive north Indians under their protection. Connecticut will protect Indians coming in.   101

June 7   Order on a complaint of Lewis du Bois as lieutenant of the watch at Hurley against Adrian Albertsen, Rowland Swartwood and Pauls Paulsen for creating a disturbance.   102

10   Orders: on a report of Mr Pell concerning the travelling across and on the Long Island sound by Wyckerscreek Indians; on a petition of Nicholas Blake concerning a difference between him and Francis Richardson master of a great flyboat brought in by stress of weather.   103

July 26   Governor and council of Connecticut write that north Indians are " tending towards Hudson's river." Orders on petitions: of Domine Laurentius Caroli of Delaware about cases in the court of Newcastle; of Peter Groenendike of the Whorekill concerning his suit with Henry Smith for tobacco; John Avery the president of the Whorekill court, and the jurymen Helme Wiltbank, Abram Clement Petite, Jeoffrey Summersford, Simon Paling, John Oakey and George Young to appear before the council. Regulations concerning butchers, shoemakers and tanners, and distilling and selling liquor to Indians (see *N. Y. col. mss,* 25:155).   104

28   Sweer Teunissen vs John Gerrittsen van Marken (see *N. Y. col. mss,* 25:149-53, 160).   107

Aug. 4   Above case continued. Order concerning taxes in Albany. Old commissaries of Rensselaerswyck to continue in office; changes to be made in Albany (see *N. Y. col. mss,* 25:144-45). Thos. Chambers, George Hall and the magistrates at Esopus to sit as a court of oyer and terminer for the trial of a negro, Balthas, belonging to George Hall accused of murder. Order concerning the duties of the sheriffs of Long Island and Delaware; Thos. Willett to be high sheriff of Long Island. Orders: on a letter of Capt. Edmund Cantwell at the Delaware about the Susquehannah Indians coming in; on a petition of the Widow Hans Block of Newcastle concerning an outdrift for cattle.   108

8   Letters received from the governor of Canada, and the commander at Albany. Caniacka a Maquae sachem reports on French movements.   113

10   Conference with Caniacka sachem of the first castle, Dekassiedagareere sachem and Tayadorus, Mohawks, Cornelis Arnout, interpreter (see *N. Y. col. mss,* 25:162).   113

11   Order rebuking Capt. Cantwell in Delaware for an unnecessary alarm because Susquehannah Indians are coming in.   115

1676   **v. 3**

Sep. 2 Permission granted to a Dutch vessel of Commander Jacob
Benckes' squadron to victual at New York.   115

3 Taxes to be laid at Esopus and Albany for expenses during
the Indian war in the East.   116

8 Application made by Massachusetts for the surrender of
north Indians denied. Order upon a letter from Abr'm
Corbett concerning sufferers from the Indian war at
Pemaquid (see Hough. *Pemaquid.* p. 8-9). Domine van
Rensselaer imprisoned at Albany for " dubious words," to
be released (see *Doc. hist. N. Y.* 3:875; Q 3:527).   117

15 Order upon complaint of Hans Juriaensen against Edmond
Cantwell; the latter to pay a fine.   118
Meeting of Gov. Andros and council with the ministers of
New York on the case between Jacob Leisler, Jacob Mil-
burne and Domine van Rensselaer (see *Doc. hist. N. Y.*
3:875-76; Q 3:527-28).   119

16 Warrant sent to the commander and magistrates at Albany
to place Jacob Milburne under bonds for his appearance
in re Domine van Rensselaer (see *N. Y. col. mss,* 25:166,
and *Doc. hist. N. Y.* 3:876; Q 3:528).   119

18 Warrant for the arrest of Jacob Leisler in re Domine van
Rensselaer (see *Doc. hist. N. Y.* 3:876-77; Q 3:528).   120

20 Order on complaint of George Hewlett constable of Hempstead for having been arrested at New York by order of
Mayor Wm. Darvall and Deputy-mayor Nich's de Meyer.   122

23 Trial of the case between Jacob Leysler and Domine van
Rensselaer (see *Doc. hist. N. Y.* 3:877; Q 3:528-29).   124

Oct. 2 Order concerning a dispute between Capt. Thos. Chambers
justice of the peace and Lieut. George Hall sheriff at
Esopus, about the powers of the sheriff.   125

3 Land on Cowneck within Hempstead limits granted to John
Cornill driven out from the East by the Indians (see *N. Y.
col. mss,* 25:204). New order about the difference between
Thos. Chambers and George Hall (p. 125). Petition of
Abr'm Corbett (see *N. Y. col. mss,* 25:163) granted.   126

11 Dep.-Gov. Treat of Connecticut present. Conference on
Indian affairs.   128

14 Wm. Darvall sworn of the council.   129

18 Order on a complaint of Justices Richard Cornell and Thos.
Hicks that Thos. Rushmore, Nath'l Piersall, Abr'm Smith,
Joseph Langden, Adam Mottsen, Blue John Smith, Joseph
Williams, Jonas Wood, Robert and John sons of Robert
Beagles, John Mervin, Tim Halsteed, Sam. Denton etc.
have destroyed the newly begun settlement of John Cornell
at Cowneck (see *N. Y. col. mss,* 25:225-34).   129

1677   **v. 3**

to be called to meet the governor at Albany in August.
Letter to be sent to Mon. la Salle at Cataresky. Frenchmen to be escorted as prisoners to Father Bruyas.   146

19   Order concerning lawyers. Fees for cording wood. **Letter**
to Mon. la Salle read.   148

28   Rensselaerswyck affairs. Land matters on Staten Island in
dispute between Mr Thatcher, his sister widow of Nath'l
Davenport and others (see *L. P.* 1:118).   148

June 6   Henry Courcy of Maryland, Martin Gerritsen of Albany, and
Stephanus van Cortlandt present. Indian affairs.   151

9   Pemaquid to be again taken possession of for the duke and
peace to be made with the Indians there (see Hough.
Pemaquid. p. 14-15).   153

11   The drums to beat for raising soldiers to go to the eastward. 154

p. m.   News received from Albany that Maquaes have robbed and
captured Mahicanders and north Indians at Philipp Pieter's
[Schuyler] bowery and at the Half Moon; also that they
have killed some of Uncas men.   154

1676

Nov. 15   Examination of Joseph Knott a prisoner under charge of
having shipped unculled staves (see *N. Y. col. mss*, 25:249-
52).   155

16   Examination of Knott continued and sentence of the mayor's
court affirmed.   156

1677

July 2   Order concerning a dispute about land between Hempstead
and the Indians.   158

16   Punch Jansen committed to prison for saying that John
Harding and all others sent east had been killed by the
Indians. The sloop Hope alias Blue Cock of New York,
Simon Barnsen master, John Shackerly part owner, con-
demned for infringement of custom-house rules. Advice of
council on letters received from Capt. Salisbury and Col.
Henry Courcy at Albany with Indian news.   158

27   Case between Mrs Block and Johannes de Haes about an
outdrift (p. 144) referred to the court at Newcastle. Order
in re Walter Wharton vs Edmund Cantwell.   162

Aug. 2   Orders upon receipt of a letter from Capt. Anthony Brockholes at Pemaquid; he or Ensign Knapton to remain there
as commander; Mr Joseline or other justice of the peace
to settle differences between inhabitants and fishermen
(see Hough. *Pemaquid.* p. 16-18). Capt. Salisbury's letter
and the answer of the Onondagas and Oneidas to Col.
Courcy (see *N. Y. col. mss*, 26:69) not to be answered as the
Governor will soon go to Albany.   163

1677	**v. 3**

3	Orders: upon several letters from Nantuckett; Thos. Macy to continue as chief magistrate etc. (see *N. Y. col. mss,* 26:77); on a petition of Samuel Moore who has infringed custom-house rules (see Hough. *Nantucket.* p. 113-14).	164

4	Permission to land, proceed to Delaware and settle on unimproved land there, granted to Thos. Olive, Daniel Willes, John Penford, Joseph Helmely, Robt. Stacy and Benj. Scott, arrived from England in the ship Kent, Gregory Marlow master (see *Doc. rel. to col. hist. N. Y.* 12:579).	166

5	Order in the case between John Hendmer mariner, and Thos. Bray master of the ship Canary Merchant (see *N. Y. col. mss,* 26:79).	168

Sep. 11	Orders for the government of Pemaquid (see Hough. *Pemaquid.* p. 18-19).	169

27	New York is taxed by Connecticut on account of some mischief done by Indians at Hatfield. Letters received from Ensign Caesar Knapton at Pemaquid, and the French at St Johns and Penobscot (see Hough. *Pemaquid.* p. 19-23).	170

28	Answer to Connecticut read and approved.	170

Oct. 5	Capt. Thos. de la Vall and Nath. Silvester present. Gov. Andros has leave to go to England. Garrison of New York to be increased.	170

19	Warrant for the commitment of Edward Griffeth merchant charged with scurrilous speeches and reflections on the government.	172

Nov. 7	Petition of Elizabeth Gibbs (see *N. Y. col. mss,* 26:92) tabled. Former order regulating price of wheat suspended. Flour barrels to be marked when shipped (see *N. Y. col. mss,* 26:147). Order regulating fees for anchorage; Joseph Lee wharfinger. Gov. Andros ready to sail for England; Capt. Anthony Brockholes to be commander in chief, Capt. Mathias Nicolls to command the militia of Long Island and dependencies; rules concerning the council.	173

10	Letter received from Albany by Claes Luck and two Englishmen from Boston, Benj. Waite and Stephen Jenning who declare that they did not say Schenectady belonged to Boston, and that they were on their way to Canada to find their wives and children.	176

Council minutes for the intervening period are to be found in *N. Y. col. mss,* 26:157; 27:2, 34-35, 44, 54-55, 57-58, 64, 66, 84-85, 108, 120, 125-26, 176.

1678   **v. 3**

Aug. 17 Brief granted to the church officers for collecting money to
ransom people captured by the Turks in Jacob Leysler's
pink. Regulations for the trade to and at Albany.   178

20 Martin Gerritsen and Dirck Wessels commissaries, with
Robert Livingston their secretary, complain of French
intrigues among the New York Indians.   179

22 Appeal of Major John Fenwick from the court of assizes to
the king not allowed. The French intrigues among the
Maquaes, Mahicanders and north Indians to be counter-
acted.   179

23 Pemaquid affairs; Gov. Andros to go there in the spring
(see Hough. *Pemaquid.* p. 32-33). Sentence of the Albany
court against Wm. Loveridge jr (see *N. Y. col. mss*, 27:7)
confirmed. John Hendricks Bruyn of Albany sentenced
to imprisonment and fine for illegally trading with Indians,
released with a fine. Orders concerning the Indian trade
at Albany. Seneca Indians at war southwest of Maryland.   180

Sep. 6 Land granted opposite Schenectady to the town for a minister etc. Changes in the commissaries of Schenectady.
Order concerning a dispute between Johannes Provost
sheriff of Albany, and Ludovicus Cobet schout of Schenectady, about their jurisdiction.   182

11 Henry Jackson comes as messenger from a French man-of-
war, anchored near Sandy Hook asking permission in the
name of the French commander to come in for wood and
other supplies; granted.   184

14 Capt. Bernard le Moine commanding the Golden Fleece
French man-of-war produces his commission from his king
and from Sieur de Povancay governor of Tortudas.   184

19 Order on a deposition of Henry Clarke surveyor of the
customs charging Thos. Lewis master and owner of the
sloop Katharine of New York with illegal trading, and
Thos. Thatcher with obstructing the surveyor in perform-
ing his duties; Hendrick Arents alias Spaniard, and Jan
Teunisse alias de Pape his witnesses.   185

24 Capt. Christopher Billop dismissed from military service for
extravagant speeches.   185

Oct. 8 New commissaries appointed for Albany; Rich'd Pretty to
be sheriff there (see *N. Y. col. mss*, 27:27).   186

23 Timothy Cooper ordered to remove from Albany for having
written to Major Pincheon (see *N. Y. col. mss*, 27:18, 27-28). 186

31 Letters are written to the magistrates of Albany concerning
trade with Schenectady, the rights of the van Rensselaer
family, and ransom of the captives in Algiers (see *N. Y.
col. mss*, 27:26-27, 30).   186

1678   **v. 3**

Nov. 30   Sentence against Dr Henry Smith of the Whorekill for idly
          charging Justices Helmanus Wiltbank and Edward
          Southrin, and Clerk Cornelis Verhoofe of the court with
          crimes.   187

A ms list of books in the secretary's office in 1772, found in *N. Y. col. mss,*
99:44 shows that no v. 4 of Council minutes, Dec. 1678–Sep. 1683 existed
at that time. Various scattered minutes up to November 1680 may be
found in *N. Y. col. mss,* 28:58-59, 63, 74-75, 85-87, 120-23, 131-32, 142-43,
159-62, 168, 173-74; 29:2-3, 19, 27-28, 32, 36, 68, 117, 127, 136-37, 143, 150,
156, 169, 173, 179, 185, 187, 196, 212-13, 220, 230, 256, 258, 261.

Vol. 5   1683-88

1683

Sep. 13   John Spragge, Fred'k Flypsen, Stephanus van Cortlandt
          sworn of the council. Some of the governor's instructions
          read. Appeal of Jacob Melyn from the judgment of the
          mayor's court in an action against Stephen Cregoe to the
          court of assizes allowed. Appeal allowed Isaac Melyn (see
          N. Y. col. mss, 31:45); also Thos. Lawrence from a judg-
          ment of the Gravesend sessions (see *N. Y. col. mss,* 31:72).
          Writs of election for representatives to be sent to the
          sheriff of Long Island. Staten Island to elect one repre-
          sentative: Fishers, Silvesters and Gardiners islands to vote
          with the east riding. Writs sent to the Esopus and Albany.
          Schenectady to elect one representative. John Allen ap-
          pointed sheriff of Pemaquid and surrounding islands which
          are to elect one representative (see Hough. *Pemaquid.*
          p. 73). Matthew Mayhew to be sheriff of Nantuckett,
          Martins Vineyard, Elizabeth islands and all other islands
          east of Long Island which are to elect one representative.
          Town clerk of New York called upon for a list of free-
          holders. Canadians trading at Albany must have a pass
          from their governor; New Yorkers, going to hunt with the
          French or Indians likewise. Order regulating the valua-
          tion of coin.   I

    15   Order on a petition of Mingo Anthony a negro. Commis-
          sions to Lucas Santin as judge, Wm. Nicolls as register,
          and John Colier as marshall, for the trial of Nicolas Clough
          master of the ship Camelion read and approved. Appeal
          of the town of Hurley from a judgment of the Kingston
          sessions to the court of assizes allowed. Rules concerning
          markets to be observed. Sec. John Spragge to be clerk

1683   **v. 5**

of the assizes. John Palmer appointed high sheriff of
Staten Island. Writs of election sent to the sheriff of New
York.   2

22   Order on a petition of John Archer (see *N. Y. col. mss*,
31:42). None but freeholders to vote at the election. Case
of Mingo Anthony deferred. Order on a petition of Thos.
Willett for quiet possession of Hogs island.   4

24   Mingo Anthony adjudged to be a slave. Order on a petition
of Wm. Moore and Jeremiah Fenwyck against their former
captain, Edward Reade of the ship Golden Hind.   5

26   Conference on the case of John Archer (p. 4). Order on a
petition of Rob't Cockram, John Darvill, Arthur Davis,
Daniel Kelly, Henry Lewin, Robert Dawson, John Mer-
styn and John Hallimore, convicted of a conspiracy on
board the Camelion. Complaint of Wm. Moore (p. 5),
John Finch, Jeremiah Fenwyck and Robert Annett against
their captain referred to law.   6

Oct. 1   Petitions: of Edward Whittacres, George Meales and Richard
Hays; of Henry Alberts; of Jacob Rutgers; of Aert Peterson; of Robert Story tabled. Petition of Gerrit Egbaerts
for his son detained by his wife referred to the justices of
Staten Island.   6

4   Conference with Maquaes schems.   7
Conference continued (see *Doc. hist. N. Y.* 1:398-99; Q
1:262-63; Indian queens present.   8

9   Order on a petition of Tackpousha sachem of Mashpeage
L. I. (see *N. Y. col. mss*, 31: 82).   13

12   Orders: on petition of Richard Ponton, Wm. Richardson and
Joseph Palmer all of Westchester against molestations by
John Archer (p. 4, 6); on letters from the governor of Canada with complaints against Mon. Ville Roy; on petition
from Eastchester asking for separation from Westchester;
John Hinksman, Richard Stockin, Phil. Pinkney to appear for Westchester, Francis Brown of Rye and Robert
Blomer for Eastchester; on petition of Edward Hubbert
and Dirck Garretsen for protection against John Archer.   13

22   Petition of Tackpousha (p. 13) referred to the court of assizes. Daniel Carty complaining against his master re-
ferred to the mayor.   15

Nov. 5   Petition of J. Palmer married to the widow of John Winder for a quietus referred on objections by Mr Pinhorn.
Petition of John Rider referred until the arrival of Thos.
Lewis. Thos. Coker sworn in as collector of excise
money.   16

1683   v. 5

10　　Petition of the mayor and aldermen of New York for a
confirmation of their ancient priviledges; order thereon.
Petition of J. Palmer for a quietus (p. 16) granted Pinhorn having withdrawn his objections.　　　　　　　　　16

12　　Gov. Dongan absent; Capt. Anthony Brockholes presides.
Instructions to Edward Antill merchant to sail for England
in the Camelion, Nicholas Clough master and consult in
England with Sir Benjamin Bathurst concerning affairs of
the Royal African company.　　　　　　　　　　　　20

16　　Examination of the case of Paulus Richards vs Stephen
Gaineau for debt; Mon. Minvielle and Paul la Valloy witnesses.　　　　　　　　　　　　　　　　　　　　22

20　　Gov. Dongan returned.　Petition of Dirck Dyc for return
of money paid for the release of his son John from cap-
tivity in Algiers granted as the son was dead before the
money reached its destination.　　　　　　　　　　　23

22　　Instructions and orders for the governing of Pemaquid
(see Hough. *Pemaquid.* p. 75-81).　　　　　　　　　23

23　　Petition of Fredk. Ellis (see *N. Y. col. mss*, 31: 93) referred
to Capt. J. Youngs, Capt. John Howell and Isaac Arnold.
Petition of mayor and aldermen referred to Mr West.
Cornelis Steenwyck appointed mayor, Nicholas Bayard,
John Iniaus, Wm Pinhorne, Guline Verplanck, John Rob-
inson and Wm Cox aldermen.　　　　　　　　　　27

25　　Governor of Connecticut Robert Treat, Sec. John Allyn,
Major Nathan Gold and Mr Pitkin before the council on
boundary matters.　　　　　　　　　　　　　　　27

28　　Articles of agreement between New York and Connecticut
about the boundary line.　　　　　　　　　　　　28

30　　Capt. J. Colier late high sheriff of New York to give an account of monies paid by Fr. Flypsen for two sailors of
the ship Rebecca.　　　　　　　　　　　　　　　31

Dec. 6　Petition of mayor and aldermen of New York (see *N. Y.
col. mss*, 31: 95); answer.　　　　　　　　　　　　32

9　　Orders of the weigh money read and signed.　　　　35

15　　Orders on petitions: of Winnaquaheag sachem of Connecticut on the south side of Long Island for remittance of
a fine in a suit with Richard Smith; of the inhabitants
of Madmans Neck (see *N. Y. col. mss*, 31: 96). Ralph
Cardall's deed.　　　　　　　　　　　　　　　35

20　　Orders on petitions: of the inhabitants of Rye for confirmation of their lands in Connecticut etc.; of Nathaniel
Baker sr (see *N. Y. col. mss*, 31: 98).　　　　　　　36

1684

Jan. 3　Order on petition by the inhabitants of Madnans Neck
(see *N. Y. col. mss*, 31: 100).　　　　　　　　　　37

1684   v. 5

10 Orders on petitions: of Johannes Sanders Glen of Schenectady asking that no one but himself be allowed to plow the Mohawks sachems' land, granted; of Anna van Borsum against Jacques Cortiliau (see *N. Y. col. mss*, 31: 102); by the inhabitants of Hurley against Henry Pawling about fences (see *N. Y. col. mss*, 31:97). Answer to a letter from the commissaries at Albany on Indian affairs and estates of deceased persons.   38

19 Inhabitants of other colonies not to plead in New York without the governor's license. Order to Robert Roberts master of the Rebecca to appear before the council on complaint of Archill Martlie mate, John Cochart boatswain, and others of the same ship.   41

15 Capt. Roberts and the above complainants present; the captain settles the matter.   41

17 The matter between Anna van Borsum and Jacques Cortiliau (p. 38) referred to John Brown, Peter Jacobs, Nich's Bayard and Guline Verplanck. Order on petition of Peter Jacobs Marius (see *N. Y. col. mss*, 31:103). Case of John Rider administrator of the estate of Roger Rugge deceased referred to the mayor and aldermen. Col. Lewis Morris made a member of the council.   42

28 Petition of Robert Wright (see *L. P.* 2: 26) tabled. Wisquoscheak Indians renew their allegiance. John de Fries and Harlem lands. Report in re Anna van Borsum vs. Jacques Cortiliau received (see *N. Y. col. mss*, 31: 107).   43

31 Orders on petitions: of Samuel son of Richard Smith of Nesaquake about land matters; of Balth. Bayard and Hans Kiersted sons-in-law of Govert Lockerman deceased for an accounting by Francis Rumboutse and Johannes van Brugh executors of Maritie Jansen widow of G. Lockerman. Mr White summoned before the council in re Peter Jacobs Marius (p. 42). Recorder of New York city to give the charge to the grand jury; members of the council may sit as justices of the peace in the quarter sessions of New York county; John West to be clerk of the sessions; instructions for the recorder's charge.   44

Feb. 7 Nich's de Meyer, Guline Verplanck and Peter de la Noy to examine the books of Govert Lockerman (see *N. Y. col. mss*, 31: 111) on the petition of Bath'z Bayard etc. (p. 44). Orders on petitions: of Nich's de Meyer against John Young (see *N. Y. col. mss*, 31: 110); of Paulus Richards for a quietus as administrator of Tyse Barnse deceased; of Richard Cornell against Robert Wright and Francis Pew. Commissions of Mathias Nicolls and John Palmer as judges read and amended.   46

1684   **v. 5**

Order granting the petition of Josias and Paulus Marlitt
for a survey and division of their inherited land part of
which has been sold to Paulus Richards.   59

22 Rules for the purchase of land from the Indians. Action on
a petition of Peter Losser for land at Esopus postponed.   60

24 Order on a petition of John Hansen, Jeronymus Rappalle
and John Tunissen (see *L. P.* 2: 32). Letters of administration to be granted to Volkertie Pieters (see *N. Y. col.
mss,* 31: 130). Jacobus de Haert asking a confirmatory
patent for land at Haverstraw is told he cannot have one
for various reasons given.   61

25 Inhabitants of Hempstead appear against the petition of
John Hansen etc. (p. 61).   62

31 Petition of George and Harmanus Burger for land at Maspethkills rejected.   Order for Paulus Richards administrator of the estate of Tyse Barnsen deceased to settle
certain debts of the estate with Nich's de Meyer before he
can have a quietus (p. 46). Order on a letter from Albany concerning bolting of flour. A member of the council present at the court of sessions in New York to sit
as presiding judge. Patents for land on Staten Island to
be called for; the villages of Harlem, Boswyck, Brookland, Bedford, Flatbush, New Lots, Gravesend, New
Utrecht, Newtown, Maspethkills, Hempstead, Jamaica,
Flushing and Oysterbay to produce their patents and Indian deeds before the council. Laws and orders made
by the mayor etc. of New York approved with amendments. Petition of John Palmer, James Graham, Thos.
Coddrington and John Royse (see *L. P.* 2: 34) granted.   62

Ap. 9 Reasons for making the petition about bolting (p. 58) presented by the mayor and aldermen (see *N. Y. col. mss,*
31: 134). Letter from Gov. Broadstreet brought by Gov.
Cranfield of New Hampshire. Conference with Minisink
Indians.   65

11 A letter from Gov. Broadstreet brought by Messrs Dud-
ley and Shrimpton about a probable Indian war discussed;
Gov. Cranfield present (see Hough. *Pemaquid,* p. 91-93).
Letters to the council of New Hampshire (see Hough.
Pemaquid. p. 93-94); and to Gov. Simon Broadstreet of
Boston.   66

12 Orders on petitions: of John Cooly;   of Richard Hayes
about land matters; of Arent Tunissen; of Henry Desbrow
(see *N. Y. col. mss,* 31:136); of Thos. Bayles vs Samuel
Willson about papers of his wife the widow of Ralph
Cardall; of Obadiah Holmes (see *L. P.* 2:42); of John

1684   v. 5

19   Order concerning customs duties.   83

21   J. Kingsland agent for the deputy-governor of Barbadoes
complains of badly packed flour being exported from New
York; order thereon. Custom-house fees on Long Island
complained of.   83

22   Order on a petition of Jacob Meleyn for land on Staten
Island. N. de Meyer complains against Joseph Lee executor of the estate of Sam. Hitchcock, John Betts and
Sarah Veale for not making returns. Orders on petitions:
of John Houmbs; of Thos. Youngs about pilotage fees.   84

29   Clause inserted into the patent for Mr Mayhew and Mr
Gardiner. Orders about packing flour and customs duties
approved.   85

27   License to purchase Indian lands west of Nippro creek
granted to Fred. Flypsen. Order on petition of Thos.
Crandall jr for an attachment on the goods of English
Smith and George Lockhart on board the Seaflower,
Wallsall Cobbie commander.   85

28   Indians acknowledge their sale of land to Fred. Flypsen.
Order on a complaint of Rev. Mr Hobard minister at
Hempstead about his salary.   86

30   J. Palmer appointed judge, John Spragge register, and John
Cavalier marshall of the admiralty. Vacancies in the various offices to be filled.   86

June 5   Petition of Jo. Hobart of Easthampton vs Giles Silvester
for opposing officers referred to the court of oyer and
terminer. Order concerning customs duties on Long
Island. Enlistments in Capt. Hobard's troop approved.   87

20   Case of the Seaflower, Wallsall Cobbie com'r (p. 85). Action on the petition of Fred'k Ellis postponed. Petition
of Ryck Abrams & Co. rejected. Order on petition of
Gabriel Minvielle for letters of administration on the estate of Joshua L'Osseur late of Bordeaux deceased. Petition of Dirck Jansen Hoogland rejected. Order on a
petition of Mrs Rider for a quietus.   88

24   Orders on petitions: of Thos. Willett, Elias Doughty, Thos.
Hickes, Richard and John Cornell (see *N. Y. col. mss,*
31:153); of Jacob Meleyne (see *L. P.* 2:46). Answer to
a letter from the governor of Canada (see *Doc. hist. N. Y.*
1:100-1; Q 1:68).   89

July 9   Order on petition of George Wood (see *N. Y. col. mss,*
31:155, 172). Action on a petition of Wm. Loveridge for
land at Katskill postponed. Petition of Wm. Beekly for
land south of Crabb island, Harlem river granted. Action on a petition of Jacob Kipp (see *N. Y. col. mss,* 31:155;

1684   v. 5

and, *L. P.* 2:50) postponed. Mrs Rider to have a quietus
for her late husband's administration on the estate of
Roger Rugge (p. 88). Capt. Nicolls' bond as vendue
master exchanged.   91

28   Gov. Dongan at Albany; Capt. Anthony Brockholls presides. Minisink Indians before the council with presents
for the governor (see *N. Y. col. mss,* 31:158). Quietus
granted to Mrs Rider (p. 88).   93

Sep. 6   Petition of the inhabitants of Kingston (see *N. Y. col. mss,*
31:180) referred. Order on a petition of Thos. Atkinson
and other sailors against their captain, Wallsall Cobbie.
Petition of the Lutheran congregation (see *N. Y. col. mss,*
31:173) referred (see *Doc. hist. N. Y.* 3:406; Q 3:246).
Elisha Hutchinson to be legally prosecuted for unlawful
settlement on Rowsac island (p. 70). Action on a
petition of the inhabitants of Pemaquid (see *N. Y.
col. mss,* 31:181) postponed. Boundaries between Hempstead and Jamaica settled. Order on a complaint of
Caleb Carman, Elizabeth widow of Peter Smith, Wm.
Creed and Wm. White vs the town of Flushing about
land. Thos. Atkinson, Nich's Luist, Wm. Taylor, Wm.
Gutheridge, Essex Knethell sailors of the Seaflower
to have their private chests, etc. although the ship had
been seized as not free under the navigation act.   91

13   Order in re Daniel Turneer vs Lewis Morris (see *N. Y. col.
mss,* 31:156). Orders on petitions: of Capt. Cobby; of
the inhabitants of Kingston (p. 91).   95

Oct. 3   Petition of Phil. Wells referred. Orders on petitions: of
Gertruyde widow of Jochem Wessells for land at Albany;
of Edward Hornet and his wife Mary (see *N. Y. col. mss,*
32:14); of John Gilbert for pay; of Mr Denton.   96

21   Town of Hempstead, and Isaac Horner for Oysterbay be-
fore the council about their boundaries; Capt. Thos.
Townsend and Henry Townsend sr ordered to appear for
Oysterbay.   97

29   Order on a petition of John Williams and others, sailors
of the ship Beaver against their captain, Jacob Maurice.   97

Nov. 1   Thos. Townsend, Nath'l Cole, John Wicks, Isaac Horner for
Oysterbay, John Seamans, John Jackson, Simon Saring
for Hempstead settle their boundary quarrels before the
council. All justices of the peace and sheriffs continued
in their respective offices.   98

3   Mayor and aldermen to hold the court of sessions and
mayor's court.   100

1684   v. 5

15   Mr van Clyffe and Mr Stautenburgh to have letters of ad-
      ministration under the will of Dirick Jans van Deventer
      (see *N. Y. col. mss*, 31:154). Gervase Marshall and brother
      granted letters of administration on their grandfather's
      estate. Petition of Dirick Hoogland rejected. Order on
      a petition by the inhabitants of Jamaica (see *N. Y. col. mss*,
      32:25).   100

Dec. 1   John Palmer sworn of the council. Order concerning vic-
      tualling houses. Settlers on Staten Island, at the Younck-
      ers, Spiting Devil, Broncx river, Rye, and Bedford to
      produce their land titles. Petition of Wm. Morris referred. 101

15   Major A. Brockholls presiding. Yonckers, 'Spiting Devil,
      Broncx river, Staten Island patents examined. Petition of
      Neely rejected.   101

24   Gov. Dongan present. Answer to a letter from Isaac Ar-
      nold; order to the same for searching after smuggled
      goods and unlicensed liquordealers. Answer to a letter
      from Josiah Hobard, Jo. Fordham and Thos. Mapes.
      Letters of administration granted to Mr Willson and Mr
      Rider on the estate of Ralph Cardall.   102

1685

Jan. 8   The governor absent. Mr Horton brings the Indian deeds
      of Rye, Joseph Theale the same for Bedford. Orders on
      petitions: of John Inians (see *N. Y. col. mss*, 32:40); of
      Gervasse Marshall and John Smith.   103

16   Dirck van Clyffe and Peter Jacob Marius oppose the grant-
      ing of letters of administration on the estate of Dirck
      .Wogertse to Marshall and Smith (p. 103).   104

Feb. 11   Gov. Dongan present. The case of Dirck van Clyffe etc. vs
      Gervasse Marshall (p. 104) referred to arbitrators. Hen-
      drick Gillus appointed administrator on the estate of
      Jacob uyt den Bogard vice Petrus Bayard and Marinus
      de Witt who have left the province. Time to purchase
      Indian lands north of his father granted to Philipp Phil-
      ippsen.   105

Mar. 2   Regulations for preventing the running away of servants
      and debtors. Mr West appointed to claim the towns on
      the west side of Connecticut river for New York. Post
      office to be established. Order on a petition of Thos.
      Trowbridge (see *N. Y. col. mss*, 32:51). Gervasse Mar-
      shall referred to the court of mayor and aldermen. Sheriff
      of New York county to take up the body of a negro buried
      at Corlears Hook.   106

23   Proclamation to issue about pedlars and concealed weapons.
      Same about landing goods at the bridge. Rule about
      giving the freedom of the city.   107

1685   **v. 5**

31   Yonckers patent, etc. produced. John Robinson and Paulus
       Richards appointed arbitrators, Capt. J. Palmer umpire,
       between Ansell Sam'l Levy and Simon Valentine van der
       Wilde.   107

Ap. 3   Proclamation to issue forbidding all vessels to trade at other
       ports than New York. Stephan van Cortlandt and Wm.
       Creed to be arbitrators for Flatbush, Nicholas Bayard
       and Roeloff Murtens for Breucklyn. Petition of Jan Clute
       (see *L. P.* 2:66) rejected.   108

7   Indians of Murthers creek acknowledge the sale of their
       land. Capt. Jonathan Selleck deposes having received
       clipped money from Benj. Blagge.   109

9   Petition of George Heathcot referred to the law.   109

21   Solemnities on receipt of the news of the death of King
       Charles 2. King James 2 to be proclaimed.   109

24   Fortifications of New York city to be repaired. Petition of
       Arent Schuyler (see *L. P.* 2:93) granted. Robert Ham-
       mond clerk of the representatives ordered to deliver acts
       of assembly. Létters of administration granted to Jane
       Rider (see *N. Y. col. mss,* 32:68). Indians acknowledge
       a sale of land to Jacob de Key. Flushing patent pro-
       duced.   111

25   Order to seize and prosecute the sloop of Rich'd Patishall
       upon information of Major Wm. Dyre. Order on a pe-
       tition of Hugh Riddall (see *N. Y. col. mss,* 32:61, 69).   112

29   John Lawrence, John Brown, and Mathias Harvy for Flush-
       ing vs Wm. Creed, Wm. White and widow of Peter Smith
       (see *L. P.* 2:92). Order of the court of record in New
       York city in re the brigantine Edmond and Martha,,
       Rich'd Patishall master; Major Wm. Dyre called upon for
       further report in the case (p. 112). Order on a petition
       of Nicholas Garrett (see *N. Y. col. mss,* 32:63).   112

May 13   Writs of election for representatives of N. Y. city, Staten
       Island, Kings county and Westchester to be sent out.
       Quitrents for N. Y. county to be collected. Order sum-
       moning Mrs Steenwyck before the council. Order on a
       petition of Margaret Steenwyck (see *N. Y. col. mss,* 32:70). 115

June 3   Gervase Baxter sworn of the council. Captain le Sage of
       the ship Trompeuse allowed to come in for provisions.
       The ship Charles, belonging to Fr. Flypsen, and seized
       for having broken bulk contrary to law, is discharged.
       Land granted to Robert Livingstone (see *N. Y. col. mss,*
       32:75).   116

6   Inhabitants of Albany to bring in stockadoes for repairing
       the fort there.   117

1685   v. 5

8   Letter received from Walter Clark, deputy governor of
    Rhode Island. Caveat of Peter de la Noy against the
    grant to Robert Livingston. Order on a complaint of
    Richard Codner master of the ketch Adventure (see *N. Y.
    col. mss*, 32:78). Thos. Case of Long Island summoned
    before the council   117

15 Appeal brought by Sam'l Winder for Jacob Mauritz against
    the petition of his sister-in-law, Margaret Steenwyck
    (p. 115) read: order thereon. Orders: in re de la Noy vs
    Livingston (p. 117); on a petition of Wm. White, Wm.
    Creed and Sam'l Rosa, vs Dan'l Whitehead.   118

18 Peter Neve and Sarah Skidmore ask for patents (see *L. P.*
    2:68, 71). Thos. Walton, Mary Britton and François
    Martineau to be taken in custody by the sheriff of Staten
    Island.   118

25 Thos. Rudyard of counsel for Jacob Mauritz pleads on the
    above appeal, John West of counsel for Mrs Steenwyck.
    Mrs Thos. Walton for her husband, Francis Martineau
    and Mrs Mary Brittain produce their land papers (see
    L. P. 2:67, 75, 87) and their quitrent is fixed.   118

23 Thos. Chambers and Henrick Beakman before the council
    about John Ward bell-ringer at Kingston; referred to
    magistrates and inhabitants.   119

July 2 Gov. Dongan absent. Order in re Jacob Mauritz vs Mrs
    Steenwyck.   119

13 Orders on petitions: of Peter Chock (see *N. Y. col. mss*,
    32:80); of John Cornelissen (see *L. P.* 2:69); of Dirck
    Claes.   120

16 Gov. Dongan returned. Judge Palmer commissioned to
    hold a court of oyer and terminer at Martin's Vineyard
    if necessary.   120

20 Orders on petitions: of Adam, John, and Elizabeth Wright
    for letters of administration on the estate of their mother,
    Alice Crabbe; of Mary, widow of Philipp Jones of Rhode
    Island for letters on her husband's estate. Jean Basilier's
    sloop ordered to be seized for having wine and brandy on
    board.   120

23 Orders on petitions: of Fr. Flypsen (see *N. Y. col. mss*,
    32:83); of Joseph Mayhew for letters of administration
    on the estate of his father, Samuel Mayhew, vice Anthony
    Wright.   121

25 Proclamation to issue against giving information and taking
    affidavits in a clandestine manner. New orders on the
    above petition of Fr'k Flypsen.   121

Aug. 1 Maryland Indians before the council want the peace made
    last summer confirmed.   122

3   Major Wm. Dyre charged by the governor with having
     given clandestine information.   122
5   Examination of Major Wm. Dyre. The assembly to be
     dissolved and writs for the election of a new one to
     issue.   123
15   Indians acknowledge the sale of land to Fred. Flypsen.
     Petition of Jane Rider (see *L. P.* 2:135) granted. Order
     on a petition of John Boisbellau (see *N. Y. col. mss,* 32:85,
     86).   124
17   Order to David Toshack Miniveird who has settled on un-
     purchased Indian land. Jonathan Parker reprimanded for
     transporting servants to Rhode Island.   124
27   Petition of Joseph Mayhew (p. 121) denied upon production
     of Anthony Wright's papers by Isaac Horner and Mary
     Andrews his next of kin. Petition of Humphry Astly (see
     N. Y. col. mss, 32:66, 87) rejected.   125
Sep. 12 Letter from King James 2 received. Petition of Peter Lud-
     gar referred to the mayor etc. Order on a petition of
     Henry Filkin (see *L. P.* 2:132). All sheriffs of the province
     summoned before the council.   125
17   Order on a petition of Andrew Gibbs (see *L. P.* 2:141).
     Inhabitants of Tappan, Haverstraw and New Lots sum-
     moned before the council. Order on petitions: of Jacob
     Mauritz; of Aeltie Slichtenhorst. Petition of Saul Brown
     referred to ———.   126
21   Timber for repairing the fort at Albany to be brought in
     by the inhabitants. License to purchase Indian land
     granted to Peter Schuyler.   126
28   The sloop Happy Returne allowed to enter although come
     without clearing papers from Newfoundland.   127
Oct. 8   Mr Manning, Hendrick Smith, W. Alberts, George Steven-
     son, Stephen Georgson, John Buckhold, Thos. Wendall,
     Johannes Lawrensis, Peter Johnson Boeckhoult, Luke de
     Pau, Roeloff Peterson, Jan Jansen, John Albertus, John
     Allwyn, Mr Blackwell, Tho. Browne, Joseph Theale for
     Bedford; Dow Harmansen with Peter Jansen Haine,
     Tiebout Garretsen, Daniel de Clerk for Tappan; Hendrick
     Ricault, Flor Williams, John Cornelissen and Menny
     Johannes for Haverstraw produced their papers for patents. 127
p. m.   Tackapausha and Paman acknowledge at Mr van Cortlandts
     house the sale of land at Rockaway to Capt. Palmer.
     Memorandum that on the 10th of Oct. two other Indians
     appeared before the council at Capt. J. Palmer's house
     acknowledging receipt of purchase money for their two-
     thirds of Crabb meadow on Katawawmacke.   128

13 Claes Johnson Permasent, Teunis Roeloffs, Dow Harmenson, Cornelius Claussen, Peter Johnson Haring, Garret Stenmetts, Johs. Garretsen, Hubert Garretsen, Ide van Vorst, Jan Stratemaker, John Vreese, Claus Emanuel, Arian Lambertsen, Stats de Grote, Lambert Adriansen, Corn's Adriansen, Daniel de Clark and Corsen Haring granted land at Tappan. Peter Jacobs granted a confirmatory patent for land at Haverstraw formerly granted to Jacobus de Hart. John Cornelissen granted land at Apomapo, next to S. van Cortlandt. Jacobus van de Water, Jeronimus Rapallese and Teunis Guisbertsen, for Breucklyn, Jacques Corteliau and John Johnson van Dyke for New Utrecht before the council to settle their respective quitrents. Ministers and magistrates forbidden to marry Jacques Vigor alias Jacques Gallop to his wife's sister Louisa with whom he has run away from Canada. Members of the council to have the power of justices of the peace in all counties. Nicholas Bayard appointed mayor, John Knight high sheriff, Tho. Caker coroner, Nich's Bayard, James Graham, Capt. Andrew Bowne, John de la Vall, Wm. Pinhorne, J. Robinson, Gabriel Minvielle, Wm. Beakman, Abr'm de Peyster, Joh's Kipp and Jacob Leysler justices of the peace of New York; Thos. Stillwell high sheriff, Corn's Coursen, Phil. Wells, Obadiah Holmes, Richard Stillwell justices of the peace, Francis Barber coroner for Richmond county; Roeloff Martensen high sheriff, Jacques Corteliau, Nich's Stillwell, Elbert Elbertsen, —— Beakman and Mr Morris justices, Peter Johnson of Gueoos coroner for Kings county; Major Willett high sheriff, Thos. Hicks, Rich'd Cornel, Elias Daughty, Thos. Stevens, Dan'l Whitehead, Capt. Symmonds, John Jackson, —— Townsend of Jericho, —— Townsend of Oysterbay justices, Edward Stevens coroner for Queens county; Capt. Hobart high sheriff for Suffolk county; Rich'd Pretty high sheriff, all the council justices, Peter Schuyler, Jan Jansen Bleker, Henry Cuyler, Robert Sanders, —— Goatson, Marten Garretsen, —— van Rensselaer magistrates for the town, John Trapett coroner for Albany county; Capt. Sanders justice for Schenectady. Sheriffs to be sworn in before the justices of the peace and give bonds. Patent for land on Cowneck, L. I. granted to Mr Cornell, Mr Daughty and Mr Hicks. Land in Flushing township to be surveyed for Elias Doughty (see *L. P.* 2:165). Order on petitions of Isaac Swinton and of Dr Henry Taylor for land in Flushing township (see *L. P.* 2:135).

1685   **v. 5**

22 Patent to John Williams of Rhode Island and associates made
void Mayhew's patent being precedent. Warrant of survey
granted to Wm. Creed et al (p. 118). Order concerning
land purchased by Cornwall and Willet. Warrant of survey granted to Dr Henry Taylor (p. 128); to John Lawrence (see *L. P.* 2:133); to Jasper Smith all for land in
Flushing. Order on a petition of Adrian Gerretts about
the estate of Teunis Willemse. Patent granted to Peter
Schuyler (see *L. P.* 2:136).   133

23 Orders on petitions: Philipp Lawrence (see *N. Y. col. mss,*
32:111). Ansell Sam'l Levy (see *N. Y. col. mss,* 32:110).
James Lloyd (see *L. P.* 2:139).   134a

29 Orders on petitions: of Francis, Charles, and Elias Doughty
for land (see *N. Y. col. mss,* 32:112). Lt.-col. Youngs referred to the house of representatives. Bartholomew Mercier (see *N. Y. col. mss,* 32:113). Elias Doughty (see
N. Y. col. mss, 32:114). John Palmer (see *L. P.* 2:140).
Francis Cooley for land in Flushing.   135

Nov. 3 J. Tuder appears for the town of Flushing against the petitions of Doughty and Swinton for land. Nath'l Pearsall
likewise for Hempstead against the grant of land to Capt.
J. Palmer at Rockaway.   136

10 Thomas Willett appears for Flushing to settle about the
quitrents; grant of land to the petitioners recommended by
the governor. Orders on petitions: of Dirick van der
Clyffe and Peter Stoutenburgh in a will case, of T. Cooley 137

12 Day of thanksgiving for the victories over the rebels in England and Scotland appointed. Estate of Gabriel l'Asseur
to be delivered by Gabriel Minvielle to the governor.   137

19 Orders on petitions: Regnier Williams and Barent Lewis
(see *N. Y. col. mss,* 32:125). Andrew Gibb (see *L. P.*
2:142). Petition of Hendrick Thompson (see *N. Y. col. mss,*
32:124) rejected.   138

20 Special commission to be given to the judges for the trial
of Philipp Lawrence. Lucas Santen collector of the
province to produce all books and papers relating to the
revenue. Proclamation giving notice of the suppression
of the rebellion in England and appointing a day of prayer
and thanksgiving for "the good success of the Ottoman
forces."   138

24 Patent for Flushing read and passed. License to purchase
Indian land near Oysterbay granted to Henry Townsend
sr and jr, John Underhill, Matthew Prior, Job Wright,
Joseph Dickenson, James Townsend, and John Townsend.
Mr Swinton allowed to draw up an information against
Rye and Bedford about their land titles.   140

26 Deputies from Newtown, Bushwyck, and Brookland before the council about their boundaries. Order on petitions: Thos. Higby (see *L. P.* 2:143). Dirck van Clyffe (see *N. Y. col. mss*, 32:126).   140

30 Recorder James Graham sent for. Philipp Lawrence to be punished according to the duke's laws.   141

Dec. 1 Patents to be issued to Newtown and Bushwyck.   142

3 Quietus desired by Dirck van Clyffe (p. 140) not to be granted until Jacob Leisler's return. Petition of Phil. Lawrence (see *N. Y. col. mss*, 32:115) granted. Mrs Engeltie Burger and Thos. Parcell desiring patents for the same land the case is deferred: Gabriel l'Asseur's estate.   142

10 James Graham appointed and sworn attorney general of the province, Isaac Swinton appointed clerk of the chancery, John Cavalier messenger of the court of chancery. Order on a petition of John West (see *L. P.* 2:144).   142

12 Warrant for Wm. Nicolls to go to Martins Vineyard, Nantucket, Elizabeth islands in Dukes county and inquire into the illegal trading there.   143

14 Order concerning revenues and quitrents and establishing a court of exchequer. Orders on petitions: Fred. Flypsen (see *N. Y. col. mss*, 32:128); of Wm. Merrit (see *N. Y. col. mss*, 32:129).   144

17 Mayor Nicholas Bayard sworn of the council, Isaac Swinton and John Knight as clerks of chancery. Philipp Lawrence to be transported to the West Indies (p. 141). Orders on petitions: Daniel Whitehead (see *L. P.* 2:146). Thos. Wenham for a bill of store. A new street to be made above the Smith's garden through the land of George Heathcote.   145

18 Mrs Engeltie Burger and Thomas Parcell (p. 142) referred to the courts.   146

1686

Jan. 7 Gov. Dongan absent. Order on a petition of Andrew Gibbs (see *L. P.* 2:147, and *N. Y. col. mss*, 33:1).   147

Feb. 19 Gov. Dongan present. Order on petitions: Morgan Jones (see *N. Y. col. mss*, 33:3). Claes Bickers. Commission for the court of exchequer read and approved.   147

20 Patent for Newtown passed; all township patents to be drawn like it. Motion of the attorney general that the inhabitants of New York may have the vacant land to low water mark and the liberty of granting licenses. Richard Hartshorne to be arrested for taking up a whale in the sea.   147

22 Patent of New York considered and referred. A paper called a remittment given by Gov. Lovelace to David Gardiner not thought sufficient to release Gardiner from paying quitrent.   148

1686   **v. 5**

Mar. 11   Petition of David Scudder referred to the law. Orders on
petitions: Inhabitants of Boshwyck. Wm. Beekly (see
L. P 2:124, 128). John Tuder (see L. P. 2:152). Order concerning Westchester patents.   149

15   Order in re Jonathan Wright and Jasper Smith (see L. P.
2:154) vs Major Thos. Willett, Capt. Hicks and Justice
Cornell.   149

18   Daniel Turneer appears against the petition of Wm. Beekly
(p. 149); postponed. Order on a petition of John Tuder
(see L. P. 2:155). Petitions of some Newtown people and
of J. Knight referred.   150

25   Orders on petitions: Richard Gibbs (see L. P. 2:157). Jacob
Loockermans. James Lorkan (see L. P. 2:156). Henry
Filkin. Aeltie Leisler (see N. Y. col. mss, 33:5).   150

Ap. 1   Warrant for opening a new street to be issued by the mayor
and damages paid. Sheriffs of Long Island to be sued in
the court of exchequer. Petition of Samuel Rusgoe referred to law. Land on Roeloff Jansen's kill granted to
Philipp Schuyler (see L. P. 2:158).   151

7   Mr Woodhull and Capt. Tucker appear for Seatalcott against
the grant of a patent to Andrew Gibbs; the latter's name
to be inserted in the patent of Seatalcot. Orders on petitions: The Easthampton overseers of the poor (see L. P.
2:161). Jacobus Scalenger against sheriff Joseph Fordham
of Suffolk county. Jacobus Scalenger and Sam'l Mumford vs the same (see N. Y. col. mss, 33:27). Richard
Woodhull for pay for clearing a highway.   152

15   T. Hicks, Elias Doughty and Thos. Willetts to take out the
patent for Cowneck as petitioned for (p. 128). Orders on
petitions: of Tachanick an Indian (see L. P. 2:169): of
John de la Val, John White, John Knight, John Tuder,
and John West (see L. P. 2:168). Order concerning trade
with the Indians.   153

22   Order on a petition of Elizabeth Coppin widow of John
Whight (see N. Y. col. mss, 33:28).   154

26   Patent of New York city passed. Order on a petition of
Joseph Brown and Isaac Gibes (see N. Y. col. mss, 33:29). 155

29   John Pell justice of the peace in West Chester county reprimanded for making pounds to take stray horses; he is
advised to satisfy the Indians. Address of Elizabeth Coppin
widow of John Whight.   155

June 10   Capt. J. Palmer to proceed to Pemaquid and settle the quitrents there (see Hough. Pemaquid. p. 107). Sheriffs to
collect the quitrents take out their commissions at New
York etc.   156

1686   **v. 5**

11   Orders on petitions: Thos. Brooks (see *N. Y. col. mss*, 33:32);
     of White and others of Jamaica vs Daniel Whitehead.   157
14   Order on representation of Mr Betts and Mr Stephens of
     Newtown concerning their patent.   158
20   Newtown votes on the patent question received. Paulus
     Johnson granted letters of denization.   158
22   Order on a petition of Paulus Schrick (see *N. Y. col. mss*,
     33:36).   158
30   Gawen Laurie deputy governor of east New Jersey and John
     Skene deputy governor of west New Jersey in council state
     that they intend to run the lines between the three govern-
     ments; George Keith, Andrew Robinson, and Phil. Wells
     to be the surveyors.   159

July 7   Orders on petitions: John Persons Weaver, Simòn Hillyer,
     Jacob Dayton et al (see *L. P.* 2:192). Mary widow of
     Samuel Davis (see *N. Y. col. mss*, 33:39). Edw'd Antill
     (see *N. Y. col. mss*, 33:37). Case of Peter Chock vs Mr
     Fordham referred to the court of chancery. Samuel Day-
     ton, Samuel Tyrrell, Jonathan Rose, and Walter Jones ap-
     pear before the council about the petition of the Indian,
     Tachanick (p. 153). Order on a petition of Thos. Tall-
     madge for the inhabitants of Easthampton (see *N. Y. col.
     mss*, 33:38; and, *L. P.* 2:193).   160
29   Robert Cody, John Parsons, Jacob Dayton, John Field,
     Sam'l Sherry, Oliver Norris, Wm. Hamilton, Daniel Kief,
     Simon Hillyer, John Richardson, inhabitants of East-
     hampton complain that the town would lay out no land
     for them; order thereon (see *Doc. hist. N. Y.* 3:351;
     Q 3:213). Order on a petition of Jacobus de be Abois (see
     N. Y. col. mss, 33:42). Stephan van Cortlandt and Mr
     Rumbouts vs Peter Lansingh about Indian lands.   161

Aug. 9   The inhabitants of Hempstead and Oysterbay appearing ac-
     cording to order referred to the courts. Order on a peti-
     tion of John Hendrick de Bruyne (see *N. Y. col. mss*,
     33:43).   162
7   Conference with Minisink and Tappan Indians.   162
12   Order on petition of Stephen Hussey (see *N. Y. col. mss*,
     33:44). Joris Jacobson and others appear for Brookhaven
     and give reasons for their caveat against the grant to
     Rich'd Gibbs of the land bought by him from Robert Lea-
     cock. Jacobus de be Abois appears on his petition (p. 161). 164
30   Assembly prorogued. Mr Garton ordered to come to New
     York and give an account of the revenues in his hands.
     Sheriffs to give bonds.   164

1686   v. 5

Sep. 1   Conference with five nations of Indians; Arnold interpreter. 165
Conference continued (see *Doc. hist. N. Y.* 1:403-5; Q 1:265-
66). Instructions given to surveyor-general Phil. Wells
for running boundary line with east New Jersey. Order
on a petition of Hendrick Kyler (see *L. P.* 2:197).   167

2   Attorney-general James Graham to draw an address on the
state of the province. Question as to signing a writ of
error decided.   171

6   Address delivered by the attorney general. Indians acknowledge a deed. Richard Hulse forbidden to build on land
south of Seatalcot. Richard Cornell, John Jackson, and
Daniel Whitehead to view the land called Unkechalk
where Samuel Dayton, Samuel Tyrrell, Jonathan Rose, and
Walter Jones live. Land on Cowneck to be reserved out
of Hempstead patent.   171

14   Governor Dongan receives a commission as captain general
and governor in chief of New York and takes the oath.
Anthony Brockhalls, Fred. Flypsen, S. van Cortlandt, J.
Spragge and Gervase Baxter nominated by the king as
council, are sworn in. The swearing of Luke Santen postponed. The governor reads some of his instructions.
Order concerning trade and navigation.   172

16   Order to Major Nicholas de Meyer for an inspection of the
companies of foot in the city. Order to Major Patrick
Mackgregorie muster master to muster all companies in
the province. General order to the militia. Capt. Lucas
Santen to report with his troop of horse.   175

18   Order on a complaint of Mathias Nicolls judge of the admiralty against John Smith a custom house officer; Thos.
Coker and Richard Rogers testify.   176
John Smith is fined and dismissed the service; the governor
remits the fine.   180

20   Christopher Billop deposes that Luke Santen has spoken
scurrilously of the governor. A vessel to be bought for
revenue service at the east end of Long Island. Lucas
Santen to hand in his books and papers for audit and to
turn in revenue moneys weekly. Petitions of George
Battersby late master of the Mariners Adventure and of
Christ Rennolls, Chas. Conner, Phil. Neason, Corn's
Creek, Hogen Neale, and Thos. Salvage referred to the
judge of admiralty.   180

23   Lucas Santen sent for and reprimanded. Edward Antill,
Paulus Schrick, and Thos. Coker recommended for custom
house officers (others wanting).   181

1686   **v. 5**

Nov. 18   Petition of Capt. Colbache's men vs their master rejected
           (see *N. Y. col. mss*, 33:65). Thos. Jeames minister of East-
           hampton to be arrested for preaching a seditious sermon
           (see *N. Y. col. mss*, 33:66-70). Josiah Hubbard subpoenaed.
           Samuel Mullford, Robert Dayton, Sam. Parsons, Benj.
           Concklin, Thos. Osborne, and John Osborne of East
           hampton to be arrested for preaching a seditious sermon
           N. Y. col. mss, 33:71-75): also Thos. Osborne, Stephen
           Hedges, and Mary Perkins for the same offense (see *N. Y.
           col. mss*, 33.76 for all of the above entries; see also *Doc.
           hist. N. Y.* 3:355-56; Q 3:216): order to Mr Hubbart con-
           cerning it. Henry Peirsall appears for Southampton about
           land matters; order thereon. Mr Woodhull appearing for
           Seatalcot about land is referred to the court of exchequer.
           Isaac Platt and Thomas Powell for Huntington referred to
           the same. Notice to be sent to Major Winthrop about his
           land on Long Island. Joab Wright appearing for Oyster-
           bay the town is ordered to purchase all unpurchased lands.
           Order on the difference between Rev. Mr Prudden and his
           parishioners (see *Doc. hist. N. Y.* 3:356; Q 3:216).   183

     20   Report of Messrs Cornhill, Hicks, John Jackson, and Daniel
           Whitehead concerning Southampton lands; John Laughton
           of South'n, Rev. Mr Ebourne of Seatalcot, and John
           Arreson their guides. Shinnecock and Unquechage In-
           dians examined as to their land sales; Sequetagie, Conut-
           cana, and Maersepege sachems likewise.   185

     21   Warrant to issue for the seizure of a ship which coming
           from Ireland has entered at Amboy, N. J.   186

     22   Isaac Swinton clerk of the council sworn to secrecy.
           Charges of John West against Lucas Santen read. Ordi-
           nary keepers to take out licenses.   186

     25   Charges of the attorney-general vs Lucas Santen read.
           John Walwin appointed sheriff, Nich's Manning collector
           and receiver for Cornwall county; military commissions
           there to be made out according to Capt. Palmer's recom-
           mendations. Orders for Capt. Manning concerning trade
           in Kennebec river. Majors Brockholls and Baxter to try
           mutineers on Staten Island. Orders on the petitions of
           Abr'm Corbett (see *N. Y. col. mss*, 33:87) and Rev. Mr
           Jeames (see *N. Y. col. mss*, 33:79); referred.   187

Dec. 6   Petition of Abr'm Corbett granted. Patents for Southamp-
           ton and for Joseph Sackett signed. John Pell to buy un-
           purchased Indian lands in his bounds. Order on a motion
           of Mr Tudor on behalf of Thos. Kelly master of the Ad-

1686   v. 5

venture for a speedy trial. Mr Arnold hands in his
accounts.   187

9   Revenue and other laws to remain in force unless repealed.
Order in re Adventure of Youghall, Thos. Kallan master
(p. 187). Act against pirates and privateers to be prepared.
Lucas Santen charges persons not named with "imbez-
ling" and is ordered to give names. Patents for East-
hampton and for Francis Pero signed.   188

13 Monday to be council day for the kings affairs, Thursday for
public business. Order on the report against Lucas Santen.
Order on a petition of Rev. Mr Ebourne (see *N. Y. col.
mss*, 33:86). Order in re Adventure, Thos. Kelly master
(p. 188). Collector Lucas Santen's accounts to be audited. Patents to Samuel Eborne for Snakeneck and to
John Cornhill for land on Cowneck passed.   189

27 [17?] Brookhaven to lay out and set apart land for the minister.
Patents for Andrew Gibbs, Sam'l Eborne and for Seatalcot
passed.   189

20 Act against privateers read the first time. Order for the
seizure of goods, imported by Crawford and Campell,
Scotch merchants, into East and Southampton. Lucas
Santen brings his answer to the last order about him.   189

23 Simon Sareing, John Treadwell and Jonathan Smith commissioners for Hempstead brought by Henry Filkin before
the council for contempt; clear themselves and are ordered
to set apart land for their minister, Jeremy Hobbart. Same
order sent to Jamaica. Patents for John Seamans, John
D. Bruyne and Andries Camons passed.   190

1687

Jan. 3 Petition of Samuel Rusco referred to the law. Order concerning Francis Stepney a dancing master from Boston (see
N. Y. col. mss, 35:7).   191

6   Order on a petition of Francis Stepney (see *N. Y. col. mss*,
35:3, 8). Patents for town of Westchester, for John
Chrushron, and John Pullon passed.   191

10 Capt. Billop appointed surveyor of highways on Staten
Island. Wm. Beakman's patent passed.   192

13 Lucas Santen suspended from the office of collector and receiver, and to be arrested; Peter de la Noy appointed col-
lector pro tem.   192

Lucas Santen ordered to deliver to S. van Cortlandt all books,
and to the governor all money in his hands.   194

Lucas Santen refuses to deliver the books and Isaac Swinton
is ordered to search for and seize them with the help of the
sheriff of New York.   194

1687   **v. 5**

Minutes from this date to July 6, exclusive may be found in *N. Y. col. mss,* 35:14, 18, 19, 21, 22, 23, 24, 31, 33, 36, 37, 39, 42, 43, 45, 48, 50, 52, 54, 58, 60, 61, 62, 64, 65, 66, 67, 70, 71, 72.

July 7   Gov. Dongan absent at Albany; Major van Cortlandt to take charge of the seals, Major Flypsen of the keys of the presses containing the books and records, John Knight of the books etc. and to act as deputy secretary vice Isaac Swinton deceased.   195

19   Major Brockholls comes from Albany and Schenectady for men and provisions (see *Doc. hist. N. Y.* 1:244; Q 1:150). Major Willett to raise 60 men in Queens, and Col. Bayard the same number in New York counties.   195

26   Charles Lodwyck, John de la Val, and George Mackenzie to take an inventory of the books and records in the secretary's office with a view of opening it for public business. Copies of proclamations and acts of council to be made.   196

30   Above copies to be sent to the sheriffs of all counties; rules for receiving and opening them.   196

Aug. 1   Keys of the secretary's office to be delivered to John Knight the inventory having been taken.   197

2   Petition of Richard Perrott of Middlessex county, Va., to allow Judge Nichols to testify for him in a land matter granted, and the judge testifies.   197

18   Gov. Dongan returned. Account of expenses in the war against the French read (see *Doc. hist. N. Y.* 1:252; Q 1:154). Order on a petition of Daniel Duchemin et al. (see *N. Y. col. mss,* 35:92).   198

19   Taxes to be laid for paying the war expenses; bills to be drawn for that purpose (see *Doc. hist. N. Y.* 1:252; Q 1:154-55). Assessors to hasten their work. Matthew Mayhew ordered to deliver the prisoners lately taken in Dukes county with the plate etc. in their possession to Ensign Sharp.   198

20   Bill for raising a penny in the pound on the estates in Kings, Queens, Dukes, Dutchess, Richmond, Orange, Westchester, and Suffolk counties passed (see *Doc. hist. N. Y.* 1:252; Q 1:155).   199

26   Order calling Joseph Harwood and Samuel Windor as evidences for Thos. Hawarden vs Rob't Allison (see *N. Y. col. mss,* 35:93) about a ketch, Mich'l Vaughten master.   199

27   Robert Allison examined and ordered to give security for his good behavior.   200

Sep. 2 Instructions to Judge Palmer going to England read and approved. Bill to raise one half penny in the pound on the estate in New York, Albany, and Ulster counties passed. Order concerning assessors. Bill for regulating the collection of excise money passed. Patents for George Lockhart and Thos. Hawarden signed. Petition of Harman Dowsen for land granted. 200

5 Time for making assessments in Suffolk county extended. Letter to be sent to the governor of Canada about Major McGregory a prisoner of the French (see *Doc. hist. N. Y.* 1:265; Q 1:162). 201

6 Letter to the governor of Canada read and approved. 202

7 Letters from Gov. de Nonville of Canada, from Robert Livingston, and from Mayor Peter Schuyler of Albany received. Judge Nichols to translate Gov. de Nonville's letter. Examination by Rob't Livingston of John Rosee an inhabitant of Albany who was in Canada with Anthony Lis Pinar read; ordered that the mayor of New York examine Anth'y Lis Pinar, Dirck van der Heyden, Fred'k and Naning Harmsen who escaped from prison at Quebec. Schenectady to be fortified; Indian scouts to be kept towards Corlaers lake; Christian Indians, coming from Canada to the five nations, to be sent to New York. No Indian corn or peas to be exported from Albany or Ulster counties. Inquiries to be made at Albany how long ago trade was carried on with the Indians who have straws or pipes through their noses and the farther Indians (see *Doc. hist. N. Y.* 1:266; Q 1:162-63). Carpenters to work on the Albany fortifications. Anthony Lispinar or la Fleur to be sent to New York from Albany if suspected that they have kept any intelligence with Canada. Petition of Donald Coffee vs John Palmer (see *N. Y. col. mss,* 35:98). 202

9 Translation of Gov. de Nonville's letter and Gov. Dongan's answer read. Mr Laprary to take the governor's letter to Canada. The French are reported as preparing 1500 pairs of snowshoes; women, children and old men of the five nations to be sheltered against a French invasion at Catskill, on Livingston's land, and along the river (see *Doc. hist. N. Y.* 1:272; Q 1:166). 204

11 Militia of the province to be put in readiness to meet the French (see *Doc. hist. N. Y.* 1:272; Q 1:866). Col. Nich's Bayard for New York, Capt. Thos. Stillwell for Richmond, Major Stephanus van Cortlandt for Kings, Major Thos. Willett and Capt. John Jaxon for Queens, Col. Thos.

Young, Major John Howell and Capt. Joseph Fordham, Major Fred. Flypsen for Westchester to be in command and appoint subaltern officers. 205

22 Letter from Rob't Livingston received with propositions of the Oneidas and Maquaes and answers of the mayor of Albany (see *N. Y. col. mss*, 35:99). Order on a petition of Phil. Smith for land at Tappan near Dr Lockhart's, Bill for naturalizing Daniel Duchemin et al (p. 198) passed. Order directing Major Chambers to have his men ready and mounted for a march to Albany. 205

27 Resolves of the court of lieutenancy in New York city confirmed (see *N. Y. col. mss*, 35:103). Men who cannot go on military service to Albany to send substitutes. 206

29 Order on a petition of Wm. Merrit (see *N. Y. col. mss*, 35:104). Steph. van Cortlandt appointed mayor, Robert Hammond sheriff of New York. 206

Oct. 8 Col. John Young suspended from the council because he and Major Howell have mustered in the Suffolk militia men unfit for service. James Graham sworn of the council vice Young. Bill to prevent abuses in the excise read. Col. Young and Major Howell to pay for the clothing and arms issued to Capt. Fordham's company of Suffolk. Measures to be taken to restore Spaniards kept as slaves in the province to freedom. Patent to John de la Val for land in Ulster county passed. James Graham and Wm. Nichols to audit the accounts of George Brewerton (see *N. Y. col. mss*, 35:107). —— Provoost, John Trompeet, and partners to pay quitrent for their land in Albany county. Order on a petition of Henricus Selyns and his wife Margaret (see *N. Y. col. mss*, 35:106). Letters of administration not to be granted to the executors named in the will of Mary Mathews deceased. 207

11 Order on petition of the mayor etc. of Albany (see *N. Y. col. mss*, 35:114) [Marginal note, that this entry belongs to the 25th of October]. Bill to prevent abuses and frauds in the excise passed. Patent to Wessel ten Brook for land at Esopus passed. Thos. Walton's quitrent for land on Staten Island fixed. Sheriffs of all counties to continue in office, Peter Schuyler likewise as mayor of Albany. Order concerning the shoemaking and tanning trade. Sherrif of Albany to collect the quitrents due by Provoost, Trompeet et al (p. 207). Christian Indians and children of Christian parents brought from Campeache and Laverde Cruisa (Vera Cruz) as slaves, to be set free. 209

25 Above order on petition of mayor etc. of Albany repeated
(p. 209). Order for the pay of George Brewerton. Petition of Richard Tinker (see *N. Y. col. mss*, 35:116) rejected.
Patents passed: John Knight for land on Rondout creek,
called Knightsfield between Anna Beek's and Jacob
Rudsen's land; John Pell for Pellham manor; John Lansing
for land on the plain south of Albany; Johannes Wandall
and Johannes Lansing for land on Ruttenkill, Albany;
Harman Dowsen and Theunis Dowsen for land called
Pessatinck in Orange county; Thos. Lovelace for land on
Staten Island. Petition of Dirck Johnson Hooglandt vs
Peter Lott (see *N. Y. col. mss*, 35:115) referred. Major
Anthony Brockholls empowered to sign warrants, passes
etc. during Gov. Dongan's absence in Albany.   210

Nov. 10 Major Brockholls presiding. Order on a petition of Samuel
Burt brother of Richard Burt deceased, master of the ship
Robert of London (see *N. Y. col. mss*, 35:118); Pierre
Peyre, Peter Reverey and Michael Peck testify as to the
manner of his death by drowning.   211

19 Inventory of books and papers on board the Robert, Richard Burt late master made by Abr'm de Peyster, John
de la Val and Samuel Burt to be recorded. Letters come
from England for the governor to be forwarded to Albany, Messrs. Graham and van Cortlandt paying the
charges.   212

21 Duplicate of a letter from the commissioners of plantations,
brought by Gov. Hamilton of East New Jersey to be recorded.   212

25 Orders for collecting duties on imported goods brought to
East New Jersey. Application of Jacob Leisler for permission to enter a wreck granted.   213

29 Order on petition of Henry Willis and Edward Titus,
quakers of Hempstead (see *N. Y. col. mss*, 35:122). Samuel Burt appointed administrator of his brother's effects
by the mayor's court confirmed.   213

Dec. 3 Order on being informed by Daniel Mackreig that David
Toshack of Orange county is dead without heirs in the
country.   214

5 Jacob and David Robles referred to the governor with their
petition for denization (see *N. Y. col. mss*, 35:123). Report
of the proceedings between the governor of East New Jersey and Mr Graham about a port of entry to be recorded.   214

24 Order on the petition of John Robinson for letters of administration on the estate of Phil. Jones (see *N. Y. col. mss*,
35:125).   215

1687   **v. 5**

26   Order on the petition of Thos. Meech late master of the ship
      Johanna; John Joost and Hendrick ten Eyck to assist
      him.   215

1688

Jan. 3   George Brown to go to the east end of Long Island about
           the transportation of whale-oil out of the province.   215

      7   Order on petition of Richard Smith against Samuel Eborne
           (see *N. Y. col. mss*, 35:127). S. van Cortlandt and James
           Graham receivers of the revenue to pay George Brown
           (p. 215) on account for his services.   216

      8   Warrant to impress sloops issued to Thos. Hawarden for
           raising the brigantine Richmond aground on the shoals
           near Thos. Walton's place on Staten Island.   216

      23   Trial of the case between Richard Smith and Saml. Eborne. 216

Feb. 2   Thos. Stevens justice of the peace dismissed from office and
           with his brother Edward committed for having fraudu-
           lently procured a marriage licence for Wm. Norris and
           Jane Hayes their niece and the daughter-in-law of Norris.
           Indian post to Albany.   217

      13   Letters of administration on the estate of Mrs Elizabeth
           Graveratt granted to Pieter de Riemer. George Brown
           called back from east Long Island.   218

      18   Order on information given by Richard Hartford com-
           mander of the Royal James, that Simon Grover master
           of the sloop Primrose carries on an illegal trade. Augur's
           sloop and goods, seized at Easthampton to be sent to
           New York.   218

      27   Petition of Elias Doughty, Richard Cornhill and Thos.
           Hicks, justices of the peace of Queens county (see *N. Y.
           col. mss*, 35:130) referred.   219

Mar. 6   Order on petition of Richard Blacklidge (see *N. Y. col. mss*,
           35:132). Order on petition of Thos. Roberts (see *N. Y.
           col. mss*, 35:131).   220

      13   Major Baxter comes from Albany with the governor's in-
           structions that the council shall provide for the war ex-
           penses; other colonies to be called upon for assistance (see
           Doc. hist. N. Y. 1:273-74; Q 1:167). George Brown (p. 218)
           paid off. Order on petition of Samuel Eborne (see *N. Y.
           col. mss*, 35:133).   220

      28   Gov. Dongan returned. Letter from the king received;
           copies to be sent to the other colonies. Proceedings be-
           tween Gov. Dongan and the French agents Father Valiant
           and Mon. Demon at Albany read; also letters between
           Gov. Dongan and Gov. de Nonville. Address to the king
           to be drawn (see Hough. *Pemaquid*. p. 132).   221

1688   **v. 5**

30 Letter to neighboring governors read and approved. Salaries of judges of oyer and terminer to continue (see *N. Y. col. mss*, 35:134). Act for instructing negroes in Christian religion to be drawn. Christ'r Garvy to carry the governor's letters to Maryland etc.   222

Ap. 2 Proclamation to issue for a public thanksgiving that the queen is with child. Stephanus van Cortlandt appointed deputy auditor of the revenues by Wm. Blathwayt and sworn in. Order on a petition of Domine Henricus Selyns (see *N. Y. col. mss*, 35:136). John Cavalier messenger of the council to summon the jurors who tried the case of Josia Hubbert sheriff of Suffolk county, ex dem Rex vs the sloop Brothers' Adventure, Jonathan Hall master. Order on a petition of Daniel Verveelen (see *N. Y. col. mss*, 35:135).   222

9 Justices of the peace who have not made a return of the names of assessors sworn in by them called before the council. Order in re Cornelius Barnes, John Okey, Theophilus Probasco, John Stryker, yeomen of Flatbush vs Adrian Bennet and Jocabus van de Water of Brooklyn in error. Order in re Thos. Lamberts, Randolph Evans, Jacobus van de Water, Jeronimus Rapalie and Adrian Bennet vs Corn's Barnes and John Okey in error. Order on petition of Matthew Midleton (see *N. Y. col. mss*, 35:137).   223

12 Warrant of survey for land on Staten Island granted to Richard Mitchel (see *N. Y. col. mss*, 35:138). Order on petition of Benj. Collier (see *N. Y. col. mss*, 35:145). Order on petition of Capt. Robert Augur (see *N. Y. col. mss*, 35:139). Order on petition of Dom'e Henricus Selyns (p. 222).   224

16 Order on petition of John Okey and John Hegeman (see *N. Y. col. mss*, 35:146). Mathias Harvy and Edward Griffin of Flushing, Nathaniel Denton and Joseph Thorston of Jamaica, Abr'm Smith and Rich'd Valentine of Hempstead, Nath'l Cooley and Job Wright of Oysterbay are returned by Justice Daniel Whitehead as refusing to take the prescribed oaths as assessors, and are summoned before the council. Col. Young and Isaac Arnold summoned on charges preferred by Daniel Whitehead ranger of Long Island. Inhabitants of Kings and Queens counties to repair the Stony hill and the highway between Bedford and Jamaica. Justices to lay out highways between the respective towns. Mathias Nichols, Elias Dowty,

Thos. Hicks and John Townsend to sit as court of oyer
and terminer for the trial of Wm. Jones of Queens county,
accused of sodomy.   225

21 Jurors summoned by John Cavalier (p. 222) examined;
affidavit of Thos. Howard in the same case; Isaac Arnold
summoned (see *N. Y. col. mss,* 35:147).   226

26 Assessors for Queens summoned (p. 225) and committed
for trial before a special court of oyer and terminer; and
new assessors to be elected for the respective towns.
Mode of collecting assessments prescribed. John Pell,
John Palmer, Wm. Richardson justices, and Joseph Lee
clerk of the peace for Westchester county appear on the
petition of Benj. Collier (p. 224). Order concerning accounts of, and actions before the justices; all towns and
liberties to maintain their own poor and pay for the killing of wolves.   227

30 Letters received and read from Gov. de Nonville of Canada, and from Dirck Wessells. Propositions of Gov. Dongan to the six nations (see *N. Y. col. mss,* 35:148) read
and approved. Major McGregory's accounts for traveling
expenses from Canada allowed. Accounts of Robert Livingston for disbursements to the soldiers, Indians, French
prisoners (see *Doc. hist. N. Y.* 1:274; Q 1:167); and for
repairs of the fort at Albany read.   228

May 3 A new levy to be made, as the taxes lately ordered are
not sufficient; quota expected from every county; the attorney-general to draw an act accordingly (see *Doc. hist.
N. Y.* 1:274-75; Q 1:167-68). Order on petition of Joseph
Fordham (see *N. Y. col. mss,* 35:149). Col. Young and
Isaac Arnold answer the charges of Daniel Whitehead (p.
225); order thereon. Proceedings in the trial of the sloop
Brothers' Adventure, Jonathan Hall master read (p. 226).
Isaac Arnold appointed searcher and surveyor of customs
for Suffolk county. Robert Lapraire to run the line between Breucklin and Flatbush. Fine of Abr'm Corbett
(see *N. Y. col. mss,* 35:151).   229

6   Gov. Dongan to go to Albany; scouts to lie in the Indian
castles and the governor to send if necessary for the Boston forces and make presents to the Indians.   231

7   Minissink Indians to be called to Albany for cooperation
with the six nations.   231

14 Order against destroying trees on the high roads. John
Cavalier's account of expenses as messenger allowed.
Orders on petitions: of Dow Johnson (see *N. Y. col. mss,*
35:153); of John Hoagland (see *N. Y. col. mss,* 35:154);

1688	v. 5

of Mathias Harvy (see *N. Y. col. mss,* 35:156); of Weyntil Teunis, widow of Tierck Kiberts for a survey of her land adjoining the lot of Abr'm Rycken in Queens county. Col. Bayard, Major van Cortlandt and Robert Lepraire to run the lines between Breucklin and Newtown. Col. John Young late high sheriff of Yorkshire on Long Island prays for a quietus.	232

17	Order on complaint of Col. Lewis Morris against sheriff Benj. Collier of Westchester county. Letter to be sent to the president and council of Pennsylvania about quitrents in the three lower counties on the Delaware. Sheriffs to bring in the money raised under the late tax-acts. Attorney-general Wm. Nicholls to receive pay for services. Patent to the town and corporation of ―― town, Ulster county, passed. Major Flypsen and Col. Bayard to audit the accounts of Major Stephanus van Cortlandt and James Graham as receivers of the revenue; their report to be the receivers' discharge. Acts for raising £2555 and for continuing the salary of judges passed. Acts for the religious education of Indian and negro slaves; to prohibit shoemakers from "using the mistery of tanning hides" read.	233

30	Gov. Dongan absent at Albany. A military watch to be kept in New York city, privateers being repotted off the coast. Peter Bogardus to carry Long Island Indians to Albany. Governor's instructions to the members of council remaining in New York, Majors van Cortlandt and Philippse, and Col. Bayard read and to be recorded.	234

June 2	Order on petition of Thos. Walton against the sheriff of Richmond county. Copies of the act for raising £2555 to be sent to all counties.	235

6	John Knight late deputy secretary delivers the records, etc. to the council (see *N. Y. col. mss,* 35:162). Accounts of Josiah Hobart sheriff of Suffolk county for the collection of taxes allowed.	235

July 26	Order on petition of Domine Henricus Selyns (see *N. Y. col. mss,* 35:167).	236

28	Gov. Dongan returned. Confirmatory patents granted: Elizabeth van Dyke for land at Kattskill; Maria van Rensselaer, Hendrick van Nesse, Gerrit Teunissen and Jacobus van Cortlandt for land at Hossick; Jan van Loane, Joachem Staats and Johannes Provoost for Louenenburge, Albany county; Lewis de Boyce for land near the Palls, Ulster county; Wm. Cox for a lot in New York city. Patents to Wm. Nicolls for all the islands on the south side of

1688   v. 5

Long Island; to Peter Schuyler for land opposite Med-
lyne island at the Long reach, Dutchess county; to Garret
Aertsen, Arien Rose, John Elton, Hendrick Kipp and
Jacob Kipp for land in Dutchess county. Gov. Dongan
to deliver the seals of the province to Sir Edmond Andros.
Consideration of paying the war debts deferred until the
new governor has arrived.   236

30   Spanish Indian slaves professing Christianity to be released
and sent home. Col. Bayard and Major van Cortlandt
to make up the accounts of the officers and soldiers of the
expedition to Albany. New York being annexed to the
government of New England the collection of the £2555
tax is suspended. Order concerning the pay of officers
and soldiers. Quakers referred to the courts with their
petition (see *N. Y. col. mss*, 35:168, 169). Petition of
Robert Ellison (see *N. Y. col. mss*, 35:169) rejected.   237

Aug. 2 Major Brockholls presiding. Order on the report of Col.
Bayard, Major van Cortlandt and Robert van Gunlin about
Breuklin and Flatbush. Act about tanning hides (p. 233)
passed. Patents to the town of Huntington, L. I.; to
Godfrid Deelius for the pasture at Albany; to Jochem
Staats for land in Ulster county passed.   238
Paytable of the officers and soldiers of the Albany expe-
dition.   239

1686

June 3   Order from the committee of trade and foreign plantations
Whitehall   to the governor and council of New York, to transmit
quarterly reports on the state of the colony.   241

1683

Jan. 27   Royal commission appointing John Spragge secretary of the
St James   province.   242

1684

Oct. 10   Report of the Connecticut commissioners, Volkin Gold,
Stanford   Jonathan Sellick, Dan'l Sherman, John Hariman, of their
meeting with the New York commissioners, Lt. Col. John
Young, Capt. John Pell and Surveyor Phil Welles, and
fixing the boundaries from Lyons point on Byram river;
approved by Governors Thos. Dongan of New York and
Robert Treat of Connecticut at Millford, February 10,
1685.

Vol. 6 1691-93

1691

Mar. 19   Arrival of Gov. Henry Sloughter; he takes the oaths and
publishes his commission (see *Doc. hist. N. Y.* 2:358-59;
Q 2:202). Major Ingoldsby brings before the council
Joost Stool with a letter from Jacob Leisler. Leisler, Mil-
bourne and his council called, but only the latter with
Delancey appears; Leisler refusing.   1

20   Joseph Dudley, Fred. Philipps, Stephanus van Cortlandt,
Gabriel Minvielle, Chidley Brooke, Thos. Willett and Wm.
Pinhorne sworn in as members of the council. Papers
relating to Leisler delivered to the secretary. Col. Nich's
Bayard and Wm. Nicolls sworn of the council. Jacob
Leisler brought in as prisoner, also Abr'm Governeur,
Gerard Beeckman, Wm. Churcher, Corn's Plevier, Hen-
rick Jansen van Boerton, Wm. Lawrence, Thos. Williams,
John Coe, Myndert Coarten, Rob't Leacock and Johannes
Vernillie (see *Doc. hist. N. Y.* 2:359; Q 2:202). John
Lawrence commissioned and sworn in as mayor of the
city, Thos. Clarke as coroner of the city and county of
New York.   2

21   Sheriffs appointed; Thos. Lyndell for New York, Gerard
Strycker for Kings, John Jackson for Queens, Josias
Hobbard for Suffolk, Thos. Stillwell for Richmond, Benj.
Collier for Westchester, Cornelius Bogardus for Ulster
and Dutchess, Gasper Teller for Albany counties. Day of
meeting for the general assembly fixed, and writs of election sent out. Thos. Stillwell sworn in as sheriff.   3

23   Col. Dudley, van Cortlandt and Ch. Brooke appointed a
committee for the examination of the prisoners (see *Doc.
hist. N. Y.* 2:362; Q 2:204). Fred. Philipps, Gabr. Monvielle and Col. Willett to be a committee for taking account of the stores in the fort and of the necessary repairs to it. Foot companies of the garrison. Salary due
to James Graham for service in the collector's office.
Thomas Newtown appointed attorney-general. Jasper
Teller and Corn. Bogardus sworn in as sheriffs.   4

24   Andrew Gibb to be clerk of the peace for Queens. Thos.
Fort Wm.   Lyndall sworn in as sheriff of New York county. Joseph
Henry   Lee to be clerk of the peace in Westchester county. Sir
Robert Robinson, Col. Wm. Smith, Wm. Pinhorne, John
Lawrence, Jasper Hicks, Major Richard Ingoldsby, Col.
John Young and Capt. Isaac Arnold to hold a special
court of oyer and terminer for the trial of the prisoners
(see *Doc. hist. N. Y.* 2:362; Q 2:204). Wm. Beekman,
Joh's Kipp, Wm. Merritt, Brant Schuyler, Balt. Bayard

and John Merritt, sworn in as aldermen. Mr De Lansee,
Eben Wilson, Thos. Coker, Teunis de Key and Thos.
Clarke as councilmen. Capt. John Tuder to be register
of the admiralty and notary public. Wm. Pinhorne to
be recorder of the city of New York. Capt. Wm. Kidd
complains against Capt. Jasper Hicks commander of the
man of war Archangel for imprisoning one of his men.
Valuable services of Capt. Kidd.   5

25 Col. Wm. Smith takes the oath as councillor. James Barrey
brought in a prisoner and admitted to bail. Capt. Rich'd
Forster's petition granted. Asher Levy's bail. Court of
admiralty to be held. John Joost to give bail; also Daniel
Lawrence. Act to be proposed to the next assembly authorizing members of the council to act as justices of the
peace.   7

26 George Lockhart appointed to be clerk of the market. Fran-
cis Blin and another Frenchman prisoners to be sent on
board of the Archangel man of war. Joseph Dudley and
Thomas Johnson sworn in as judges of the admiralty.
Leisler and fellow prisoners (see *Doc. hist. N. Y.* 2:362;
Q 2:204). James Graham's salary as collector.   8

30 Nicolas Bayard, Steph. van Cortlandt and Wm. Pinhorne
to be a committee for preparing evidence against prisoners; Wm. Nicholls, Geo. Farewell and James Emmett to
be king's counsel in the case (see *Doc. hist. N. Y.* 2:363;
Q 2:205). Tramps to be arrested.   9

Ap. 1 Richard Smith sworn in as justice of the peace for Suffolk
county. Account of Macgregerie's burial (see *Doc. hist.
N. Y.* 2:363; Q 2:205). Col. Dudley's account paid. Elias
Makelson of Aquihanon in East New Jersey and John
Capitaine of Bergen, N. J. to be arrested.   9

2 Tacapain sachem of Masepeeg, L. I. with other Indians before the council.   10

p. m. Presents given to the Indians. Day of thanksgiving. Mc-
Gregory's purchase of Indian lands on John Peache's
creek, Hudson river, confirmed.   11

4(?) Col. Smith and Chidley Brook to swear in the assembly.
Proclamation to go out concerning the late troubles.   12

10 Petition of widow Anna Schuyler, concerning some beavers
considered. Isaac Arnold sworn in as justice of the peace
for Suffolk county.   13

13 Order on petition of the daughters of Dr Hanmore deceased.
Opinion of council concerning Leisler's authority to act
upon a letter addressed to Lt. Gov. Nicholson (see *Doc. hist.
N. Y.* 2:365-66; Q 2:207).   13

1691   **v. 6**

pairs to the fort by order of Leisler referred to a committee.   23

6 Robert Livingston's account for Indian presents ordered paid.   24

9 Thos. Carhart to have the land claimed by Widow Stillwell.   24

11 Arms taken from citizens of New York during the late troubles to be returned.   24

12 Payment of charges for the governor's journey to Albany and of his salary ordered.   25

13 Salary of Jarvis Marshall as doorkeeper of the council ordered paid.   25

14 Council advise that it is necessary the sentence against Leisler etc. be carried out (see *Doc. hist. N. Y.* 2:374; Q 2:212).   26

15 John Thompson ordered to be released from prison. Joseph Dudley appointed chief justice; Thos. Johnson, Wm. Smith, Steph. van Cortlandt and Wm. Pinkhorne justices of the supreme court. Col. Smith appointed judge of the prerogative court for Suffolk county; salary of the supreme court justices fixed.   26

16 Opinion of the house of representatives coinciding with council in the Leisler affairs (see *Doc. hist. N. Y.* 2:375; Q 2:212).   27

18 Fred. Philipps, Nichs. Bayard, Chidley Brooke and Gabriel Monvielle appointed a committee to audit certain public accounts.   28

27 Peter Schuyler, Dirck Wessells, Evert Bancker, John Beecker,
Albany Jan Janse Blycker, Gerrit Ryerson, Gerrit Teunissen, Kilian van Rensselaer, Martin Gerritsen, Derick Teunissen, Sander Glenn, Peter Vosburgh, Claes Ripse and Egbert Teunissen sworn in as justices of the peace for Albany city and county; Peter Schuyler also as judge of the common pleas. Proclamation to issue against exportation of provisions out of the county.   28

June 3 Col. Dudley to go to the New England colonies and ask
Albany for assistance against the French.   29

5 A company of volunteers to be raised for cooperation with the Indians against Canada.   29

29 Troops for the defense of Albany to be raised in New Jersey.
Ft. William Call on the southern colonies for assistance in defending
Henry Albany, " the key and centre of all their matye's territories on the main of America."   30

July 4 Col. Bayard, Col. Smith, Major Ingoldsby, Capts. Cortlandt, Wm. Merritt, Schuyler, de Key, Wilson and Gore to be a committee for inspecting the fortifications of New York city. Fred. Philipps, Col. Bayard and Major Minvielle to examine Jan Cornelisse having misbehaved in an expedition to the eastward. Flour borrowed at Albany for the Canada expedition ordered paid. Representation of the state of the province to be sent to England. Augustine Graham to be surveyor-general vice Alex. Boyle deceased. Order on a petition by John Smith against the corporation of New York. Order granting land on Staten Island to Wm. Britton yeoman.   32

7   Warrants to impress seamen for the Archangel issued. Highland Indians before the council. Jarvis Marshall to be marshall of the admiralty, and water baily.   33

8   French Indians near Albany. Adolph Philipps sent to Connecticut for troops. Acts of assembly to be sent to the sheriffs.   33

11   Packets for southern colonies delivered to John Perry's post; for Connecticut to Mr Newtown.   34

14   Public moneys collected in Leisler's time to be accounted for.   35

18   Peter de la Noy's account for money disbursed as receiver by Leisler's order not accepted and he is ordered to refund. 35

21   Orders on petitions: by Nich's de Mauritz for restitution of or payment for guns taken from him during the Leisler troubles and now in the blockhouse at Albany; by Mr Antill. Payment to Christ'n Laurier for the hire of his sloop Grace ordered.   36

23   Gov. Sloughter dead; proceedings of council relating to it; Doctors Thornhill, Karbyle, Brett, Gaudineau, Tienhoven and Lockhart to hold a post mortem examination.   36

24   Wm. Nicolls, Mr Graham, Judge Johnson and the sheriff to examine the governor's papers; Col. Bayard, Judge Johnson and Mr Lyndale to make arrangements for the governor's burial in Stuyvesant's vault.   37

25   The secretary to inform New England governors of the death of Gov. Sloughter. Public papers, taken out of the governor's returned.   38

26   Major Richard Ingoldsby to act as commander-in-chief; he is sworn in and proclamation to that effect issued.   38

28   Capt. Jasper Hicks refused to acknowledge the authority of the commander-in-chief; order of council thereon. Philipp French, Thos. Wenham, Jonathan Selleck and Capt. Alloway to inspect provisions sent ashore by Capt. Hicks as unfit. Mr Broadbent to receive part of Leisler's salary. 40

29   Rip van Dam appointed in place of Phil. French. Letters by Gov. Sloughter to the king, to Mr Blathwayte etc.

1691   **v. 6**

referred to a committee.   The attorney general to write
letters to the lord president and Lord Nottingham on behalf of the commander-in-chief and council.   Order on a
petition by shipmaster for dispatch.   Treasury affairs.   40

30   Charges of Mr Graham for his journey to Albany ordered
paid.   Report of the doctors as to the cause of the governor's death.   Money to be sent to Albany for Mr
Schuyler's expedition to Canada.   42

31   Order on petition by Cornelius Jacobs master of the sloop
Planter against Capt. Hicks of the Archangel for detention
of his men.   Shipmasters refuse convoy by the Archangel
for only 20 leagues.   42

Aug. 1   Capt. Hicks refused permission to leave the station to convoy
ships to England.   43

3   Warrant ordered to issue for the payment of men discharged
from the sloop Planter Corn. Jacobs master.   44

6   Papers for England signed and Capt. Alloway put under
bonds for their safe delivery or to sink them if necessary. 44

8   Provisions etc. taken for Major Schuyler's expedition to
Canada ordered to be paid.   Public accounts.   Order on
complaint by Joseph Lee against Robert Bloomer sr and jr.
Day for meeting of council on ordinary business fixed.
Order on Francis Huling's report concerning escaped
French prisoners.   44

13   Chidley Brooke to have credit for money sent to Albany for
Major Schuyler's expedition.   Beer measures fixed.
Money advanced for the Canada expedition ordered to be
repaid.   Robert Bloomer sr and jr to be arrested for non-
appearance on the charge made by Joseph Lee, Wm
Laughter and Lieut. John Horton.   45

15   Wm Blankistein appears before the council as representative
of the committee of Maryland.   46

17   Capt. Kidd's prize not to pay customs duties.   47

20   R. Livingston of Albany before the council reports that the
Mohawks are uneasy on account of the running away of
some French prisoners to Esopus; orders sent to Esopus
for their apprehension.   Matthew Mayhew reports disorders
at Martins Vineyard and Nantuckett.   New officers to be
appointed.   Dirck Wessells of Albany to be rewarded for
his good services in Indian affairs.   47

24   Rumors of a French invasion.   Major Beekman of Esopus
to send troops to Albany; Col. Treat of Connecticut to do
the same.   Major Peter Schuyler presents to council the
journal of his expedition against Canada.   48

1691   **v. 6**

Mott. Order on a petition by Edward Antill for land on
Staten Island.   60

29   Elizabeth Mott. Inhabitants of Plunderneck, L. I. complain
that as their lands lie between Flatbush and Newtown they
do not know to which militia company they belong.
Christian Snydacker to be under the captain of Flatbush,
and Joris Kimball under Newtown. Order on a petition of
Barent Vempe, Sanders Glenn and Johannes Glenn sons-
in-law of Snert Teunissen van Velsen killed at Schenec-
tady for land.   61

Nov. 9   Salary of Judge Johnson to be paid.   62

13   Extremely cold weather. Clothing for the soldiers at Al-
bany. Collection of taxes urged again.   63

19   Expenses of Hendrick Gerritse wounded in the Canada expedition ordered paid. Petition of Barent Vempe, etc.
(p. 62) granted. Jeremiah Tothill to be paid for piloting
the Archangel.   63

Dec. 30   The attorney-general to write a letter to the secretary of
state on the military forces sent to Albany and the bad
behavior of the other colonies.   64

31   Hendrick Gerritse (p. 63) to receive a pension. Salary of
collector, his employes, and of gauger fixed.   65

1692

Jan. 8   Letters to Lord Nottingham and Mr Blathwaite signed.
Petition of Edward Antill granted.   65

11   Caleb Heathcote's bill for 6 watchcoats for the garrison to
be paid. Thos. Wenham's bill for supplies furnished the
sloop Planter to be paid. Letter from Albany by the land
post announces an Indian defeat by the French at Corlaers
lake. Present to the five nations ordered for which the
deputy-receiver at Albany is to give the money. Johannes
Kipp and Jacobus Cortlandt to be administrators of Mary
Loockerman's estate vice Joh's Vanbrugh. John Perry's
post to Virginia.   66

28   Order on petition by William Thompson for expenses in
nursing Nicholas Reynolds a sick soldier. Custom house
in bad repairs. Leisler's widow to find other quarters.   68

Feb. 11   Order on a petition by Philipp Philipps for land on Tapan
creek. Bill of John Pelletreaux for candles for the garrison
ordered paid. Salary etc. of John Clapp clerk of the Assembly to be paid. Order on petition by John Williamse
Rome surety for his brother Jacob Williamse Rome.   68

22   Thos. Garton to be judge of the common pleas for Ulster
county. Capt. Bradshaw at Albany to discourage his
soldiers from deserting. Serg't Windiford to be court-

1692   **v. 6**

martialled.   Mathew Plowman's accounts as collector.
Salary of doorkeeper Jarvis Marshall ordered paid.   Peter
Delanoy's debts to government (p. 35).   Custom house to
be repaired.   69

25   Audit of Mathew Plowman's accounts ordered.   Payment to
James Moody for "navigating" the woodboat of the
garrison.   Payment to Jacobus Cortlandt.   Order in a suit
for ejectment of Fred. Philipps against the tenant of
Papirinimon.   71

28   Fortifications of New York to be repaired but the mayor etc.
refuse assistance.   Carmen to do duty for the fort.   72

Mar. 3   Albert Bos, Isaac Sandford, George Stoffell and Peter D'Milt
accused of having spoken disrespectfully of the government
at the house of Peter King.   Lieut. Hutchins suspected of
correspondence with disaffected persons to be removed to
Albany.   Day of thankgiving ordered.   Proclamation to
issue for insuring the peace disturbed by "factious and
seditious persons at Boston."   Examination of Albert Bos,
Peter D'Milt and Jan de Forrest ordered.   Ducking stool
and pillory for women to be provided.   73

9   Jarvis Marshall ordered to bring before the council James
Berry and his servant Daniel Lawrence of Queens county
for resisting the justices of the peace.   75

Richard Ponton and Robert Bloomersen, of Westchester
county to be arrested by John Jennings for seditious words.
Capias to issue against James Berry and Daniel Lawrence.   76

17   Payment for making copies of revenue acts passed by the
assembly ordered.   Ashton's bill for firewood for the
garrison to be paid.   Fred. Philipps, Lieut. Col. Monviele
and Chidley Brooke offer to pay the soldiers, the collector
to refund their advances.   Orders on petitions: by Andrew
Gibb for land on the south side of Long Island between
Winganhappagne and Orowake; by Thos. Barker for land
on Cowneck, L. I.; of Miles Forster for renewed lease
of one of Leisler's houses.   Audit of Robert Livingston's
bills ordered.   76

19   Letters from Albany full of alarm because Onondagoes have
been defeated by the French and the soldiers are about to
be disbanded; order thereon to Capt. Bradshaw.   Proclamation to issue calling upon inhabitants of Albany to
act in their self-defense.   Revenue of the weigh-house to
be applied for repairing the fortifications of New York.
Order on petition by Ellis Duxbury for the plantation of
Gov. Lovelace whose niece he has married.   78

27   Disorders committed by the pinnace's crew of the hired ship
Archangel.   80

31 Revenue of the weigh-house and fortifications. Justices of the peace to be commissioners for administering the oaths of allegiance and supremacy. Payment ordered to Thos. Coker.   81

Ap. 11 Warrants of impress to complete the crew of the Archangel to be issued. Trouble about provisioning the ship. Prisoners indicted for treason to give bail for their appearance before the supreme court. Thomas Johnson and John Lawrence sworn of the council.   81

16 Provisions for the Archangel. A lunatic son of John Lawrence married to Sarah widow of Charles Bridges. Taxes to be collected quickly for the payments of the soldiers at Albany.   83

18 Order on petition by Edward Wislake concerning the sloop Hopewell saved by him and seized by Capt. Hicks. Payment of salary to Thos. Johnson ordered.   84

20 Copies of acts of assembly and minutes of council to be sent to England in place of those formerly sent and lost. Orders on petitions: by the constables of New York for remuneration of services in collecting taxes; by Rinea Pepar's wife about abuses by soldiers.   85

21 Defective warrants issued by Gov. Sloughter on the collector for payment of public moneys made valid. Case of Mrs Lawrence formerly Mrs Bridges referred to the prerogative court (p. 83). Rinea Pepar's wife. Capt. Hicks refuses to give up the men of all the Hopewell detained by him (p. 84). Payment of Secretary Mathew Clarkson's bill ordered.   86

22 Payment to Dirck Wessells of sum voted him ordered (p. 47). Audit of military accounts ordered. Letter to be sent to Jamaica concerning the complaint for nonpayment of salary made by John Prudden minister there.   88

25 Order on a bill of Attorney-general Newtown for expenses. Allowance to the secretary for copying papers to replace other copies lost with Capt. Alloway of Bristol.   88

27 Order on a letter from the justices of Suffolk county who cannot collect taxes because the acts sent to them have not been signed. Stoffell Probasco and Peter Cortilian to be justices for Kings county. Payment ordered to Harpert Jacobs for going express to Albany. Order on a petition by Ellis Doughty and Samuel Height for license to purchase land near Orowake river called Appletree Neck. Payment of various sums for military purposes ordered.   89

May 2 Capt. Chante commander of the station ship Albrought inquires for a victualler; Stephen van Cortlandt recommended. Messengers to Albany ordered paid.   91

1692   v. 6

24   Jeremiah Tothill's bill for pilotage ordered paid.   Bill of
     Jan Cornelis and Major Merritt to be paid.   Bill for
     charges of a sick seaman.   Disorders in Queens county.   100

26   Detachment from Suffolk county.   No escort for the com-
     mander-in-chief.   101

28   Thos. Coker to be paid for grain out of the credit of the two
     companies established in England.   102

June 9   New York city in arrear with taxes.   David Kennedy ap-
     pointed administrator of the estate of John Anderson mer-
     chant at Barbados deceased.   102

     Hue and cry to issue after David Jellisen, Abr'm Montaigne,
     Johannes Lawrens and Harman Meyer deserters from the
     Albany detachment.   Justices of Kings, Queens and West-
     chester counties to be summoned to answer for their negli-
     gent collection of taxes.   Committee of council to examine
     into the report made by Mrs Lyndall that Clapper's wife
     had called the commander-in-chief a murderous rogue.   102

13   The mayor of New York explains why the taxes are collected
     so slowly.   103

16   The commander-in-chief returned from Albany reports on his
     expedition: fort very much out of repairs; alarm caused
     by skulking [scouting] parties of French Indians; meeting
     held with the five nations who are firm in the British in-
     terest; troops stationed at Schenectady and at the Half
     Moon, some needed for Cannestigaioenna.   Address by
     the mayor etc. of Albany concerning the fortifications to be
     sent to the king.   Wm. Morris, John Teunnisse, Roeloff
     Martins, Joseph Hegeman and Nicholas Stillwell, justices
     of Kings county brought before the council by the sheriff;
     Jacques Cortiliau another justice absent because sick abed;
     also John Pell and Wm. Barnes justices of Westchester
     county concerning slow collection of taxes.   103

18   Letter to be sent to Col. Dudley for Sir Wm. Phips regard-
     ing the Chevalier D'Eaux.   Incidental charges allowed to
     the collector.   Payment ordered to James van der Spegel
     and mate for trying to catch three French prisoners.   Col.
     Cortlandt will no longer be deputy to Mr Blathwayte the
     auditor.   106

23   John Perry's post to be paid for carrying dispatches to Vir-
     ginia.   Petition of Daniel Waldron for pension on ac-
     count of wounds received in his majesty's service during
     the Leisler troubles granted.   106

28   Order in regard to damages done during the Leisler disturb-
     ances.   John Lawrence's lunatic son (p. 86).   107

30 Peter Schuyler sworn of the council; moves the needs of the
garrison at Albany, and that military guards are required
by the harvesting farmers. Payment of his expenses ordered.   108

July 1 Accounts of Peter Schuyler and Dirck Wessells audited and
ordered paid.   109

14 Public accounts; expenses £5182, 12sh 8½d, and still due by
government £1984, 6sh, ¾d. Hendrick Gerritse's maintenance (p. 63 and 65). Expenses of Gov. Sloughter's funeral. Schuyler's accounts. Dr Thos. Thornhill to be
paid for surgical services to men wounded in the Leisler
troubles.   110

16 Joost de Bane to have a license as schoolmaster of New
Utrecht, L. I. and no other allowed to teach school there.
Nathaniel Silvester relieved from paying taxes for his
island in Suffolk. Debts due by government to be paid.   111

26 Accounts of provisions for the Albany garrison to be paid. 112

Aug. 9 Letter received from Col. Dudley at Roxbury, N. E. that
Sir Wm. Phips "shifts" and delays the surrender of the
French prisoners escaped from New York; order thereon.
Payments for various charges to be made to the col-
lector, to Caleb Heathcote and to Abr'm De Peyster.
Order on a petition by Dirck Hansen Hooglandt of Flat-
bush, L. I. against Peter Lott.   113

12 Col. Lyonell Copley, governor of Maryland, and Lt. Gov.
Nicholson of Virginia send each £100 for the defence of
the frontiers and request that passes be given to New York
Indians going south of Virginia. Mayor of Albany ordered to issue such passes. Major Mayhew of Martin's
Vineyard reports uneasiness in Duke's county on account
of Boston officers serving papers there; order that the
county still belongs to New York. Capt. Arent Schuyler
to bring in some Sattaras Indians coming to make peace;
warrant issued on the collector for Capt. Schuyler's
charges. Warrant issued on the collector for beer furnished at Albany to the soldiers by Albert Ryckman and
Harmen Rutyart.   113

17 Bill of Pieter de Reymier for mending glass windows in the
fort ordered paid. Bill for provisions to the garrison at
Albany ordered paid.   115

18 Capt. Arent Schuyler with the far Indians called Showannios
and some Senecas, before the council; Malisit chief of the
Senecas reports a French port at the head of the lakes
where he met Capt. Tontye; Showannios want to make
peace. John Gardner makes a deposition against Gerrit

Duykinc for railing against the commander and council. Robert White's account for firewood ordered paid. Dirck Hansen Hooglandt and Peter Lott referred to common law with their quarrel.   116

19   Reply to the far Indians with presents.   117

22   Proclamation to issue for a day of thanksgiving for a naval victory over the French and discovery of a plot against the king and queen. Indian presents to be paid for. Accounts of Dirck Wessells for military and Indian charges to be audited. The far Indians going home to have an escort under command of Capt. Arent Schuyler. Dirck Hansen Hooglandt's land to be resurveyed (p. 116).   117

23   Report of a conference between Peter Schuyler and 350 Indians on the warpath against Canada read. Payments to the Indians ordered. Dirck Wessell's accounts audited and ordered paid.   118

30   Benjamin Fletcher appointed governor takes the oaths, publishes his commission and administers the oaths to the council. All officers civil and military continued in office.   119

31   Oath administered to Wm. Smith of the council absent on the preceding day. Peter Delanoy's accounts. Committee of council to view the fort as to required repairs. James Graham wants to be restored to the place of attorney-general and recorder of the city which latter office is held by Wm. Pinhorne of New Jersey; Pinhorne summoned before the council. David Jamison sworn as clerk of the council.   120

Sep. 1   Prisoners petition for pardon; order thereon. Wm. Pinhorne not being a resident of the province is not allowed to take the oath of office and is dismissed; James Graham reappointed as recorder. Orders concerning the ship Francis and Thomas claimed by Jacob Mauritz and Fred. Philipps respectively. Persons under bail for connection with Leisler discharged.   121

2   Resolution as to a provincial agent in England, John Povey appointed agent. Prisoners pardoned. Public accounts of Major Ingoldsby to be examined.   123

6   Major Ingoldsby called upon to account for public moneys received. Daniel Honan appointed accountant-general of the province. Order upon petitions by Wm. Churcher, Wm. Lawrence, Joost Stool and John Coe prisoners for high treason, and of Rich'd Ponton also a prisoner.   124

7   Petition by the inhabitants of Suffolk county for a port denied. Advice from Gov. Copley of Virginia concerning Indian outrages.   125

murdering another. Allowance to Rev. Godfr. Dellius continued. Account of Rob't Livingston for disbursements to Capt. Schuyler's company of fusileers at Albany.   133

11 Inhabitants of Schenectady excused from paying taxes. Salary to Hellegont the female interpreter fixed. Various salary payments etc. ordered.   135

13 New election of representatives ordered for the city and county of New York on account of dissatisfaction with the former election. Herman Jansen, Elias Burger, and John Clute, prisoners of war, escaped from Canada, to receive pay.   135

14 Abr'm de Peyster sworn in as mayor and Stanley Handcock as sheriff of New York city. Thos. Codrington late sheriff discharged from the indenture given to his predecessor Thos. Lyndall for some prisoners.   136

15 Order on petition by Augustine Grassett weighmaster relating to dues. Payments ordered to Wm. Welch servant of the assembly, and Hendrick Gerritsen a pensioner.   136

19 Council advises that the governor personally visit the field where the election of representatives is to be held.   137

24 A barge for boarding vessels at Sandypoint to be procured and the house on Nutten Island to be rebuilt. David Murray paid for transporting artillery to Albany.   137

25 Peter Schuyler sworn of the council. Committee appointed to receive the reports on valuation of estates. Allowance to Peter Mase and Joshua Mashloe for transporting soldiers to Albany. Salary of Rev. Godfr. Dellius ordered paid. Col. Courtandt to provide beds for the Albany garrison.   138

26 Order on petition by John Hoglandt about a bond given to Capt. George Lockhart and Edw. Buckmaster. Order that the treasury warrants should be numbered. Payment of salaries ordered to: Peter Schuyler as captain of fusileers, John Schuyler lieutenant, Thos. Sharpe, lieutenant, Sanders Glen lieutenant in Capt. George Bradshaw's company of fusileers. Robert Livingston's account for incidental military and Indian expenses to be paid. Peter Schuyler's account for Indian disbursements at Saraghtogue to be paid.   139

27 Order on petition by Samuel Kniffin of Rye regarding taxes. Capt. George Lockhart and Edward Buckmaster before the council in re John Hooglandt.   140

28 Petitioners for a port in Suffolk to appear the following morning.   141

appointed: John Harrison for Queens county, Gerrit
Strycker for Kings, Josiah Hobbart for Suffolk, John
Stillwell for Richmond, Corn's Bogardus for Ulster and
Dutchess, John Apple for Albany, Benj. Collier for Westchester. Petition by Gerritt Jansen Roose for land fenced
in and added to the governor's garden referred to a committee. Peter Strycker and Joseph Sackett reported as
having public money in their hands raised in Leisler's time
summoned before the council.   149

3   John Warren commander of the barkantine John's Adventure petitions for a letter of marque; granted.   150

8   Order on a petition of Anthony Tyce for land on Staten
Island; granted. Committee report that Gerrit Jansen
Roose has been wrongfully deprived of his land; ordered
restored. Account of Capt. Arent Schuyler for travelling
with Showannoes ordered paid. Account of Casper Teller
for transporting soldiers etc. to Albany ordered paid.   150

15 Account of Jonah Thomas for entertaining a sick soldier ordered paid. Warrants issued: to Lieut. Beckford for the pay
of Capt. Bradshaw's company; to Nich's Bayard for gun-
carriage wheels. Order on petition by the inhabitants of
Boswyck, Brooklyn and Flatbush against Newtown for intrusion upon their lands. Warrant issued to John Clapp
for salary as clerk of the assembly.   151

22 Accounts of Gov. Sloughter and Major Ingoldsby to be
examined. Fort to be viewed. Warrant issued to Col.
Steph. Cortlandt for fort, Indian and French prisoners'
charges. Peter Strycker and Joseph Sackett before the
council (p. 149) and discharged of responsibilities. Order
concerning Boswyck etc. against Newtown.   152

29 Order concerning commissions to be taken out of the secretary's office by civil and military officers. Order on petitions: of Melle Caspars for land; of Jacob Lockermans
for confirmatory patent of ground in New York. Warrant issued: to David Jamieson for salary as clerk of the
council; to Daniel Honan for salary as accountant-general.   154

1693

Jan. 5   Advice of council concerning an inflammatory letter written at Boston by Abr'm Governeur a Leislerian condemned
for murder, and pardoned. Jasper Nissepatt father-in-law
of Governeur, and Gerard Beeckman summoned before the
council. Capt. Thos. Clarke to fetch Abr'm Governeur
from Boston. Warrant to the surveyor for laying out land
of Richard and Thomas Willet and of Col. Courtlandt according to Indian deeds. Quietus granted to Henricus

Salinus husband of the widow of Cornelius Steenwyck as administrator of John Shackerly's estate. Warrant issued to Jacob Phenix for transporting soldiers to Albany. Order on petition by Miles Forster for payment of a warrant given by Major Ingoldsby. Letter from Gov. Fletcher to Sir Wm. Phips about Abr'm Governeur. Governor Fletcher wants to heal the dissensions. Proclamation to issue for pacifying the people.   155

12 Warrant to issue to Stephen Courtlandt for presents to the far Indians; to James Graham for services as attorney-general; to Thos. Munsey for Indian presents; to John Pelletreaux for candles; to sundries for Indian presents. Edw. Stevens and Thos. Betts appear on behalf of Newtown (p. 153). Order on a petition by Thos. Fullerton. Duplicate of warrant issued to Abr'm de Peyster for lost original.   157

16 Letter from Sir Wm. Phips concerning Martins Vineyard read with Gov. Fletcher's answer.   158

19 Joseph Burroughs of Queens county to be bound over to the next supreme court. Thos. Fullerton to have a patent for the land of Robert Fullerton deceased. Manor of Phillipsborough erected with duty to maintain Kingsbridge and tolls fixed. Petitions of Jane Berryman for confirmatory patent of land on Staten Island, and of George Brown for land on the same island referred to the attorney-general. Augustine Graham sworn in as surveyor-general. Committee appointed to supervise the running of boundary lines between Boswyck and Newtown.   159

26 Order on the petition of Jane Berryman for land. Report on Major Ingoldsby's account kept in the governor's custody. William Blathwayte auditor-general of the revenues allowed 5% of all the revenues as salary. Warrants to issue to Chidley Brooke for his salary as collector and receiver-general.   160

31 Major Ingoldsby reports the stockadoes of the fort at Albany in a rotten condition; council advises to build a stone fort there. Circulars sent out to hasten the collection of taxes. Committee to audit Gov. Sloughter's accounts of moneys given for extraordinary expenses. Committee on finances appointed.   161

Feb. 2. Petition of Laurence Cornifleau & Co. vs Gabriel Monviele referred to Lt. Col. Lodwyck, Mr Barbaree and Mr De Lancy, merchants. Petition of Sarah Burger referred to the attorney-general. Warrant issued to Dirck van der Burgh bricklayer for work on the fort. The governor to have his expenses for coming to New York refunded.   162

9 Peter de Lanoy's accounts audited and sent to England.
Committee appointed to consider an address by the mayor
of New York for a confirmatory charter. Warrants to
issue: for payment of carpenter's work done in the fort by
Henry Ford before and another for work after Governor
Fletcher's arrival; to Joseph Bueno for powder and goods
furnished to the fusileers at Albany; to Jarvis Marshall
for salary as attendant upon the council; to Abr'm de
Peyster as administrator of the estate of Thos. Johnson late
justice of the supreme court; to Dirck van der Burgh for
work done in the fort before the governor's arrival. Petition of Isaac Forrest for repayment of money advanced at
former dates referred to committee.   162

10 Capt. Clarke reports that Sir Wm. Phips encourages and
will not deliver Abr'm Governeur. Council agree to send
an address to their majesties anent the matter.   164

13 Reports from Albany and Esopus that a body of French
and Indians has been seen within 36 miles of Schenectady.
Troops to be sent to Albany. Letter of Sir Wm. Phips.   165

14 First and second castles of the Maquaes in the hands of the
French. Governor to go to Albany with Col. Bayard.
Lieut. Jeremiah Tothill to get sloops ready. Express from
Albany and Esopus to receive a reward. Appropriation
made for the governor's journey to Albany. Opinion and
advice of the council concerning Martins Vineyard. Address of council to their majesties.   165

15 The governor absent on his way to Albany with 200 men.
Southern and New England colonies to be informed of
state of affairs.   171

17 Provisions for the detachment gone to Albany provided for.
Powder to be issued to some of Col. Willet's men gone to
Albany.   171

25 Capt Edw. Chant commander of their majesties' ketch Albrought advised to career her bottom for repairs in
"Jefferys cove through Hellgate," where Robert Darkins
can pilote him.   172

26 Gov. Fletcher reports the escape of the French; his letter
from Schenectady, Feb. 21, and Albany, Feb. 23.   173

Mar. 3 Gov. Fletcher returned reports on his expedition. Neighboring colonies to be informed and their assistance asked. 175

10 Report on the condition of the fort at Albany. Council are
of opinion, other colonies ought to contribute to building
a stone fort. Committee to consider Indian speech that
they want to see the governor "when the bark is loose
upon the trees." Connecticut people complain of arbitrary

Ap. 3   Wm. Pinhorne, Chidley Brooke and John Laurence take the
         oaths as judges of the supreme court. Warrant to Jeremiah
         Tothill for traveling express to Maryland and Virginia.
         Accounts of fusileer companies to be audited.   185
     7   Permission to come in granted to a privateer. Governor
         reports his appointment as governor of Pennsylvania and
         New Castle, and committee of council is to go with him
         to his new government. Assembly to be adjourned.   185
     8   Production of flax, hemp, tar and other naval stores in the
         province under consideration. Supplying the royal squad-
         ron under Sir Francis Wheeler, and Col. Foulkes land
         forces in the West Indies referred to a committee. Taxes
         on Staten Island. Proclamation to issue concerning free-
         holders who desert their farms on account of taxes.
         " Smart money " granted to Andrew Roos wounded in the
         expedition against the French. Petition of John Stillwell
         for a patent of land on Staten Island occupied by his father
         without patent granted. Quitrents to be paid in money.
         Warner Wessells whose son, and Antie Christians whose
         husband are prisoners of the infidels at Salley granted per-
         mission to collect money for ransom. Taxes in Ulster
         and Dutchess counties to be paid in wheat to Rob't Liv-
         ingston. Dirck Wessells, Livinus van Schaick and Kilian
         van Rensselaer to muster the four fusileer companies at
         Albany. Warrants to Rob't Livingston for Indian
         presents and for subsisting fusileer company.   186
    10   Pennsylvania to pay for the expenses of Gov. Sloughter's
         journey to that province. Warrants: to Col. Andrew
         Hambleton for expenses on his journey to Piscataqua river
         and to Capt. Thos. Clarke for same to Boston; to Wm.
         Smith for salary as chief justice.   188
    13   Warrants: to Amon Bonan for firewood; to Rob't Livingston
         for disbursements to the soldiers at Albany; to sundries for
         expenses of the expedition against the French.   189
    14   The Maryland bill of exchange for assistance on the frontiers
         protested. Pecuniary difficulties of the government. Gov-
         ernor's object in going to Pennsylvania; David Jamieson
         to go with him.   190
    19   Indians reported by Appollonia Welch as intending to
         revenge Leisler.   191
    20   Order on petition by Sarah Burger for land. Warrants: to
         Caleb Heathcote for a pinnace; to the secretary for clerical
         work in his office; to Stephen Courtlandt for subsisting
         soldiers on their way to Albany; to Dirck Wessells for
         Indian presents.   192

27 The ship Elizabeth of Berwick to be seized for not clearing. Letter to be written to Gov. Fletcher about a ship from Martinico, and time of his meeting the Indians at Albany. Martinico ship suspected of unlawful intentions. Money sent to Rob't Livingston for the payment of soldiers. 201

June 1 Dissensions in Newtown about taxes. 202

3 Newtown taxes. Warrant to Capt. Ebenezar Wilson for a drum delivered to Capt. Peter Matthews a᷎ Albany. 202

5 Gov. Fletcher, returned, reports on Pennsylvania affairs. His journey to Albany. Virginia has given money for the defence of the frontiers on credit which Stephen Courtlandt accepts and will pay in the money. Revenue laws. Jonathan Marsh's invention of a new mold of vessel to be tried. 202

6 Letters from Virginia and Maryland read. Order upon a petition by Soveraine Tienhout for land at Showangunck, Ulster county. Revenue laws. Act for settling the militia. Indian presents. Gertrud Bruyn petitions for the same lands as Sov. Tienhout. Report by Barent Egbertsen from Nassau about Frenchmen passing in canoes between Cowneck and New Rochelle. 204

7 Rumors of an Indian insurrection on Long Island; investigation ordered. The ketch Albrought to go to Albany with the governor if possible. Lt. Col. Lodwyck to represent to the authorities in England the state of affairs in New York. The ship Elizabeth released. 205

8 Suffolk detachment still wanting. Col. Wm. Smith to supercede Col. John Young as commander of Suffolk county militia. Warrant to Peter Waldron for having been wounded in the late expedition. Sir Wm. Phips' complaint vs Capt. Edw. Chant. Warrants: to Rob't Livingston for disbursements to Albany troops; to Jarvis Marshall for salary. 207

10 Wm. Pinhorne come to live in New York reinstated as member of the council. Warrant to John Cooley for blacksmith work in the fort. Wm. Nicolls to oversee the sodwork of the fort. Measure adopted for paying the debts of the government. 208

12 The governor is ready to go to Albany. Arrears of taxes to pay discharged officers. Warrant to Mrs Margaret Sharp in part of her husbands pay as gunner at Albany. Money given by Virginia and Maryland for the defence of the frontiers applied. Warrant for the expenses of the governor's journey to Albany. Col. Stephen Courtlandt pays in the money for the Virginia bills of credit. War-

rant to Rob't Livingston for incidental military charges at
Albany.   Allowance for military substance fixed.   Warrant
to- Francis Ber, Mattys Fayette and four other French
prisoners allowed to return to Canada being exchanged.   209

13   Warrant for payment of discharged officers.   Instructions
for Col. Lodwyck.   210

July 14   The governor, returned from Albany, reports the Indians
well satisfied; French troops on their way to Cadaracqua
and to an unknown place; Indians sent out on a scout;
Major Schuyler stationed at Schenectady; the governor is
willing to return to Albany if he could find forces; Sir
Wm. Phips has promised 200 men but none have come;
Mohawks held prisoners by Sir William and Col. Pincheon
on suspicion of having committed murders at Deerfield
although it is proved French Indians have done it.   Warrant to Col. Nich. Bayard for money advanced for Indian
presents.   Col. Abr'm de Peyster to view the fortification.
Gov. Copley of Maryland sends money to assist in the
defense of the frontiers.   211

17   Sir Francis Wheeler having arrived at Boston with the West
Indies squadron, Chidley Brooke is sent there to congratu-
late him on his safe arrival and consult about an attack on
Canada.   Commissioners from all the English colonies
invited to come to New York and concert measures for the
defence of the frontiers.   Collection of taxes urged.   Question raised as to the necessity of a court of exchequer.   213

20   Warrant to Daniel Honan for subsistance of a French
prisoner Jean Lebord.   Surveyor to lay out and map land
on the Kill van Kull, late Gov. Lovelace's petitioned
for by Philipp Welles.   License to purchase land in Orange
county granted to Ryck Abrahamse.   Salaries ordered
paid: to Rev. Godfr. Dellius; to David Jamison; to Wm.
Pinhorne.   Petitions by Kilian van Rensselaer and by
Schenectady for remission of quitrents granted.   Wm.
Appeel wounded at Schenectady in 1689 excused from paying excise.   Salary to John Povey ordered paid.   215

27   Proclamation to issue concerning public moneys in private
hands.   No court of exchequer needed in the province.
Assembly to be dissolved and new election ordered.   Capt.
Edw. Chant to have a silver tankard for services to Albany.
Salary to Daniel Honan to be paid.   Warrants: to John
Peterse Bank for going express to Albany; to Henry Ford
for carpenter work on the fort.   Chapel in the fort in
ruinous condition to be pulled down.   216

Reversed side
v. 6

1687

Aug. 19 Order extending the time for collecting taxes in Dukes
county.   1
Order directing the surrender of pirates taken and im-
prisoned in Dukes county to Ensign Thos. Sharpe for
transportation to New York.   2

26 Warrant for the arrest of Robert Allison on a complaint by
Thomas Hawerden.   4

Sep. 7 Order to the mayor and aldermen of Albany requiring them
to ask that the five nations of Indians deliver over all
Christian Indians from Canada; to inquire about far
Indians with straws or pipes through their noses and about
Anthony Lispinard, Lafleur or other Frenchmen having
correspondence with Canada.   5
Order directing Robert Livingston to hurry up the work
on the fort at Albany.   6
Order concerning the fortifications at Albany and at
Schenectady.   7

9 Order to mayor of Albany to offer shelter in the neighbor-
hood to Indian women, children and old men, the French
apparently intending to renew the war against Senecas.   8
Order to Thomas Buttler to take charge of and bring to
New York the ship Joanna of Piscattaway seized for illegal
trading.   9

14 Dedimus potestatem to administer the oath of assessors for
Kings and Orange counties to Major Stephan van Cortlandt and Justice Beeckman, for Queens to John Jackson
and Daniel Whitehead, for Huntington to Ebenetus Platt,
for Seatalcott and Smithstone to Andrew Gibb, for
Southold to Isaac Arnold, for East and Southampton to
Major John Howell, for Westchester to John Pell and John
Palmer, for Richmond to Thos. Lovelace and Justice Stilwell, for Dutchess to Rob't Livingston, for Ulster to Major
Chambers and Justice Beeckman; for Albany county to
the mayor of the city. Rules for the collection of taxes.   10

26 Order to Major Thomas Chambers to have his troops ready
for marching to Albany and Schenectady.   12

Oct. 8 Order to Col. John Young and Major John Howell of Suffolk county to reimburse Capt. Joseph Fordham for arms
etc. delivered to their detachment.   13

11 Warrant: sheriff of Richmond county to levy on Thos.
Walton for arrears of quitrent.   14
Order: sheriffs in the various counties to continue in office
for another year.   15
Warrant: sheriff of Albany county to levy on John Trum-
pett et al. for arrears of quitrent.   15

1687		**v. 6**
25	Order on petition by Dirck Jansen Hooglandt against Peter Lott.	16
	Order on petition by the mayor of Albany for continuance of a local duty on rum etc.	17
Nov. 10	Order: Samuel Burtt, brother to Richard Burtt master of the ship Robert of London drowned during the voyage, to act in the place of his brother with the mate and boatswain.	18
	Order: Abr'm de Peyster, John Delavall and Samuel Burtt to take an inventory of Richard Burtt's accounts.	19
25	Order in the governor's absence that S. van Cortlandt and James Graham appoint a collector and receiver for the province of East Jersey.	20
Dec. 3	Order: Daniel Mackreyck servant to the late David Tossach to take an inventory of his deceased master's estate.	21
5	Order on petition by Daniel and Jacob Robles for denization and permission to land goods from the ship Phenix James Duncan master.	22
1688		
Jan. 7	Order on petition by Richard Smith vs Samuel Eborne.	23
Feb. 9	Order for the arrest and dismissal from office of Thos. Stevens justice in Queens county, he having surreptitiously obtained a marriage license for Wm. Morris of the ferry and Jane the step daughter of Morris and niece of Edward Stevens.	25
18	Council minute on the report by Richard Hartford commander of the shallop Royal James that the sloop Primrose Symon Grover master has been seized for illegal trading. [26]	24
	Order: Robert Augur's sloop and goods seized at Easthampton to be sent to New York for trial.	27
	Order: Stephen Bailey to appear before the council for denying the authority of Capt. Rich'd Hartford.	27
Mar. 6	Order on petition by Richard Blackridge on behalf of the towns of Stratford, Milford and Fairfield for leave to purchase whale oil for soap boiling.	28
13	Order on petition by Samuel Eborne, to traverse the petition of Rich'd Smith (p. 23).	28
Ap. 12	Order on petition by Benj. Colier high sheriff of Westchester county vs Joseph Lee the county clerk.	29
	Order on petition by Robert Augur for release of his sloop Endeavour he paying fees.	31
16	Order: inhabitants of Kings and Queens counties to clear the road over the stony hill between Brooklyn and Jamaica. General order for laying out and clearing highways for wagon, carts etc.	31

Reversed side

1688   **v. 6**

26   John Pell, John Palmer and Wm. Richardson before the
      council with Joseph Lee county clerk of Westchester.
      Accounts examined and order thereon.   32
      Order: assessors Mathias Harize and Edw'd Griffin for the
      town of Flushing, Nath'l Denton and Joseph Thurston of
      Jamaica, Abr'm Smith and Richard Valentine of Hemp-
      stead, Nath'l Coles and Jacob Wright of Oysterbay dis-
      missed from their offices for refusing to take the legal oath.
      The towns to elect new assessors.   33

July 30   Order: Jarvis Marshall to bring in the Spanish Indian slaves
      of Cornelis Fredricks Druger, Dirck van der Burgh, Joh's
      Clapper, Giles Shelley master of the ketch Prosperous, and
      Robert Allison, with a view of liberating them; the Indians
      must be able to say the Lord's prayer.   35

The remainder of "reversed side" is legislative minutes of the council
separately paged 1-77, and published in *Journal of the legislative council of
the colony of New York.* 1:1-39.

Vol. 7   1693-97

1693

July 28   A messenger from Albany reports that the man sent to
      Canada by the Jesuit Milett a prisoner at Oneida has re-
      turned with a peace belt and letters for Domine Dellius.
      Dissatisfaction with proceedings of five nations.   Major
      Dirck Wessells sent to Onondaga to counteract French
      intrigues.   1

31   Letter to the five nations read and approved.   2

Aug. 3   Warrant for the payment of the messenger from Albany.
      Account of the governor's journey to Albany and of Indian
      presents, audited and ordered paid.   New chapel in the
      fort.   Confirmatory grant of lots in New York city to
      Peter Stoutenbergh.   Warrant to Jarvis Marshall for re-
      calling ships from Sandyhook.   Fort at Albany.   War-
      rants: to Secretary Matth. Clarkson for clerical work and
      part salary of David Jamison; to Rob't Livingston for
      rebuilding the Mohogs fort.   2

10   Warrants: to Elisha Parker for firewood for the garrison;
      to Matthew Clarkson for cloaths given to the Indian boy
      Christian; to Gabriel Monviele for writing paper; to Jarvis
      Marshall for salary; to John Pelletreaux tallow chandler for
      candles.   Survey of plantations on the Kill van Kull filed
      in the secretary's office.   4

17 Patent granted to Ryck Abrahamse for land near the High
Lands purchased from the Indians. Warrants: to Joseph
Bueno for powder; to Rev. Godfr. Dellius for maintenance
of 3 Indian boys; to Wm. Nicolls for sodwork on the fort.
John Comp and Gert. Bruyn's lands. Payment to Mrs
Margaret Macgregere for the services in 1688 of her late
husband Major Hugh Macgregere. Warrant to Nicholas
Bayard for iron to mount the great guns.   4

18 Report from Boston of an attack feared from a French
squadron. Militia of New York to be in readiness for a
march to Boston. Ten of the greatest guns to be mounted
at Sandypoint.   5

19 Proclamation to issue forbidding the exportation of provisions until further orders because they may be needed
for the troops summoned to defend New York.   6

24 Report of the governor concerning fortifications at the lower
bay. Expenses of the governor's journey to Sandypoint
ordered paid. Report of Chidley Brooke on his journey
to Boston and conferences with Sir Francis Wheeler and
Sir Wm. Phips; he also produces a new patent as collector
and receiver-general, allowing him deputies. Warrant to
John Pelletreaux for candles.   7

25 Fortifications; assembly to raise funds for building them.
Militia camps. Beacons.   8

30 Permission granted to Samuel Burgesse to export flour.
Report from Albany of Mons. Crevier being brought in
as prisoner.   9

Sep. 1 John Comp and Gertrud Bruyn; the latter to have the land
in Ulster county. Fort at Albany. New battery in New
York. Peter Waldron. Warrants: to Nich's Bayard for
wheels to the great guns; to Wm. Beckley for ropes.   10

4 Dirck Wessells reports that the five nations will not make
peace with Canada and refer the governor of Canada to
Cayenquiragoe (Swift Arrow, Gov. Fletcher's Indian
name) whom they own as their master.   11

7 Warrants to Sec. Matthew Clarkson and Rev. Godfrey
Dellius for salary.   11

11 Connecticut and Rhode Island to assist at Albany. Pecuniary
assistance by Maryland. County treasury of Kings county
in the hands of Gerard Beeckman condemned for high
treason.   12

12 Land granted on Staten Island to Anthony Tyce as petitioned
for.   13

13 Expenses of the governor's journey to Albany. Warrants:
to Rob't Cranell for salary as coxon of their majesties
pinace; to Mangel Jans for firewood.   13

1693 v. 7

14 Warrants: to Miles Forster for locks etc. for the fort; to
Peter de Rimier glazier for glass for the fort. 14

19 Financial transactions. Dom. Dellius reports on the activity
of the French. Governor thinks his presence at Albany
is required. Order on a petition by Joachimintie Elting
for leave to purchase Indian lands in Dutchess county.
Weighhouse affairs and revenues. 14

20 Connecticut refuses to assist at Albany but will send a commissioner. 15

21 John Comp and Gertrud Bruyn. Warrant to David Jamison
for salary. 16

25 Commissioners called from the other colonies; Sir Wm.
Phips refuses to send any or give assistance. Post office.
Warrant to Sergt. John Bulkeley for funeral expenses of
Walter Woolford a grenadier. Order on petition by
Hendryck Arianse for leave to purchase Indian land in
Dutchess county. 16

28 Warrants: to Lieut. Enoch Fithian for expenses of the Suffolk county detachment; to Thos. Munsey for subsistance
of soldiers. Governor inquires whether he shall go to
Albany for the winter. Warrants: to Chidley Brooke for
his own and his employees salaries; to Dirck Wessells for
expenses on the journey to Onondaga. License granted
to Claas Evertse commander of the Dutch ship King David
to purchase provisions. 17

Oct. 2 Governor Fletcher appointed commander of the Connecticut
militia. Taxes in New York city. Mrs Sloughter. 18

5 Accounts of Chidley Brooke as collector etc. audited and
passed. Order on petition by Col. Wm. Smith to have
his land on Long Island erected into a manor (St
Georges). John van Comp and Gert. Bruyn. Warrants:
to Peter Melett for blacksmith work in the fort; to Evert
Bogardus for transporting soldiers to Albany. 19

7 Salary for James Graham attorney-general fixed. Warrant
to John Clapp clerk of the assembly, for house rent, etc.
Further accounts of Chidley Brooke passed. Col. John
Young's accounts of taxes on Long Island. Gertruy
Bruyn and John van Comp. 20

10 A French privateer, John Reaux formerly of New York commander, riding at anchor in Muskitoe cove; the commander
arrested and Capt. Evans to capture his ship. Reports of
French doings in Canada and consequent preparations in
New York. Fortifications of New York. Examination of
Jacob Dennis taken prisoner with Reaux who is likewise
examined. 22

1693 v. 7

6 Report by Major Schuyler of French intentions. Governor to go to Albany with troops. Gov. Andrew Hamilton of New Jersey writes about troops. Warrants: to Stephen van Cortlandt for pay of New Jersey troops; to Daniel Honan for expenses of the governor's journey. 25

12 Capt. Evans reports that he could not catch Reaux' ship in the sound. Governor may go to Connecticut by land. Nathaniel Cole's connection of John Reaux; suspended from his office of justice at Oysterbay. John Reaux' confession as to a naval attack on New York. Fortifications. Warrants: to Wm. Bradford printer for salary; to Wm. Pinhorne justice. Payment ordered to Mrs Margaret Macgregere. John Reaux' men disposed of. Account of Wm. Merritt for pilotage of the Albrought. 26

18 Letter of credit to be sent to Major Peter Schuyler and Rob't Livingston for defraying expenses of scouting parties etc. Pension to Peter Waldron wounded at the frontiers. Bedding for the soldiers at Albany. 28

23 Isaac Brashen and John Pero carpenters to finish work on the barkantine Greyhound, James Norman master, ordered to pursue John Reaux' privateer before they go to work on the station ship Richmond. 29

Nov. 7 Governor returned from Connecticut reports on the opposition of the general court of Connecticut in regard to assistance on the frontiers; men from there to be *ordered* out. Governor's presence at Albany not absolutely necessary. Anthony Crepel of Ulster county to have a confirmatory patent. Warrants to the attorney-general and the secretary for clerical work. 2ç

9 Philipp French, Jeremy Tothill, Miles Forster and Robert Downs, merchants to be a committee for supervising the provisioning of the Dutch ship King David. Storage allowed conditionally to Capt. John Evans and Purser Wm. Gannoway of their majesties' frigate Richmond. 31

16 Dissolution of the assembly agreed upon. Musterrolls of Albany companies produced. Nath'l Cole jr, to be released on bail because he might perish from cold in Queens county jail. Warrant to Chief Justice Smith for salary. Dr Thos. Thornhill asks for his pay due by Gov. Sloughter. 32

23 Report from Albany that the Mohawks are cut off; the Jerseymen have run; Gov. Hamilton asked to replace the runaways but cannot get soldiers. New York city detachment to go to Albany. Lieut. Abraham Schuyler resigns in order to go to sea and is paid off. Warrant for

1693   **v. 7**

soldiers bedding. Accounts of Rob't Livingston to be
audited. Warrants: to doorkeeper Jarvis Marshall for
salary; to Evert Bogardus for transporting Col. Ingoldsby
and soldiers to Albany.   33

30   Writs of election for the general assembly to issue. Accounts
of the government to be laid before the next assembly.
Stockadoes for the fortifications. John Reaux to be freed
from his irons and the jail being insufficient have the
liberty in city limits. Small arms in store to be fitted for
use. Warrants: to Isaac Dechamp merchant for locks;
to Fred. Philippse for iron and bunting; to same for kettles
and an hourglass for the Albany soldiers; to Thos. Coker
on behalf of Lieut. Sharp gunner at Albany. Surveyor to
lay out land for Isaac Billian as petitioned for.   34

Dec. 2   Order from Whitehall in regard to Gov. Sloughter's accounts. 35

7   Warrants: to Daniel Honan for pay of express messenger
from and of Jerseymen going to Albany; to same for incidental charges; to John Pelletreaux for candles used in the
fort. Expenses of the governor's last journey. Gov.
Sloughter's accounts. Fortifications.   35

11   Report from Albany that Count Frontenac is still endeavor-
ing to make peace with the five nations; Major Peter
Schuyler to go to Onondaga and prevent it. Council are
opposed to the governor's journey to Albany. Special
court of oyer and terminer to be called for the trial of some
soldiers.   36

14   Mayor etc. of New York summoned before council about
the fortifications. Widow Sloughter. Woodboat of the
garrison. Warrants: to Abr'm Schuyler for transporting
men from Ulster county to Albany; to Dirck Benson; to
Jacob van Tilborough; to Robert Livingston for subsistance of soldiers at Albany. Indentures of William Bryan
to Capt. Christ. Billop cancelled. Members of the council sworn in as justices of the peace.   37

15 • Mayor and aldermen before the council but not enough of
the latter to make a quorum; adjourned.   38

18   Speeches of governor, council and aldermen, regarding fortifications and the city's liability to pay for them. Mayor,
aldermen and common council doubt their authority to
levy money for such purposes but will give money from
their private purses.   38

28   Members of council sworn in as justices of the peace. Order
on petition by Peter King vs the sheriff of New York for
releasing the goods of Robert Brett.   43

1694   v. 7

3   Report from Gov. Andrew Hamilton of the Jerseys that 100
    French and 50 Indians are in the Minissink county de-
    bauching the Indians; Arent Schuyler sent to investigate.   52

5   Arrangements made for defense upon new reports of an in-
    tended French attack on Kingston.   52

8   Accounts of Daniel Honan accountant-general to be audited
    by a committee.   53

15 Warrant to Daniel Honan for expenses of the governor's
    journey to Long Island " in arms " and for the militia to
    drink their majesties' health.   Expenses of the governor's
    journey to Pennsylvania audited and allowed.   Expendi-
    tures of Daniel Honan for the fort.   Warrants: to Wm.
    Bradford for printing sundry public papers and the book
    Seasonable considerations offered to the good people of
    Connecticut; to Simon Schermerhoorn for transporting
    soldiers to Albany; to Wm. Mosse and company of porters.
    Chaplain John Miller not considered entitled to the church
    living in New York.   53

22 The governor reports on his journey to Long Island.
    Boundary line between New York and New Jersey.   54

27 Correspondence about the protested Maryland bills of ex-
    change.   Surveyor Aug. Graham to make a plan of the
    proposed fortifications and of New York city.   55

Mar. 1 Warrants: to Daniel Honan for governor's journey to Long
    Island; to same for incidental expenses; to Dirck Wessells
    for expenses on his journey to the five nations; to Mrs
    Eliz. Wandell for Indian corn given to Indians; to John
    van Inbrough for a canoe; to John Mosse for subsisting
    soldiers at the house of Mary Downs his wife; to Arent
    Schuyler for journeying to the Minissink country.   New-
    town, L. I. to elect a collector vice Joras Abramse in-
    capacitated.   John Evans to have a patent for land up
    Hudson's river purchased from the Esopus Indians.   Order
    on petition by Widow Pauling for land.   Warrant to Major
    Wm. Merrit for charges of collecting taxes.   55

2   Order on petition by Widow Ann Richbell for survey.   War-
    rant to Stanley Handcock for a horse lost on the journey
    to Connecticut.   57

3   Proclamation for a day of humiliation, fasting and prayer to
    issue.   57

6   Order on petition by Jacques Guyon for land on Staten
    Island.   57

8   Warrants: to Daniel Honan for incidental office expenses;
    to Henry Ford for carpenter work in the fort.   Order on

1694   **v. 7**

Miller and Daniel Honan. Warrants for salaries: to William Smith chief justice; to Rev. Godfr. Dellius. Petitions for land by Daniel Shotwell and by Tjerck Caus de Witt granted. Order on petition by the owners and freighters of the barkantine Orange. Robt. Livingston to continue victualling the troops at Albany.   65

15 Maryland bills of exchange. Warrant to Evert Bancker for pay of Capt. George Bradshaw's company. A riding collector of taxes to be appointed. Warrants to Hend. van Dyck surgeon to the Albany troops. Suffolk taxes. Warrants: to Robert Livingston for firewood, candles etc; to Col. Nichs. Bayard for disbursements to officers at Albany; to Robt. Livingston for pay of soldiers; to Joseph Yeats for firewood to Albany garrison.   66

16 Capt. John Evans commander of the Richmond allowed to fill his crew by impressing sailors. Expenses of the governor's journey to Albany audited and allowed. Warrants: to Daniel Honan for advances made; to Col. Bayard for the payment of troops; to Jarvis Marshall for salary; to Daniel Waldron for curing his wounds. Capt. John Evans to have a patent for land. Crexier the French prisoner at Albany redeemed from the Indians by Major Schuyler, dead.

p. m. Virginia sends money. Governor going to Pennsylvania makes recommendations to the council.   66

21 French Indians throw a warclub over the stockadoes into the city of Albany and pursue inhabitants. Money and hourglasses to be sent to Albany.   68

26 Dirck Stone appointed justice of the peace for Maynoth in Westchester county. Gerrit Strycker sheriff of Kings county dead; Jacobus Kiersted appointed in his place. Hourglasses for Albany.   69

June 13 Militia men uselessly detained at Albany. Warrant to Henry Ford for carpenter work in the custom house.   69

July 2 The governor returned disappointed. Report from Col. Treat that it is removed. Gov. Fletcher intends to make war on the five nations. Order on petition by Phil. French regarding importation of goods. Justices of the peace careless about collecting taxes to be summoned.   70

5 Warrant to Col. Nich. Bayard for gun carriages. John Comp and Gertruy Bruyn. Warrant to Robert Livingston for salary of Hilleke the interpretress. Committee to view the governor's house in the fort as to repairs. Custom-house cellar to be leased. Warrants for salaries: to Matthew

28   Indian presents. Governor about to start for Albany to meet the Indians selects a committee of council to go with him. Mohawks before the council.   79

30   Committee to consider what presents are to be provided for Indians at Albany.   8o

Aug. 2   Col. Lodwick to receive the thanks of council for services in England. . Belt sent from the Senecas and Onondagas to the Delawares in Pennsylvania disturbs the latter. Warrants: to Col. Nich. Bayard to defray charges of agency in England; to Chidley Brooke for salaries. Barracks in the fort to be taken down and rebuilt. Warrant to Stephen van Cortlandt for sundry expenses for clothing to Indians come from Canada, for firewood etc. in the fort. Warrant to pay fusileers. Additional land grant to Wm. Barker. Regulations of money scales and weight read and Jacob Boelen with Corn. van der Burgh appointed money adjusters. Warrant to Col. Lodwyck for expenses in England. Orders on petitions: by Abrm. Luteine; by Richard Harvey; by Dorland Swebringh, all for land: and by Joris Remse. Warrants to Daniel Honan for a chest with utensils for the governor's journey to Albany and for Indian presents.   80

3   Warrant to James Spencer carpenter for work in the fort. Additional land grant to Paul Richards. Petition of Cornelius Jacobs for release of the barkantine Orange under bail granted. Capt. Henry Tergeny, Capt. Thos. Gleaver, Thos. Wenham, and Stephen de Lancey to appraise the Orange. Warrant to Thos. Gleaver for transporting guns from England. Market to be moved back to the green before the fort.   82

6   Address of thanks to their majesties. News from Boston. Expedition to Albany. Provisions.   83

9   Orders on petitions for land: by Simon Simonse; by Geo. Brown. Warrants: to Col. Andrew Hamilton for apprehending deserters; to Daniel Honan for expenses of the governor's journey to Albany; to Arent Schuyler for entertaining Mohawks; to Matthew Clarkson for the son of Christagie. Orders on petitions for land: by Arent Prael; by Paulus Richards; by Guy Bodein. Payment of fusileers at Albany.   84

13   Massachusetts presents to Indians to be given by the governor of New York not by Massachusetts commissioners.   85

p. m.   Governor of New Jersey, Majors Pincheon and Sewell, and Capt. Townsend from Boston, Capts. Allein and Stan-

1694   **v. 7**

Nov. 1 Warrant to John Clapp clerk of the assembly for salary,
house rent etc. Order on petition by John Hoden concerning
taxes. Thos. Baxter and Justice Wm.
Barnes of West-
chester county to appear in Hoden's tax case.
Warrants:
to Daniel Honan for firewood; to John Crooke cooper for
work in the fort; to John Pelletreaux for candles; to
Stephen van Cortlandt for presents to Long Island Indians; to Robert Livingston for incidental military expenses at Albany, and for subsisting soldiers there.   103

3 Celebration of the king's birthday.   105

8 Exportation of pipestaves etc. prohibited by New Jersey and
a free port established at Amboy. Capt. Thos. Thew commander of the sloop Amity granted a letter of marque
against the French. Address to the lords of committee on
behalf of Col. Ingoldsby receiving the pay of lieutenant-
governor. Governor signs accounts of Chidley Brooke.
Accounts of Daniel Honan approved. Wm. Barnes justice
of the peace in Westchester county ordered to refund the
taxes paid to him by John Hadon, and costs. Order on a
complaint by Thos. Baxter collector of Westchester.   105

15 Account of the money from Virginia approved. Reissue
of a warrant to Jacob Dickison the original being lost.
Complaint against sloop from Bermuda selling salt by re-
tail in the road.   107

22 John Ward granted a confirmatory patent. Accounts of Gov.
Sloughter.   108

29 Warrant to Col. Andrew Hamilton for salary as postmaster.
Col. Nich. Bayard to have the flag mount etc. paved.
Warrant to Col. Ingoldsby for clearing away the brush
around the fort at Albany.   109

Dec. 9 Daniel Shotwell's petition for land granted. A Long
Island Indian complains against John Smith and others
in Hempstead for cutting his timber. The plantation of
Lewis Morris at Harlem erected into a manor. Warrant
to Capt. Thos. Clarke for services as tax collector on
Long Island.   109

13 Petition of James Emott for land on Staten Island granted.
Warrant to James Spencer for carpenter work in the fort.
John Reaux conditionally allowed to serve as mate on
board a merchant vessel. Accounts of Daniel Honan for
firewood to be audited.   110

31 Letter from Col. Henry Beeckman complaining against Capt.
Thos. Garton and Capt. Haasbrook for neglect in fortifying their parts of Kingston; order thereon.   110

Jan. 3   Warrants: to government officials not named; to Daniel
Honan as per audited accounts. John Reaux. Col. Cortlandt to provide fire buckets for the fort. Order on complaint of Gabriel Le Beauteaux vs Peter De Lanoy. Inhabitants of Westchester county assessed for taxes in Ulster and Dutchess counties. Maryland refuses to assist
New York in the defence of the frontiers.   111

10   Licences to purchase land in Suffolk county granted: to Wm.
Nicoll; to Ebenezar Wilson. Petition of Arent Praal for
survey granted. Peter De Lanoy before the council.
Troubles about the act of assembly establishing a ministry. Paving the flag mount. Wandall vs Cooke.   112

17   The Two Brothers islands near Hellgate granted to James
Graham. Warrants: to Margaret Selinus for iron furnished to the fort; to Nich. Bayard for material for the
barracks. Report on the accounts of Gov. Sloughter.
Cellar under the custom-house let to Mich'l Howdon.   113

24   Letter to the governor of Maryland read and signed. Accounts for work in the fort to be audited. Warrants: to
Col. Heathcote for material furnished to the fort and
for taking up two deserters; to John Appel of Schenectady wounded though not in the king's service to go beg-
ging hereafter. Cooke vs Wandell. Gov. Sloughter's accounts.   115

31   Boundaries between Newtown and neighbors.   116

Feb. 7   Order on petition by Mayor Charles Lodyck about the drink-
ing houses. Cooke vs Wandell.   117

14   Assembly prorogued. Boundaries of Newtown and neighbors.   117

28   Confirmatory patent for land at Bushwick granted to Michael
Parmitier. Boundaries of Newtown and Brooklyn. Warrants: to Dirck van der Burgh for brick layers work on
the chapel; to Daniel Honan for material to the barracks;
to James Spencer for carpenter work on the fort; to Col.
Stephen Cortlandt for provisioning soldiers; to Daniel
Honan for firewood; to Mayor John Abeel of Albany for
repairs to the fort there.   117

Mar. 7   Pinhorne's account for shingles for the fort referred to a
committee. Col. Andrew Hamilton's memorial for in-
creased allowance to the post office referred to a full board.
Confirmatory grant of land on Manhattan Island to Wm.
Beeckman. Petition for land on Staten Island by Mark
Dusachoy granted. Order on petition by Lawrence and
Francis Wessells for permission to carry away oyster shells
from Marshall's and Welch's land. Indians speak boldly

1695   **v. 7**

15 Collection of taxes and disposition of the money collected.
Printing of public papers. Confirmatory patent for land
at Harlem granted to John Low.   127

16 Measures for the defence of the frontiers. Military accounts
referred to a committee.   128

18 Various accounts referred to a committee for examination.
Order on a petition by Henry Ranslear about the barkantine Orange.   129

22 The assembly dissolved.   129

23 The field officers in the province called together to delib-
erate on measures for the defence of the frontiers.   130

24 Opinions of the field officers to be printed. Col. Caleb
Heathcote of Westchester thanked " for his care and plain-
ness " in bringing the militia of his county to a right un-
derstanding of the governor's doings.   130

25 Some members of the council interested in accounts referred
to them for audit request that others be appointed. Warrants: for payment of officers on the frontiers; to Henry
van Rensselaer for transportation of soldiers. Arnout
(Viele's) petition referred to the mayor of Albany. Warrants: to Peter de Rimier for glass windows in the fort;
to Elisha Parker for firewood. Military accounts and muster rolls.   131

May 2 Patent for lands above Antonios Nose on Hudson river
granted to Theunis Dekey. Warrants: to Dirck Wessells
for entertaining sachems of the five nations; to James
Spencer for carpenter work on the barracks. Electioneer-
ing.   132

9 Forces coming from Nassau (L. I.) to have free ferriage.
Order upon a petition of Thos. Coker. Assembly to be
called. Orders: on petition by Dirck Schepmoos about
land;summoning Gerard Beeckman upon a complaint of
the justices of Kings county. Warrant to John Theuniss
for a " sean for the use of the fort."   133

13 Unofficial report of the death of the queen; order in consequence.   134

16 Accounts of the collector and receiver-general read and
signed. Warrants to the collector for his and other officers' salaries. Accounts of John Abeel mayor of Albany,
Daniel Honan, Joachim Staats and Peter Bogardus referred
to a committee. Patent for land on Staten Island granted
to Daniel Perrin.   134

17 Writs of election for members of the assembly to be issued.   135

20 Death of the queen confirmed; address of condolence to be
sent to the king.   135

1695   **v. 7**

23 Warrants: to Joachim Staats and to Peter Bogardus for
    military transportation; to Daniel Honan for firewood;
    to John Abeel for bricks to the Schenectady blockhouse
    and repairs of the fort at Albany. Queens county Indians
    renew their allegiance.   136

30 Address to the king signed and sent to Mr Blathwayte.
    Quartering of soldiers in New York and Albany. Two
    negroes belonging to widow Susannah Elliot pardoned.
    Survey of John Vincent's meadow ordered. Moses Levi
    granted denization. Patent for land at Southampton, L. I.
    granted to Josiah Hobbart. Account of Giles Gaudineau
    surgeon to the grenadeers referred to a committee. Lucas
    Tienhoven and John Cornelius granted license to purchase
    Indian land on David de Marez creek in Orange county.   137

June 13 Connestagioena and Half Moon to be regarrisoned with
    troops from the other colonies. Col. Bayard to buy the
    necessary pots, spoons, etc. for Albany soldiers. Warrant
    to Stephen Cortlandt for money advanced for public use.
    Attorney-general to prosecute in the court of exchequer
    people refusing additional duties. Committees appointed:
    to consider custom-house rules; to examine carpenters' ac-
    counts for work done in the fort. Order on petition by
    the owners of the Orange for remission of fines. Patent
    for land on Staten Island granted to John Vincent.   138

18 Address of thanks to the king for sending over troops. The
    officers and soldiers to receive a present to drink the king's
    health.   139

p. m. Reports from Col. Ingoldsby of the French marching to-
    wards Albany and from Maryland of a French fleet coming
    to attack New York. One of the two companies arrived
    from Boston under Capts. Weems and Hide to be sent
    to Albany. Military accounts.   140

20 Military accounts. Patent for land in New York granted to
    Tobias Stautenburgh. Survey of Indian land purchased
    by Lucas Tienhoven and John Cornelius ordered. Order
    on petition by Francis Pape regarding customs duties.   140

27 Account of Surgeon Giles Gaudineau audited; others referred
    to a committee. Warrants: to Capt. Benjamin Phips and
    Peter Matthews for pay of their companies, dismissed May
    1st; to Major Peter Schuyler for subsistence of four com-
    panies and for incidental charges; to John Abeel for re-
    pairing the fort at Albany; to James Spencer for material
    etc. to the barracks. Patent for a house and lot in New
    York city granted to Warner Wessells and John William-
    sen Neering. Form of a commission for holding courts of
    judicature to be framed.   141

1695

28   Connecticut refuses to send troops and is again requested
        to do so. Warrants to Daniel Honan for incidental ex-
        penses. Addition to the governor's lodgings in the fort.   142

July 4 Warrant to Stephen Cortlandt for money advanced to the
        troops in the late revolution.   143

11   New England and Pennsylvania refuse to assist New York
        against the French. Le Reaux to be tried. Governor's
        lodgings to be enlarged. Governor not to go to Albany.
        Warrants: to Daniel Honan for firewood; to John Clapp
        clerk of the assembly for salary. Michael Hawdon's ac-
        count for entertaining Capt. Paxton's pinace crew and for
        going express to Albany referred. Warrants for salaries
        of government officers. Patent for land in Marbletown
        granted to John Ward. Salary of printer increased. War-
        rant to David Jamison clerk of council for incidental and
        clerical charges.   144

15   Correspondence with Connecticut about military assistance.
        Conference with five nations and river Indians at Albany.
        Schachkook Indians desire assistance to build a fort;
        granted. River Indians not to go hunting in New Eng-
        land.   145

25   Rhode Island offers other than military assistance; not ac-
        cepted men must come. Punishment for deserting. War-
        rant to Stephen Cortlandt for things furnished to soldiers.
        Capt. Peter Matthews called upon for an account of things
        furnished to his company. Peter Schuyler to get the same
        from the other companies. Warrant to John Pelletreaux
        for candles used in the fort. Daniel Honans accounts.
        Memorials of Major Anthony Brockholls, Widow Ber-
        riman and Nich's Blanck referred to a committee. War-
        rants: to Michael Hawdon for his account (p. 144); to John
        Abeel for payment of loyalists in Leisler's time.   147

Aug. 1 Deserters from New York troop caught at Fairfield, Ct.,
        and rescued by the mob. Soap for the soldiers. Care of
        sick soldiers at Albany. Warrant to Robert Smith for
        transporting timber to the fort.   148

5   A French privateer reported on the coast; reports of depreda-
        tions at Martins Vineyard; the royal ship Richmond sent
        after her; the brigantine Charles, —— Huxford commander
        sailing for a wreck on the Isle of Sables to take reinforce-
        ments for the Richmond but cannot.   149

8   Le Reaux acquitted. Money collected for redeeming the
        prisoners in Algiers to be used for the chapel in the fort.
        Accounts of Major Brockholls, Widow Berriman and
        Nich's Blanck audited; warrants issued to them. Petition

of Lieut. David Schuyler and accounts of Jacob Monen,
Cooley the blacksmith, and Capt. Peter Matthews referred to a committee. Officers' lodgings in the fort need
new furniture.   150

15   Virginia will send troops to New York. Warrant to Jacob
Moenen for armourer work. Report on furniture in officers' lodgings. Permission granted to Marten Cregyer
to build a house at Albany. Military accounts of Captains
Weems and Hide, Majors Schuyler and Howell referred to
a committee. Warrants: to Peter Schuyler and Col. Ingoldsby for pay of their companies; to Col. Ingoldsby for
firewood; to John Cockburn for paving bastions in the
fort; to Dirck van der Burgh for travelling on public service
to Maryland; to John Rosie for like travel to Canada; to
Chaplain Alex. Innes for salary. Survey of land purchased
by Lucas Tienhoven and John Cornelius shows they want
100,000 acres; considered too much; may have 1000 each.
Patent granted to Martha Ashfordby and her daughters,
Susan, Mary, Helen, Ann and Katherine for land at Marbletown originally patented to her husband. Confirmatory
patent granted to Hendrick Hansen. Gov. Fletcher to go
to Albany and meet the five nations who are to be called
by Major Schuyler.   151

18   French intend to resettle Cadaracqui and Indians want help
to prevent them. Troops sent to the Mohawk castles.
Connecticut repeats its refusal of assistance against the
French; again written to.   153

24   Warrants: to Major Peter Schuyler for victualling troops;
and for pay of his company; to Capt. James Weems and
Wm. Hide for incidental military charges; to John Terevitt
for military transportation. Various accounts referred to
a committee. The governor to start for Albany on the
7th of September.   154

29   Letter from Gov. Nicholson of Maryland accrediting Thos.
Tasker, read and answered. Petition of Capt. Ebenezar
Wilson referred to a committee. Charges for the governor's journey and Indian presents. Thos. Tasker treasurer of Maryland offers pecuniary assistance in place of
troops; accepted. Old Maryland bills of exchange. Form
of a commission for holding courts considered. Isaac
Naptali granted denization. Warrant to Capt. Peter
Matthews for incidental charges. Accounts for firewood
and " rascarricks " referred. License to purchase Indian
land in Westchester county granted to John Harrison.   155

1695   v. 7

Sep. 1   Report from Albany that the French have retaken Cadaracqui. Five nations cannot come to Albany and the
governor is not to go there. Indians want 500 men to
help them; other colonies to furnish troops but none expected from New England.   157

5   Warrants: to Capt. Thos. Clarke for military transportation
in Leisler's time; to Major Peter Schuyler for Indian provisions; to Dan'l Honan for firewood and deal boards for
the fort; to Joseph Johnson for gun whals. Expenditures
to be examined. Warrants: to Col. Rich'd Ingoldsby for
firewood at Albany; to Robert Livingston for salary as
sub-collector. Salary of the sub-collector at Albany
changed. Warrant to Dirck van der Burgh for bricklayer
work in the fort. Accounts of carpenters and porters
referred. The governor to grant commissions for holding
courts of king's bench, common pleas, and exchequer according to act of assembly. Warrant to Wm. Pinhorne
for expenses of governor's journey to Albany. Maryland
bills to be sold.   157

24   The governor reports on his journey to Albany; the French
have again settled at Cadaracqui but cannot be driven out
without help from other colonies; proposes to send an
agent to England to represent state of affairs; conference
held with Indians at Albany. Warrant to Domine Dellius
for repairing a house for the Indians. Petition of soldiers
from Major Baxter's company referred. Capt. Sanders
Glenn's account referred. Warrant to Col. Stephen Cortlandt for expressage paid to Albany.   159

28   Measures to be laid before the assembly. French protestants (not named) granted denization. Land 20 miles
above Schenectady granted to Nich's Bayard. Survey of
boundary lines in Flatlands ordered.   159

29   Wm. Merritt nominated mayor of New York. Celebration
of English victories and of capture of Namur.   160

Oct. 1   Petition for land in Ulster county by Thomas Noxon referred
to representatives from the county. Returns of collected
taxes called for.   161

3   Warrants: to Wm. Mosse for porterage; to Capt. John de
Peyster for lead given to Indians. Accounts of Robert
Livingston, of Thos. Winne and governor's expenses to
Albany referred to committees. Lt. Gov. Stoughton of
Boston sends money for Indian presents. Warrant to Ed-
ward Graham and James Wells for carpenter work in the
fort.   161

1695   **v. 7**

10 Patent granted to Thos. Noxon. Warrants: for the payment
of Major Baxter's company; to Thos. Robinson for work
in the fort. Patent for land at Sequatage granted to Thos.
and Rich'd Willett.   162

11 License to purchase Indian lands in Ulster county granted to
Thos. Anthony and Bernard Swartod, Elias Hun, Peter
Ginand and Isaac Cadebeck. Warrant to John Abeel for
repairs in the fort of Albany. Petition of Lieut. Thos.
Sharpas referred. Warrant to Robert Weight for boat hire. 162

14 Chidley Brooke and Domine Dellius to go as provincial
agent to England; committee appointed to draw up instructions for them.   163

16 Buildings near the blockhouse not to be allowed and the
blockhouse to be repaired.   163

17 Account of Daniel Honan for furnishing officers quarters
referred. Warrants: to James Wells for carpenter work in
the fort; to Daniel Honan for firewood. Order on petition
of Bathstina Wessells against her brother John Pell.
Survey of land at Coxsinck in Ulster county ordered for
Tjerck Claes de Witt. Warrant to Lieut. Thos. Sharpas
for salary.   163

18 Warrants: to Daniel Honan for officers furniture and for
incidental expenses; for salaries of government officers.   164

24 Arrears of taxes for Suffolk called in. Accounts of the receiver-general signed; warrants to same for salaries of himself and employees; appointments of deputies by the same
during his absence in England as agent.   164

25 Warrants: to Wm. Pinhorne for expenses of governor's last
journey to Albany and Indian presents; to Robert Livingston for incidental expenses in the Albany fort. John Pell
and his sister Wessells to be examined by a committee (p.
163).   165

30 Warrants: to Chidley Brooke for salary; to Daniel Honan
for maps of Canada and the lakes prepared by Aug.
Graham; for pay of the agents in England.   166

31 Warrants to John Clapp clerk of the assembly for fees etc.   166

Nov. 1 Indian affairs. Warrant to Thomas Monsey for expenses
as deputy collector.   167

4 Correspondence with Gov. Nicholson of Maryland about
assistance sent to England. Warrant to Chidley Brooke
for Maryland bills.   167

14 Order on petition by Thos. Milton master of the dogger
ketch Success bound from Jamaica to Madera. Warrant
to John Pelletreaux for candles. New Utrecht boundary
line. Lieut. Sharp's petition referred. Six French

1695   v. 7

protestants from Ulster county granted extension of purchasing licenses. Various accounts referred. Warrant to
Daniel Honan for incidental charges in the fort.   168

21   Warrants: to James Virtue for cutting the kings arms in
brass; to Lt. Col. Gabr. Monvielle for soap to the soldiers;
to Joseph Johnson for gun wheels; to James Wells and
to James Spencer for carpenter work in the fort; to Lieut.
Thos. Sharp for salary as gunner at Albany; to Jacob
Moenen for gunsmith work; to And'w Hamilton for the
post office. Pennsylvania accounts referred. Petition of
John Mila referred to the mayor and elders of the French
church. Warrants: to John Cockburn for paving the
bastions; to Major Peter Schuyler for making a well at
Onondaga. Scarcity of corn in the province. The ketch
Success to be surveyed as to its seaworthiness by Fred.
Philipps and Caleb Heathcote of the council, John Scrougy
and Thos. Gleaves masters of ships, Elias Puddington, Wm.
Hellaker, Benj. Herring, and Clement Elsworth master
builders. Patents for land granted to Ellis Duxbury, Mark
Dusachoy and Jacob Lockermans.   169

28   Various accounts referred to committees. Josiah Hobbarts
patent for land in Easthampton corrected. Orders on petitions: for land at the Gowannos by Ariaen Bennet; by
Jeremiah Smith and others for remission of a fine. Seamen of the ketch Success to be discharged for the winter.
Amount of grain and flour in the city.   170

Dec. 2   Report from New England that 1500 Canadians intend to
attack Albany. Connecticut troops to march over land.   171

4   Warrants: to Aert Elbertse for boat hire; to Stephen Cortlandt for soldiers' provisions. Buildings round the blockhouse. License to purchase land in Orange county granted
to Claes Janse and seven others.   171

12   Order upon petition by John Laurence. Gerrit Duycknighs
account referred. Manor of Kingsfield at Schoharie.
Correspondence from Maryland about assistance. Action
on petition by the mayor etc. deferred.   172

14   Gov. Treat of Connecticut wants provisions for the troops
coming from his colony.   172

19   Court of oyer and terminer in Ulster county. Col. Henry
Beeckman appointed judge of the common pleas for Ulster
county vice Thos. Garton refusing to sit. Captain George
Lockhart appointed surgeon-general.   173

1696

Jan. 9   Warrant to Nichs. Bayard for freight of gun wheels. Carpenters account. Petition for incorporation by the minister
and elders of the Dutch church granted. Jonathan Wright

town.   Warrant to Col. Cortlandt for timber in the fort.
John Harrison's purchase of land.   Mr Emott to act as
attorney for Miles Forster vs Lockermans.   178

12   Case between Ettie Leisler and Miles Forster deferred.   Petition of Thomas Noxon to be sheriff of Ulster county referred.   Petition of Timothy Halstead and others for
remission of fine not granted.   Saviott Broussard alias
Dechamps and his wife Marie Chintrier granted denization. 179

19   Warrant to Dirck van der Burgh for work on the chapel;
assembly to be asked for money to finish it.   Warrants:
to John Wessells for transporting timber to it; to Mr
Forster for locks in the fort.   Order on petitions by John
Kip and Thos. Wenham.   Sheriff of Ulster county.   Petition of members of the church of England for license to
purchase land between the kings garden and the burying
ground granted (Trinity church).   Petition of Gerrit
Travis deferred at the request of Humphrey Underhill.
Town of Rye to have a patent.   Town of Westchester to
be incorporated as a city.   Leisler and Forster.   180

26   Warrant to Capt. John Kip for pay of his company.   Accounts referred and acted upon.   Survey of land on Staten
Island in the rear of Curtis ordered for Nath'l Brittain.
Fortifications.   Petition of Caleb Heathcote for land between the kings garden and low water mark referred to a
committee.   181

Ap. 2   Warrant to Col. St. Cortlandt for incidental expenses.   Peter
Melott's account referred.   Petitions for land patents by
Jan Harmense and by Gerryt Jansen Roos granted.   Quit-
rents.   Gerryt Jansen Roos receives a confirmatory grant
of the slaughterhouse.   Patent and lease for 41 years to
Caleb Heathcote.   Charter for the Dutch church granted.
Patent to Capt. Kip granted.   182

9   No corn to be exported from Albany.   Order for the arrest
of Ryer Schermerhorn on complaint of Capt. Sanders
Glenn for obstructing repairs to the fortifications.   Dutch
church charter.   183

10   Order on petition by John Cuyler for license to export corn
from Albany.   Ground behind the wind mill granted to
Capt. Kip.   Warrant to John Glenn for incidental charges
at Schenectady.   Major Schuyler's accounts referred.   183

15   Mr Ranslear's accounts referred.   Warrants: to Andrew
Hamilton for the post office service; to justices for salaries.
Goods brought from Boston by Isaac Le Noir and family
admitted duty free.   Warrants to Major Peter Schuyler for
pay of his company for victualling, for disbursements in

express messenger. Blacksmith account. David Lloyd
and Isaac Norris granted letters of administration on the
estate of Thos. Lloyd deceased. Arrears of taxes in New
York city. Capt. Wm. Hyde and Lieut. Roger Wright.
Order on petition by Nich's Bayard for confirmatory
patents. License to purchase land on Byram river granted
to John Brundage. John Harrison's patent. Petition by
Capts. Wilson and Clarke concerning Half Moon granted.
Officers' quarters in Albany.   191

22 Letters from Sir Edmond Andros governor, and Mr Byrd
auditor, of Virginia with money for the campaign received.
Arrears of taxes in Queens county.   192

26 Celebration ordered for discovery of the plot in England.
Connecticut evades giving assistance.   193

28 Petition by Gabriel Ludlow and John Sipkins referred to a
committee. Survey of land petitioned for by William
Tillier ordered. Warrant to Peter Melott for blacksmith
work in the fort. Capt. Hyde's account to be sent to
England. Officers' quarters in Albany. Warrants: to
Dirck van der Burgh for leathers in the fort; to John
Cobrun for stone cutter's work in the fort; to Capt. Wm.
Hyde for charges in pursuing deserters. Order relating to
the purchase of land by Rutsen & Co. and by Swartod &
Co. at Waghhackemmick, Ulster county. George Ryer-
son's petition referred.   193

June 11 Petition of Ludlow and Sipkins granted. Warrants: to Wm.
Nicoll; to Stephen Cortlandt for Mr Povey; to Daniel
Honan for firewood. No corn to be exported from New
York. Warrant to Col. Rich'd Ingoldsby for garrison
firewood at Albany. Arrears of taxes. Petitions for land
granted: by Abr'm Lakeman on Staten Island near Barker
and Bartlett; by Aug. Graham. Taxes in Suffolk county.
Eliza Williamse granted license to collect money for the
redemption of her husband from slavery in Salee. Order
to disarm and imprison all Roman catholics. Receiver-
general's accounts signed. Showanoes complain against
the Senecas. Address of congratulation to the king
signed.   194

18 Order on petition by Samuel Bayard for land in Orange
county. Hendrick Tenyck granted license to purchase
land. Order on petition for land by Daniel Honan and
Mich'l Howdon.   196

19 Orders and rules for quartering officers in Albany. Simon
Young to be sheriff of Albany county vice John Apple
superseded for neglect of duty.   196

1696   v. 7

25   Warrants: to Robert Livingston for incidental charges in
     Fort Albany; to John Clapp for salary. Patent petitioned
     for by John Harrison granted to Wm. Nicoll, Eben. Wil-
     son, David Jamison, John Harrison and Samuel Height.
     Law-suit between Arian Bennet and Simon Aertsen, Emott
     and Tudor attorneys. Petitions for land: by Nathaniel
     Brittain; by Abr'm Lakeman; by Col. Cortlandt and
     Jacques Pullion granted.   197

26   License to export grain granted to Philipp Schuyler. Price
     of bread.   198

29   Lt. Gov. Stoughton of Massachusetts is granted permission
     to export a sloop load of provisions (see N. Y. col. mss,
     40:173). Exportation of grain considered.   198

July 2   Appointments: Wm. Pinhorne to be judge; Wm. Sharpas
     register, and Richard Stoaks marshall of the admiralty
     court. Lieut. Roger Wright vs Capts. Weems and Hyde.
     Gov. Hamilton of New Jersey wants Capt. Peter Matthews
     to beat the drum for recruits in his colony. Survey of
     land for Wm. Barker ordered. Prohibition to export grain
     taken off for 8 days (see N. Y. col. mss, 40:178).   199

9   Rob't Sanders granted a license to purchase land. Salary
     of Robt. Livingston as sub-collector at Albany. Informa-
     tion by Lieut. George Sydenham vs Capt. Hyde read.
     Taxes in Suffolk county. News from Albany about French
     movements (see Doc. hist. N.Y. 1:323; Q 1:207). Military
     quarters at Albany.   200

11   Petition by prisoners made by Capt. William Kidd com-
     mander of the galley Adventure, granted (see N. Y. col. mss,
     40:179-80). Taxes in Suffolk county.   201

16   Quotas of men from Virginia and Maryland to be substituted
     by quotas of money. Charges made against Gov. Fletcher
     in England referred to the council. Royal present to the
     Indians received. Money collected for redemption of
     slaves at Salee to be applied for Trinity church (see N. Y.
     col. mss, 40:182). Lieut. Sydenham vs Capt Hyde.   201

20   Maryland disputes pecuniary liabilities. Act for trade and
     navigation to be enforced. Exchange of French prisoners.
     Gov. Fletcher on the charges against him and on " Mr
     Livingston's case."   202

23   French prisoners of war. Trinity church. Warrant to the
     chief justice for salary. Lieut. George Sydenham resigns
     and Lieut. Reeckford or Young are recommended for his
     place in Capt. James Weems company.   203

27   Reports from Connecticut and Onondaga about French
     movements (see Doc. hist. N. Y. 1:323-24; Q 1:207-8).
     Lieut. Roger Wright resigns.   204

31   Five nations call for assistance against the French (see *Doc. hist. N. Y.* 1:324; Q 1:283). Governor wants to go and members of the council raise money on their personal security.   205

Aug. 2 Trade and navigation act. French movements. Proclamation to issue warning people to have their arms in order. Militia to be called out. Letter from the governor to the council with instructions how to act during his absence at the frontiers.   205

3   People near the highlands of Neversink to be on the lookout for French ships. Fortifications.   206

4   Embargo laid upon all outward bound ships till September 1. 207

7   News from Delaware of a ship taken in the bay by the French.   207

9   Capt. Evans of the station-ship Richmond wants a sloop. Mr Graveradt reports having been chased by French ships while going to Delaware.   207

18   The governor returned and his proceedings at Albany on Aug. 7th are entered as follows: 207

Speech of the governor on the situation (see *Doc. hist. N. Y.* 1:341-45; Q 1:217-19). Oneida sachems in town sent for. Report of committee on Indian affairs. Commission and instructions for Peter Schuyler, Rev. Godfrey Dellius, Major Dirck Wessells and the mayor of Albany to treat with the five nations. Money to be paid to Rev. Mr Dellius for the charges of the commissioners. Connecticut men marching to Albany. Onondaga and Oneida Indians to be supplied with corn. Taxes in arrears.   207

23   Pemaquid fort taken by two French ships (see Hough,
New York *Pemaquid.* p. 134). Count Frontenac reported to have orders for the taking of Albany and Schenectady. The governor expresses his readiness to take the field. Winter clothing for troops at Albany. More men wanted from Connecticut and New Jersey. Council object to the governor's going. The Richmond to cruise between Delaware and Block Island.   213

27   Petition of Peter Chock against the sheriff (see *N. Y. col. mss,* 40:190) referred. Arrears of quitrents in Schenectady remitted. Patent granted to Giles Shelley. Warrant to Evert Bancker and Domine Dellius for Indian charges. Thos. Wenham, Jeremiah Tothill, Rob't Lurting and John Morris, in charge of the ship Sarah and Ellinor lately captured by the French and driven to New York by distress are granted leave to unload her duty free but not to sell

1696　　　　　　　　　　　　　　　　　　　　**v. 7**

her goods. Chaplain Smith to examine Peter Mingo as
to being fit for baptism. Rene Sunard purser of the French
man of war.　　　　　　　　　　　　　　　　　　213

Sep. 3　Warrants: to Hendrick van Rensselaer for military transportation; to John Cobrun for paving the magazine mount.
Land granted to Domine Dellius. License to Col. Beeckman. Supply for the provincial agents. Capt. Brant
Schuyler and Capt. Laurence Read to distribute money
among the fusileers.　　　　　　　　　　　　　214

10　Petition of Elizabeth Green referred to the overseers of the
Sarah and Ellinor. Warrants: to John Pelletreaux and to
James Wells for charges against the fort; to Corn's Low
for military transportation. Petitions: of John Kesham;
of Rob't Livingston, referred. Additional duty accounts.
Report on a memorial of Capt. Weems approved (see
N. Y. col. mss, 40:193).　　　　　　　　　　　215

12　The governor to go to Albany and meet the five nations.
Indian presents increased. Major Schuyler to victual
Albany troops. Assembly to adjourn. Clothing for the
soldiers. Proclamation for taking deserters to issue (see
N. Y. col. mss, 40:196).　　　　　　　　　　　216

15　Col. Willet complains against Justice Thos. Stevens, Capt.
Francis Doughty and Lieut. Edward Stevens for refusing
to sign the association. Soldiers' clothing. Warrants: to
Henry van Dyck for salary as surgeon at Albany; to Lieut.
Thos. Sharp for salary as gunner (see *N. Y. col. mss*, 40:192).
License to purchase land granted to Henry Filkin. Robert
Livingston. Mayor of New York city to be continued in
office.　　　　　　　　　　　　　　　　　　217

17　Robert Livingston's commission; he is temporarily suspended
from office as Indian agent (see *N. Y. col. mss*, 40:197).　218

Oct. 12　The governor reports on his doings at Albany. Journal to
be printed. Measures to be laid before the assembly.
Accounts. Petitions granted: of Joseph Holmes for land
in the rear of Vincent fountain granted; of Peter Minne
and Anthony Tyce for land on Staten Island; of Col.
Heathcote for license to purchase land between Scroton
river and Harrison's purchase.　　　　　　　　218

14　Mayor and sheriff of New York sworn in. Account of public
money in the receiver's hands called for.　　　　219

15　Warrants: to Nich's Bayard, to Stephen van Cortlandt, to
Fred. Philippse, to Gabriel Monvielle for moneys advanced
by them for military expenses; to Jacobus van Dyck for
salary as surgeon at Schenectady. Surveyor Henry
Cornelius Bogard to survey land: for Col. Smith; for John
Pew and Thos. Morgans.　　　　　　　　　　　220

1696   **v. 7**

22   French prisoners to be sent for exchange to England. Order
      on petition by Katherine Salway for exchange. Patent
      for land granted to Mr Barker. Sheriffs ordered to collect
      quitrents. Payment to Dirk van der Burgh. Rob't
      Livingston. Land in Westchester county to be surveyed
      for Caleb Heathcote according to Indian deed.   221

26   Gov. Stoughton of Connecticut reports a squadron of French
      ships has gone to Pettiguavas. Petition of French and
      Livingston for importation of certain goods granted.   222

28   Mayor of New York to have the city taxes collected and paid
      to the receiver-general.   222

30   Letters of denization granted to Erasmus Harrison. War-
      rants: to Harpert Jacobse for military transport; to Daniel
      Honan for Indian disbursements and military clothing; to
      Wm. Pinhorne for material in the fort.   222

Nov. 2 Execution of an act of assembly to be enforced. Soldiers
      to be paid. Land near the governor's garden to be leased
      to Caleb Heathcote for 41 years. Patent for land granted
      to Gerrit Roose. Surveys of land ordered on petitions by
      Col. Cortlandt and by Mr Tillier. Patents granted to
      —— Pullion, Col. Cortlandt, Simon Aertsen, and Elizabeth
      Peacock.   223

3   Warrant to Col. Abr'm de Peyster for Col. Rich'd Ingoldsby's
      charges on the frontiers.   224

5   Good news from Albany of a successful expedition against
      the French. Pay of soldiers. Col. Cortlandt, Col. Heathcote,
      and Daniel Honan advance money at 10% to the govern-
      ment. Justice Stevens, Capt. Doughty, and Lieut. Stevens
      arrested for refusing to sign the association. Warrant to
      Eliz. Butler for nursing —— Dowick a sick soldier.   224

6   Revenues fall short. Justice Stevens etc. have turned quakers
      and are dismissed from service. Pay of soldiers. Patent
      granted to Melle Caspers.   225

10   Warrant to Dan'l Honan for soldiers' pay. Money advanced
      by Cortlandt and others returned.   225

20   Gov. Fletcher absent on the frontiers. Pennsylvania sends
      by David Loyd money for the New York Indians.   226

27   Payment ordered to Giles Shelley for transporting Reyne
      Sinard of the French man of war.   226

Dec. 29 Flints for muskets required at Albany. Taxes. Jacob
      Rutsen justice of the peace refuses to account for taxes
      collected. Connecticut called upon for troops. Mr Nicoll
      wants more land.   227

1697

Feb. 2 Punishment to be inflicted upon the body of a dead negro
      sentenced for murder before his natural death.   227

Morris. Johann Provoost and Marg't Mauritz. Land granted to Gulick and Lake. Various accounts referred. Warrants: to John Pelletreaux for candles to the fort; to Francis Leconte for subsisting two French female prisoners; to Daniel Honan for money advanced by him, Col. Cortlandt, and Col. Bayard.   235

10   Connecticut's claim to Rye and Bedford. Indian affairs. James Stevens master of the ship Swift of Bristol before the council and allowed free entry. Taxes at Rye and Bedford. 237

17   Supply of firewood to the garrison at Albany by John Barker and Isaac Caspers.   238

20   Lot in Queen street, N. Y. granted to Major Merret. Lot granted to the secretary. Land in the Minissincks granted to Capt. Arent Schuyler. Excise at Albany. Dr Van Dyck's memorial referred. Various accounts referred. Warrants: to Lt. Col. Gabr. Monvielle for incidental charges; to Tames Wells for carpenter work in the fort; to Lieut. John Bulkeley for firewood to the garrison. Excise of New York to be let to the highest bidder at vendue in Geo. Rascarrick's house. Arrearages of taxes. 238

22   Justice Theale of Rye reports that the inhabitants of Rye and Bedford do not want to belong to New York. Embargo laid on all vessels because of privateers on the coast. Supply of bread for the city to be considered.   239

24   Rob't Livingston has failed to deliver letters from England. Rumors at Albany of a French attack. Fireships. Annexation of New York to Massachusetts.   240

27   Fireships. Warrants to Daniel Honan for levy money, and for expenses of governor's journey to Albany. Indian presents and soldiers' pay. Furniture for officers at Albany. Warrants: to Col. Nich's Bayard for Indian charges; to John Clap clerk of the assembly for charges. Expenses of the governor's journey to Pennsylvania. Warrants: to Stephen van Cortlandt for soldiers clothing and for incidental charges; to John Ashton storekeeper for firewood to the fort; to Thos. Monsey for sea charges; to Dirck van der Burgh for mason work in the fort; Daniel Honan resigns as accountant-general. Warrant to Jacob Moene armorer. Patent for land in Dutchess county granted to Caleb Heathcote, Augustine Graham, Henry Filkin, David Jamison, Henry Tenyck, John Aertsen, Wm. Creed, Jarvis Marshall and Jas. Emott, (Great nine partners). Survey of land for Thos. Laurence ordered, and for Thos. Codrington. Order on petition by John Cuyler. Land granted to Theunis Eghbertse. Survey ordered for Joost van Metere.   243

1697

Cases not tried: John Kiersted vs Walter Marshall; John
Delavall vs Walter Marshall; Walter Marshall vs James
Barbor; Joseph Lee vs Walter Marshall; David Dufoy vs
the same, all in ejectment.   33
Judgment in re Wallsall Cobbie vs Dr George Lockhart and
English Smith of London merchant.   33
Judgment in re Wm. Hallett vs Simon Valentine van der
Wilden.   43
Judgment in re Lucas Santen vs George Heathcote.   45
Order of court: Capt. Wallsall Cobbie discharged by virtue
of a habeas corpus; Hugh Ridell to give bail for having
stabbed Mich'l Vaughton; appraisal of the sloop Lancaster
Joseph Hopper master, and Geo. Heathcote owner, ordered.   50
October   Judgment in re Matthew Taylor vs John Crooke for trespass
and ejectment.   53
Judgment in re Amsell Samuel Levy vs Simon Valentine
van der Wilden for debt.   57
Judgment in re Darby Bryant vs Wm. Griffeth and John
Smith for trespass.   76
Judgment in re Wm. Creed vs Peter Delanoy for ejectment.   78

—————————

The remainder of "reversed side" is legislative minutes of the council,
separately paged 1-129, and published in *Journal of the legislative council of
the colony of New York*, 1:41-109.

—————————

Vol. 8, pt 1   1697-98

June 2   Carriages for field pieces to be provided. Embargo on outgoing vessels raised. Land granted to Stephen Cortlandt.   1
      3   Warrants: to John Cobrun stone cutter for paving the am-
munition mount; to Evert Janse, Volkert van Hoose,
Peter Bogardus and Francis Winne for military transportation; to Henry Ranslaer for transporting military provisions; to Thomas Monsey for charges in letting the excise; to Caleb Heathcote and Nich's Bayard for lime and
firewood; to the same for loss on Maryland bills. Survey
of land for Humphry Davenport ordered. Orders on petitions: by Henry Francis Brestead; by Robert Griffin
master of the ship Johanna, and Mathew Ling attorney for
Richard Willet factor to the creditors of Tyrens and Cruger.
Robert Livingston denies having received letters for the
governor.   1

1697   v. 8

5   Case of Robert Griffin and Mathew Ling vs Onzel van
    Swieter and Cruger considered out of the jurisdiction of
    council.   2

7   Permission given to export grain and provisions for the
    fleet and land forces at Newfoundland.   2

10 Orders on petitions: of Thomas Wenham; of White & Co.;
    of Mr van Rensselaer, and of others. Various accounts
    referred. Van Swieten and Cruger.   2

17 Order on petition by Mr Honeyman. Crew for the station
    ship Richmond. Small iron guns to be restored to Col.
    Lodwyçk. Land granted: in Orange county and in New
    York city to Samuel Bayard; in Flushing to Samuel
    Height. Licenses to purchase land: on the Mohawk river
    to Col. Schuyler, Domine Dellius, Mr Wessells, Mr Banker
    and Judge Pinhorne; near Rockenkoway pond to Wm.
    Nicoll. Patents for land: between Southampton, South-
    old and Brookhaven, to be added to St Georges manor
    granted to Wm. Smith; at the highlands to Adolph Phil-
    ipps. Confirmatory patent for land on Staten Island to
    Leonard Lewis. Patents for land in Orange county
    granted: to Lucas Tienhoven; to Matthias Blanchan. An
    Indian wife murderer to be tried by the Suffolk court of
    oyer and terminer. Order on petition by Matthew Plow-
    man. Patent for Cortlandt manor granted.   3

21 Patent for land granted to Col. Bayard. Orders on peti-
    tions: by Capt. van Rensselaer and by inhabitants of Ulster
    county for remission of quitrents. Queries by the lords
    of trade to be answered.   4

24 Payment of scouts. Orders on petitions: by Martin Cregier;
    by Gab. Monvielle; by Nicholas Stuyvesant. Warrants:
    to pay for work in the chapel; to Col. Stephen Cortlandt
    for soldiers pay and for timber to the fort; to Daniel Honan
    for plate in the chapel. Daniel Honan's resignation as ac-
    countant-general recommended to be accepted. Warrant
    to Col. Schuyler and Major Wessells for levy money. Capt.
    Joyner's petition referred. Livingston's petition referred.
    The secretary ordered to translate some papers from Dutch
    into English.   4

28 Permission given to take provisions to Curaçao. River In-
    dians on the Merrimack in New England. Pay of officers'
    servants.   5

July 1 Warrants: to Chidley Brooke for salary as receiver-general
    and auditor-general; to Nich's Stuyvesant for a bell bor-
    rowed from him and broken; to Col. Peter Schuyler for
    incidental expenses. Bond for Mathew Plowman late col-

lector given by Cols. Cortlandt and Bayard.   Warrants:
to Miles Forster for ironwork in the fort; to Isaac
Dechamps for same; to Col. Peter Schuyler and Major
Dirck Wessells for money advanced; to Rob't Livingston
for salary as sub-collector; to Col. Peter Schuyler for
soldiers' pay.   Confirmatory patent for lots in the city
granted to Wm. Huddleston and John Rodman.   Patent
granted to Anth'y Tyse and Peter Minne.   6

8   Orders on petition: by Dirck Hoghlandt; by Melle Casperse;
by Christina Venvoos.   Land granted to Matthias Hoogh-
telingh.   Report on repairs in the fort approved.   Money
granted by Pennsylvania in 1693.   Warrants: to Col. Peter
Schuyler for soldiers' blankets and for firewood; to Col.
Cortlandt for firewood to the Albany garrison.   No money
in the treasury.   Kings farm to be let for the benefit of
Trinity church.   7

10   Col. Schuyler and Major Wessells report that they cannot
raise money in Albany for support of the Indians.   Rumors
of a new governor coming and annexation to Boston prevent New York merchants from lending money.   Warrant to Francis Winne for the use of Col. Schuyler and
Major Wessells in paying scouts.   Prompt payment of
taxes urged by circular letters.   8

15   Mr Laurence opposes a grant to the Widow Venvoos.   The
wreck of the bark Swallow on Long Island.   Warrant to
Fred. Philipps for timber to the fort.   9

22   Indian affairs.   Defence of the frontiers.   Christina Venvoos.   Patents granted to Harrison & Co. and to John de
Bruyn.   Warrant to Johannes van Zant for turners work
in the fort.   Warrant formerly issued to Dirck van der
Burgh recalled and four new ones issued each for ¼ of
the original.   9

23   Indian affairs.   Col. Cortlandt to supply the New York
garrison with firewood.   10

29   Various accounts referred.   Warrants: to Harpert Jacobse
for transporting soldiers to Albany; to Col. Peter Schuyler
to pay Isaac Casperse and Johs Bleecker for firewood.
Land on Staten Island ordered to be surveyed for Richard
Morrell.   Warrants for salaries.   10

31   Patent for land on Mohawk river granted to Col. Schuyler
and partners.   Col. Schuyler's account referred.   Major
Dirck Wessells to collect all taxes and arrearages of taxes
in Ulster and Dutchess counties.   Confirmatory patent
granted to Widow Venvoos.   11

Aug. 4   Rumors from Rhode Island and Boston of an attack intended
by the French; precautions taken.   11

5 Warrants: to Peter Jacob Marius for money advanced; to Col. Peter Schuyler for a debt due him by a soldier; to Stephen Cortlandt for firewood. Excise at Albany. Joseph Smith not to be tried by special commission. Warrant to David Jamison clerk of the council for this book of minutes. Dirck Hooghlandt's petition for land not granted, it being in Gravesend patent. 12

19 Confirmatory patents granted to Abr'm Lakeman; and to Egbert Teunisse and Barent Albertse Bradt. Survey of land for Anthony Bagley ordered. Warrants: to Peter Bogardus for transportation of soldiers; to Capt. John Merrett for a recruiting journey to Connecticut. Survey of land for Jan Swebringh ordered. Warrant to Col. Peter Schuyler for salary as commissary. Lease of Kings farm for 7 years to be given to Trinity church. Warrant to Col. Nich's Bayard to pay express messengers from Ulster county. 12

Sep. 2 Patent for land granted to John Cuyler. Warrants: to Daniel Honan as overseer of the workmen in the fort; to Giles Gaudineau for nursing a French prisoner. Accounts referred. Warrants: to Col. Stephen Cortlandt for pay of express messengers from Albany; to Giles Shelley for passage of Reyne Sinard a French prisoner. Orders: on petition by Jacob Lockermans; on a memorial relative to arrears of quitrents in Ulster county. 13

7 Order relative to an examination into prizes and privateers by Mr Jennings and Mr Robinson. 14

9 Patent for city lots granted to Thomas Roberts. Order on petition by Balthazar Bayard. 14

20 Order on petition by Ebenezar Dennis and Edward Streete quartermaster of the bark Dorothy privateer against Capt. John Evans of the Richmond. Patents granted: to Wm. Nicoll for Raconckonny pond and land on Mannetasquett river; to John Cornelius for his son Benjamin for land at Ramepogh, Orange county. Order on a petition of Patrick Waldron a sick soldier. 14

21 Capt. John Evans defends his proceedings against the bark Prophet Daniel, and Dorothy. 15

28 Order on petition by David Collins concerning the pink Blossom. Land in Orange county granted to Cornelius Clausen. The case of the Prophet Daniel. 15

29 Major William Merrett nominated for mayor of New York and Capt. Ebenezar Wilson for sheriff. 16

30 Warrant of survey granted to Aeltie Slegtenhorst. French prisoners. The case of the bark Prophet Daniel decided.

1697   v. 8

Payment ordered to Col. Peter Schuyler for a debt due by
Serg't Berryford.   Warrants: to Lieut. Thos. Sharp for
salary as gunner at Albany; to David Hendrix for transporting the governor's baggage from Pennsylvania.
Order on a memorial by Col. de Peyster relative to stores
imported by Griffith.   The attorney-general to prosecute
delinquent taxpayers.   16

Oct. 14   Collection of taxes to be enforced, the earl of Bellomont
not having arrived with money for the soldiers as expected.   Petition of Joseph Smith referred.   Mayor and
sheriff sworn in.   Proclamation by the mayor etc. of Albany against the exportation of grain approved.   Land at
Waghaghkemek granted to Codeber & Co.   Order on
petition for land by Peter Hendrix de Haas.   License to
purchase land granted to the secretary.   Warrant of survey
granted to Wm. West.   Letters of denization granted upon
the petition of Rev. P. Pieret, to six protestant French
men taken prisoners (see *N. Y. col. mss*, 41:120).   Order
on petition by Claus Evertse for leave to proceed to
Curaçao.   Warrants for salaries of judicial and civil officers.   17

21   Coats for the sentries to be provided.   Warrant to Ann
Bowen for keeping two sick soldiers, Patrick Waldron and
John Ormson.   Land near Saratoga granted to Peter
Hendrix de Haas.   Warrant to Col. Henry Beekman for
express charges.   Order on account of Mrs Macgregere
vs Col. Dongan.   Warrants: to Adam Wallice for pay;
to Capt. James Weems for a coat to Ephraim Pangborne;
to Omy de Lagrange for transporting soldiers to and from
Albany; to John Crooke cooper for work in the powder
magazine.   Assembly to be prorogued.   18

26   Collection of taxes.   French prisoners.   Taxes on Long
Island to be collected by Capt. Thos. Clarke, in Richmond
county by Major Wessells, in New York and Orange
counties by the mayor.   19

28   Lieut. Abr'm Beeckford of Col. Ingoldsby's company to have
furniture like other officers.   Taxes of New York city.
Lord Bellomont expected daily to arrive.   Financial
difficulties about soldiers' pay.   20

Nov. 4   Warrants: to John Pelletreaux for candles to the fort; to
Col. Peter Schuyler etc. for pay of scouts; to Daniel Honan
for locks to the fort.   Land granted: to John Cassee; to
Jacob Corbett.   Proclamation to issue concerning desertions.   Warrant to Col. Peter Schuyler for salary as commissary.   20

12   Land granted: to Richard Smith; to Isaac Billian.   Order
     on petition by Edw. Livingston.   Warrants: to Col.
     Stephen Cortlandt for incidental charges and for firewood;
     to the mayor of Albany to pay for work on the new bar-
     racks.   Mrs Fletcher and many " gentlewomen of the best
     quality " obtain a reprieve for four deserters condemned to
     death.   21

18   Complaint of the church officers at Kingston against their
     minister, Domine Johs. Petrus Nucella read.   Warrant
     of survey for Widow Dorothy Clark's meadow issued.
     Order on report upon Edw. Livingston's petition for free
     admission of sugar.   22

25   Claus Evertse granted permission to purchase provisions for
     his ship Meerman.   Warrants of survey granted: to Roeloff
     and Daniel Swebringh; to Hendrick van Dyck and to
     Thomas Stillwell.   Warrant to John Ashton for painting
     in the chapel.   Reward granted to Lieut. Abr'm Beeckford
     for catching deserters.   Quitrents on Long and Staten
     islands and in Westchester to be collected.   22

Dec. 2 Tax of one penny per pound.   Account books of the ac-
     countant-general.   Warrant for the salaries of the
     accountant-and the auditor-general.   Captives in Algier
     with the exception of Barthold Rolfton having been
     redeemed or died, the money collected for that purpose to
     go to Trinity church; order to the trustees Stephen van
     Cortlandt, Peter Jacobs [Marius], Dr John Kerbyle and
     Johs. Kipp concerning it (see *Doc. hist. N. Y.* 3:419;
     Q 3:254).   Order on a petition for land by Daniel Honan
     and Mich'l Howden.   Warrant to Major Wm. Merret
     for account of Col. Young.   Order on petition by Dirck
     van der Burgh for interest.   Warrant to Major Wm.
     Merret for incidental charges in Gov. Sloughter's time.
     Order in re Simeon Soumaine (Sonman) vs Wm. Prusher.
     Warrant to Col. Abr. de Peyster for wine given to the
     soldiers to drink the king's health.   23

29   Confirmatory patent granted to Peter Peterse and Gillis
     Inyard.   Tax of one penny per pound.   Rewards to
     Capt. Weems and Lieut. Bulkeley for catching de-
     serters.   Census for New York, Kings and Queens
     counties ordered.   Warrant to Onzeel van Swieten for
     painting and glass in the chapel.   Capt. Thos. Clarke
     appointed collector of quitrents in New York, Orange,
     Westchester and Richmond counties and on Long Island.
     Nicholas Feilding appointed landwaiter vice Wood
     resigned.   24

1697   v. 8

20   Advice of a peace with France received from Boston and
     orders sent to Albany to persuade the Indians to bury the
     hatchet.   Lord Bellomont reported on the coast, Gov.
     Fletcher surrenders the plate for Kings chapel to the clerk
     of the council.   Confirmatory patent granted to Sarah
     Scidmore.   25

23   Col. Cortlandt's account of money sent to Albany for pay-
     ment of scouts.   Daniel Honan's account for incidental
     charges.   Warrant to Daniel Honan for work in the
     chapel.   Preparations for the reception of Lord Bellomont.   26

28   Warrants: to Dirck van der Burgh for work in the fort; to
     John Chavalier for carpenter work in the fort; to Col.
     Stephen Cortlandt for incidental charges; to Daniel Honan
     for accountant work before he was appointed; for salaries
     of officers.   Confirmation by the lords justices of a number
     of laws relating to the Leisler affair, militia, town govern-
     ment, taxes, intestates estates, etc., passed in 1695.   Quar-
     ters for Lord Bellomont.   26

30   Auditing of Col. Dongan's accounts deferred.   27

1698

Jan. 6   News from Albany of an alarm (see *N. Y. col. mss*, 41:139).
     Canadian prisoners to be released.   Trial of a soldier for
     killing an Indian deferred.   Trial of Gerrit Teunissen
     for accidentally killing a small daughter of Col. Schuyler
     deferred (see *N. Y. col. mss*, 41:138).   Warrants: to Col.
     Schuyler, Major Wessells and Captain van Rensselaer for
     soldiers pay; to Major Wm. Wessells for incidental
     charges and taxes on the kings house.   28

20   Order on petition of Dirck Jansen Hooghlandt.   Warrants:
     to Wm. Sharpas for clerical duties; to Thomas Wenham
     for powder to Capt. Mitchell's sloop.   Order on complaint
     of Peter Chock against Justice Hicks.   29

Feb. 10   Accounts referred.   Warrant to Major Wm. Merret for
     house rent.   Indian affairs.   Phil. Ketcham of Newtown
     appointed collector vice Edward Stevens who asks to be
     relieved.   Gallery in Trinity church for the governor and
     council at government expense.   29

Mar. 4   Council meet in the house of a member confined by gout.
     Warrants: to John Pelletreaux for candles; to Savoy
     Dechamps for ironwork to the fort; to Nich's Bayard for
     incidental charges; to Williamke Schermerhoorn for trans-
     porting provisions to Albany; to Johannes Sanders for
     repairing blockhouse at Schenectady; to Gerardus van der
     Beeck for grave cloths and to John de la Montague for
     burying soldiers.   John Lawrence appointed guardian of
     his insane son, John.   Order for printing certain papers.   30

17 Warrant to Col. Stephen Cortlandt for firewood and for
clothing for Wahauá the Indian. Orders: on petition by the
agents of the city of Albany; on an Indian deed to Mr
van Rensselaer. Petitions of Johannes Cuyler and James
Bobin referred. Land granted to Andrew Cannon.   31

24 Act of parliament relating to trade via Maryland read.
Ann Bowen's payment for taking care of Patrick Waldron
a sick soldier. Warrant to Capt. Peter Matthews for incidental charges. Address to the king to be drawn up
and the assembly to join. Petition of Dr Tienhoven and
Daniel Waldron referred (see *N. Y. col. mss*, 41:146).   31

29 Warrant to Abr'm Schuyler and John Rosie for expenses
on their journey to Albany (see *N. Y. col. mss*, 41:148).
Patent granted to Hendrick van Rensselaer.   32

31 Memorials of Capt. Hyde and of Mr Brooks referred. Payment of Edward Antill as captain under Sir Edm. Andros ordered. No funds to pay George Scott armorer
under Andros. Collection of taxes.   32

Ap. 1 Warrants: to Chidley Brooke for agency expenses; to John
Perry carpenter for the gallery in Trinity church. Committee appointed to meet Lord Bellomont. Warrants: to
Lt. Col. Gabr. Monvielle for wine on thanksgiving day;
to Capt. Peter Mathews for repairs of the barge; for
official salaries. Ann Bowen's memorial referred.   33

2 Richard, earl of Bellomont the new governor, and Capt.
John Nanfan lieutenant governor present. Lord Bellomont has his commission read, the seals are delivered to
him, the oaths administered to him and the lieutenant
governor, and he swears in the council. Proclamations
to be drawn: 1) For dissolving the assembly (see *N. Y.
col. mss* 42:1); 2) Against vice and profaneness; 3) To
confirm all officers in their positions. Writs prepared for
a new assembly.   34

5 Attorney-general James Graham and Sec. Mathew Clarkson
sworn in. The new assembly to meet May 18th. Special
commission to sit for the trial of three sailors accused of
murdering their captain and supercargo.   34

21 Commissioners to be sent to Canada with the articles of
peace and to treat for an exchange of prisoners. Col.
Peter Schuyler sworn in as councillor. Col. Peter Schuyler and Mr Godfrey Dellius to be commissioners to
Canada. Warrant for their expenses.   35

May 8 Extraordinary meeting of council. Oath of secrecy administered to the lieutenant governor, also to Edward Randolph and Thomas Weaver who are not members of the

1698   **v. 8**

council. Investigations into Gov. Fletcher's and Wm
Nicoll's connection with pirates. Wm Nicoll suspended
from the council and with Capt. Evans put under bail.   35

17　Measures to be laid before the assembly. Committee appeared to swear in the assembly. All excise except that
of Albany to be farmed.   39

18　Order on petition of Lieut. Young for his pay.   39

19-23　Legislative minutes (see *Jour.* 1:111-13).   40-43

24　The lords of trade deny the right of a port of entry at Perth
Amboy, N. J.; proclamation to issue to that effect because
many people think of moving there. Another proclamation against enlisting under foreign princes. Clothing to
be provided for Mohawk proselytes.   43

June 1　Legislative minutes (see *Jour.* 1:113-14). Warrant to Brandt
Schuyler for payment of provisions in Albany.   43

4　Present to be given to Wappingnes and Wighquighskeck
Indians come to welcome the new governor.   45

7　Order for the trial of Barent Albertse Bradt accused of having killed an Onondaga sachem. Owners of vessels going
to Madagascar to give bail, that they will not trade with
pirates; this measure referred to the assembly. Wm Pinhorne suspended from the council. Chidley Brooke likewise from the office of receiver-general, and collector of
the customs; and from the council. Col. Stephen Cortlandt and Thos. Monsey jointly appointed to be receiver-
general and collector. Chidley Brooke removed from his
office as judge, and the governor's reasons for the suspension signed by E. Randolph surveyor-general.   45

8　Legislative minutes (see *Jour.* 1:114): Order on petition by
George Philipps minister of Jamaica. Salaries of the
French ministers, Pieret of New York and Bondet of New
Rochelle, increased. Petitions of Joseph Smith for salary
as comptroller of ordnance, and George Scott as armorer
referred.   47

9　Indian presents. The governor proposes to visit the frontiers. Warrant to Robt Livingston for expenses of the
governor's journey. Buildings in the fort to be finished.
The gate-house to be enlarged to admit the governor's
coach. Legislative minutes (see *Jour.* 1:115).   48

10　Legislative minutes (see *Jour.* 1:115): Fees allowed to the
judge of the admiralty.   49

14　Chidley Brooke ordered to pay over the public money to
Col. Stephen Cortlandt. Legislative minutes (see *Jour.*
1:115): Agent for the province to reside in England.   50

16　Order on petitions; by Widow Mary Milbourne; by Onzeel

van Swieten. Geo. Philipps against Jamaica. Order on petition by Robt. Livingston jr and David Schuyler, opposed by Robt. Livingston sr.   51

18   Letter from Gov. J. Basse of New Jersey to Lord Bellomont refusing to surrender some pirates imprisoned in New Jersey, and answer. Order relating to a sloop seized for not being qualified according to act of parliament. Warrant to John Perry for carpenter work in the fort. John Ashton storekeeper to oversee the work in the fort. Defence of Wm Pinhorne.   52

25   Accounts referred. Rye and Bedford. Confirmatory patent granted to Major General Winthrope. Petitions of Agustie Keyser and Hendrick Janse referred. Order on petition by Jan Hooghtdingh for release of his condemned sloop. Major Selleck and other commissioners of Connecticut admitted. Henry Beeckman examined as to his connection with an act against unlawful by-laws (bolting act) for which Gov. Fletcher is reported to have received £400.   55

July   4   The governor about to go to Albany recommends to the mayor and aldermen the peace of the city. Canada claims the five nations. Orders on petitions: by Mrs Delanoy; French protestants on Staten Island; Anna Bowen; Jacob Codeberand; Johs. de Graves. Warrants: to Chidley Brooke for charges of 2 Indians returned from England in the Fowey; to the same for charges in letting the excise to farm, for office expenses, for salary; to Robt. Anderson for porterage.   56

6   Order on complaint of Jacob Leisler against the sheriff's high charges. Warrants for official salaries.—Parmiter appointed sheriff of New York vice Capt. Wilson suspended on charges.   57

22   Lord Bellomont absent. New Jersey asserts her right to a free port at Amboy; New York customs officers to go to Amboy and watch.   58

23   The governor of New Jersey demands a clearance to Amboy for the ship Dispatch, Stephen Jerome master; he reasserts the right to a free port.   58

Aug.   5   Security to be taken for the Dispatch until the government in England decides the New Jersey claim.   59

15   Lord Bellomont returned, reports on his transactions with the Indians. Petitions of inhabitants of Albany and Schenectady for payment of government debts granted. Col. Wm Smith in the name and by order of the council compliments the governor on his " successful pains with

1698   **v. 8**

the Indians." Canada and the five nations. Schenectady
barracks to be repaired.   59

16   Constables of New York sharply reprimanded for neglect of
duty. Warrant to Col. Peter Schuyler for firewood.
Agreement to be made for delivery of firewood to Albany
garrison. Wm Shaw searcher at Albany. Excise at Albany. Pay to Dr van Dyck and Dr Staats for salary as
surgeons to the Albany companies. Order on petition by
Andries Coeyman (see *N. Y. col. mss,* 42:48).   61

17   Indian affairs. The mayor of Albany and John Baptista the
interpreter, to go to Onondaga. Messenger sent to
Canada.   61

Sep. 2   Lord Bellomont sick. A pirate ashore at Lewis in Delaware bay; Capt. Cullford of the Fowey man-of-war refuses to go in pursuit having orders to return to England.
Deserters from his ship sheltered in East Jersey. Pilotage
for the Deptford man-of-war demanded by Capt. John
Trevitt. Embargo on outward bound ships.   63

21   Lord Bellomont sick. Indian news.   63

28   Barne Cosens appointed clerk of the council vice David
Jamison dismissed. Nichs. Bayard, Gabriel Minvielle and
John Lawrence suspended from the council; Abr. de
Peyster, Robt. Livingston and Samuel Staats appointed
in their places and sworn in. Thomas Willett and Richd.
Townley also suspended. Warrant for salaries of civil
officers.   64

29   Fredk. Philipps relieved from the council at his own request,
he being 73 years old; Robert Walters appointed in his
place and sworn in; Capt. John de Peyster appointed
mayor, and Isaac de Reymer sheriff of New York.   64

Oct. 4   Abrm. de Peyster appointed justice of the supreme court of
judicature and sworn in. James Spencer innholder committed for slandering the governor. Warrant to Lieut.
Thomas Sharp for salary as gunner at Albany.   65

6   Report by John Schuyler and John Rosie on their journey
to Canada. Journal of John Schuyler read (see *N. Y. col.
mss,* 42:69-70). Accounts of John Schuyler, of Lieut.
Daniels, and of Richard Staats referred. Proclamation to
issue for a day of prayer. Warrants: to Abrm. de Peyster
for expenses of governor's journey to Albany, Indian presents etc; for Indian presents to Onzeel van Swieten; to
Samuel Bayard; to Johs. van Cortlandt; to Rip van Dam
for a travelling chest; for Indian presents to Gabriel Minvielle; to Peter Morin brazier; to Steven de Lancey; to
Moses Levi; to Arent the turner for gun carriages; for

Indian presents and governor's charges to Robert Livingston; for use of his sloop to Harpert Jacobse; to Abrm.
Provoost; for provisions to Indians and French prisoners
to R. Livingston; to Dr James Brodie for salary as
surgeon to the govenor; to R. Livingston for expenses of
governor's journey to Albany; to the same for care of
sick soldiers and repairing blockhouses; for expenses in
Albany fort and for Indian charges; to John Clapp for
salary as clerk of the assembly; to Isaac Caspersen for firewood to Albany garrison; to Robert Livingston for
soldier's pay.   66

7   Hendrick Hanson appointed mayor, and John Groenendyck
sheriff of Albany. Warrants: to Capt. John Schuyler, John
Rosie, Dirck van der Heyden, John Livingston, David
Schuyler for their journey to Canada; to Lieut. Daniel
Hunt for repairing barracks and blockhouses at Schenectady; to Richard Staats messenger of the council for horsehire.   68

10   Little Minissinck Indians before the council offer their land
for sale. Orders on petitions: by Mary Milburn (see N. Y.
col. mss, 42:73-74); by John Middag (see N. Y. col. mss,
42:73-74; 75); by Dirck vander Heyden (see N. Y. col. mss,
42:72). Order on a representation by Col. Wm Smith relating to his property near the fort.   70

14   Licenses to purchase Indian land granted: to Widow Rim-
derig Quick (see N. Y. col. mss, 42-76); to Wm. Tietsoor
(see L. P. 4:104). Mayor John de Peyster, and Sheriff
Isaac de Reymer sworn in. Warrants: to John Peter
Melett blacksmith for work in the fort; to Dirck Benson
for transportation of prisoners from Albany; to Miles
Forster for candles sent to Albany; to Col. Peter Schuyler for salary as victualler; to Col. Stephen Cortlandt for
timber, firewood and work in the fort and presents to Long
Island Indians; to Robert Livingston for outfit and provi-
sions to French prisoners; to Major Dirck Wessells for
Indian expenses; to Anne Bowen for keeping two sick
soldiers, Patrick Waldron and John Armston; to Robt.
Livingston for John Schuyler's journey to Canada; to John
Peter Melett for ironwork in the chapel; to Ryer
Schermerhoorn, and to Robt. Livingston for military
transportation.   71

22   Accounts of Robert Livingston, Col. Romar's (see N. Y. col.
mss, 42:89) and others referred. Orders on petitions: by
John Simpson (see N. Y. col. mss, 42:88); by Claus Clause
Slyter for land (see N. Y. col. mss, 42:84); by Thos.

Parmyter and Peter Chock for land in Queens county.
Warrant to Aug. Graham surveyor-general for a map of
the province made by him. Bedding for soldiers. Indians.
Orders: on the account of Capt. Joachim Staats; on the
petition of Lieut. Math. Shanke (see *N. Y. col. mss*, 42:85);
on the petition of John Trevitt (see *N. Y. col. mss*, 42:86);
on the accounts of Surgeon Jacob Staats and of Hendrick
and Jacobus van Dyck.   73

Nov. 7   Soldiers quarters at Albany. French prisoners. Order on
petition by Capt. John Smith of the brigantine Swift and
of Capt John Blake of the bark Concord (see *N. Y. col.
mss*, 42:101). Sheriff to be appointed for and Representatives chosen in Orange county, as in other counties. Warrants: to Robt. Livingston for money advanced; to Abrm
de Peyster for freight of military stores from England.
Lieut. Mathew Shanke to be provided with bedding. Warrants: to Robert Livingston for sundries to the Indians
and French prisoners, also for salary as commissary; to
Surgeons Hendrick and Jacob van Dyck for salary; to
Harpert Jacobse and Evert Bancken for rum to the
Indians; to Joachim Staats for the use of his sloop; to
Col. Wm Romar for expenses in viewing fortifications at
Albany and Schenectady; to Dr Jacob Staats for attend-
ing sick soldiers.   74

10   Three representatives to be elected for Albany city and
county. Order on petition by Barent Pieterse Coeman.
Warrants: to Abrm de Peyster for wine given to the
soldiers; to Richard Stocks messenger of the council, for
horsehire.   76

17   Order on representation by Ducie Hungerford surveyor of
the customs that the mayors court has no jurisdiction beyond low water mark.   76

23   Proclamation against boarding vessels before the customs
officers to issue. The ship Hester ready to sail from Perth
Amboy without clearance from New York to be seized.
Order on petition for bedding by the soldiers at Albany.
Warrant to Gabriel Ludlow for clerical work. Proclamation to issue relating to the oath of allegiance (see *N. Y.
col. mss*, 42:117).   77

24   Order for the seizure of the ship Hester at Amboy by Ducie
Hungerford; instructions to Capt. Peter Matthews for that
purpose: 78

26   Order on petition by Capt. Adam Baldrige and Wm Taylor
owners of the Swift, and of Capt. Blake of the Concord
for release of their vessels. Warrant to John Nanfan for

1699   **v. 8**

20   Order on petition by Richard Wyse. John Lawrence sheriff
      of Queens county, reports tumultuous behavior in his
      county; his petition dismissed.   Order on petition by Johs.
      Beeckman (see *N. Y. col. mss,* 42:140).   88

28   Warrants: to Abrm Gouverneur for expenses on journeys
      for the public service (see *N. Y. col. mss,* 42:142); to Martin
      Wenham for salary as postrider (see *N. Y. col. mss,* 42:141);
      to Thos. Wenham for sauce. Accounts referred.   Warrant
      to Abrm de Peyster for wine given to the trainbands.   88

Mar. 9 Petition of Dirck Jansen Hooglandt referred.   Col. Isaac
      Arnold commissioned to make seizures on Long Island
      under the provincial acts, or trade and navigation acts;
      his salary.   John Townsend to be surveyor of the customs
      and searcher at Oyster bay, Huntington and Musketoe
      cove. Henry Jourdains account referred (see *N. Y. col. mss,*
      42:152).   89

13   Order granting the petition of Joseph Langdon.   Warrants:
      to Col. Stephen Cortlandt for expenses in seizing the ship
      Hester; for candles and coals to the fort, timber, Indian
      presents and money advanced for lieutenant governor's
      salary; to Joachim Staats for bringing the lieutenant
      governor from Albany; to Barne Cosens for stationery;
      to Miles Forster for candles to the fort; to .Col. Wm
      Romar inginieir-general for fireworks etc; to Col. Stephen
      Cortlandt and Ducie Hungerford commissioners of the
      customs for incidental charges.   89

14   Orders received from England for the prosecution of Adam
      Baldridge accused of harboring and trading with pirates
      at the Island of St Marie near Madagascar.   91

16   New custom-house barge to be built.   Officers' quarters.
      Proclamation against lotteries to issue (see *N. Y. col. mss,*
      42:152).   Richard Floyd jr of Suffolk county summoned
      before the council on a charge of having cut up a drift
      whale, and justices Richd. Whodle and Thos. Holmes
      ordered to seize the blubber. Order in the suit of Tyrans
      and Cruger vs de Peyster.   91

20   Same case continued. Lord Bellomont's commission for the
      vice-admiralty read.   Thomas Parmyter late gunner sum-
      moned before the council.   92

21   Order concerning the pay due to Thomas Parmyter late
      gunner and supervisor of buildings.   92

22   Capt. John Nanfan's commission as lieutenant governor
      read.   He and the governor take the prescribed oaths.
      John Townsend wishes to surrender his commission of sur-
      veyor of customs at Oysterbay.   The matter is laid be-
      fore the assembly.   93

1699   v. 8

13   Agreement with Jan Baptist van Eps for a journey to On-
      ondaga reported.   101

19   Memorials by Ducie Hungerford and by John Evetts re-
      ferred. Reward to be paid to John Morrey for intercepting
      a letter from Broadish the pirate, to Col. Pierson.   102

22   Accounts of seizing etc the ship Hester audited and ad-
      justed.   102

25   Thomas Palmer comptroller of the customs suspended for
      misbehavior.   103

26   Petition by Garret van Trift referred to the mayor and alder-
      men for report.   103

27   Col. Dongan's accounts. Execution to issue against Valen-
      tine Cruger surviving partner of Francis Tyrens in re de
      Peyster. Inventory of a bag of jewels given by Joseph
      Broadish the pirate to Lt. Col. Henry Pierson.   104

May 4 Return of the execution against Val. Cruger "non est in-
        ventus." Petitions of Duncan Campbell (see *N. Y. col.
        mss*, 43:1) referred.   105

5   Warrant to Lieut. John Riggs for pursuing deserters to the
      Jerseys and for shifting powder.   105

8   Revenue accounts to be audited. Excise in Kings, Queens,
      Richmond, Westchester and Ulster counties.   105

10   Order on petition by Wm Shackerly.   106

11   Return of scire facias in re De Peyster vs Cruger. Case of
      the ship Adventure Joseph Broadish pretended master.   106

12   Indian presents. Inventory of papers belonging to the
      estate of — Shackerly deceased ordered to be made. War-
      rants: to Col. Abrm de Peyster for wine given to the
      soldiers; to Col. Wm Smith for express messengers sent
      on public service; to Samuel Staats for Dumont pòstrider
      in Ulster county.   107

13   Hearing of the case de Peyster vs Cruger. Execution to
      issue against Cruger's bail.   108

14   Proclamation to issue against holding correspondence with
      the Scotch ships fitted out for making a settlement in
      America (Caledonia).   109

15   Warrants: to Wm Bradford for printing the votes of the
      assembly; to Robt Livingston for soldiers' pay.   109

p. m. Warrants: to Gabriel Ludlow for salary as clerk of the as-
        sembly; to Gabriel Thompson for salary as assembly door-
        keeper; to Wm Bradford for stationery; to James Gra-
        ham for services as speaker of the assembly. Additional
        instructions for the governor, and the governor's instruc-
        tions for the lieutenant governor, entered verbatim. War-

1699   v. 8

rants: to Barne Cosens for government services; to David
de Bon Repos for pension. Order on petition by Col.
Abrm de Peyster relating to the ship Fortune (see *N. Y.
col. mss*, 43:43-44).   109

16   Audit of Robt. Livingston's accounts ordered by the lords
of the treasury. Petition by Benj. Feneile (Faneuil)
granted (see *N. Y. col. mss*, 43:43-44).   114

19   Lord Bellomont absent in Boston. Decision of the attorney-
general that a certain oath relating to the plantation trade
cannot be administered to the lieutenant governor. Warrant to Arnout Cornelise Viele for expenses on his journey
to Onondaga. Indian affairs; Mr Dellius suspended from
his ministerial function. Order on petition by Jacob
Gerriot.   115

25   Review of the accounts of Gabriel Ludlow clerk of the assembly ordered. Wm Lawrence and John Barbaree to
be guardians of John Lawrence, non compos mentis.
Order on petition of Lawyer Antill for appeal to the King's
council in England in re Wandall vs Alsopp.   116

31   John and Wm Bulckley's demurrer read. Order on petition
by Wm Creed (see *N. Y. col. mss*, 43:23). Warrants to
Robert Livingston for payments to soldiers at Albany and
Schenectady, to Indians, to French prisoners, to sick
soldiers and for salary as commissary.   116

June 5   Letter (verbatim) of Col. Jeremiah Basse governor of the
Jerseys, relating to Capt. Shelley a pirate arrived at Cape
May. Capt. Giles Shelley summoned before the council.
Indian affairs.   117

7   Indian affairs. Edward Buckmaster who confessed to have
been in the ship Nassau, Giles Shelley captain at Madagascar and Ste Marie committed.   118

14   Otto van Toyle also accused of piracy likewise committed.   118

21   Domine Dellius and the Indians. Custom-house barge.
Order on memorial by Paroculus Parmyter and a petition
by Mary Drew (see *N. Y. col. mss*, 43:26).   119

22   Warrants to Daniel Bondet French minister of New
Rochelle, and Peter Peret French minister of New York.
Order on petition by Sarah van Feurden.   119

28   Warrants for salaries of civil officers. Indians. Case of the
ship Nassau found abandoned at Redd Hook.   120

July 5   Order from Lord Bellomont at Boston for the commitment
of Capt. Giles Shelley and crew of the Nassau; no piracy
being charged against them it cannot be done. Petition
of John Gerretse Decker referred.   121

8   Indian affairs.   121

1699   **v. 8**

16   Lt. Gov. Nanfan takes the oath to observe the acts of trade.
      Companions of Capt. Kidd offer to turn informers if
      assured of their own safety.   127

18   Orders on petitions: by the mayor of New York (see *N. Y.
      col. mss*, 43:42); by Michael Hawdon (see *N. Y. col. mss*,
      43:41); by Rich. Voizy. Warrants: to Jean Rosie, Abrm
      Schuyler, and Fraer Armot, for expenses on journey to
      Canada (see *N. Y. col. mss*, 42:40); to Jan Baptist van Eps
      for journey to Onondaga. Accounts of the ship Fortune.
      Order on complaint by Peter Villeponteaux vs Mr Bondet.
      Scheme for erecting courts of judicature drawn u~ by Col.
      Wm Smith, John Guest, and James Graham approved. An
      Indian of Suffolk county to be tried for barn burning.
      Warrants: to Stephen Cortlandt for carpenter work in the
      fort; to Capt. Brandt Schuyler for nails to the fort; to
      Jacobus van Cortlandt for boards etc to the fort.   128

23   Warrant to Col. Abr'm de Peyster for purchasing the ship
      Fortune (see *N. Y. col. mss*, 44:43-44). Letter received
      from Sec. Vernon directing Capt. Kidd and his crew to be
      seized. Order for seizure of James Gillam repeated
      (p. 125). Orders on petitions: by Wm Paterson; by John
      Granada a Spaniard; by Thos. Worden. Order for the
      discharge of Rich'd Voizy from Capt. Robert Drummond's
      Scotch ship. Accounts of Alletie Doornes widow, and
      George Sydenham to be audited. Habeas corpus act not
      to be in force in the colonies.   130

25   Cornelius Quick mariner gives information concerning Capt.
      Kidd's treasure.   130

26   Proclamation to issue for the capture of Edward Buckmaster
      (see *N.Y. col. mss*, 43:50). John Tuthill before the council. 130

29   Proclamations to issue: for the arrest of James Gillam,
      Humphrey Clay, and English Smith; for proroguing the
      assembly.   131

30   Wm Murray and David Munro allowed to land from the
      Scotch ship Unicorn. Schaakhook Indians. Onondaga
      Indians trade in Pennsylvania, Daniel Tay to be land and
      tidewaiter vice John Parmyter declined.   131

Sep. 7 Indian affairs. James Gillam the pirate. Pirates' goods.
      Domine Nucella and John Martin refuse to surrender the
      letter sent from Canada to Domine Dellius. Orders on
      petitions: by Samuel Wood of Suffolk county; by free-
      holders of Brookland; by mayor of New York for demoli-
      tion of two bastions; to Elias Nean for his sufferings as a
      protestant in France. John Barbarie is at his own request
      relieved from the guardianship of John Lawrence (p. 116).

1699   **v. 8**

Crew of the pinnace. Revenue accounts. Trial of Indian
barn burner. Highways to be laid out in Richmond
county.   132

11   Thomas Clarke to be arrested for connection with Capt.
Kidd. Powder for the Schaakhook Indians.   133

13   John Chiampanti appointed agent of the province vice
Weaver returning to New York. Samuel Vetch, Robert
and Thomas Drummond summoned before the council.
John Tuthill also. Order on complaint of Capt. Thos.
Wenham vs deputy naval officer John Parmyter for ille-
gally seizing the ship Speedwell.   133

14   Naval officer Paroculus Parmyter informs the council that
an information against the Speedwell has been filed in
the court of admiralty. Michael Harding wants to hire
part of the custom-house.   134

21   Firewood for Albany garrison. Part of the custom-house
leased to Michael Hawdon (Harding) (p. 134). Letters
of denization for Surgeon Peter Bassett. Capt. Lancaster
Syms has bought a negro boy from Capt. Kidd. Order on
petition by Elizabeth Worshend.   134

22   Proclamation to issue against the destruction of pine trees
on the Mohawk river.   135

27   Warrants for salaries of civil officers. Captains Robert
Sinckler, John Smart and Isaac Brasier to appraise the
sloop William. Lancaster Syms paid £15 for the negro to
Capt. Kidd.   135

29   David Provoost to be mayor, Charles Oliver sheriff of New
York; Peter van Brugan to be mayor of Albany city, and
John Williams sheriff of Albany county. Sheriffs ap-
pointed: John Elbertsen for Kings; Peter Berian for
Queens; John Wick for Suffolk; Jacob Cowlson (Cous-
seau) for Richmond; Edmund Ward for Westchester;
John Petersen for Orange; Stephen Gasserce for Ulster
and Dutchess counties. John Coe and other justices of
Queens to appear before the council.   135

Oct. 4   Queens county justices. James How, Nicholas Churchill,
Daniel Dooley and John Eldridge suspected pirates have
broken jail in New Jersey. Accounts referred. Warrant
to Col. Stephen Cortlandt for entertaining French agents
from Canada. Carsten Luersen's securities discharged.   136

5   Robert Walters to be justice of the supreme court for trial
of cases in which Abr'm de Peyster has an interest.   137

6   Order concerning informations filed, or to be filed in courts
of law, or of admiralty.   137

1699   v. 8
17   Case of Robert and Ann Everndon settled. Warrants: to
     Barne Cosens for stationery; to Gabriel Minvielle for wine
     to the soldiers. Surveyor of customs Ducie Hungerford
     and the seized ship Adventure.   142
29   Robert Everndon is reconciled to his wife and his bond for
     alimony cancelled.   142
Dec. 7   Soldiers' barracks etc to be viewed. Jonah Tome's account
     for nursing John Berry a sick soldier referred.   142
14   Order on petition of Engelbert Lott and other inhabitants
     of Flatbush against Daniel Polhemus, Rouloff Verkirk,
     John Vleit, and Isaac Hegeman.   142
21   Flatbush case. Export of horses to Canada forbidden. Bed-
     ding for soldiers. Warrants: to Paroculus Parmyter
     naval officer for office stationery; to Jonah Thomas for
     nursing (p. 142).   143

1700
Jan. 4   Petition of Samuel Wood (p. 132) dismissed upon report of
     justices of Suffolk county.   143
16   Warrants: to Robert Walters for soldiers' bedding; for
     salaries of civil officers.   143
20   Queens county justices refuse to issue warrants under £2000
     act. Account for candles to the fort referred.   144
Feb. 16 Order against exporting horses to Canada to be enforced.
     Warrant to Cornelius van der Beek for soldiers' burial-
     cloth. Examination of Daniel Latham a quaker as to his
     connection with Capt. Kidd's crew.   144
Mar. 14 Proclamation to issue forbidding the export of horses to
     Canada. Order on complaint of Mrs Davis vs John Rod-
     man for intending to pull down a party wall between her
     house and the city hall. John Latham shipwright author-
     ized to cut ships timber for the public service. Warrant to
     David Hendrickse for a boat lost in assisting the Newport
     man-of-war, Captain Morris commander aground at the
     Narrows. Order on petition by Benj. Fenuille. Wm
     Sharpas reports on his mission to Pennsylvania and Mary-
     land about pirates.   145
23   Proclamation to issue for proroguing the assembly.   146
29   Order on petition by Thos. Lawrence vs Content Titus (see
     N. Y. col. mss, 43:105). Proclamation about horses read
     and approved.   146
Ap. 3   Robert Walters appointed and sworn in as justice of the
     supreme court vice Cortlandt sick.   147
5   Indian affairs.   147
8   Orders on petitions: by Engelbert Lott (see N. Y. col. mss,
     43:110); by Paul Richard (see N. Y. col. mss, 43:108).
     Proclamation to issue offering a reward for the discovery

of the murderer of Hester wife of Marcus Lefort and daughter of Richard. Orders on petitions: by Martinus Lamberse (see *N. Y. col. mss*, 43:109); by Thomas Lawrence and on a motion made by Mr Emett in re James Fullerton vs Wm Creed.   147

16 Content Titus justice of Queens county defends himself against the charges made by Engelbert Lott whose complaint is dismissed. Wm Creed to file a bill of errors. Two acts of parliament to be published.   148

17 Warrants: for salaries of civil officers; to Wm Sharpas for expenses of a journey to Maryland (see *N. Y. col. mss*, 43:113). Hendrick Hansen's accounts referred (see *N. Y. col. mss*, 43:114-15). Excise. Long Island Indians renew their allegiance.   148

18 Engelbert Lott vs Ducie Hungerford. Order on petition by Mich'l Hawdon (see *N. Y. col. mss*, 43:116). Warrants to Hendrick Hansen for sundries to the Indians. Shenacock Indians renew their allegiance.   150

27 Proclamation to issue about unlicensed sale of liquor. 150

May 1 Martinus Lamberse suspected of the murder of Hester Lefort to be tried by special commission of oyer and terminer. Frederick Platt also for killing his slave. Examination of Fort Wm Henry ordered. Ryer Schermerhorn to be assistant judge of the common pleas at Albany. Survey of land ordered for John Hutchins et al: (see *L. P. 3*:1). 150

9 Order of the king in council in re Val. Cruger vs Abr'm de Peyster. £2000 tax. Order on petition by Thos. Morgan and Gerrit Vechte. Warrants: to Jonathan Davis for sweeping chimneys in the fort (see *N. Y. col. mss*, 43:120); to John Rodman for building a wall between his house and the kings house. Stephen Cortlandt, Abr'm de Peyster, Samuel Staats, and Robert Walters to be justices of a court of oyer and terminer for the trial of Mart. Lambertse; also justices of the peace in Westchester for the trial of Fred. Platt.   151

15 Lt. Gov. Capt. Nanfan, takes an oath concerning the property taken from the pirates. Col. Abr'm de Peyster to go the circuit of Ulster county, the judge appointed being suspended.   153

16 Justices of Richmond county and Ellis Duxbury summoned before the council. Commission of oyer and terminer issued to Stephen Cortlandt etc.   153

20 Proclamation to issue for proroguing the assembly. 153

30 Warrants: to Cornelius de Peyster and Garrit Banker for charges of the judge on circuit in Ulster county (see *N. Y. col. mss*, 43:127); to Col. Stephen Cortlandt for candles

to the fort. Bill of sale to George Anderson for the ship
Adventure to be given. Warrant to John Carter for reading prayers to the soldiers. Commissions issued for the
trial of Frederick Platt.   154

June 6   Accounts referred. Order on petition by Hendrick and
Dirck Caursen (see *L. P.* 3:3). Warrant to Robert Livingston for providing wheelbarrows to be used in the fortifications of Albany and Schenectady.   154

20   Proclamation to issue for the arrest of Ducie Hungerford
(see *N. Y. col. mss,* 43:128). Warrant of survey of land
in New York city for Peter de la Noy. Accounts of
Engelbert Lott and Abr'm de la Noy to be audited. Order
on petition by Evert Byvanck (see *L. P.* 3:2). Warrant
to Dirck van den Burgh for work and material to the
fort.   155

22   Cruger vs de Peyster. Survey of land for Amarens, widow
of John Stout ordered (see *L. P.* 3:6).   155

July 2   Warrants for salaries of civil officers. Proclamation to
issue for proroguing the assembly.   156

3   Order on petition by Henry Fowler (see *L. P.* 3:7). Petition of Evert Byvanck (p. 155) dismissed.   156

14   Proclamation to issue for convoking the assembly.   156

16   Indian affairs. Warrant to Barne Cosens for stationery.
Accounts of Robert and John Livingston referred.   157

25   Lord Bellomont returned. Governors in America forbidden
to give letters of denization by order of the king in council. Proclamation ordered by the lords of trade for the
arrest of Henry King a pirate who has plundered Henry
Munday master of the ship John Hopewell of London.
Warrant to Lawrence Claese for a journey to Onondaga
(see *N. Y. col. mss,* 43:139-140).   157

26   Warrant to Isaac Taylor for Indian hatchets. Accounts referred.   159

29   Lord Bellomont wants his expenses to and from Boston
paid; warrant to Isaac Taylor for that purpose.   160

31   Monsieur Maricour and Father Bruyas, S. J. reported as
tampering with the five nations. Warrant to Johs. de
Waudell and two others for coming express from Albany.   160

Aug. 2   Letter from the lords of trade relating to East Jersey read.
Accounts referred.   161

3   Accounts of James Wells and Jean Le Chevalier referred.
Warrants: to Robert Livingston for wheelbarrows to the
forts at Albany and Schenectady, for stocks for Indian
guns, for Indian provisions, for Indian disbursments, for
sundries to the fort at Albany; to Col. Stephen Cortlandt

for cleaning lodgings in the fort; to James Wells for carpenter work in the fort; to Henry Meason blacksmith for work in the fort.   161

5 Commission of oyer and terminer to issue to Peter van Brugh, Hendrick Hansen, Dirck Wessells and Jan Janse Bleecker for the trial of Thos. Long and John Plats accused of felony (see *N. Y. col. mss,* 43:145). Warrants: to John Livingston for catching deserters; to Isaac Taylor for the governor's expenses in catching James Gillam the pirate.   162

7 Warrants: to John Allen and John Reynolds sawyers for work in the fort; to Col. Wm Smith for presents to Long Island Indians and for official charges; to Garrit Luykase, Hendrick Rooseboom, Nicholas Bleecker and Jan Baptist van Eps for going with Col. Peter. Schuyler to Onondaga; to Rob't Livingston and Hendrick Hansen for expenses of this expedition; to Cornelius de Peyster and Gerrit Banker to pay Clem Ellswordt for carpenter work in the fort.   163

8 Warrant to Hendrick Hansen for firewood to the Albany garrison. Account referred.   164

9 Warrants: to Abr'm Gouverneur for services as speaker of the assembly; to Dirck van der Burgh for mason work in the fort; to Col. Peter Schuyler and Hendrick Hansen for a journey to Onondaga; to Ryer Schermerhorn for public transportation. The ship Fortune condemned in admiralty as foreign built, to go to England.   164

Sep. 13 Rye and Bedford. Indian affairs. Proclamation to issue for convoking the assembly. Robert Livingston confirmed by royal order as collector of the excise, receiver of quitrents, town clerk, clerk of the peace, and clerk of the common pleas at Albany.   165

18 Mediterranean passes. Wayt Winthrop produces his commission as judge of the admiralty. Expenses of the governor's journey to Albany to be audited. Warrants: to Duncan Campbell for money advanced; to Robert Livingston for entertaining French agents.   167

19 Wayt Winthrop sworn in as judge of the admiralty.   167

23 Soldiers coming from Ireland (see *N. Y. col. mss,* 43:122). Proclamation to issue concerning Mediterranean passes. 167

27 Above proclamation read and approved. Nomination of mayor and sheriff of New York.   168

28 Isaac de Riemer appointed mayor, Peter de Mill sheriff of New York; John Bleecker sr mayor, and Jonathan Broadhurst sheriff of Albany. Sheriffs: Benj. van de Water

1700   **v. 8**

for Kings; Zachariah Mills for Queens; John Mulford for
Suffolk; Bernard van Benthuysen for Dutchess' and Ulster;
Teunis Dowisson for Orange; Jeremiah Fowler for West-
chester; Christian Corsen for Richmond counties.   169

Oct. 2 Warrants: to Rob't Livingston for Indian provisions, for
disbursements to the fort and to the Indians; to Francis
Winne for use of his sloop by the governor; to Cornelius
Low for his sloop; to Jan Baptist van Eps for services as
Indian interpreter; to Peter van Brugh for Indian presents;
to Wm Morris for presents; to Fred Oathout for beer to
the governor; to Alexander Mason for necessaries on the
governor's journey to Albany; to Thos. Noell for Indian
presents; to Col. Cortlandt for candles to the fort; to
Abr'm de Peyster for Indian presents; to Abr'm Staats
for hire of his sloop; to Anthony Rogers for his expenses
to Albany with the governor. Capt. James Weems' petition referred.   169

7 Warrant to Col. Cortlandt for expenses of governor's
journey to Albany. Military furnishings. Surgeon Jacob
Staats appointed to Capt. Weems' company, and Hendrick
van Dyck to Mayor Rich'd Ingoldsby's. Warrant to Wm
Mumford for stonecutters work on the fort. Indian affairs. 171

8 Order on petition by Dirck Jansen Hooglandt. Soldiers
bedding. Order on petition by Jacob Manritz and Johs.
Provoost. Warrant to John Bleecker for Indian interpret-
ing. Order on petition by Michael Hawdon. Albany
excise. Petition by James Kinard sergeant dismissed (see
N. Y. col. mss, 43:171).   171

11 Commission for a trading expedition to be prepared for
John Peroo owner and master of the sloop Three
Brothers (see *N. Y. col. mss*, 43:168). Capt. Shelley and
his crew suspected of piracy. Warrants for salaries of civil
officers.   172

12 Suffolk county excise.   173

14 Isaac de Riemer, John Johnson Bleecker and Peter de Milot
sworn in as mayors of New York and of Albany and as
sheriff of New York. Warrant to Thos. Farmer for transporting John Williams a deserter.   173

15 John Hughes, Wm Webb, Patrick Waldrop, Daniel Lath-
well, John Denny, and other old and decrepit soldiers
to be sent to England in the galley New Port. Warrants:
to Francis Vincent for sails to the custom-house barge; to
Cornelius Lodge for paint etc to the same; to John
Latham for carpenter work on the same; to Robert Crannell for rum to the pinace workmen; to Jean le Chevalier

for carving work; to John Coolley for blacksmith work
on the barge; to John Owen for joiners work on the same;
to Aert Elbertsen for use of his sloop on public service;
to John Ellison for sundries to the fort and the barge.   174

16   Governor's house to be examined for repairs. Indian affairs.
Scow ashore near South-hold.   175

19   Aug. Graham the surveyor-general a man not to be de-
pended upon, Pieter Cortileau appointed surveyor for the
province.   176

22   Warrant to Bowdewyn de Witt for going express from
Esopus, to Albany (see N. Y. col. mss, 43:175).   177

23   Warrants: to John Riggs for his trouble in escorting
pirate prisoners from Burlington, N. J. to New York (see
N. Y. col. mss, 43:178); to Hendrick van Dyck for salary
as surgeon (see N. Y. col. mss, 43:177).   177

24   Warrant, to Francis Chappell for rent of committee room.
Samuel Clews appointed surveyor (see N. Y. col. mss,
43:179). Warrant to Johannes Vinhagen for going express
to Albany.   177

25   Additional instruction to the governor concerning courts-
martial. Warrant to Col. Stephen Cortlandt for work in
the fort. Samuel Clews sworn in as surveyor.   177

26   Abr'm Gouverneur appointed recorder of New York city
vice Graham illegally acting as such, and sworn in.   179

29   Wine imported by the French advocate-general of Petit
Guavas as a present to the governor admitted free of duty.
Warrants: to Gabriel Ludlow for salary as clerk of the
assembly; to Gabriel Thompson for salary as doorkeeper.   179

30   Stephen Cortlandt appointed chief justice and sworn in.
Stephen Cortlandt, Abr'm de Peyster, Rob't Livingston
and Rob't Walters, of the council, with Capt. Peter
Matthews, Lt. Chs. Ashfield, and Lt. Henry Holland to
be judges of the court-martial, Paroculus Parmyter judge
advocate, Barne Cosens clerk, and Rich'd Stokes marshal,
under act of legislature.   [179]

31   Warrant to Gabriel Ludlow for copying council papers.
Wm Bradford displaced as government printer. Warrant
to Abr'm Gouverneur for copying council papers which
should have been printed.   [179]

Nov. 5   Warrant to Johs. Sanderse Glen for repairing Schenectady
barracks. Albany firewood. Warrant to Hendrick Hansen for same. Furniture for officers lodgings at Albany. 180

6   Warants: to Peter van Brugh for Indian disbursements and
a journey to Onondaga with Col. Romar; to Hendrick
Hansen for expenses of Col. Romar's journey (see N. Y.

col. mss, 44:4); to Dirck Wessels for Indian expenses; to Garrit Viele for the same; to Henry Meason for blacksmith work in Fort Wm Henry; to Abr'm Gouverneur for services as speaker of the assembly; to Abr'm de la Noy and Engelbert Lott for material to the fort; to Dirck Wessels for journeys on public service; to Col. Peter Schuyler for provisions to French prisoners etc; to Lieut. Thos. Sharp for salary as gunner at Albany; to Capt. John Schuyler for provisions to Indians sent to Ottowawa; to Abr'm de Peyster for pay of Ryer Schermerhorn and John Latham, sent for ships timber.   180

12   Order of the king in council confirming Robert Walters as member of the council in New York. Barracks to be built outside the fort. Watch coats for soldiers. £2000 tax. Warrant to Ryer Schermerhorn for firewood to Schenectady garrison (see *N. Y. col. mss*, 44:8). Order on address by the house of representatives (see *N. Y. col. mss*, 44:6).   182

13   Affidavits of John Parmyter, Robert Crannel, and Daniel Toy taken against Ducie Hungerford for malfeasance in office. Albany excise.   184

27   Sloop Batchelors Delight, John Roberts master seized for breach of the laws at Oysterbay. Warrant to Nicholas Blank for blacksmith work done by John Petersen Melott his debtor fled to East Jersey (see *N. Y. col. mss*, 44; Ib 15–19). John de Peyster commissioner of customs to furnish bedding for the soldiers (see *N. Y. col. mss*, 44:17). Correspondence and orders concerning courts of law. Warrants for work and materials to the ship Fortune to Benj. Faneuil, Aaron Bloom, Abr'm de Peyster, Isaac Brazier, Samuel Phillips, Nichs. Jemain, John Sipkins, Daniel Roberts, Capt. Wm Collvitt, Frederick Philipps, Barent Rynderson, Isaac de Mill, Rich'd Willett, Francis Vincent, George Elswordt, Isaac de Peyster, John Davie, Abr'm Kipp and Sam'l Staats (see *N. Y. col. mss*, 44:9-14).   186

Dec. 12   Warrants: to Paroculus Parmyter, Barne Cosens and Richard Stokes, for services in the court-martial; to Surgeon Henry van Dyck for services under the Indian commissioners.   188

28   Orders: on information by Richard Shute justice in Westchester county concerning Peter Villepontoon suspected of the murder of David Burgett; on memorial by the mayor etc of New York (see *N. Y. col. mss*, 44:23); concerning a bill of exchange drawn by Thos. Weaver; on a petition by Jacob Mauritz and Johs. Provoost.   189

Jan. 2   Thomas Weaver sworn in as collector and receiver-general;
his salary. Freight for military stores by the Thomas and
Elizabeth, Thos. Ogden master. Peter and Mary Villepontoon, son and daughter of Peter Villepontoon to be
arrested (p. 189).   190

7   Proclamation to issue offering a reward for the discovery of
David Burgett's murder (see *N. Y. col. mss*, 44:24).   191

8   Case of the ship John and Henry. Edward Antill and the
mayor etc of New York.   191

21   Nathaniel Coles appointed surveyor and searcher of the
customs at Oysterbay. Chief justice and attorney-general
superseded under orders from England to appoint able
lawyers to these places. Mr Atwood appointed chief justice, and Mr Broughton attorney-general coming from
England. Warrants for salaries of civil officers. Payment to Dr Jacob Staats. Warrants: to Jacob van Noorstrandt for iron in the fort; to —— Mayou for sailors'
coats; to Jonathan Davis for sweeping chimneys; to Daniel
Mesuard for fitting out the governor's sloop to Thos.
Swiney for work in the fort; to Jacob Mauritz and Johs.
Provoost for money illegally levied upon them (see *N. Y.
col. mss*, 44:25).   192

27   Thomas Weaver appointed to and sworn of the council.
Demands under act of assembly the books and accounts,
of the revenue. Alien shipmasters cited before the council.
Warrant to Abr'm Gouverneur for expenses on a journey
to the east end of Long Island about pirates. Albany
excise.   194

30   Captain Jacob van Cortlandt and Johannes van Cortlandt,
brother and son, of the late Col. Stephen van Cortlandt
testify concerning account books. Warrant to Rob't
Livingston for salary as secretary of Indian affairs not to
be signed. Warrant to Abr'm de Peyster for wine given
to the soldiers.   195

Feb. 3   Denization of aliens. Dirck van der Burgh's accounts to
be audited. Order on petition of Boaz Bell late master
of the John and Henry of Carolina against John Hold-
critz present master (see *N. Y. col. mss*, 44:31). Barne
Cosens to act as kings counsel before the court of sessions. 196

7   Order on petition by John Tollman and Nath'l Pearsall (see
N. Y. col. mss, 44:33). Petition of Magdalena Pelletreaux
dismissed. Accounts of Ducie Hungerford to be audited. 197

11   Accounts of Col. Stephen Cortlandt produced to be audited.
Tide mill to be set up by John Marsh. Warrant to John
Rodman for building a wall to the kings house.   197

1701   v. 8
12 Answer of the justices of Queens county to the petition of
    John Tollman and Nath'l Pearsall (p. 197).   198
15 Orders of the king in council, approving and vetoing laws
    passed in 1699. Mathew Plowman. Audit of Col. Cort-
    landt's accounts. Government warrants to be legal tender
    for customs duties.   198
18 Memorial of commissioners to examine the public accounts.
    Memorial of Thos. Weaver collector and receiver-general.
    Deposition by the same. Order to search for Col. van
    Cortlandt's books refused by his widow.   202
19 Deposition by Barne Cosens concerning Mrs Gertrude van
    Cortlandt. Deposition by Ann Chappell tavern keeper.
    Proclamation to issue forbidding payment of excise money
    to Gertrude van Cortlandt.   209
20 Widow Gertrude van Cortlandt and her son Johannes and
    John Basford before the council relative to Col. A. van
    Cortlandt's books. Firewood for the fort.   210
Mar. 5 Death of Lord Bellomont. Lt. Gov. Nanfan absent in
    Barbados. Proclamation to issue announcing Lord B's
    death (see *N. Y. col. mss*, 44:48). Absent members called
    to town. Abr'm de Peyster the eldest member to act as
    president until the return of the lieutenant governor, or
    Col. Wm Smith. Letters to be sent to Massachusetts and
    New Haven announcing the death (see *N. Y. col. mss*,
    44:49-50). Council to wait on Lady Bellomont.   211
6   Hendrick Hansen and Peter van Brugh of Albany to be
    asked to advance money for the pay and subsistance of
    the Albany garrison (see *N. Y. col. mss*, 44:52).   213
13 Wm Smith presiding. Discussion on the powers of the
    council. Military stores to be examined. Pay for the
    soldiers to be provided.   213
14 Clause of a letter from the lords of trade concerning legis-
    lative acts. Bills of stores to be given by the collector.
    Warrants: to Anne Bowen for nursing a sick soldier,
    Patrick Waldron; to Mary Thomas for taking care of sick
    soldiers. Order on petition by Peter Berrian. Proclama-
    tion to issue convoking the assembly (see *N. Y. col. mss*,
    44:55).   217
15 Col. Wm Smith refuses to sign and is directed to affix his
    signature to the preceding proclamation. Supreme court.
    Order on petition by Edward Folwell, Mathew Howel and
    Henry Pierson to be judges of the common pleas for the
    trial of Folwell vs Giles Sylvester, Judge Arnold being a
    party in said cause. Candles for Fort Wm Henry. Order

1701   **v. 8**

2   Order on petition by Lieut. Mathews for power to command
     in the fort.   227
3   Military stores. Capt W. Caldwell of the Advice man-of-
     war. Soldiers. Proclamation to issue about deserting.
     Capt. James Weems denied leave to go to England and
     ordered back to Albany· (see N. Y. col. mss, 44:78); his
     memorial concerning the garrisons at Albany and Schenec-
     tady to be laid before the assembly. Warrants: to Wm
     Sell for salary as tidewaiter; to Daniel Toy and Nicholas
     Feilding for same; to James Evitts for salary as searcher;
     to John Crooke gauger of liquors; to Barne Cosens for
     salary as clerk of the council; to Rich'd Stokes messenger
     of council. Assembly advised to adjourn.   228
4   Answer of Peter Schuyler and Robert Livingston to the me-
     morial of the commissioners of accounts read and ordered
     thereon (see N. Y. col. mss, 44:81). No quorum in the
     assembly yet.   230
8   Military stores by the Advice. Order on petition by Barne
     Cosens (see N. Y. col. mss, 44:88). Warrant to Jan Janse
     Bleecker for blockhouses and officers lodgings at Albany
     (see N. Y. col. mss, 44:91–92). Mayor etc of Albany to
     rent officers' lodgings: Wm Lawrence before the council
     on behalf of Susannah Lawrence. Order on application
     by John Lawrence concerning East India goods seized in
     Queens county. Assembly advised to adjourn and give
     council time to prepare bills.   230
9   Paper signed by Thos. Weaver, Abr'm de Peyster, Samuel
     Staats, and Robert Walters all of the council (see N. Y.
     col. mss, 44:94).   231
10   Col. Wm Smith not ready with his answer to the foregoing
     paper. Coronation day.   233
14   Col. Wm Smith's answer read; reply by the above four mem-
     bers of council (see N. Y. col. mss, 44:100).   233
15   Quarrel between Col. Wm Smith and the council as to the
     former's authority to act as governor continued.   238
16   Capt. Wm Caldwell of the Advice man-of-war asked to meet
     the council.   239
17   Orders to Capt. Caldwell. Dispute between the collector of
     customs and the naval officer. Warrant to Wm Davis for
     disbursments.   239
18   Warrant to Col. Wm Romar for fitting out messengers to
     the Ottowawas and other far nations. Leave to go to
     Boston denied him. Warrants: to Gabriel Ludlow and
     Gabriel Thompson for salary as clerk, and messenger, of
     the assembly; to Robert Crannell matross for pay due him;

1701   **v. 8**

23   Accounts referred. Warrant to Barne Cosens for attend-
         ing the commissioners of accounts.   248

30   Order of the king in council declaring Rye and Bedford to
         belong to New York. Letter from the King to Lord
         Bellomont about Rye and Bedford. Proclamation to that
         effect to issue. Letters from the king about suppression
         of pirates, and about fortifications and the quota of the
         various colonies to be furnished for the defense of the
         frontiers. Matthew Plowman. Accounts of Robert Living-
         ston referred. Petition of Jacob Isaac referred. Court of
         chancery authorized.   248

June 1 Proclamations concerning Rye and Bedford read and ap-
         proved; also about establishing a court of chancery (see
         N. Y. col. mss, 44:132); also for dissolving the assembly.
         Writs for a new election to issue. Indians made uneasy
         by Mon. Maricour's intrigues; Capt. John Bleecker to go
         to Onondaga to quiet them and call a meeting at Albany.
         Proclamation to issue confirming all civil and military
         officers (see *N. Y. col. mss*, 44:130). Account of the £1000
         tax for building a fort at Onondaga. Proclamation to issue
         about elections and returns.   256

5   Indian affairs. Order on petition by Robert Livingston (see
         N. Y. col. mss, 44:140). No returns of the £1000 tax re-
         ceived. Orders on petitions: by Capt. Sincklair; by Wm.
         Richardson and John Crooke. Returns of the £2000 tax
         called for.   258

17   Census to be taken. Warrant to David Jamison for salary
         as clerk of the council in 1698. David Jamison sworn in
         as deputy surveyor-general.   259

26   Indian affairs. Barne Cosens sworn in as clerk and register,
         of the court of chancery. Warrants: to Jean le Chevalier
         for joiner work in the fort; to John Schuyler for repair of
         Albany blockhouses; to Peter de Riemer for glass to the
         fort; to Barne Cosens for salary as clerk, and Richard
         Stokes as messenger, of the council; to Jacobus van Dyck
         as surgeon to Schenectady garrison; to Joachim Staats for
         transporting soldiers; to Hendrick Hansen for firewood to
         Albany garrison. Orders: on petition by Abr'm de la
         Noy concerning Peter de la Noy's will; in regard to Jacob
         Isaac's goods; on a petition by Mando a free negro
         woman (see *N. Y. col. mss*, 44:147). Col. Romar refused
         permission to leave Boston.   260

27   Report on the petition of Capt. Robert Sinclair of the ship
         Resolution, and warrant to the same for freight of military
         stores in Gov. Fletcher's time. Warrant to Jean Bachand

for blacksmith work in the fort. Payments ordered: to
John Maddock for disbursments in the fort; to expresses
from Albany. Accounts of the governor's expedition to
Albany.   262

Aug. 4   Wm Atwood sworn of the council and as judge of the
admiralty. Sampson Shelton Broughton sworn as attorney-general of the court of admiralty. Atwood to be
chief justice, and Broughton attorney-general of the province.   263

     5   Wm Atwood and S. S. Broughton sworn in as chief justice,
and attorney-general respectively. Letter from the king
relating to Trinity church. Court of oyer and terminer
to sit for the trial of a negro woman and John Johnson
accused of felony. Abr'm de Peyster and Robert Walters
to be associate judges of the supreme court.   264

     7   Patent for five small islands given to John Baptist van Eps
and Lawrence Claese by the Indians granted (see L. P.
3:13). Warrant to John Baptist van Eps for services as
interpreter.   265

    14   Petition of the negro woman Mando against Sam'l Denton
referred to John Coe justice for Queens county.   266

    15   Proclamation relating to pirates received from England.
Thos. Weaver's salary as receiver-general not to be paid
for the time of his absence in England. Abr'm de Peyster
appointed deputy auditor-general. Special session of the
supreme court ordered for the trial of Capt. Wake's ship.   266

    18   Statement of quitrents called for.   267

    19   Proclamation to issue concerning the treaty with Algiers.   268

    22   Indian affairs; French intrigues. Journal of Capt. Bleecker
and David Schuyler during their late stay at Onondaga
read. Order on petition by Adolph Philipps and Stephen
de Lancey (see N. Y. col. mss, 44:158).   268

    26   Warrant to Elizabeth Whanewright for nursing sick soldiers.
Letters about the census and the £1000 and £2000 taxes to
be sent out. Warrants to Hendrick Hansen for firewood.
Col. Gabriel Minvielle called in re Philipps and de Lancey.   269

    28   Soldiers' pay. Ordinance for establishing a court of chan-
cery (see N. Y. col. mss, 44:161). Weaver and Livingston
(see N. Y. col. mss, 44:156). Accounts referred.   270

    29   The lieutenant-governor and council take the oaths ap-
pointed in the chancery court ordinance.   273

    30   Weaver and Livingston (see N. Y. col. mss, 44:163). Ac-
counts of Lady Bellomont referred.   273

Sep. 2   Thos. Noell and John de Peyster to be masters, Barne
Cosens register and examiner also purse and seal bearer,

1701   v. 8

and sealer of writs, Abr'm Gouverneur and Richard Harris
clerks of the court of chancery. The petition by Robt.
Livingston read (see *N. Y. col. mss*, 44:165).   273

9   Thos. Weaver's accounts as agent of the province in England referred.   274

11 Justices of the peace summoned before the council for
neglecting to send in census lists.   274

16 Leigh Atwood appears on behalf of Capt. Wake and his
ship Elizabeth and Catharine, Rip van Dam offering his
bond; order in regard to it. Order on petition of Wm
Creed vs Daniel Whitehead.   274

18 Order on petition by Thos. Baxter justice in Westchester
county against Thos. Hunt and John Hunt also justices of
the peace (see *N. Y. col. mss*, 44:164). Case of the ship
Elizabeth and Catharine. Letter received from Gov.
Francis Nicholson of Virginia about men for the defense
of the frontiers. Creed vs Whitehead. Robert Livingston sworn in as judge of the court of chancery. Patent
to be drawn to Abr'm de la Noy for lots in Stone and
Bridge streets, New York city.   275

22 Petition by Robert Livingston read (p. 273). Journal of
John Bleecker and David Schuyler of their Onondaga
expeditions read. Widow Gertrude van Cortlandt empowered to receive debts due for customs at her husband's
death. Order on petition of Mathias Mott (see *L. P.* 3:20).
Baxter vs Hunt. Proclamation to issue for the arrest of
John Hunt (see *N. Y. col. mss*, 44:166). John Hunt superseded as justice of the peace.   276

29 Warrant to Barne Cosens for the lieutenant governor's sal-
ary. Mayors and sheriffs appointed: Thomas Noell mayor
of New York, John Bleecker jr of Albany; Isaac de Riemer
sheriff of New York; Jonathan Broadhurst of Albany;
Benj. van de Water of Kings; Zachariah Mills of Queens;
John Mulford of Suffolk; John de Pue of Richmond;
Boudewyn de Widt of Ulster and Dutchess; Isaac Denham
of Westchester; Teunis Dowisson of Orange counties.
John Johnson Bleecker to be recorder of Albany city.
Order on petition by Edw'd Hodges.   277

Oct. 2 Thomas Hunt placed under bonds to keep the peace.
Weaver vs Parmyter.   278

4   Warrant to Thomas Sharp for salary as gunner (see *N. Y.
col. mss*, 44:167). Orders on petitions: by Samuel Height,
John Way and Robert Feild, Quakers (see *N. Y. col. mss*,
44:169); petition for a public landing place between Wall
street and Burgers path. Creed vs Whitehead.   279

1701   **v. 8**

10   Agreement between Leigh Atwood & Co. and Dirck van
den Burgh produced (see *L. P.* 3:17). Warrant to Lady
Bellomont for money due her late husband.   286

13   Wm Smith, Samuel Staats, Robert Walters and Thos.
Weaver, of the council, Capt. Wm Caldwell of the Advice
man-of-war, and George Larkin appointed commissioners,
Wm Sharpas register of the court of admiralty for the trial
of pirates, and sworn in. Land called Maskake near Shaw-
angunk in Ulster county to be surveyed for Mathias Mott. 287

20   The ship Elizabeth and Catherine released under condition
of being insured. Warrants for salaries: to John de Peyster surveyor, and James Evitts searcher, of the customs,
and to Wm Sell, Daniel Toy and Nich's Feilding tidewaiters; to Barne Cosens clerk, and Rich'd Stokes messenger, of the council. Salary of the chief justice and attorney-
general fixed. Warrant to Lt. Gov. Nanfan for Indian
expenses.   288

21   People of Rye and Bedford refuse to pay taxes as reported
by justices Henry Fowler, Thos. Baxter and Thos. Pinckney of Westchester. Warrant to John Maddock for incidental expenses in the fort. John Bachand's account referred to John Ellison and Abr'm Ketteltasse. Patents
granted: to Brandt Schuyler (see *L. P.* 3:18); to Jacobus
de Key (see *L. P.* 3:19).   289

Dec. 1   Ordinance to be drawn concerning the sessions of the supreme court (p. 280; see *N. Y. col. mss,* 45:33).   289

8   Vetch's sloop ashore on Long Island and Lieut. Charles
Oliver sent to take charge of her prohibited goods. Accounts referred. Sessions of the supreme court.   290

16   Thos. Weaver appointed collector of duties and sworn in.
Sessions of the supreme court.   290

18   Gov. Elias Haskett of the island of Providence attends the
council and swears to the truth of his memorial (see *N. Y.
col. mss,* 45:38); his memorial. Capt. John Wake's ship.
Order on petition by Deliverance Brown (see *N. Y. col.
mss,* 45:39).   290

18(?) Order to the sheriff for the arrest of John Graves, James
Crawford and Roger Predent, on complaint of Gov. Haskett.   292

22   The sheriff produces his three prisoners and they are re-
manded.   292

24   Col. Stephen van Cortlandt's accounts. Warrants: to Lady
Bellomont for the balance of her late husband's salary;
to Mrs Gertrude van Cortlandt for money due her late
husband. Quit rent of Abr'm de la Noy's patent. Soldiers'
quarters. Patent granted to Mathias Mott.   292

1702   **v. 8**

24   Order on petition by Johannis Hardenbrook and others not
named. Proclamation ordered on January 22d read.   304

26   Rip van Dam, Philipp French and Thos. Wenham again
refuse to deliver certain papers; Philipp French is superseded as justice of the peace and all three are to be tried
at the next supreme court. Orders on petitions: by Severeyn ten Hout (see *N. Y. col. mss*, 45:67); by Susannah
Vaughton (see *L. P.* 3:28); by Samuel Staats (see *L. P.*
3:29). Warrants: to Abr'm de Peyster for provisions to
the ship Fortune; to Thos. Weaver for incidental charges;
to Gabriel Ludlow for salary as clerk of the assembly;
to Wm Teller for hire of his sloop; to John Schuyler for
fitting out messenger to the Onagongos (see *N. Y. col.
mss*, 45:68).   305

29   Warrants: to Gabriel Thompson for entertaining Frenchmen from Canada and Indians (see *N. Y. col. mss*, 45:28);
to Lady Bellomont for salary of Thos. Weaver as agent
of the province; to Robert Walters for pay of Judith Pemberton nurse of sick soldiers, Henry Povey and Jonas
Thomas. Proclamation to issue concerning commissions
(see *N. Y. col. mss*, 45:69).   306

Feb. 2   Wm Creed summoned before the council. Susannah Vaughton summoned. Order on petition by John Hutchins (see
L. P. 3:30). Escheator of the province called.   307

4   Commission of oyer and terminer to be prepared to try
Nich's Bayard and John Hutchins for high treason.   308

5   Thos. Weaver appointed solicitor-general. Susannah Vaughton before the council. Indian purchase by Pauling produced by Mr Emott to be recorded.   308

9   Orders on petitions: by Matthew Clarkson, Lancaster Syms,
Robert Walters, Rich'd Slater, John Chollwell, Cornelius
de Peyster, Leigh Atwood, Barne Cosens and Caleb Heathcote (see *L. P.* 3:31); by Nich's Bayard and John Hutchins
(see *N. Y. col. mss*, 45:70). Books and accounts of Paroculus Parmyter late naval officer called for. Sheriff of
Westchester county, Jonathan Scriben, John Horton and
Joseph Purdy called before the council.   308

p. m.   Paroculus Parmyter refuses to produce his books; sheriff of
of New York ordered to seize them.   309

10   Books seized by the sheriff delivered to Thos. Weaver and
James Evitts for examination and report.   309

12   Order of the king in council in re Cruger vs de Peyster,
Commission of oyer and terminer prepared, the justices
sworn and the accused notified. Execution against Wm
Creed for costs of appeal ordered.   310

1702 v. 8

14 Petition of Barne Cosens (see *N. Y. col. mss,* 45;73) referred.
Petition of Col. Caleb Heathcote (see *L. P.* 3:31) granted. 311

17 Orders: for writ of ad quod damnum on the petition of Caleb
Heathcote; on petition of Caleb Heathcote, Joseph Theule
and others; on petition by John de Peyster and others (see
L. P. 3:32) for license to purchase Indian lands. 312

19 License to purchase Indian lands granted to Samuel Staats,
Cornelius Claesen, Abr'm Provost, Garrit Gerritse and
Barent Staats (see *L. P.* 3:33). Order on petitions by John
de Puy and Daniel Lake. Warrant to Jacob Staats for salary as surgeon. Cruger vs de Peyster. Jon'n Scrifen and
others of Westchester (p. 308) examined in relation to
libels signed by them. 313

28 Capt. Thos. Clarke swears that everything on board Capt.
Kidd's sloop has been delivered to the governor with inventory. Thos. Davis to be riding messenger of the council on Long Island. 314

Mar. 2 Proclamation to issue proroguing the assembly (see *N. Y.
col. mss,* 45:74). Order on petition by Robert Walters and
others for land in Westchester county (see *L. P.* 3:33). 314

5 Cruger vs de Peyster. License to purchase Indian lands in
Ulster county granted David Provoost and others (see
L. P. 3:35). 315

10 David Jamison called before the council cannot be found.
Proclamation of amnesty etc. to issue (see *N. Y. col. mss,*
45:76). 316

11 Henry Ludlow, John Wick, and Dr Nath'l Wade to appear
before the council concerning the sloop run ashore on
Long Island and seized by Charles Oliver. Payment to
Justice Hobart ordered for expenses in seizing the sloop.
Col. Heathcote's manor of Scarsdale, and report of the
sheriff. 317

12 Report of the solicitor-general on the manor of Scarsdale,
and order to prepare letters patent for it. Rip van Dam
promised he shall not be prosecuted. License to purchase
Indian lands granted: in Dutchess county to Capt. Wm
Caldwell, Isaac Gouverneur, Robert Sanders, Henry Beekman and others (see *L. P.* 3:38); in Westchester to Samuel
Staats, Dirck Vanden Burgh and Barne Cosens (see *L. P.*
3:34); in Ulster county to John Hardinbergh, Albert Rosa,
John Middagh (see *L. P.* 39-41). Patent for land on Staten
Island granted to Marc Dusachoy. Mate of the sloop
stranded in Suffolk county ordered before the council. 317

17 Order on petition of Col. Nicholas Bayard condemned for
high treason. 320

1702

18   James Mott objecting to the grant of Scarsdale manor to be heard by the council. Order on memorial by the officers in Fort Wm Henry (see *N. Y. col. mss*, 45:77). License to purchase Indian lands in Suffolk county granted to Isaac de Riemer (see *L. P.* 3:43).   320

19   Corporation of Kingston (see *N. Y. col. mss*, 45:78). John Balck (see *N. Y. col. mss*, 45:79).   321

21   Agreement made by James Mott and Henry Disbrowe with Caleb Heathcote concerning the manor of Scarsdale. John Balck endenized.   321

26   Public accounts. Rev. Bernardus Freeman to be induced to remain at Schenectady. Proclamation to issue convoking the assembly (see *N. Y. col. mss*, 45:86). Survey of land on Staten Island ordered for Peter Corteleau (see *L. P.* 3:44, 46). Order about Severeyn ten Hout's caveat against a patent for land to Mathias Mott. Cruger vs de Peyster. Drift whales in Suffolk county.   322

30   License to purchase Indian lands in Ulster county granted to Abr'm Gouverneur and others (see *L. P.* 3:45). Proclamation to issue for discovery of the person who cut down the gallows (see *N. Y. col. mss*, 45:88).   323

Ap. 2   Warrants: for salaries of civil officers; to Abr'm de Peyster for wine to the soldiers; to John de Peyster for firewood to the garrisons; to Garrit Viele for lead to Indians; to Jonathan Davis for sweeping chimneys in the fort; to John Sharp for carpenter work done in the fort by John Perry; to John de Peyster for money due him. Order on petition by Samuel Staats. Accounts. Vote of thanks to Thos. Weaver solicitor-general for services in the Bayard trial; and of disapproval of attorney-general Broughton for his negligence in the case.   324

6   Cruger vs de Peyster. Court of exchequer. Proclamation to issue offering a reward for discovery of the person who wrote under a former proclamation next to the words, " God save the king," " and hang John Nanfan."   325

9   Dr Samuel Staats vs Caleb Heathcote about land. Money for the Onondaga fort. George Clarke denounces Eden Burroughs as having written the above words; he, George Marriner, Andrew Marriner, and Edw'd Rosum are summoned before the council.   326

13   Barne Cosens appointed escheator-general. Warrants to Lady Bellomont and Lt-Gov. Nanfan for moneys due to them under act of assembly. £2000 tax not paid yet. Patent for land granted to Thos. Parcell of Great Barnes island (see *L. P.* 3:53). Petition of Susannah Vaughton

v. 8
referred. Surveys of land ordered: for Francis Martino
(see *L. P.* 3:54); for Thos. Stillwell (see *L. P.* 3:51). Patents for land granted: to Peter Cortileau; to Adrian Lane
(see *L. P.* 3:52). Surveys: ordered for Abr'm Luteine; for
Nath'l Brittaine (see *L. P.* 3:57). Patent for land on Staten
Island granted to Peter le Conte (see *L. P.* 3:49). Survey
of lands on Staten Island near Mr Oselton, on Smokers
point near Jean Rigoult, west of Thos. Pusling, and in
front of Breville ordered for John de Puy and others; for
Thos. Weaver and Marc Dusachoy (see *L. P.* 3:55). Patent
for land in Ulster county granted to David Provoost and
others (see *L. P.* 3:48). Attorney-general Broughton acknowledges his neglect of duty and is pardoned. Eden
Burroughs (p. 326) is committed.   328

14   Order on petition by Susannah Vaughton. Letter from the
lords of trade and plantations with opinion of Attorney-
general Thos. Treavor, and Solicitor-general Jo. Hawles
on denization. Wine and beer to be laid in for Lord Cornbury. Salaries formerly paid to Wm Pinhorne and John
Guest as assistant judges to be paid also to present Asst.
Judges de Peyster and Rob't Walters. House in the fort
to be put in order for Lord Cornbury. Thos. Longworth
to be clerk of Suffolk county vice Henry Smith term ex-
pired. Petitions of Nich's Bayard and John Hutchins to
be printed. Letter to the lords of trade in regard to Bayard and Hutchins. Warrants: to Attorney-general Sampson Shelton Broughton for salary; to John Laurence for
bringing pirates from Oyster bay to New York; to Lawrence Claesen interpreter for journeys to Oneida and Onondaga; to Thos. Williams for bringing back Mon. Bat-
tailey going to Canada without pass; to Thos. Weaver for
contingent expenses; to Ryer Schermerhorn for firewood
to Schenectady garrison; to John van Zandt for mending
pump in the fort; to John Crooke for work in powder
magazine; to John Bachaud for blacksmith work in the
fort; to Gabriel Ludlow for official work done for Lord
Bellomont; to Robert Walters for firewood to Fort Wm
Henry; to Dirck Wessells for candles to Albany garrison;
to Jonathan Broadhurst for excise work at Albany; to
Rob't Walters for linen to officers; to Gabriel Thompson
for salary etc.   331

15   Survey of land ordered for Leigh Atwood and Richard Slater.
Edw'd Antill temporarily disbarred for refusing to take
the proper oaths. Act of assembly to be enforced against

1702   v. 8

Robert Livingston. Survey ordered for Isaac and Cornelius de Peyster. Warrants to Abr'm de Peyster and
Robert Walters for salaries as assistant judges.   336

16   Caleb Heathcote answers the allegations of Dr Samuel
Staats. Edward Antill takes the oath.   337

17   Resolutions of council to be communicated to Rev. Bern.
Freeman.   338

18   Roger Baker discharged on giving bail. Patent granted for
land in Ulster county to Robert Sanders, Thomas Sanders,
Johs. Bush, Wm Sharpas and Joseph Cleator (see L. P.
3:60). Warrant to Isaac de Riemer for fitting out the
barge crew. Indian acknowledgment of land sale to Robert Sanders. John Groenendyck appointed deputy receiver
of quitrents in Albany county. Edward Burroughs of
Queens county to be arrested for speaking disrespectfully
about the governor. Warrants to George Clarke and Andrew Marriner for discovering the writer of the words
" hang John Nanfan."   338

21   John Barberie appointed to do the work of Col. Nich's Bayard on the accounts of Mrs van Cortlandt. Accounts.
License to purchase Indian lands in Suffolk county granted
to Isaac de Riemer, John Cornelise, John Evotse, John
Plevier, Barent Christyanse, Wm Creed and Rich'd Cornwall.   339

22   Confiscation of Robert Livingston's estate. Abr'm de Peyster offers to assist the government in financial difficulties.   340

23   Patents for land on Staten Island granted: to Daniel Lake
and Joseph Holmes (see L. P. 3:63); to Anthony Tyssen
(see L. P. 3:62).   340

27   Rob't Livingston suspended from the council (see N. Y. col.
mss, 45:98). Memorandum taken by the lieutenant governor. Edward Burroughs. Warrants: to the sheriff of Suffolk
county for expenses in arresting John Mulford; to John
Owen for joiner work and to Peter de Riemer for glaziers
work in the fort; to Zachariah Mills for incidental expenses; to Burger Myndersen for blacksmith work and to
Jacob van Noorstrandt for nails etc to the fort; to James
Wells for carpenter work in the fort; to John van Veighten
for military freighting; for contingencies to Jacob Blom,
Myndert Schuyler, Jeremiah Collcutt, Jacobus van Duersen
and Rutgert Waldron.   341

28   Survey of land for John Shadwell ordered.   343

30   Petition of Hannah Hutchins referred (see N. Y. col. mss,
45:99). Order on petition by John Gonsales.   343

1702   **v. 8**

May 1   Abr'm Gouverneur appointed corrector of the press. Linen-
press and chimney-back in the fort. Warrants: to Gov.
Nanfan for salary: to Abr'm Gouverneur for services as
speaker of the assembly; to David Provoost for expenses
as commissioner of accounts; to Abr'm de Peyster for
wine to the soldiers.   344

2   Acts of assembly to be sent to England. Warrant to Robert
Walters for firewood.   345

3   Edward, Lord Cornbury arrives and publishes his commission as captain-general, governor-in-chief, and vice admiral; is sworn at the house of the sick Chief justice
Atwood. New council: Wm Atwood, Wm Smith, Peter
Schuyler, Abr'm de Peyster, Sam'l Staats, Robert Walters,
Thos. Weaver, S. S. Broughton, W. W. Romar, Wm Lawrence, Gerardus Beeckman, and Rip van Dam; such of
them as are in town take the oaths. Barne Cosens sworn
as clerk of the council. Proclamations to issue, 1 for dissolving the assembly, and 2 for all officers in their posts.
Governor's commission published at the city hall.   345

p. m.   Lord Cornbury sworn to observe the laws of trade.   346

The remainder of this volume is legislative minutes separately paged 1-93
and printed in *Journal of the legislative council of the colony New York*, 1:117-75.

Vol. 9   1702-6

Pages 1 to 18 inclusive are a repetition of pages 338 to 346 of volume 8.

1702   **v. 9**

May 4   War with France expected. State of the province to be represented to the home government. Neighboring governors to be notified of Lord Cornbury's arrival. Proclamations: to issue calling upon creditors of the province to
present their claims; for the encouragement of religion
and virtue and the suppression of vice.   19

5   Census to be taken. Wm Lawrence sworn of the council.
Wm Carter appointed collector of the customs and sworn
in.   20

7   Proclamation to issue calling upon debtors of the province
to pay. The collector and receiver-general wants copies
of provincial laws concerning duties of import and export.
The governor, Abr'm de Peyster, Samuel Staats, Robert
Walters, Wm Lawrence and Rip van Dam are sworn in as
judges of the court of chancery. Patent for land in Flushing to Samuel Haight to be set aside (see *L. P.* 2:248).
Warrants: to Lawrence Claesen interpreter for expenses on
journey to Onondaga; to Harpert Jacobse for military
freighting; to John Bleecker for Indian presents; to Cor-

nelius Schermerhorn for transporting soldiers; to Ryer
Schermerhorn for presents to Indians given for liberty to
cut ship timber; to Wm Hall for firewood to Schenectady
garrison; to Ryer Schermerhorn for repairs to Albany and
Schenectady forts; to John Johnson Bleecker and Hendrick
Hansen for same.   21

8   Abstract of duties under act of assembly called for. Severeyn
ten Hout vs Mathias Mott heard and referred. Petition
of Philipp French and Thos. Wenham (see *N. Y. col. mss,*
45:114) referred. Proclamation to issue concerning the
oaths of allegiance and supremacy. Warrant to Barne
Cosens for expenses of the supreme court in the trial of
Wm de Myer late collector of excise in Ulster county.   23

13 Letters directed to Monsieur Pascoutal at Montreal delivered
to the governor by Daniel Cromline to be opened. Papers
relating to Col. Willett, Mr Whitehead, and Mr Jacobson
called for. Complaints against Col. Willett received.
Orders on petitions: by Abr'm Gouverneur recorder, John
de Peyster, Jacob Boelens and Martin Clock aldermen,
Abr'm Brasher and Abr'm Mesier assistant aldermen (see
N. Y. col. mss, 45:115); by Mary Burroughs for discharge
of her son Eden (see *N. Y. col. mss,* 45:118).   25

14 Address by the mayor etc of New York to the governor read
(see *N. Y. col. mss,* 45:122). Wm Atwood sworn in as
judge of the chancery court. Warrant to Lucas Kierstead
master of the sloop Sarah and Mary for assistance to the
Jersey man-of-war at Sandy Hook (see *N. Y. col. mss,*
45:119). Petition of Peter van Brugh and Hendrick Hansen referred.   26

15 Warrant to Lord Cornbury for salary.   27

18 Wm Smith and Peter Schuyler sworn of the council and as
judges of the court of chancery. Col. Thos. Willett before
the council. Paper from members of the house of representative delivered by Capt. Nanfan.   28

19 Sheriff of New York suspended after receipt of a petition by
Mrs John Hutchins. Pay to express messengers.   29

20 Five nations to be called to Albany for a meeting with the
governor. Accounts referred.   29

21 Gerardus Beeckman sworn in as judge of the court of chancery.   30

26 Wolfgang Wm Romar sworn of the council. Memorial of
Chief justice Atwood in answer to complaints by Philipp
French and Thomas Wenham read (see *N. Y. col. mss,*
45:125-26). Inspection of the garrison and military stores
ordered.   31

1702   **v. 9**

28   Roger Baker summoned before the council. Order on the
      answer of the mayor etc of New York to the complaint of
      the recorder. Powder vault to be built. Orders: on
      memorial by Thos. Weaver and Wm Carter (see *N. Y. col.
      mss*, 45:128); on petition by James Graves and Roger
      Prideaux, and by Onzeel van Sweeten on behalf of Valen-
      tine Cruger of London (see *N. Y. col. mss*, 45:129). War-
      rants to Peter Schuyler for firewood. Accounts referred.
      Warrants: to John Abeel for the use of Elizabeth van de
      Thoft; to Wm Ketelhyn and Harman Rutgers for house
      rent to officers at Albany; to Peter Schuyler and Dirck
      Wessels for expenses on a journey to Onondaga.   31

June 1   Waganhaes Indians in the Seneca country are to be asked to
      come to Albany. Order on statement by the collector con-
      cerning warrants.   34

4   Warrants to Thos. Weaver for wampum belts to the Wagan-
      haes. Orders on petitions: by Bern. Freeman (see *N. Y.
      col. mss*, 45:134); by John Champion; by the collector and
      comptroller; by Bartholomew Feurt. Accounts referred.   35

5   John Graves and Roger Prideaux discharged (see *N. Y. col.
      mss*, 45:135).   36

9   Charges preferred against Chief justice Atwood, Collector
      Weaver and councillors Abr'm de Peyster, Sam'l Staats
      and Robert Walters (see *N. Y. col. mss*, 45:138-40).
      Wm Smith appointed chief justice and sworn in; Caleb
      Heathcote, Thos. Wenham and Peter Fauconier to man-
      age the office of collector and receiver-general after receipt
      of books etc from Thos. Weaver. Attorney-general to
      prosecute Thos. Weaver in the supreme court. Accounts.   36

10   Orders on petitions: by Wm de Meyer late collector of ex-
      cise in Ulster county; by David Maddox (see *N. Y. col. mss*,
      45:141); by Severeyn ten Hout (see *L.P.* 33:67). Orders: on
      a statement by Wm Smith concerning two sloops seized in
      Suffolk county; on a petition by Robert Livingston. Pro-
      clamation to issue against paying public moneys to Thos.
      Weaver. Decision on the complaint by the recorder etc
      against the mayor etc (p. 31); concerning the freedom of
      the city given to soldiers. Proclamation to issue granting
      pardon to deserters who return within three months.
      Order on petition by Wm Bradford. Account of expenses
      for Col. Peter Schuyler's journey to Canada (see *N. Y. col.
      mss*, 45:142). House rent allowed to Rev. Wm Vesey.   38

11   Examination of charges against ex-Chief justice Wm Atwood
      and Thos. Weaver ordered. Orders on petitions: by Judith
      Pemberton; by Peter van Brugh and Hendrick Hansen.

1702   v. 9

Rob't Livingston's accounts referred. Proclamation about
deserters read. Warrant to Peter Schuyler for a journey
to Canada in 1698. Order on petition by Samuel Vetch.   42

p. m.   Warrant to the sheriff for the arrest of Thos. Weaver ab-
sconded. Order for appraisal of Capt. Samuel Vetch's
sloop. Ebenezer Wilson sworn in as high sheriff of New
York. Proclamation to issue offering a reward for the apprehension of Thos. Weaver and letters to neighboring
governors to be written about him (see *N. Y. col. mss*,
45:144).   44

13   Warrants: to Hendrick Hansen and Peter van Brugh for
expenses on a journey to Onondaga (see *N. Y. col. mss*,
45:143); to Chief justice Smith for salary; damage done to
his house to be appraised. Bridge wharf in the rear of the
fort to be built. Accounts of Robert Edward and John de
Honneurs referred.   46

p. m.   John Bridges appointed second justice of the supreme
court and judge of the admiralty court. Orders on petitions: by Kilian van Rensselaer (see *L. P.* 3:68); by Johannis Lydius minister at Schenectady. Commission for
managing the office of collector and receiver-general to be
renewed. Ordinance to issue concerning cases in the court
of chancery. Proclamation to issue about the excise.   47

15   Ryer Schermerhorn called before the board. Order on petitions by Ellis and Mary Duxbury (see *L. P.* 3:69). Mrs
Thos. Weaver intercedes for her husband. Report and
order on the petition of Wm de Meyer. Wm Hodgson to
build the powder vault. Salary of coxswain and crew of
of the barge fixed. Expenses of governor's journey to
Albany.   50

p. m.   John Bridges doctor of law sworn in as judge of the
supreme court; the same and Caleb Heathcote appointed to
and sworn of the council. Petitions by Johs. Lydius,
Bern. Freeman and Lawrence Claese, and account of Capt.
Weems referred to the governor for investigation at Albany. Expenses of the journey.   52

16   Petition by John Trevitt pilot referred. Order on petition by
Peter le Roux concerning his father's sloop Susannah.
Warrant to Ryer Schermerhorn for bringing ship timber
from Albany. Agent in England to be appointed. Joseph
Winshop's account referred. Petition of Lieut. John Ben-
net disallowed. Jacob Rutsen judge of common pleas in
Orange county, and Boudewyn de Witt sheriff of same
county, dismissed. Order on petition by John Collins.
Papers of Thos. Weaver to be examined by Dr John

Bridges and S. S. Broughton. Warrants: to Joseph Winshop and five others for going express to Albany (see *N. Y. col. mss*, 45:151); to Johs. Schuyler for charges in settling the eastern or Onagongaes Indians at Schackhook (see *N. Y. col. mss*, 45:151); to Edw'd Corbett for firewood to Lieut. Rich'd Brewer at Albany; to Thos. Williams for firewood to Albany blockhouse; to Francis Wynne for public transportation.   54

p. m. Order concerning a difference between Vincent Tillon a Frenchman, and Jacob Kierstead. Rip van Dam offers to supply government with money.   58

18 News of the accession to the throne of Princess Ann of Denmark; proclaimed as queen (see *N. Y. col. mss*, 45:153). Stephan van Cortlandt's accounts.   60

19 Warrant to John Freeman for coming express from Maryland. Expenses of proclaiming Queen Ann to be audited. Charges against Boudewyn de Witt late sheriff of Ulster county to be examined. Protection assured to Thos. Weaver. Presents for Indians to be provided. Thos. Weaver. Governor about to go to New Jersey.   62

29 Writs to issue for calling the assembly. Orders on petitions: by tavernkeepers of New York (see *N. Y. col. mss*, 45:158); by Edw'd Antill attorney for John Savine against Capt. Vetch; by Thos. Weaver (see *N. Y. col. mss*, 45:155). Salary to be again paid to the minister at New Rochelle (see *Doc. hist. N. Y.* 3:931; Q 3:563). Warrants for salaries of civil officers.   63

30 Papers of Thos. Weaver. Papers of Stephen van Cortlandt to be restored to his widow. Surveys of land ordered: for Stephen Gasherie; for Paul Samuel du Foir brother-in-law of Peter Albert of London merchant (see *L. P.* 3:71). Patent for land on Staten Island granted to Joseph Billop and Abr'm Lakeman (see *L. P.* 3:69). Order on petition by Rob't Livingston. Caleb Heathcote and Rip van Dam to be superintendants of work in Fort Wm Henry. Firewood for the fort. Warrants: to Wm Hudson for making powder vault in the fort; to Robert Livingston for Indian disbursements etc; to Rev. Wm Vesey for house rent. Estate of Boudewyn de Witt an alien. List of patents, quitrents, etc. called for. Governor about to go to Albany. Thos. Weaver.   64

Aug. 5 Governor in Albany. John Bleecker jr mayor, John Abeel recorder of Albany, Rob't Livingston sr, Major Dirck Wessells, and Capt. Evert Bancker to sit as court of oyer and terminer for the trial of four negroes accused of murdering the chief of the river Indians.   67

1702   v. 9

27   Proclamation to issue for a day of fasting and public prayer
        on account of sickness in city of New York.   69
Sep. 8   Governor present. Burrough of Westchester to choose a
Cheer Hall   representative. War with France and Spain declared.
Orange co.   Order on petition by Rev. John Lydius of Albany for
        salary; granted and warrants issued to him. Warrants: to
        Lawrence Claese for services as Indian interpreter; to Rev.
        Bern. Freeman for salary as Indian missionary. Excise of
        Albany. Survey of land near Kattskill ordered for Helme
        Jansen (see *L. P.* 3:75). Petition of Isaac Switz referred.
        Quitrents in Ulster county (see *L. P.* 3:79). Patents for
        land near Schenectady granted: to Adam Vrooman (see
        L. P. 3:74); to John Pieterse Mebie (see *L. P.* 3:73). Sy-
        mon, Johannes and Nicholas Westphale, Teunis and Jurian
        Quick, Hendrick Jan Decker and others to be tried for
        rioting at Waggackemeck, Ulster county. Orders on peti-
        tions: for land in Suffolk county by Mrs Gertruy van
        Cortlandt (see *L. P.* 3:83); for a patent by Bedford town-
        ship; by Dirck Benson (see *L. P.* 3:81); by Wm and Phil.
        Merrell (see *L. P.* 3:80). Sam'l Blackman master of the
        Jersey man-of-war and Beverley Latham to value Ryer
        Schermerhorn's ship timber. Thos. Weaver. Licenses to
        purchase land: in Suffolk county granted to Dr John
        Bridges and Rip van Dàm; in Dutchess county to S. S.
        Broughton (see *L. P.* 3:82). Revenue sloop to cruise for
        smugglers. Caleb Heathcote, Thos. Wenham and Peter
        Fauconier sworn in as commissioners of the receiver-gen-
        eral's office. Daniel Honan appointed secretary of the
        province vice Clarkson deceased.   70
12   Orders on petitions: by sailors of the Elizabeth and
Kingsbridge   Catherine for wages, Capt. John Wake being dead (see
Westches-   *N. Y. col. mss*, 45:180); by Garret Aertsen (see *L. P.* 3:84).
ter co.   Robert Livingston's accounts referred. Order on petition
        by Lawrence Thomase (see *N. Y. col. mss*, 45:181). Salary
        of Rev. Mr Bondett of New Rochelle. Proclamation to
        issue concerning the collection of taxes. Orders on peti-
        tions: by inhabitants of Hurley, Marbletown and Mam-
        backus in Ulster county (see *L. P.* 3:86); by David Schuy-
        ler (see *L. P.* 3:77); by Rob't Livingston jr (see *L. P.* 3:78);
        by Gerardus Comfort (see *L. P.* 3:72); by Wm Notting-
        ham (see *L. P.* 3:87). Indian affairs. Order for survey of
        land near Huntington for Charles Congreve (see *L. P.*
        3:85); Daniel Honan sworn in as secretary. Lady Bello-
        mont to refund the money given for building the Onon-
        daga fort. Warrant to Thos. Davis as salary for riding
        messenger on Long Island. Ship timber.   78

1702   **v. 9**

17   Proclamations to issue: convoking the assembly to meet at
      Jamaica, L. I. on account of sickness in New York; ad-
      journing the supreme court to the same place. Order con-
      cerning courts of common pleas. Orders on petitions: by
      Johannes Cuyler; by Lieutenants Henry Holland and Rich-
      ard Brewer. Fire wood accounts of Albany garrison.
      License to purchase Indian lands near Kattskill granted: to
      Henry and Gerardus Beeckman and Daniel Honan; to Dr
      John Bridges. Capt. Nanfan's warrants (see *N. Y. col. mss,*
      46:1). Philipp French to be mayor, clerk of the market,
      coroner, and water bailiff of the city, and Ebenezer Willson
      high sheriff of the county of New York. Governor intends
      to go to Albany. Proclamations to issue: about quick
      burial of persons dying from "malignant distemper";
      about other sanitary measures and about a weekly day of
      fast and humiliation. Bedford township.   83

Oct. 20   Edward Cole appointed doorkeeper and messenger of the
Jamaica   council, vice Rich. Stokes deceased. Legislative minutes
L. I.   (see *Jour.* 1:176). Order upon petition by the elders of
           the four Dutch churches in Kings county (see *N. Y. col. mss,*
           46:66), and calling Johs. Schenck town clerk of Flat-
           bush before the council (see *Doc. hist. N. Y.* 3:141; Q
           3:90-91).   89

21   Legislative minutes (see *Jour.* 1:177).   89

22   Petition by Johannes Groenendyck rejected (see *N. Y. col. mss,*
      46:64). Petition by Jas. Evitts referred. Legislative min-
      utes (see *Jour.* 1:177). Aries van der Belt ordered before
      the council in re Dutch churches of Kings county (see *Doc.
      hist. N. Y.* 3:142-43; Q 3:91-92). Legislative minutes (see
      Jour. 1:177).   92

23   Legislative minutes (see *Jour.* 1:178).   94

24   Legislative minutes (see *Jour.* 1:178).   95

27   Proclamation to issue for a day of thanksgiving with a clause
      for incouraging virtue etc.   96

28   Legislative minutes (see *Jour.* 1:179). Salary of Thos. Davis
      riding messenger. Matthew Ling, Capt. John Corbett and
      Samuel Blackman to examine the sloop Mary (see *N. Y.
      col. mss,* 46:89-101). Petition by Nich's Bayard referred.
      Bayard to give bail for his appearance before the queen in
      council. Legislative minutes (see *Jour.* 1:179). Wrecks
      and drifts in Suffolk county.   97

29   Report and order on the petition by Nich. Bayard. Sur-
      vey of land ordered for Francis Vincent, Jacques Pullion
      and Macc Desachoy (see *L. P.* 3:88). Capt. Weems' ac-
      counts referred. Capt. Nanfan before the council in regard
      to two sloops wrecked in Suffolk county.   100

1702   v. 9
    30   Bail of Col. Nich's Bayard received.   Petitions, accounts
          and memorials referred.   Benj. van de Water late sheriff
          of Kings county, to be prosecuted for obstructing Richard
          Stillwell, present sheriff in the performance of his duties
          (see *N. Y. col. mss*, 46:73).   102
Nov. 3   Stillwell against van de Water.   104
    4   Order on an address by the inhabitants of Schenectady.   104
    5   Legislative minutes (see *Jour.* 1:180). Benj. van de Water
          called before the council.   105
    6   Legislative minutes (see *Jour.* 1:181).   Survey of land in
          Richmond county ordered for Caleb Heathcote (see *L. P.*
          3:91). Legislative minutes (see *Jour.* 1:181). Col. Nich's
          Bayard discharged from prison. Prosecution against Benj.
          van de Water (p. 102) stopped.   106
p. m.   Capt. Nanfan and Lieut. Oliver before the council about the
          sloops Society, and Mary, run ashore in Suffolk county;
          order relating to them.   108
    7   Legislative minutes (see *Jour.* 1:181).   Survey of land for
          Dirk Benson ordered (see *L. P.* 3:81). Sloop Mary to be
          bought by government for revenue service. Memorial by
          Capt. John Tudor referred.   Peter Lott called before the
          council on petition by Dirck Jansen Hooghlandt. Legis-
          lative minutes (see *Jour.* 1:181).   109
    10   Capt. Nanfan to give an account of the goods taken from
          the sloops Society, and Mary. Order regarding the pay-
          ment of warrants. Legislative minutes (see *Jour.* 1:182).
          Order on petition by John Hutchins who is admitted to
          bail for his appearance before the queen in council. War-
          rants: for salaries of civil officers; to Capt. James Weems
          for candles to Albany garrison; to David Schuyler, Dirck
          Wessells, and John Rosie for expenses on journey to
          Canada; to Peter Schuyler for firewood to Albany gar-
          rison; to John Abeel for same furnished by Edward
          Corbett; to Hendrick van Dyck and Jacob Staats for
          surgeons' services.   111
    11   Legislative minutes (see *Jour.* 1:182). Orders on petitions:
          by Edward Antill; by George Hadley son of Mary Hadley
          deceased; by trustees of Westchester (see *L. P.* 3:92); by
          inhabitants of Oysterbay (see *N. Y. col. mss*, 46:110-11);
          by Peter Villeponteaux (see *N. Y. col. mss*, 46:109); by
          Capt. Jas. Weems and Lieut. Matthew Shank (see *N. Y.
          col. mss*, 46:108, 113).   115
p. m.   Legislative minutes (see *Jour.* 1:182). Order on an address
          by quakers.   Committee on Rob't Livingston's petition
          enlarged. Quarters of officers at Albany. License to pur-
          chase Indian lands granted to Col. Wm Smith, Caleb
          Heathcote, Peter Schuyler and others. Necessary articles

to be furnished to Albany garrison. Order on petition by
Lieut. Rob't Gwyn (see *N. Y. col. mss,* 46:112). Warrant
to Edward Antill for guns (see *N. Y. col. mss,* 46:114).
Abr'm Schuyler's account referred.   116

12   Legislative minutes (see *Jour.* 1:182). Accounts referred.
French priests in the Onondaga and Seneca country.
Capt. Watkins' brigantine taken by the French. Paulus
van Vleck wanders about the country preaching without
a license (see *Doc. hist. N. Y.* 3:894; Q 3:538-39). Warrant
to Abr'm Schuyler for journeys to the Indian country.   118

p. m. Audit of Rob't Livingston's accounts. Warrant to John
Abeel for Indian and military disbursements and for John
Rosie's journey to Canada. Sheriff's fees.   120

13   Lieut. Oliver. Capt. Nanfan. Long Island ferries. Legis-
lative minutes (see *Jour.* 1:183). Warrants: to Thos.
Williams for firewood to Albany blockhouse; to John
Luykasse and Wm Robie for journeys to Onondaga; to
Daniel Bondett French minister for salary.   121

14   Sloops Mary, and Society. Legislative minutes (see *Jour.*
1:183).   125

p. m. Bedding allowed to Lieut. Chas. Oliver. Militia of
Queens and Kings counties to attend the governor from
Jamaica to the ferry. Capt. Nanfan and the sloops seized
by him.   126

17   Legislative minutes (see *Jour.* 1:184).   128
Ft Wm Henry

19   Sloops Mary, and Society: Legislative minutes (see *Jour.*
1:184). Indian affairs. License to purchase Indian lands
in Dutchess county granted to Rob't Lurting and Sampson Broughton (see *L. P.* 3:93).   130

p. m. Legislative minutes (see *Jour.* 1:184). Capt. Nanfan delivers papers regarding the sloops seized by him (see *N. Y.
col. mss,* 46:123-35).   131

20   Legislative minutes (see *Jour.* 1:185).   132

21   Legislative minutes (see *Jour.* 1:185). Petition by the chap-
plain and the surgeon of the New York garrison referred.
Duplicate of warrant to Barne Cosens for salary.   134

24   Report on Rob't Livingston's accounts received. Legislative minutes (see *Jour.* 1:186). Petition by Rob't Allison
referred. Salary of Jas. Evitts doubled (see *N. Y. col. mss,*
46:141). Order on the memorial of Col. Wm Smith about
wrecks and drifts.   135

p. m. Capt. Nanfan swears to his accounts of the sloops seized
by him. Rich'd Slaten to be prosecuted for embezzlement.
Warrant to Rev. Alex. Innes for salary as chaplain to the

foot companies (see *N. Y. col. mss,* 46:142). Rip van Dam,
Lt. Col. Wenham, Stephen de Lancey and Samuel Bayard
offer to lend money to government. Warrant to Rev. Wm
Vesey for salary.   137

25   Legislative minutes (see *Jour.* 1:186).   139

p. m. Petitions by Mrs Gertrude van Cortlandt, by Dirck van den
Burgh, Ebenezer Willson, Daniel Honan, Philipp Rokeby
and Wm Sharpas (see *L. P.* 3:96) and by Wm Carter and
Jas. Evitts (see *N. Y. col. mss,* 46:144) referred. Legislative minutes (see *Jour.* 1:187.   141

26   Legislative minutes (see *Jour.* 1:187). Firewood for Ft
Wm Henry.   144

p. m. Legislative minutes (see *Jour.* 1:188).   145

27   Legislative minutes (see *Jour.* 1:188).   146

Dec. 1 Rob't Livingston's accounts to be audited. Warrants: to
Gabriel Ludlow for salary as clerk, and to Gabriel Luff
for same as doorkeeper of the assembly; to Daniel Whitehead for house rent to the assembly at Jamaica; to Michael
Handon for same in New York.   [147]

10   Johannis van Alen, Coenradt Borghghrd, Abr'm van
Alstyne and Harmen van Jansen summoned before the
council concerning Paulus van Vleck. Order on petition
by Daniel Case (see *L. P.* 3:100). Warrants for salary to
Rev. Peter Peiret (see *N. Y. col. mss,* 46:147). Order on
petition by Peter and Magdalen Fauconier (see *L. P.*
3:99). Accounts referred. Order on petition by Wm
Lawrence (see *L. P.* 3:101).   [148]

11   Survey of land in Suffolk county for Daniel Case ordered.
Report on the papers and trial of John Hutchins received
(see *N. Y. col. mss,* 46:149-78). Petitions: of Elias and
John Pelletreaux referred; of Samuel Staats (see *L. P.*
3:102); of Isaac de Riemer, (see *L. P.* 3:104); of Abr'm
Lakeman and Peter le Conte (see *L. P.* 3:103); all referred. Warrants to Rip van Dam and Caleb Heathcote
for firewood to the garrison.   149

18   Proclamation to issue forbidding the distilling of rum in
New York city, and within a mile from the city hall.
Warrant to John Hudson for brickwork on the powder
vault.   150

19   The chaplain and the surgeon in Fort Wm Henry to have
furniture for their lodgings. Warrant to Rob't Livingston
for salary as military storekeeper at Albany.   151

24   Accounts of Mrs Van Cortlandt. Order on part of petition
by Margaret van Schayck executrix of Matthew Clarkson.
Warrants: to Christopher Denn for carpenter work in the
fort; to James Evitts for bricklayers work there. Petition

1702 v. 9

by Samuel Bayard referred. Survey of land for Charles Congreve ordered. Peter Fauconier and Dr Rokeby to examine into the allegations of certain distillers. Time for allowing distilling extended to January 10th. 151

31 Petition by Paroculus Parmyter complaining against Wm Lawrence (see *N. Y. col. mss*, 47:12), and order thereon. Order concerning licenses to purchase Indian lands and warrants of survey. Survey of land in Suffolk county ordered for Dr John Bridges and Rip van Dam. Accounts referred. David Jamison called before the council on petition by Oloff van Cortlandt (see *L. P.* 3:106). Petition by Cornelia Allison referred (see *N. Y. col. mss*, 47:10). Warrants for salaries of civil officers. Order on petition by Edward Cole (see *N. Y. col. mss*, 47:9). 154

1703

Jan. 8 Accounts. Warrants: to Rob't Edwards for bricklayers work in the fort; to Isaac Lenoir for use of his house in Jamaica to the governor and council. 157

14 Parmyter vs Lawrence. License to purchase lands in Orange and Ulster counties granted Philipp French, John Corbett, Matthew Ling, Caleb Cooper and Stephen de Lancey (see *L. P.* 3:107). Samuel Denton and his negro woman (p. 60). Quakers. 158

21 Parmyter vs Lawrence. Orders on petitions: by John Chadeague [Chadaine] (see *L. P.* 3:108); by Jacob Garriott; by Margaret Stokes (see *N. Y. col. mss*, 47:22). Rip van Dam's accounts for building the powder vault referred. Order to the secretary to produce all caveats entered. Census. 160

28 Justice John Tallman of Queens accused of irreligious utterances, suspended from office, and to be prosecuted (see *Doc. hist. N. Y.* 3:199; Q 3:124). Quakers. List of caveats received. Accounts referred. Petition by Sam'l Blackman rejected (see *N. Y. col. mss*, 47:26). Parmyter vs Lawrence. Payment to Jacobus van Duersen for conducting a detachment to Albany. 162

Feb. 2 Estate of Robt. Livingston restored to him. Peter Berrian called before the council. Warrants: to Robt. Livingston jr and John Baptist van Eps for a journey to Onondaga; to Barne Cosens for office furniture and stationery; to Wm Bradford for salary as printer etc.; to John d'Honneur for going express; to Elias and John Pelletreaux for candles to the fort; to Capt. Peter Matthews for expenses on governor's journey to Albany etc.; to Servas Morrisett for smith work in the fort; to Nanning Harmesen for hire of his sloop. 164

4   Sampson Shelton Broughton continued as attorney-general of the province by orders from England and sworn in. John Coe, Content Titus and Wm Hallet, and the quakers. Content Titus, Edward Hunt and Peter Berrian, trustees of Newtown, to be prosecuted for illegal methods in raising funds to build a meeting house for an independent minister.   167

5   Parmyter vs Lawrence, Schenectady. Hearing ordered on caveat by John Hutchins against a patent for land in Orange county to Melle Caspar, alias Springstead. Orders on petitions: by Wm Bradford; by Thomas Sanders; by David de Bon Repos; by Oloff van Cortlandt; by Isaac de Riemer; by Oliver Besley; by inhabitants of Schenectady; by Nichs Bayard; by Henry Filkin. Parmyter vs Wm Hallet sr.   168

11   Trustees of New Haven want guns sent to New York in 1689 returned. Lancaster Syms and Michael Hawdon, by Oloff van Cortlandt their attorney against —— Mowbray, by Edward Antill and Wm Nicoll in land matters.   171

12   Robt. Livingston called before the council about his accounts. Myndert Harmense called on Henry Filkins petition. Accounts referred. Warrants: to Jacob van Duersen for military transportation; to Caleb Heathcote for firewood.   172

15   Warrant to Robert Sinclair issued June 27, 1701 to be annulled as obtained under false pretenses. Capt. Nanfan's certificate to Mrs Stokes' account required. Revenue marine service. New Haven guns.   173

18   Persons having filed caveats to be called before the council. Parmyter vs Lawrence. Orders on petitions: by Wm Nottingham; by Robt. Livingston. Excise. Jonathan Whitehead. Warrants to Sam'l Bayard for firewood.   175

19   Letters received from Lieut. Thos. Sanders of the Jersey man-of-war, and tidewaiter Wm Sell informing that Edw'd Pette, Joseph Conckline and Wm Bradley of Southold have helped impressed sailors to desert; order for their arrest (see *N. Y. col. mss, 47*:47-48). Accounts of commissioners of revenue. Care of sick soldiers.   177

p. m.   Capt. Nanfan refuses to certify Mrs Stokes' account. Petitions by Paroculus Parmyter (see *N. Y. col. mss, 47*:49-50) referred.   179

20   Paroculus Parmyter to be prosecuted on report upon his petitions. Petitions: by Robt. Livingston; by Robert Milward; by Robert Walters referred.   179

25   The chief and the second justice report on the court of chancery. Capt. Nanfan reports on Mrs Stokes' account.

Escheator-general to find an office of the estates of Jaspar
Nessepatt an alien, and of Onzel van Sweeten an alien,
both deceased without heirs. Warrant to Robt.
Milward for services as prosecuting attorney at Albany. Duplicate
of warrant issued to Robt. Walters for firewood and as-
signed to Barth'w le Feurt. Proclamation to issue con-
cerning deserters.   180

Mar. 1   Isaac Arnold, Thomas Mapes and Thos. Young, justices of
Suffolk summoned before the council on information by
Major John Merritt. Edw'd Pette arrested (p. 177) con-
fesses that he participated with Symon Grover, Stephen
Bayley, Benj. Youngs, Lott Johnson and Daniel Terry in
a riot on board of the seized sloop Discovery at Southold;
Pette bailed not to leave the city; the others to be arrested. John Drake, Thos. Pinckney and Gregory Gud-
geon, justices of Westchester county called before the
council on an address by church wardens and vestry of the
Westchester division.   183

4   Hearing on caveat by John Hutchins vs Melle Caspar postponed. Edw'd Pette's bail approved. Parish of Eastchester. Order on petition by Joseph Sackett on behalf of the
town of Newtown (see *N. Y. col. mss*, 47:61). John Parcell elected collecter of Newtown discharged on camplaint
of Thomas Wickenham that he is an illiterate person.
John Mulford, Thos. Chatfield, Josiah Hobart and John
Wheeler to be arrested on a report by Thos. Cardale
deputy surveyor-general. Jonathan Horton to give bail
for not leaving the province. Caveat against Sam'l Staats
and others to be heard.   185

6   Rich'd Shaw, Nath'l Baker, Josiah Edwards, Enoch Tiffin,
Wm Scallenger, Dan'l Bishop, John Gardner and Mama-
seth Kempson to be arrested on a deposition by Thos.
Cardale. Order to the sheriff of Suffolk county for the
delivery of the sloop Discovery to Thomas Longworth.
Bail of Jonathan Horton approved. Accounts for nursing
sick soldiers referred. Warrant to Rip van Dam for work
in the fort. Petition by Wm Bradford referred.   187

11   Johs. van Alen and others discharged. Albany quitrents.
Report of commissioners on tavernkeepers' petition
referred. Wawayanda patent. Accounts referred. Gun
carriages to be provided. John Hutchins vs Melle Caspar again postponed. Petition by Hendrick Johnson van
Dyck and account of Elias and John Pelletreaux referred. 188

p. m.   Order on petition by the mayor etc. of New York (see
N. Y. col. mss, 47:65). Albany quitrents. Petition by Mrs

Gertrud van Cortlandt referred. Warrant to Francis
Wynne for firewood.   190

18   Patent for land in New York city granted to Jacob de Key
upon deed from the mayor etc. Sloop Discovery affair.
Petition by Daniel Honan referred. Barent Staats' account referred. Myndert Harmense to appear before the
council. Wawayanda patent. License to purchase lands
from the Minissink and Waghakemeck Indians granted to
Phil. French and others. Excise. Orders on petitions:
by Barne Cosens (see *N. Y. col. mss*, 47:69); by Rich'd
Sackett (see *L. P.* 3:115) and by Cornelia Allison.   191

22   Isaac Arnold and Thos. Mapes put under bail not to leave
the province. Nath'l Bishop and the high sheriff of Suffolk county to be arrested on information by Thos. Cardale (see *N. Y. col. mss*, 47:71-73). Orders on petitions:
by Rob't Livingston; by Benj. Aske and by Charles Congreve (see *L. P.* 3:105, 116). Warrants: to John Schuyler for sundries to Indians; to John Abeel for same; to
Bern. Freeman for salary as Indian missionary; to Lawrence Claese for salary as Indian interpreter.   193

p. m. Writ to the escheator-general in regard to the estate of Jaspar Nessepatt revoked.   195

25   Caveat by the town of Brookland against patent to the city
of New York discussed; Emott for Brooklyn, Buckley
for New York. Paroculus Parmyter formerly disbarred
again admitted to the bar. Warrants to Mrs Gertrud van
Cortlandt on accounts of her late husband. Order on
petition by the same and her son Oloff van Cortlandt.
Thos. Cardale swears to his reports of doings in Suffolk
county.   195

p. m. License to purchase land in Suffolk county granted to Benj.
Aske. Warrants for salaries of civil officers.   196

Ap. 1 Dr John Bridges appointed chief justice by the queen.
Proclamation to issue for a day of thanksgiving. Warrants: to the wife of Jon'n Davis for chimney sweeping;
to Samuel Blackman for going express; to Rob't Walters for firewood; to Elias and John Pelletreaux for candles to the fort.   197

2   Major Dirck Wessells to go to Onondaga about French
priests. Memorial by Peter Schuyler referred. Proclamation read and approved. Warrants to Peter Schuyler for
firewood.   198

5   Dr John Bridges sworn in as chief justice. Dates for holding courts in Orange county fixed. Petition by David de
Bon Repos, minister of Staten Island referred. Inhabitants

of the out farms in Albany county, especially of Half Moon,
desert their places. 199

6   Robert Milward appointed second justice of the supreme
court and sworn in. Thos. Wenham appointed justice of
the same court and sworn in. 201

8   Warrant to Thos. Longworth for services with the sloop
Discovery. Salary of secretary fixed. Warrant to Peter
Schuyler for Dirck Wessel's journey to Onondaga. 202

p. m.   Patent for land called Kadarode in the Mohawk country
granted to John Petersen Mebie. 203

13   Petition by Wm Carten referred (see *N. Y. col. mss,* 47:88).
Josiah Hobart, Thos. Chatfield, Manassah Kempton, John
Wheeler, Rich'd Shaw, Wm Scallenger, Daniel Bishop,
Josiah Edwards, Joseph Conklin and Wm Bradley reported
arrested, the others (p. 185) not to be found. Order on petition by Lucretia widow of Denyse Hegeman. Warrant for
the commitment to the New York jail of the above prisoners (see *N. Y. col. mss,* 47:90). 203

p. m.   Legislative minutes (see *Jour.* 1:189): Joseph Conckline
and Wm Bradley admitted to bail. Richard Greenes account referred. Surveys of land ordered: for Cornelius
Dykman (see *L. P.* 3:118); for Andries Gardner (see *L. P.*
3:90). Warrants: to Peter Schuyler for victualling the
forces at Albany in 1697 and 1698; to Daniel Honan
for salary as secretary; to Thos. Davis for expenses as
riding messenger; to Richard Greene for guarding the
pink Hope. Forts at Nestigione and Half Moon.
Myndert Harmense discharged. 204

14   Order on petition by Joseph Conckline and Wm Bradley
(see *N. Y. col. mss,* 47:93). Hearing of caveats. 208

17   Conckline and Bradley (see *N. Y. col. mss,* 47:94). Capt.
George Rogers, Lieut. Henry Long and Thos. Sanders,
Purser John Francklin and Surgeon John Longford, all
of the Jersey man-of-war sworn in. Hearings of differ-
ences: between New York city and Brooklyn; between
John Hutchins and Melle Caspar deferred. Orders on
petitions: by John Abeel; by Jacobus van Dyck; by John
Baptist van Eps; by John Gilbert. Account of Harpert
Jacobse referred. Jonathan Owen and the quakers. St
George manor and Brookhaven. Joseph Conckline and
Wm Bradley discharged. 209

20   John Wheeler discharged; the others to be prosecuted. 213

21   Warrants for quartering soldiers in 1700 to Mary Harris,
John Davids, Robt Crannell, Anth'y Farmer, Thos. Carell,
Cornelia Allison, Berkley, Wm Mosse and Susannah
Robert. Fort for the Schaakhook Indians. 214

22 New York city vs Brooklyn. Wawayanda patent. War-
rants: to John Abeel for balance of expenses of Gov.
Fletcher's expedition to Albany; to John Baptist van Eps
for a journey to Onondaga; to Surgeon Jacobus van
Dyck for salary. Accounts of Lawrence Claese and John
Osburne referred. Ulster county taxes and quitrents.
License to purchase Indian lands near Schenectady and
Saratoga granted to S. S. .Broughton (see *L. P.* 3:122).
Petition of George Hadley granted (see *L. P.* 3:121).
Order on petition by Benj. Faneuil (see *L. P.* 3:120).   215

26 John Gardner, Nath'l Baker, Josiah Edwards and Nath'l
Bishop arrested in Suffolk county and committed to jail
in New York.   219

27 Legislative minutes (see *Jour.* 1:190). Patent to Dr John
Bridges (Wawayanda) signed. Kings county taxes.   220

p. m. High sheriff of Suffolk county defends himself (see
N. Y. col. mss, 47:106). Order on memorial of Dame Mary
Sloughter widow of Gov. Sloughter (see *N. Y. col. mss,*
45:182). Legislative minutes (see *Jour.* 1:190).   221

28 Legislative minutes (see *Jour.* 1:191). Ulster county quitrents. Warrants to Rip van Dam and Caleb Heathcote
for firewood.   222

29 Legislative minutes (see *Jour.* 1:191).   223

May 4 Legislative minutes (see *Jour.* 1:191). High sheriff Wm
Herrick of Suffolk county put under bail not to leave the
province.   225

6 Suspension of Wm Atwood, Thos. Wenham, Abr'm de
Peyster, Sam'l Staats and Rob't Walters approved by the
queen. Sentence of Nich's Bayard and John Hutchins re-
versed by the queen. Acts repealed. Susannah Vaughton
complains that Capt. Nanfan detains her Indian deed for
land at Crown Elbow in Dutchess county. Hutchins vs
Caspar heard. Caveats to be heard: by Jacob Rutsen vs
Hurley, Marbletown and Mumbackus; by Magdalena
Rosekrans against a patent for Leendert Cooll; of Caleb
Heathcote against a patent to people of Bedford; of
Isaac de Riemer about Crop Meadow and Half Hollow
hills; of Albert Manasse and Florus Wmse Cromelin; of
John Cosier; of Claus Clause Slyter; of Sam'l Mulford;
of Thomas Noxon vs. Leendert Cooll; of Samuel Paul
du Four; of Leendert Cooll; of Nath'l Brittain.   226

7 Legislative minutes (see *Jour.* 1:192). Montaukett lands. 229

8 Hearing of caveat by Claus Clause Slyter vs Capt. Thos.
Garton. Patent granted to Garton. Legislative minutes
(see *Jour.* 1:192): Warrants: to Wm Bradford for paper

etc.; to Gabriel Ludlow for salary as clerk of the assembly. Accounts of the sloops Mary, and Society. Wreck at Brookhaven. Accounts referred. Wm Lawrence and Gerard Beeckman called before the council. Wm Herrick's bail received. Petition by Lawrence van Schayck and Lawrence van Aele referred (see *L. P.* 3:124). Order on petition by Wm Nicoll and And'w Gibb. Warrant to Daniel Bondet for salary as minister at New Rochelle. Amount of quitrent to be paid by Severeyn ten Hout for the land called Masscaks, Ulster county, fixed.   231

11   Montauket lands. Wm Nottingham. Escheat of Onzel van Sweeten. Legislative minutes (see *Jour.* 1:192). Newtown.   234

12   Excise of New York city to be taken into the hands of government. Newtown (see *L. P.* 3:126). Daniel Smith of Smithtown, Suffolk county, to be arrested and tried for assaulting a justice of the peace.   235

13   Montaukett lands. Jacob Rutsen, Jacob Aertsen and Abr'm Haasbrook to be arrested for failing to report on Ulster county quitrents; John Heermans reports and is discharged. Hearing of caveat by Rutsen vs Marbletown deferred. Petition by Rob't Livingston jr referred. Warrant to John Abeel for sundries to soldiers and Indians at Albany. Legislative minutes (see *Jour.* 1:193).   236

14   Legislative minutes (see *Jour.* 1:193). Proclamation to issue contradicting false rumors. Order on petition by Nicoll and Gibb (p. 231). Newtown. Petition by Phil. French referred (see *N. Y. col. mss,* 47:126).   238

17   Legislative minutes (see *Jour.* 1:193). Prosecution of Thos. Weaver late collector suspended.   241

18   Legislative minutes (see *Jour.* 1:194). Special commission to issue for the trial of an accidental murder.   242

19   Legislative minutes (see *Jour.* 1:194). Abr'm Haasbrook discharged. Quota of Maryland and Virginia for forts in New York not forthcoming.   243

20   Legislative minutes (see *Jour.* 1:194).   245

22   Legislative minutes (see *Jour.* 1:195).   246

25   Legislative minutes (see *Jour.* 1:196). Indian affairs. Order on petition by John and Daniel Lawrence. Newtown. Nicoll and Gibb (p. 231, 238). Petitions: by Barent Vrooman; by Johs. Sanderse Glen; by Cornelius Dykman (see *L. P.* 3:118, 127); and account of Francis Wynne, all referred. Legislative minutes (see *Jour.* 1:196): Report on Barne Cosens' account approved. Warrant to Peter Schuyler for pay to Indian messengers.   248

26   Legislative minutes (see *Jour.* 1:196): Warrant to Rob't
       Livingston jr for salary as clerk of a special court of
       oyer and terminer at Albany.   249

27   Legislative minutes (see *Jour.* 1:196). Order on petition by
       Jacob Rutsen and Jacob Aertsen prisoners. Legislative
       minutes (see *Jour.* 1:196).   251

29   Ulster county taxes. The above prisoners are discharged.   253

31   Legislative minutes (see *Jour.* 1:197).   254

June 1   Legislative minutes (see *Jour.* 1:198). Peter Schuyler's ac-
       counts referred. Hurly, Marbletown and Mumbackus.
       Newtown. Legislative minutes (see *Jour.* 1:198). Mon-
       tauket lands. Acts confirmed and repealed.   257

2   Marbletown bounds. Legislative minutes (see *Jour.* 1:198).
       Proceedings of Queens county court of sessions to be ex-
       amined. Warrant to Peter Schuyler for Indian presents
       in 1688.   259

3   Legislative (see *Jour.* 1:199). Montauket lands. Hurley and
       Marbleton: Legislative (Ib): House of office for the gar-
       rison to be removed as a nuisance: Order concerning
       John and Daniel Lawrence (p. 248).   261

9   Legislative minutes (see *Jour.* 1:200).   264

10   Legislative minutes (see *Jour.* 1:200). Warrants: to Johs.
       Sanderse Glen and to Barent for firewood to Schenectady
       garrison; to Lawrence Claese for journeys to Onondaga;
       to Dirck Wessels for same; to James Spencer for recruit-
       ing services. Montauket lands. Patent for land granted
       to Helmer Janse (see *L. P.* 3:75, 130): Legislative min-
       utes (see *Jour.* 1:200): License to purchase Indian lands
       in Orange county granted to Benj. Faneuil: Legislative
       minutes (see *Jour.* 1:200). Quitrents for Marbletown and
       Mumbackus fixed.   267

11   Legislative minutes (see *Jour.* 1:201).   272

12   Legislative minutes (see *Jour.* 1:202).   273

15   Legislative minutes (see *Jour.* 1:202).   274

16   Legislative minutes (see *Jour.* 1:202). Patents granted: to
       Mumbackus (see *L. P.* 3:132); to Marbletown (see *L. P.*
       3:131). License to purchase Indian lands granted to David
       Schuyler and Rob't Livingston jr. Patent for land in
       Dutchess county granted to Henry Beekman. Legisla-
       tive minutes (see *Jour.* 1:202).   275

17   Legislative minutes (see *Jour.* 1:203). Dutch privateer from
       Curaçao allowed to refit. Legislative minutes (see *Jour.*
       1:203).   277

18   Legislative minutes (see *Jour.* 1:203). Order on petition by
       Henry Beekman (see *L. P.* 3:133). Legislative minutes
       (see *Jour.* 1:203).   278

19   Order on petition by Caleb Heathcote mayor of the borough
of Westchester (see *N. Y. col. mss,* 47:178, 180). Legislative minutes (see *Jour.* 1:204).   280

24   Accounts of Thos. Wenham and Peter Fauconier referred.
Hearing of caveat by Isaac de Riemer deferred. Orders
on petitions: by Philipp French and others (see *L. P.*
3:136); by Florus Crom; by Richard Greener; by John
Fort alias Libertee; by Peter Laesseing; by John Embree.
Sloop Discovery seized and condemned for illegal trade
to be used in the revenue service. Petition by Dirck
van der Burgh referred (see *N. Y. col. mss,* 47:183).
Caveats by Jacob Rutsen vs Marbletown, Hurley and
Mombackus dismissed. Warrant to Wm. Anderson.
Newtown books to be examined. Clauses about fishing,
fowling etc. to be inserted into the patents for Marbletown and Mombackus. Mombackus to be called
Rochester. Accounts of the governor's journey to Albany
to be audited. Petition by Schenectady church rejected
(see *N. Y. col. mss,* 47:168, and *Doc. hist, N. Y.* 3:143-44;
Q 3:92).   282

July 1 Difference between Phil. French and Eben'r Wilson to be
examined. Survey of Half Hollow hills to be made.
Order on petition by Florus Crom. Patent granted to
Wm. Nottingham. Warrants: for salaries of civil officers;
to Wm. Vesey rector for house rent; to Gabriel Ludlow
for salary as clerk and to Gabriel Luff as doorkeeper, of
the assembly; to Michael Hawdon for rent of his house
by the assembly. Vincent Tillon vs Jacob Kierstead
(p. 58).   285

15   Shawannas Indians before the council make propositions.
Presents to be given to them.   288

16   Presents delivered to the Shawannas. Schaakhook Indians
leave their country to live among the Mohawks.   289

20   Roger Mompesson arrives from England with a commission
of judge of the admiralty and is sworn in. Report on the
petition of John Embree (see *N. Y. col. mss,* 47:186).
Indian affairs. Warrants to Peter Fauconier and Thos.
Wenham for disbursements for the fortifications. Fortification accounts. Warrants to Wenham and Fauconier
for contingent public charge.   289

27   £1800 tax. No assessment of the £2000 tax made in Hempstead. More taxes than called for by the act collected in
Gravesend. Riot at Jamaica stirred up by Mr Hubbard
a dissenting minister (see *Doc. hist, N. Y.* 3:202; Q 3:126). 292

29   Collection of taxes in Queens county. Clerks of the peace
in Suffolk, Westchester, Richmond, Orange and Dutchess

counties summoned before the council for not sending collected taxes to the receiver-general. Collectors of the £1000 tax for building the Onondaga fort to be appointed (see *N. Y. col. mss,* 48:6). Major Wm. Lawrence called before the council. Justices of Kings county also called.   294

30   Order of the queen in council received approving the act for granting unto her majesty £2000. Thos. Wenham appointed of the council and sworn in. Lord Cornbury appointed captain-general and governor-in-chief of the province of New York, and sworn in (p. 16). Wm. Smith, Peter Schuyler, S. S. Broughton, W. W. Romar, Wm. Lawrence, Gerard Beekman, Rip van Dam, John Bridges, Caleb Heathcote, Thos. Wenham, Matthew Ling and Kilian van Rensselaer appointed to, and some of them sworn of the council. Freedom of debate and vote in all cases granted to the council. Thos. Byerley appointed and sworn in as collector and receiver-general. George Clarke sworn in as secretary of the province. Proclamation to issue adjourning the supreme court on Long Island.   296

Aug. 3   Wm. Smith and Peter Schuyler sworn of the council. Order on petition by Wm Lawrence vs John Embree (see *N. Y. col. mss,* 48:14). Collectors of the £1500 for erecting batteries at the Narrows to be summoned. Report on the petition by Wm Nottingham called for (p. 175). Ulster county taxes; Jacob Rutsen called before the council (p. 253). Accounts referred. Warrants: to Wm. Hodgson for bricklayers work in the fort; to Elias and John Pelletreaux for candles; to Francis Wynne for firewood to Albany garrison; to Henry van der Spiegel for window glass in Fort Anne; to Rip van Dam and Stephen de Lancey for Indian presents; to Robert Livingston, John Barbarie and Sam'l Bayard, executors of Gabriel Minvielle deceased; to Ebenezer Wilson; to Hellegauda de Key; to Margaret widow of Rich'd Stokes for articles furnished for the governor's journey to Albany; to Nanning Harmense; to Harpert Jacobse; to Wm Teller and to Dirck van den Burgh for hire of their sloops on the same occasion. Repairs to the fort. Petition by Capt. Jas. Weems granted (see *N. Y. col. mss,* 48:20). Accounts to lie on the table. Warrants: to Anne Bowen; to Judith Pemberton; to Elizabeth Smith; to Mary Thomas; to Susannah van Bonnel; to Susannah Churcher; to Elizabeth Stokes; to Elizabeth Letts; to Catherine Mansaile and to Hannah Graves, all for nursing sick soldiers. Report and

order on an account of Sheriff Jon'n Broadhurst of Albany
(p. 67). Daniel Honan ordered to turn over to George
Clarke the records etc. of the secretary's office.   300

5   Order on petition by the inhabitants of Bedford. Kings
county taxes. Phil. French et al. vs Ebenezer Wilson
et al. Indian affairs. Peter Schuyler's accounts. Warrants: to Peter Schuyler for Indian payments; to Matthew
Ling for provisions to the Indians. Wm. Lawrence vs
John Embree. Warrants of the 20th of July signed.   308

6   Order on petition by Jacobus van Cortlandt (see *L. P.*
3:141). Phil. French vs Eben'r Wilson. License to purchase land granted to Thos. Wenham. Petition by Phil.
French rejected. Warrants: to Wm. Smith for express
messengers; to Peter Schuyler for firewood to Albany garrison and for Indian disbursements.   311

9   Caleb Heathcote sworn of the council. Order on memorial
by Thos. Byerley collector and receiver (see *N. Y. col. mss,*
48:42). Quitrents. Boat for the custom-house service to
be purchased. The collector can draw salary only from
the day of his arrival. Patent granted to Jacobus van
Cortlandt. Attorney-general's accounts referred. Warrant
to Peter Schuyler for a journey to the Onondagas and
Oneidas, whom he is to call to meet the governor at
Albany. Survey of the land claimed by Phil. French and
by Eben'r Wilson to be made. Proclamation to issue forbidding the boarding of vessels before the customs officers
have visited them.   313

10 Hendrick Hansen, Peter Vosburgh and Lammert Jansen
summoned before the council. Election of a representative for Rensselaerswyck ordered vice Kilian van Rensselaer
appointed to the council. Repairs to the custom-house
to be made. Bedford. Orders on petitions: by Thos.
Cardale (see *L. P.* 3:142) and by Dirck Jansen Hooglandt
(see *L. P.* 3:143). Lord Cornbury intends to go to New
Jersey in order to proclaim his commission.   316

17 Peter Schuyler presides. Capt. Henry Claver of the Dutch
privateer Castle Roy not allowed to sail until he has given
bonds that he will not take on board debtors etc.   318

31 Lord Cornbury returned. An Indian murdered. Legislative minutes (see *Jour.* 1:205): Patent for Bedford to be
drawn up. Jacobus Kierstead discharged of his bond.   318

Sep. 2.   Wm. Carter appointed controller of the customs and sworn
in. Letter from the queen forbidding governors to accept
presents voted by the assembly, and fixing their salary.
Letter from the lords of trade concerning courts of judi-

1703   **v. 9**

cature. Letter from Lord Nottingham containing information of the declaration of war in the West Indies and
about trade with the French. Orders: on memorial by
Thos. Byerley (see *N. Y. col. mss,* 48:53); on petition by
Jacob Rutsen (see *N. Y. col. mss,* 48:54).   320

6 The governor and members of the council present take the
"protestant succession"·oath. Barne Cosens sworn in as
clerk of the council. Warrants: to Marg't Stokes for
services by her late husband; to John Osburne for sweeping chimneys in the fort. Reports referred. Warrants:
to John Clapp for carpenter work in the fort by John
Perry; to Thos. Byerley for fitting out a revenue cutter,
etc.; to Lucretia Hegeman for services done by her
husband among the eastern Indians; to Wm. Vesey for
salary as rector of Trinity church and house rent; to Dan'l
Bondet as minister at New Rochelle; to Peter Peiret as
minister in New York; to Caleb Heathcote, Thos. Wenham and Peter Fauconier for salaries as commissioners of
the revenue.   327

13 Capt. Henry Claver. Kinderhook affairs (see *N. Y. col. mss,*
48:9-12, 62). Wm. Peartree to be mayor, and Ebenezer
Wilson sheriff, of New York. Order on petition by Wm.
Bond master of the galley Cole and Bean. Warrants to
Peter Fauconier and Thos. Wenham exchanged for others.
Newtown books. Governor intends to go to Albany to
meet the five nations.   330

Oct. 5 Governor absent in Albany sends directions for issuing a
proclamation to adjourn the assembly.   333

8 Governor returned. Supreme court to sit longer than provided in the ordinance establishing it.   333

14 Mayor Wm. Peartree and Sheriff Eben'r Wilson take the
oaths. Legislative minutes (see *Jour.* 1:205): Oaths of
allegiance and supremacy administered to the officers of
the independent companies; Capt. Peter Matthews, Lieuts.
John Riggs, Matthew Shanke, Rich'd Hopson, Capt. Jas.
Weems, Lieuts. Henry Holland, John Peirson and Surgeon Phil. Rokeby; and to naval officer Peter Fauconier. 334

15 Supreme court. Edward Petty discharged from his bail.   336

18 Legislative minutes (see *Jour.* 1:206). Collector Thos.
Byerley, Sec. Geo. Clarke, and Doorkeeper Edw'd Cole
sworn in. Legislative minutes (see *Jour.* 1:206).   338

19 Lease of the custom-house. Legislative minutes (see *Jour.*
1:206). Patent for Jacobus van Cortlandt signed. Fort
at Albany to be repaired. Warrants: to Thos. Byerley
for carpenter work in the fort done by Christopher Denn;

to Barne Cosens for stationery; to Capt. Jas. Weems for candles. Bedford patent. Orders on petitions: by Abr'm Lakeman as guardian of Susannah le Conte daughter of John le Conte (see *N. Y. col. mss*, 48:84); by Albert Rykman (see *N. Y. col. mss*, 48:86). Warrants for salaries: to Hendrick van Dyk as surgeon; to Jacob Staats; to Jacobus van Dyk; to Fred. Mynderse as armorer in Albany.   339

20   Warrants to Henry Holland for firewood. Caleb Heathcote, and Judge Roger Mompeson take the oath of abjuration; also Mayor Wm. Peartree and recorder S. S. Broughton. Warrants for Thos. Wenham and Peter Fauconier signed. License to purchase Indian lands granted to Richard Sackett (see *L. P.* 3:115, 149). Lease of the custom-house. Order on petition by John Cloet.   342

21   Legislative minutes (see *Jour.* 1:207): Orders on petitions by Dirck van den Burgh, Nanning Harmense, John Abeel and Capt. Jas. Weems. John Braddick's account referred.   343

22   Daniel Honan, Wm. Smith, Michael Hawdon, Jacob de Key and Lieut. Lancaster Syms subscribe the abjuration oath and the first four are also sworn in as justices of the peace.   345

23   Warrants: to Henry Holland for candles; to John Abeel for officers' lodgings at Albany. Legislative minutes (see *Jour.* 1:20). Petition by Jane widow of Richard Greener sadler rejected (see *N. Y. col. mss*, 48:82). Report on Florus Crom's petition to lie on the table. Warrants: to Lancaster Syms for wine to the soldiers on the queen's birthday; to Dirck van den Burgh for wine at Indian treaty in Albany.   345

27   Kilian van Rensselaer sworn in as member of the council. Order on petition by Lieuts. John Riggs and John Person (see *N. Y. col. mss*, 48:88). Warrants: to Gabriel Ludlow clerk, and to Gabriel Luff doorkeeper of the assembly for salaries; to Michael Hawdon for use of his house by the assembly. Petition by Jacobus van Dyck referred.   347

Nov. 3   Proclamation to issue assuring sailors of privateers that they shall not be impressed for the royal navy. Orders on petitions: by Jannetie Cregier; by Gerard Beeckman; by Paroculus Parmyter; by officers stationed at Albany (see *N. Y. col. mss*, 48:77). Warrant to Thos. Byerley for expenses of repairing the custom-house. Orders on petition by Kilian van Rensselaer (see *L. P.* 3:153). Lieuts. Riggs and Person to have bed linen.   348

4   Confirmatory patent granted to Kilian van Rensselaer. New order on the petition by Jannetie Cregier. Orders on petitions: by Andrew Dupuy master of the sloop Jacob by

Barne Cosens. Custom-house. Hurley (see *L. P.* 3:154).
Proclamation to issue to discourage desertions from the
Jersey man-of-war, and from the army. Petition of Lieut.
Henry Holland rejected (see *N. Y. col. mss*, 48:100). Orders
on petitions: by Thos. Byerley; by Hilletie van Olinda.
Warrants: to Wm. Chambers for salary as gauger of the
excise; for salaries of civil officers; to Peter Schuyler
for firewood and for expenses of a journey to the Indian
country; to Thos. Wenham for guns to Shatteras Indians;
to Wm Sell for expenses on a revenue cruise. Bedford
patent.   349

6   Wm Smith takes the abjuration oath. James Evetts searcher
of the customs, Wm Chambers gauger of the excise, Wm
Sell, Nich's Feilding and Daniel Toy land and tidewaiters,
Richard Stillwell high sheriff of Kings county swear the
abjuration oath. Newtown records. Warrants: to the
attorney-general for fees; to Barne Cosens for expenses
in the escheator-general's office; to Wm Chambers for
salary. Ulster and Dutchess county taxes. Jacob Rutsen
to be arrested. Col. Wm. Smith and the sloops Mary, and
Society. Firewood for Albany garrison. Warrants to
Mrs Gertrud van Cortlandt for moneys due to her late husband.   354

9   Governor absent in New Jersey. Wm Smith presides. Wm
Lawrence complains of having been assaulted on the street
by one John Kincker who is to be arrested. Jacob Willse
complains of having been assaulted by Wm Lawrence (see
N. Y. col. mss, 48:106).   361

22   Lieut. Charles Congreve ordered to conduct military detachments to the frontiers is provided with money and provisions.   363

Dec. 4 Jacob Rutsen discharged from arrest upon giving security
for making up the tax accounts.   364

23   Lord Cornbury returned. Proclamation to issue concerning
pay-warrants. Collection of the £1000 and £1500 taxes (see
N. Y. col. mss, 48:115). Jacob Rutsen's accounts. Warrant to Lieut. John Riggs for bed linen. License to purchase land granted to Robert Lurting and Sampson
Broughton (see *L. P.* 3:158). John de Peyster, Samuel
Staats and Isaac de Reymer called before the council.   365

24   Three above men ordered to produce the power of attorney
from Mr Weaver late collector. License to purchase land
granted to Wm. Peartree, Jacobus van Cortlandt and
John van Horne (see *L. P.* 3:155). Warrant to Lieut.
Charles Congreve for military expenses. Permission given

to John Willsee to prosecute Wm. Lawrence of the council for assault (p. 361). Order on petition by Phil. French
and others (see *L. P.* 3:159).   366

1704

Jan.   6   Warrants: to civil officers for salaries; to Rev. Wm. Vesey
for his salary; to S. S. Broughton for fees as attorney-
general; to Benj. Aske for wine, and to Jeremiah Tathill
for articles provided for the governor's journey to Albany;
to John Crook for bacon etc.: to Matthew Ling, Benj.
Aske and Caleb Cooper, administrators of the estate of
Onzel van Sweeten for wine and rum on the governor's
journey to Albany in 1702; to John Vincent for mending
pump of the garrison; to Thos. Noxon for wine for the
governor's journey to Albany in 1702. Special court of
oyer and terminer to sit in Queens county for trial of a
quaker accused of blasphemy. Orders on petitions: by
Wm Bradford (see *N. Y. col. mss,* 48:147); by Thos.
Williams, by Stephen de Lancey, by Richard Sackett, by
Tierck Harmense, by S. S. Broughton (see *L. P.* 3:115,
149, 157, 160, 161). Warrant for Lieut. Chas. Congreve
signed. Wm Bradford to receive his salary quarterly as
other civil officers. Complaint of Paroculus Parmyter
against Wm Lawrence of the council referred to two " in-
different " persons. Newtown books. Orders on petitions: by Philipp Rokeby surgeon to the land forces (see
N. Y. col. mss, 48:148); by Phil. French et al. Jacob
Willsee vs Wm Lawrence.   367

13   License to purchase lands granted to Peter Fauconier and
others (see *L. P.* 3:164). Minissinck patent (see *L. P.*
3:163). Newtown books. Order on petition of Tierck
Harmense p. 367). Jacob Willsee vs Wm Lawrence.
Proclamation ordered on December 23 signed and to be
printed.   371

20   Orders on petitions: by Lieut. Richard Hc̗son; by Peter
Fauconier. Newtown affairs and books. Phil. Rokeby
before the council in regard to his petition (p. 367). Warrant to Rev. Johs. Lydius for missionary services. Edw'd
Cole messenger of the council. Jacob Willsee vs Wm Lawrence.   373

27   Order on petition by Mary Lawrence (see *N. Y. col. mss,*
48:158). Division of Minissinck patent. Warrants: to
Stephen de Lancey for guns to the Indians; to Wm Bradford for stationery. Report on confirmed and repealed
acts read. Survey of land ordered for Thos. Cardale et al.
(see *L. P.* 3:165). Jacob Willsee vs Wm Lawrence. Collector's accounts referred.   375

1704   **v. 9**

Feb. 10 Newtown books. Mary Lawrence vs Wm Lawrence.
Minissinck patent.   376

17 £1000 tax for building the Onondaga fort in Kings county.
Petition by Margarett van Schayck referred (see *N. Y. col.
mss*, 48:163). Warrants: to Lieut. Rich'd Hopson for furniture; to Thos. Byerley for a custom-house boat and incidental charges; to Rev. Wm. Vesey for salary and house
rent; to John Abeel for repairs of block-houses and of the
Indian house at Albany; to Dirck van den Burgh for
mason work in the fort; to Gabriel Luff for hire of wagons
on Long Island; to John Braddick for use of his sloop in
the revenue service; to Daniel Honan for incidental expenses on the fort; to Dr Phil Rokeby for medicines; to
S. S. Broughton for fees in the case of the sloops Mary,
and Society. Order on petition by Richard Sackett and
others (see *L. P.* 3:166). Report on the petition of Thos.
Byerley (p. 349) approved (see *N. Y. col. mss*, 48:104-5).
Petition by John Hutchins et al. referred.   Accounts of
the governor's journey to New Jersey (see *N. Y. col. mss*,
48:172). Parmyter vs Lawrence (p. 367). Minissinck patent, Lawrence vs Lawrence.   377

24 Justice Robert Milward sworn in. Accounts of Albany expedition referred. Petition by Benj. Aske et al. granted
(see *L. P.* 3:168). Minissinck patent. Supreme court for
Orange county to be appointed (see *N. Y. col. mss*, 48:170).
Montauket lands. John Bachand's accounts referred.   382

Mar. 9 Minissinck patent. Orders on petitions: by Daniel Honan
and Mich'l Hawdon (see *L. P.* 3:169; by John Hutchins
(see *L. P.* 3:171); by Thos. Worden. Quitrents. Warrants for things furnished for the governor's journey to
Albany by John Abeel, Daniel Honan, Peter Fauconier.
Fort Anne to be inspected as to repairs. Warrants for the
governor's salary to be prepared.   383

23 Report on Jacob Rutsen's accounts to lie on the table.
Orders on petitions: by Thos. Wenham; by Barent
Pieterse Coeyman (see *L. P.* 3:176); by John Vincent; by
Anth'y Badgley (see *L. P.* 3:172); by justices of Kings
county; by Christopher Rousby (see *L. P.* 3:173); by
Jacob Regnier (see *L. P.* 3:175); by Rob't Lurting (see
L. P. 3:174).   385

24 Richard Ingoldsby appointed lieutenant governor and sworn
in. Petition by Christopher Rousby (p. 385) granted.
Patent for land granted to Barent Pieterse Coeyman (p.
385). Warrant to Lancaster Syms for Bristol stones to
the fort. Orders on petitions: by Jacob Rutsen (see *N. Y.*

col. mss, 49:15); by Thos. Worden; by Elias and John Pelletreaux. Warrants to Peter Fauconier for the governor's salary. Survey of land for Anth'y Badgley signed (p. 385). Warrant to Jacob van Duersen for journeys to Albany. Lancaster Syms and Chris'r Denn intend to put up lading cranes; permission given.   386

Ap. 3   Ordinance for establishing the supreme court to be issued. Warrants: to civil officers for salaries; to John Trevitt for services on board the revenue sloop William in 1702. Orders on petitions: by Math. Ling et al (see *L. P.* 3:179); by Isaac de Reymer; by Mary Lawrence (see *N. Y. col. mss*, 49:18). Warrant to Francis Winne for firewood to Albany garrison. Division of Flushing common lands forbidden.   388

     8   Ordinance concerning the supreme court signed. License to purchase land in Orange county granted to Lieut. John Riggs (see *L. P.* 3:180).   390

    13   Legislative minutes (see *Jour.* 1:207). Warrant of survey granted to Hendr. Martinse Witts (see *L. P.* 3:187). Andries Coeyman called before the council. Flushing common. Patent for Chris'r Rousby and wife Sarah to be prepared.   390

p. m.   Legislative minutes (*Jour.* 1:208). Hearing of caveat by Barent Pieterse Coeymans vs Kilian van Rensselaer deferred. Orders on petitions: by Capt. Peter Matthews (see *N. Y. col. mss*, 49:20); by John de Morest (see *L. P.* 3:182). Patent for Chris'r and Sarah Rousby.   391

    15   Warrant to Lieut. Charles Congreve for military expenses. Flushing matters. Orders on petitions: by Peter Lansing; by Arent Danielse; by Lieut. Charles Oliver. Warrants: to Johs. Sanders and Jellis van Voorst for firewood to Schenectady garrison; to Peter Schuyler for incidental expenses at Albany. Order on the report concerning the petition of Thos. Worden pipemaker to dig clay in Flushing township.   393

    20   Minissinck patent. Confirmatory patent granted to Peter Schuyler (see *L. P.* 3:184). Petition by Helletie van Olinda referred. Legislative minutes (see *Jour.* 1:208). Petition by John Baptist van Eps referred. Warrant of survey for Anth'y Badgley to be executed. Accounts referred. Ordinance for establishing a supreme court in Orange county to issue (see *N. Y. col. mss*, 49:26-27). Collector of quitrents in Albany to pay John Abeel for officers' house rent. Petitions referred. Warrant to Col. Wm Smith for services in seizing the sloop Society.   394

21   Order on petition by the trustees of Westchester (see *L. P.* 3:187). Warrant to Arent Danielse for repairing the Schenectady blockhouse. Orders on petitions: by Effie Hanse (see *L. P.* 3:185); by Richard Sackett & Co.; by the inhabitants of Schenectady (see *L. P.* 3:186). Ulster and Dutchess county taxes. Daniel Honan's petition referred. Warrant to Peter Schuyler for pay of soldiers. Wm Smith wants rent for his house used for quartering soldiers.   396

25   Legislative minutes (see *Jour.* 1:209). Flushing commons may be divided. Warrants to Peter Schuyler and to Jacob Turck for candles to Albany and Schenectady garrisons.   398

26   Legislative minutes (see *Jour.* 1:209). Westchester affairs. Edw'd Burroughs, justice of Queens county, Sam'l Clows and Sam'l Mills summoned before the council on the petition of John Grice. Account of Dan'l Ebbetts bricklayer referred. Minissinck patent. Warrant to Isaac Caspersen for firewood at Albany. Dirck van den Burgh sworn in as justice of the peace in Orange county. Quitrents.   399

28   Tierck Harmense vs Effie Hanse. Anne Daniell's account referred. Minissinck patent. Order on petition by Wm Nicoll and Andrew Gibb (p. 231). Legislative minutes (see *Jour.* 1:209). John Grice's affair (p. 399). Warrants given in October to Capt. Weems cancelled the originals having been found. Coeymans vs van Rensselaer. Orders on petitions: by Wm Peartree (see *L. P.* 3:189); by Wm Davis (see *N. Y. col. mss*, 49:32). Jacobus van de Water called before the council. Accounts referred.   401

May 3   Petitions by James Spencer and by Mrs Gertrud van Cortlandt to lie on the table (see *N. Y. col. mss*, 49:48-49).   403

4   Warrants: to Rev. Wm Vesey for salary and house rent; to Wm Hall for firewood to Schenectady garrison; to Barne Cosens for stationery; to Barent Staats for military freighting; to Thos. Williams for services in Indian affairs; to Daniel Honan for clerical work. Salary of Wm Davis as clerk in the custom-house fixed. Warrants: to Peter Schuyler, Rip van Dam and Caleb Heathcote for firewood to Albany, Schenectady and New York garrisons; to Lawrence Claese for salary as Indian interpreter. Patent to Hendrick Johnson van Dyck deferred. Warrants to Wm Smith for use of his house as soldiers' quarters. Patent granted to Peter Lansing (see *L. P.* 3:183). Capt. Nanfan's accounts referred. Order on petition by Jonathan and Samuel Smith (see *L. P.* 4:2). Warrants: to Peter Fauconier for wine etc. on account of the governor's journey to Albany in 1702; to John Crook for

salary as gauger; to commissioners of the revenue for fitting up chaplain's and surgeon's quarters in the fort, for timber sent to England by the Benjamin in 1702, for carpenter's work in the fort done by Christopher Denn, for payments to Derick Wessells and Isaac le Noir, for mending the governor's barge (see *N. Y. col. mss*, 49:52-54).   404

6 Schenectady. Brooklyn taxes. Legislative minutes (see *Jour.* 1:211). East- and Westchester.   409

8 Coeyman vs van Rensselaer. Warrants: to Caleb Heathcote for firewood; to Daniel Ebbetts for bricklayers work in the fort; to Anne Daniels for nursing John Harris a sick soldier; to Elizabeth Stokes for nursing Edward Clayton and other sick soldiers. License to purchase land granted to Thos. Wenham and George Clarke (see *L. P.* 4:4). Warrants to Margaret van Schayck for the salary of the late Sec. Matthew Clarkson. Capt. Nanfan's accounts (see *N. Y. col. mss*, 49:55). Report on the condition of Fort Anne read. Montaucket lands.   410

9 Legislative minutes (see *Jour.* 1:211). Schenectady matters. Brooklyn taxes. Warrants of the day before signed. Warrant to Lieut. Charles Oliver for firewood to Albany garrison. Warrant for survey of land between Great Nuttenhook and Swartahook, Albany county granted to Effie Hanse (see *L. P.* 4:3). Order on petition by Rob't Livingston (see *N. Y. col. mss*, 49:68). Warrant of survey granted to Wm Nicoll and Andrew Gibb (see *L. P.* 4:5). Repairs to Fort Anne ordered. Warrant to Wm Davis for salary as custom-house clerk.   414

10 East- and Westchester. Schenectady. Jeronimus Rapale and Brooklyn taxes.   416

11 Warrant to Peter Schuyler for a journey to Onondaga. Montaucket lands. Legislative minutes (see *Jour.* 1:211). Petition by Rich'd Sackett referred. Quitrents. Schenectady. Petition by Barent Pieterse Coeyman rejected (see *L. P.* 4:6). Order concerning firewood for the different garrisons. Jeronimus Rapale. Warrants: to Peter Schuyler for pay of soldiers; to Abr'm Schuyler for same and for scouting services; to Lieut. Charles Congreve for contingent military charges.   417

13 Patent granted to Matthew Ling et al. (see *L. P.* 4:8). Warrant to Capt. Abr'm Schuyler for military expenses. Taxes. Order on petition by Tierck Harmense (see *L. P.* 4:7). Peter Schuyler, John Sanders Glen, Adam Vrooman, Daniel Johnson and John Baptist van Eps appointed first trustees of Schenectady. Peter Schuyler's patent.   419

1704   v. 9

16   Minissinck quitrents. Patent for land granted to Andries
      Gardineur. Land to be granted to Tierck Harmense must
      first be surveyed. Warrants of May 13 to Peter Schuyler
      to be exchanged for others; another warrant to him
      signed. Warrant to Rob't Livingston for salary as store-
      keeper.   421

19   Accounts of Thos. Weaver late collector. East- and West-
      chester. Orders on petitions: by John Abeel (see N. Y.
      col. mss, 49:73); by David de Bon Repos (see L. P. 4:10);
      by Daniel Toy (see N. Y. col. mss, 49:72). Jeronimus
      Rapale to be prosecuted. Schenectady and Ryer Scher-
      merhorn (see L. P. 4:9). Legislative minutes (see Jour.
      1:212). Petitions by George Clarke and by John Hutchins
      (see N. Y. col. mss, 49:75) referred. Date for election of
      trustees in Schenectady fixed.   423

23   Legislative minutes (see Jour. 1:212). Schenectady quitrents.
      Warrants: to John Abeel for provisions to the Indians; to
      Capt. John Riggs for fencing Fort Anne.   425

24   Legislative minutes (see Jour. 1:212). Warrant of survey
      granted to Hendrick Martinse Wittz (see L. P. 4:11).   427

25   Legislative minutes (see Jour. 1:213). Orders on petitions:
      by Lieut. Henry Holland (see N. Y. col. mss, 49:80); by
      Jacob Regnier & Co. (see L. P. 4:13).   427

26   East- and Westchester. Legislative minutes (see Jour. 1:213).   429

30   Legislative minutes (see Jour. 1:214). New Rochelle bounds.
      Orders on petitions: by Robert Milward (see L. P. 4:15);
      by David de Bon Repos (see L. P. 4:16); by Jacob Reg-
      nier (see L. P. 4:13). Petition of John Hutchins (p. 423)
      granted. George Duncan vs Chris'r Rousby (see N. Y.
      col. mss, 49:86). Order on petition by Daniel Kirkpatrick
      and Thos. Ford.   430

31   The survey of Flushing commons. Legislative minutes
      (see Jour. 1:214).   432

June 1 Legislative minutes (see Jour. 1:215). East- and Westchester. 434

2   Legislative minutes (see Jour. 1:216). Flushing commons.
      Accounts of Thos. Weaver late collector.   435

6   Legislative minutes (see Jour. 1:216). Supreme court to be
      adjourned on account of Chief Justice Bridges' illness.
      Warrant to Peter Schuyler of May 16 to be exchanged for
      another; also that to Hendr. Hansen of June 13, 1702.   437

9   Legislative minutes (see Jour. 1:216). Petition by John Abeel
      rejected (see N. Y. col. mss, 49:96). Samuel Smith vs Benj.
      Ask. Accounts of the late earl of Bellomont re-
      ferred. Survey of land for Rich'd Sackett called in ques-
      tion. Order on petition by Capt. Nanfan (see N. Y. col.
      mss, 49:97). Legislative minutes (see Jour. 1:216).   439

chief justice vice Bridges deceased. £1300 tax; justices of
the peace in Richmond and Kings counties to be prosecuted for neglect in collecting it; Samuel Clows clerk of
the peace in Queens county to be committed for the same.
New patent for Minissinck lands to be prepared.   455

18 Roger Mompeson sworn in as chief justice. Order on petitions: by Thos. Byerley (see *N. Y. col. mss*, 49:142); by
Nanning Harmense; by Thos. Hunt jr; by rector and
wardens of Trinity church (see *N. Y. col. mss*, 49:137); by
Peter Fauconier (see *N. Y. col. mss*, 49:143); by S. S.
Broughton (see *L. P.* 4:21). Militia detachments to march
to Albany. Accounts of Capt. Nanfan (see *N. Y. col. mss*,
49:141). Governor goes to Albany.   457

26 A French privateer lands at Sandy Hook and plunders the
inhabitants; the Dutch privateer of Capt. Adrian Claver
and Capt. Evertse to pursue and capture him.   461

27 Ten large ships supposed to be French are reported to have
come within Sandy Hook. Militia called out. The ships
are found to be prizes of Capt. Claver.   461

28 Capt. Claver's men refuse to attack the enemy when in
sight. Enlistment on board Capt. Claver's and Capt.
Evertse's ships encouraged. Capt. Thos. Penniston given
permission to cruize for the French privateer. Prizes of
Capt. Claver allowed to come into port. Provisions for the
three ships procured on credit of the council.   462

30 Capt. George Rogers of the Jersey man-of-war refuses to
obey an order for cruizing but will do so when requested
in writing.   463

31 Letter to Capt. George Rogers signed.   464

Aug. 1 Warrant to Abr'm Provoost master of the sloop Elizabeth for
transporting militia to Albany. John le Roux lately on
board of a French privateer examined and committed on
suspicion of piracy (see *N. Y. col. mss*, 49:153).   464

7 The French privateer intends to go toward Boston; Gov.
Dudley of Massachusetts warned; the Jersey goes in pursuit.   465

24 Lord Cornbury returned. Minutes of council during his absence read. He reports on Albany and Schenectady forts
and on the five nations. Report on the petition by rector
and wardens of Trinity church. Warrant of survey granted
to Thos. Hunt jr (see *L. P.* 4:22). Justices of Richmond
county pay the county quota of the £1300 tax and are discharged. Collector's accounts of the revenue petition by
John le Roux (see *N. Y. col. mss*, 49:169) referred. Survey of Richmond county to be expedited. Memorial by

1704   **v. 9**

Robert Milward referred (see *N. Y. col. mss,* 49:167). Wm
Lawrence called.   466

28   Quitrents of land granted to Rich'd Sackett fixed. Land in
controversy between Susannah Vaughton and Jacob Regnier granted to the latter. Capt. Praa of Piscataqua needed
as witness against John le Roux. Warrant to Thos.
Sharp for salary as gunner at Albany. Orders on petitions: by Thos. Lacey (see *N. Y. col. mss,* 49:177); by Barne
Cosens; by Peter Fauconier (see *N. Y. col. mss,* 49:175).
Governor goes to New Jersey.   468

p. m. George Clarke's name to be inserted in the Minissinck patent
vice Edmund Mott deceased. Warrant to Thos. Wenham
for expenses during the late alarm. Wm Peartree to be
mayor, and Ebenezer Wilson sheriff, of New York. Warrant to Rev. Wm Vesey for salary.   470

Sep.   2   Order on petition by David Provoost, Leonard Lewis, Johannes Tiebout and Abr'm Ketteltas vs Capt. Claver (see
N. Y. col. mss, 49:180-181).   471

4   Mr Regnier appears for Capt. Claver on the preceding complaint.   472

6   A French privateer supposed to be off Sandy Hook.   473

8   The ship is brought up to the city.   473

10   The crew of the same to be examined.   473

12   The ship proves to be a prize, taken by Capt. Rene Tongreton commander of a private man-of-war, from one L'Roux
trading illegally with the Spaniards. The ship is released and
a letter written to Capt. Tongreton (see *N. Y. col. mss,*
49:182). Capt. Peter Ramon receives assistance for the recovery of deserters from his ship (see *N. Y. col. mss,*
49:182).   474

16   Matthew Ling dead; Rich'd Willett and Walter Thong to
take charge of his estate (see *N. Y. col. mss,* 49:183).   475

20   Mary Sloughter widow of Gov. Sloughter to be buried in the
fort (see *N. Y. col. mss,* 49:184).   475

Oct.   2   Proclamation to issue adjourning the assembly.   475

6   Lord Cornbury returned. Legislative minutes (see *Jour.*
1:22). Adrian Claver, John de Peyster, Isaac de Riemer,
Abr'm Wendell and Abr'm Gouverneur summoned before
the council. Absent members called.   476

12   Legislative minutes (see *Jour.* 1:221).   476

14   Wm Peartree and Ebenezer Wilson sworn in as mayor and
sheriff respectively.   477

17   Warrants: to civil officers for salaries; to surgeons for
salaries. Accounts and petitions referred: by John Abeel;
by Capt. John Nanfan; by Myndert Fredericks0; by

Francis Winne. New patent to be prepared for Jacob Regnier substituting the name of John Peirson for that of Peter Fauconier. New patent for Rich'd Sackett et al. leaving out the names of Wm. Corlyout and Rich'd Blacklock. Order on petition by Adrian Claver captain, and Wm Nazareth quartermaster, of the private man-of-war El Castel del Rey (see *N. Y. col. mss*, 50:9).   477

20   Petitions by James Davis (see *N. Y. col. mss*, 50:16), and by John le Roux (see *N. Y. col. mss*, 50:15) referred. Wm Lawrence and Gerard Beeckman called to attend the council. Petitions: by Margaret Stoaks (see *N. Y. col. mss*, 50:17) and by Jan Bronck, Jonas Dow, Francis Salisbury of Katskill (see *L. P.* 4:25) referred. Warrant to Nanning Harmense for use of his sloop in 1703 (see *N. Y. col. mss*, 50:12).   480

24   Warrants for the governor's salary exchanged for others. Petitions and accounts: by Hilletie van Olinda (see *L. P.* 4:27), by Mary Thomas, by Cornelius Cool (see *L. P.* 4:26) referred. Patent granted to Hilletie van Olinda. Sheriff of Queens county summoned before the council. Justice Mott of Queens dismissed for malfeasance. Warrants: to John Abeel for military and Indian disbursements; to Myndert Frederickse for salary as armorer at Albany; to Abr'm Provoost for government freighting. Court of chancery to sit. Montauket lands.   481

26   Legislative minutes (see *Jour.* 1:222). Date fixed for the trial of John le Roux; Capt. Samuel Sands of Queens county to be a witness. Wm Lawrence of the council arrested at the suit of Paroculus Parmyter; ordered to be discharged and Parmyter summoned before the council (see *N. Y. col. mss*, 50:18). Warrant to Thos. Byerley for military provisions furnished by Abr'm Provoost. Legislative minutes (see *Jour.* 1:222). Petition by Samuel Pray and various accounts referred.   483

27   Warrants: to Samuel Pray for expenses of a journey from Piscataqua as witness against John le Roux; to Lieut. John Riggs for pay to under sheriff of Queens county for services in securing deserters. Duplicate warrant to the deputy auditor to replace one that is lost. Legislative minutes (see *Jour.* 1:222). P. Parmyter vs Wm Lawrence.   485

Nov. 1   Order concerning Peter Schuyler's accounts (see *N. Y. col. mss*, 50:22). Warrants: to Peter Schuyler for firewood to Albany and Schenectady garrisons; to Thos. Byerley for incidental expenses in the custom-house; to George

4:38); by Jacob Regnier (see *L. P.* 4:39); by Mary
Broughton widow of S. S. Broughton (see *L. P.* 4:42); by
James Mott (see *L. P.* 4:40); by Joseph Hedger; by Mrs
Anne Bridges (see *L. P.* 4:41); by Johs. Sanderse Glen
(see *N. Y. col. mss*, 50:54); by John van Loon (see *L. P.*
4:43. Warrants: to Peter Fauconier for Lord Cornbury's
salary; to civil officers for salaries.   504

31 Robert Coe church warden, John Talman, Henry Wright,
Sam'l Carpenter, Sam'l Highby, Anth'y Waters, John
Everett, John Coe, Jon'n Hazard and Daniel Lawrence
vestrymen of Jamaica, examined concerning their neglect
or refusal to provide for the salary of their minister (see
Doc. hist. N. Y. 3:208; Q 3:130). Warrant to Lord Corn-
bury for expenses on his journey to Albany. Glebe at
Hempstead to be surveyed.   506

Ap. 5 Orders on petitions: by Dr John Rodman (see *N. Y. col.
mss*, 50:56); by Margaret Peiret (see *N. Y. col. mss*, 50:57).
Joseph Hedger vs Flushing. Quitrent for John van
Loon's land partially remitted. Orders on petitions: by
Robert Luddington; by Cornelius Dyckman; by John
Auboineau (see *L. P.* 4:44). Fees of the naval officer
regulated. Warrant to Peter Fauconier naval officer for
incidental charges. Admiralty court fees.   507

12 East- and Westchester. Salaries of admiralty court officers
fixed. Ordinance to issue regulating the admiralty court.
Fees of vendue masters and appraisers of the court.   510

14 Orders: on petition by Peter Fauconier (see *N. Y. col. mss*,
50:55, 58, 62); on memorial by Robert Milward (see *N. Y.
col. mss*, 50:63, 65); on petitions: by Daniel Kirkpatrick
and Thos. Ford; by Isaac de Riemer (see *L. P.* 4:50); by
Cornelius Dyckman (see *L. P.* 4:47); by John Clapp (see
L. P. 4:48); by Mary Broughton (see *L. P.* 4:49). Ordinance regulating the admiralty court signed.   511

16 Warrants to Peter Fauconier for candles to the fort. Report
on Rob't Milward's memorial (p. 511) confirmed. Petition of Dr John Rodman referred. Order on petition by
collector and custom-house -officers (see *N. Y. col. mss*,
50:67).   514

p. m. Thos. Byerley collector and receiver-general suspended for
illegally granting a " bill of store " to Capt. Chollwell.   515

17 Commission of nisi prius to issue on petition by Barent
Pieterse Coeyman (see *N. Y. col. mss*, 50:66). Peter
Fauconier appointed to act as commissioner of the col-
lector's office and sworn in (see *N. Y. col. mss*, 50:70).
Warrants to Peter Fauconier and other former commis-

sioners for balance of dues. Proclamation to issue forbidding the importation of " chipt " bitts and double bitts. Governor intends going to Albany. 516

May 8 Zachariah Roberts justice of Bedford, arrested on a complaint by John Thompson and Benj. Wright (see *N. Y. col. mss*, 50:74-76). John Jones a dissenting minister of Bedford arrested (see *N. Y. col. mss*, 50:77-79). Report on Thos. Weaver's accounts referred (see *N. Y. col. mss*, 50:81). Warrant to Thos. Byerley for incidental customhouse charges. Excise. Orders on petitions: by Dirck Egbertsen (see *N. Y. col. mss*, 50:80); by Hendrick van Dyck (see *L. P.* 4:51). Lord Cornbury goes to New Jersey. Thos. Byerley swears to his accounts. 517

17 Thos. Odell a forger of Boston bills of credit apprehended by Jno. Cawley, Nicholas Thomas Jones and Robert Sanders, to be sent as prisoner to Massachusetts. Guard rooms for the town militia to be prepared in the city hall. 520

June 9 Lord Cornbury returned. Legislative minutes (see *Jour.* 1:224). 521

11 Legislative minutes (see *Jour.* 1:224). 521

14 Legislative minutes (see *Jour.* 1:224). 522

15 A French privateer off the coast near Barnegat; measures to capture him. 525

p. m. The ship Elizabeth Capt. Jones, the brigantine Return Capt. Potter, the sloops Peartree Capt. Dunscomb and Seaflower Capt. Cawley, to be fitted out for a cruize against the French privateer. 526

16 Volunteers called for; none coming a proclamation is issued offering a reward to those, who will go on the cruize.

25 Accounts of John Abeel referred. Warrant to Rev. Wm Vesey for salary. Indian propositions laid before the board. 526

28 Legislative minutes (see *Jour.* 1:225). New patent granted to John Petersen Mebie (see *L. P.* 4:52). Warrants to Nanning Harmense exchanged for new ones. Order on petition by Hilletie van Olinda (see *N. Y. col. mss*, 50:103), and warrant to her for pay as Indian interpretress. Peter Schuyler's accounts referred. Indian affairs. Agreement to build a fort at Schenectady laid before the council (see *N. Y. col. mss*, 50:104-107). 527

29 Letter received from Col. Peartree commanding expedition against the French privateer (p. 525-26). The Return and the Peartree to be recalled. Warrants: to be prepared to John Abeel for expenses in building Schenectady fort; to

Lawrence Claesen for pay as Indian interpreter; to Peter
Schuyler for building fort at Schenectady.   529

July   3   Warrants: to Lord Cornbury for salary; to civil officers for
salaries; to Hilletie van Olinda and Lawrence Claese for
pay as Indian interpreters; to John Abeel for officers'
house rent, Indian disbursements and repairs to forts at
Albany and Schenectady. Act for settling the militia to
be prepared. Indian accounts of Peter Schuyler referred.
Warrant to Caleb Heathcote for firewood.   530

5   Legislative minutes (see *Jour.* 1:226). License to purchase Indian lands for Thos. Wenham renewed. Warrant to Peter
Schuyler for Indian disbursements. Orders on petitions:
by inhabitants of Rye; by Jannetie Kendall (see *N. Y. col.
mss*, 50:114), Account of Indian expenditures. Legislative minutes (see *Jour.* 1:226).   532

6   Legislative minutes (see *Jour.* 1:226). Account for firewood
referred.   534

7   Legislative minutes (see *Jour.* 1:227). Order on petition for
patent by John Clap.   535

10   Legislative minutes (see *Jour.* 1:227). Warrants: to John
Crook for salary as gauger; to Rob't Livingston for salary
as storekeeper at Albany. Petition of Mrs Gertrud van
Cortlandt to lie on the table. Legislative minutes (see
Jour. 1:227).   536

11   Legislative minutes (see *Jour.* 1:228).   538

12   Legislative minutes (see *Jour.* 1:228). Orders on petitions:
by Nanning Harmense (see *N. Y. col. mss*, 50:116); by
John and Hope Williams of Oysterbay (see *L. P.* 4:53). 539

13   Legislative minutes (see *Jour.* 1:229). Warrants to Rip van
Dam for firewood to be prepared. Caveat by George
Booth against John Clap to be heard. Report on the
petition of John and Hope Williams (p. 539).   540

14   Legislative minutes (see *Jour.* 1:229). Booth vs Clap heard
and referred.   541

17   Legislative minutes (see *Jour.* 1:229). Patent for Westenhook lands granted to Peter Schuyler (see *L. P.* 4:54). 542

18   Legislative minutes (see *Jour.* 1:230). Warrant to Peter
Schuyler for work done on Schenectady fort by Daniel
Johnson. Patent to Trinity church for the queen's farm
and queen's garden to be prepared. Accounts of tax collectors called for.   543

19   Legislative minutes (see *Jour.* 1:230). Booth vs Clap decided. John and Joseph Williams.   544

26   The Lowestaffe man-of-war arrives and brings acts of parliament to be published. Letter from the lords of trade con-

1705   **v. 9**

cerning the assembly. Legislative minutes (see *Jour.* 1:230).
Orders on petitions: by Barne Cosens (see *N. Y. col. mss,*
50:119-20); by George Booth (see *L. P.* 4:55).   545

27   Legislative minutes (see *Jour.* 1:232). Account of Wm Bradford referred (see *N. Y. col. mss,* 50:122).   550

30   Legislative minutes (see *Jour.* 1:232). Warrant to Wm Bradford for stationery. Orders on petitions: by Cornelius
van Texel (see *L. P.* 4:56); by Peter Fauconier (see
N. Y. col. mss, 50:125).   551

31   Legislative minutes (see *Jour.* 1:233). Order on petition by
Ebenezer Wilson for himself and Peter Schuyler (Westenhook, p. 542, see *L. P.* 4:57). Stores in Fort Anne to be
examined.   553

Aug. 1   Legislative minutes (see *Jour.* 1:233).   554

2   Report on Peter Fauconier's accounts [incomplete].   555

3   Legislative minutes (see *Jour.* 1:233).   556

4   Order on petition by Sackamawigra a Westchester Indian
(see *L. P.* 4:58). Legislative minutes (see *Jour.* 1:233). 556

9   Warrants: to Rip van Dam for firewood; to Gabriel Ludlow for salary as clerk of the assembly; to Rev. Wm Vesey
for salary.   558

16   Patents to be prepared: for Peter Schuyler, for Corn's Dyke-
man. Account of repairing passage between the chapel
and fort distilling room referred. Bids for firewood invited. Warrant to Gabriel Luff for salary as doorkeeper
of the assembly.   559

18   Warrants: to John Hutchins for entertaining Spanish prisoners of war; to Rev. Daniel Bondet for salary; to Thos.
Wenham for Indian disbursements. Platforms of the fort
at Albany to be repaired. No bids for firewood received. 560

22   Account of damage to the ship Elizabeth Capt. Jones commander. Capt. Lancaster Syms agrees to furnish firewood for the fort. Memorial by Peter Fauconier concerning duties on goods brought in by privateers laid on
the table. Duplicate of a warrant issued to Mrs de Forest.
Lord Cornbury goes to Amboy.   561

30   Warrants: to Adolph Philipps for repairing passage (p. 559);
to Wm Sell for damages to the Elizabeth (p. 561). Inhabitants of Schenectady against Ryer Schermerhorn.   562

Sep. 6   Proclamations to issue: for adjourning the assembly; prohibiting the entertainment of mariners. New provincial
seal received. Petition of Lieut. Charles Oliver referred.
Governor goes to Long Island.   562

17   Peter Rolland master of the sloop Catharine receives permission to take to Jamaica two Spanish prisoners, John Gonsales de Riviera and Anthony Rosales.   563

1705   **v. 9**

26   Lord Cornbury returned.   Legislative minutes (see *Jour.*
      1:234).   563
27   Patent for John Clap & Co. to be prepared (see *L. P.* 4:61).
      License to purchase land granted to Eben'r Wilson (see
      L. P. 4:60).   564
Oct. 4   Legislative minutes (see *Jour.* 1:235).   Wm Peartree and
      Ebenezer Wilson renominated mayor and sheriff of New
      York.   565
5   Legislative minutes (see *Jour.* 1:235).   565
6   Legislative minutes (see *Jour.* 1:235).   Patent to be prepared
      for Anne Bridges, John Clapp and others.   Draft of sur-
      vey of land petitioned for by Cornelius van Texel called
      for.   566
11   Legislative minutes (see *Jour.* 1:235).   566
12   Legislative minutes (see *Jour.* 1:236).   Patent to be prepared
      for Mrs Broughton.   Warrants: to Peter Schuyler for fire-
      wood to Albany garrison; to Caleb Heathcote for fire-
      wood to New York garrison.   567
13   Legislative minutes (see *Jour.* 1:236).   Warrants to the gov-
      ernor and civil officers for salaries.   Wm Davis appointed
      vice Evitts deceased to attend the searchers duties with
      Mr Chambers.   John Crook to be land- and tidewaiter and
      gauger vice Tay removed for negligence.   Governor in-
      tends to go to New Jersey.   Order on petition by Joseph
      Mallison (see *N. Y. col. mss*, 50:163).   568
15   Wm Peartree and Eben'r Wilson sworn in as mayor and
      sheriff of New York.   569
30   Carpenters to be impressed by the mayor for making re-
      pairs to the Deal Castle man-of-war.   Capt. Ogle com-
      mander.   Hue and cry after a marine Simon Loundsdale
      deserted from the detachment of Lieut. Williams on the
      Lowestoffe.   570
Nov. 15   Orders on petitions by Peter Fauconier and by trustees of
      Westchester (see *L. P.* 4:63).   Warrants: to Ann Evitts
      for salary of her dead husband; to civil officers for salaries. 570
Dec. 6   Letter from lords of trade received by the Triton Prize man-
      of-war concerning coin.   Letters from the queen approv-
      ing the appointment of Roger Mompesson, John Barberie
      and Adolph Philipps to the council.   Proclamation to issue
      for a day of thanksgiving for victories by the duke of
      Marlborough.   Canadians reported as intending an attack
      on Albany; measures to prevent it.   571
13   Proclamation (p. 571) signed and to be printed.   Warrant
      to Rev. James Laborie French minister at New York for
      salary.   Patent to be prepared for Mrs S. S. Broughton

and her son Sampson (see *L. P.* 4:62). New York cannot agree to sign the articles of peace made by Gov. Dudley of Massachusetts and New Hampshire with Canada. Quitrents unpaid and to be discovered. Orders on petitions: by Barne Cosens (see *N. Y. col. mss*, 50:179); by Hendrick Hansen. " Chipt " bitts and double bitts still imported contrary to order (p. 516). 573

20 Order on memorial by Peter Fauconier (see *N. Y. col. mss*, 50:177). Quitrent for the land granted to Broughton & Co. fixed. 575

27 Order on petition by George Booth, Mrs Anne Bridges and others (see *L. P.* 4:64). Accounts of Thos. Weaver. Order on petition by George Booth, Wm Bond and others (see *L. P.* 4:65). Account of Geo. Booth referred. 576

1706

Jan. 3 Duties on prize goods. 576

11 Warrants to the governor and civil officers for salaries. Caveat by town of Rye against patent for Ponofield dismissed. Duties on prize goods. Warrant to James Laborie for salary. 577

17 Warrant to John Crook for fees in gauging liquor. Thos. Weaver's accounts. 578

24 Warrant to John Crook signed. Report on the petition from Rye referred. Order on petition by Geo. Booth, Wm Bond et al. (see *L. P.* 4:66). 578

Feb. 21 Time to sue out a patent extended for Geo. Booth. Warrant of survey granted to Geo. Booth, Wm Bond and others. Patent for Isaaç de Riemer & Co. for land in Suffolk county signed. Patent to John Clapp & Co. to be signed (see *L. P.* 4:67). Duty on prize goods. 579

26 Indian murderers on Long Island to be tried by their tribe. Orders on petitions: by Robert Puddington (see *L. P.* 4:69); by Richard Harris (see *N. Y. col. mss*, 51:79). Quitrents. 580

28 Patent for John Clapp signed. Warrants: to Roger Mompesson judge, Sampson Broughton advocate, John Tudor register, and Jarvis Marshall of the admiralty, for salaries; to customs officers; to Rev. Wm Vesey. Caveat by Eastchester vs Westchester. Bickley vs Emott. 581

Mar. 1 Petition by Lancaster Symes referred (see *N. Y. col. mss*, 51:81). Duty on prize goods (see *N. Y. col. mss*, 51:80). Warrants: to Richard Harris for escheat fees; to Jacob Staats for soldiers' pay. Hallet vs Wm Lawrence. Eastchester vs Westchester. 582

11 Patent for Mrs Mary Broughton signed. Eastchester vs

Westchester (see *L. P.* 4:70). Hallett vs Wm Lawrence (see *N. Y. col. mss,* 51:83). Wm Lawrence suspended from the council. Indian affairs.   583

20   Warrants issued to and lost by Mr Bondet duplicated (see *N. Y. col. mss,* 51:88). Order on petition by Mich'l Hawdon (see *N. Y. col. mss,* 51:92). Warrant of February 28 to Rev. Wm Vesey exchanged. Hearing of caveat of Capt. Wilson vs Rye deferred. Warrant to Barne Cosens for fees in escheat cases. Isaac Arnold discharged from his bail. Order on memorial by Judge R. Milward (see *N. Y. col. mss,* 51:91). Kilian van Rensselaer sworn " one of the court of chancery."   585

28   Warrants for salaries: to civil officers; to Barne Cosens. Peter Fauconier reports on payment of warrants. Warrant to Robert Millward duplicated. John Wildy arrested. 588

Ap.   4   Duties on prize goods (see *N. Y. col. mss,* 51:98). Warrants to issue to Lancanster Symes for firewood. Sampson Broughton's name to be substituted for his mother's in a patent for land (see *L. P.* 4:72). Wilson vs Rye.   589

Vol. 10, 1706-11.

Ap.   11   Warrants to Rev. Daniel Bondet signed. Warrants delivered to Dan'l Foy (see *N. Y. col. mss,* 51:103). Warrants to Lancaster Symes for firewood signed. Order on petition by Jacob Rutsen (see *N. Y. col. mss,* 51:105). Wilson vs Rye. Excise. Petition by John Crook (see *N. Y. col. mss,* 51:102) referred.   1

18   Wilson vs Rye. Excise of Albany. Treaty of 1665 with the Esopus Indians to be renewed. East- and Westchester. Petition by Dirck Jansen Hooghlandt (see *N. Y. col. mss,* 51:105) referred. Riot in Queens county.   2

23   Controversy between Newtown and Bushwick, L. I. License to purchase land in Suffolk, granted to Peter Fauconier, renewed (see *L. P.* 4:73). Order on petition by Paroculus Parmyter (see *N. Y. col. mss,* 51:114). Legislative minutes (see *Jour.* 1:236). Dumner's packet boats to the West Indies.   4

25   Boundaries of Newtown and Bushwick. License for P. Fauconier (p. 4) signed. Warrants for salaries to admiralty officers. Accounts of Geo. Clarke referred. Parmyter given permission to sue Edw'd Cole. Patent for kayaderosseras to be prepared. Governor going to New Jersey.   5

May   9   Fortifications for New York city necessary. Proclamations to issue concerning powder in town and concerning the militia.   7

1706 v. 10

14 Lord Cornbury defers his journey to New Jersey. Legislative minutes (see *Jour.* 1:237). Means for fortifying the city to be raised. 8

15 Citizens of New York will lend money for fortifying the city, and Lawrence Reed, David Provoost, Robert Lurting and Abr'm de Peyster to be managers for buying material. 9

23 Petitions by John Abeel and by Harpert Jacobsen referred (see *N. Y. col. mss,* 51:133-34, 136). Proposal to bring powder from Curaçao. 10

29 Legislative minutes (see *Jour.* 1:237). Order on petitions by John Abeel (see *N. Y. col. mss,* 51:137-139). 10

June 13 Legislative minutes (see *Jour.* 1:238). Warrants to issue: to John Abeel for money advanced; to Harpert Jacobson for hire of his sloop; to Peter Schuyler for Indian disbursements and for firewood for Albany and Schenectady garrisons. Petitions by Lieut. Phil. Schuyler (see *N. Y. col. mss,* 51:145) and by Rev. Lydius referred. 13

14 Legislative minutes (see *Jour.* 1:238). Warrants signed. Patent for land above Schenectady granted to Eben'r Wilson and John Abeel (see *L. P.* 4:75). 15

18 Legislative minutes (see *Jour.* 1:239). Warrants to issue: to Peter Schuyler for Indian disbursements; to Phil. Schuyler for work done on Schenectady fort. 17

20 Legislative minutes (see *Jour.* 1:239). Petition of Johannes Mynderse (see *N. Y. col. mss,* 51:148-149) referred. Quitrent for land granted to Wilson and Abeel fixed. Warrants to Peter and Phil. Schuyler (p. 17) and to Rev. Wm Vesey for salary signed. 18

21-22 Legislative minutes (see *Jour.* 1:239). 20-22

24 Indian affairs; far Indians at Albany; French Indians gone to New England; Virginia Indians want to make an alliance with the five nations. Present to the Indian messenger. Abr'm Schuyler to go to the meeting at Onondaga. 22

27 Legislative minutes (see *Jour.* 1:240). 24

July 4 Advice received of a French fleet coming to this coast. License to purchase land granted to Dirck van den Burgh and Thos. Saunders (see *L. P.* 4:76). Warrants for salaries to issue. Report on Barne Cosens' accounts referred. Florus Crom. 25

11 Warrants signed. Warrants for salaries to Rev. James Laborie and Daniel Bondet. Florus Crom. License to D. van den Burgh (p. 25) signed. 27

18 Warrants to Hendrick van Dyke, Jacobus van Dyke, surgeons to Hilletie van Olinda Indian interpretress, for pay

1706   v. 10

signed. License to purchase land granted to Johs. Hardenbergh (see *L. P.* 4:77). Order on petition by Hendrick
Hansen (see *N. Y. col. mss,* 5:154).   29

Aug. 7 Five nations want the governor to meet them at Albany.   30
22 Warrants signed. License to Johs. Hardenburgh signed.
Warrant to Dr Phil. Rokeby for curing a French Indian.
Sampson Broughton to be appointed attorney-general after
the session of the supreme court. Legislative minutes (see
Jour. 1:241).   31

29 Warrant to Dr Rokeby signed. Books for the register of
admiralty needed. Legislative minutes (see *Jour.* 1:241).   32

Sep. 2 Money for the governor's journey to Albany appropriated.
Petition of John Abeel and Eben'r Wilson (see *L. P.* 4:78)
referred.   33

27 Lord Cornbury returned. Legislative minutes (see *Jour.*
1:241).   34

Oct. 3 Warrants to issue: for salaries of the governor, civil and cus-
tom-house officers; to Peter Schuyler for firewood; to
Fred'k Minderse for pay as armorer; to Lieut. Holland for
house rent at Albany; to Lieut. Gwyn for same; to Albert
Slingerlandt for hire of his house at Albany to Lieut.
Brewer. Quitrent for land granted to Wilson and Abeel
reduced (see *L. P.* 4:78). Petition of Col. Beeckman (see
N. Y. col. mss, 51:168-169) referred. Order on petition by
B. Rynders concerning duty on prize goods.   39

14 Wm Peartree and Eben'r Wilson renominated mayor and
sheriff of New York and sworn in. David Schuyler appointed mayor, and Henry Holland sheriff of Albany; the
latter sworn in. Warrants signed. Warrant to issue to
Lieut. Chas. Oliver (see *N. Y. col. mss,* 51:163, 177-178).
Order on reappointment of Robert Livingston to the offices of town clerk, clerk of the peace, clerk of the common
pleas for Albany city and county, and secretary of Indian
affairs. Legislative minutes (see *Jour.* 1:242).   43

15 Legislative minutes (see *Jour.* 1:243). Patent to Wilson and
Abeel to be prepared (p. 33, 39). Order on report by the
justices of Richmond county concerning Jacob Garriott's
petition (see *N. Y. col. mss,* 51:165). Custom-house needs
repairs. Patent for Nanning Harmense to be prepared
(*L. P.* 4:79).   47

16 Legislative minutes (see *Jour.* 1:243). Warrants to issue: to Col.
Beeckman (p. 39); to Lawrence Claesen Indian interpreter
for salary and journeys to Onondaga; to Johs. Mynderse
for blacksmith work in Schenectady fort; to George Booth
for joiner work in secretary's office (record cases). War-
rant to Lieut. Oliver signed.   49

1706   **v. 10**

17   Legislative minutes (see *Jour.* 1:243).   Warrants signed.
      Petitions referred: of Lieut. Chas. Oliver; of Capt. Wm
      Bond (see *N. Y. col. mss*, 51:174); of Sampson Broughton
      (see *L. P.* 4:80); of Lawrence Claese. Warrants to issue
      to surgeons Hendrick and Jacobus van Dyke for salary.   51

18   Legislative minutes (see *Jour.* 1:243). Warrants to issue: to
      Lieut. Oliver for house rent; to Lawrence Claese for pay
      as Indian interpretèr and a journey to Onondaga. Peti-
      tions and accounts referred; of Phil. Schuyler (see *N. Y.
      col. mss*, 51:78); of Nanning Harmense. Warrants signed.   54

19   Legislative minutes (see *Jour.* 1:244).   Warrants signed.   57

21   Legislative minutes (see *Jour.* 1:244).   Newtown and Bush-
      wick. License to purchase land granted to Isaac Switts
      (see *L. P.* 4:81). Rules for paying salaries of officers of
      the admiralty court. Wenham's memorial concerning duty
      on burnt wines and brandy referred to England (*N. Y.
      col. mss*, 51:179).   59

p. m. Legislative minutes (see *Jour.* 1:245).   64

Dec. 5 Warrants to be prepared for salaries of assembly officers and
       of Rev. Wm Vesey.   65

19   Warrants to issue: to Lancaster Symes for firewood; to Phil.
      Schuyler for work on Schenectady fort: to Nanning Har-
      mense for hire of his sloop in 1704. Newtown and Bush-
      wick.   65

23   Newtown and Bushwick.   67

1707

Jan. 2 Newtown and Bushwick.   68

9   Newtown and Bushwick. Warrants for salaries of the gov-
     ernor, civil officers and Rev. Wm Vesey signed.   68

16   Newtown and Bushwick. Warrant to Register Tudor of the
     admiralty for books.   70

23   Petitions referred by Nanning Harmensen (see *L. P.* 4:85);
     Mrs Anne Bridges, Lancaster Symes et al. Wilson vs Rye.   71

Feb. 6 Thos. Byerley restored to the office of collector and receiver-
       general (see *N. Y. col. mss*, 52:9).   72

13   Petition by Peter Fauconier with accounts referred (see
     N. Y. col. mss, 52:21-25).   73

27   Petition by Mrs Anne Bridges (see *L. P.* 4:86) referred
     (Cheesecocks patent). Rye and Wilson. Warrant to
     Nanning Harmensen.   74

Mar. 6 Warrant to Peter Fauconier (p. 73). Reports on accounts of
       contingent expenses of Fauconier and Barne Cosens refer-
       red. Quitrent on Cheesecock patent reduced. Order on
       petition by Benj. Faneuil and Duncan Campbell (see *N. Y.
       col. mss*, 52:16). License to purchase land at Oysterbay

granted to Thos. Jones and John Townsend. Account of Edward Cole referred. Petition and accounts of Lancaster Symes referred (see *N. Y. col. mss*, 52:35-37). Wilson and Rye.   75

20   Warrants signed: for salaries to civil officers; to Peter Fauconier for candles; to Phil. Schuyler for work on Schenectady fort; to officers of the assembly for salaries. Petition by Peter Fauconier referred. Warrant to issue to Fauconier for contingent expenses. License for Thos. Jones and John Townsend (p. 75) to issue. Warrant to issue to Lancaster Symes for firewood. Warrant for drawing Cheesecock patent signed. Petition by Hendrick Tenike referred (see *L. P.* 4:89). Excise to be let. Wilson and Rye.   76

22   Warrants signed. Rules for paying salaries of admiralty officers and warrants, to them to issue. Warrants to issue to Peter Fauconier for disbursements (see *N. Y. col. mss*, 52:26-34, 38-39). Petition of John Lovell referred (see *L. P.* 4:108). Governor goes to New Jersey.   80

May 5   Order on petition by André Fresneau master of the brigantine St John of St Thomas (see *N. Y. col. mss*, 52:43).   82

16   Abr'm Sandford mariner reports, that Peter Cock master of a French privateer intended to cruize on the coast of Virginia and New England. The Tritons Prize man-of-war, Capt. Davis, commander, needs men for the crew; sailors from other vessels temporarily put on board. Vessels in port embargoed.   83

17   Soldiers put on board the Tritons Prize.   84

31   The Tritons Prize returns from the cruize and reports, that no French privateer has been seen.   84

June 4   Seamen to be impressed to fill the complement of the Tritons Prize. Embargo taken off.   85

5   Volunteers to be called for the present cruise of the Tritons Prize and seamen to be impressed in Kings and Queens counties. Sheriffs of same counties to provide horses for Edw. Cole on public service. Sloop for public service to be hired or impressed by Mr Hull master of the Tritons Prize. Wm Chambers to receive pay for boat hire.   86

19   Lord Cornbury returned. Petitions referred: by inhabitants of Hurley; by Johs. Hardenberg (see *L. P.* 4:91-93); by Margaret Stokes; by Hendrick Hansen (see *N. Y. col. mss*, 52:48); by Jacob Galliott (see *L. P.* 4:94); by John Rolland (see *N. Y. col. mss*, 52:47); by John Abeel (see *N. Y. col. mss*, 52:46). Patent granted to Nanning Harmensen (see *L. P.* 4:95). Rombouts vs Crabtree.   87

26   Warrant for patent to Nanning Harmensen signed. Collector Byerley ordered to pay the warrants given to John Abeel. Jacob Galliot to be allowed a road through the land of Wm Tillier on Staten Island (p. 87). Newtown and Bushwick. Rombouts vs Crabtree. Order on petition by Sampson Broughton (see *N. Y. col. mss,* 52:48).   90

July 3   Warrants for salaries of civil officers signed. Warrants to Lieuts. Brewer and Holland for house rent to be prepared. License to purchase land in Albany county granted to John Abeel and Eben'r Wilson (see *L. P.* 4:101). Warrant for Kayaderosseras patent to be prepared. Petition of Wm Sell referred. Collector Byerley to pay messengers from Virginia. Order on petition by Jacobus van Cortlandt, Wm Peartree and John van Horne (see *L. P.* 4:100). Rombouts vs Crabtree.   93

8   Warrants signed. Warrant to Jacobus Staats for salary as surgeon. License for John Abeel and Eben'r Wilson signed. Rombouts vs Crabtree.   96

10   Warrants to Peter Schuyler for firewood to be prepared. Petition of Lieut. Oliver referred (see *N. Y. col. mss,* 52:51).   98

17   Warrants signed. Petition of Capt. Jas. Weems referred (see *N. Y. col. mss,* 52:56-57). Order on petition by Lancaster Symes. Rombouts vs Crabtree. License to purchase land in Albany county granted to Isaac Switz. Warrant to Lieut. Rich'd Hopson for bed linen (see *N. Y. col. mss,* 52:55-56).   99

23   Warrants and license signed. Hendrick Tenike to be heard on his petition (p. 76), opposed by John Hutchins. Rombouts vs Crabtree. Collector Byerley ordered to pay warrants issued to Lancaster Symes. Public accounts of Peter Fauconier to be examined. Warrant to Lieut. Thos. Sharpe for salary as gunner at Albany to be prepared.   101

Aug. 14   Warrants signed. Warrant to be drawn to Capt. Jas. Weems for work on Albany fort. Confirmatory patent granted to Lydia Rose (see *L. P.* 4:103). Accounts of Lancaster Symes for firewood, of Mr Anderson in behalf of Phil. Schuyler for sweeping chimneys in Schenectady referred. Orders on petitions: by Capt. Tuder (see *N. Y. col. mss,* 52:60); by John Hutchins vs Tenike (see *L. P.* 4:102). Rombouts vs Crabtree.   103

Sep. 1   Lieut. Brewer arrives from Albany with Capt. Sheldon of New England and French prisoners (see *N. Y. col. mss,* 52:63-64). Appropriation for the governor's journey to Albany. Accounts of Mr Bogardus referred.   105

1707   **v. 10**

5   Warrants signed.   Hutchins and Tenike.   Newtown and
     Bushwick.   Order concerning Collector Byerley's refusal
     to pay warrants given to Rip van Dam.   107
10   Newtown and Bushwick.   Petition by Wm Tietsoort (see
     L. P. 4:104) to lie on the table.   Wm Chambers called
     before the council.   Hutchins and Tenike.   109
11   Hutchins and Tenike; patent granted to Tenike.   Wm
     Chambers testifies about custom-house rules in re
     van Dam.   Hearing of caveat by Gravesend vs Dirck
     Hooghland & Co. ordered.   Orders: on petition by offi-
     cers of the forces for bedding; on a memorial of officers
     of the admiralty court for salaries (see *N. Y. col. mss,*
     52:66-67).   Byerley testifies in re van Dam.   110
Oct. 4   Lord Cornbury at Albany.   Ebenezer Wilson nominated
         mayor and Wm Anderson sheriff of New York.   114
14   Lord Cornbury returned.   Warrants for salaries to civil
     officers signed.   Warrant to the widow of Edw'd Cole for
     her late husband's salary.   Eben'r Wilson and Wm. Ander-
     son sworn in as mayor and sheriff of New York.   Lord
     Cornbury reports having found everything quiet on the
     frontiers, also a great deal of smuggling to Canada.   114
Nov. 20   Petitions by Peter Schuyler et al., by Capt. Weems, Lieut.
          Hopson et al. about Sarachtoga patent, referred.   War-
          rants to Peter Schuyler for firewood to Albany and
          Schenectady garrisons.   117
21   Saratoga patent.   Warrants to Lancaster Symes for firewood.
     Patent for Hellgate rock granted to John Lovell (see *L. P.*
     4:108).   Collector Thos. Byerley under arrest and bond
     not to leave the province; examination of his accounts
     ordered; Peter Schuyler, Peter Fauconier and Robert
     Walters appear against him.   Account of John Cross for
     lodging Indians referred.   Gravesend vs Hooglandt de-
     ferred.   118
27   Orders on petitions: by Peter Fauconier (see *N. Y. col. mss,*
     52:81-85); by Nanning Harmensen & Co.   Salaries of
     admiralty officers.   Accounts of Thos. Wenham, Adolph
     Philipps, Robert Walters, Barth'w Feurt and Johs.
     Burgher (see *N. Y. col. mss,* 52:88-89) referred.   Warrants:
     to Elizabeth Cole for the salary of her late husband; to
     Rev. Wm Vesey for salary and house rent.   Report on
     Collector Byerley's books read.   Order on petitions: by
     George Booth (see *L. P.* 4:110); by Sampson Broughton.
     Rombouts vs Crabtree.   124
Dec. 18   Patent to John Lovell signed.   Petition of Lancaster Syms
          on behalf of Bernardus Verveulen for a patent for land

1707   **v. 10**

formerly granted by Phil. Carteret referred. Warrants to
Thos. Wenham etc. (p. 124). Gravesend vs Dirck Hooglandt heard and decided.   129

1708

Jan. 8   Patent granted to George Booth (p. 124). Petition of admiralty officers against Peter Fauconier. Warrants
signed.   131

22   Orders on petitions: by Lancaster Syms (see *N. Y. col. mss,*
52:92); by Mayor Evert Bancker, and corporation of
Albany (Saratoga patent; see *L. P.* 4:111). Accounts of
Geo. Clarke referred.   134

29   Warrants for salaries to civil officers. Reply of Peter Fauconier to petition of admiralty officers read (see *N. Y.
col. mss,* 52:94). Order on petition by Cornelius Seabring
(see *N. Y. col. mss,* 52:98). Collector Byerley appears on the
petition of Lancaster Symes (p. 134). Rip van Dam vs
Byerley.   135

Feb. 5   Order on petition by Johs. Hardenbergh & Co (see *L. P.*
4:112). Warrants: to Adrian Beeckman for provisions to
sea expedition in 1705; to George Clarke for office expenses. Order on petition by mayor and corporation of
New York against Cornelius Seabring (see *N. Y. col. mss,*
52:99). Warrant to Barne Cosens for expenses as clerk
of the council. Expenses in that office fixed. Rip van
Dam vs Byerley.   137

12   Account of Henry Swift referred. Maurice Newenhuysen
reports that letters are sent to France concerning the condition of New York. Corporation of New York vs Seabring.   140

26   Report on M. Newenhuysen's information (see *N. Y. col.
mss,* 52:101-104). Capt. Faneuil called. Warrants: to
Robert Crannel for pay as coxwain of the barge; to
Adrian Beeckman (p. 137). Warrant for patent to George
Booth signed. Peter Fauconier and his accounts. Firewood warrants to be taken in payment for custom-house
duties. New York vs Seabring.   141

Mar. 4   Order on petition by Wm Anderson on behalf of Hurley,
Ulster county. Warrant to Wm Chambers for use of his
sloop in 1705. Capt. Faneuil not to be suspected of sending information to France (see *Doc. hist. N. Y.* 3:431-32;
Q 3:261-62). Peter Fauconier's accounts.   144

18   Order on petition by Tjerck Harmensen Fisher (see *L. P.*
4:113). Saratoga patent (see *L. P.* 4:114). Warrants to
Rev. D. Bondett for salary. Order on petition by Corn's
Coole and Adrian Garritse of Hurley (see *L. P.* 4:115).
Patent for Johs. Hardenbergh to be prepared.   146

25   Warrant of survey for Harmensen Fisher signed. Petition
     of mayor etc of New York referred. Copies of deposi-
     tions and of council minutes regarding him to be given
     to Capt. Faneuil.   148

Ap. 8 Report on the petition of Corn's Cool (p. 146) received.
     Petitions referred: by Wm Cullen (see *N. Y. col. mss,*
     52:124); by Lancaster Symes (see *N. Y. col. mss, 52:*115);
     by mayor etc of Albany (see *L. P.* 4:124). Patents
     granted: to mayor etc of New York (see *N. Y. col. mss,*
     52:119); to Bern'd Verveulen for land on Peecks creek.
     License to purchase lands granted to Lawrence Claese
     (see *L. P.* 4:117). Orders on petitions: by Peter Schuyler
     and John Abeel (see *N. Y. col. mss,* 52:122); by John Abeel
     on behalf of Jacob Staats and Hendrick van Dyke (see
     N. Y. col. mss, 52:120-121); by Eliazbeth Cole (see *N. Y.
     col. mss,* 52:123); by Anne Newkirk (see *N. Y. col. mss,*
     52:118); by Corn's Seabring and Henry Filkin (see *L. P.*
     4:116).   148

15   Warrants and licenses signed. Patent granted to Lancaster
     Symes (see *L. P.* 4:118). Report on the petition of mayor
     etc of Albany confirmed. Warrants: to Lancaster
     Symes for firewood; to Wm Cullen for hire of his sloop
     in the revenue service. Orders on petitions: by Wm.
     Apple (see *L. P.* 4:119); by Cornelius Swits (see *L. P.*
     4:120); by Wm .Carter controller of the customs (see *N. Y.
     col. mss,* 52:127); by John Rosie and others of Nestigione
     (see *L. P.* 4:121). Warrants for salaries to civil officers.
     New patent to be prepared for George Booth (p. 141).
     Farmers of the excise at Albany to pay the warrants to
     John Abeel and Peter Schuyler notwithstanding Collector
     Byerley's orders. Petition of Anne Newkirk (p. 148)
     granted. List of admiralty fees called for.   153

22   Patents granted to Lancaster Symes & Co., and to John
     Rosie (p. 153) signed. Patent for George Booth and for
     Cornelius Swits. Warrants for salaries and for firewood.
     Petition of Peter Praa and others of Bushwick (see *L. P.*
     4:83, 122) to lie on the table. Admiralty officers' fees
     reported. French privateers and New York fortifications. 158

23   Controversy between Newtown and Bushwick decided for
     the latter. Warrants to the chief justice to be taken in
     payment for excise dues.   161

27   Lord Cornbury and the lieutenant-governor absent. Benj.
     Cooper master, and John Leroux passenger, of the sloop
     Endeavour report having been chased by a French ship
     off Sandy Hook. Vollenteers called to man the Tritons
     Prize, Capt. Norbury for a ten day cruize.   162

29   Deposition by Francis Jones (see *N. Y. col. mss*, 52:130)
      heard and an order issued to Capt. George Fane com-
      mander of the Lowestaffe man-of-war for a cruize. Infor-
      mation sent to Lord Cornbury.   162

May 15 Nicholas Tinchoven to be pilot for the Lowestoffe. Order
        for a cruize by Capt. Fane.   164

June 1 Indian affairs. Lawrence Claese reports, that the French
        intend to build forts at Skowkase and at Ohoryagre.
        Indians want an English fort in their country. Payment
        of expenses to Lawrence Claese ordered.   165

4   Deposition of George Moore mariner concerning the tak-
     ing of the ship Experiment from Barbados near Sandy
     Hook and his escape. Order to Capt. Fane for a cruize. 166

13   Letter to Capt. Fane about a French privateer with two
     prizes having been at Sandy Hook.   167

22   Lord Cornbury returned. Saratoga patent. Act of assem-
     bly declaring the proceedings against Bayard and
     Hutchins illegal confirmed by the queen; order of the
     queen in council at Kingston Jan. 8, 1708 is on p. 172. 168

July 1 Warrants for salaries to civil officers. Patent for Bushwick
        signed. Patent granted to Wm Apple and heirs of Har-
        manus Higedaam to be notified. Collector Byerley re-
        fuses to pay warrants issued to Register Tuder of the
        admiralty and to Lawrence Claese Indian interpreter.
        Warrant to Lawrence Claese for expenses in New York.
        Loan by Wm Peartree to be returned.   170

6   Indian affairs. Petition by Lawrence Claese referred. Quit-
Fort Anne rent to be paid by Bushwick fixed. Proclamation to issue
        convoking the assembly.   174

8   Petition of Fred'k Minderse referred. Warrant to the same
     for pay as armorer at Albany. Petition of Peter Fau-
     conier (see *N. Y. col. mss*, 52:140) granted. Land peti-
     tioned for by Wm Apple to be patented to him and to
     heirs of Heigedorn (p. 153, 170).   175

9   Additional instruction concerning the president of the coun-
     cil received and entered. Indians desire the governor to
     meet them at Albany. Warrant for expenses of the gov-
     ernor's journey signed. Saratoga patent. Warrant to
     James Parker for express charges from Albany. Writs
     for election to issue.   176

Aug. 5 Quitrent for land granted to Wm Apple fixed. Orders on
        petitions: by Adam Vrooman; by Elias Boudinot (see
        L. P. 4:127); by Ellis Duxbury (see *L. P.* 4:126). Com-
        plaint of Tuder vs Byerley to be heard.   178

1708   **v. 10**

16   Measures to be proposed to the assembly. Orders on petitions: by Peter Fauconier; by Francis Vincent. Warrant for patent to Ellis Duxbury signed.   180

19   Custom-house affairs examined. Warrants signed. Legislative minutes (see *Jour.* 1:246).   182

20   Legislative minutes (see *Jour.* 1:246). Custom-house affairs. Warrant to Rev. Wm Vesey for salary. Petition of Mr Vincent referred. New patent granted to Adam Vrooman for a creek and a mill above Albany. Patent granted to Tjerck Harmensen (see *L. P.* 4:129).   183

21   East- and Westchester. Fauconier and Byerley (see *N. Y. col. mss*, 52: 146-147).   184

24   Order of the queen concerning attendance of the council. Patent granted to Fr. Vincent (see *L. P.* 4:130). Order on petition by Eben'r Wilson (see *L. P.* 4:132). Warrant to Lieut. Henry Holland for house rent. Provisions for volunteers on the Triton's Prize. Examination of Peter Fauconier concerning custom-house affairs (see *Jour.* 1:247).   185

26   Collector Byerley charged with breach of trust. Fauconier's accounts. Legislative minutes (see *Jour.* 1:248). Petition of John Jackson sr and jr referred. Quitrent to be paid by Francis Vincent fixed. Accounts of the £1800 tax called for. Patents granted: to Eben'r Wilson; to Peter Fauconier (see *L. P.* 4:131). Warrant to Domine Lydius for services as Indian missionary (see *N. Y. col. mss*, 52:148). Collector Byerley refuses to accept for duties warrants issued to Peter Schuyler for firewood.   188

27   Legislative minutes (see *Jour.* 1:248). Warrant signed. Warrant for patent to John Jackson sr and jr.   189

30   Examination of Peter Fauconier's accounts continued. Quitrent for Adam Vrooman's patent fixed; also for John Jackson's. Schuyler and Byerley. Van Dam and Byerley. 190

Sep. 2 Time for settling land above Schenectady extended for Wilson and Abeel. Quitrent for Eben'r Wilson's house in Wall street New York fixed. Warrant to Capt. Jas. Weems for moneys advanced by him (see *N. Y. col. mss*, 52:155-158). Patent granted to Mrs Anne Bridges et al. (see *L. P.* 4:134). East- and Westchester decided in favor of the former.   191

3   Legislative minutes (see *Jour.* 1:249). Order on the report of council about the £1800 tax (see *N. Y. col. mss*, 52:149-50). Custom-house investigation (see *Jour.* 1:249).   193

7   Legislative minutes (see *Jour.* 1:250). Warrants signed. Payment to Lawrence Claesen to be made out of the quit-

rents of Albany and excise of Ulster counties. Byerley's
answer to lie on the table (see *N. Y. col. mss*, 52:161).
£1800 tax. Thos. Weaver's accounts. Commissions of
Robert Livingston recorded.   197

9   Wilson and Rye. Thos. Byerley. Orders on petitions: by
Eben'r Wilson; by Philipp Rokeby. Legislative minutes
(see *Jour.* 1:250). Duplicate warrant given to Rev. D.
Bondet canceled.   200

10   Legislative minutes (see *Jour.* 1:250). Wilson and Rye decided in favor of the former. Confirmatory patent granted
to Phil. Rokeby. Order on petition by Rob't Livingston. 202

11   Legislative minutes, and breaches of trust by Collector
Byerley (see *Jour.* 1:251); Byerley suspended from office;
Col. de Peyster to act in his place. Patent granted to
Col. Wm Peartree.   203

13   Legislative minutes, and examination of Peter Fauconier
concerning custom-house affairs (see *Jour.* 1:253). Fauconier exonerated.   207

15   Legislative minutes (see *Jour.* 1:262). Mistake in entry of
warrants. Warrants signed. Proclamation to issue empowering Peter Fauconier to receive the excise dues. Orders on petitions: by Rip van Dam (see *L. P.* 4:135); by
Wm Bradford (see *N. Y. col. mss*, 52:163); of Nanning
Harmen (see *L. P.* 4:138); by Robert Livingston (see
N. Y. col. mss, 52:165).   221

16   Legislative minutes (see *Jour.* 1:262). Orders on petitions:
by Claude Buissonet (see *L. P.* 4:140); by John Berry and
James Wright (see *L. P.* 4:136). Warrant signed.   223

17   Legislative minutes (see *Jour.* 1:262). Petition by Claude
Bouissonet referred. Order on petition by Anne Bridges
and others (see *L. P.* 4:139). Warrant signed. Order on
petition by Major Thos. Jones (see *N. Y. col. mss*, 52:167-
168). Warrants to Rev. Bondett for salary.   224

p. m.   Legislative minutes (see *Jour.* 1:263).   225

18   Legislative minutes (see *Jour.* 1:263). Petition of Elizabeth
Cole referred (see *N. Y. col. mss*, 52:170-172). Warrant
for patent to Anne Bridges signed. Petitions by Thos.
Jones, Wm Bradford and Mich'l Hawdon (see *N. Y. col.
mss*, 52:169) referred.   225

22   Legislative minutes (see *Jour.* 1:263). Petition of Anne
Bridges (see *L. P.* 4:139) referred. The collector called
on Thos. Jones' petition, and Hendrick Hansen on that
of Tierck Harmensen.   226

23   Legislative minutes (see *Jour.* 1:264). Orders on petitions:
by John Bodine (see *L. P.* 4:141); by Jacques Guyon (see

L. P. 4:143). Thos. Jones' rum released (p. 224-25). Tierck Harmensen's petition granted. Memorial by Aug. Graham surveyor-general, to lie on the table.   227

24   Legislative minutes (see *Jour.* 1:264). Patents granted: to Claude Bouissonet; to Jacques Guyon; to John Bodine. Warrant to Henry Swift for entertaining Indians. Two Brothers islands granted to Wm .Bond (see *L. P.* 4:142). Legislative minutes (see *Jour.* 1:264).   228

27   Legislative minutes (see *Jour.* 1:264). Warrants signed. Patent for Kayaderosseras granted to Nanning Harmense & Co. Petition for land on Staten Island by Lancaster Symes referred. Legislative minutes (see *Jour.* 1:265).   229

28   Legislative minutes (see *Jour.* 1:265). The Lowestoffe man-of-war and an armed sloop to cruize for a privateer. Memorial by Aug. Graham and Wm .Bond (see *L. P.* 4:152) referred.   230

29   Legislative minutes (see *Jour.* 1:265). Confirmatory patent granted to Wilson and Abeel (see *L. P.* 4:148). Mayor and sheriff of New York reappointed. Warrant for Westenhook patent signed.   230

30   Legislative minutes (see *Jour.* 1:265). Warrants: for salaries to civil officers; to George Clarke secretary, and to Barne Cosens clerk of the council for office expenses. Order on petition by Peter Schuyler & Co. (see *L. P.* 4:153). Account of Mr Bachand referred. Capt. Fane cannot go to sea.   bis 230

Oct. 1   Legislative minutes (see *Jour.* 1:266). Order on petition by Elias Pelletreau (see *N. Y. col. mss,* 52:177).   231

4   Legislative minutes (see *Jour.* 1:267). Orders on petitions: by Anne Bridges (see *L. P.* 4:154); by Peter Fauconier (see *N. Y. col. mss,* 52:178).   234

6   Legislative minutes (see *Jour.* 1:267).   234

8   Legislative minutes (see *Jour.* 1:267). Orders on petitions: by Jacobus van Dyck; by Johs. de Peyster (see *N. Y. col. mss,* 52:180). Warrants: to Lawrence Claesen for pay as Indian interpreter; to Lieut. John Collins for house rent. Accounts and petitions: by John Abeel (see *N. Y. col. mss,* 52:179); by Peter Schuyler & Co. (see *L. P.* 4:163); by John Mowbray; by Andries Gardiner (see *L. P.* 4:155). Warrants: to Wm van Ale for hire of his sloop; to Hans Cross for entertaining Indians.   235

11   Legislative minutes (see *Jour.* 1:268). Patent granted to Andries Gardiner. Warrants: to John Abeel for work on Albany fort; to Jacobus van Dyck for salary as surgeon; to Lieuts. Brewer and John Collins for house rent. War-

rants signed. Petition by Lieut. Brewer (see *N. Y. col. mss*, 52:181) referred. Patent granted to John Mowbray (see *L. P.* 4:156). Address to the queen concerning coins to be prepared. Custom-house affairs.   237

12 Legislative minutes (see *Jour.* 1:269). Warrant signed.   240

14 Ebenezer Wilson and Wm Anderson sworn in as mayor and sheriff of New York. Warrants signed. Patent granted to Cornelius Cool and others of Hurley (see *L. P.* 4:157). Quitrent for patent to Andries Gardiner fixed. Legislative minutes (see *Jour.* 1:269).   241

15 Legislative minutes (see *Jour.* 1:269). Quitrent for John Mowbray's land in Suffolk county fixed. Patent granted to Lancaster Symes (see *L. P.* 4:158).   241

16 Legislative minutes (see *Jour.* 1:270).   242

18 Warrant to Cornelius van Dyck for the salary of his late father surgeon Henry van Dyck (see *N. Y. col. mss*, 52:183). Thos. Byerley's accounts (see *N. Y. col. mss*, 1:182); he is suspended and a proclamation to that effect is to issue.   243

21 Order on petition by Thos. Wenham (see *L. P.* 4:159). Warrant signed. Legislative minutes (see *Jour.* 1:270). Custom-house books and papers to be inventoried.   244

22 Legislative minutes (see *Jour.* 1:270). Patents: for Saratoga granted to Peter Schuyler (see *L. P.* 4:163-65); for Kayaderosseras to Nanning Harmensen (see *L. P.* 4:161-62); to Thos. Wenham (p. 244). Warrant to Johs. de Peyster for firewood.   245

23 Legislative minutes (see *Jour.* 1:271). Warrants signed. Warrant to Peter Schuyler for firewood to Albany and Schenectady garrisons.   246

25 Legislative minutes (see *Jour.* 1:271). Joseph Hunt jr, John Ferris jr, Edw'd Griffin sr, Robert Heustis, John Oakly, Jas. Crumwell, James Ferris summoned before the council for opposing the survey of land granted to Wm Peartree in Westchester county. Quitrent for Saratoga patent fixed. Petition by Mr Anderson on behalf of Jac. van Dyck referred.   247

26 Duplicate of patent warrant for Norwalk island signed. Legislative minutes (see *Jour.* 1:272). Account of Peter Schuyler for candles referred (see *N. Y. col. mss*, 53:3). Warrant to the same for firewood. Account of Peter Schuyler for a journey to Albany (see *N. Y. col. mss*, 53:2). Quitrent for land on Staten Island granted to L. Symes fixed. Complaints against Lord Cornbury declared groundless.   248

p. m. Legislative minutes (see *Jour.* 1:272).   250

27   Legislative minutes (see *Jour.* 1:272).   Warrants to Peter
     Schuyler for expenses to Albany, and for candles.   Declar-
     ation of council concerning complaints against Lord Corn-
     bury.   Warrant signed.   Petition by Mark Dusasway (see
     L. P. 4:167) referred.   250

p. m. Legislative minutes (see *Jour.* 1:273).   252

29   Legislative minutes (see *Jour.* 1:274).   Warrants signed.
     Petition by Goosen Gerritse referred.   Joseph Hunt jr et al.
     (p. 247) discharged.   254

p. m. Legislative minutes (*Jour.* 1:274).   255

30   Legislative minutes (see *Jour.* 1:274).   Warrant to Adolph
     Philipps (p. 131) canceled.   Others for like services also
     to be cancelled, payment made by act of assembly.   255

Nov. 1 Warrants to Peter Schuyler for moneys advanced and ser-
     vices rendered.   Rip van Dam's rum to be resurveyed.   257

2   Warrants signed.   Lord Cornbury intends going to New
     Jersey.   John Abeel's account referred.   258

16   Lorn Cornbury returned.   Petitions referred: by Henry
     Beeckman (see *L. P.* 4:169-170); by Bernardus Freeman
     (see *N. Y. col. mss,* 53:7); by John Bachan (see *N. Y. col.
     mss,* 4:4-5, 30).   259

18   Legislative minutes (see *Jour.* 1:275).   259

24   Orders on petitions: by Isaac Mercier and others of New
     Rochelle against Peter Simon and wife, and on a counter
     petition by Barth'w le Roux (see *L. P.* 4:171); by Henry
     Taylor.   259

26   Legislative minutes (see *Jour.* 1:275).   260

27   Legislative minutes (see *Jour.* 1:275).   261

Dec. 2 Warrants to Elizabeth Cole.   Report of S. S. Brough-
     ton late attorney-general on public money in the hands of
     Jeronimus Rapalie referred to attorney-general May Bick-
     ley.   Weighmaster Grassett to pay "clipped" money into
     the treasury.   261

3   Accounts of Thos. Weaver late collector settled.   262

10   Warrants signed.   Warrants to Gabriel Ludlow clerk and to
     Wm Churchill doorkeeper of assembly, for salary.   Patent
     granted to Goosen Adriaense (see *L. P.* 4:168).   Warrant
     to Col. Wm Peartree for advances under act of assembly.   263

11   Warrants signed.   Petition of Wm Anderson (see *L. P.*
     4:172) referred.   264

15   Lord Lovelace arrives on Long Island and expects to be in
     New York the following day.   Warrants for salaries
     signed.   Petitions by Gertrud van Cortlandt (see *N. Y. col.
     mss,* 53:11; and, *L. P.* 4:173) referred; barge accounts.
     Petition by Judge Milward concerning Byerley's bonds
     referred.   264

1708   **v. 10**

17   Dinner to be prepared for Lord Lovelace.   266
18   Lord John Lovelace publishes his commission and takes the
      oaths and swears in the council. Proclamation to issue
      confirming all officers in their posts.   266
23   Wm Peartree and David Provoost appointed by the queen
      to the council and sworn in; Abr'm de Peyster likewise ap-
      pointed, but refuses to be sworn. Communications re-
      ceived from England concerning Indian presents, pala-
      tines, rate of foreign coins and trade, and requiring an ac-
      count of ordnance stores. Proclamation to issue for ap-
      prehending straggling seamen.   267
30   Order on petition by Richard Harris (see *N. Y. col. mss,*
      53:12).   268
1709
Jan. 5   Powder magazine to be repaired. Proclamation to issue dis-
      solving the assembly and writs for election of a new one;
      also of coroners. List of debts of the government called
      for. Is security given by sheriffs? Servants imported by Mr
      Keeble for making potashes to be hired out, Mr Keeble
      not having come in the ship Globe with them. Ordinance
      establishing the court of chancery called for. Warrant to
      Abr'm de Peyster to pay Rip van Dam for repairs on the
      new magazine.   269
13   Prosecutions in excise cases to stay (p. 268). Anderson to
      lay his list of government debts before the council. Lord
      Cornbury to be asked for Thos. Weaver's bond, and other
      public papers. Security to be given by the sheriffs. Peti-
      tion of Johannis Romer referred. Assembly to meet
      April 17. Orders on petitions: by Samuel Staats and
      Robert Walters (see *N. Y. col. mss,* 53:14-15), and by Mag-
      telt Messepatt. Warrant to Lord Lovelace and civil offi-
      cers for salaries.   270
20   Peter Fauconier's recognizances. Execution against Rich'd
      Harris stopped (p. 268). Lord Cornbury wants time in
      which to deliver the papers called for; granted, and peti-
      tions for his salary (see *N. Y. col. mss,* 53:19-20). Orders
      on petitions: by Johs. Roomer (see *N. Y. col. mss,* 53:17-18); by
      Isaac de Riemer (see *N. Y. col. mss,* 53:29); by Wm An-
      derson (see *N. Y. col. mss,* 53:27). Debts of the govern-
      ment. Warrant to Rip van Dam for repairing the new
      magazine. Magtelt Messepatt's affair settled (see *N. Y.
      col. mss,* 53:15). Orders on petitions: by Lancaster Symes
      and Eben'r Wilson (see *N. Y. col. mss,* 53:28); by Robert
      Livingston (see *N. Y. col. mss,* 53:24); by John Bachau; by
      Daniel Ebitts and by Elias Pelletreau (see *N. Y. col. mss,*
      53:25-26).   275

27   Lord Cornbury to answer in writing to the complaint of
      Samuel Staats and Robert Walters (p. 270). Messrs.
      Symes and Huddleston accepted as sureties of Sheriff An-
      derson. Order on petition by elders and deacons of the
      Dutch reformed church of Brooklyn (see *N. Y. col. mss*,
      53:3; and *Doc. hist. N. Y.* 3:148-49, Q3:95). Petition of
      John Harris et al. (see *N. Y. col. mss*, 53:33-34) referred.
      Thos. Byerley restored to his office of collector and re-
      ceiver-general upon orders from England; proclamation to
      issue to that effect.   278
Feb. 3 Answer to Staats and Walter's complaint (p. 270, 278) re-
      ceived from Lord Cornbury (see *N. Y. col. mss*, 53:37).
      Answer to Lord Cornbury from Thos. Byerley (p. 275; see
      N. Y. col. mss, 53:35). Brooklyn church and Bern. Free-
      man (see *Doc. hist. N. Y.* 3:150-51; Q3:96). Orders of the
      queen in council approving acts of assembly. Additional
      instructions to the governor concerning land grants. Let-
      ter from the queen in regard to palatines and their min-
      ister Joshua de Kocherthal. Report on ammunition re-
      ceived. Petition of Mrs van Cortlandt (see *L. P.* 4:173-74)
      referred.   280
11   Col. Heathcote sworn of the council and George Clarke as
      clerk of the council. Reply of Dr Staats and Rob't Wal-
      ters to Lord Cornbury to be sent to England (see *N. Y.
      col. mss*, 53:41). Lord Cornbury and Thos. Byerley (see
      N. Y. col. mss, 53:38). Symes and Wilson vs Thomas
      Byerley (see *N. Y. col. mss*, 53:42). Petition by Lord
      Cornbury (see *N. Y. col. mss*, 53:43) to lie on the table.
      Petition by John Abeel (see *N. Y. col. mss*, 53:44) to lie on
      the table. Petition by Henry Swift (see *N. Y. col. mss*, 53:40)
      referred. Petition by Rob't Livingston (see *N. Y. col. mss*,
      53:45) referred.   286
24   Lord Lovelace in New Jersey. Order on petition by Lord
      Cornbury (see *N. Y. col. mss*, 53:46). Thos. Byerley is given
      time to make ready his answers to complaints. Accounts
      and petition of Lord Cornbury (see *N. Y. col. mss*, 53:47-48)
      referred. Order on petition by Margaret widow of Pat-
      rick Magregory (see *L. P.* 4:175). Refunding money
      loaned by Wm Peartree in 1702.   287
Mar. 14 Useless ordnance stores to be sold and fort to be repaired.
      Ship Unity Will Patience commander reported at Ber-
      mudas on her way to New York with a rich cargo; the
      Maidstone man-of-war to cruize against French privateers
      for protecting the Unity and other ships.   289
19   The Kinsale, and Maidstone men-of-war ordered out for a
      cruize of three weeks towards Barnegat.   290

20   Capt. George Gordon of the Maidstone ready to sail pro-
      vided he can get 40 men for his ship. Capt. John Clifton
      of the Kinsale refuses to obey orders of the council not
      signed by Lord Lovelace. Capt. Nich's Tienhoven is will-
      ing to be pilot of the Maidstone. Letter and orders to be
      sent to Capt. Clifton.   291

22   Quarrel between the council and Capt. John Clifton con-
      tinued: Wm. Calleway swears to an affidavit concerning it.
      Capt. Gordon with the Maidstone ordered to Bermudas as
      convoy of the Unity. Letters sent to Lord Lovelace at
      Perth Amboy, N. J., by the Pennsylvania post.   292

23   Capt. Clifton needs 50 to 60 men for his ship who are de-
      tailed out of the garrison. Warrant issued to Nich's
      Tienhoven for piloting the Kinsale (see *N. Y. col. mss,*
      53:52). Capt. John Rolland of the sloop Lark reports hav-
      ing sailed from Bermudas in company with the Unity; the
      Maidstone to cruize for her. Charles German offers to
      carry the men aboard the Kinsale.   293

Ap. 6   Lord Lovelace returned. Col. Schuyler sworn of the coun-
      cil. Legislative minutes (see *Jour.* 1:276).   295

     7   Legislative minutes (see *Jour.* 1:276).   296

    14   Legislative minutes (see *Jour.* 1:277). Letter from Gov. Sal-
      tonstall of Connecticut about five nations received.   298

    19   Legislative minutes (see *Jour.* 1:277). Expense account of
      the government called for. Order on petition by Peter
      Schuyler. Memorials from Messrs Winthrop and Leverett
      of Massachusetts and Messrs Hamlin and Whiting of
      Connecticut (see *N. Y. col. mss,* 53:57) received. Indian
      affairs (see *N. Y. col. mss,* 53:56).   299

    20   Expense account of the government received and to be laid
      before the house of representatives. Answer to the me-
      morials of Massachusetts and Connecticut given to the
      agents. Answer to propositions made by Indians (see
      N. Y. col. mss, 53:58). Legislative minutes (see *Jour.* 1:277).
      Indian presents to be sent to Albany.   300

    25   Shawanoes Indians in New York make propositions, and are
      given presents.   301

    26   Indians. Legislative minutes (see *Jour.* 1:278).   302

May 6   Col. Ingoldsby to be informed of the death of Lord Love-
      lace. Officers to continue in their posts. Mr Cockrill
      Lord Lovelace's secretary asked for the governor's instruc-
      tions which are entered in the minutes. Capt. Matthews
      to command the garrison; the keys to be delivered to Col.
      Schuyler. Papers sent by Lady Lovelace. Letters to be
      sent to Gov. Saltonstall, Col. Vetch, Col. Nicholson and

1709   **v. 10**

the governor of Pennsylvania. Play acting and prize
fighting forbidden. Instructions.   302

p. m.   Col. Schuyler presides. Instructions to two Indians going
to Montreal and Quebec on a scout. Instructions for Mr
van Renselaer and Robert Livingston with presents to the
Indian spies. Col. Schuyler to keep the keys of the stores
until they are examined and inventoried.   338

7   Lord Lovelace to be buried in New York. Warrant to Lady
Lovelace for her husband's salary. New York regiment
ordered out for the funeral and furnished with powder etc.   340

8   Vessels not to be cleared to prevent news of the intended
expedition reaching the enemy. Col. Redknap not to
leave the province till further orders. Warrants to Lady
Lovelace for public expenses by her husband. Stores to
be examined. Letters to be sent to Col. Dudley and to
Mr Shackmapple about the privateer.   341

The entries on pages 342-457 are rough minutes of council; the fair and
more complete copy of them is paged 645-733.

9   Lt. Gov. Rich'd Ingoldsby present and sworn in after reading his commission. Proclamation to issue continuing all
officers. Mr Cockerill called upon to deliver the seals.
Stores to be surveyed. Lady Lovelace called upon for public papers. Proclamation to issue for an embargo.   645

10 Legislative minutes (see *Jour.* 1:278). Lord Cornbury called
upon for public papers. Stores to be inventoried.   645

14 Legislative minutes (see *Jour.* 1:278). Order on petition by
Joshua Cockerthal. Masters of merchant vessels refuse to
lend men for the man-of-war to go on a cruize after a
privateer.   646

17 Legislative minutes (see *Jour.* 1:278). The queen's instructions to Col. Vetch. Letter from the queen to Lord Lovelace about the expedition against Canada.   647

18 Legislative minutes (see *Jour.* 1:279). Proclamation to be
published by Cols. Vetch and Nicholson similar to their
Boston proclamation.   653

19 Legislative minutes (see *Jour.* 1:279). Palatines. Order on
petition by Lord Cornbury (see *N. Y. col. mss*, 53:66).
Writ of ne exeat against Thos. Byerley to issue. Expenses
of repairing the fort. Indian presents.   653

20 The sloop Diamond allowed to take aboard provisions for
the fleet at Boston. Legislative minutes (see *Jour.* 1:280).
Warrants: to Peter Schuyler for firewood to Albany and
Schenectady garrisons; to Thos. Byerley for money paid
for fort repairs.   655

21 Legislative minutes (see *Jour.* 1:280). Canada expedition
and Indian affairs. John son of Robert Livingston ordered

1709   v. 10

to Canada has a bond of the court of chancery extended.
Sloops with provisions and hospital stores to be sent to
Quebec and Montreal. Peter Schuyler to be second in
command under Col. Nicholson. Colonels Saltonstall and
Gookin will go with their detachments as far as Albany.   655

p. m.   Legislative minutes (see *Jour.* 1:281).   657

23   Command of Canada land expedition settled. Proclamation
        to issue for the arrest of Thos. Byerley. Legislative
        minutes (see *Jour.* 1:281). Arms to be inspected (see *N. Y.
        col. mss*, 53:78, 83). Connecticut regiment (see *N. Y.
        col. mss*, 53:75). Col. Schuyler to command the Indians
        (see *N. Y. col. mss*, 53:80). Articles of war. Staff officers
        to be appointed for the expedition. The colonel, lieuten-
        ant-colonel and major of each regiment to have a com-
        pany.   658

24   Legislative minutes (see *Jour.* 1:282). Canada expedition.
        Col. Nicholson wants a certificate of his appointment to the
        command-in-chief and recommends that a general day of
        fasting be set. Memorial to Gov. Gourdon Saltonstall of
        Connecticut, Lt. Gov. Charles Gookin of Pennsylvania
        and Lt. Gov. Ingoldsby from Col. Sam'l Vetch. Address
        by Cols. Ingoldsby, Saltonstall, Gookin with the council
        and assembly of New-York, to Col. Francis Nicholson;
        both about the expedition.   660

25   Peter Schuyler presides. Accounts of the Kinsale man-of-
        war Capt. John Clifton to be audited. Arms to be dis-
        tributed to the garrison.   663

26   Capt. John Riggs to command the Connecticut detachment
        (see *N. Y. col. mss*, 53:85). Capt. Clifton to cruize for a
        topsail vessel off Sandy Hook and Neversink. Proclamation
        about arms of volunteers. Order on petition by Joshua
        Kocherthal and Herman Schuneman on behalf of the pal-
        atines (see *Doc. hist. N. Y.* 3:544-45; Q3:329).   663

27   Arms for the expedition to be cleaned and repaired. Pre-
        siding officer of the council designated during the absence
        of the lieutenant governor and president. Capt. Clifton of
        the Kinsale cannot sail for want of men.   665

28   Capt. Clifton to take men out of the Maidstone.   666

30   Garret van Horne and other owners of the Content privateer
        called before the council concerning Henry Hutchins and
        ——— Loper two men impressed for the men-of-war.   666

31   Affidavit of Abr'm van Duersen, Jost Leysen and John Par-
        myter concerning the impressing of seamen for the Tri-
        tons prize man-of-war. Order on petition by Nich's
        Brower (see *N. Y. col. mss*, 53:87).   666

1709   v. 10

June 3 Lt. Gov. Ingoldsby returned. Mr Cockrill called before the
        council. Legislative minutes (see *Jour.* 1:282). Lord Love-
        lace's commission and other public papers called for.   668
     4 Lady Lovelace is reluctant to give up her late husband's
        papers. Legislative minutes (see *Jour.* 1:282).   669
     6 Legislative minutes (see *Jour.* 1:282). Boston post to be
        stopped until further orders. Canada expedition.   670
  p. m. Legislative minutes (see *Jour.* 1:283).   670
     7 Legislative minutes (see *Jour.* 1:283).   671
     8 Legislative minutes (see *Jour.* 1:284). Joint committees on
        Canada expedition to meet at the Coffee house (see *N. Y.*
        col. mss, 53:92-93).   672
  p. m. Legislative minutes (see *Jour.* 1:284).   673
    13 Col. Ingoldsby absent. Letters from Peter Schuyler recom-
        mending officers for the Albany and Ulster county detach-
        ments (see *N. Y. col. mss*, 53:95), on Indian affairs, and
        covering a journal of John and Abr'm Schuyler sent to the
        lieutenant governor. Canada expedition; rendezvous for
        the county detachments fixed.   673
    15 Canada expedition.   674
    16 Lt. Gov. Ingoldsby returned. Address to the queen to be
        prepared. Letters from England to Lord Lovelace re-
        ceived. Indian affairs. Letter to be written to Capt.
        Davis of the Maidstone man-of-war about impress of sea-
        men.   675
    18 Opinion of the chief justice and the attorney-general regard-
        ing the government's power to order impressing of sailors
        asked. Palatines (see *Doc. hist. N. Y.* 3:545; Q3:329). Can-
        ada expedition.   676
    20 Order on petition by Lord Cornbury for a certificate that his
        creditors prevent his return to England. Legislative min-
        utes (see *Jour.* 1:284).   677
    21 Memorial to the queen on the lack of arms signed. Legis-
        lative minutes (see *Jour.* 1:285. Palatines called pietists
        (see *Doc .hist. N. Y.* 3:545; Q3:329). Certificate for Lord
        Cornbury signed. Long Island Indians to be called to
        serve in the Canada expedition (see *N. Y. col. mss*, 53:100).
        Arms wanting for the expedition. Delegates of the five
        nations to go to Boston and see the fleet and army, which
        is to go on the expedition. Indian presents. Post route
        between Albany and Westfield to be established.   678
    22 Militia of New York city to do guard duty at Fort Anne.
        Request to Capt. George Gordon of the Lowestaffe man-
        of-war to delay sailing signed (see *N. Y. col. mss*, 53:102).
        Indian affairs. Shoemakers to be impressed for making
        cartridge boxes.   680

23 Lt. Gov. Ingoldsby absent. New York city militia troop to make the night rounds. Clearance of vessels ordered: sloop Speedwell, Phil. Wanton master for Jamaica; brigantine Dolphine, Thos. Rudden for Barbadoes; sloop Three Brothers, Thos. Lee; brigantine Success, Dan'l Dunscombe; sloop Lark, John Bolland all for Jamaica; sloop Endeavor, John Fowles for Curaçao; sloop Seaflower, Thos. Hunt, for St Thomas; brigantine Eagle, Chas. Whitefield, for Antigua; sloop Friendship, Andrew Law, for Nevis; brigantine St John, Alex'r Woodcop for Surinam. Canada expedition (see *N. Y. col. mss*, 53:103). Legislative minutes (see *Jour.* 1:285). Guard to be kept at Albany and Schenectady. Addresses to Col. Francis Nicholson (see *N. Y. col. mss*, 53:99). 681

25 "Sayns" asked from the men-of-war for the expedition. Money for the Canada expedition. Address to the queen to be signed by the members of the council. Legislative minutes (see *Jour.* 1:285). Impressing of sailors. French prisoners to be sent to Flatbush and Hempstead, L. I. New York troop discharged from duty. Votes of New Hampshire council approving the appointment of Col. Nicholson. 684

29 Order on petition by Edw. Hardrigh a deserter from Bermudas. Duties on prize goods. 686

July 2 Lt. Gov. Ingoldsby returned. Col. Wenham to have arms repaired. Long Island Indians. Canada expedition. Legal opinion that the lieutenant-governor cannot order the impressing of sailors from privateers or merchantmen. 686

3 Garrit Ville to go to the Long Island Indians. Indian affairs Cols. Ingoldsby and Nicholson going to Albany. Station ship for New York asked for. Memorial from the commissioners of the Canada expedition to Col. Sam'l Vetch, adjutant-general of her majesties forces. List of expenditures for the expedition. Order of the queen in council disallowing the provincial act about coin. Address to Col. Francis Nicholson from governor and council of Rhode Island; with letter from Gov. Sam'l Cranston (see *N. Y. col. mss*, 53:104). 687

13 Too many officers in Col. Schuyler's regiment. 694

Albany

15 Surgeon wanted for Schuyler's regiment. Scouting parties of Albany militia and Connecticut troop to be sent out. Payments made for building storehouses, canoes etc. Indian spies rewarded. Presents made to old men, women and children of the four nations present at Albany. Account of of what is necessary for the expedition called for. 694

1709   **v. 10**

16   Arms given to the Indians to be repaired.   Grenadiers to
      have red caps.   Methods for transporting provisions to
      Wood Creek to be arranged.   Disputes between commis-
      sioners of the expedition and commissioners of Indian
      affairs to be settled by the council.   Indian affairs; Mini-
      sink and Jersey Indians.   695

19   Commissioners of Indian affairs.   Money advanced by Col.
      Schuyler cannot be repaid now.   Minissink Indians will
      not come.   Indian presents.   Abraham Schuyler and five
      others to go to the Senecas.   696

21   Order on petition by Lawrence Claesen and Indian interpre-
      ters for pay.   697

23   Commissioners of the expedition approve of sending Abr'm
      Schuyler to the Senecas, to stay there 14 days, and the men
      accompanying him to be selected from the military.   698

25   Oneidas want John Bleecker, Evert Wendell, Stephanus
Albany   Groesbeck, Abr'm Cuyler, John and Gerrit Rooseboom
      and Johs. Harmanse Fischer to go with them to Canada
      as interpreters.   699

Aug. 4 Affidavit by Jacob van Zutphen of Yellow Hook, L. I. con-
New York   cerning the refusal of Capt. Rodgers of the South Sea
      Castle man-of-war to release an impressed sailor.   699

18   Lt. Gov. Ingoldsby returned.   Legislative minutes (see *Jour.*
New York   1:286).   Henry van Ball vs Roger Bret on a writ of error.
      Orders on petitions: by Peter Matthews, Wm Sharpas
      and Wm Davis for land near the paltz in Ulster county;
      by Alex. Griggs (see *L. P.* 4:182).   700

25   Complaint of Col. Beekman vs Col. Wenham.   Patent
      granted to Matthews, Sharpas and Davis.   Orders on peti-
      tions: by Christopher Rousby; by Wm Sunderland and
      Wm Chambers (see *L. P.* 4:179); by Peter Fauconier; by
      John Conrad Codweis (see *N. Y. col. mss,* 53:109); by
      Joshua Kocherthal (see *N. Y. col. mss,* 53:107-8).   Proc-
      lamation to issue empowering P. Fauconier to receive cer-
      tain public moneys.   Iron and steel to be sent to Albany
      for the expedition.   701

Sep. 6 Recommendation to the queen for J. C. Codweis and
      J. Kocherthal signed.   Warrants for land patents signed.
      Order upon petition by Lord Cornbury.   701

8   Communications received from the expedition dated Wood
      creek.   Order on petition by Gerardus Beekman et al. (see
      L. P. 5:1).   Legislative minutes (see *Jour.* 1:286).   Order
      on petition by Joseph Hegeman, Peter Navius and Jero-
      nimus Remsen on behalf of elders of Dutch church at
      Flatbush (see *N. Y. col. mss,* 53:111; and, *Doc. hist. N. Y.*

3:156; Q 3:99). Letter received from Sec. Stanley of Connecticut concerning Hannah Taylor (see *N. Y. col. mss,* 53:110). Account of stores to be taken. 702

12 Arthur Knight and King owners of the sloop Seahorse vs Henry van Ball (see *N. Y. col. mss,* 53:112). Caienquirago a five nations Indian to be lodged and fed while in town. Legislative minutes (see *Jour.* 1:286). 703

15 Legislative minutes (see *Jour.* 1:286). Bret vs van Ball in error. Isaac Mercier and other French protestants of New Rochelle vs Rev. D. Bondet. Wm Sunderland and Wm Chambers. Crabtree vs Rombouts. Trinity church. 704

16–20 Legislative minutes (see *Jour.* 1:287). 705–6

21 Order on address from the mayor etc. of Albany for securing the frontiers. Legislative minutes (see *Jour.* 1:288). Patent granted to Sunderland and Chambers. 706

22 Legislative minutes (see *Jour.* 1:288). Van Ball vs Bret in error. French church at New Rochelle. 707

Joint committee meeting on the address from Albany at the Coffee House. Address to the queen to be prepared. 708

24 Legislative minutes (see *Jour.* 1:288). 708

26 Col. Vetch asks the governors of colonies interested in the Canada expedition to meet at New London. Report of sick soldiers at Wood creek received. Opinion of the council that the congress of governors should meet at New York. Legislative minutes (see *Jour.* 1:289). 709

29 Eben'r Wilson and Wm Anderson renominated as mayor and sheriff of New York. 711

Oct. 6 Legislative minutes (see *Jour.* 1:289). Report on difficulties between Rev. Antonides and Freeman read (see *N. Y. col. mss,* 53:121). Orders on petitions: by Cornelius Seabring and Corn's van Brunt of the Dutch church in Kings county; by Dorus Polhemus and elders of the same; by John Auboineau for land back of New Wark; by David Provoost, Rip van Dam and Lawrence Jansen (see *L. P.* 5:2); by Wm Peartree. 711

8 Legislative minutes (see *Jour.* 1:289). 712

10 Letters received about congress of governors and Indian affairs. Palatines (see *N. Y. col. mss,* 53:122). Opinion of the council about the lieutenant-governor's going to the congress. 714

11 Legislative minutes (see *Jour.* 1:290). 714

12 Legislative minutes (see *Jour.* 1:290). The queen's forces to be posted at Albany and 100 provincials to be raised in addition. 715

1709   v. 10

13   Legislative minutes (see *Jour.* 1:290). Orders on petitions:
      by Rev. Dan'l Bondet; by Gerardus Beekman; by Caleb
      Heathcote (see *L. P.* 5:3).   715
14   Mayor Wilson and Sheriff Anderson of New York sworn
      in.   716
18   Orders on petitions: by John Barberie (see *L. P.* 5:5); by
      Peter Fauconier (see *N. Y. col. mss,* 53:123-25, 129). Forts
      on Wood creek and Canada expedition.   717
19   Legislative minutes (see *Jour.* 1:291). License to purchase
      Indian land near New Wark for John Auboineau signed.
      Resolve of assembly about congress received.   717
20   Rev. Daniel Bondet. Congress of governors. Land
      granted to Gabriel Ludlow and Wm Bradford (see *L. P.*
      5:4). Van Ball vs Crabtree. Col. Ingoldsby intends going
      to the congress in Rhode Island and wants money (see
      Jour. 1:291). Order concerning the dispute between
      Antonides and Freeman (see *Doc. hist. N. Y.* 3:162; Q
      3:103).   718
22   Letters to Lord Lovelace received, read and to be laid be-
      fore the assembly. Opinions and order on petition by
      Peter Fauconier (see *N. Y. col. mss,* 53:129).   719
27   Order on petition by George Norton that the sheriff of New
      York give security. Opinions and order concerning the
      dispute between Antonides and Freeman (see *N. Y. col.
      mss,* 53: 127-28). Peter Fauconier. Order concerning
      petitions for land and land grants. Petitions by John
      Smith (see *L. P.* 5:6); by Lawrence Cornelisen; by Henry
      Oblinus (see *L. P.* 5:27) referred. Legislative minutes (see
      Jour. 1:291). Order on petition by Judge Robert Milward
      (see *N. Y. col. mss,* 53:130).   721
Nov. 1 Legislative minutes (see *Jour.* 1:292). Orders on petitions:
      by Peter Fauconier; by Peter Barberie (see *L. P.* 5:4);
      by Wm Anderson (see *N. Y. col. mss,* 53:131).   723
4   Legislative minutes (see *Jour.* 1:292). Warrants cancelled.
      Order on petition by Peter Fauconier. French church at
      New Rochelle. Land granted: to John Smith, Nath'l
      Ma ——, John Sellwood and Corn's Lodye (see *L. P.* 5:6);
      to Lawrence Cornelissen, John Cornelissen, Abr'm Myre
      and Arent Quackenbush. Henry Oblinus (p. 721) to give
      names of his partners. Land granted: to Peter Barberie
      (p. 723); to Barent Waldron (see *L. P.* 5:12). Thos.
      Weaver's accounts.   725
9   Legislative minutes (see *Jour.* 1:293). Petition of New York
      merchants received (see *N. Y. col. mss,* 53:137).   727
10   Order on petition by Judge Milward (p. 721). Legislative
      minutes (see *Jour.* 1:293). Order on petition by John van
      Horne, John Theobald and Chas. Crombline (see *L. P.* 5:9). 728

1709 v. 10

11 Legislative minutes (see *Jour.* 1:294). The Kinsale, and Maidstone men-of-war to sail to Barbados and convoy merchant men from there. Order on petition by Rev. Vincent Antonides (see *N. Y. col. mss,* 53:139). 729

12 Legislative minutes (see *Jour.* 1:294). Exchange of prisoners (see *N. Y. col. mss,* 53:140). 731

Dec. 3 Audit of Capt. Clifton's accounts ordered. 732

1710

Feb. 15 Pay of soldiers. Land granted: to Mrs Margaret McGregory and Thos. Toshack; to Chas. Huddey and Phil. Brooke (see *L. P.* 5:31). Fort Anne needs repairing. Revenues. Dr Johnson reports on Mr Cockerill's estate, as connected with pay of soldiers. Orders on petitions: by Thos. Jones & Co. (see *L. P.* 5:33); by Johs. Beeckman (see *N. Y. col. mss,* 53:155); by Henry Beeckman (see *L. P.* 5:32). Proclamation to issue adjourning the assembly. Rev. V. Antonides. Judge Milward. Peter Fauconier and the sheriff to attend. 457

20 Patent granted to Huddy and Brooke. Land granted to Roger Mompesson (see *L. P.* 5:34). Revenues. 459

23 Warrant signed. Revenues. Patent granted to Augustine Graham (see *L. P.* 5:36). Petition of Roger Mompesson referred (see *L. P.* 5:35). Patent granted to Henry Beeckman (see *L. P.* 5:32). Petition by Abr'm Hasebrook et al. for confirmatory patent for New Paltz referred. Order on petition by Melchior Gulch (see *N. Y. col. mss,* 53:157). Land granted to Judge Robert Milward. 459

27 Patent granted to Marc Dasway [Dusachoy] (see *L. P.* 5:38). Warrant of survey granted to John Auboineau. Land granted to Daniel Crombine, Paul Droilhet and two others (see *L. P.* 5:7). Patents granted: to Rip van Dam & Co. (see *L. P.* 5:37); to Thos. Jones & Co. (see *L. P.* 5:33); to Roger Mompesson (p. 459); to Eben'r Wilson & Co. (see *L. P.* 5:39). Thos. Weaver's accounts and bonds. 461

Mar. 2 Flag of truce from Canada with prisoners for exchange at Albany. 463

4 Father Maneuil a French priest and others to be exchanged. Warrants for patents and surveys signed. Patents granted: to Wm. Peartree and others (see *L. P.* 5:45); to John Barberie; to Peter Barberie (see *L. P.* 5:42). Warrant to Thos. Byerley to pay Rip van Dam for charges of transporting French prisoners to Albany. Wm. Davis and Wm Chambers appointed by Col. Quary, searcher of the customs, and tide surveyor respectively sworn in (see *N. Y. col. mss,* 53:159). 463

7   Warrants for patents signed. Father Mareuil called before
the council. Orders on petitions: by Gerardus Beeckman
et al. (see *L. P.* 5:49); by Ebenezer Wilson and Lancaster
Symes (see *L. P.* 5:40). Warrants to Thos. Byerley for
repairs of the fort made by Rip van Dam, Mr Philipse
and Major Provoost. Order on petition by Lord Cornbury. Land granted: to Charles Congreve (see *L. P.*
5:50); to John Lawrence; to Obadiah Hunt (see *L. P.*
5:43). Petition of Abr'm Hasbrouck and Paltz patentees
referred (see *L. P.* 5:48).   465

9   Warrants signed. Orders on petitions: by Jacob Beeckman,
Anthony Luick et al.; by Wm Bradford and Gabr'l
Ludlow.   467

14   Pass for French prisoners signed. Warrant for patent to
Ger. Beeckman signed. Report of committee on the peti-
tion of Abr'm Hasbrouck (p. 465) confirmed. Petition of
Chas. Congreve (see *L. P.* 5:53) laid on the table. Order
concerning lands resumed by the crown from Capt. Evans.
Expenses of transporting Father Mareuil to Albany.   467

21   Orders on petitions: by Wm Aertsen (see *N. Y. col. mss,*
53:161-62); by Lancaster Symes (see *L. P.* 5:62); by Wm
Anderson (see *L. P.* 5:52); by Robert Read (see *L. P.*
5:54). Proclamation to issue for adjourning the assembly.
The Maidstone man-of-war ordered on a cruize.   470

24   Report on the petition of Lancaster Symes confirmed. Orders on petitions: by Thos. Lawrence (see *L. P.* 5:55);
by Obadiah Hunt (see *L. P.* 5:56); by Wm Glencross
(see *L. P.* 5:44, 63); by Wm Provoost (see *L. P.* 5:58); by
John Thomas (see *L. P.* 5:57); by Wm Bond (see *L. P.*
5:61); by Dirck Bensing (see *L. P.* 5:59); by Joost
Palding (see *L. P.* 5:51); by Henry Swift (see *N. Y. col.
mss,* 53:163); by Abr'm de Peyster (see *L. P.* 5:60).   470

25   Warrants for patents: to Charles Congreve; to Augustine
Graham (p. 459) and Alex'r Griggs; to Obadiah Hunt.
Land granted to Wm Glencross   472

Ap. 10 Gerardus Beeckman presides in the absence of the lieutenant
governor, whose commission is revoked. Order of the
queen stopping all further grants of lands until the arrival
of the new governor Robert Hunter received and to be
published. Proclamation to issue for continuing officers
in their places.   473

10   Col. Ingoldsby has locked up the seals and public papers.
Lewis Morris not recognized as president of the New
Jersey council. Col. Ingoldsby called before the council.
Letter of the queen concerning land grants.   474

p. m.   Complaint of Myndert Schuyler, Johs. Cuyler and others of Albany against Col. Matthews and his soldiers and order thereon. Indian affairs. Albany to be stockaded. No more certificates for land to be signed.   476

13   Orders on petitions: by Stephen de Lancey and others (see *N. Y. col. mss*, 53:170); by mayor etc. of New York concerning scarcity of breadstuffs. Embargo of all vessels ordered for three months, and proclamation to issue to that effect. Riot in Jamaica (see *N. Y. col. mss*, 53:168; and, *Doc. hist. N. Y.* 3:214-15; Q 3:133-34).   478

17   Col. Ingoldsby before the council. Letter of the queen revoking his commission.   480

18   List of names of Indian commissioners at Albany called for. Orders on petitions: by Rev. V. Antonides (see *N. Y. col. mss*, 53:169); by justices of the peace of Queens county (see *N. Y. col. mss*, 53:172; and, *Doc. hist. N. Y.* 3:170-71; Q 3:107-8). Wm Anderson willing to give security as sheriff (see *N. Y. col. mss*, 53:173).   481

20   Myndert Schuyler and Johs. Cuyler of Albany before the council ordered to make their representations in writing. Order on petition by Benj. Faneuil (see *N. Y. col. mss*, 53:176). Capt. Richard Davis of the Maidstone man-of-war to have soldiers in place of some men whom he must leave ashore sick. Wm Anderson. Order concerning the riot in Jamaica (see *Doc. hist. N. Y.* 3:216; Q 3:134).   483

21   Kilian van Rensselaer, John Abeel, Evert Bancker, Hendr. Hansen and Johs. Roseboom appointed Indian commissioners at Albany. John Harmense Vischer commissioned ensign in Capt. Myndert Schuyler's company, Col. Peter Schuyler's regiment. Orders: on memorial of Myndert Schuyler and Johs. Cuyler (see *N. Y. col. mss*, 53:177-78); on petition by John Braddick (see *N. Y. col. mss*, 53:175).   485

22   The Kinsale man-of-war, Capt. Clifton ordered on a cruize. Order to victual the soldiers put on board given to Capt. Davis (p. 483). Order on petition by John Cruger and others (see *N. Y. col. mss*, 53:179). Col. Heathcote and Roger Mompesson ordered to attend the council.   486

27   Roger Mompesson cannot attend having been ordered to come to New Jersey. Palatines and provisions. Opinion of Attorney-general Bickley on the petition of John Cruger et al. Commission for Indian affairs signed. Alterations made in the order of April 21 on the memorial of M. Schuyler. The chief justice called.   488

28   Pass granted to John Braddick (p. 485). Powder in the fort. Capts. Congreve and Symes and Dr Rokeby or-

dered to appear before the council. Orders on petitions:
by Benj. Faneuil and And'w Fresneau (see *N. Y. col. mss,*
53:180); by Joseph Lymen. Boats going to the mills with
wheat to give bonds. Account of public stores in Albany
called for. Stores in New York to be examined. Orders
on petitions: by Daniel Remsen et al (see *N. Y. col. mss,*
53:182; and, *Doc. hist. N. Y.* 3:172; Q 3:109); by Phil.
Headman (see *N. Y. col. mss,* 53:181).   489

29 Account of provisions in the city received. Capt. Congreve,
Symes and Mr Rokeby ordered on duty with the city
companies. Attorney-general Bickley delivers his opinion
in writing (see *N. Y. col. mss,* 53:186). Letter received
from Lord Clarendon. Petition of Benj. Faneuil and
And'w Fresneau (see *N. Y. col. mss,* 54:2, 8) rejected.
Palatines. Vessels going to New Jersey may be cleared.
Order on petition by Wm Anderson (see *N. Y. col. mss,*
53:184-85).   490

May 5 Capt. Matthews defends himself against the charge made
by Myndert Schuyler (p. 476, 483). John Everet appointed
sheriff of Queens county vice Wm Creed jr deceased.
Petition of John Lymen for clearance of the ship Gloster
with pork and peas rejected because of the expected arrival of 3000 palatines. Embargo continued. Orders on
petitions: by And'w Gibson (see *N. Y. col. mss,* 54:4); by
John Abeel (see *N. Y. col. mss,* 54:3); by Garret Uncle-
bag (see *N. Y. col. mss,* 54:5).   492

6 New Jersey asks that Lewis Morris be arrested and New
York refuses. Military punishment. John Everet sworn
in as sheriff of Queens county, John Coe and Anthony
Waters being his securities. Andrew Gibson allowed to
sail.   494

10 Provisions for the palatines. Mr Rednap and fortifications
in the province. Letter to New Jersey to be written concerning the embargo. Advertisements for the supply of
pork to the palatines. Palatines.   495

11 Pork for the palatines to arrive.   496

15 Orders on petitions: by Abr'm Daiton of Brookhaven for
a brief for charity; by Art, Matthew and David Arsen
(see *L. P.* 5:64). Pork for the palatines.   497

18 Lewis Morris denies having opened a letter as charged by
the council of New Jersey. The Kinsale again ordered
on a cruize. Headman vs Regnier. Mill at Jan Martyn's
hook may be erected by Art Arsen (p. 497). Vote on
the question whether the embargo is to be taken of.
Bread in the hand of commissioners at Albany to be sent
to New York and sold.   498

19   Order on petition by George Woolsey, Hope Carpenter
      and others (see *N. Y. col. mss,* 54:7). Ship Glocester to
      be cleared on giving certain bonds.   500

23   Order on petition by John van Horne (see *L. P.* 5:65).
      Fines of George Woolsey etc (p. 500) remitted (see *Doc.
      hist. N. Y.* 3:217; Q 3:135).   501

25   Soldiers pay. John Arms (see *N. Y. col. mss,* 53:183). Capt.
      Clifton of the Kinsale man-of-war peremptorily ordered
      to cruize. Order in re Headman vs Regnier (p. 498).
      Benj. Faneuil and And'w Gibbs granted permission to
      export wheat in the ship Friendly Galley.   502

June 1 Subsistence of soldiers in Albany. Proceedings of Indian
      commissioners read. Orders on petitions: by Tierck
      Harmense Fisher (see *N. Y. col. mss,* 54:10); by Luis
      Gomes (see *N. Y. col. mss,* 54:9); by Garret Unclebag
      (p. 492).   506

8   Order on memorial by Lancaster Symes and Phil. Rokeby
      concerning pay and subsistence of the governor's com-
      pany (see *N. Y. col. mss,* 54:13) and on the reply to it by
      Dr Johnstone one of Mr Thos. Cockerill's executors.
      Luis Gomes & Co. granted permission to export wheat
      consigned to Francis Lewis de Vas conselos of Madeira
      (see *N. Y. col. mss,* 54:11). Forts at Albany and Sche-
      nectady to be repaired.   507

12   The council rebukes the president for refusing to grant a
      petition of Rev. V. Antonides (see *N. Y. col. mss,* 54:14)
      and breaks up (see *Doc. hist. N. Y.* 3:173; Q 3:110). 509

13   Palatines arrived in the ship Lyon to be examined by
      Doctors Law, Moone and Garran and quarantined on Nut-
      ten island where Johs. Hebon and Peter Williamse car-
      penters are to fit up buildings (see *Doc. hist. N. Y.* 3:551-
      52; Q 3:333-34). Capt. Davis of the Maidstone man-of-war
      ordered to cruize.   510

14   Gov. Robert Hunter arrived; his commission read and
      published; he and the members of the council present are
      sworn in. Dr Samuel Staats reinstated to the council
      hesitates accepting. Proclamation to issue continuing
      officers in their places.   512

15   Dr Samuel Staats sworn of the council. Wm. Peartree dis-
      missed from the council. Orders of the queen in council
      confirming acts of assembly passed in 1708. Letter of the
      queen reinstating Dr Staats. Lands on the Mohawk river
      to be viewed for the palatines.   [514]

16   Scheme for the government of the palatines to be drawn up
      (see *Doc. hist. N. Y.* 3:552-53; Q 3:334). Proclamation to
      issue for their protection against extortions. Abr'm de
      Peyster sworn in.   518

17   Officers for the palatines to be appointed (see *Doc. hist.*
      N. Y. 3:533; Q 3:334). Letter from the queen regarding
      a new seal.   519
20   Gov. Hunter intends to go to Albany to meet the five
      nations. Palatine orphans to be provided for and an ad-
      vertisement to that effect to be published. Meeting of the
      assembly fixed.   521
22   Thomas Walters reinstated, David Provost appointed to the
      council; they and Caleb Heathcote sworn in. Letter
      from the queen reinstating Thos. Walters. List of officers
      in the militia regiments called for; also list of civil officers
      in the counties. Ordinance for courts on Nutten island
      read and to be published (see *N. Y. col. mss,* 54:32).
      Order on petition by Nich's Tienhoven and Jacob Mau-
      ritz (see *N. Y. col. mss,* 54:24-25). Palatine orphans.   522
29   Journal of Evert Bancker and David Schuyler on a treaty
      between the five nations and the Waganhaes read. Orders
      on petitions: by George Elseworth (see *N. Y. col. mss,*
      54:21); by Melchior Gulch (see *N. Y. col. mss,* 54:23).   525
July 5 Indian affairs; five nations want to come into the covenant
      chain. Ships which have brought the palatines have to
      pay tonnage dues. Lewis Gomez and Abr'm de Lucena
      granted permission to export wheat in the ship Expedi-
      tion, George Cock master. Pilots warrants of Nich's
      Tienhoven and Jacob Mauritz renewed (p. 522).   526
13   Indians will not allow the land at Schoharie to be sur-
      veyed. Opinion of council on the powers of the presi-
      dent. George Elseworth.   528
20   The Mohawks consent to have the Schoharie land surveyed.
      Order on petition by John Livingston. Length of service
      of May Bickley as attorney general attested.   529
27   Orders on petitions: by Wm Stokes and others (see *N. Y.
      col. mss,* 54:43); by Anna Gravenraet (see *N. Y. col. mss,*
      54:41). Palatine children. Order on petition by Elias
      Pelletreau (see *N. Y. col. mss,* 54:42).   530
31   Order on petition by Thos. Byerley (see *N. Y. col. mss,*
      54:44). Wm Anderson suspended from office as sheriff
      of New York on petitions; Francis Harrison appointed in
      his place and sworn in, Lewis Morris and John Johnston
      his sureties.   531
Aug. 28 Gov. Dudley of Massachusetts wants the five nations to go
      to war against the French Indians. Indian affairs (see
      N. Y. col. mss, 54:51).   533
31   Orders on petitions: by Moses Gilbert (see *N. Y. col. mss,*
      54:52, 60); by George Cock.   533

1710   **v. 10**
Sep. 1   Schoharie lands and Indian affairs. Revenue, and canceling
          bills of credit.   534
   p. m. Legislative minutes (see *Jour.* 1:296).   535
      9   Orders on petitions: by Peter Rose and Robert Bensing (see
          N. Y. col. mss, 54:61); by Thos. Higbee (see *N. Y. col. mss,*
          54:63). Table of fees submitted. Legislative minutes (see
          Jour. 1:297).   539
  11–14   Legislative minutes (see *Jour.* 1:298).   540–41
     14   Order on petition by Jannetie Cregier for land at Canesta-
          gione.   541
     18   Order on petition by Abr'm de Lucena (see *N. Y. col. mss,*
          54:64). Moses Gilbert's petition granted (p. 533). Legis-
          lative minutes (see *Jour.* 1:298).   541
  21–25   Legislative minutes (see *Jour.* 1:298-99).   542–43
     29   Thos. Byerley swears to his accounts. Mr Davis also swears.
          Jacobus van Cortland nominated mayor and Francis Har-
          rison sheriff, of New York. Petitions by Jannetie Cregier,
          by Johannis Schuyler, by Elizabeth Sydenham to lie on
          the table.   544
Oct. 12   Legislative minutes (see *Jour.* 1:299).   545
     14   Legislative minutes (see *Jour.* 1:300). Jacobus van Cortland
          sworn in as mayor, Francis Harrison as sheriff, of New
          York; Robert Livingston jr as mayor, and Johannis Cuy-
          ler as recorder, of Albany.   546
     18   Legislative minutes (see *Jour.* 1:300).   550
     19   Legislative minutes (see *Jour.* 1:301). Petition of Nicholas
          Bayard (see *L. P.* 5:70) to lie on the table.   551
     21   Legislative minutes (see *Jour.* 1:301). Letter received from a
          Spanish governor prisoner of war at Boston, concerning
          the sale of other Spanish prisoners as slaves. Indian
          affairs.   553
  26–30   Legislative minutes (see *Jour.* 1:301-2).   554–56
Nov. 2   Order on petition by Mary widow of Capt. John Tudor (see
          N. Y. col. mss, 54:92). Legislative minutes (see *Jour.*
          1:303).   558
      4   Legislative minutes (see *Jour.* 1:303). Mrs Tudor. 559
      8   Legislative minutes (see *Jour.* 1:303). Thos. Byerley pro-
          duces orders from England concerning certain revenues. 560
   9–15   Legislative minutes (see *Jour.* 1:304-5).   561–66
     16   Expedition against Canada. Legislative minutes (see *Jour.*
          1:306).   567
     18   Legislative minutes (see *Jour.* 1:306). Orders on petitions:
          by the trustees of Hempstead (see *L. P.* 5:71); by Abr'm
          Santford (see *N. Y. col. mss,* 54:100).   569
  21–22   Legislative minutes (see *Jour.* 1:307-8).   571–73

1710 v. 10

23 Legislative minutes (see *Jour.* 1:308)., Order on petition by
Margaret Macgregory (see *L. P.* 5:72). Court of chancery.
Liabilities of members of the council to be arrested deter-
mined. 574

p. m.–25 Legislative minutes (see *Jour.* 1:308-9). 575–77

27 Dispute between Rev. Antonides and Freeman settled (see
Doc. hist. N. Y. 3:176; Q3:111-12). Gov. Hunter intends to
go to New Jersey. 578

1711

Feb. 22 Roger Brett vs Van Ball in error deferred. 579

Mar. 1 Order on petition by Wm Lawrence (see *N. Y. col. mss,*
54:168). Brett vs van Ball. 580

22 Wm Lawrence. Brett vs van Ball. Executors of Rombouts vs Crabtree. 580

29 Order on petition by Myndert Scutt (see *L. P.* 5:84). Indian
affairs; New York Indians want to make war on the Waganhaes; disapproved. 587

Ap. 12 Legislative minutes (see *Jour.* 1:310). Jane Tothill vs
Helena de Key, in error. Barnes on the demise of Peartree vs Hunt in error. 583

18 Capt. Walter and Major Provost sworn of the council under
a wrong Christian name; approved in England. Clause
directed to be inserted in land patents; letter from the
queen to that effect. 586

20 Legislative minutes (see *Jour.* 1:311). Accounts of Rip van
Dam (see *N. Y. col. mss,* 54:190) and of Mrs Abeel for
work on Albany fort referred. 588

24 Indian affairs; a French detachment at Onondaga; Col.
Schuyler to go there. Spanish prisoners sold as slaves
to Mr Frew and Mrs Wenham petition for liberty to go
into the queen's service. 590

27 Plate belonging to the chapel to be delivered to Mr Sharpe
chaplain to the forces. Order in re Wm Lawrence (p. 580). 592

30 Order concerning Rev. Freeman and Antonides (see *Doc.
hist. N. Y.* 3:177; Q3:112). 593

May 3 Examination in re Wm Lawrence (p. 580, 592). Tothill vs
de Key. Fullerton vs Hunt. Roberts vs Frost. 594

10 Table of fees called for by the lords of trade. Writs to issue
for calling the assembly. Wm Lawrence's case to be
decided by arbitrators. 595

June 16 Canada expedition. Gov. Hunter is going to New London
to meet other governors; assembly to be prorogued. Embargo laid on outgoing vessels. Indian affairs. 597

27 Orders concerning the expedition; carpenters to be impressed for work on bateaux. Provisions not to be exported. Long Island Indians for the expedition. Account
of provisions called for. 598

28   Gov. Hunter communicates the resolutions of the council of
      war at New London (see *N. Y. col. mss*, 55:42). Annapolis
      Royal. Bakers to bake bread for the public service. No
      supply of men can be sent to Col. Vetch. Permission
      granted to the Fevershams Prize to sail under convoy of
      the Tritons Prize, Capt. Garlington (see *N. Y. col. mss*,
      55:57). Express messengers. Market houses except that
      at Burgers path to be used for building bateaux. Account
      of breadstuffs in Albany called for.   599

30   Order on petition by bateaux carpenters (see *N. Y. col. mss*,
      55:65). Indians on the Susquehannah called upon to join
      the five nations (see *N. Y. col. mss*, 55:73). John Walters
      to procure materials for building bateaux. Independent
      companies to be formed into a regiment. Reply to. me-
      morial of Col. Gookin (see *N. Y. col. mss*, 55:71-72). List
      of things wanted for the expedition presented. Account of
      military in Albany called for.   602

July 2   Indian affairs. French officers sent from Albany to be en-
      tertained by Mr Bradford. Legislative minutes (see *Jour.*
      1:312).   604

4   The ship Two Brothers allowed to sail under convoy of
      Capt. Garlington (see *N. Y. col. mss*, 55:94). Money for the
      expedition.   607

10   Provisions for the expedition. Constables' watch to be rein-
      forced. Gov. Hunter intends to go to New Jersey. De-
      fence of the coast.   608

11   Legislative minutes (see *Jour.* 1:313).   609

17   Order on petition of René Het (see *N. Y. col. mss*, 55:113).
      Military establishment. Legislative minutes (see *Jour.*
      1:313). Provisions to be collected in the country.   611

19-21 Legislative minutes (see *Jour.* 1:314).   613

23   Legislative minutes (see *Jour.* 1:315). Order on petition by
      merchants of New York (see *N. Y. col. mss*, 55:180).   616

25-Aug. 1 Legislative minutes (see *Jour.* 1:315-19).   618

Aug. 2   Legislative minutes (see (*Jour.* 1:319). Order on petition by
      Charles Forestier (see *N. Y. col. mss*, 56:6).   632

3-4   Legislative minutes (see *Jour.* 1:319-20).   633

8   Gov. Hunter intends to go to Albany with Lt. Gen. Nichol-
      son. Order on petition by Rev. V. Antonides (see *N. Y.
      col. mss*, 56:15).   635

15   Gov. Hunter absent. Order on petition by militia officers
      of Kings county (see *N. Y. col. mss*, 56:47).   636

20   Order on petition by Abr'm Schellenger (see *N. Y. col. mss*,
      56:50). Order to Francis Vincent gunner concerning the
      position of guns about the city. John Carter a deserter to
      be put in irons.   637

1711   v. 10

29   A French privateer off Sandy Hook; the Fevershams Prize
      man-of-war, Capt. Paston, disabled cannot go on a cruize;
      Capt. Rainer and Capt. Tynes offer to go in their ships.
      Volunteers for the expedition called for.   638

31   Volunteers entered on board Rainer's and Tyne's ships re-
      fuse to go because Capt. Paston has ordered the jacks and
      pendants to be lowered. Capt. David Tynes to be commis-
      sioned as commander of the sloop Swan and to hoist the
      jack ancient and pendant. Deposition of Capt. Samuel
      Thornton late master of the sloop Hopewell captured by a
      French privateer.   640

p. m. Letter from Capt. Robert Paston concerning the hoisting of
      the jack and pendant; he has taken them from the Swan.   643

The remaining pages of this volume, 645-733, are identical with 342-457.

Vol. 11—1711-19

1711

Sep. 3 Act of parliament received and published for establishing a
      general post office in the colonies. Thos. Byerley sworn of
      the council; queen's letter directing it to be done; another
      letter from the queen concerning his salary. Memorial re-
      ceived from Mr Polhampton about abuses in mustering.
      Embargo on vessels taken off. Minutes sent to England.   1

13   Warrant of survey granted to John Parcell (see *L. P.* 5:86).
      Court of chancery. Warrants for salary to Wm Davis and
      Wm Chambers, customs officers (see *N. Y. col. mss*, 56:77).
      Order on petition by Thos. Woodmansey (see *N. Y. col.
      mss*, 56:75). Inglebert Lott enters a caveat against grant-
      ing a charter to some Dutch churches on Long Island (see
      Doc. hist. N. Y. 3:180; Q3:114).   6

18   Opinion of council regarding a rumor about misdemeanor
      and neglect of duty by the captains of men-of-war.   7

18(?) News received from Gen. Hill that the naval expedition
      against Canada has failed; to be sent to Gen. Nicholson
      (see *N. Y. col. mss*, 56:94-95).   8

24   Fortifications of Albany reported weak; to be laid before the
      assembly. Court of chancery (see *N. Y. col. mss*, 56:100).   9

29   Land expedition against Canada about to return to Albany.
      Caleb Heathcote nominated mayor, Francis Harrison
      sheriff of New York. Report on the caveat entered by
      Inglebert Lott confirmed (see *N. Y. col. mss*, 56:103; and
      Doc. hist. N. Y. 3:180-81; Q3:114). Report concerning a
      court of chancery confirmed. Conveyance of a pew in
      Trinity church to Col. Bayard and Heathcote called for.   10

Oct. 2 Legislative minutes (see *Jour.* 1:321).   11

1711 v. 11

4 Legislative minutes (see *Jour.* 1:321). Order on petition by Wm Lawrence (see *N. Y. col. mss,* 56:114-18). Officers of the court of chancery appointed; masters, van Dam and Philipse, register Wileman, examiner Harison, clerks Sharpas and Broughton. Proclamation to issue announcing session of court. 13

5 Letter received from Lt. Gen. Nicholson (see *N. Y. col. mss,* 56:113) to be laid before the assembly. Legislative minutes (see *Jour.* 1:322). Account of powder in magazine called for. 15

15 Mayor Heathcote, Sheriff Harrison, the recorder and justices of the peace [aldermen] sworn in. 16

17 Legislative minutes (see *Jour.* 1:322). Contract for building forts in the Indian country read (see *N. Y. col. mss,* 56:124). Address from the magistrates etc. of Albany on the condition of the frontiers to be sent to England with the above contract. Account for preparing sloops against the French privateer to be laid before the assembly. 16

18 Petition of Wm Barber convicted of felony, for pardon to lie on the table. Officers of the court of chancery sworn in. Deserters to be hunted up and tried. Legislative minutes (see *Jour.*1:322). Indian affairs. 17

20 Legislative minutes (see *Jour.* 1:323). Provisions remaining over from the expedition. Commission of jail delivery for Westchester county to be made out. 19

23 Legislative minutes (see *Jour.* 1:323). 20

25 Legislative minutes (see *Jour.* 1:323). Deed of conveyance of a pew in Trinity church produced and ordered to be recorded. Rombouts vs Crabtree. 20

26 French Indians have killed David Kettelyn and family. Legislative minutes (see *Jour.* 1:323). Order on petition by New York merchants (see *N. Y. col. mss,* 56:140). 21

30 Legislative minutes (see *Jour.* 1:324). 22

Nov. 1 Legislative minutes (see *Jour.* 1:324). Letters received from Col. Dudley, Lt. Gen. Nicholson and Col. Vetch. Address to the queen to be prepared. Accounts of Peter Arkell referred. 23

2-5 Legislative minutes (see *Jour.* 1:325). 27

8 Legislative minutes (see *Jour.* 1:326). Pay of managers of the expedition to be fixed. Unused provisions to be sold. 30

9 Legislative minutes (see *Jour.* 1:326). Report on manager's pay approved (see *N. Y. col. mss,* 56:161). 31

12 Legislative minutes (see *Jour.* 1:327). Warrants signed. 33

15-16 Legislative minutes (see *Jour.* 1:327-28). 34

17 Legislative minutes (see *Jour.* 1:328). Order on petition by merchants of New York (see *N. Y. col. mss,* 56:159). 38

1711   **v. 11**

19   Legislative minutes (see *Jour.* 1:329). Petition of Daniel Bon-
     det for patent of a church lately erected " in the street of
     New Rochelle " referred (see *N. Y. col. mss*, 57:73).   41
20–24 Legislative minutes (see *Jour.* 1:330-31).   43
26   Report on answer to a letter from Governors Dudley, Salton-
     stall and Cranston.   49
29   Reply to the assembly in answer to message of November
     17th to be drawn up. Resolves of the assembly communi-
     cated concerning establishment of courts (see *Jour. assem-
     bly N. Y.* 1:308). Van Ball and Rombouts vs Crabtree in
     error.   51
Dec. 6   Letter to the lords of trade approved.
13   The letter to the lords of trade.   53
20   A French prisoner sent from Boston to Albany to be retained
     at the latter place. Rombouts vs Crabtree.   61
1712
Jan. 3   Rombouts vs Crabtree in error.   62
10. Case continued.   62
17   Order on petition by Dr Staats (see *L. P.* 5:87). The French
     prisoner to be kept at Albany notwithstanding Col. Dud-
     ley's request for his liberation. Rombouts vs Crabtree.   62
24   Warrant of survey granted to Dr Staats (p. 62). Order on
     petition of Peter Arkell (p. 23).   63
31   Report on the petition of Daniel Bondet (p. 41) approved
     (see *N. Y. col. mss*, 57:74). Rev. Mr Vesey, the clerk of the
     assembly, and the address to the queen. Patent granted to
     Daniel Bondet and his church at New Rochelle. Hunt vs
     Fullerton.   64
Feb. 14 Orders on petitions: by Henry Swift (see *N. Y. col. mss*,
     57:80, 82); by John van Horne and Evert Duycking (see
     N. Y. col. mss, 57:81). Van Ball vs Crabtree.   65
21   Henry Swift's petition (p. 65) to be laid before the assembly.
     Order on petition by Thos. Byerley for books and papers
     in the hands of Peter Fauconier (see *N. Y. col. mss*, 57:118). 66
Mar. 7   The attorney-general ordered to enter a nolle prosequi in re
     van Horn and Duycking (p. 65).   67
20   Thos. Byerley and Peter Fauconier called before the council
     (see *N. Y. col. mss*, 57:119). Report on the estate of John
     Lawrence filed (see *N. Y. col. mss*, 57:116). Roger Mompes-
     son admitted to practice in the court of chancery. Letters
     received from lords of trade. Census to be taken.   67
27   Order on petition by Jane le Chevalier. Thos. Byerley and
     and Peter Fauconier (see *N. Y. col. mss*, 57:121).   68
Ap. 3   Forts in the Indian country. Mr Bonvenier a French pris-
     oner has gone to Canada with Lieut. Kettelhuyn who is

1712   v. 11

Indian commissioners to be laid before the assembly.
Thanks to be given to the five nations for stopping war
between Tuscaroras and North Carolina. Petition of Wm
Bond referred (see *L. P.* 5:100). Legislative minutes (see
Jour. 1:333).   81

15 Legislative minutes (see *Jour.* 1:334). Petition of Harman
Jorise (see *L.P.* 5:99) referred. Warrants of survey granted.
Henry Wileman and Henry van Bael (p. 79); to Wm Bond
p. 81). Proclamation to issue concerning arrears of quitrents.   83

22 Petition of Peter Macgregory (see *L. P.* 5:128) referred.
Patent granted to Harman Jorise (p. 83). Patent to Lancaster Symes for all vacant land on Staten Island to be in-
vestigated.   86

23 Indian affairs. Cacknewaga Indians send a belt to atone for
murders and desire an open path from Albany to Canada;
Indian commissioners to decide the matter (see *N. Y. col.
mss,* 57:152-53). Patent granted to Roger and Pinhorne
Mompesson (p. 71). Depositions of Jacob D—— and
James Spennick in regard land in Ulster county to be entered in the council minutes [not done]. Legislative minutes (see *Jour.* 1:335).   87

29 Legislative minutes (see *Jour.* 1:335).   89

31 Legislative minutes (see *Jour.* 1:335). Quitrent for Harman
Jorise's land on Staten Island fixed. Petition of palatines
settled at Quaseck creek [Newburgh] referred. Order on
memorial by Dirck Jansen Hooglandt (see *L. P.* 5:102).   89

June 3 Petition of John Macklain and Richard Winfield (see *L. P.*
5:102) referred.   90

5 Quitrent to be paid by Dutch church in Kingston fixed.
Petitions: of John Rutsen and Jacob Bruyn (see *L. P.*
55:105); by Hugo Frere sr and jr, Isaac Frere and Simon
Frere (see *L. P.* 5:103); by Jacob Rutsen (see *L. P.* 5:104),
all referred.   91

6 Legislative minutes (see *Jour.* 1:336).   92

7 Legislative minutes (see *Jour.* 1:336). Reports on petitions of
June 3d and 5th confirmed.   95

12 Legislative minutes (see *Jour.* 1:336). Petitions: of Peter
Johnson (see *L. P.* 5:113); of minister etc. of episcopal
church on Staten Island for incorporation, both referred.
Warrants of survey granted: to Jacob Rutsen; to John
Rutsen and Jacob Bruyn (p. 91, 95); to Henry Wileman
and Henry van Bael (p. 83); to Wm Bond (p. 83); to Hugo
Frere et al. (p. 91); to John Macklain and Rich'd Winfield
(p. 90).   96

25 Legislative minutes (see *Jour.* 1:344). Petitions by freehold-
    ers of Richmond county (see *L. P.* 5:92, 121) and by
    Hendrick Hansen (see *L. P.* 5:121) referred.   133
27 Memorial by Thos. Byerley concerning quitrents read and
    referred (see *L. P.* 5:123). Legislative minutes (see *Jour.*
    1:344).   133
29 Caleb Heathcote mayor, and Francis Harrison sheriff of
    New York, renominated. Robert Livingston jr nomi-
    nated mayor, and Thos. Williams sheriff, of Albany.   134
30 Legislative minutes (see *Jour.* 1:344).   135
Oct. 1 Opinion of council on application from Antigua for assist-
    ance against a French invasion. Legislative minutes (see
    Jour. 1:345).   136
4-7 Legislative minutes (see *Jour.* 1:345-46).   138
13 Legislative minutes (see *Jour.* 1:346). Memorial of Benj.
    Faneuil (see *N. Y. col. mss*, 58:33-34) referred.   141
14 Mayor Heathcote ill in the country cannot come to be
    sworn in. Letter from the earl of Dartmouth read. Legis-
    lative minutes (see *Jour.* 1:347). Patent granted to John
    Macklain and Richard Winfield (p. 104).   142
16 Warrant of survey granted to David Provost jr (see *L. P.*
    5:124). Legislative minutes (see *Jour.* 1:347).   143
18 New York merchants to be asked to carry French prison-
    ers taken by Capt. van Burgh under flag of truce to the
    French West Indies.   144
20 Legislative minutes (see *Jour.* 1:347).   145
22 Mayor and sheriff of New York and several justices of the
    peace sworn in. Legislative minutes (see *Jour.* 1:348).   146
23 Legislative minutes (see *Jour.* 1:348). Petition of Rich'd
    Merrell (see *L. P.* 5:125) referred. Warrants of survey
    granted: to David Provost jr (p. 143); to Hendrick
    Hansen (p. 133). Report on the petition of palatines
    (p. 89) confirmed.   147
27 Royal proclamation announcing cessation of arms between
    England and France received. News to be sent to Canada.   148
29-30 Legislative minutes (see *Jour.* 1:348-49).   149
31 Legislative minutes (see *Jour.* 1:350). Report on the peti-
    tion of Benj. Faneuil (p. 141) confirmed (see *N. Y. col.
    mss*, 58:35).   153
Nov. 6 Legislative minutes (see *Jour.* 1:351). Petition of John Dove
    and John Bellue (see *N. Y. col. mss*, 58:53) referred.   154
7-15 Legislative minutes (see *Jour.* 1:351-52).   154
20 Legislative minutes (see *Jour.* 1:352). Petition of Peter
    MacGregory referred.   157

1713   v. 11
26   Writs for election of the new assembly made returnable May
       12th following.   169
Ap. 2   Report on the petition of Rich'd Marcell [Merrell] con-
       firmed (see L. P. 5:125); patent granted to him. Letter
       from Gov. Vaudreuil of Canada about peace received.
       Report on ferriage fees to Staten Island confirmed (see
       N. Y. col. mss, 58:110). Patent for 21 years granted to
       Dove and Bellue for the Staten Island ferry (see L. P.
       5:137). Petitioners against Capt. Wright (p. 168) to pay
       charges before their second petition is read.   170
9   Order on petition by Elias Boudinot (see L. P. 5:139).
       Letter of Indian commissioners (see N. Y. col. mss, 58:109)
       to be laid before the assembly.   171
30   Warrants of survey granted: to the palatines at Quasseck
       creek [Newburg] (see L. P. 5:142); to Rich'd Marcell
       (see L. P. 5:155). Petition of Leonard Lewis and John
       Cruger (see L. P. 5:140) referred.   171
May 7   Indian affairs; Tuscaroras defeated in North Carolina; five
       nations must not help them. No provisions to be ex-
       ported.   172
21   Petition of Cornelius van Texel and others (see L. P. 6:16)
       referred.   173
27   Legislative minutes (see Jour. 1:354).   174
28   Indian affairs. Patent granted to Barth'w Feurt (see L. P.
       5:143). Petition by Peter Wilcock and others of Flushing
       against Capt. Jon'n Wright not cognizable before the
       council. Petition of Samuel Bayard referred (see L. P.
       5:144).   180
June 2   Legislative minutes (see Jour. 1:355). The collector ordered
       to inspect outward bound vessels in regard to provisions
       loaded in them.   181
4   Legislative minutes (see Jour. 1:355). List of vessels with
       provisions on board and of vessels cleared laid before the
       council. Petition by Abr'm de Lucena and Justus Boss
       (see N. Y. col. mss, 58:125) rejected. No more vessels
       with provisions to be cleared.   182
10   Action on petition by John Burroughs master of the galley
       Albany (see N. Y. col. mss, 58:128) deferred. Legislative
       minutes (see Jour. 1:355).   183
11   Legislative minutes (see Jour. 1:356). Order on petition of
       New York merchants for leave to export provisions.   184
15   Legislative minutes (see Jour. 1:356). Vessels to be allowed
       to load provisions, but not to be cleared.   185
17   Legislative minutes (see Jour. 1:356).   186
18   Legislative minutes (see Jour. 1:357). Order on petition by
       Jacob Rutsen (see L. P. 5:146, 150-151).   186

1713   **v. 11**

19–20 Legislative minutes (see *Jour.* 1:357).   187
23   Legislative minutes (see *Jour.* 1:358). Warrant of survey
      granted to Elias Boudinot (p. 171). Report on the peti-
      tion of Samuel and Lewis Du Bois (see *L. P.* 5:153) con-
      firmed.   190
25   Legislative minutes (see *Jour.* 1:358). Cadden to be cleared
      for Rhode Island, Bryan for Boston. Report on the peti-
      tion of Kennedy and Bayly (p. 167) confirmed. Jacob
      Mauritz jr to give bonds for his good behavior.   191
27   Legislative minutes (see *Jour.* 1:359).   192
29   Legislative minutes (see *Jour.* 1:359). Five nations Indians
      spread terror in Massachusetts. Patent to be made for the
      episcopal church on Staten Island (see *N. Y. col. mss,*
      58:132, 137; and, *L. P.* 5:158). Petition of Johannes Vedder
      (see *L. P.* 5:159) referred. Order concerning vessels
      loaded.   193
30   Legislative minutes (see *Jour.* 1:360). Vessels may be
      cleared. Question concerning liberty of Spanish slaves
      (see *N. Y. col. mss,* 58:134-35) referred to common law.   194
July 1 Legislative minutes (see *Jour.* 1:360).   195
2   Legislative minutes (see *Jour.* 1:361). Petitions: by Adam
      Vroman; by Mathias de Mott (see *L. P.* 5:161); by Hen-
      drick and Hans Hansen (see *L. P.* 5:163); by Henry
      Beeckman referred.   198
4–6   Legislative minutes (see *Jour.* 1:361-63).   199
17   Legislative minutes (see *Jour.* 1:363). License to purchase
      land granted to Johs. Vedder (p. 193). Patents granted:
      to Hendrick and Hans Hansen (p. 198); to Henry Beeck-
      man. Petition by Lancaster Symes (see *L. P.* 5:166) re-
      ferred. Order on petition by Henry Holland (see *L. P.*
      5:171).   204
23   Report on Lancaster Symes' petition (p. 204) confirmed.
      Order on petition of Peter Oblinus and others of Harlem
      (see *L. P.* 5:167).   207
Aug. 3 Indian affairs: letters from Lieut. Chas. Huddy, command-
      ing Mohawk castle, and from Indian commissioners re-
      port five nations about to take up arms against the
      English.   207
6   Order on petition by Josuah Wroe and Wm Hampton (see
      N. Y. col. mss, 58:147). Patent granted to Rich'd Merrett
      (see *L. P.* 5:174). Indian affairs: Tuscaroras not to settle
      among the five nations. Confirmatory patent granted to
      Lancaster Symes (p. 204; see *N. Y. col. mss,* 58:157).   208
13   Indian affairs (see *N. Y. col. mss,* 58:155-56).   210
18   Proclamation for publishing the peace between England
      and France received from England.   210

1713   **v. 11**

27   Proclamation to issue for a day of thanksgiving. Petitions:
      by Myndert Schuyler (see *L. P.* 5:175); by Isaac de Pey-
      ster and others (see *L. P.* 5:179) referred.   211

Sep. 18   Indian affairs. Petition of Jacob Hendrick Hasting (see
          L. P. 5:178) referred. Court fees. Order on petition by
          Stephen Domingo (see *N. Y. col. mss*, 58:166).   211

29   Caleb Heathcote and Francis Harrison renominated as
      mayor and sheriff, of New York; Rob't Livingston jr and
      Thos. Williams as mayor and sheriff, of Albany. Warrant
      of survey granted to Andries Coeymans (see *L. P.* 5:180).
      Petitions: by Rev. V. Antonides vs Freeman (see *Doc.
      hist. N. Y.* 3:182; Q 3:115); by Rev. J. Kocherthal for
      land, referred.   213

Oct. 1   Petitions: by Francis Harrison, John Fatham, Thos. Braine,
          Jas. Graham and John Askoll; by Samuel Bayard (see
          L. P. 5:181), referred. Confirmatory patent granted to
          Lancaster Symes to correct a mistake (p. 208).   214

8   Indian affairs. Warrant of survey granted to Chas. Mott,
      Corn's Cooper and Thos. Barker (see *L. P.* 6:1). Order
      on petition by Samuel, John, Henry and Benj. Soaper
      (see *N. Y. col. mss*, 58:168).   215

14   Caleb Heathcote and Francis Harrison sworn in as mayor,
      and sheriff of New York; also some justices of the peace.   216

15   Legislative minutes (see *Jour.* 1:364).   217

21   Legislative minutes (see *Jour.* 1:365). Memorial by Thos.
      Byerley referred.   219

22   Journal of Hendrick Hansen (see *N. Y. col. mss*, 58:169; and,
      Doc. rel. col. hist. N. Y. 5:372-76), received and referred.   221

p. m.–23   Legislative minutes (see *Jour.* 1:366-67).   221

28   Legislative minutes (see *Jour.* 1:367). Letter from the queen
      concerning trial of cases in which the church is concerned.   224

29   Letters from lords of trade received, with treaty of peace;
      about sending prisoners to England for trial; about quit-
      rents. Petitions: of Peter van Brugh (see *L. P.* 6:3); of
      Lawrence Clause and Fred'k Vroman (see *L. P.* 6:4) re-
      ferred. Treaty of peace to be printed.   227

30–31   Legislative minutes (see *Jour.* 1:367).   228

Nov. 19   Alterations made in the commission of the peace for Queens
          county. Petition by Myndert Schuyler, Arent van Putter
          and John Dellemont for license to purchase land referred.
          Petition by Rob't Livingston (see *L. P.* 6:6) to lie on the
          table (see *Doc. hist. N. Y.* 3:686; Q 3:411). Warrant of
          survey granted to Jacob Pullion. Petition of Robert Mil-
          ward for warrant of survey referred. Order on petition
          by Thos. Hunt jr (see *N. Y. col. mss*, 59:2-3, 5). Petition
          of Johs. Vedder referred (see *N. Y. col. mss*, 59:1).   229

1713   **v. 11**

20   Gov. Hunter intends to go to New Jersey. Robert Milward
      suspended from office as judge of the supreme court.   231

1714

Mar. 24   Legislative minutes (see *Jour.* 1:368).   231

Ap. 1   Rumor that Lord Slane has been appointed governor of
      New York and Mr George makes comments disrespect-
      ful to Gov. Hunter. Petition by Jonathan Whitehead and
      other justices of Queens county referred to the assembly
      (see *L. P.* 6:10).   232

3   Mr George reprimanded declaring that what he said at
      Swift's was said, while he was drunk. Legislative minutes
      (see *Jour.* 1:368). Petitions by John Schuyler (see *L. P.*
      6:11) referred.   233

7   Legislative minutes (see *Jour.* 1:369).   234

8   Petition by Francis Harrison et al. (see *L. P.* 6:8) referred.
      Quarantine measures.   235

10   License to purchase Indian lands granted to Adam Vroman
      (see *L. P.* 6:12-14). Warrants of survey granted: to Johs.
      Vedder (see *L. P.* 6:15); to Francis Harrison et al., the
      name of John Tatham's widow to be inserted in place of
      her dead husband's (p. 214, 235). Legislative minutes (see
      Jour. 1:369).   235

22   Petition by Peter Schuyler and others for license to pur-
      chase Indian lands in the Mohawk country referred. Re-
      ports on petitions: by Myndert Schuyler (p. 229, see *L. P.*
      6:19); by Corn's van Texel (see *L. P.* 6:16); by Isaac
      de Peyster (p. 211); by Jacob Hendrick Hasting con-
      firmed. Petition by Col. Weems about deserters referred.   236

29–May 13   Legislative minutes (see *Jour.* 1:369-70).   237

18   Legislative minutes (see *Jour.* 1:370). Petitions: by Myn-
      dert Schuyler (see *L. P.* 6:24); by Col. Rutsen and Col.
      Beekman about quitrents. Warrant of survey granted to
      Henry Holland.   239

20   Petition of Peter Schuyler for land in the Mohawk country
      referred. Inquiry to be made concerning measures.   241

25   Order on memorial by Thos. Byerley (p. 219). Indian af-
      fairs; Schackhook Indians; five nations and southern
      Indians intend to hold a secret meeting (see *N. Y. col.*
      mss, 59:47).   241

June 3   Legislative minutes (see *Jour.* 1:371). Order on application
      by Mr Maxwell agent for the prize of the Sorlings man-
      of-war: Survey ordered for Myndert Schuyler (see *L. P.*
      6:25).   243

8   Legislative minutes (see *Jour.* 1:371).   243

12   Warrant of survey granted: to Myndert Schuyler (see *L. P.*
      6:32). Patent granted to Johs. Vedder (see *L. P.* 6:28-29).

1714   v. 11

Petitions: by Adam Vrooman (see *L. P.* 6:34); by Samuel
Babington (see *L. P.* 6:55); by Adert Timenson and
Cornelius Christiansen (see *L. P.* 6:31); by Hendrick
Anthony, all referred. Legislative minutes (see *Jour.*
1:372).   245

17   Opinion of council called for in regard to giving a con-
     firmatory patent to Gilbert Marcellis (see *L. P.* 6:44).
     Legislative minutes (see *Jour.* 1:372). Petitions: by
     Leonard Lewis; by Jannetie Cregier; by palatines at
     Quassek creek (see *L. P.* 6:39), referred.   247

20   Legislative minutes (see *Jour.* 1:373).   248

23   Legislative minutes (see *Jour.* 1:373). Report on granting
     patent to Gilbert Marcellis confirmed (p. 247; see *L. P.*
     6:45).   249

24   Indian affairs. Fauconier in error vs the queen. Tothill
     vs de Key.   250

27   Peace with Spain proclaimed.   251

July 1 Legislative minutes (see *Jour.* 1:374). Nissepat in error vs
         Harris and wife.   252

5   Indian affairs (see *N. Y. col. mss,* 59:66). Legislative minutes
     (see *Jour.* 1:374).   252

6–7 Legislative minutes (see *Jour.* 1:374-75).   253

10   Legislative minutes (see *Jour.* 1:375). Patent granted to
     Francis Harrison and others (see *L. P.* 6:48-49).   254

13–22 Legislative minutes (see *Jour.* 1:375-77).   255

23   Legislative minutes (see *Jour.* 1:377). Petitions: by several
     inhabitants of the province (see *N. Y. col. mss,* 59:81); by
     John Johnston et al. attorneys for Lady Lovelace, re-
     ferred. Orders: on memorial by the agents of the
     Sorlings prize; on petition by John Conrad Codwise (see
     N. Y. col. mss, 59:82).   257

27   Legislative minutes (see *Jour.* 1:377). Revenue accounts to
     be examined.   258

29   Legislative minutes (see *Jour.* 1:378). Order on memorial
     by Abr'm Wendall and other agents of the Sorlings prize
     concerning dollar bills. Salary warrants to be prepared.
     Mr Regnier answers to the petition of J. C. Codwise
     (p. 257). Rousby in error vs de Riemer.   259

31   River Indians before the council renew and brighten the
     covenant chain. Salary warrants signed.   261

Aug. 5 Petition of John Dongan (see *L. P.* 6:54) referred. Orders
        on petitions: by Jannetie Cregier (see *L. P.* 6:50-51); by
        Hendrick Anthony and others (p. 245); by Leonard Lewis
        (p. 247); by Elbert Timenson and others (p. 245); by
        Samuel Babington (p. 245); by Andries Coeman (see

1714　　　　　　　　　　　　　　　　　　　　　　　　　**v. 11**

L. P. 6:65). Petition: of Cornelius Seabring (see *L. P.* 6:61); of Dirck Benson; of Margaret Mac Gregory (see *L. P.* 6:53), referred. Messpott vs Harris and wife.　264

6　Legislative minutes (see *Jour.* 1:378). Five nations to be called to Albany to meet the governor.　265

12　Arrears of taxes and excise to be collected. Patent granted to George Lockstadt and other palatines at Quasseck creek, with special lot for Rev. Joshua Kocherthal (see *L. P.* 6:57).　266

19　Brief of charity granted to the widow of Francisco Pavia, for his services in the English expedition against Cadiz. Warrants of survey granted: to Corn's Seabring (p. 264); to Robert Milward (see *L. P.* 6:58-60); to Samuel Babington (p. 245, 264). Proclamation to issue concerning English measures (see *N. Y. col. mss,* 59:72).　266

26　Legislative minutes (see *Jour.* 1:378). Patents granted: to Adam Vrooman (p. 235, 245; see *L. P.* 6:64); to Abr'm Coeyman (see *L. P.* 6:66). Warrant of survey granted to Lewis Morris (see *L. P.* 6:68). Petition of Corn's van Brunt (see *L. P.* 6:63) referred. Rousby vs de Riemer.　267

31　Legislative minutes (see *Jour.* 1:379).　268

Sep. 2　Legislative minutes (see *Jour.* 1:379). Fauconier vs the queen. Tothill vs Gouverneur.　270

3-4　Legislative minutes (see *Jour.* 1:379-80).　271

4 p. m. Minutes sent to England.　271

9　Legislative minutes (see *Jour.* 1:380). Warrants of survey granted: to Corn's van Brunt (p. 267); to Dirck Ben on (p. 264; see *L. P.* 6:69). Rousby vs de Riemer.　273

29
Albany　Dr John Johnston nominated mayor, Francis Harrison sheriff of New York; Rob't Livingston jr mayor and Thos. Williams sheriff, of Albany.　273

Oct. 4
Fort Anne　Gov. Hunter returned from Albany informs the council of Queen Anne's death and the accession of George, duke of Brunswick.　274

5　King George to be proclaimed "in the most solemn manner" on the following Monday　274

7　Journals kept at Albany read. Warrants of survey granted to Samuel Staats (see *L. P.* 6:73).　274

11
Ft George　King George proclaimed at the fort and the city hall. Governor, council and secretary take the oaths.　275

14　Oaths administered to Mayor John Johnston, Sheriff Francis Harrison, the recorder, and to aldermen as justices of the peace; also to Gerard Beeckman and Adolph Philipse of the council.　275

1714   **v. 11**

21   Patent granted to the English church at Albany (see *N. Y.*
      col. mss, 59:101-2). Petition of John Collins (see *L. P.*
      6:75) referred. Patent granted to Rob't Milward (see
      L. P. 6:74).   276

25   License to purchase Indian lands granted to John Collins. 276

Nov. 3 Patents granted: to Meyndert Schuyler for land at Schoharie
      (see *L. P.* 6:78-79); to Meyndert Schuyler, Avent van
      Petten and John Dellemond (see *L. P.* 6:81-84). Warrant
      of survey granted to John Collins (see *L. P.* 6:86-87). Peti-
      tions: by Robert Walter (see *L. P.* 6:93); by Evert
      Bancker (see *L. P.* 6:71); by Dirck Wessells (see *L. P.*
      6:70); by Philipp Livingston (see *L. P.* 6:72), all referred.
      Legislative minutes (see *Jour.* 1:381).   276

4   Petition of Sam'l Staats and Rip van Dam (see *L. P.* 6:96)
      referred. Patent granted to John Collins (see *L. P.* 6:88-
      92).   278

11   License to purchase Indian land granted to Samuel Staats
      and Rip van Dam (p. 278). Recompensation voted to
      the commissioners of the late Canada expedition. License
      to purchase Indian land granted to Robert Walter (p. 276).
      Petition of Harman van Slike referred.   280

18   License to purchase Indian land granted to Harman van
      Slike. Petition of Abr'm de Peyster a. o. (see *L. P.* 6:98)
      referred.   281

22   Letters come from England by the sloop Hazard cast away
      on the New England coast. Royal proclamation for con-
      tinuing all officers in their places published at the city
      hall.   281

Dec. 2 Petition by Alex. Baird a. o. referred. License to purchase
      Indian lands granted to Abr'm de Peyster (p. 281). War-
      rant for the governor's salary drawn.   282

14   Legislative minutes (see *Jour.* 1:381). Warrants signed.
      Petition by Peter Schuyler (see *L. P.* 6:102) referred.
      Warrant of survey granted to Alex'r Baird (p. 282).   283

16   License to purchase Indian land granted to Peter Schuyler
      (p. 283). Order concerning Indian deeds, deeds of gift
      or other conveyances from the Indians. Account of duties
      and customs to be examined. Warrants for pay of fire-
      wood signed. Fauconier vs the queen. Tothill vs Gouv-
      erneur ex dem. de Key.   284

1715

Jan. 13 Petition by Lewis Morris et al for 3600 acres in Ulster
      county referred. Proclamation for adjourning the assem-
      bly to issue. Tothill vs Gouverneur. Fauconier vs the
      queen.   286

1715   **v. 11**

John MacLane (see *L. P.* 6:114-15). George Clarke sworn
in as secretary of the province.   304

June 2 Legislative minutes (see *Jour.* 1:385).   Bill of costs of Mr
Bickley in re Fauconier referred.   305

9 Legislative minutes (see *Jour.* 1:385).   306

14-15 Legislative minutes (see *Jour.* 1:386).   307

17 Legislative minutes (see *Jour.* 1:387).   Affidavits of Thos.
Gleone and John Foster received that Capt. Jonathan
Wright had been elected " common whipper." John Conrad Wiser to be arrested (see *N. Y. col. mss,* 60:3). Order
of the king regarding a grant of land to Gregory Gaugeon
(see *L. P.* 6:105) referred. Petition by Hugo Frere et al.
(see *L. P.* 6:118) referred.   309

20 Legislative minutes (see *Jour.* 1:387).   312

22 Legislative minutes (see *Jour.* 1:388).   Warrant of survey
granted to Harman van Slipk [Slyke].   313

23 Legislative minutes (see *Jour.* 1:388).   Warrant of survey
granted to Archibald Kennedy (see *L. P.* 6:121). Petition
of John Crook and others (see *L. P.* 6:122) referred. Peter
Hoof, Eliakim Hedger and John Foster reprimanded for
insult to Capt. Jon'n Wright (p. 309).   314

30 Legislative minutes (see *Jour.* 1:388).   Map of Rosendale
lands called for. Patent granted to Hugo Frere (see *L. P.*
6:119-20). Petition of Maudlin Rosencrans and Mariane
van Aken (see *L. P.* 6:125) referred. Petition of Servas
Feeraboom (see *L. P.* 6:123-24) granted.   315

July 1-5 Legislative minutes (see *Jour.* 1:389-90).   316

7 Legislative minutes (see *Jour.* 1:391). Stephen Gasherie called
before the council on the petition of Hendrick Anthony.   320

13 Legislative minutes (see *Jour.* 1:392-93).   323

15 Legislative minutes (see *Jour.* 1:393).   Warrants for salary
signed. Account of Geo. Clarke for expenses and petition

19 Legislative minutes (see *Jour.* 1:394).   Warrant of survey
granted to Evert van Ness (see *L. P.* 6:126). Warrant to
Geo. Clarke for incidental expenses (see *N. Y. col. mss,*
60:5). Account of Mr Byerley's incidental expenses to be
examined. John Conrad Wiser has gone to Boston; the
governor there requested to arrest him. Laws against riots
to be executed in Albany.   328

20 Legislative minutes (see *Jour.* 1:394). Warrants: to Mr Byerley for incidental expenses; to Martha Mompesson for her
late husband's salary.   330

21 Legislative minutes (see *Jour.* 1:395).   331

23 Letter of instruction to Mr Champante provincial agent in
London read (see *N. Y. col. mss,* 60:28).   334

1716   **v. 11**

Memorial of Col. Lodewick about Col. Schuyler and Lewis
Morris' appointment to the chief justiceship read. Prisoners
taken in South Carolina to be returned. Orders on petitions: by Abr'm de Lucena (see *N. Y. col. mss*, 60:96); by
Zacharias Hofman; by John Christian Garlach and others
(see *L. P.* 6:138), referred. Account of stationery furnished
by Wm Bradford referred. Warrants: for salaries of civil
officers signed; to Charles le Reaux for engraving plates
of bills of credit.   346

6   Warrants for salaries of civil officers signed. Account of
Mr Lurting and others for signing bills of credit referred
(see *N. Y. col. mss*, 60:97). Instructions for the governor
received. Ordinance to be prepared for establishing courts
in Dutchess county. Jacob Morris and Wm Kerten to be
pilots.   349

9   Warrant to Col. Lurting and others for signing bills of
credit. Ordinance concerning . Dutchess county courts
(see *N. Y. col. mss*, 60:99) to issue. Petitions: by Elias
Boudinot & Co. (see *L. P.* 6:139); by Phil. Schuyler and
heirs of Dr Staats, referred. Governor goes to New
Jersey. Report on the petition of Abr'm de Lucena (p. 346)
confirmed.   351

May 30   King George's letter appointing George Clarke of the council; Geo. Clarke sworn in vice Mompesson deceased. Thos.
Byerley sworn in as collector. King's letter appointing
Lewis Morris chief justice. Gov. Hunter appointed vice-
admiral. Lieut. John Scott treats with the Mohawks about
land without license and is reprimanded. Warrant of sur-
vey granted to Zacharias Hofman.   352

June 5   Proclamation to issue for thanksgiving on account of the victories over the rebels in England. Legislative minutes (see
Jour. 1:397).   354

6   Legislative minutes (see *Jour.* 1:398).   356

14   Order on petition by Richard Lawrence (see *L. P.* 6:140).
Account of incidental expenses by Thos. Byerley referred. 357

28   Warrants for salaries of civil officers signed. Legislative
minutes (see *Jour.* 1:398). Order on account of work on
Indian guns. Petitions: by Robert Walter & Co. (see *L. P.*
6:144); by Noah Parton & Co. (see *L. P.* 6:147); by Samuel
Odell (see *L. P.* 6:146); by John Shotwell; by James Jenkins (see *N. Y. col. mss*, 60:112), referred. Petition by Richard Lawrence (p. 357) dismissed.   357

27–29 Legislative minutes (see *Jour.* 1:398-99).   360

30   Legislative minutes (see *Jour.* 1:400). Report on accounts
of Thos. Byerley confirmed. License to purchase land
granted to Phil. Schuyler (p. 351).   364

1716   **v. 11**

Aug. 18   Letter from the king appointing Dr John Johnston to the
          council; he is sworn in vice Samuel Staats deceased. In-
          dian presents received from the king.   367

     21   Legislative minutes (see *Jour.* 1:401).   Indian affairs (see
          N. Y. col. mss, 60:121).   368

     22   Legislative minutes (see *Jour.* 1:401).   License to purchase
          land granted to Robert Walter (p. 357).   Patent granted
          to John Shotwell.   Minutes sent to England.   370

     24   Legislative minutes (see *Jour.* 1:402).   Patents granted: to
          Zacharias Hofman (p. 352); to Samuel and Eliza Babing-
          ton (see *L. P.* 6:148).   Petitions: by Henry Beekman (see
          L. P. 6:166); by John Harmanse Fisher; by Daniel van
          Olinda (see *L. P.* 6:162), referred.   371

     28   Legislative minutes (see *Jour.* 1:402).   373

     30   Legislative minutes (see *Jour.* 1:403).   License to purchase In-
          dian lands granted to John Harmanse Fisher (p. 371).   374

     31   Legislative minutes (see *Jour.* 1:403).   Indian affairs. 375

     31   Legislative minutes (see *Jour.* 1:404).   376

Sep. 1   Legislative minutes (see *Jour.* 1:404).   Patent granted to Har-
          man van Slyke (see *L. P.* 6:153).   378

      3   Examination of Robert Lurting in regard to a sloop fitted
          out by him and supposed to be intended against the
          Spaniards in Florida.   380

     13   Warrants for salaries signed.   Indian affairs.   383

     27   Account of incidental expenses by clerk and doorkeeper of
          the assembly referred.   Warrant of survey granted to Thos.
          and Walter Dongan (see *L. P.* 6:154-55).   385

     29   Dr John Johnston, Francis Harrison, Robert Livingston jr
          renominated as mayor and sheriff, of New York; and mayor
          of Albany, Samuel Babington nominated as sheriff of Al-
          bany.   385

Oct. 4   Indian affairs (see *N. Y. col. mss*, 60:130-31).   Order on peti-
          tion by the justices of Suffolk county (see *N. Y. col. mss*,
          60:136).   386

     15   John Johnston and Francis Harrison sworn in as mayor and
          sheriff, of New York.   387

Nov. 1   Warrant of survey granted to John Harmanse Fisher (p. 374).
          Petition of Henry Beekman son and heir of Henry Beek-
          man referred.   Order on petition by Richard Wilson (see
          N. Y. col. mss, 60:137).   Warrants: to John Cuyler and
          Hendrick for firewood to frontier garrison; to Indian
          commissioners for expenses. Tothill in error vs de Key.   387

      8   Orders received from England for examination into a rob-
          bery on the marquis de Navarres (see *N. Y. col. mss*, 60:143-
          44).   389

1716   v. 11

9   Report on the above examination read and approved. War-
     rants signed.   390
15   Order on letter from Capt. Wm Owen of the Solebay man-
     of-war. Capt. Jeffers to take Wm Glover to London.
     Hearing on caveat by Col. Rutsen against patent to Capt.
     Hosman deferred.   391

1717

Jan. 31 Warrants for salaries signed. Quarantine measures.   391
Feb. 7   Murders and rape committed at Albany. Indian affairs.   392
    14   Patent granted to Johannes Harmanse Fisher (see *L. P.*
         6:157).   393
    28   Arrears of taxes called in. Patent granted to Alex'r Baird,
         Abr'm van Vlerg and Harman Johnston (see *L. P.* 6:158).   394
Mar. 14 Warrants for salaries signed.   395
    21   Committee appointed to examine the accounts of John
         Graham the weighmaster.   395
Ap. 4   Indian affairs (see *N. Y. col. mss,* 60:157). Petitions by Con-
         rad Borghart (see *L. P.* 6:159); by Caspar van Housen; by
         Wm Bradford (see *N. Y. col. mss,* 60:158), referred.   396
    11   Warrants of survey granted: to C. Borghardt and Elias van
         Schaaks; to Caspar van Housen. Warrant to Wm Brad-
         ford for stationery. Caveat entered by Col. Rutsen dis-
         missed (p. 391).   396
    25   Legislative minutes (see *Jour.* 1:405). Memorial by justices
         of Kings county referred. Orders: on memorial of Robert
         Jenney master of the grammar school; on petition by
         widow Jannetie Cregier.   397
29–May 1 Legislative minutes (see *Jour.* 1:405).   398
    2   Order on petition by Jacob Mauritz and Wm Hurtin [Kur-
         tin] pilots (see *N. Y. col. mss,* 60:160, 162). Memorial of
         Thos. Byerley (see *N. Y. col. mss,* 60:161) referred. Stephen
         Gasherie and trustees of Marbletown to come before the
         council on the petition of Hendrick Anthony.   399
    7   Order on memorial of Thos. Byerley (p. 399). Warrant of
         survey granted to Daniel van Olinda (p. 371; see *L. P.*
         6:165).   401
    9   Legislative minutes (see *Jour.* 1:406). Petition of Jacob Rut-
         sen and justices of Ulster county (see *N. Y. col. mss,* 60:163)
         referred.   401
11–14   Legislative minutes (see *Jour.* 1:406-7).   403
    16   Legislative minutes (see *Jour.* 1:407). Proclamation about
         pilotage signed. Order on petition of Thos. Porter and
         John Fred (see *N. Y. col. mss,* 60:164).   405
    21   Legislative minutes (see *Jour.* 1:408). Account for repairing
         forts at Albany and on the frontiers referred.   406

1717   **v. 11**

23   Legislative minutes (see *Jour.* 1:408). Order on petition of
Lewis Gomez concerning duty on wine. Indian presents.   407

p. m.   Legislative minutes (see *Jour.* 1:409).   410

24   Legislative minutes (see *Jour.* 1:409). Indian presents sent to
Albany.   411

27   Legislative minutes (see *Jour.* 1:410).   413
Legislative minutes (see *Jour.* 1:410). Order on petition by
John Dunk (see *N. Y. col. mss,* 60:166).   414

p. m.   Legislative minutes (see *Jour.* 1:411).   415

June 24   Gov. Hunter returned from Albany reports on his conferences with the Indians. Mr Bridger appointed surveyor of
the woods in the colonies. Capt. Wm Owen, of the Solebay man-of-war reports from Jamaica that he is to sail
with 20 merchant men under his convoy for England.   416

25   Richard Caverley master, and Jeremy Huggins boatswain
of a pirate sloop examined. Warrant to the governor for
salary.   417

July 4   Warrants for salaries signed. Question debated and sub-
mitted to the chief justice and lawyers, whether Wm Dobs
and Samuel Vincent connected with pirates can be bailed.
Report on the petition of Lewis Gomez confirmed (p. 407).
Order on memorial by David Provost (see *N. Y. col. mss,*
60:167). Petition by Benj. Faneuil referred. Hearing of
Hendrick Anthony and brother vs Stephen Gasherie and
Depuy.   418

11   Report on petition of Benj. Faneuil confirmed. Francis Harrison sworn in as surveyor and searcher of all rates, duties
and impositions. Opinion of the chief justice, attorney-
general, and lawyers H. Wileman, H. Vernon and Rob't
Livingston in re Dobs and Vincent (p. 418). Petition by
Patrick McKnight (see *N. Y. col. mss,* 60:171) referred.   421

16   Money and valuables taken from Jeremy Huggins boatswain,
and Richard Caverley master, of the pirate sloop Mary
Ann delivered to the governor.   423

23   Francis Harrison resigns his office as sheriff of New York,
and Thos. Farmer is appointed in his place and sworn in.
Richard Caverley the pirate names Capt. Lessley, Capt.
Hornigold, also Capt. Laboos, of the sloop Postillion as
fellow pirates and the River Plate, Banisters Key, the Ba-
hama islands, Exnine, Providence, Richmond island and
Damaries cove as piratical rendezvous. Minutes sent to
England.   424

Aug. 22   Report on petition of Patrick McKnight (p. 421) confirmed.
Warrant of survey granted to Rip van Dam, Phil. Schuy-

1717   **v. 11**

ler and heirs of Samuel Staats. Patent granted to Henry
Beekman. Warrant to Thos. Byerley for moneys ad-
vanced.   425

Sep. 4   Council advises Gov. Hunter not to attend the meeting of
governors at Philadelphia proposed by Col. Spotswood of
Virginia because it might increase the Indian uneasiness.   426

5   Legislative minutes (see *Jour.* 1:411). Gov. Hunter writes to
Gov. Spotswood etc. as advised.   427

16   Indian affairs. Warrants for salaries signed. Legislative
minutes (see *Jour.* 1:412). Order on petition of Jannetie
Cregier (p. 397). Time for report on petition of Hendrick Anthony extended (p. 418).   428

26   Indian affairs. Legislative minutes (see *Jour.* 1:412). Report
on the weighmaster's accounts to lie on the table (see
N. Y. col. mss, 60:175). James Dixon appointed by royal
order collector and receiver general of the revenues; also
collector of the customs, and sworn in vice Thos. Byerley
removed. Petitions: by Johs. Hardenbergh (see *L. P.*
6:167); by Jacobus Bruyn (see *L. P.* 6:168), referred.   430

28   Letter received from secretary of state Addison relating to
the rebellion at Martinico.   432

30   Mayors and sheriffs of New York, and of Albany renominated. No vessels to be cleared for Martinico.   432

Oct. 10   Col. Peter Schuyler sworn in as councillor and justice of the
peace. Legislative minutes (see *Jour.* 1:413). Warrants
of survey granted to Johs. Hardenbergh and to Jacobus
Bruyn (p. 430). Ordinance for altering time of sessions
of the supreme court to be prepared.   432

12   Legislative minutes (see *Jour.* 1:413).   433

14   Commissions delivered and oath administered to Mayor John
Johnston and Sheriff Thos. Farmer. Aldermen sworn in
as justices of the peace.   434

17   Legislative minutes (see *Jour.* 1:413). Report on the account of Hendrick Hansen and Johs. Cuyler for repairs to
the fort at Albany confirmed.   435

21   Proclamation issued forbidding protection to be given to
rebels of Martinico. Legislative minutes (see *Jour.* 1:414).   436

24   Legislative minutes (see *Jour.* 1:415). License to purchase
Indian land granted to Rob't Walter (see *L. P.* 6:144, 172).
Warrant of survey granted to the trustees of Kingston (see
L. P. 6:170).   438

26   Legislative minutes (see *Jour.* 1:415). Warrant of survey
granted to Col. Schuyler at Kinderhook.   439

30   Legislative minutes (see *Jour.* 1:415).   440

1717   **v. 11**

31   Legislative minutes (see *Jour.* 1:416). Capt. Pearce of the
      Phoenix man-of-war reports that he and the Lyne on the
      Virginia station, and the Squirrell on the New England
      station have orders to reduce pirates.   441

Nov. 1–3 Legislative minutes (see *Jour.* 1:416-17).   442

7   Opinions as to mode of procedure in trial of pirates. Legis-
      lative minutes (see *Jour.* 1:417). License to purchase In-
      dian land granted to Johs. Hallenbeck (see *L. P.* 6:176). 444

8–9   Legislative minutes (see *Jour.* 1:418).   446

14   Opinion of council that the pirates cannot be tried under the
      commission of King William.   448

21   Legislative minutes (see *Jour.* 1:419). Warrant of survey
      granted to Omy La Grange sr and Johannes Symmonsen
      (see *L. P.* 6:180).   449

29   Legislative minutes (see *Jour.* 1:419). Opinion of councilor
      and order relating to letter from Justice Robert Hudson
      of Suffolk county about seditious sentiments.   451

30–Dec. 23 Legislative minutes (see *Jour.* 1:420-22).   452

Dec. 31 Letter received from lords of trade about illegal trade with
      French plantations; proclamation to issue forbidding it.
      Letters from Secretary Addison and from the lords of trade
      relating disorders in New Jersey.   461

1718

Jan. 9 Order on letter from Capt. Vincent Pearce of the Phoenix
      man-of-war relating to ship supplies.   463

14   Theod. Howell dismissed from his office of justice of the
      peace in Suffolk county. Richard Floyd accused of "ill
      practices" in the same county.   464

27   Royal proclamation granting pardon to pirates who surren-
      der within a given time received by Capt. Pearce; the cap-
      tain offers and is ordered to sail to the Bahamas and dis-
      tribute the proclamations.   465

Feb. 10 Letter received from Gov. Saltonstall of Connecticut about
      the boundary line.   466

20   Quarantine measures. Petition of Benj. Peck to lie on the
      table (see *N. Y. col. mss*, 60:152). Petition of Rich'd Alsop
      and Alex. Baird for monopoly of oyster fishing in Mes-
      path creek referred (see *L. P.* 6:183).   466

Mar. 13 Warrants for salaries signed. Order on petition by Lewis
      Gomez relating to duty on goods shipped from London in
      the Neptune, Thos. Gallop master.   468

25   Petition by New York merchants (see *N. Y. col. mss*, 61:7-8)
      referred. Account of commissioners for signing bills of
      credit referred. Palatines at Huntersfield mutinous.

1718   **v. 11**

Pirates surrender. Patent granted to John Schuyler for
woodland at Canastagione.   469

27   Warrant to Rob't Walter and other commissioners for expenses in signing bills of credit. Petition of New York
merchants (p. 469) granted. Gov. Hunter is going to New
Jersey and the assembly is adjourned. Minutes sent home. 471

Ap. 19   Complaint made by inhabitants of Rye about Connecticut
officials sent to the governor of Connecticut with remon-
strations.   473

May 9   Weighmaster John Graham ordered to pay all public money
in his hands to the treasurer.   474

27   Capt. Pearce returned from Providence reports that he has
seized and brought with him the ship John and Elizabeth,
John Sipkins master on suspicion of piracy.   474

p. m.   Legislative minutes (see *Jour.* 1:423).   475

June 11   Indian affairs; Flatheads reported as marching against the
five nations. Legislative minutes (see *Jour.* 1:424). Gov.
Hunter goes to New Jersey.   477

17   Legislative minutes (see *Jour.* 1:424). Certificate concerning
rate of exchange signed for Capt. George Gordon, of the
Pearle man-of-war. Warrants for salaries signed.   478

19   Legislative minutes (see *Jour.* 1:424). Order on petition by
Hendrick Anthony and brothers vs Stephen Gasherie.   481

23-25 Legislative minutes (see *Jour.* 1:425-26).   484

27   Legislative minutes (see *Jour.* 1:426). Warrant of survey
granted to Johs. Hallenbeck (p. 444). Patents granted to
Johs. Hardenbergh and to Jacobus Bruyn (p. 430, 432; see
L. P. 6:186-87).   489

30-July 1 Legislative minutes (see *Jour.* 1:427-28).   491

July 2   Legislative minutes (see *Jour.* 1:429). Geo. Clarke appointed deputy auditor general by Mr Walpole.   500

3   Legislative minutes (see *Jour.* 1:430).   504

10   Letter from Gov. Saltonstall and petition of Sam'l Mills et al.
relating to disturbances along the boundary line received,
and order thereon. Petition by Rev. Christ. Bridge rector
of Rye for letters patent referred.   507

19   Patent granted to Rev. Christ. Bridge. Warrant of survey
granted to Anne Mullinder (see *L. P.* 7:1-2).   509

Aug. 23   Indian affairs; governor to meet the five nations and quiet
their uneasiness. Arrears of quitrents called in. Certificate of good behavior to be given to Joshua Kocherthal
and John Fred'k Hager ministers of the palatines. Order
of the king in council approving an act of assembly.
Patent granted to Joshua Kocherthal and palatines at
Quasseck creek (see *L. P.* 6:188).   509

1718   **v. 11**

Sep. 9 Gov. Hunter reports on his meeting with the five nations
          (see *N. Y. col. mss*, 61:54). Thos. Byerley reinstated in his
          offices of collector and receiver general.   512
     19 Warrants for salaries signed.   513
     24 Legislative minutes (see *Jour.* 1:431).   514
     29 Mayors and sheriffs of New York, and of Albany renomin-
          ated.   516
Oct. 7 Legislative minutes (see *Jour.* 1:432). ˙   518
      8 Legislative minutes (see *Jour.* 1:432). Petitions: by John
          Haskall (see *L. P.* 7:4); by Cadwallader Coldin, James
          Kennedy and James Alexander (see *L. P.* 1:6); by Andrew
          Johnston, Patrick McKnight, John Lawrence and Phineas
          McIntosh (see *L. P.* 7:10); by Patrick McGregor (see *L. P.*
          7:3); by Christian Henke on behalf of the palatines at
          Quasseck creek, all referred.   518
      9 Piracy committed on the Delaware river. Legislative min-
          utes (see *Jour.* 1:432). Warrants of survey granted to John
          Haskall and to Cadw. Colden et al. (p. 518). Petition of
          Rebecca and Hunter Scott (see *L. P.* 7:8) referred.   520
p. m.   Legislative minutes (see *Jour.* 1:433).   522
     10 Legislative minutes (see *Jour.* 1:436). Warrant of survey
          granted to Alexander Johnstown et al (p. 518). Petition
          of Rebecca and Hunter Scott (p. 520) rejected. Surveyor
          General Augustine Graham ordered to survey the land for-
          merly granted to Capt. John Evans and since vacated and
          resumed.   537
     14 Legislative minutes (see *Jour.* 1:437). Mayor, recorder,
          aldermen, sheriff and clerk of New York sworn in.   539
     15 Legislative minutes (see *Jour.* 1:437).   540
     16 Legislative minutes (see *Jour.* 1:438). Wm Bradford to de-
          liver all blank bills of credit printed by him, to the com-
          missioners for destruction.   541
p. m.   Legislative minutes (see *Jour.* 1:438).   543
     20 Letter received from the lords of trade complaining of bad
          tar and pitch imported from the colonies. Petition of
          James Dixon (see *N. Y. col. mss*, 61:65) referred.   546
     23 Warrant to James Dixon for arrears of salary.   547
     25 Letter from lords of trade concerning a petition against an
          act of assembly and papers referred to a committee. War-
          rant to James Dixon signed
     27 Letter received from lords of trade concerning pardon to
          pirates who surrender. Proclamation issued to that effect
          and published at the city hall. Rich'd Caverly and Jeremy
          Huggins to be pardoned.   549
     28 John Lewis a pirate to be pardoned on the application of his
          wife Anne Lewis. Adolph Philippse, Caleb Heathcote,
          George Clarke, Isaac Hicks and William Willett to be
          commissioners for running Connecticut boundary line.   550

1718   **v. 11**

Nov. 1 Affidavit of Gabriel Ludlow clerk of the assembly against
Wm Bradford for neglect of printing assembly votes. Examination of Dennis Downing one of the signers of an address to the king against an act of assembly. Answer to
the address and the letter from lords of trade (p. 547).
Minutes sent home.   551

13 Connecticut boundary. Dr Colding weighmaster to call in
arrears of weigh accounts. License to purchase land
granted to Cap't. Walter et al. (see *L. P.* 7:12).   569

Dec. 26 Gov. Hunter goes to New Jersey. Warrants for salaries
signed.   570

1719

Ap. 7 Warrants for salaries signed.   572

9 Patents granted: to John Haskoll (see *L. P.* 7:33-34); to
Ann Mullender (see *L. P.* 7:13-14); to Archibald Ken-
nedy (see *L. P.* 7:41-42); to Cadwallader Colden (see *L. P.*
7:32); to James Alexander (see *L. P.* 7:39-40); to Andrew
Johnston (see *L. P.* 7:21); to Phineas McIntosh (see
L. P. 7:30-31); to John Lawrence (see *L. P.* 7:27-29); to
Patrick McKnight (see *L. P.* 24-26). Petitions: by
Patrick McGregory (see *L. P.* 7:3, 46); by David Gala-
tian; by Peter Schuyler (see *L. P.* 7:22), referred.   575

16 New Jersey boundary line. Warrants: to Benj. Burt for
salary of Andrew Bagg deceased, late land and tidewaiter;
to Thos. Fell land and tidewaiter for salary. Order on
petition by Thos. Allison et al. (see *N. Y. col. mss*, 61:80). 580

23 New Jersey boundary line. Warrant of survey granted to
Kilian van Rensselaer (see *L. P.* 7:44-45).   581

28 Legislative minutes (see *Jour.* 1:439).   582

29 Petition by Messire Christopher de Rossel (see *N. Y. col.
mss*, 61:82) read.   585

30 Legislative minutes (see *Jour.* 1:440). List of persons in
arrears for quitrents to be made and the attorney general
to prosecute them. Proclamation to issue calling for
speedy payment of quitrents (see *L. P.* 7:15).   586

May 2 Rob't Walter and Isaac Hicks appointed commissioners,
and Allen Gerard surveyor to ascertain the New Jersey
boundary line; warrant to them for expenses. Warrants
of survey granted to David Galatian and to Patrick
McGregory (p. 575).   589

5 Declaration of war against Spain received from the governor of Maryland. Warrants signed.   591

14 Ordinance for altering sessions of the courts of common
pleas in Kings county signed and ordered to be printed.   592

21 Legislative minutes (see *Jour.* 1:441).   592

1719   v. 11

8   Warrants signed for Thos. Brazier and for Widow Katherine
     Post. Order on petition of Capt. de Rossel (see *N. Y.
     col. mss*, 61:158). Petition of Archibald Kennedy for a
     lot in New York city referred.   650
9   Indians affairs (see *N. Y. col. mss*, 61:157).   651
13   Gov. Hunter turns the government over to Col. Schuyler,
     as president of the council. Petition of Wm Bradford (see
     L. P. 7:63) referred. Minutes sent home.   653

Vol. 12, 1719-20

1719

July 21   Peter Schuyler presides and is sworn in after reading of
          Gov. Hunter's commission and instructions.   1
     23   Order on petition of Thomas Grents on behalf of André
          Saens de Pietry (see *N. Y. col. mss*, 61:165).   2
     24   Order on petition by Henry Dewildey master of the brigan-
          tine Elizabeth and Catherine (see *N. Y. col. mss*, 61:161).
          Petition of Jacob Rutsen and Adrian Gerretsen (see *N. Y.
          col. mss*, 61:167), and memorial of Col. John Riggs and
          Capt. Henry Holland commanders of the independent
          companies at Albany about bedding etc, referred.   3
     30   Col. John Riggs authorized to repair the barracks at Albany.   5
Aug. 6   Orders on petition: by John Johnston, Gabriel Ludlow and
          Wm Bradford (see *L. P.* 7:65-66); by Kilian van Rens-
          selaer (see *L. P.* 7:64). Commission of oyer and terminer
          to issue for the trial of Jordan, who the sheriff of New
          York fears will escape from jail. Order on petition by
          Garret Vielly (see *N. Y. col. mss*, 61:172). Order on Mr
          Noxon's report that the sheriff of Orange county has
          removed.   6
     20   Report on petition of John Johnston, Gabriel Ludlow and
          Wm Bradford (p. 6) confirmed. Petition of Wm Brad-
          ford and Gabriel Ludlow (see *L. P.* 7:67) referred. Jus-
          tice Cornelius Haring of Orange county reports that
          Sheriff Timothy Halstead has been absent for two months;
          another sheriff to be appointed. Petitions: by Mary
          Ingoldsby (see *L. P.* 7:69); by Stephen de Lancey et al.
          (see *L. P.* 7:68) referred.   10
     27   Order on petition by Christ. de Rossel commander of the
          ship Victory (see *N. Y. col. mss*, 61:174). Account of
          debts to the weighhouse and porters presented by Dep.
          weighmaster Heath, to lie on the table.   15
     28   Jonathan Jordan and a negro belonging to Harmanus
          Burger both sentenced to death, reprieved for a week.   17
Sep. 3   Account of the military storekeeper referred. Petition by
          Thos. Byerley (see *L. P.* 7:74) referred. Patent granted

1719   **v. 12**

to Jacob Rutsen and Adrian Gerretsen (p. 3). Orders on
petitions: by Melchoir Gellis (see *L. P.* 7:78); by Servas
Fleraboom (see *L. P.* 7:70).   18

10   Orders on petitions: by merchants of New York (see *N. Y.
col. mss*, 61:177); by Jacques Christoph Duplessis (see
N. Y. col. mss, 61:180). Warrant of survey granted to
John Cluit of Canestagione. Order on petition by Francis
Furlong (see *N. Y. col. mss*, 61:179).   21

11   Order on petition of Jacques Christoph Duplessis (p. 21).   23

15   Order on petition of Gabriel Dubois Jourdain (see *N. Y.
col. mss*, 61:181).   24

17   Petition of Evert van Ness of Canestagione (see *L. P.* 7:90)
referred.   25

24   Orders on petitions: by inhabitants of the province (see
N. Y. col. mss, 61:191); by Allan Jarratt [Gerard] (see
N. Y. col. mss, 61:187); by Patr. McGregory; by Daniel
van Olinda (see *L. P.* 7:76); by Jacques and Peter Cortelyou (see *N. Y. col. mss*, 61:190). Connecticut act of
assembly concerning boundary line received (see *L. P.*
7:87). Account of New Jersey boundary line commission-
ers referred. Warrants for salaries signed.   26

29.   Jacobus van Cortlandt appointed mayor, Thomas Farmer
sheriff of New York; Myndert Schuyler mayor, and
Garret van Scak sheriff of Albany.   32

Oct. 1   Orders: on petition by Wm Ranking and Peter Porter (see
N. Y. col. mss, 62:6); on memorial by Allan Gerard.
Francis Harrison says he has no objection to make to
the petitions of Servas Fleraboom and of Melchoir Gellis
(p. 18). Capt. Miller, commanding privateer allowed to
sail.   33

8   Order on petition by Thos. Ellison, Wm. Ranking and Peter
Porter (see *N. Y. col. mss*, 62:7). Patents granted: to
Daniel van Olinda (p. 26); to Servas Fleraboom and to
Melchoir Gellis (p. 18, 33).   35

14   Mayor, sheriff, recorder, and aldermen as justices of the
peace sworn in.   38

15   Minutes of the Indian commissioners (see *N. Y. col. mss*,
62:1-2). Report on petition of J. and P. Cortelyou confirmed (see *N. Y. col. mss*, 62:8). Petition of John Stevenson for a ferry from Throggs point to Whitestone (see
N. Y. col. mss, 62:15). Memorial of Lt. Col. James
Weems and Capt. Lancaster Symes (see *N. Y. col. mss*,
62:9). Petitions: by Rich'd Floyd and Wm Smith (see
N. Y. col. mss, 62:10, 12); by Burger Mynderts (see *L. P.*
7:80), referred. Sheriff of Suffolk county before the council. Petition of Peter Hoganboom referred.   38

22   Johannes Apple before the council on the complaint of
      Kilian van Rensselaer (p. 6). Order on petition of Thos.
      Codman. Patents granted: to Johannes, Peter and
      Catherine, children of Peter Johnson deceased (see *L. P.*
      7:70, 77); to Melchoir Gellis (see *L. P.* 7:79).   46

29   Petitions: by James Christ. Duplessis owner, and Bernard
      Capela master, of the sloop St Michael (see *N. Y. col. mss,*
      62:17-19); by Edw. Gatehouse (see *L. P.* 7:92), referred.   48

30   Rob't Walter, Rob't Lurting, John Cruger, Lancaster
      Symes and Phil. Cortlandt appointed to audit the accounts
      of Capt. John Rose of the Seaford man-of-war (see *N. Y.
      col. mss,* 62:16). Petition of Wm Eier for land referred.   49

Nov. 6   Hearing on the petition of Rich'd Floyd and Wm Smith
         (p. 38, see *Doc. hist. N. Y.* 3:389; Q 3:235). Order on
         petition by Henry Lane, John Spratt and James Ricaut.   51

9   Warrant to John Riggs for repairing fort at Albany. Let-
      ter received from Mr Popple secretary of the lords of
      trade concerning smuggling, and pitch and tar making, to
      be printed.   52

12   Allan Jarratt [Gerard] to be appointed surveyor general
      (see *N. Y. col. mss,* 62:27). Orders: on memorial of
      Francis Harrison and Gilbert Livingston (see *N. Y. col.
      mss,* 62:25); on the accounts of New Jersey boundary
      commissioners. Warrant for Col. John Riggs signed.
      Dep. weighmaster Heath to collect arrearages of debts.
      Petition of Nicholas Westfall and others of Orange county
      (see *N. Y. col. mss,* 62:24) referred.   54

13   James Christopher Duplessis allowed to sell some of his
      goods (see *N. Y. col. mss,* 62:20), and list of stores which
      he may buy.   58

16   Minutes of Indian commissioners at Albany November 7
      and 9 to be sent to the southern Colonies. Petition of
      Rev. Petrus Vas et al. (see *N. Y. col. mss,* 62:28, 36) re-
      ferred.   61

17   Patent of incorporation granted to Rev. P. Vas. Petition
      of Jacobus Bruyn (see *L. P.* 7:81) referred.   71

26   Petitions: of Jacobus Kip, John Cruger, Oliver and John
      Schuyler, John Cruger, Phil. van Cortlandt and David
      Provost (see *L. P.* 7:86); of Francis Vincent (see *L. P.*
      7:88) referred. Patent granted to Johs. Hardenbergh
      (see *L. P.* 7:83-84).   72

Dec. 3   Patent granted to Francis Vincent. Warrant of survey
         granted to Jacobus Kip et al. (p. 72). Petition of J. C.
         Duplessis and Bernard Capela (see *N. Y. col. mss,* 62:34);
         of Elizabeth Bridge widow of Christ'r Bridge (see *N. Y.*

1719   **v. 12**

col. *mss*, 62:37) referred. Letter from Gov. Sam'l Shute of
Boston (see *N. Y. col. mss*, 62:33) referred.   74

7   Report on the petition of J. C. Duplessis (see *N. Y. col. mss*,
62:35-36, 51).   78

10   Isaac Bobin sworn in as deputy secretary. Letter from Col.
Riggs about bad condition of the fort at Albany referred.   81

17   Warrant of survey granted to Edw. Gatehouse (p. 48).
Petitions: by Jeremiah Schuyler, Jacobus van Cortlandt,
Fred'k Philippse, Wm Sharpas and Isaac Bobin (see *L. P.*
7:94); by Andries Volk and Jacob Weber palatines (see
L. P. 7:93), referred. Warrants for salaries signed.   82

27   Patent granted to Andries Volk and Jacob Weber (p. 82).
Warrant of survey granted to Jere. Schuyler et al. Peti-
tions: by Thos. Brazier (see *L. P.* 7:111); by Egbert van
Bursum (see *L. P.* 7:96) referred.   84

1720

Jan. 22   Petition by Cornelius Low, Gerard Schuyler and John
Schuyler (see *L. P.* 7:98-99) referred. Patents granted:
to Edw. Gatehouse (see *L. P.* 7:104); to Jere. Schuyler
et al. (p. 82, 84). David Jamison appointed and sworn in
as attorney general vice John Raynes deceased. Orders
on petitions: by Thos. Clarke & Co. for wharf extension
on the East river; by Cornelius Kuyper (see *N. Y. col.
mss*, 62:57).   86

28   Letter from Sec. Josiah Willard of Boston with Massachusetts charter (see *N. Y. col. mss*, 62:56) referred. Warrants
of survey granted: to Thos. Brasier (see *L. P.* 7:112); to
Corn's Low et al. (p. 86). Order on caveat by mayor etc
of New York against patent to Thos. Clarke & Co. Petition by Mary Ingoldsby and Mary Pinhorne (see *L. P.*
7:114) referred.   89

Feb. 18   Order on caveat against the patent to Thos. Clarke (p. 89).   91
Mar. 3   Hearing on caveat against the patent to Thos. Clarke et al.
Ordinance concerning sessions of the supreme court to be
printed (see *N. Y. col. mss*, 62:70). Petition of James
Anderson presbyterian minister for patent of incorpora-
tion referred.   92

17   Warrant of survey granted to Corn's Low et al. (see *L. P.*
7:120). Patent granted to Thos. Brasier (see *L. P.* 7:117).
Petitions: by Thos. Noxon (see *L. P.* 7:119); by Wm
Bond (see *L. P.* 7:125), referred. Pardon granted to Hannah Travis (see *N. Y. col. mss*, 62:72). Caveat entered by
May Bickley on behalf of Trinity church against patent
of incorporation for the presbyterian church. Corn's Kuyper and the sheriff of Orange county called before the
council (p. 86); also Charles Broadhead with trustees of

Marbletown and Justice Jacob Rutsen (see *L. P.* 7:116).
Petition by John McGregory, Katherine Evans, Jane
Lawrence, children of Patrick McGregory, and Thos.
Toshack (see *L. P.* 7:115) referred. Warrants for salaries
signed.   94

21   Warrant of survey granted to Thos. Noxon.   99

31   Hearing on May Bickley's caveat (p. 94) deferred. Peti-
tions: by Wm Huddleston (see *L. P.* 7:128); by Johs.
Hey and others (see *L. P.* 7:122) referred. Mayor etc of
New York against Thos. Clarke.   99

Ap. 16   Letter from Indian commissioners at Albany with affidavit
of Jacobus Vedder (see *N. Y. col. mss*, 62:80-81). Financial
affairs. Warrants of survey granted to Wm Huddleston
(p. 99) and to Wm Bond (p. 94).   101

21   Francis Harrison appointed to the council; king's letter to
at the   that effect; he is sworn in. Letter from Sec. Craggs
president's   about changes of officers. Proclamation to issue proro-
chamber.   guing the assembly (see *Jour.* 1:449). Letter from Sec.
Craggs with the appointment of Dr Cadw. Colden to be
surveyor general. Judge, justices etc of Orange county
and Corn's Kuyper called before the council.   108

29   Petition of Charles Cromline (see *L. P.* 7:123) referred.
Ft. George   Mayor etc of New York vs Thos. Clarke.   112

May 5   Letters received from Nicholas Laws governor of Jamaica
complaining of John Hickford master of the privateer
sloop Hunter. Pardon granted to Wm Smith.   113

p. m.   Letters and papers from Jamaica referred to the court of
admiralty. Order on petition of James Commerford late
commander of the sloop Samuel and Elizabeth (see *N. Y.
col. mss*, 62:91).   115

12   Order on petition by Joseph Loyd and Bernard Schaats
(see *N. Y. col. mss*, 62:89). Chs. Broadhead et al. vs Jacob
Rutsen. Petitions: by Richard van Dam (see *L. P.* 7:132);
by Vincent Matthews (see *L. P.* 7:137); by Phil. Schuyler
jun. and Christ. Abeel (see *L. P.* 7:133), referred. Petition by Wm Lake (see *N. Y. col. mss*, 62:92) granted.   117

19   Warrants of survey granted: to Charles Cromline (p. 112);
to Rich'd van Dam (p. 117); to Vincent Matthews; to
Phil. Schuyler (p. 117).   119

28   Petitions: of Gerard Beekman, Rip van Dam, Adolph
Philippse and Anne Peartree (see *L. P.* 7:146); of Francis
Harrison, Oliver Schuyler and Allan Jarrat (see *L. P.*
7:149); of Philipp Schuyler, Johs. Lansing jr, Henry Wileman and Jacobus Bruyn (see *L. P.* 7:148), referred. Patent granted to Thos. Noxon (see *L. P.* 7:139). Thos.

1720   **v. 12**

        Farmer appointed escheator general vice Aug. Graham
        deceased.   121

June 2   Warrants of survey granted: to Gerard Beekman et al.; to
        Phil. Schuyler et al.; to Francis Harrison et al. (p. 121).
        Patent granted to Wm Huddleston (p. 99, 101). Petition
        of Wm. Baker (see *N. Y. col. mss,* 62:87) dismissed. Dep-
        uty weighmaster Heath's report referred (see *N. Y. col.
        mss,* 62:97).   122

     6   Proclamation to issue proroguing the assembly.   124

     9   Indian affairs. Journal of Myndert Schuyler and Rob't
        Livingston jr, while at the Sennekies castle. Order on
        petition by Bernardus Swartwout (see *L. P.* 7:131). Corn's
        Kuyper before the council (p. 86, 94). Minutes sent
        home.   [123]

   17   Patent granted to Vincent Matthews (p. 119). Order on
        petition by Mary Ingoldsby and Mary Pinhorne for them-
        selves and for Mary and John Pinhorne, infants (see *L. P.*
        7:158). Petitions: by Jos. Budd, John Hoit, and Daniel
        Purdy son of Joseph Purdy deceased (see *L. P.* 7:159);
        by Henry Beeckman and John Stoutenburg (see *L. P.*
        7:157); by Wm Chambers (see *L. P.* 7:162), all referred.
        Orders on petitions: by Isaac Anderson (see *L. P.* **7:156**);
        by Rich'd Merril (see *L. P.* 7:155). Petition of Lewis
        Morris, Vincent Pearce, James Graham, Andrew Nicholls
        and Robert Kennedy referred. Warrants for salaries
        signed.   133

   30   Patent granted to Richard van Dam. New warrants
        of survey granted to Phil. Schuyler et al. (p. 121-22; see
        L. P. 7:165); to Francis Harrison (see *L. P.* 7:164); to
        Wm Bond (see *L. P.* 7:160). Petition of Patrick McGreg-
        ory (see *L. P.* 7:163), referred. Orders on petitions: by
        Dan'l Purdy, Sam'l and Benj. Brown (see *L. P.* 7:171);
        by John Kelly (see *L. P.* 7:184); by Lewis Morris (see
        L. P. 7:166). Indian affairs; letter from Indian commis-
        sioners, and journal of Lawrence Claesen on a journey
        to Octjagara.   136

July 7   Patents granted: to Francis Harrison et al. (p. 136); to
        Phil. Schuyler et al.; to Wm Bond. Petitions: by James
        Commerford (see *N. Y. col. mss,* 62:109); by John Kelly
        (see *N. Y. col. mss,* 62:110), referred. Warrant to Rob't
        Walters and New Jersey boundary line commissioners for
        expenses. Petition of Capt. Jos. Budd, John Hoit and
        Dan'l Purdy (see *L. P.* 7:180) referred.   142

   14   Warrant of survey granted to Wm Chambers (p. 133).
        Petition of Rob't Walter (see *L. P.* 7:186-87) referred.

Patents to Joseph Budd et al. (p. 142); to Mary Ingoldsby and Mary Pinhorne (p. 133). Warrant of survey to
Peter McGregory (p. 136). Order on petition of Lewis
Morris et al. (p. 133). Petition of Wm. Baker (see *L. P.*
7:188) referred. Warrant to Rob't Walter et al. (p. 142)
signed. Samuel Odell having entered a caveat against
the patent to Dan'l Purdy et al. (p. 136; see *L. P.* 7:190)
called before the council. Proclamation to issue proroguing the assembly. Indian affairs; five nations to come
to Albany for a meeting.   145

21   Warrant of survey granted to Robert Walter (p. 145). Caveat entered against the patent to Wm Baker (p. 145) by
Thos. Byerley (see *L. P.* 7:188). Petition of Isaac de
Peyster, Abr'm de Peyster jr, John and Jacob Walter (see
L. P. 8:1) referred. Patent granted to Mary Ingoldsby
and Mary Pinhorne (p. 145) exchanged for a warrant of
survey. Orders: on representation by James Commerford
against the privateer sloop Hunter; on petitions by Corn's
van Horne et al. (see *N. Y. col. mss*, 62:115); by Abr'm
Wendell and Rodrigo Pacheco (see *N. Y. col. mss*, 62:117).
Petition by Rob't Walter et al. (see *N. Y. col. mss*, 62:116)
referred. Warrant to John Little doorkeeper and messenger of the council for salary. Letter and minutes of
Indian commissioners.   148

28   Letter from Gov. Keith of Pennsylvania about Indian affairs received. Warrants of survey granted: to Patrick
McGregory (see *L. P.* 7:202-3); to Isaac de Peyster et al.
(p. 148). Petition of James Graham referred. List of
Indian presents and prices. Warrant for the expenses of
the Indian conference at Albany to be prepared. Caveat
entered by Cadwallader Colden against patent to Joseph
Budd and others of Rye (see *L. P.* 8:4). Patents granted:
to Joseph Budd et al. (p. 142, 145); to Gerard Beekman
et al. (p. 121, 122; see *L. P.* 7:199-200). Hearing on caveat
of Thos. Byerley and petition of Dan'l Purdy (see *L. P.*
7:171, 190) referred. Surveyor general to lay out land
for Wm Chambers as per warrant.   154

30   Warrant of survey granted to Daniel Purdy, Sam'l and
Benj. Brown for land on Byram river.   158

Aug. 4   Warrant for expenses of Indian conference signed. Order
on petition by Leah Courant (see *N. Y. col. mss*, 62:100,
127). Petitions: by Abr'm Wendell (see *N. Y. col. mss*,
62:128); by Rodrigo Pacheco (see *N. Y. col. mss*, 62:132);
by Wm Chambers, referred.   159

1720   v. 12

6 Patent granted to Patrick McGregory (see *L. P.* 8:11-12).
Petitions: by Robert Walter et al. (see *N. Y. col. mss,*
62:136); by Rev. Petrus van Driessen (see *N. Y. col. mss,*
62:136; and, *Doc. hist. N. Y.* 3:911-12; Q3:548) referred.   161

8 Orders on petitions: of Robert Walter; of Abr'm Wendell;
of Rodrigo Pacheco (p. 159, 161). Patent granted to Wm
Baker (see *L. P.* 8:13).   162

9 Patent of incorporation granted to the Dutch protestant
church at Albany (see *N. Y. col. mss,* 62:137, 139).   163

11 Patent granted to Mary Ingoldsby and Mary Pinhorne (see
L. P. 8:14-16). Jacobus van Cortlandt vs Joseph Hunt in
error. Patent granted to Daniel Purdy, Sam'l and Benj.
Brown (see *L. P.* 8:17-19).   ·164

Sep. 9 President Schuyler returned from Albany reports on the
meeting with the five nations; minutes entered. Account
of expenses; petition of Indian commissioners (see *N. Y.
col. mss,* 62:146); and of John Clute (see *L. P.* 8:20), referred.   165

15 Patent granted to Jacobus Kip, John Cruger, Phil. Cortlandt,
David Provost, Oliver and John Schuyler (see *L. P.* 8:24).
Jacobus van Cortlandt vs Jos. Hunt in error. Proclamation to issue proroguing the assembly. Warrants for salaries signed.   182

Vol. 13, 1720-22

1720

Sep. 17 Gov. Wm Burnet's commission read and the oaths adminis-
tered to him. King's approval of an act of assembly.
Proclamation to issue continuing all officers in their places.
Seal and keys of the magazines delivered to the governor.   1

19 Order on petition by Rev. James Anderson et al. (see *N. Y.
col. mss,* 62:157). Warrant for firewood to issue.   4

20 Letter received from Indian commissioners and representation from mayor etc. of Albany concerning French encroachments. Indian affairs.   5

29 Robert Walter nominated mayor, Thos. Farmer sheriff of
New York; Myndert Schuyler mayor, Henry Holland
sheriff of Albany. Warrants signed for expenses of repairing Fort George and barracks and for firewood to Albany,
Schenectady and Fort Hunter garrisons. Warrant to be
prepared for Indian expenses. Account of Indian expenses
by Pres. Schuyler referred.   8

Oct. 3 Report on Pres. Schuyler's account confirmed (see *N. Y. col.
mss,* 62:148). Warrant signed.   10

6 Capt. Henry Holland to prepare a statement of the repairs
necessary to Albany and Schenectady fortifications. Mr

1720   **v. 13**

Livingston writes about trade with Canada from Albany.
Petition of James Commerford (see *N. Y. col. mss,* 62:166)
referred.   11

13 Legislative minutes (see *Jour.* 1:451). Capt. Henry Holland
hands in the required statement.   12

14 Mayor, sheriff etc. of New York sworn in. Petition of Wm
Townsend and others (see *N. Y. col. mss,* 62:169) referred..   18

27 Legislative minutes (see *Jour.* 1:452).   19

28 Legislative minutes (see *Jour.* 1:453). Petition of Wm Provoost, John vander Hule and others (see *N. Y. col. mss,*
62:167) referred.   23

Nov. 3 Legislative minutes (see *Jour.* 1:454). Account of incidental
charges by Thos. Byerley (see *N. Y. col. mss,* 62:173); and
application by Mr Harrison on behalf of Isaac Hicks and
Wm Willett Connecticut boundary commissioners referred.
Order on petition by Mary van Rensselaer (see *L. P.* 8:30).
Petition of Coenrat Bogart and Elias van Schaick (see
L. P. 8:35) referred; that of Wm Warner and others (see
N. Y. col. mss, 62:174) dismissed. Legislative minutes (see
Jour. 1:454).   25

4 Legislative minutes (see *Jour.* 1:454).   29

12 Peter Schuyler, Hend'k Hansen, John Cuyler, Peter van
Brugh, Evert Banker, Henry Holland, Phil. Livingston,
John Collins, John Wendell of Stone Rawbey [Stone
Arabia] and John Bleeker appointed Indian commission-
ers. Legislative minutes (see *Jour.* 1:455). Warrant to
Isaac Hicks and Wm Willet for expenses as Connecticut
boundary commissioners.   31

14-16 Legislative minutes (see *Jour.* 1:456-58).   35-39

16 Warrant to I. Hicks and Wm Willett signed.   39

17 Legislative minutes (see *Jour.* 1:459-60).   43

18 Legislative minutes (see *Jour.* 1:460). Petition of widow Catherine Brett (see *L. P.* 8:39) referred.   50

19 Legislative minutes (see *Jour.* 1:461).   52

22 Warrants signed: to George Baimfield for public expenses;
to Thos. Brasier for firewood and candles to the assembly;
to Lewis Morris for services in the assembly; to Cath.
Post for use of her house by assembly committee; to Gabriel Ludlow clerk of the assembly for stationery etc.; to
Rob't Crannel for salary as sergeant at arms. Warrant to
be prepared for Thos. Byerley.   60

28 Petition of John Haskall (see *L. P.* 8:40) referred. Warrant
for Thos. Byerley signed. Minutes sent home.   61

Dec. 21 Surveyor general C. Colden ordered to examine a quadrant
used by Allan Jarrat for the New Jersey boundary survey.
Warrants for salaries signed.   62

1720   **v. 13**

27   Oath of chancellor taken by the governor; and Rob't Walter,
     Rip van Dam, Rob't Lurting, Cadw. Colden appointed
     masters in chancery, Gilbert Livingston register, Francis
     Harrison examiner, Wm Sharpas and Rob't Livingston jr
     clerks, and John Gara messenger.   63

1721

Jan. 19   Account of commissioners for signing paper money bills (see
          N. Y. col. mss, 63:31) referred.   64

Feb. 2   Warrant to issue for paying account of commissioners for
          signing bills.   65

     9   Order on petition of deputy weighmaster Samuel Heath con-
          cerning pay due to porters. Warrant signed.   66

     14   Gov. Burnet goes to New Jersey. The assembly is ad-
          journed.   67

May 9   Letter from the lords of trade about assembly sessions and
          Indian presents. Indian affairs; five nations repulsed by
          Virginia Indians; Governor of Canada lays claim to
          Niagara. Warrants for salaries signed.   68

     19   Legislative minutes (see Jour. 1:464). Depositions received
          about ships commanded by Capt. Braddick and by Capt.
          Norton seized at Southold (see N. Y. col. mss, 63:72). Gov.
          Spotswood of Virginia reports that Roberts the pirate is
          on the coast with two ships; Capt. Braddick called before
          the council. Warrant to Rob't Walter for salary as second
          judge of the supreme court.   71

p. m.   Examination of Capt. John Braddick. Affidavits by Claus
          Benning, Bastin de Keyser and George du Ref, Tunus
          Goverson. John Braddick committed for complicity with
          pirates.   75

     23   Letter from Chief justice Lewis Morris about Braddick.
          Opinion of council on bailing Braddick. Warrant of sur-
          vey granted to Henry van Rensselaer (see L. P. 8:43). 85

June 9   Legislative minutes (see Jour. 1:465).   88

     12   Legislative minutes (see Jour. 1:465). Opinion of council on
          a letter from the governor of New England relating to a
          naval rendezvous; Sandy Hook considered preferable to
          Nantasket.   89

     15   Legislative minutes (see Jour. 1:466). Warrants for salaries
          signed.   91

     23   Legislative minutes (see Jour. 1:467).   96

     29   Legislative minutes (see Jour. 1:467). Warrant of survey
          granted to John Haskall (p. 61). Order on petition of
          Jacob Rutsen on behalf of the trustees of Hurley (see N. Y.
          col. mss, 63:87-88).   97

1721   v. 13

July   1   Legislative minutes (see *Jour.* 1:468). Patents granted: to
           Lewis Morris (see *L. P.* 8:52); to Vincent Pearce (see *L. P.*
           8:51). The French are building a fort at Niagara.   100
       6   Legislative minutes (see *Jour.* 1:468). Ordinance establishing
           a court of common pleas in Dutchess county read, and to
           be printed (see *N. Y. col. mss,* 63:95).   104
       7   Legislative minutes (see *Jour.* 1:470).   109
       8   Rip van Dam to go to Madame Cortlandt in relation to Mrs
           Bretts purchase (see *L. P.* 8:52).   111
      12   Legislative minutes (see *Jour.* 1:470).   112
      13   Legislative minutes (see *Jour.* 1:471). Inquiry to be made into
           the security given by the treasurer.   115
   14-27 Legislative minutes (see *Jour.* 1:472-75).   118-30
      27   Order on memorial by Thos. Byerley (see *N. Y. col. mss,*
           63:106).   130
   p. m.   Legislative minutes (see *Jour.* 1:475).   133
Aug.   3   Letter from the king appointing Cadw. Colden and James
           Alexander to the council vice Peter Schuyler and Adolph
           Philippse removed; they are sworn in.   137
      24   Warrants of survey granted: to John Haskall (see *L. P.*
           8:59-60); to Andrew Nickells (see *L. P.* 8:55). Patent of in-
           corporation granted to Robert Walter, Corn's de Peyster,
           Lancaster Symes and Peter Fauconier (see *L. P.* 61-62).
           Gov. Burnet is going to Albany.   139
      26   Ordinance for changing sessions of the supreme court read,
           and ordered printed. Confirmatory patent granted to Ger-
           ard Beekman, Rip van Dam, Ad. Philippse and Ann Pear-
           tree.   140
      31   Proclamation against selling liquor to the Indians. Trade
Albany   carried on from Sarattogue to Canada to be stopped.   141
Sep. 2-9 Palatines at Skoharee. Indian conference and list of presents
           given.   143
       9   Palatines.   162
      11   An officer and 20 men to be stationed at Saratoga for stop-
Livingston ping trade to Canada; how to be paid; blockhouse to be
manor   erected. Indian affairs. Lawrence Claesen to be paid for
           extraordinary services in the Seneca country; Mrs Mon-
           tour interpreter at Saratoga to be paid. Peter Schuyler jr
           to be captain of the company sent to live among the Sen-
           ecas. Indian presents. Purchase of land. Instructions for
           Capt. Peter Schuyler jr.   163
      15   Measures proposed for preventing horse disease from spread-
Ft George   ing. Gov. Burnet reports on Indian conference at Albany. 173
      16   Proclamation concerning horse disease to be printed. Letter
           received from the governor of Canada on Indian affairs.   174
      19   Letter received from the governor of Boston on Indian af-

fairs. Order in relation to duty on Indian presents. Indian affairs. Warrants for salaries signed. Minutes sent
home.   175

20   Report on permission given to neighboring governments for
treating with New York Indians, and letter from Sec.
Josiah Willard of Boston. Letter in reply from Deputy
Sec. I. Bobin denying treaty right.   178

29   Robert Walter renominated mayor, Thos. Farmer sheriff of
New York; Peter van Brugh nominated mayor vice Myndert Schuyler, Henry Holland renominated sheriff of Albany. Inventory of king's stores at Livingston manor referred. Petitions: of John Waldron (see *L. P.* 8:57); of
Patrick Hume (see *L. P.* 8:58); of Wm Bradford (see *L. P.*
8:64); of James Smith (see *L. P.* 8:63), referred. Warrant
to Cath. Post for use of her house by assembly committee
signed.   181

Oct. 2   Royal mandamus appointing Lewis Morris jr to the council
vice Caleb Heathcote deceased; he is sworn in.   184

3   Stores at Livingston manor to be brought to Fort George
and some to be sold (see *N. Y. col. mss*, 63:153). Reports
on petitions: of John Waldron; of Patrick Hume; of James
Smith; of Wm Bradford (p. 184), are approved. Petition
of James Henderson (see *L. P.* 8:69) referred.   185

4   Report on the petition of James Henderson approved.   189

5   The Swartwouts and Westphalias before the council; they
enter into recognizances for their good behavior. Division line between Orange and Ulster counties to be settled.   190

9   The Swartwouts' [Thomas, Bernardus, Jacobus jr Swartwout, Peter Gamerse, Harm. Bernh. van Weigh] and the
Westphalias [Nicholas, Nicholas jr. Johannes Westphalia,
Corn's Dutcher, Corn's Conckendal] before the council.
Report of the attorney general on running the division line
between Orange and Ulster counties. Letter to be written to Indian commissioners of Massachusetts at Albany,
that they cannot treat with the five nations. Palatines.   191

14   Mayor and sheriff of New York sworn in.   197

Nov. 2   Petitions: by Thos. Garland (see *L. P.* 8:74); by Rich'd Ashfield and Evert Wendell (see *L. P.* 8:75), referred. Account of incidental office charges etc. by George Clarke referred. Rules for carrying out an act for supervising in-
testates' estates to be prepared.   197

7   Report on Sec. Clarke's account confirmed (see *N. Y. col. mss*,
63:162). Reports on petitions of Thos. Garland, of Rich'd
Ashfield and Evert Wendell (p. 197) approved. Petition of
Lewis Morris, Cadw. Colden, James Alexander, Abr'm
Horne, John Collins and Marg't Fether (see *L. P.* 8:76)

1721   **v. 13**

referred. Warrants to George Clarke for incidental
charges signed.   199

9   Report on the act for supervising intestate estates approved
(see *N. Y. col. mss*, 63:169). License to purchase Indian
lands granted to Lewis Morris et al. (p. 199).   203

p. m. Letter from Capt. John Waldron, commanding the Greyhound man-of-war (see *N. Y. col. mss*, 63:170) referred.   204

28   Report on Capt. Waldron's letter approved. Petitions: of
Henry Lane (see *L. P.* 8:79); of John van Horne (see *L. P.*
8:80); of Corn's van Horne (see *L. P.* 8:78); of Jacobus
Bruyn and Henry Wileman (see *L. P.* 8:84-85); of Richard
Alsup (see *L. P.* 8:81); of Gilbert Willet and Edw. Gatehouse (see *L. P.* 8:86), all referred. Boston reported very
unhealthy; quarantine measures.   205

Dec. 2 No quarantine against Boston considered necessary; only
smallpox raging there. Reports on the petitions: of Gilbert Willet and Edw. Gatehouse; of Jacobus Bruyn and
Henry Wileman (p. 205) approved. Salaries fixed.   209

14   Public money paid to the late treasurer to be accounted for.
Petitions: of John du Puy (see *L. P.* 8:95); of Stephen du
Blois (see *L. P.* 8:93); of Peter van der Lyn and Thos.
Fell (see *L. P.* 8:94), referred. Reports on petitions: of
John van Horne; of Corn's van Horne; of Henry Lane
(p. 205), approved. Warrants for salaries signed.   211

21   Order on petition by Joseph Budd, John Hoit, Caleb Willet,
Humphrey Underhill, Joseph Horton, George Lane, Daniel
Lane, Moses Lop, David Horton, John Turner, Johath
Lynch, Peter Hatfield, James Travis, Isaac Covert, Benj.
Brown, John Horton, David Ogden and Wm Yeomans
(see *L. P.* 8:91).   216

1722

Jan. 11 Petitions: of Lancaster Symes (see *L. P.* 8:98); of Samuel
Hunt and Dan'l Brondage (see *L. P.* 8:92, 100); of Robert
Walter, Rip van Dam, David Provoost, Hendrick Hansen,
And'w Coeymans, Abr'm Gouverneur, Lawrence Claesen,
Stephen Groesbeck and John Dunbar (see *L. P.* 8:99), referred. Reports on petitions of Jas. Budd et al. (p. 216)
of Stephen du Blois; of Peter van der Lyn and Thos. Fell
(p. 211); of Rich'd Alsup (p. 205); of John du Puy (p. 211),
approved. Account of public moneys delivered by Cath.
de Peyster wife of the late treasurer Abr'm de Peyster,
and orders concerning it.   217

18   Petition of Garret van Horn, John Read, Thos. Bayeux,
Stephen Richards, Thos. Clarke, Rip van Dam jr, Henry
Cuyler, Peter Bristed et al (see *L. P.* 8:103); mayor and

corporation to be heard on this petition. Reports on petitions: of Hunt and Brondage (p. 217); of Rob't Walter et al.; of Lancaster Symes, approved. Petition of Francis Harrison, Lewis Morris jr, John Spratt, John Schuyler, Abr'm Wendell and John Haskall (see *L. P.* 8:106) referred.   223

22   Report on petition of Francis Harrison et al (p. 223) approved.   226

23   Order on petition of Thos. Jansen and Thos. Cock in behalf of themselves and inhabitants of Marbletown (see *L. P.* 8:110). Warrant of survey granted to Garrit van Horn et al (p. 223).   227

Feb. 1   Letters from Albany received. Petitions: of mayor etc. of of New York (see *L. P.* 8:111); of Abr'm Ketteltas, Thos. Lynch, Rynier Hild and Anth'y Duane (see *L. P.* 8:115), referred. Memorial of Abr'm de Peyster jr treasurer (see *N. Y. col. mss,* 64:23) referred. Map of the soil on East river petitioned for by Garret van Horne submitted by the surveyor general (see *L. P.* 8:114).   229

8   Order on petition of Gabriel Ludlow, Fred'k Seabring, Andrew Clarke, and Thos. Fell customs officers, concerning their salaries. Report on petition of Garrit van Horn et al. (p. 223, 227, 229) referred to mayor etc. of New York. Council to meet in a fortnight. List of persons indebted to the weighhouse called for. Surveyor general to survey Capt. John Evans' patent, and a committee to hear testimony about it.   231

23   Report of testimony given by John d'Honneur 40 years old, Francis Wessells 70 years old, Charles Philippse 33 years old, Cornelius Low 52 years old, and Wm Bond 67 years old, concerning the highlands and boundary of Evans' patent; surveyor general to survey accordingly. Order concerning public moneys. Hearing on the petitions of Abr'm Ketteltas and mayor etc. of New York against grant to Garrit van Horn (see *L. P.* 8:103, 111, 115). Petitions: of Rob't Walter and Henry Beekman (see *L. P.* 8:119); of Edw. Blagg and Johs. Hey (see *L. P.* 8:127); of Robert Crook (see *L. P.* 8:121); of Thos. Braine (see *L. P.* 8:118); of George Burnet (see *L. P.* 8:122), referred.   235

24   Patents granted: to Robert Walter and Henry Beekman; to Thos. Braine; to George Burnet (p. 235). Petitions: of John Chambers (see *L. P.* 8:130); of John Teller and Jacobus Stoutenburgh (see *L. P.* 8:129), referred. Survey of White Plains laid before the council and referred (see *L. P.* 8:124-25).   240

1722   **v. 13**

Mar. 1   Report on White Plains claims (see *L. P.* 8:126) approved.
          Patent granted: to John Chambers (p. 240); to Edw. Blagg
          and Johs. Hey (p. 235). Account of Phil. Livingston for
          public expenses (see *N. Y. col. mss,* 64:39-40) referred.
          Orange and Ulster county boundaries. Gov. Burnet in-
          tends to go to New Jersey. Accounts of the weighhouse
          referred.   244

      3   Ordinance for altering sessions of the court of common pleas
          in Ulster read and ordered printed. Petition of Godfried
          de Wulfen (see *L. P.* 8:142) referred. Letter from the com-
          missioners of Indian affairs at Albany; opinion of council
          on it; persons tampering with the Indians to be punished. 246

     24   Report on Phil. Livingston's account to be further consid-
          ered. Patent granted to Godfr. de Wulfen (p. 246). Peti-
          tion of Hugh Munro (see *L. P.* 8:144) referred. Warrants
          for salaries signed.   253

May 17   Order on memorial of Andrew Fresneau and René Hett (see
          N. Y. col. mss, 64:57). Warrants: to Phil. Livingston for
          public expenses; to John Schuyler for same (see *N. Y. col.
          mss,* 64:47). Petition of Phil. Livingston (see *N. Y. col.
          mss,* 64:56) referred. Account of Lawrence Claesen (see
          N. Y. col. mss, 64:60-61) referred.   255

p. m.   Report on memorial of Andrew Fresneau and René Het con-
          firmed. Warrants signed.   257

     30   Memorial of And'w Fresneau and René Het (see *N. Y. col.
          mss,* 64:62) referred. Map of Evans' patent laid before the
          council. Legislative minutes (see *Jour.* 1:479).   258

June 1   Report on memorial of Fresneau and Het (p. 258) approved
          (see *N. Y. col. mss,* 64:64), and order thereon. Report on
          accounts of Phil. Livingston and of Lawrence Claesen
          (p. 255); warrants to issue.   263

      8   Warrants to Phil. Livingston and to Lawrence Claesen
          signed. Minutes sent home.   265

     14   Legislative minutes (see *Jour.* 1:480). List of patents granted
          before 1709 called for; also list of quitrents. Public papers
          in the hands of the late surveyor general to be delivered to
          Dr Colden. Table of fees for the admiralty court to be es-
          tablished. Warrants for salaries signed.   266

     16   Proclamation to issue forbidding traffic to Canada. War-
          rant to Thos. Wildman for expenses on a journey to the
          Seneca country. Legislative minutes (see *Jour.* 1:480).   270

     21   Legislative minutes (see *Jour.* 1:480). Warrant signed. Order
          on petition of Gasper Springsteen et al. (see *N. Y. col. mss,*
          64:84).   271

     22   Legislative minutes (see *Jour.* 1:480).   273

1722   **v. 13**

26   Legislative minutes (see *Jour.* 1:481). Petition of Charles
Congreve (see *L. P.* 8:162) referred.   276

28   Legislative minutes (see *Jour.* 1:482). List of patents granted
before 1709 to be examined. Order on petitions of Joseph
Sackett and William Doughty (see *N. Y. col. mss,* 64:91-92)
in reply to Gasper Springsteens (p. 271). Patent granted
to Charles Congreve (p. 276).   278

July 3   Legislative minutes (see *Jour.* 1:483).   283

5   Legislative minutes (see *Jour.* 1:484). Hearing on the northwest line of Evans' patent (see *L. P.* 8:185) postponed to
obtain affidavits of Peter Cortelyou, Corn's Cuyper and
Peter Herring; Hanns and Johannes Hey, Adrian and Gisbert Crum, Albert Mine et al. summoned as witnesses.
Table of fees in the admiralty court referred.   287

6-7   Legislative minutes (see *Jour.* 1:484-86).   291

7   Mr Clows called before the council to show by what author-
p. m.   ity he acts as surveyor.   298

12   Report on patents granted before 1709. Mr Clows makes
his submission and is dismissed after a reprimand. Proclamation to issue revoking all commissions given and appointments made by former governors, except of militia
officers, clerks of the council and assembly, and revenue
officers. Witnesses to be examined under oath concerning
bounds of Evans' patent.   301

16   Time of supreme court sessions changed (see *N. Y. col. mss,*
64:103). Table of fees in the admiralty court to be printed
(see *N. Y. col. mss,* 64:72-73, 102).   304

28   Letter received from the governor of Boston relating to Indian affairs.   304

Aug. 2   Order concerning report on patents granted before 1709 (see
N. Y. col. mss, 64:100, 107). David Provoost and others
[not named] to be examined about Evans' patent. Memorial of Capt. Edw'd Smith, commanding the Greyhound
man-of-war referred (see *N. Y. col. mss,* 64:110-11).   306

8   Archibald Kennedy appointed collector and receiver general
of the revenues, and collector of customs vice Thos. Byerley, and sworn in. Order on memorial of Capt. Edw.
Smith (p. 306; see *N. Y. col. mss,* 64:113, 118). Hearing on
the northwest line of Evans' patent fixed.   308

9   Caveat against the surveyor general's return of the northwest line of Evans' patent dismissed (see *L. P.*8:185). Order
on petition of Jacobus and Samuel Swartwout on behalf of
themselves and Thos. Swartwout, Peter Gamer, Harmanus
van Wege and Bernardus Swartwout against Johannes
Westphalia (see *N. Y. col. mss,* 64:152).   310

1722   v. 13

13   Minute of commissioners relating to the bounds of Evans'
      patent. Letters from Gov. Alex. Spotswood on board the
      Enterprize man-of-war at Sandy Hook and from Gov.
      Sir Wm Keith of Pennsylvania about Indian affairs; confer-
      ence to be held with them.   311

14   Order on petition of Jacobus and Samuel Swartwout vs
      Edw'd Blagg. Account of Thos. Byerley's disbursements
      (see *N. Y. col. mss*, 64:121-26) referred. Conference between
      Gov. Burnet, the governor of Virginia with Mr Robinson
      and Mr Harrison, and the governor of Pennsylvania with
      Mr French and Mr Hambleton about treating with the five
      nations at Albany.   326

15   Stores of the governor of Virginia to be free from duty.   334

27   Propositions to be made by Gov. Burnet to the five nations;
Albany   approved by council. Propositions to be made by gover-
      nors of Virginia and Pennsylvania.   335

p. m. Indian conference. Gov. Burnet makes his propositions.   344

28   Address of the justices and inhabitants of Schenectady. Peti-
      tion of Johann Christian Garlach, Wm and Nicholas York,
      and Elias Garlach for license to purchase land at Skoharee
      referred. Major Abr'm Schuyler to live among the Senecas
      for one year.   345

29   Gov. Spotswood of Virginia makes his propositions to the
      five nations.   346

30   Hearing on the caveat of Hendrick van Rensselaer vs
      Coenrat Borgharet and Elias van Schaick postponed. John
      Baptist van Eps arrested for spreading false reports among
      the Indians.   347

31   License to purchase land granted to Johann Christ. Garlach
      et al (p. 345). Order on address of the justices etc. of
      Schenectady (p. 345). John B. van Eps to be prosecuted.
      Petition of Lieut. John Scott (see *L. P.* 8:188) referred.   347

p. m. License granted to Lieut. John Scott. Petition of Coenrat
      Borghaert and Elias van Schaick (see *L. P.* 8:35, 156) dis-
      missed.   348

Sep. 4   John Baptist van Eps admitted to bail in the sum of £500.
      Instructions for Major Abr'm Schuyler.   349

      8   Indian conference; Gov. Spotswood [Assarigoe=cutlass],
      Gov. Sir Wm Keith [Onas=pen], Gov. Burnet [Corlear]
      and five nations. Minutes sent home.   354

Vol. 14, 1722-25

1722

Sep. 25   Additional Instructions to Gov. Burnet relating to trade;
Fort George   proclamation to issue thereon. Boundaries between the
      five nations and Virginia Indians established.   Receiver

1722   **v. 14**

general to join the committee on patents granted before
1709. Petitions of Christ'r Denn (see *L. P.* 8:198) and of
Anne Hooglandt (see *L. P.* 8:145) referred. Warrant to
issue to Thos. Byerley for disbursements. Warrants for
salaries signed.   1

29 Mayor and sheriff of New York and mayor of Albany renominated; Philipp Verplanck sheriff of Albany.   9

Oct. 3 Legislative minutes (see *Jour.* 1:487). Petitions: of Lewis
Morris, Cadwallader Colden, James Alexander, Abr'm van
Horn, John Collins and Marg't Veder, wife of Harm.
Veder (see *L. P.* 8:189-190, 193); of Francis Harrison et al
(see *L. P.* 8:194); of Lieut. John Scott, commanding at
Fort Hunter (see *L. P.* 8:197), all referred.   10

10 Patents granted: to Lewis Morris et al.; to Francis Harrison
et al.; to John Scott (p. 10); to Christ'r Denn (p. 1). Memorial of Cadw. Colden (see *N. Y. col. mss*, 64:151) referred. Legislative minutes (see *Jour.* 1:488). Warrant to
issue to Peter Schuyler jr, Jacob Verplanck, Johs. Visger
jr, Harmanus Schuyler, Johs. van den Bergh, Peter Gro-
endyk and Peter van der Heyden, for residing in the
Seneca country (see *N. Y. col. mss*, 64:135-36). Warrant to
Wm Pinthrop and Charles Burn for serving as smiths
in the Seneca country. Swartwout vs Blagg.   13

14 Mayor, sheriff etc. of New York sworn in. Warrants signed.   18

17 Legislative minutes (see *Jour.* 1:488).   19

18 Legislative minutes (see *Jour.* 1:489). Complaint of Swartwout vs Blagg dismissed with a reprimand to the latter.   23

p. m. Legislative minutes (see *Jour.* 1:489). Warrant to issue to
Cadw. Colden for expenses (p. 13).   25

23 Legislative minutes (see *Jour.* 1:490). Petition of Stephen
du Blois (see *L. P.* 9:3) referred.   29

24 Legislative minutes (see *Jour.* 1:491). Patent granted to
Stephen du Blois (p. 29).   32

25-27 Legislative minutes (see *Jour.* 1:492-93).   35

27 Vessel with palatines arrived from Holland; quarantine
measures. Time for order in regard of Indian presents
from Boston extended.   41

31-Nov. 1 Legislative minutes (see *Jour.* 1:495).   45

1 Order on petition by Lancaster Symes (see *L. P.* 9:6).   47

29 Petition of Wm Burnet jr, Gerardus Beekman, Arch'd
Kennedy and David Provoost (see *L. P.* 9:9) referred.
Order on petition of justices and inhabitants of Richmond
county (see *N. Y. col. mss*, 65:29). Warrants signed: to
Gabriel Ludlow clerk of the assembly for drawing bills;
to Robert Elliston custom house clerk for examining

1722   **v. 14**

revenue entries; to Wm Bradford for stationery to the
assembly.   51

Dec. 1 License to purchase Indian lands granted to Wm Burnet jr
et al (p. 51). Report on the petition of justices etc of
Richmond county (see *N. Y. col. mss*, 65:30). Minute of
the council of Virginia about Indian boundaries. Report
on the petition of Garrit van Horn et al.   53

7 Claims of George Clarke on behalf of Horatio Walpole
auditor-general, allowed; warrants to him to issue (see
N. Y. col. mss, 65:3). Memorial of Archibald Kennedy receiver-general on quitrents referred (see *N. Y. col.
mss*, 65:44). Warrants for salaries of Francis Harrison
judge of the admiralty, James Alexander attorney-general,
and Cadw. Colden surveyor-general, signed.   60

11 Warrants to Horatio Walpole signed. Account of Sec'y
Clarke for incidental expenses (see *N. Y. col. mss*, 65:33)
referred.   65

14 Letter received from Sec'y Willard of Boston on Indian affairs, and referred; report of council on it (see *N. Y. col.
mss*, 65:35). Petition of Lewis and Mordecai Gomez (see
N. Y. col. mss, 65:37) referred.   66

20 Reports: on the receiver-general's memorial (p. 60); on
petition of Lewis and Mordecai Gomez (p. 66); on Sec.
Clarke's accounts recommitted. Orders on petitions: of
Francis Child (see *L. P.* 9:13); of Wm Bradford (see
N. Y. col. mss, 65:34). Warrants for salaries signed. Order
concerning the salary of the clerk of the council (13:209). 72

1723

Jan. 11 Report on the petition of Francis Child (p. 72) to lie on the
table. Petition of Francis Harrison et al (p. 10; see *L. P.*
9:21) granted. New warrant signed for Wm Bradford
(p. 72).   79

17 Petition of John Jost Petri and Conrad Rickert (see *L. P.*
9:21) granted. New warrants signed for Wm Bradford

Feb. 7 Memorial of Archibald Kennedy concerning needed repairs
of the customhouse referred. Petition of Cornelius Low
for land under water dismissed and prayer of Fran. Child
(p. 72, 79) to be granted to them jointly. Warrant to
Sec. Clarke (p. 65, 72) signed. Attorney-general's and
chief justice's opinion on land grants; council's report
thereon.   83

28 Wm Dugdale high sheriff of New York gives bonds for
due execution of his office; David Provoost and Abr'm
van Horn sureties. Letter from Gov. Wm Dummer of
Boston. Instructions to Wm Sailer, Elisha Cooke, Spencer

1723   v. 14

Phips and John Stoddard, Massachusetts commissioners
to treat with the five nations at Albany; opinion of council thereon. Petitions referred: of Robert Walter, Rip
van Dam and Hendrick Hansen (see *L. P.* 9:34); of Phil.
Schuyler and David Provoost (see *L. P.* 9:35).   102

Mar. 7   Patents granted: to Robert Walter et al; to Phil. Schuyler
and David Provoost (p. 102).   Petitions referred: of
J. Christ. Garlick, Wm York, Joh. Lawyer, Joh. and
Hendrick Schuffer (see *L. P.* 9:8, 28); of Wm York,
Jacob Fred'k Lawyer and Nich's York (see *L. P.* 8:136;
9:23); of Joh. Conr. Weiser, Peter Wagoner and Peter
Fick (see *L. P.* 9:37); of Edw. Bromhead (see *L. P.* 9:36);
of Dederick Martinstock (see *L. P.* 9:38). Order on peti-
tion by Rip van Dam, Paul Richards, Helena de Key,
Jean Tothill, Abr'm de Peyster for himself brothers and
sisters, Garrit van Horn, Henry Cuyler, Isaac Gouverneur,
John Read, Peter Bristed, Thos. Bayeux, Sam'l Payton,
Corn's Low and Francis Child (see *L. P.* 9:39); granted.
Petition of Ger. Beekman (see *L. P.* 9:41) referred.   111

9   Reports on petitions: of Joh. Christ. Garlick et al; of Joh.
Conrad Weiser et al; of Edw. Bromhead; of Ded. Martinstock (p. 111) approved and petitions granted.   120

14   Richard Bradley sworn in as attorney-general vice John
Rayner deceased. Warrants for salaries signed.   124

21   Letter from Gov. Gordon Saltonstall of Connecticut; and
act of Connecticut assembly concerning the boundary line;
report of council thereon. Thos. Bayeux appointed um-
pire in re Lt. Edw. Smith and Lewis Gomez.   125

28   Petition of Wm Bowen, Henry Huff, Arent Potman, Wau-
ter Swart, Wm Sixbury, Sarah Grout and Thos. Wildman,
who have spent a long time at hard labor among the
Indians, for license to purchase land on Canada creek referred. Order on petition of Robert Walter and other
officers of the admiralty court (see *N. Y. col. mss*, 65:63).
Minute of council of Boston. Quarantine against Jamaica.
License granted to Wm Bowen et al.   135

Ap. 18   Gov. Burnet again takes the oath as chancellor. Memorial
of Arch'd Kennedy (see *N. Y. col. mss*, 65:69) referred.
Accounts of Abr'm Schuyler (see *N. Y. col. mss*, 65:66)
referred. Petition of Martha Heathcote, Jacobus van
Cortlandt, Nehemiah Palmer and Henry Fowler (see *L. P.*
9:52) referred.   140

19   Order on report on Arch. Kennedy's memorial (p. 140).
Warrants to issue: to Arch. Kennedy for paying Mr
Hamilton employed by him in suits for quitrents; to

1723   **v. 14**

Abr'm Schuyler for Indian expenses. Report on the petition of Martha Heathcote (p. 140) approved.   144

22 Warrant for paying Andrew Hamilton signed. Gov. Burnet is going to New Jersey.   147

May 9 Patent granted to Lewis Morris et al (13:199, 203; see *L. P.*
9:55). Deposition of Sam'l Clows, coroner of Queens
county, concerning Thos. Lynstead a counterfeiter received (see *N. Y. col. mss,* 65:78); order to search the
houses of Sherrard, Thos. Kable and Deborah Wright the
supposed wife of Thos. Lynstead, at Oysterbay, also the
house of Thomas Pullen in New York. Order on an affidavit of Jacob Cuyendall and Thos. Quick of Minisinck
in Orange county concerning Indian robberies. Warrant
to Lawrence Claesen for expenses on a journey to the
Senecas. Petition of Joseph Loyd for remission of duty
on slaves referred. Indian presents from Boston to be
admitted free from duty.   148

14 Legislative minutes (see *Jour.* 1:495). Sheriff of New York
reports that he has not found any thing in Thos. Pullen's
house, about counterfeit bills (see *N. Y. col. mss,* 65:81).
Warrant for Lawrence Claesen (p. 148) signed.   153

15 Thos. Sherrard, Thos. Kable and Thos. Pullen examined
about Thos. Lynstead (see *N. Y. col. mss,* 65:82-83) and
dismissed. Orders to examine Samuel Burcham of Oysterbay and others. Order on petition of Joseph Loyd (p.
153).   158

17 Legislative minutes (see *Jour.* 1:496). Memorial of Arch'd
Kennedy concerning incidental expenses in the receiver-
general's office referred.   160

23 Legislative minutes (see *Jour.* 1:496). Petition of Daniel
Chubb (see *L. P.* 9:64) to lie on the table. Warrant to
issue to Arch'd Kennedy for incidental expenses (p. 160).
Petition of Richard Bradley and Isaac Bobin for land
referred.   162

25-30 Legislative minutes (see *Jour.* 1:497).   167

30 Petition of Corn's Low (see *N. Y. col. mss,* 65:89) referred. 167

June 6 Legislative minutes (see *Jour.* 1:498). Petition of Francis
Harrison for confirmatory patent to his share of 5000
acres granted in 1714 to Mary Tatham, Thos. Braine,
James Graham and John Haskall referred. Memorial of
Jeremiah Schuyler, Joannis jr, and Joannis C. Cuyler for
their and Lawrence Claesen's and Jurian Hogan's services in the Seneca country (see *N. Y. col. mss,* 65:93) referred. Petition of Rich'd Jerrard and Wm Bull (see
L. P. 9:70) referred. Petition of Lewis and Mordecai

1723   **v. 14**

Gomez concerning import duties referred. Petition of
Peterse Mebee (see *L. P.* 9:69) to lie on the table.   169

13   Legislative minutes (see *Jour.* 1:498). Patent granted to
Francis Harrison (p. 169). Warrants to issue to Jeremiah
Schuyler et al (p. 169). Petition of Rich'd Bradley and
Isaac Bobin (p. 162) granted. Warrants for salaries etc
signed.   171

14   Legislative minutes (see *Jour.* 1:499). Petition of Lewis
and Mordecai Gomez (p. 169) granted. Patent granted
to Rich'd Jerrard and Wm. Bull (p. 169).   175

20   Legislative minutes (see *Jour.* 1:501). Patent granted to
Conrad Weiser jr, Johs. Lawyer jr, and Peter Wagoner
(see *L. P.* 9:58).   181

27   Legislative minutes (see *Jour.* 1:501). Memorial of Archibald Kennedy concerning public funds; and, petition of
John Pieterse Mebee (see *L. P.* 9:80) referred.   183

28–July 6   Legislative minutes (see *Jour.* 1:502-6).   184–97

18   Allowance for the company of one captain, two lieutenants
and eight men who are to go to the Seneca country for
a year fixed. Warrants: to Jacob Verplanck for services
in the Seneca country; to Derick Egbert doorkeeper,
Robert Crannel sergeant at arms and Catherine Post for
services to the assembly.   197

Aug. 10   Royal mandamus appointing Abr'm van Horn and William
Provoost to the council; they are sworn in and take their
places. Further allowance for the men going into the
Seneca country; premium set on knowledge of the Indian
language. Petition of Wm Apple relating to land in the
city dismissed. House and lot of Richard Elliot, cooper,
of New York city, escheated and granted to Lewis Rou
(see *L. P.* 9:85).   200

15   Report of the committee on boundary act of Connecticut;
order of council thereon. Report on table of fees in the
chancery court and in the court of appeals, of governor
and council referred.   208

22   Ordinance of fees reported and to be printed (see *N. Y.
col. mss,* 65:120). Ordinance relating to the recording of
deeds to be sent to county clerks (see *N. Y. col. mss,*
65:121). Ordinance of fees in the court of appeals (see
N. Y. col. mss, 65:117) to lie on the table.   233

Sep. 12   Petition of Wm Bowen et al (see *L. P.* 9:63) referred.
Order on memorial by Capt. Henry Holland (see *N. Y.
col. mss,* 65:131). Accounts of the auditor and treasurer
(see *N. Y. col. mss,* 65:128) referred. Robert Walter renominated mayor, Wm Dugdale sheriff of New York,

1723   **v. 14**

Peter van Brugh mayor, Thos. Williams sheriff of Albany.

Indian trade from Albany to Canada.   234

14   Patent granted to Wm Bowen et al (p. 234). Report on
treasurer's accounts (see *N. Y. col. mss*, 65:130) approved.
Petition of Archibald Kennedy for land referred (see *L. P.*
9:105). Warrants for salaries signed. Warrant to George
Clarke for Horatio Walpole. Gov. Burnet is going to
New Jersey.   238

16   Journal of Abr'm Schuyler in the Seneca country received;
warrant to him for expenses signed.   241

Oct. 14   Mayor and sheriff of New York sworn in.   242

Dec. 12   Additional instructions for Gov. Burnet relating to his assent
to private acts. Letter from Gov. Saltonstall and resolution of Connecticut assembly about boundary line received
and referred. Copy of an order of council to be sent to
the receiver-general. Memorial of Archibald Kennedy
about incidental office expenses (see *N. Y. col. mss*, 66:26)
referred. Warrants for salaries etc signed.   243

13   Report on letter of Gov. Saltonstall about the boundary line.
Warrant to issue to Arch'd Kennedy for office expenses.   248

p. m.   Warrants for salaries etc signed. Warrant to Charles
Burns Indian interpreter for services at Mount Burnet,
certified to by Lieut. Wm Helling stationed there.   251

16   Order on petition of Robert Willasy (see *N. Y. col. mss*,
66:30).   254

30   Commissioners for running the Connecticut line to meet at
Rye in February following.   255

1724

Jan. 23   Order of the king in council for restitution of Spanish
property taken in the war. Time in which to buy
Indian land as per license granted to Wm Burnet jr et al
extended (see *L. P.* 9:90-91). Warrant to Charles Burns
(p. 251) signed. Instructions for Connecticut boundary
commissioners to be prepared.   257

27   Letter from Gov. Saltonstall concerning the boundaries
received. Report on instructions to commissioners approved; allowances to them fixed; commissions for them
to be prepared.   263

31   Warrants to Francis Harrison, Cadw. Colden, David Provoost and Johs. Jansen, Connecticut boundary commis-
sioners for expenses signed.   266

Mar. 19   Petition of And'w Fresneau and John du Puy (see *L. P.* 9:94)
referred. Connecticut commissioners fail to meet the New
York commissioners; new meeting fixed. Warrants for
salaries signed.   267

1724 v. 14

Ap. 2 Report on the petition of John Pieterse Mebee (p. 183) approved and warrants of survey granted. Account of Geo. Clarke for enrolling laws referred. Resolution concerning the Connecticut boundary line; allowance to commissioners fixed and instruction for them. 271

8 License to purchase Indian land granted to Hartman van Deker, Roolof Stayley, Gerrit Spender, Ryndert Skeefort, Christ'r Hillse, Charles Aker, Lambert Stenbergh, Johannes Lager, Derick Login and Nicholas Aker, palatines (see *L. P.* 9:95-96). Gov. Burnet is going to New Jersey. 274

May 1 Royal assent to the New York act for running the Connecticut boundary line. Report of the Connecticut boundary commissioners. 275

15 Legislative minutes (see *Jour.* 1:507). Opinion of council on a letter from Capt. Peter Salgard commanding the Greyhound man-of-war relating to the issue of rum to shipwrights, stopped by the admiralty board. 291

June 13 Petition of Jacob Sharp, Christ'r Hagatorn, Jacob Shoemaker and other palatines (see *L. P.* 9:101) referred. Address of Justices Wm Willet, Isaac Hicks and Richard Floyd of Westchester county (see *N. Y. col. mss*, 66:80) referred. New license to purchase land granted to Wm Burnet jr, to include the name of Rob't Livingston jr (see *L. P.* 9:99). Petition of John Haskoll (see *L. P.* 9:108) referred. Warrant to Lawrence Claesen for services in the Seneca country (see *N. Y. col. mss*, 66:77). Petition of Rich'd Jerrard (see *L. P.* 9:98) referred. Warrants for salaries signed. Report on the petition of Jacob Sharp et al approved and order thereon (see *Doc. hist. N. Y.* 3:722-23; Q 3:431-32). Patents granted to John Hasskoll and to Richard Jerrard. 298

15 Order on petition of Stephen and Paul Richards, Jacob Leisler et al (see *N. Y. col. mss*, 66:79). Letter from Gov. Wm Dummer of Massachusetts on Indian conference received; also instructions from him to John Schuyler and John Stoddard deputies for Massachusetts at the Indian conference; opinion of council thereon. 305

23 Legislative minutes (see *Jour.* 1:509). Answer of mayor of New York to the petition of Stephen and Paul Richards (p. 305) referred. Petition of Wm Bull (see *L. P.* 9:106) referred. 308

24 Answer of mayor etc of New York (p. 308) withdrawn. Legislative minutes (see *Jour.* 1:509). Connecticut boundary line. 311

1724   **v. 14**

29   Legislative minutes (see *Jour.* 1:510). Patent granted to Wm
      Bull.   314
July 9   Legislative minutes (see *Jour.* 1:510-11).   317
      11   Order on the account of Sec. Clarke for incidental expenses.
           Warrant of survey granted to Philipp Pipoon and Abr'm
           Gouverneur (see *L. P.* 9:110).   318
13-16 Legislative minutes (see *Jour.* 1:511-12).   320
      16   Petition of Marc Legaur (see *N. Y. col. mss*, 66:97-98) referred.
           Allowance to officers employed in the trial of pirates to be
           fixed. Warrant to John Haskall for carrying notice of
           intended survey to Connecticut (p. 311) signed. Order on
           new answer of mayor etc of New York to the petition of
           Stephen and Paul Richards et al (p. 305, 308, 311; see *N. Y.
           col. mss*, 66:99).   323
      18   Legislative minutes (see *Jour.* 1:513). Report on allowances
           to Marc Legaur, Joseph Whittemore and John Callean
           (see *N. Y. col. mss*, 66:97-98, 100, 114) approved and war-
           rants signed.   326
      21   Legislative minutes (see *Jour.* 1:514). Warrants to officers
           employed in the trial of pirates to be made out according
           to report (see *N. Y. col. mss*, 66:104). Johs. Glen and
           Johs. Wemp to clear the road from the Mohawk river car-
           rying place to Wood creek going into Oneida lake.   330
22-24 Legislative minutes (see *Jour.* 1:515-17).   333-40
Aug. 6   Royal approval of acts of assembly. Warrants to issue: to
           James Alexander for drawing bills of assembly; to Gabriel
           Ludlow clerk of the house, for incidental charges; to Henry
           Vernon for drawing bills; to David Le Tellier for translat-
           ing Mrs Montour's deposition; to the doorkeeper of the
           assembly for whitewashing the chamber etc; and to Cath.
           Post for use of her house by assembly committees. Peti-
           tion of Lewis Morris jr and Andries Coeymans (see *L. P.*
           9:119) referred. Warrants to James Alexander advocate-
           general, Richard Nicholls register, Wm Dugdale provost
           marshall, Robert Crannell marshall of the admiralty court,
           Isaac Bobn deputy secretary, Abr'm Gouverneur French
           interpreter, and Rodrigo Pacheco Spanish interpreter,
           signed.   342
      27   Warrants to James Alexander etc. signed. Petitions re-
           ferred: of Jacob Sharp et al (see *L. P.* 9:114-16); of Wm
           Bradford (see *N. Y. col. mss*, 66:121); of John Scott jr (see
           L. P. 9:118). Report on petition of Jacob Sharp (see *Doc.
           hist. N. Y.* 3:725-26; Q 3:434-35).   346
      3   Patent granted to Lewis Morris jr and Abr'm Coeymans (p.
           342). Warrants to issue: for paying account of commis-

sioners to sign bills of credit (see *N. Y. col. mss*, 66:130);
to Jacobus Kip and Corn's van Horne for material to repair Fort George. Account of the auditor-general referred (see *N. Y. col. mss*, 66:128). Gov. Burnet intends
to go to Albany and renominates now Robert Walter to
be mayor and Wm Dugdale sheriff of New York, mayor
and sheriff of Albany are renominated. Warrant to issue
for the salary of the auditor-general. Warrants signed.　　349

Oct. 1　Memorial of Wm Bradford concerning unprinted laws of
Gov. Dongan's time referred. Warrants for salaries
signed. Minutes sent home per Capt. Downing.　　351

　　8　Edward Blood commanding at Mount Burnet reports on illegal trade to Canada carried on by Nicholas, son of
Philipp Schuyler and Jacob, son of Hermanus Wendell,
with affidavit concerning it by Charles Buckley, sergeant
at Mount Burnet; minutes of Indian commissioners about
it received and council's opinion on it. Gov. Burnet communicates the propositions made by him to the six nations
on Sep. 14, 15, 17, 19 and 20.　　353

　14　Robert Walter sworn in as mayor, Wm Dugdale as sheriff
and both as justices of the peace of New York.　　374

　15　Petition of Abr'm van Horne, Wm Provoost, Wm Burnet jr
and Phil. Livingston (see *L. P.* 9:125) referred. Warrant
to issue to Johs. Glen and Johs. Wemp for improving the
carrying place to Wood creek, upon certificate of Major
Goose van Schaick and David van der Heyden (see *N. Y.
col. mss*, 66:140). License granted to Abr'm van Horne
et al.　　374

　29　Letter from Allured Papple, secretary of the lords of trade
(see *N. Y. col. mss*, 66:110-12) with a petition of London
merchants trading to New York; king's order on the petition; extract from the minutes of the board of trade.
Memorial of Rip van Dam and other merchants of New
York (see *N. Y. col. mss*, 66:143) referred. Petitions referred: of Thos. Noxon (see *L. P.* 9:126); and of John
Mebee (see *L. P.* 9:129).　　375

Nov. 6　Report on petition of London merchants (p. 375).　　[385]

　19　Accounts of Jacobus Kip and Corn's van Horn, managers
for repairing Fort George referred.　　402

　26　Report on the memorial of Rip van Dam et al (p. 375).
Warrant to Jacobus Kip and Corn's van Horn signed. Dr
Colden's report (see *N. Y. col. mss*, 66:124) to be filed in
the secretary's office. Petition of Nathaniel Osborn (see
L. P. 9:131) referred.　　402

1724   v. 14

Dec. 16   Letter from Lt. Gov. Wm Dummer of Massachusetts, about
           war against the eastern Indians (see *N. Y. col. mss*, 66:161)
           referred. Warrants for salaries signed.   408
p. m.   Report on Gov. Dummer's letter (see *N. Y. col. mss*, 67:1). 413
1725
Jan. 14   Petition of Corn's Low, Thos. Bayeux, Peter Bristed and
           Samuel Payton (see *L. P.* 9:133) referred. Order on peti-
           tion of members of the French church (see *N. Y. col. mss*,
           67:5; and, *Doc. hist. N. Y.* 3;469; Q 3:284).   415
28   Order on the petition of Corn's Low et al (p. 415). Answer
           of Mr Moulinar and rest of consistory of French church
           (see *N. Y. col. mss*, 67:8-10); order thereon. Petition of
           Wm Sharpas and Rob't Livingston jr, clerks of the court
           of chancery about fees (see *N. Y. col. mss*, 66:16) referred.
           Sec. Clarke's accounts of incidental expenses referred.
           Petition of the heirs of Gerard Beekman and others (see
           L. P. 9:136) referred.   416
Feb. 11   Executors of David Provoost to hand in the accounts of the
           tonnage office. Proclamation to issue for the better ob-
           servance of the laws of trade (see *N. Y. col. mss*, 67:12).
           Secretary's fee-table to be scrutinized.   419
18   Report on petition of members of the French church (see
           N. Y. col. mss, 67:14-15; and, *Doc. hist. N. Y.* 3:474-75; Q
           3:286-87). Patent granted to the heirs of Gerard Beek-
           man et al (p. 416). Fees allowed to the clerks of the court
           of chancery (see *N. Y. col. mss*, 67:17).   420
Mar. 5   Report on the reply of Mr Moulinar etc (p. 416) to petition
           etc (see *N. Y. col. mss*, 67:20; and, *Doc. hist. N. Y.* 3:479-80;
           Q 3:289-90) and order thereon.   423
18   Warrants for salaries signed.   425
25   Additional instructions for Gov. Burnet about assenting to
           bills. Petition of Rodolph Stehle and Nich's Eckerd (see
           L. P. 9:138) referred and warrant of survey granted.   426
Ap. 3   Order on petition of Wm Halliday commanding the ship
           Princess Carolina (see *N. Y. col. mss*, 67:25). Isaac Hicks
           appointed Connecticut boundary commissioner, vice David
           Provoost deceased.   429
8   Instructions to be prepared for the commissioners appointed
           to survey the Connecticut boundary line. Instructions.   431
14   Warrants for expenses of surveying said line signed. Peti-
           tion of James Alexander, Andries Coeymans and heirs of
           Samuel Staats etc for land in the Mohawk country re-
           ferred. Archibald Kennedy's account of incidental
           charges in the receiver-general's office referred.   436

1725 v. 14

15 Francis Harrison, Cadw. Colden and Isaac Hicks sworn in
as commissioners to run the Connecticut line. Patent
granted to James Alexander et al (p. 436). Warrants: to Geo. Clarke for incidental office expenses; to
Archibald Kennedy. 438

19 James Livingston resigns as deputy to Surveyor-General
C. Colden. Colden proposes that either John Haskoll,
Robert Crooke, John Verkerke or Cornelius Low be appointed to survey the Connecticut line. Orders referred:
on petition of Peter Vallette, merchant of New York city,
about duty on negroes belonging to Capt. Rowden; on
memorial of William Bradford (see *N. Y. col. mss, 67:28*).
Order directing Mr Wileman, formerly deputy secretary
to search for missing acts of assembly (see *N. Y. col. mss,
67:29*). 440

29 Accounts of David Provoost late tonnage officer, handed in
by Mr van Wyck executor of his will; order thereon.
Petitions referred: of Robert Letice Hooper (see *N. Y.
col. mss, 67:33*); of Wm Burnet jr, Arch'd Kennedy, Rob't
Livingston, David Provoost, Catharine van Wyck and
Helena Santford, children and grandchild of David Pro-
voost deceased (see *L. P. 9:143*). Minutes sent home by
Capt. Downing, master of the ship Alexander. 442

May 13 Mr Wileman writes that he cannot find the missing acts (see
N. Y. col. mss, 67:29). Patent granted to Wm Burnet jr
et al (p. 442). Memorial of Jacobus Kip and Corn's van
Horne (see *N. Y. col. mss, 67:44-46*) referred. 444

20 Memorial of Francis Harrison, Cadw. Colden and Isaac
Hicks, Connecticut boundary commissioners; discussion
of it. Warrants signed: to Jacobus Kip and Corn's van
Horne for repairs in Fort George; to Mr Cuyler for re-
pairing the fort at Albany and the blockhouse at Sara-
toga (see *N. Y. col. mss, 67:42*); to boundary commission-
ers for expenses in surveying Connecticut line. Widow
Goose van Schaick appointed to furnish firewood to the
Albany garrison, vice Widow Hendrick Hansen. Gov.
Burnet is going to New Jersey. 445

Vol. 15, 1725-29

1725

May 25 Capt. Robert Walter presides. Capt. Woodside, master of
the brigantine Hopewell from Madeira to be examined as
to smallpox on that island; his mate Henry Fuller has
been carried sick to Goalets, a painter in Maiden Lane.
Quarantine measures. 1

1725

26-31   Quarantine measures (see *N. Y. col. mss*, 67:55, 57).   2-3

June 4   A pirate reported near Rockaway on Long Island. Order
for a cruize etc (see *N. Y. col. mss*, 67:48-49).   4

7-16   Quarantine measures.   4-6

16   A son of Sir Richard Everett and the children of Mr Good-
win passengers of the ship Samuel from London have been
ill with smallpox (see *N. Y. col. mss*, 67:56).   6

18   Letters received from Gov. Cranston of Rhode Island and
from Gov. Burnet in relation to John Drake.   6

23   Gov. Burnet returned. Passengers of the Hopewell allowed
to land on Bedlows island. Warrant to Barent Rynders
and John van Horne, owners of the Hopewell for provisioning quarantine guard put on board her. Warrants
signed: for salaries; to John Cuyler and Catharine van
Schaick for firewood and candles to Albany garrison; to
Rynders and van Horne; to John Moore, Thos. Shebow,
George Southal and John Gifford for services as quarantine guard.   6

Sep. 2   Legislative minutes (see *Jour.* 1:518). Marg't Codrington,
executor of Tho. Codrington in error vs Adolph Philippse
executor of Phil. French. Warrant to Wm Dugdale for
services in connection with quarantining the Hopewell.   8

15   Legislative minutes (see *Jour.* 1:519). Memorial of Jacobus
Kip and Corn's van Horne (see *N. Y. col. mss*, 67:62-64)
referred.   9

16   Warrant for their expenses signed. Warrants to issue to
Phil. Livingston for paying Herm. Vedder and company,
also the smith sent to the Onondaga country.   11

23   Warrants signed: for salaries; to Phil. Livingston for
Herm. Vedder, Isaac Staats, Andries Bradt jr, Hendrick
Wempt and Herm. van Slyck.   12

29   Legislative minutes (see *Jour.* 1:520). Order on petition of
Jan Mebee son of Jan Peterse Mebee (see *L. P.* 9:148).
Johannes Jansen nominated mayor, Wm Dugdale sheriff
of New York; Johs. Cuyler mayor and Thos. Williams
sheriff of Albany.   13

Oct. 14   Royal order appointing Phil. Livingston to the council vice
Gerard Beekman deceased. He is sworn in and takes his
seat. Mayor and sheriff sworn in. Legislative minutes
(see *Jour.* 1:520). Repairs needed, and to be made on the
fortifications of Schenectady, Fort Hunter and Mount Burnet; also new gun carriages at Albany. Minutes of Indian
commissioners received; they have had meetings with
some of the six nations and with Caghnawaga, Skawninada
and Roudix Indians.   15

1725   v. 15

19   Legislative minutes (see *Jour.* 1:521). Minute of the Indian
     commissioners laid before the council (see *N. Y. col. mss*,
     67:47). Warrant to issue to Lawrence Claesen for ser-
     vices in Onondaga country. Samuel Burchild to be re-
     leased from jail, James Smith the sole witness against him,
     not being a credible person.   17

27   Legislative minutes (see *Jour.* 1:521). Warrant to Lawrence
     Claesen signed.   18

28   Petitions referred: of Lewis Morris jr and Andries Coey-
     mans (see *L. P.* 9:155); of Wm York for himself and other
     palatines (see *L. P.* 9:151); of Lewis York and Wm York
     (see *L. P.* 9:152); of Robert Crannell jr (see *N. Y. col. mss*,
     67:79).   19

Nov. 2 Licenses to purchase land granted: to Wm York and pala-
     tines; to Lewis Morris jr and A. Coeymans; patent to
     Wm and Lewis York (p. 19). Warrant to issue to Rob't
     Crannel for keeping Samuel Burcham in jail. Legislative
     minutes (see *Jour.* 1:521). Order on deposition by Dr
     Johnson relating to Lettice Hooper's negroes (see *N. Y.
     col. mss*, 67:74). Smiths to be sent to the Onondagas and
     Senecas. Road from the carrying place to Wood creek.   21

4   Legislative minutes (see *Jour.* 1:522). Petition of Lewis
     Morris jr and Andries Coeymans (see *L. P.* 9:156) granted.
     Rob't Crannel allowed additional charges for keeping
     Sam'l Burcham.   23

8   Legislative minutes (see *Jour.* 522). Warrant for Robert
     Crannel signed.   25

9–10 Legislative minutes (see *Jour.* 523).   26–27

10   Minutes sent home by Peter Waye master of the brigantine
     Prince Fredik.   27

Dec. 16 Order on petition by Wm Sharpas town clerk and clerk of
     the peace of New York (see *N. Y. col. mss*, 67:86). War-
     rants for salaries signed.   28

1726

Feb. 10 Jacob Moene in error vs John Everson.   29

Mar. 17 Warrants for salaries signed. License to purchase Indian
     land granted upon petition of Abr'm van Horne, Wm
     Provoost, Mary Burnet jr and Phil. Livingstone (see *L. P.*
     9:159).   30

Ap. 6 Legislative minutes (see *Jour.* 1:524).   31

15   Order on petition of Johs. Roseboom and Hendrick Ten
     Eyck (see *L. P.* 9:164). Legislative minutes (see *Jour.*
     1:525).   33

21   License to catch porpoises granted to Lewis Hector Piot de
     Langloiserie (see *N. Y. col. mss*, 67:101). Legislative

1726   v. 15

minutes (see *Jour.* 1:526). Warrant of survey granted on
petition of Jacob Rutsen (see *L. P.* 9:168).   37

28   Legislative minutes (see *Jour.* 1:526). Petition of Johannes
Fisser (see *L. P.* 9:172) referred.   40

May 18   Legislative minutes (see *Jour.* 1:527). Petition of Evert
Wendell, Jan Janse Bleecker, Phil. Schuyler, Joannis ten
Broeck, David Abeel and others (see *L. P.* 10:4) referred.   41

p. m.-23   Legislative minutes (see *Jour.* 1:527).   42

23   Petitions referred: of George Burnet (see *L. P.* 10:9); of
Wm Jevon (see *L. P.* 10:10). Account of the auditor-
general referred.   43

24   Warrant to the auditor-general for auditing treasurer's accounts signed. Patents granted to Wm Jevon and to
George Burnet (p. 43). Legislative minutes (see *Jour.*
1:528).   45

June 7-8   Legislative minutes (see *Jour.* 1:530-31).   50

8   Order on petition of Moses Gombeaux (see *N. Y. col. mss,*
67:107).   51

9-14   Legislative minutes (see *Jour.* 1:532).   55

14   Warrants for salaries signed. Order on petition by Moses
Gombeaux (see *N. Y. col. mss,* 67:109).   56

15-16   Legislative minutes (see *Jour.* 1:534-35).   60-63

17   Order on petition of Charles and Francis Doughty (see
N. Y. col. mss, 67:110) and table of ferriage fees.   65

p. m.   Legislative minutes (see *Jour.* 1:536).   66

23   Warrants to Tunis Tiebout, Adrian Koning and Christ'r
Duyckin for work in Fort George signed. John Everson
in error vs Jacob Moene.   69

29   Wm Newman, Thos. Marsh, Wm Ward, Thos. Atkinson
and Robert Yates arrested on suspicion of piracy; on examination they say they are sailors of the ship Pleasant
from London, James Morris master, sprung a leak at sea.
Petition of Evert Wendell etc (p. 41) referred to the governor of Connecticut. Gov. Burnet is going to New
Jersey.   70

July 11   Capt. Walter presiding. Jacob Fleerboom vs Fred. Morris
in error.   71

28   Gov. Burnet returned. Jacob Fleerboom vs Fred. Morris
ex dem. Honan. John Everson vs Jacob Moene in error.
Wm Kirten and Andrew Law appointed pilots. Petition
of Henry Hoffe (see *L. P.* 10:12) referred. Warrant to
the clerk of the assembly for incidental charges signed.   72

Aug. 11   Assembly dissolved; writs to issue for election of a new one.
Gov. Burnet is going to Albany.   73

Sep. 27   Gov. Burnet returned. Legislative minutes (see *Jour.* 1:539).   74

1726   v. 15

29   Robert Lurting nominated mayor, Wm Dugdale sheriff of
     New York, Rutger Bleecker mayor, Thos. Williams sheriff
     of Albany. Legislative minutes (see *Jour.* 1:540).   77

Oct. 14 Mayor and sheriff of New York sworn in. Legislative
         minutes (see *Jour.* 1:541).   80

15–21 Legislative minutes (see *Jour.* 1:542).   82–83

21   Minutes of the Indian conference at Albany, Sep. 7, 9, 13,
     14.   83

25–27 Legislative minutes (see *Jour.* 1:543-44).   111

27   Order on petition of Dorothy Barclay for pay of expenses
     in taking care of Michael Montour the son of Montour the
     Indian. Accounts of Peter van Brugh for work on the
     fortifications of Albany etc referred. Warrants to issue
     for services in the Indian country, to Jacob Brewer, Herm.
     Vedder jr, Jurian Hogan, Phil. Livingston and Gertrud
     Schuyler on behalf of Abr'm Schuyler deceased, Johs.
     Mulder, Jacob Maase, Cornelius Cuyler and Lawrence
     Claesen; allowances fixed for services there in the follow-
     ing year to Evert Bancker, Jost van Sysen and Nicholas
     Wemp. Legislative minutes (see *Jour.* 1:544).   113

29   Warrant to issue to Peter van Brugh (p. 113). Legislative
     minutes (see *Jour.* 1:545).   117

Nov. 2 Legislative minutes (see *Jour.* 1:545). Warrants signed. 119

p. m.–3 Legislative minutes (see *Jour.* 1:546).   120

3   Indian deed for the beaver hunting country as far west as
     Tegerhunkserode (Detroit, Mich.) received and ordered to
     be recorded (see *L. P.* 10:13).   122

5–11 Legislative minutes (see *Jour.* 1:547-50).   124–30

15   Warrants to pay for work done in Fort George to Tunis
     Tiebout and Adrian Koning signed.   132

24   Warrants for salaries signed. Petition of Henry Hoofe (p.
     72; see *L. P.* 10:13-14) referred. Minutes sent home by
     Capt. Downing master of the ship Alexander.   132

1727

Jan. 5 Warrants for salaries signed. Patents granted: to Johannes
        Fischer (p. 40; see *L. P.* 10:25-28); and to Hy. Hoofe
        (p. 132).   133

Mar. 2 Ordinance establishing courts in Dutchess county passed.
        Letters and resolutions received from Massachusetts con-
        cerning Westenhook patent and boundaries; referred.
        Fort to be built at the mouth of Onondaga river
        (Oswego).   134

9   Fort at the mouth of Onondaga river; palatines to help in
     building it; how to be paid for; Indian consent to be ob-
     tained.   135

1727   v. 15

16 Warrants for salaries signed. A garrison of soldiers to be
    sent to the mouth of the Onondaga river.   137

Ap. 13 Royal mandamus appointing Archibald Kennedy to the
    council vice Thos. Byerley deceased; he is sworn in and
    takes his seat. Orders on the answer of the Westenhook
    patentees to the letter from Massachusetts (p. 134).
    Massachusetts boundary matter to be referred to the as-
    sembly. Orders upon letters sent from Massachusetts to
    the Indian commissioners at Albany, Oswego. Service in
    the Indian country.   138

27 Preparations made for the garrison to be sent to Oswego.
    Instructions for Capt. Lancaster Symes and Lieut. Nicholls
    who are to command the detachment to Oswego.   141

May 6 Indians object to the building a fort at Oswego. Account
    of the auditor-general referred and a warrant for it signed.
    Petition of Robert Livingston jr and Lancaster Symes jr
    (see L. P. 10:30) referred.   146

June 15 Warrants for salaries etc signed. The Indians have given
    their consent to build the Oswego fort.   147

20 License to purchase land granted to Rob't Livingston jr and
    Lancaster Symes jr (p. 146).   149

July 31 The governor of Canada has summoned the garrison at
    Oswego to stop building the fort and to leave; opinion
    of council that they are to remain and continue their work;
    Mr Bancker to treat with the five nations about it.   149

Aug. 4 Letter from Gov. Beauharnois of Canada; French expedi-
    tion reported ready to go against Oswego; answer to the
    letter from Canada discussed.   151

10 Answer to Gov. Beauharnois. Caghnawaga Indians want to
    come and live at Saratoga. A few Indians and smiths to
    live at Oswego.   155

21 Proclamation to issue of the accession of George II (see
    N. Y. col. mss, 68:17-18) and to be sent to the sheriffs of
    all the counties. Writs for election of a new assembly.   160

24 The governor and members present take the oaths. Proc-
    lamation to issue requiring all officers to take the oaths
    to King George II. Additional instructions to Gov. Bur-
    net concerning appeals to the king in council.   161

Sep. 14 The six nations have agreed to defend Oswego against the
    French. Warrants signed: for salaries; to Susanna Par-
    myter and Egbert van Borsom for boarding the messen-
    gers from Canada. Order in regard to illegal trade from
    Albany to Canada.   163

29 Warrant to issue to Mr Bancker for Indian service (see
    N. Y. col. mss, 68:20). Petitions of Johannes Hornebeck

1727   v. 15

(see *L. P.* 10:31) and of Jacob Fisher (see *N. Y. col. mss,*
68:16) referred. Robert Lurting and Wm Dugdale renominated mayor and sheriff of New York, Rutger
Bleecker and Thos. Williams of Albany.   165

30   Warrants signed. Legislative minutes (see *Jour.* 1:554).   166

Oct. 7   Legislative minutes (see *Jour.* 1:555). Petition of Lewis
Francis Fauchere commander of the ship Vigilant Postillion
of Nantes (see *N. Y. col. mss,* 68:51-52) referred and
granted.   168

14   Duplicate orders from the privy council to proclaim King
George II. Royal proclamation continuing all officers in
their places received (see *N. Y. col. mss,* 68:13). Mayor
and sheriff of New York sworn in. Legislative minutes
(see *Jour.* 1:555).   170

18-19   Legislative minutes (see *Jour.* 1:555-57).   171-73

26   Dr Colden takes the oaths to King George II. Warrant to
John Rose for supplies to messengers from Canada signed.
Legislative minutes (see *Jour.* 1:557). Petition of Abr'm
van Horne and Wm Provoost (see *L. P.* 10:33) granted.   174

Nov. 1   Legislative minutes (see *Jour.* 1:558). Petition of Lewis
Francis Fauchere for leave to sell enough of his cargo to
pay his debts in New York (see *N. Y. col. mss,* 68:53-54)
referred. Warrants to pay for Indian services to issue to
Phil. Livingston, Stephanus Groesbeck, Lawrence Claesen,
Joseph van Sice and to Joseph Clement. Petition of
Jannetie Cregier (see *L. P.* 10:41) granted.   176

2   Legislative minutes (see *Jour.* 1:558). Report on the petition
of Capt. Lewis Francis Fauchere approved.   177

11   Legislative minutes (see *Jour.* 1:559). Warrants signed.
Warrants to pay for Indian services to issue: to Peter
Schuyler, Gaishort van Brockel and Kilian Reader (see
N. Y. col. mss, 68:21-22); to Myndert Schuyler; to Stephen
Groesbeck; and to Herm. Wendell (see *N. Y. col. mss,*
68:25). John Cuyler reappointed Indian commissioner.   179

15-18 Legislative minutes (see *Jour.* 1:560-61). Warrants signed. 180-82

18   Petition of Sarah Varick, Wessell Wessells jr, Abr'm Laker-
man, Corn's van Horne (?), And'w Teller, Stephen Bayard, Jacobus van Cortlandt, John Lemontes, Phebe Out-
man and Antie Ten Eyck (see *L. P.* 10:38) referred. Royal
approbation of an assembly act. Patent granted to Sarah
Varick et al (see *N. Y. col. mss,* 68:33).   182

24-25 Legislative minutes (see *Jour.* 1:561-62).   185-86

25   Petitions referred: of Joseph Sacket and Nath'l Hazard (see
L. P. 10:42); of Rip van Dam, Thos. Thong, Helena de
Key, John Searle, Garret van Horne, Henry Cuyler Gou-
verneur and John Read (see *L. P.* 10:43).   186

1727		v. 15

p. m.   Patent granted to Joseph Sacket and Nath'l Hazard (p. 186).
Petition of Rip van Dam et al (p. 186) granted.   191

27   Committee on resolutions of the last assembly authorized to
send for persons and papers.   192

Dec. 5   Report of the above committee (see *N. Y. col. mss*, 68:34-39).
Memorial of Att'y-General Bradley (see *N. Y. col. mss*,
68:28) referred.   192

19   Report on the ordinance relating to fees in the court of
chancery (see *N. Y. col. mss*, 68:44). Order directing the
attorney-general to prosecute land suits (see *N. Y. col. mss*,
168:43). Patents granted: to Johannes Hornebeck (see
L. P. 16:37): to Wm York, Phil. Moor, John Peter Zenger,
Hans George Baringer and Jacob Burst, palatines (see *L.
P.* 10:51). Warrants for salaries signed. Minutes sent
home by Capt. Thos. Smith of the Beaver.   200

1728

Feb. 12   The French of Canada reported as intending to attack
Oswego. Writs of election to issue quickly.   212

28   Ordinance of fees in the court of chancery approved and to
be printed. Ordinance concerning procedure in the court
of chancery to be prepared. Petitions of Corn's Low et al
(see *L. P.* 10:50) referred and order thereon. Petition of
Martha Heathcote (see *L. P.* 10:52) referred. Van Cortlandt and Philippse vs Palmer, Quinby et al.   213

Mar. 2   Van Cortlandt and Philippse vs Palmer et al. Patent granted
to Corn's Lowet et al. Petition of Martha Heathcote
granted (p. 213).   216

7   Van Cortlandt and Philippse vs Palmer et al. Report on
the ordinance for procedure in the court of chancery (see
N. Y. col. mss, 68:60).   218

20   Warrants signed: for salaries; to Tunis Tiebout, Abr'm
Alstine and Adrian King for work on Fort George.   221

28   Petition of Peter van Brough, Jonas Douw, John Wittbeene,
Petrus Douw, Wm Dugdale and Gerard Beekman (see *L.
P.* 10:56) referred. Van Cortlandt and Philippse vs Palmer
et al. License to purchase Indian land granted to Peter
van Brugh et al.   223

Ap. 5   License to purchase Indian land granted' to Abr'm van
Horne, Wm Provoost, Mary Burnet and Phil. Livingston
see *L. P.* 10:57; and, *N. Y. col. mss*, 68:63). Petitions of
Dederick Masterstock (see *L. P.* 10:59, 62), and of John
Spratt and Andries Marschalck for land referred, and sub-
sequently granted. Order on complaint of the mayor of
Albany (see *N. Y. col. mss*, 68:61).   224

1728 v. 15

15 Gov. John Montgomerie takes the oaths after the reading of his commission. Members present sworn in. Seals delivered to Gov. Montgomerie by Mr Burnet. Proclamation to issue continuing officers in their places (see *N. Y. col. mss,* 68:65). Governor's commission published at the city hall. 226

18 Lewis Morris jr and Wm Provoost sworn in. Letter received from the Indian commissioners concerning batteaux at Oswego; order thereon. Phil. Livingston hands in his answer to the complaint of the mayor of Albany (see *N. Y. col. mss,* 68:70, 72) referred. Assembly to be dissolved and writs for election of a new one to issue. 227

25 Order on Phil. Livingston's answer. 229

May 2 Robert Walter sworn in. Warrant to Wm Burnet for balance of his salary signed. 229

30 Return of writs of election fixed. Mayor etc of Albany vs Phil. Livingston. 230

June 4 Lt. Gov. Wm Dummer writes about Indian designs against Oswego; order thereon. 231

20 George Clarke confirmed by the king in his office of provincial secretary. 232

21 Royal disallowance of an act of assembly. Capt. Bagley commanding at Oswego reports on repairs and provisions needed there; referred to Indian commissioners. Warrants for salaries signed. 232

27 Accounts of the auditor general referred; warrant signed. 236

July 23–Sep. 21 Legislative minutes (see *Jour.* 1:563-81).*a* 237–74

Sep. 18 Phil. Livingston and Derick ten Broeck farmers of the excise swear to their accounts. 265

21 Gov. Montgomerie is going to Albany. President of the council to announce nominations of mayor and sheriff. 274

29 Robert Walter presiding. Letter nominating Robert Lurting mayor, Henry Beeckman sheriff of New York. 278

29 Gov. Montgomerie presiding. Robert Lurting and Henry Beeckman nominated as above, Rutger Bleecker as mayor and Goosie van Schaick sheriff of Albany. 279

Oct. 12 License to purchase Indian land granted to Rutger Bleecker, Nich's Bleecker, James de Lancey and John Haskoll. Order on petition of Francis Salisbury et al (see *N. Y. col. mss,* 68:97). Warrants for salaries signed. 280

14 Mayor and sheriff of New York sworn in. Minutes of the Indian conference, Oct. 1, 4, 5, 7. Proclamation prohibiting the sale of liquor to the Indians. 282

---

a Legislative minutes of Aug. 31, Sep. 5, 10, 11, 12 and 13, given in the *Journal,* are missing in this mss of Council minutes.

1728   v. 15

Nov. 7   Nolle prosequi to be entered in re Francis Salisbury et al
(p. 280). Petitions of Richard Bradley and Wm Jamison
(see *L. P.* 10:72) referred. Warrants of survey granted:
to Edw. Blagge, Gisbert Crom, Derick Crom, Gerrit Blovelt, Thos. Husk, Paulus Yorkson, Flora Crom and Albert
Minnelye; to Solomon and Lewis du Bois (see *L. P.*
10:74). Petitions referred: of Andrew Nicolls, Evan
Drummond, Edward Collins, John Wemp and Corn's van
Slyck (see *L. P.* 10:75); of Johannes Christman (see *L. P.*
10:73); from Dr Colden (see *N. Y. col. mss,* 68:99) and
order thereon. Patent granted to Richard Bradley and
Wm Jamison. License to purchase land granted to And'w
Nicholls et al.   308

30   Memorial of Att'y Gen. Richard Bradley concerning his
salary referred. Petitions referred: of the owners of a tract
in Orange county (see *L. P.* 10:78); of Capt. John Riggs
(see *L. P.* 10:77); the latter subsequently granted. Gov.
Montgomerie going to New Jersey.   313

1729

Mar. 10   Gov. Montgomerie returned. Sessions of the supreme
court in New York city temporarily suspended on account
of measles; warrant to issue to that effect. Petition of
Burgher Myndertse jr (see *L. P.* 10:81) referred.   315

Ap. 10   Royal disallowance of an act of assembly. Ordinance regulating sessions of the courts of general sessions, and common pleas to be prepared on representation made by the
representatives, judges and justices of various counties.
Letter from Gov. Burnet at Boston about French designs
on Oswego. Letter from Gov. Montgomerie to Indian
commissioners on the same subject. Patent granted to
Rutger Bleecker et al (p. 280; see *L. P.* 10: [84]). License
to purchase land granted to Abr'm van Horne, Wm Provoost, Mary Burnet and Phil. Livingston (see *L. P.* 10:84).
Warrants for salaries signed. Report on Att'y-Gen. Bradley's memorial (p. 308). Patent granted to Burgher
Myndertse (p. 315). Proclamation to issue calling for the
speedy paying of quitrents.   317

21   Supreme court further adjourned, upon the opinions of
Doctors Johnson and Colden; writ to that effect to issue.   326

May 5–June 5 Legislative minutes (see *Jour.* 1:582-83).   327–29

June 5   Petition of Johan Peter Kinskern (see *L. P.* 10:88) referred.   329

12   Warrants for salaries etc signed. Mr Morris makes objections to have the warrant for the chief justice signed as
drawn. Warrant to Daniel Gautier for repairs in Fort
George signed. Legislative minutes (see *Jour.* 1:583).   331

1729   v. 15

13   Legislative minutes (see *Jour.* 1:584). Paper of Mr Morris
     concerning manner of drawing warrants (see *N. Y. col. mss*,
     68:110) rejected. License to purchase Indian land granted
     to Johan Peter Kinskern (p. 329).   335

19   Legislative minutes (see *Jour.* 1:584).   338

26   Royal mandamus appointing James de Lancey to the coun-
     cil; he is sworn in and takes his place. Legislative minutes
     (see *Jour.* 1:585). Lewis Morris jr suspended from the
     council for reading a scandalous paper before it (see *N. Y.
     col. mss*, 68:117, 121).   341

27   Legislative minutes (see *Jour.* 1:585). Petition of Fred'k
     Pellinger (see *L. P.* 10:89) referred.   345

30–July 2 Legislative minutes (see *Jour.* 1:586).   346

July 2   Order upon representation by the clerk of the council con-
         cerning his fees for engrossing private acts.   347

p. m.   Legislative minutes (see *Jour.* 1:587). License to purchase
         Indian lands granted to Fred'k Pellinger (p. 345).   350

4–9   Legislative minutes (see *Jour.* 1:587-88).   352–55

9   Memorial from members of the assembly concerning the
      ordinance regulating sessions of the county courts referred. 355

10   Legislative minutes (see *Jour.* 1:589). Report on the above
      memorial recommending some alterations in the ordi-
      nance, approved and a new ordinance to issue.   356

11   Legislative minutes (see *Jour.* 1:590).   360

12   Auditor-general's account referred; subsequently warrant to
      him signed. Legislative minutes (see *Jour.* 1:590).   361

Sep. 10 Warrants for salaries signed. James Alexander objects to
         the signing of the warrant for the chief justice. Warrant to
         Daniel Gautier for repairs in Fort George signed. Petition
         of Vincent Matthews, John Cornwell, Samuel Heath and
         Abr'm Lodge (see *L. P.* 10:90-91) referred, and subse-
         quently granted.   364

29   Petition of Rutger and Nicholas Bleecker (see *L. P.* 10:96)
      referred and patent subsequently granted. Warrants
      signed to pay for firewood and candles to the frontier gar-
      risons; for Johannes Cuyler, Peter van Brugh and Stephen
      van Rensselaer. Robert Lurting and Henry Beeckman
      renominated mayor and sheriff of New York; John de Pey-
      ster mayor, Goose van Schaick sheriff of Albany.   367

Oct. 14 Mayor and sheriff of New York sworn in.   309

18   Deposition of Richard Murphy master and owner of the
      galley Jenny of Dublin about mutiny of his chief mate
      with John McCullock and crew; order thereon.   369

Vol. 16, 1729-34

1729

Oct. 20   Mr Ashfield agent for Richard Murphy, and Dr Richard
Davis report that Murphy is too ill to appear before the
council for further examination.   Examination of Wm
McKinley, chief mate of the galley Jenney, of John Mc-
Kinley second mate, of John McCullock supercargo, of
James McCarroll and Wm Espy passengers.   1

21   Examinations continued; of Peter Hagan mariner, Peter
Stanley apprentice, Richard Carroll cabin boy, John Forbes
passenger, Patrick McGan, Nich's English apprentice: case
referred.   8

22   Report on the case of the galley Jenney and vote; accused
discharged.   12

29   The entry of the above in the minutes of council not to establish a precedent.   Court of chancery opened.   Petitions
granted: of John de Peyster (see *L. P.* 10:100); of Richard
Colburn Riggs (see *L. P.* 10:101); of Johan Peter Kinskern
(see *L. P.* 10:98).   15

1730

Mar. 5   Warrants signed: for salaries; to Daniel Gautier for work
in Fort George.   Order concerning sessions of the supreme
court.   Petition of Thos. Williams, Corn's Jacobus Schermerhorn and Lendert Conyne jr (see *L. P.* 10:105) referred.   Warrant of survey for land in Westchester county
granted to Rich'd Warman, Wm Anderson, Lawrence
Gardiner, Joshua Hanlock, John Clapp and John Ferris.   17

Ap. 23   Gov. Montgomerie takes the oath as chancellor.   Royal
mandamus dismissing Lewis Morris from and appointing
Phil. van Cortlandt to the council (see *N. Y. col. mss*,
68:145); the latter is sworn in and takes his seat.   Letter
received from Henry Smith with examinations at Southold
and Southampton concerning Samuel Booth firing at the
sloop of John Baker; order that Judge Francis Harrison
make inquiries about it.   Petition of Abr'm van Horne,
Wm Provoost, Mary Burnet and Phil. Livingston (see
L. P. 10:114) referred.   Gov. Montgomerie intends going
to New Jersey.   Petition of Isaac Bobin and Abr'm Lodge
(see *L. P.* 10:113) referred.   Order on petition of Thos.
Williams et al (p. 17; see *L. P.* 10:116).   Petitions of Abr'm
van Horne et al and of Isaac Bobin granted.   [18]

July 23   Warrants for salaries signed.   Royal order for the restoration
of all Spanish prizes (see *N. Y. col. mss*, 68:144).   Letter
from the duke of Newcastle to the same effect.   Translation
of the cedula of the king of Spain ordering the restoration
of all English prizes (see *N. Y. col. mss*, 68:141); to be

v. 16

printed in the *New York gazette*. Indian commissioners
report that Jacob Brower has been murdered by an Onondaga Indian near Oswego; order thereon. Order on petition of Charles Butler (see *L. P.* 10:122).   22

Aug. 6 The Indian murder not to be meddled with until the governor goes to Albany. Hearing on caveat by Mathias van
Alstyn vs patent to Thos. Williams (p. [18]). Petition of
mayor etc of New York (see *L. P.* 10:130) referred. Petition
of Jacob Burst and other palatines for a patent of purchased Indian lands referred and granted.   30

     13 Report on the petition of mayor etc of New York (p. 30).   32

     7 Discussion on the above petition. New charter granted to
the city of New York. Hearing on the caveat of the city
of Albany against a patent to Charles Butler (p. 22).   32

     26 Legislative minutes (see *Jour.* 1:591).   36

Sep. 3 Warrants for salaries signed. Patent granted to Thos. Hen-
ley, Nathan St John, Samuel Smith, Benj. Benedict, Rich'd
Olmstead, Thos. Smith, Ebenezer Smith, Daniel Sherwood,
Benj. Burt, Thos. Hyatt, Benj. Willson, Joseph Lee, Jos-
eph, Timothy and Jonah Keiler, James Benedict, Rich'd
Osburn, Daniel Olmsted, Matthew Seymour, Joseph
Northrup, James Brown, Adam Ireland, John Thomas,
Benj. Birdsell and others of Ridgefield. Connecticut line
to be run; Cadw. Colden, Vincent Matthews and Gilbert
Willett to be commissioners; Jacobus Bruyn jr deputy
surveyor.   37

     16 Legislative minutes (see *Jour.* 1:592). Petitions referred and
subsequently granted: of Gabriel and Wm Ludlow (see
L. P. 10:134); of Corn's Cuyler and Wm Ketlyn (see *L.
P.* 110:136); of Hartman Wendeker, Coenrad Contreman
and Caspar Leng, distressed palatines (see *L. P.* 10:135).   40

     24 Legislative minutes (see *Jour.* 1:592). Petition of David
Jamison (see *L. P.* 10:137) referred.   43

     25 Legislative minutes (see *Jour.* 1:593). Order on petition of
the Westenhook patentees about encroachments by Connecticut.   44

     29 Mayors and sheriffs of New York and of Albany renomi-
nated.   48

Oct. 1 No more licenses to purchase Indian lands on the Mohawk
river to be given, on representation of Indian commissioners (see *N. Y. col. mss*, 69:99). Legislative minutes (see
Jour. 1:594).   49

     8 Legislative minutes (see *Jour.* 1:595).   50

     9 Order on petition of Peter Caverly (see *L. P.* 10:145). Legis-
lative minutes (see *Jour.* 1:595). Warrant of survey granted
to David Jamison (p. 43).   51

1730   v. 16

p. m.   Legislative minutes (see *Jour.* 1:596). Fred'k Morris sworn
in as deputy secretary. Petition of Arent Bratt jr (see *L.
P.* 10:146) to lie on the table.   54

14   Legislative minutes (see *Jour.* 1:597). Mayor and sheriff of
New York sworn in; also aldermen John Cruger, Herm.
van Gelder, Fred'k Philippse, Gerardus Stuyvesant, An-
thony Rutgers and John Rosevelt and Recorder Francis
Harrison as justices of the peace. Petition of Benj.
Blagge (see *L. P.* 10:147) referred.   56

15   Legislative minutes (see *Jour.* 1:597). Petition of Elias Pipon
(see *L. P.* 10:148).   57

16   Legislative minutes (see *Jour.* 1:598). Petition of Joseph
Sackett and Joseph Sackett jr (see *L. P.* 10:150) referred.   59

17   Legislative minutes (see *Jour.* 1:598).   61

21   Petition of Thos. Standard and Thos. Hammond (see *L. P.*
10:151) referred. Legislative minutes (see *Jour.* 1:599).   63

22-23 Legislative minutes (see *Jour.* 1:599-600).   64-65

23   Patents granted: to Benj. Blagge (p. 56); to Joseph Sackett
and Joseph Sackett jr (p. 59); to Thos. Standard and Thos.
Hammond (p. 63).   65

24-28 Legislative minutes (see *Jour.* 1:600-1).   67-69

p. m.   Proclamation to issue for the arrest of Solomon Jennings a
horse thief (see *N. Y. col. mss*, 69:102).   69

29   Auditor-general's accounts referred and warrant subsequently issued and signed. Legislative minutes (see *Jour.*
1:601). Minutes sent home.   70

Dec. 3   Warrants for salaries and services signed. The French reported as intending to build a fort at Tiederondequat.
Jean Coeur among the Senecas. French fort at Crownpoint
building. Order on these news.   72

1731

Jan. 4   John Connor convicted of felony pardoned. Petition of the
Hon. Charles Boyle (see *N. Y. col. mss*, 69:111) referred,
and patent subsequently granted.   75

Feb. 11   Charter of the city of New York delivered to Robert Lurting the mayor; John Cruger appointed deputy mayor. Address to the governor by Recorder Francis Harrison.   76

Ap. 7   Warrants for salaries signed. Barracks in Fort George need
repairing; Daniel Gautier to make the repairs and warrant
for paying signed. Additional instructions received by
Gov. Montgomerie concerning destruction of the woods.
Letter from the duke of Newcastle concerning piracies
committed by Spaniards; order thereon. Petition of John
Avory, Corn's van Ness, John Lyndesay, Gerardus Stuyvesant, Stephen van Rensselaer and Fred'k Morris for license

to purchase Indian land on the east side of Hudson's river referred and granted. Additional instruction communicated by the governor concerning ecclesiastical jurisdiction to be exercised by the bishop of London or his commissaries.   79

May 19 Gov. Montgomerie at Albany, Capt. Walter presides. Capt. Fred is reported as having brought negroes sick with smallpox from Jamaica and is examined; order thereon.   84

25 Quarantine measures.   87

June 3 Gov. Montgomerie returned. Warrants for salaries etc signed. James Coden and Mathias de Hart appointed pilots. Warrant of survey granted to Johs. van Alst (see *L. P.* 10:154). Petition of John Lindsay et al (see *L. P.* 10:155) referred; date fixed for hearing a caveat by the corporation of Albany against it. Petition of James Wallace (see *L. P.* 10:162) referred. Order on petition of John Fred (see *N. Y. col. mss,* 69:124). Indenture between New York and Connecticut concerning the boundary line; also description of monuments.   87

24 Patent granted to James Wallace (p. 87). Petitions referred: of Petrus van Driesen and Johs. Ehl (see *L. P.* 10:162); of Corn's Cuyler and Wm Kettelhuyn (see *L. P.* 10:164); of Daniel Kettelhuyn and Thomas Sharp (see *L. P.* 10:167); of Charles Boyle (see *L. P.* 10:166). Quitrent for land granted to Chas. Boyle fixed. Caveat being entered against a patent to Daniel Ketelhuyn and Thomas Sharp by John Lindsay, petition to lie on the table. Patent granted to Corn's Cuyler and Wm Kettelhuyn. License to purchase land granted to Petrus van Driesen and Johs. Ehl. Capt. John Fred's vessel to be sunk for the purpose of cleaning it from infection (see *N. Y. col. mss,* 69:127). John Kirten son of Wm Kirten deceased appointed pilot.   107

July 1 Gov. John Montgomerie dead; Rip van Dam presides; commission of the late governor and his instructions read; proclamation to issue announcing the death and confirming all officers in their places. Members not present called to attend. Seal of the province etc delivered to Rip van Dam. George Clarke, Arch'd Kennedy, James de Lancey and Charles Hume [Home] to take an inventory of Gov. Montgomerie's estate.   111

2 Messrs Kennedy and van Cortlandt to inspect the stores and make an inventory of them. Rip van Dam sworn in as president; James de Lancey as second justice, and Fred'k Philippse third justice of the supreme court. [This page follows p. 122 in the manuscript minutes].   113

1731   **v. 16**

6   No will made by Gov. Montgomerie to be found, letters of
    administration are to be given to Charles Home.   113

10 Charles Boyle, Capt. Wm Dick and John Scott to be sureties
    for Charles Home.   114

27 Order on memorial of Peter Soumans (see *N. Y. col. mss,*
    69:137). Legislative minutes (see *Jour.* 1:602). Order on
    petition of Mary Price, widow of Lieut. John Price (see
    N. Y. col. mss, 69:138). Petition of Jenneke Creggier (see
    L. P. 10:168) referred. Warrant to John Miller the late
    governor's gardener for work in the garden; he is to con-
    tinue until the arrival of a new governor.   115

Aug. 21 Indian affairs. War rumors in Albany. Warrants: to Chas.
    Home for the late governor's salary; to Johs. Cuyler, Peter
    van Brugh, Stephen van Rensselaer and John de Peyster
    for firewood and candles to Albany, Schenectady and Fort
    Hunter garrisons. Answer of Sheriff Henry Beekman to
    Peter Soumans' complaint (p. 115; see *N. Y. col. mss,*
    69:139) delivered.   117

10 Pay of independent companies. Petitions referred: of Bur-
    ger Huick and 9 others (see *L. P.* 10:170); of the corpora-
    tion of Albany (see *L. P.* 10:169): the first subsequently
    granted and order made on the second.   118

17 Assembly adjourned. Francis Pelham justice of the peace
    in Westchester county suspended and removed from office
    (see *N. Y. col. mss,* 69:131).   121

20 Assembly adjourned.   121

24 Assembly adjourned to meet the next day at the house of
    Harmanus Rutgers in the Bowry lane, outward.   122

25 Legislative minutes (see *Jour.* 1:603). Royal instruction
    concerning attendance of members of the council. Peti-
    tions referred: of Rob't Livingston jr, Peter Livingston,
    John Cruger, Henry Cuyler and Edward Man (see *L. P.*
    10:173); of John van der Spiegel, Wm Smith and John
    Borghart (see *L. P.* 10:174).   122

Sep. 3 Legislative minutes (see *Jour.* 1:604). Petition of Thos.
    Smith (see *L. P.* 10:175) referred. Pay of independent
    companies. Salary of the president under consideration
    (see *N. Y. col. mss,* 69:146).   125

4   Report of committee on the salary of the president; ap-
    proved. Supply of gunpowder needed.   128

7   License to purchase Indian land granted to Jannetie Cregier
    (p. 115). Order on the petition of John van der Spiegel
    et al (p. 122). Patent granted to Thos. Smith (p. 125).
    Petition of Rob't Livingston jr et al (p. 122) rejected.

1731   v. 16

Account of Herm. Wendall for victualling the troops at
Oswego referred.   129
13–14 Legislative minutes (see *Jour.* 1:604-6).   131–35
14   List of papers laid before the assembly (see *N. Y. col. mss,*
69:144).   135
15–17 Legislative minutes (see *Jour.* 1:606).   137–38
17   Salary of the president under consideration; warrant to him
and for other salaries signed. Warrant to Indian commissioners and to James O'Brien surgeon at Oswego to lie
on the table. Petitions referred: of Tunis van Sleyck
and Peter Lodowick (see *L. P.* 10:178); of Hartman Windecker, Coenrat Contreman and Caspar Leyp (see *L. P.*
11:1); of Stephen van Cortlandt, Wm Provoost, Rich'd
van Dam, Rich'd Hansen, Rob't Livingston jr and Daniel
Kettelhuyn (see *L. P.* 10:177); of Johs. de Wandelaer (see
L. P. 10:176); of John van der Spiegel et al (p. 122).   138
18–20 Legislative minutes (see *Jour.* 1:607-8).   142–44
20   Warrant to Jas. O'Brien surgeon at Oswego signed.   144
21   Legislative minutes (see *Jour.* 1:608). License to purchase
Indian land granted to John van der Spiegel et al (p. 138).
Petition of Stephen van Cortlandt et al (p. 138) rejected.
Order on petition of Tunis van Sleyck (p. 138). Patent
granted to Hartman Windecker et al (p. 138). Petition of
Johs. de Wandelaer (p. 138) to lie on the table.   145
22   Legislative minutes (see *Jour.* 1:609). Petitions referred: of
Henry van Rensselaer (see *L. P.* 11:2); of Jurch [George]
Hough, Hendrick Set, Wm Foex and Roelof Steel (see
L. P. 11:5).   148
23   Legislative minutes (see *Jour.* 1:609). Petition of Henry
van Rensselaer (p. 148) granted. License to purchase
Indian land granted to Jurch Hough et al (p. 148). Warrants: to Indian commissioners for necessary expenses; to
Johs. Cuyler, Peter van Brugh, Stephen van Rensselaer
and John de Peyster for firewood and candles to Albany
garrison. Goods come for Gov. Montgomerie from England to be inventoried.   149
24   Legislative minutes (see *Jour.* 1:609). Warrant to Arent
Stevens for services as Indian interpreter at Oswego as per
certificate of Capt. Edmund Blood, commanding there (see
N. Y. col. mss, 69:125).   151
p. m. Legislative minutes (see *Jour.* 1:610). Petition of Abr'm
van Horne, Wm Provoost, Rob't Livingston and Mary
Burnet (see *L. P.* 11:3-4) referred, and subsequently
granted.   152

1731   **v. 16**

25   Legislative minutes (see *Jour.* 1:610). Petition of Petrus
      van Driesen and Johs. Ehl (see *L. P.* 11:6) referred.   154

29   Robert Lurting renominated mayor, Henry Beeckman sheriff
      and Richard Nicholls coroner of New York; Hans Hansen
      nominated mayor, coroner and clerk of the market, James
      Stevenson sheriff of Albany. Legislative minutes (see *Jour.*
      1:610). Petition of Petrus van Driesen et al (p. 154) to
      lie on the table.   155

30   Warrants signed: to Herm. Wendall for victualling troops
      at Oswego; to Arent Stevens Indian interpreter. Legis-
      lative minutes (see *Jour.* 1:611). Minutes sent home.   158

Oct. 7 Warrants signed: to Gabriel Ludlow clerk and to Dirck
      Egbertse doorkeeper of the assembly for salaries (see *N. Y.*
      col. mss, 69:154). Lancaster Symes and Corn's Cuyper
      summoned before the council on a deposition of Justice
      Edw'd Sands of Orange, that Symes had said at Cuyper's
      house " God damn King George; is he a king? no."   160

11   Warrant to James O'Brien for service as surgeon at Oswego
      signed. Supreme court adjourned on account of smallpox
      in the city. Inquiry to be made concerning warrants is-
      sued to Gov. Montgomerie for repairs in the fort etc, now
      in the hands of Charles Home.   161

14   Robert Lurting sworn in as mayor; John Cruger appointed
      deputy mayor of New York.   163

21   Lancaster Symes does not appear as ordered (p. 160) and
      new charges having been brought against him of mal-
      feasance as justice of the peace, he is again summoned.
      Affidavit of Thos. Husk against Thos. Pullen (see *N. Y.*
      col. mss, 69:160) referred to Judge Corn's Herring of
      Orange county. Order on petition of Samuel Baker and
      affidavits of Wm Henry and Thos. Fowler and Joseph
      Green (see *N. Y. col. mss,* 69:150-53).   163

Nov. 11 Petitions referred: of Jurch Miller, Hendrick Windecker,
      Peter Deygert and Coenradt Coltman (see *L. P.* 11:16); of
      Fred'k Bell and Hendrick Hager (see *L. P.* 11:24); of John
      Jurch Kast jr and Jacob Hilts (see *L. P.* 11:25). Petition
      of Abr'm van Deurson et al (see *N. Y. col. mss,* 70:5) re-
      jected.   165

13   Lancaster Symes before the council; clears himself of the
      charge of disaffection: examination to continue.   167

15   Lancaster Symes before the council. Complaints received
      from Joseph Clement of Oswego against the commanding
      officer there for wasting the provisions: Robert Dunbar
      also complains of Capt. Smith's allowing Frenchmen to
      inspect the fort at Oswego; order thereon.   168

1731   v. 16

Dec. 2 Discussion as to the president's salary. Petitions referred:
of Jurch Hough, Hendrik Sex, Wm Foex and Roeloff
Steel (see *L. P.* 11:18); of Nath'l Hazard jr (see *L. P.*
11:17).   170

9 President's salary. Proclamation to issue adjourning the
assembly.   171

13 Examination of Lancaster Symes postponed.   171

23 Petitions referred: of John Collins et al (see *L. P.* 11:26);
of Gabriel Ludlow jr (see *L. P.* 11:22). Reports on peti-
titions: of Jurch Miller & Co. (p. 165); of Fred. Bell et al
p. 165); of John Jurch Kast jr & Co. (p. 165); of Jurch
Hough (p. 170); of Nath'l Hazard jr (p. 170); of John
Collins; and of Gabriel Ludlow (p. 170).   172

1732

Feb. 4 Letter received from the governor of Boston in relation to
Crownpoint; inquiry to be made whether Crownpoint
belongs to the river Indians or to the five nations. Royal
order disallowing an act of assembly. Assembly adjourned. Petition of John van der Spiegel, Wm Smith
and John Borghghart (see *L. P.* 11:28) referred and patent
subsequently granted. Order on petition of justices of the
common pleas in Suffolk county.   173

7 Salary of the president fixed and warrants for it and other
salaries signed.   178

11 Measures to prevent French encroachments on Lake Champlain. Petition of Henry Lane, John Spratt, Rob't Elliston and Fred'k Morris (see *L. P.* 11:29) referred. Assem-
bly prorogued.   179

Mar. 13 Warrants for salaries signed. Petition of Samuel Heath,
Wm Wallace and John Kelly (see *L. P.* 11:30) referred
and patents subsequently granted to them, and to Henry
Lane et al (p. 179). Assembly adjourned.   180

Ap. 18 Warrants to Anne Wendell executor of Hermanus Wendell
deceased for victualling troops at Oswego signed.   182

28 Petitions referred: of John Lawrence (see *L. P.* 11:34); of
John Anderson (see *N. Y. col. mss,* 70:14); of Thos. Hanley
and others (see *L. P.* 11:33); reports on these petitions
agreed to. Warrant to Harme Vedder for services as
Indian interpreter at Oswego in the winter of 1729-30, certified to by Capt. Wm Helling commanding there.   183

May 5 Assembly adjourned. Order on petition of Francis Harrison
as attorney for Sir Joseph Eyles against the petition of
Thos. Hanley and others (p. 183).   185

19 Letter from Wm Cosby appointed governor of New York
relating to pay of independent companies; order thereon.   186

1732   v. 16

June 6   Warrants for salaries signed. Nolle prosequi to be entered
          in re John Wickham, justice in Suffolk county, charged
          with neglect of duty. Assembly adjourned.   188

20   Members of the assembly in town called for a conference on
          appropriations for the support of troops at Oswego. War-
          rant to Rip van Dam for firewood etc to New York gar-
          rison signed. His further accounts referred to the assem-
          bly. Petition of Petrus van Driesen and Johs. Ehl (see
          L. P. 11:38) referred.   189

21   Patent granted to Petrus van Driesen (p. 189). Stephen de
          Lancey, Adolph Philippse, Anthony Rutgers, Col. Phil-
          ippse and Col. Beekman members of the assembly meet
          in conference with the council and consult on methods for
          the support of the troops at Oswego.   190

July 3   Assembly adjourned.   191

21   Members of the council to attend promptly when the assem-
          bly meets.   192

26   Petition of Petrus van Driesen and Johs. Ehl for extension
          of time in which to make purchase of Indian lands referred
          and ordered to lie on the table (see N. Y. col. mss, 70:21).
          Order on petition of John Anderson (see N. Y. col. mss,
          70:21). Warrants signed: to the gardener of the fort for
          salary; to Johs. Cuyler, Peter van Brugh, Stephen van
          Rensselaer and John de Peyster for firewood etc to gar-
          risons at Albany, Schenectady and Fort Hunter.   192

Aug. 1   Assembly adjourned. Order on petition of Lewis Morris jr,
          clerk of the circuit (see N. Y. col. mss, 70:22). Gov. Wm
          Cosby arrives.   194

p. m.   Gov. Cosby takes the oaths after reading of his commission;
          members of the council present sworn in; seals and keys
          delivered to the new governor; proclamation to issue con-
          firming all officers in their places.   195

2   Gov. Cosby publishes his commission at the city hall.   195

3   Assembly adjourned. George Clarke, Francis Harrison,
          Wm Provoost and Phil. van Cortlandt now present are
          sworn in.   196

8   Assembly adjourned.   196

10   Legislative minutes (see Jour. 1:614). James Coden ap-
          pointed pilot.   196

23   Legislative minutes (see Jour. 1:614). Warrants to Gov.
          Cosby for Indian presents and repairs in Fort George
          signed.   201

24   Warrant to Rip van Dam for firewood exchanged for one
          to Gov. Cosby and signed. Legislative minutes (see Jour.
          1:615).   202

1732   v. 16

25   Petitions referred and subsequently granted: of Corn's van
Ness, John Lindesay, Gerardus Beekman, Stephen van
Rensselaer, Charles Williams and Fred'k Morris (see *L. P.*
11:44); of Peter van Brugh (see *L. P.* 11:43. Legislative
minutes (see *Jour.* 1:615). Certificate of Indian commissioners about David Abr'm Schuyler's services as commissary at Oswego (see *N. Y. col. mss*, 70:28) referred.   203

Sep. 15   Petitions referred: of Dan'l Kettelhuyn, Stephanus Groesbeck jr, David Abrahamsen Schuyler jr, Fred'k Morris,
Charles Williams, Joseph Worrell, Thos. Cockerill and
John Felton (see *L. P.* 11:45); of Petrus van Driesen, Johs.
Ehl, Chs. Williams and Fred'k Morris (see *L. P.* 11:45).
Legislative minutes (see *Jour.* 1:615). Report on the above
petition. Order on the certificate for David Abr'm Schuyler (p. 203). Accounts of Anne Wendell, executor of
of Herm. Wendell for victualling the troops at Oswego
examined and warrant signed (see *N. Y. col. mss*, 70:29-30). 205

21–22 Legislative minutes (see *Jour.* 1:616-17).   209–12

22   Petition of Charles Kerr for pay of services as surgeon at
Oswego granted and warrant signed. Order on petition
of John Kelly and Simon Johnson attorneys at law, for
permission to practice in the mayor's court.   212

23–29 Legislative minutes (see *Jour.* 1:618-20).   216–19

29   Rob't Lurting to be mayor, Henry Beekman sheriff, Richard
Nicolls coroner of New York; John de Peyster mayor,
John Lindsay sheriff of Albany.   219

Oct. 5–14 Legislative minutes (see *Jour.* 1:621-24).   221–28

Nov. 9   Patent granted to Dan'l Kettelhuyn et al (p. 205).   231

14   Additional instruction to Gov. Cosby concerning salary; Rip
van Dam to refund half of the salary he has received.   232

17   Warrants for salaries etc signed.   235

27   Rip van Dam does not refund; order thereon.   236

29   Attorney general to commence a suit against Rip van Dam
for salary received in excess. Rumors spreading that the
governor intends to seize the property of the Dutch
church in New York; proclamation to issue for the discovery of who started the rumor.   237

Dec. 4   Court of exchequer established. Dick a negro servant of
Abr'm van Horne convicted of felony pardoned.   238

1733

Mar. 3   Warrants signed: for salaries; to David Abr'm Schuyler for
services as commissary at Oswego; to Joseph Clement for
shingling house at Oswego; to Rip van Dam for provisions
sent there; to Phil. Livingston for building bateaux for
the troops there; to Johs. Lansingh and Jeremiah van Rens-

selaer for transporting Capt. Butler there; to Abr'm Cuyler for pay of an Indian messenger; to Thos. Braine for medicines; to Garrit van Benthuysen for passage of soldiers.   239

9   Account of auditor general referred and warrant for it signed. Petitions referred and subsequently granted: of Charles Williams and Fred'k Morris (see *L. P.* 11:53); of Wessell ten Broeck (see *L. P.* 11:52). Gov. Cosby takes the oath as chancellor and opens the court of chancery.   240

19   Letters patent for altering the times of holding supreme court approved.   242

Ap. 18   Petition of Peter Winne (see *L. P.* 11:55) referred and license to purchase Indian land subsequently granted. Order on petition of inhabitants of Orange county (see *N. Y. col. mss*, 70:52).   243

Aug. 23   Warrants for salaries signed: to commissioners of Indian affairs for Indian expenses; to John de Peyster, John Schuyler and Jurie (George) Cast for victualling the troops at Oswego. Boundaries of counties settled and ordinance to that effect to issue. James de Lancey appointed chief justice vice Lewis Morris; Fred'k Philippse appointed second justice, and both sworn in. Petitions of Charles Williams, Fred'k Morris and Samuel Heath (see *L. P.* 11:59); and of Peter Bayard et al (see *L. P.* 11:58) referred and subsequently granted.   245

28   Ordinance for running boundaries of counties (see *N. Y. col. mss*, 70:62) referred. Petitions of Peter Bayard (see *L. P.* 11:62) and of Walter Butler, John Lyndesay et al (see *L. P.* 11:60) referred and subsequently granted. Above ordinance approved.   250

Sep. 12   Conference with Mohawk sachems owners of the lands near
Albany   Fort Hunter.   253

29   Royal orders appointing Henry Lane vice Rob't Walters
New York   deceased, and Daniel Horsmander vice Wm Provoost removed to New Jersey, of the council; they are sworn in and take their places. Warrants for salaries signed. Mayor, sheriff and coroner of New York renominated; Edw'd Holland nominated mayor, John Lyndesay sheriff ferred and subsequently granted.   255
of Albany. Petition of Wm Dick (see *L. P.* 11:64) re-

Oct. 10   Ordinance regulating sessions of courts in Orange county referred and approved with an amendment.   258

16   Legislative minutes (see *Jour* 1:626). Petition of Walter Butler, John Lyndesay et al (see *L. P.* 11:65) referred and subsequently granted.   259

1733 v. 16

24 Legislative minutes (see *Jour.* 1:626). Licenses to purchase Indian lands granted: to John and Philipp Schuyler (see *L. P.* 11:72); to John Roseboom et al (see *L. P.* 11:70); to Fred'k Morris et al (see *L. P.* 11:71). 261

29–Nov. 1 Legislative minutes (see *Jour.* 1:627-29). 263–69

Nov. 3 Licenses to purchase Indian lands granted: to Jacob Glen, John Schuyler and Arent Bratt (see *L. P.* 11:75); to Abr'm Glen, Abr'm Truax and Phil. Schuyler (see *L. P.* 11:75); to Charles Williams, Paul Richards, Fred'k Morris, John Felton, Thos. Cockerill, Geo. Burnett, Rob't Lansing and Gerrit Lansing (see *L. P.* 11:74). 270

14 Patent granted to George Clarke (see *L. P.* 11:84). Warrants to Gabriel Ludlow clerk of the assembly and to the doorkeeper signed. Address of the council to the governor; and the governor's answer. 271

16 Letters received from the governor and from the intendant of Cape Breton relating to distress on the island for want of provisions; order thereon. 274

19 Petition of Messrs Dugan and Laronde (see *N. Y. col. mss*, 70:72) granted. Minutes sent home by Capt. Bryant. 275

Dec. 7 Warrants for salaries signed. 276

16 Order on petition of Richard Cornwell, Silvanus Palmer and other quakers in Westchester county (see *N. Y. col. mss*, 70:77). Patents granted to John Lindesay (see *L. P.* 11:79) and to Anthony Rutgers (see *L. P.* 11:77). 277

1734

Feb. 9 Address received from the grand jury of New York city and county (see *N. Y. col. mss*, 70:81). Warrant to Stephen de Lancey under resolution of the assembly. 280

11 Report on the petition of Rich'd Cornwell and other quakers (p. 277; see *N. Y. col. mss*, 70:78-79; and, *Doc. hist. N. Y.* 3:1010-11; Q 3:611). Phinehas Eyers appointed pilot (see *N. Y. col. mss*, 70:90). 281

15 Proclamation to issue for the discovery of who put the letter under the door of James Alexander (see *N. Y. col. mss*, 70:82). 283

27 Report concerning the above letter approved and papers to be filed (see *N. Y. col. mss*, 70:83-89). Petition of Lieut. Walter Butler, Chas. Williams et al (see *L. P.* 11:82) referred and patent subsequently granted. 284

Mar. 20 Warrants for salaries signed. Indian affairs; the French have built a house in the Seneca country. 285

25 Report of the committee on the above news (see *N. Y. col. mss*, 70:98). 286

1733   **v. 16**

Ap. 1   Mohawk sachems before the council; they are sorry that
          Gov. Cosby did not bring his family to America (see *N. Y.
          col. mss*, 70:101-2).   [286]

     4   Assembly adjourned.   290

    25   James Lyne ex dem Casper van Hoesen vs Isaac van Duerse
          in error.   290

p. m.-May 2 Legislative minutes (see *Jour.* 1:630-33).   291-95

    10   Petition of Capt. Long for land under water at Turtle bay,
          East river to lie on the table.   295

    17   Petition of Mr van Cortlandt for permission to send as mem-
          ber of the assembly a representative of Cortlandt manor
          referred. Plan of the land petitioned for by Capt. Long
          (p. 295) referred. Petition of John de Peyster, Rutger
          Bleecker et al (see *L. P.* 11:90) referred.   296

    21   Licenses to purchase land granted: to John de Peyster et al
          (p. 296); to Vincent Matthews; to Michael Dunning; to
          Daniel Denton.   297

    22   Writ for election of a representative for Cortlandt manor to
          issue.   298

    31   Legislative minutes (see *Jour.* 1:633).   298

June 18   Warrants for salaries signed. Legislative minutes (see *Jour.*
          1:633). Jas. Lyne ex dem C. van Hoesen vs Isaac van
          Duerse. Petition of the minister etc of the Dutch church
          in Schenectady (see *N. Y. col. mss*, 70:107) referred and
          subsequently granted.   299

   20-21 Legislative minutes (see *Jour.* 1:634-35).   302-4
          License to purchase Indian lands granted to David D.
          Schuyler (see *L. P.* 11:98).

p. m.-22 Legislative minutes (see *Jour.* 1:636).   305-6
          Patent granted to Thos. Froeman, Jas. Lyne et al (see *L. P.*
          11:99).   306

July 13   Warrants signed: to the clerk and the doorkeeper of the
          assembly for salaries; to Daniel Gautier for building a
          room for the assembly (see *N. Y. col. mss*, 70:108); to John
          de Peyster, John Schuyler and John Jurie Kast for victual-
          ling the troops at Oswego. Patents granted: to Jos. Wor-
          rell et al (see *L. P.* 11:103); to Jas. Lyne et al (see *L. P.*
          11:102). Patent of incorporation to the Dutch church at
          Schenectady (p. 302). Argument of Mr Murray relating
          to courts of justice allowed to be printed.   308

Aug. 23   Warrants signed: to Lieut. Nelson for salary as commis-
          sary at Oswego; to Dr Fisher for medicines and to
          Charles Kerr surgeon, there. Patents granted: to Wm
          Cosby sheriff of Amboy et al (see *L. P.* 11:112); to Peter
          de Lancey (see *L. P.* 11:107). Licenses to purchase In-

dian lands: to Capt. Wm Dick et al (see *L. P.* 11:110);
to Daniel Horsmander (see *L. P.* 11:108); to Johs. Lansingh et al (see *L. P.* 11:109). Accounts of Lieut.
Paschal Nelson for stores furnished to the troops at Oswego; of Matthew Beeckman and of Thos. Williams jr
for transporting soldiers, to be laid before the next assembly. 309

24 Warrants signed: to Lieut. Nelson to pay his account (see
N. Y. col. mss, 70:113); to Charles Kerr surgeon at Oswego
for salary. Gov. Cosby is going to New Jersey. 311

Sep. 30 Robert Lurting reappointed mayor, Richard Nicolls coroner,
and John Symes appointed sheriff of New York;
mayor and sheriff of Albany reappointed. 312

Oct. 3 Warrants for salaries signed. License to purchase Indian
lands granted: to Capt. Wm Dick, Nich's Cooper and John
Lindesay (see *L. P.* 11:113); to Thomas Williams, Edw'd
Collins et al (see *L. P.* 11:115). Patents: to Johs. Lansingh et al. (p. 309); to Vincent Matthews, Michael Dunning and Daniel Denton (p. 297; see *L. P.* 11:114). Rule
made about granting land patents. 312

17 Legislative minutes (see *Jour.* 1:637). Petitions referred: of
David D. Schuyler (see *L. P.* 11:126); of John Schuyler,
Phil. Schuyler, John Schuyler jr, and Fred. Morris (see
L. P. 11:124). 315

18 Legislative minutes (see *Jour.* 1:638). Petition of John
Schuyler et al (p. 315) granted. 316

Vol. 17, 1734-38

Oct. 24 Legislative minutes (see *Jour.* 1:638). Patent granted to
David Schuyler (16:315; see *L. P.* 11:128). Proposals
made by the secretary, the surveyor general and the
attorney general concerning the frontiers, trade and quitrents. 1

25–26 Legislative minutes (see *Jour.* 1:639). 5–6

26 Petition of Paul Richards, Lewis Johnston, Johs. Myndertse,
Johs. Coenrat Petri and Thos. Taylor (see *L. P.* 11:132)
referred. Order on petition of Gerrit Johannisen Lansing
and Robert Lansing (see *L. P.* 11:130-31). 6

29 Legislative minutes (see *Jour.* 1:640). Petition of Lieut.
Walter Butler and Arch'd Kennedy (see *L. P.* 11:138) referred. 7

p. m. Legislative minutes (see *Jour.* 1:640). License to purchase
Indian lands granted to Geo. Clarke and John Lindesay
(see *L. P.* 11:134). Patents: to Fred'k Morris et al (see

1734   **v. 17**

L. P. 11:137); to Jacob Glen, John Schuyler and Arent
Bradt (see L. P. 11:136); to Chas. Boyle (see L. P.
11:135).   8

Nov. 1   Legislative minutes (*Jour.* 1:641).   10

p. m.   Patent granted to James Stringham and Daniel Everitt (see
L. P. 11:139).   10

2–4   Legislative minutes (see *Jour.* 1:642-43).   12–14

5   Draft of a proclamation for the encouragement of immigra-
tion from Europe; approved and ordered printed. Royal
order disallowing an act of assembly.   14

6   Legislative minutes (see *Jour.* 1:643). License to purchase
Indian lands granted to Corn's van Horne et al (see L. P.
11:141). Farmers of duties on Indian goods called on for
their accounts. Accounts of treasurer called for. Proclamation to issue etc (see *N. Y. col. mss*, 70:118).   18

7   Warrant drawn June 18 to order of Johs. Cuyler etc exchanged for one to order Jeremiah van Rensselaer. Warrant to Lawrence Claesen for salary as Indian interpreter.
Legislative minutes (see *Jour.* 1:644).   19

8–11   Legislative minutes (see *Jour.* 1:644-45).   20–21

12   License to purchase Indian land granted to Wm Cosby jr,
Henry Cosby, John Felton et al (see L. P. 11:144-45).   22

13   Legislative minutes (see *Jour.* 1:645).   22

15   Account of bills of credit cancelled and outstanding called
for. Legislative minutes (see *Jour.* 1:646).   23

p. m.   Legislative minutes (see *Jour.* 1:646).   25

18   John Peter Zenger arrested for publishing seditious libels.   25

20   Legislative minutes (see *Jour.* 1:647). Patents granted: to
George Clarke (see L. P. 11:148); to Peter Winne (see
L. P. 11:149). Warrant to issue to David Abr'm Schuyler
for salary as commissary at Oswego.   25

25   Above warrant signed. Patent granted to John Hamilton,
Fred'k Morris, Thos. Hammond, Michael Laurier, John
Alson and Joseph Sackett jr (see L. P. 11:150). Legisla-
tive minutes (see *Jour.* 1:647).   27

p. m.   Legislative minutes (see *Jour.* 1:647). Petition of Elizabeth
Deane widow of Christ'r Deane (see L. P. 11:151) referred.   29

26–28   Legislative minutes (see *Jour.* 1:648-49).   31–32

Dec. 2   License to purchase Indian lands granted to Jacob Lansingh (see L. P. 11:152).   36

1735

Feb. 5   Warrants for salaries signed. Account of the revenue called
for. Proclamation to issue for the discovery of counterfeiters of bills of credit. Warrant of survey granted to
Thos. Williams and Edw'd Collins (see L. P. 11:160).   36

1735   v. 17

Mar. 6   Warrants for salaries signed. Gabriel Ludlow appointed
         clerk of the peace and of the common pleas in Orange
         county; Vincent Matthews the former clerk refuses to sur-
         render the records (see *N. Y. col. mss,* 70:126).   38

Ap. 3   Patents granted: to Wm Cosby jr, Henry Cosby, John Fel-
         ton et al (p. 22; see *L. P.* 11:165); to Fred'k Morris et al
         (see *L. P.* 11:166). Order on petition of Gerrit Johannise
         Lansingh and Robert Lansingh (p. 6). Caveat entered by
         Andries Coeymans and others against a patent to Thos.
         Williams and Edw'd Collins (p. 36).   40

5   Warrant to Mathew Beeckman for transporting soldiers to
         Oswego. Order on petition of Thos. Williams and Edw'd
         Collins (see *L. P.* 11:167). Minutes sent home.   42

June 12 Addition to the proclamation of Nov. 5 (p. 14). Accounts of
         the auditor-general examined and warrant signed. War-
         rants for salaries signed.   46

27   Additional instruction to Gov. Cosby that the surveyors
         general of customs shall be members of the councils in the
         colonies; John Peagrum present surveyor general sworn
         in and takes his seat. Patent of incorporation granted to
         the church at Hempstead (see *N. Y. col. mss,* 70:131).
         License to purchase Indian lands granted to Jacob Glen
         et al (see *L. P.* 11:177). John de Peyster and John Schuy-
         ler appointed commissaries for victualling the troops at
         Oswego.   48

July 4   Paul Richards appointed mayor vice Robert Lurting de-
         ceased. Licenses to purchase Indian lands granted: to
         John Groesbeck, Peter Wagenaer et al (see *L. P.* 11:180);
         to Wm Dick (see *L. P.* 11:181); to Lieut. Walter Butler
         and Greetje Vrowman (see *L. P.* 11:182).   51

21   Royal order confirming an act of assembly. Draft of patent
         to Hempstead church (p. 48) referred and subsequently
         approved. Gov. Cosby is going to New Jersey.   53

Sep. 2   Warrants for salaries signed. Mistake in drawing warrant
         to Matthew Beeckman on the wrong fund rectified. Gov.
         Cosby intending to go to Albany nominates Paul Richards
         as mayor, Capt. Wm. Cosby sheriff and Rich'd Nicholls
         coroner of New York; Edw'd Holland mayor and John
         Lindesay sheriff of Albany. Patent granted to Aron
         Stephens and John Lindesay (see *L. P.* 11:185).   55

29   Nominations for mayors etc of New York and Albany made
Albany   as above.   57

Oct. 17 Legislative minutes (see *Jour.* 1:652).   57
Ft George

24   Account of moneys appropriated for military purposes called
         for. Warrant to Surgeon Chas. Kerr for services at

1735   v. 17

Oswego signed. Petition of Lieut. Paschal Nelson (see
N. Y. col. mss, 70:141) referred. License to purchase
Indian lands granted to Arch'd Kennedy and Lewis John-
ston (see *L. P.* 11:189).   58

Nov. 3   Patent granted to David Schuyler and John Lindesay (see
L. P. 11:190). Report on the petition of Lieut. Paschal
Nelson (p. 58; see *N. Y. col. mss,* 70:145); order thereon.
Legislative minutes (see *Jour.* 1:652).   60

4-7   Legislative minutes (see *Jour.* 1:653-54).   64-66

7   Patent granted to Peter de Lancey and John Lindesay (see
L. P. 11:191).   66

8   Legislative minutes (see *Jour.* 1:655).   69

24   Gov. Cosby ill and the council meet in his bedroom. Rip
van Dam suspended from the council. Minutes sent home. 74

1736

Mar. 10   Gov. Cosby dead. George Clarke elected to act as president,
James Alexander not voting; he is sworn in and takes the
chair. Proclamation to issue giving notice of Gov.
Cosby's death and confirming all officers in their places.
Seal commission etc delivered to President Clarke; also
seal of New Jersey.   75

11   Communication received from Mr Home, secretary of New
Jersey, concerning the seal of that province and Cosby's
commission of it; order thereon.   77

18   Assembly adjourned. Patents granted: to Wm Bowen, Jacob
Glen and John Lindesay (see *L. P.* 12:2); to John Groes-
beck, Peter Wagenaer, David Schuyler, John Empie,
Stephen van Rensselaer and Gerardus Beeckman (see
L. P. 12:4).   77

25   Patents granted: to James Stringham (see *L. P.* 11:193);
to John Schuyler and Neltje Bradt, widow of Jochim Bradt
(see *L. P.* 12:37). Petition of John Lindesay and Phil
Livingston (see *L. P.* 12:8) to lie on the table. Order concerning purchases of Indian lands.   79

Ap. 1   Patrick Lithgow ex dem Wm Nicoll defendant in error vs
Brinley Sylvester. Patrick Lithgow ex dem Wm Nicoll
and Ruth Dwight defendants in error vs Brinley Sylvester.
Warrants for salaries signed. Order in relation to " coun-
terparts " of bills of credit found in the warehouse of Rob't
Lurting deceased.   83

15   Counterfeited dollars found in the secretary's office; order
thereon. Brinley Sylvester vs Patrick Lithgow etc in error
(see *N. Y. col. mss,* 71:14).   85

22   Petitions of Joseph Sackett (see *L. P.* 12:9) referred. Order
on petition of freeholders of Orange county complaining
against James Jackson judge of the common pleas.   86

1736   **v. 17**

27–May 4 Assembly adjourned.   87–88

6   Patents granted: to John Lindesay and Phil. Livingston
(p. 79); to Joseph Sackett (p. 86). Patrick Lithgow etc
vs Brinley Sylvester. Indian affairs; South Carolina Indians want to make a treaty with the five nations (see
N. Y. col. mss, 71:20).   89

13   Account of the revenue called for. Petition of John de Peyster and Johannes Lawyer (see *L. P.* 12:11) referred.   91

16   Report concerning the counterparts of bills of credit found
(p. 83). Patent granted to John de Peyster and Johannes
Lawyer (p. 91). Oath taken by the president as chancellor.
Tools for Oswego.   92

20   Order on petition of freeholders of Orange county against
Judge James Jackson. Petition of Adoniah Schuyler (see
L. P. 12:18) referred.   96

27   Indian affairs. Minutes sent home.   98

June 10 Provision to be made for Mrs Cosby widow of the late governor. Mrs Cosby makes a present to the government of
the queen's picture. Account of the revenue to be filed
(see *N. Y. col. mss*, 71:24). Furniture for the council chamber to be bought. Petition of Lieut. Walter Butler referred, and license to purchase Indian lands subsequently
granted (see *L. P.* 12:15-16). Accounts of the auditor-
general examined and warrant signed. Patent for a ferry
from Staten Island to Elizabethtown granted to Adoniah
Schuyler (p. 96). Warrants for salaries signed.   99

15   Letters received from the duke of Newcastle and from Mr
Oglethorpe about the settlement in Georgia and Spanish
designs; order thereon.   102

17   Proclamation against supplying provisions to the Spaniards
to be printed. Patent granted to Wm Dick, Fred'k Morris, Alex'r Colden, Elizabeth Colden, Wm Cosby, Tim'y
Bagley, Charles Williams and John Lyne (see *L. P.* 12:20).
Warrants signed: to President Clarke for council chamber
furniture; to commissaries for victualling troops at
Oswego.   104

26   Pardon granted to Marg't Glass convicted of felony on the
application of Mrs Cosby. Petition of Lieut. Walter Butler
(see *L. P.* 12:31) to lie on the table. Petition of Richard
Nicholls (see *L. P.* 12:29) granted.   106

July 1 Patent granted to Lieut. Walter Butler (p. 106).   108

15   Patent granted to Thos. Noxon (see *L. P.* 12:34).   108

24   Assembly adjourned. Draft of patent to Adoniah Schuyler
(p. 96, 99) approved. Daniel Horsmanden appointed judge
of the court of vice admiralty. Patrick Lithgow etc vs
Brinley Sylvester.   110

1736   **v. 17**

29   Patrick Lithgow etc vs Brinley Sylvester. Dan'l Horsmanden sworn in as judge of the admiralty.   III

Aug. 5   Patent granted to James Mounell (see *L. P.* 12:37). License
to purchase Indian land of John Wemp (see *L. P.* 12:38).
Warrant to issue to Dr Shuckburg surgeon of the four
independent companies for medicines furnished to the garrison at Oswego.   112

Sep. 14–15 Assembly adjourned.   113–14

23   Licenses to purchase Indian lands granted: to James Henderson and John Lindesay (see *L. P.* 12:44); to Wouter
Vrooman (see *L. P.* 12:43). Patent to Fred'k Morris and
Samuel Heath (see *L. P.* 12:41). Orders on petitions: of
John Wemp (see *L. P.* 12:40); of Thos. Hunt jr (see *L. P.*
12:42). Account of John de Peyster for supplies to Oswego
garrison (see *N. Y. col. mss*, 71:33-34) referred. Warrant to
Dr Shuckburg (p. 112) signed. Fees for reports on petitions fixed.   115

29   Paul Richard appointed mayor, Wm Cosby sheriff, Rich'd
Nicholls coroner, of New York; Edw'd Holland mayor,
John Lindesay sheriff of Albany.   118

30   Report on Oswego accounts (see *N. Y. col. mss*, 70:35) approved and warrants to pay them ordered. Rip van Dam
appoints municipal officers: Corn's van Horne mayor,
Wm Smith recorder, Rich'd Ashfield sheriff, Richard
Nicholls coroner, of New York. Alderman Johs. Burger
delivers a copy of Rip van Dam's appointments to Wm.
Sharpas. Absent members of council called to attend. Proclamation to issue to admonish all officers and to warn
them against Rip van Dam.   119

p. m.   Draft of above proclamation referred.   122

Oct. 1   Proclamation approved and ordered published. Instruction
relating to the attendance of members of the council. Gunpowder to be purchased.   122

5   Equipments and camp utensils to be bought for the garrison of Fort George.   124

6   Account of military stores to be taken.   124

7   Hearing on the objections, made by the mayor of Westchester against patent to Thos. Hunt jr (p. 115) postponed.
License to purchase Indian lands granted to James Henderson and John Jost Petri (see *L. P.* 12:44). Necessaries
to be bought for the garrison of Fort George.   125

12   Assembly adjourned.   127

13   Additional instruction to President Clarke relating to the
form of prayer for the royal family (see *N. Y. col. mss*,
71:44).   127

1736

14 Hearing of caveat by the corporation of Albany against patent to John Wemp (p. 115) postponed. Legislative minutes (see *Jour.* 1:661). 128

15 Petition of Thos. Hunt jr (p. 115) rejected. 133

16 Albany against John Wemp (p. 115, 128) heard, but not decided. 133

19 Petitions received: from settlers near Fort Hunter about building a fort at the carrying place; from Oswego traders in behalf of Surgeon Charles Kerr; both referred to the assembly. 135

30 Geo. Clarke appointed lieutenant governor, takes the usual oaths and publishes his commission at the city hall. 136

Nov. 4 Memorial of Dr Cadw. Colden concerning purchases of Indian lands (see *N. Y. col. mss*, 71:65) referred. Petition of Wm Cosby and Charles Clinton (see *L. P.* 12:49) referred. 137

5 Patent granted to Wm. Cosby and Charles Clinton (p. 137). Henry Holland and Rensselaer Nicoll appointed assistant justices of the common pleas at Albany vice Phil. Schuyler and Edw'd Holland, resigned. 137

10 Assembly to be prorogued henceforth instead of being adjourned. A freeholder to be appointed sheriff of Westchester county. Patent granted to Chief Justice James de Lancey, John Lindesay, Paschall Nelson, Jacob Glen and Wm Bowen (see *L. P.* 12:50). 139

11 License to purchase Indian lands granted to John Poole, Timothy Green, Martin van Bergen et al (see *L. P.* 12:51). 140

Dec. 2 Report on the memorial of Dr Colden (p. 137). 141

1737

Jan. 6 Patents granted: to Samuel van Horne (see *L. P.* 12:63); conditionally to Thos. Ellison, and to John Sackett and James Stringham (see *L. P.* 12:61). License to purchase Indian lands to Valentine Herman and Fred'k Romo (see *L. P.* 12:62). 143

Feb. 24 Thos. Broughton of South Carolina writes that he has news from Commodore Dent at Jamaica of Spanish designs against Georgia. Proclamation to issue forbidding the sale of provisions etc to the Spaniards. 146

25 Proclamation approved. No vessels to be cleared for St Augustine. 147

Mar. 3 License to purchase Indian lands granted to Cloude de la Metre, Thos. Nottingham, Wm. Leggitt, George Ingoldsby and Isaac van Alstyne (see *L. P.* 12:70). 148

24 The mayor of New York ordered to impress seamen for the Tartar man-of-war, Capt. Norris commanding; a committee to inquire about desertions from the ship. 149

1737   **v. 17**

29 Assembly prorogued. Proclamation to issue for a day of
     thanksgiving (see *N. Y. col. mss*, 71:78).   151

30 Mayor of New York writes to Capt. Norris that he cannot
     comply with the order of the 24th (p. 149) and the coun-
     cil decides it has no power in the matter.   153

Ap. 4 Above decision of council reiterated on a new letter from
        Capt. Norris.   154

5   Deposition of Capt. Abr'm Kipp (see *N. Y. col. mss*, 71:80).
     Legislative minutes (see *Jour.* 1:675).   155

6   Warrant of survey granted David Abrahamsen Schuyler,
     Fred'k Morris, Charles Williams, Thos. Clarke, Edw'd Col-
     lins and Sarah Williams (16:204). Petition of Simon John-
     son, John Auboyneau and James Faviere (see *N. Y. col. mss*,
     71:81) and affidavit by Johs. Martinus van Harlingen (see
     L. P. 12:65) read.   160

14 Warrant of survey granted to Thos. Ellison (see *L. P.* 12:71).
     Indian affairs; treaty between the five nations and the Vir-
     ginia Indians (Cherriquees and Cattabaws); French trying
     to get a foothold at Tierondequat; order thereon.   164

28 Assembly prorogued.   167

May 3 Assembly dissolved. Minutes sent home.   167

5   Writs for election of a new assembly to be issued. License
     to purchase Indian lands granted to Capt. Peter Warren,
     Alex'r Ramsey and Wm. Tattum (see *L. P.* 12:79). War-
     rant of survey to James Stringham and John Sackett (see
     L. P. 12:80).   168

26 Letter received from the lords of trade concerning Massachu-
     setts and New Hampshire boundaries; order thereon. Rules
     made in regard to patents for land for which purchase
     licenses had been granted (16:312). Indian affairs; the
     French have received permission to build at Tierondequat.   170

June 15 Assembly meets.   173

Aug. 2 Patent granted to Wm Corry late of Ireland for land at
         or near Aries creek, Tienonderoga creek, Godority patent
         and Schoharie.   173

June 24 Gov. Clarke's speech to the five nations about permission
Albany   given to the French to build at Tierondequat (see *N. Y.
         col. mss*, 71:85, 87).   175

Aug. 25 Letters received, from Phil. Severne English consul at Sallee
Ft George to Macky and Smith at Cadiz, and from these to Guilian
           Verplanck, about Edw'd Burrows master of the sloop
           Happy of Bermuda (see *N. Y. col. mss*, 71:90-92).   177

26 Examination of the above Edward Burrows; order thereon.   178

Sep. 2 Legislative minutes (see *Jour.* 1:681).   184

14 Order on petition of inhabitants of New York city (see
     N. Y. col. mss, 71:95).   189

1737   **v. 17**

15   Wm Cosby sheriff of New York heard on the above peti-
     tion; council advises not to intermeddle in the matter.   189

26   Petition from Albany about securing the frontiers referred
     to the assembly. Military stores to be inspected. License
     to purchase Indian land granted to Wm Corry (see *L. P.*
     12:94). Patent to John Lindesay, Jacob Roseboom, Leen-
     dert Gansevoort and Sybrant van Schaick (see *L. P.*
     12:93).   192

29   Mayor etc of New York, and of Albany renominated. War-
     rants signed: to Henry Koster for salary as commissary
     at Oswego; to Peter Schuyler as same; to Arch'd Fisher
     and to James Henderson for medicines furnished to the
     garrison there.   195

Oct. 6 Patent granted to John Wemp, the caveat by the corpora-
        tion of Albany having been withdrawn.   197

10   Warrants signed: for salaries; for supplies and incidentals at
     Oswego; all for a year past.   197

13   Order on a petition from Schenectady (see *L. P.* 12:99).
     Patent granted to John Lindesay (see *L. P.* 12:100).   204

14   Patent granted to Jacob Lansingh, Abr'm Lansingh and
     Jacob Glen (see *L. P.* 12:100).   207

18   Patent granted to Zacharias Hoffman and Evert Derwilliger
     (see *L. P.* 12:95).   208

28   Licenses to purchase Indian lands granted: to John Jurie
     Kast jr, John Wendell jr, George Seypel and Peter Sney-
     der (see *L. P.* 12:103); to Arent van Dyck, Barent van
     Beuren, Leendert Conyn jr and Johan Coenrat Petri (see
     L. P. 12:104); to Henry van Rensselaer jr, Hendrick Wemp
     and Arent Stephens (see *L. P.* 12:105).   211

Nov. 22 Patents granted: to Aaron Bradt (see *L. P.* 12:116); to Wm
         Kettelhuyn, Kilian de Ridder, Gerrit de Rider and Wal-
         raven Cluts (see *L. P.* 12:112-13); to Valentine Herman and
         Fred. Romo (see *L. P.* 12:115). Petition of Micajah Town-
         send and Wm Hawkshust (see *N. Y. col. mss,* 71:117) read.
         Order on petition of Phil. Livingston for a certificate (see
         N. Y. col. mss, 71:116). Warrants to the Indian commis-
         sioners for salaries.   213

Dec. 6   Patent granted to John Schuyler jr, Phil. Schuyler, Stephen
         Bayard, Samuel Bayard jr, James Stephenson and John
         Livingston (see *L. P.* 12:121). License to purchase In-
         dian lands to Johs. van Deurson and Johs. van der Poel
         (see *L. P.* 12:120); renewal of such license to Timothy
         Green and Martin van Bergen (see *L. P.* 12:119).   219

13   Petition of Coenrat Frank for land on the south side of the
     Mohawk river to lie on the table.   223

16   Legislative minutes (see *Jour.* 1:712).   224

1738 v. 17

Jan. 5 Sessions of the circuit courts in the various counties settled; ordinance for it to be prepared. Questions concerning the province from the lords of trade; referred to different committees. 226

18 Ordinance concerning sessions of circuit courts read and approved. 232

Mar. 16 Patents granted: to Charles Boyle (see *L. P.* 12:128); to James Henderson sr, James Henderson jr and John Lindesay (see *L. P.* 12:125); to Phil. Livingston (see *L. P.* 12:126); licenses to purchase Indian lands to Aaron Bradt, Volkert van Veghten, Gerrit Cornelise van der Bergh, Hendrick Vrooman, Myndert Wemp, Abr'm Mebee, John Hendrick Clarke jr, Arent Stephens, Leendert Helmer and Nich's Pickett (see *L. P.* 12:129); to Henry van Rensselaer jr, Hendrick Wemp, Abr'm Truax and Arent Stephens (see *L. P.* 12:127). 233

Ap. 4 Assembly to be prorogued. 238

5 Assembly prorogued. 238

6 Hearings on the petitions: from Schenectady (p. 204; see *L. P.* 12:123); Wouter Vrooman (p. 115); the first to be granted, the latter dismissed. 239

17 Royal commission received for settling the difficulties between Connecticut and the Mohegan Indians; meeting appointed. 241

May 5 Customhouse officers to search the sloops of Abr'm Kipp and Edw'd Griffith for goods forbidden to be exported. Depositions of Abr'm Kipp master of the sloop Don Carlos, of David Griffith master of the sloop Jacob, of Lewis Thibon, of John Lush master of the sloop Georgia Packet, concerning Spanish designs upon Georgia (see *N. Y. col. mss*, 72:54-57). Proclamation to issue forbidding supplies being carried to St Augustine (see *N. Y. col. mss*, 72:61). Patent granted to Arent Bradt and Jacob Glen (see *L. P.* 12:132). Petition of Joseph Carpenter and John Lattin (see *L. P.* 12:133) to lie on the table. Royal order confirming an act of assembly. 243

8 Rhode Island commissioners agree upon the date fixed by New York commissioners in the Connecticut-Mohegans matter (see *N. Y. col. mss*, 72:52-53). Sloop of David Griffith not to be cleared. Examinations of shipmasters continued; Thos. Pemiston of the sloop Eagle (see *N. Y. col. mss*, 72:58). 258

18 Sloops of Abr'm Kipp and David Griffith may be cleared under bond upon representation of their owner, Mr Walton. Chief Justice de Lancey to be present at the meeting

1738   **v. 17**

of the commissioners for settling Mohegans-Connecticut
difficulties. Order in re Burger Huyck et al (16:118).   261

19   Capt. James Tucker of the sloop Midnight, and Alex'r Hext
examined in regard to the Spanish intentions against
Georgia (see *N. Y. col. mss, 72:59-60*). Proclamation of
May 5th rescinded (see *N. Y. col. mss, 72:63*).   265

June 6   Assembly prorogued (see *N. Y. col. mss, 72:69*).   271

24   George Clarke jr appointed secretary, and Fred'k Morris his
deputy; the latter sworn in. Examination of shipmasters;
Wm Seymour of the sloop Johanna, and Joseph Hinson of
the sloop Mary concerning smallpox in the West Indies
(see *N. Y. col. mss, 72:70-71*). Quarantine measures.   271

27   John Hunt of the brigantine St Peter examined (see *N. Y.
col. mss, 72:72*). Vessels from the West Indies and from
South Carolina to be quarantined near Bedlars (Bedloes)
island.   276

Aug. 22   Indian affairs; five nations not to go to Virginia to make
treaties (see *N. Y. col. mss, 72:77-78*). License to purchase
Indian lands granted to Eben'r Holly, Solomon Carpenter,
George Wood and Wm Fin (see *L. P. 12:158*). Patents
to Cadw. Colden jr, and Coenrat Rightmeyer (see *L. P.
12:159*); to Johannes van Deurson and Johs. van der Poel
(see *L. P. 12:160*).   279

Sep. 29   Simon Johnson proposed for mayor, James Livingston for
sheriff of New York; both rejected: Wm Cosby preferred
as sheriff; Richard Nicholls nominated coroner. Patent
granted to John Lindesay (see *L. P. 12:164*). Order on
petition of Robert Hunt (see *L. P. 12:165*). Warrants
signed: to Surgeon Charles Kerr for services at Oswego;
to commissioners for victualling troops there; to Lieut.
Paschall Nelson for salary as commissary there.   282

p. m.   Edward Holland nominated mayor, John Lindesay sheriff
of Albany.   285

Oct. 5   Petition of the sachems of the Seneca country for a pastor;
referred to the assembly. License to purchase Indian land
granted to Capt. Edw. Clarke (see *L. P. 12:163*).   286

17   Patents granted: to Alex'r Montgomerie, Alex'r McNaught,
Peter McArthur, Daniel Carmichil and 26 others lately
arrived from North Britain (see *L. P. 12:170*); to John Mc-
Neal (see *L. P. 12:168*); to Ronald Campbell (see *L. P.
13:1*); to Anne, Sarah, Catherine, George, Elizabeth and
Mary Bradley, children of the late Att'y-Gen. Richard
Bradley (see *L. P. 12:167*). Petition of John Thomas (see
L. P. 12:169) tabled.   290

20   Legislative minutes (see *Jour. 1:724*).   295

1738   **v. 17**

28   Royal mandamus appointing Geo. Clarke jr to the council
      vice Francis Harrison resigned. Patent granted to Tim-
      othy Bagley, John Watts and George Lurting (see *L. P.*
      13:6). Order on petition of John Thomas (see *L. P.* 13:5).
      Warrants for military expenses at Albany, Schenectady,
      Fort Hunter and Oswego signed. Minutes sent home by
      Capt. Bryant.   301

1739

Feb. 9   Royal order repealing an act of assembly. Assembly dis-
          solved; writs for election of a new one to issue. Licenses
          to purchase Indian lands granted: to Geo. Ingoldsby,
          Timothy Bagley, Rich'd Nicholls, Fred'k Morris, Rich'd
          Shuckburgh, Alex'r Colhoun, Chas. O'Neile, Jas. Lyne,
          Arent Stephens, Leendert Lansing, John Baptist van
          Eps jr, Dow Fonda, Abr'm Truax, Rob't Todd, Wm Eng-
          lish and• Alex'r Malcolme (see *L. P.* 13:18); to Leonard
          Ganseworth, Gerrit Corn's van der Bergh, Abr'm Wen-
          dall, Abr'm Dow, Dow Fonda, Johs. Hun, Jacob Wendall
          et al (see *L. P.* 13:17). Patent to Phil. Livingston, John
          de Peyster, Cadw. Colden jr, John Joseph Petri, John
          Lindesa·· and James Henderson (see *L. P.* 13:17).   305

Vol. 18, 1736-40

Legislative minutes of council from Oct. 14, 1736 to Nov. 3, 1740 printed in
Journal of the legislative council of the colony of New York, 1:661-767.

Vol. 19, 1739-44

1739

Mar. 1   Order on petition of Capt. John Budd, Hachaliah Brown
          and Jonathan Brown (see *N. Y. col. mss,* 72:101).   1

27   Table of fees for the ferry from Rye to Oysterbay approved
          (see *L. P.* 13:24).   3

Ap. 14   Gov. Clarke not to go to Albany and meet the Indians be-
          cause of smallpox in town. Assembly to adjourn for the
          same reason. Minutes sent home.   4

May 17   Patents granted: to Corn's du Bois (see *L. P.* 13:27); to
          Edward Clarke (see *L. P.* 13:28); to Jas. Henderson and
          Philipp Livingston (see *L. P.* 13:29); to Arent Bratt et al
          (see *L. P.* 13:30). License to purchase Indian lands to
          Samuel Burn and William Helen (see *L. P.* 13:31). Peti-
          tion of James de Lancey and Edw'd Collins (see *L. P.*
          13:33) granted. Petition of Jeremiah Dunbar (see *L. P.*
          13:34). Indian affairs (see *N. Y. col. mss,* 72:107-9).   5

21   Indian affairs; French intrigues. Answer of Dr Cadw.
          Colden to the petition of Jeremiah Dunbar (see *L. P.*
          13:35-36); order thereon.   9

1739   **v. 19**

June 28   Patent granted to Edw'd Clarke (see *L. P.* 13:42). License
          to purchase Indian land to Charles Boyle (see *L. P.* 13:43).
          Order on a petition of John Auboyneau, Corn's Clopper
          and Widow Ann McKnight (see *N. Y. col. mss,* 72:117).   18
July 3   Information concerning forged bills of credit; proclamation
          to issue regarding it (see *N. Y. col. mss,* 72:118). Certifi-
          cate prayed for by John Auboyneau et al (p. 18) approved.
          Warrant to commissioners for victualling troops at
          Oswego signed.   21
      6   Above proclamation to be printed. Above certificate signed. 24
Aug. 8   Order on complaint by Walter Hetherington, schoolmaster
          at the ferry vs Justice Christ'r Codwise of Kings county
          (see *N. Y. col. mss,* 72:120). License to purchase Indian
          land granted to James Dillon (see *L. P.* 13:48).   25
     14   Patent granted to Martin van Bergen (see *L. P.* 13:50).
          Petition of Charles O'Neile, Alex'r Colden and Peter
          Matthews (see *L. P.* 13:51) tabled. Hearing of Walter
          Hetherington vs Christ'r Codwise (p. 25; see *N. Y. col. mss,*
          72:121, 125).   27
     17   Royal warrant to grant commissions of marque and reprisal
          against Spain; letter from duke of Newcastle in relation
          thereto. Proclamation to issue authorizing reprisals (see
          N. Y. col. mss, 72:122).   29
p. m.   Above proclamation read, approved and ordered printed.
          Draft of a commission of marque to be prepared.   33
     21   Form of the commission and instructions to be given to
          commanders of private men-of-war. Form of bond for
          owners of them.   33
     26   Capt. Pearce of the Flamborough, royal man-of-war wants
          carpenters impressed to clean his ship; opinion of council
          thereon.   42
Sep. 29   John Cruger nominated mayor, Wm Cosby sheriff and
          Richard Nicholls coroner of New York; Edw'd Holland
          mayor, and Henry Holland sheriff of Albany.   44
Oct. 24   Assembly matters referred to a committee.   44
     25   Report of the above committee. Petition of Benj. Faneuil,
          Peter Fauconnier and Johs. Hardenbergh (see *N. Y. col.
          mss,* 72:135-36) read. Patent granted to Peter Winne (see
          L. P. 13:59).   45
Nov. 7   Warrant to commissioners for victualling troops at Oswego
          signed. Vessels known or suspected of trade with the
          Spaniards to be cleared only under bond.   50
Dec. 6   Lieut. Walter Butler commanding at Fort Hunter to be
          commissioner for building a fort in the Mohawk country
          vice Hendrik Vrooman deceased, with Jan Wimple.

1739   v. 19

Vidonia and Malmsey vines on board the snow Restoration
Thos. Fowler master, and the ship Canary Merchant John
Plunkett master, not to be seized (see *N. Y. col. mss,*
72:146-47).   52

17   Letter received from Gov. Belcher relating to boundary matters. Commissioners to meet at Albany.   53

1740

Feb. 8   Capt. Henry Row appointed commissioner of fortifications
vice Corn's de Peyster declined.   55

Ap. 3   Petitions of Rev Henry Barclay (see *L. P.* 13:63); of Peter
Winne and James Dillon (see *L. P.* 13:64) for licenses to
purchase Indian lands referred and subsequently granted.
Petitions of Jacques Cortelyou, Jacques Cortelyou
jr, Hermanus Borkelo and Simon Simonson (see *L. P.*
13:22), and of Thos. Stillwell both for ferry rights from
Long Island to Staten Island referred. Warrants for
salaries signed. Debtors of the treasury to be prosecuted.   56

23   Fees of the admiralty court in cases of prizes considered and
an ordinance relating to them to be prepared.   62

24   Ordinance for establishing fees for the condemnation of
prizes in the admiralty court. Massachusetts boundary.
Jacques Cortelyou et al to withdraw their petition (p. 56)
and bring in another.   64

30   Proclamations to issue: against damages to the fortifications;
to recall commissions of marque. Leggit of Westchester
accused of dissuading men from enlisting against Spain, to
be prosecuted.   69

Ap. 5   Opinion of council concerning a double guard at Oswego.
Mohawks want a new chapel; referred to the assembly.   70

12   Letters received from the duke of Newcastle with the
declaration of war against Spain; proclamation to issue
announcing it and calling for volunteers. Royal order received concerning letters of marque. Order on a caveat
entered by Corn's van Brunt, Jose van Brunt, Rutger van
Brunt, Nich's van Brunt, George Lott and Thos. Pallut
against ferry right petitioned for by Jacques Cortelyou
et al (p. 56, 64).   71

May 13   Legget and Barnes not to be prosecuted for the present.
Message from the assembly about adjournment.   72

Reversed side

17   Draft of a commission of marque and reprizal and instructions to commanders of private men-of-war. Form of bond
to be given by owners. Terret Lester appointed pilot.   1

29   Embargo laid on all provisions.   14

June 23   Instructions to Gov. Clarke for the expedition against the
Spanish colonies. Proclamation to issue for the encouragement of volunteers (see *N. Y. col. mss,* 73:1-2).   15

24   Proclamation to invite volunteers to come forward and
      enlist. " Method and form " to be subscribed by volun-
      teers received from Col. Blakeney.   23
27   Col. Blakeney present in council. Letters to be written to
      enlisting officers (see *N. Y. col. mss*, 73: 3-4).   30
28   Account of available moneys in the treasury called for.
      Minissink affairs. Assembly to be asked to provide means
      for the expedition.   31
July 5   Order on a letter from Anth. Lispenard jr, John Ward,
          David Ogden and Wm Fowler about the command of a
          company raised by them; Anthony Lispenard to be captain.
          Affidavit of Solomon Davis about Minissink matters
          referred.   32
12   Opinion of council concerning the pay to be given to the
      volunteers.   33
22   David Provoost jr to be captain of a company raised by
      him; the lieutenancy is offered to Hinman who refuses to
      accept; he is to be persuaded to take it.   35
26   Robert Kennedy appointed 2d lieutenant, Wm Nicolls
      ensign in Capt. Provoost's company. Answer from the
      burgomasters of Amsterdam (see *N. Y. col. mss*, 72:142).
      Warrants for salaries signed. Patent granted to Valkert
      Oothout, John de Wit, James Gardiner, Chas. Williams,
      Rich'd Nicholls, Wm Jamison et al (see *L. P.* 13:68).   36
Aug. 4   Embargo on provisions raised sufficient quantities having
          been secured for the expedition.   38
5   Translation of letter from the burgomasters of Amsterdam
      (p. 36). Thos. Stillwell granted the sole ferry right from
      Yellow Hook, Kings county, to the mouth of the Kill van
      Kull on Staten Island. Minutes sent home.   39
Sep. 29 Indian conference at Albany, Aug. 16-17. Royal approbation
          of an act of assembly. John Cruger nominated mayor,
          Wm Jamison sheriff, Rich'd Nicholls coroner of New
          York; John Schuyler jr mayor, Henry Holland sheriff of
          Albany. Warrants for salaries signed.   41
Oct. 14 Warrant to commissioners for victualling troops at Oswego
          signed.   58
20   Patent granted to Jacob Mase, John Rutger Bleecker and
      Jacobus Rutger Bleecker (see *L. P.* 13:67).   66
Nov. 3   Warrant to commissioners for victualling troops at Oswego. 59
6   Additional instruction to Gov. Clarke relating to the value
      of foreign coins; proclamation to issue promulgating it.   59
Dec. 2   Proclamation relating to foreign coin read, approved and
          to be printed. Paul François Cebe surgeon, and wife, both
          from Languedoc, France, granted letters of denization. 64

Reversed side
1740   v. 19

4   Letter from the lords of trade about the boundary line between Massachusetts and Rhode Island. Patent granted to
Stephen Bayard et al (see *L. P.* 13-70). Warrants for
salaries signed.   67

1741

Jan. 19   Letter received from Admiral Vernon regarding Spanish
and French naval movements. No provisions to be exported to foreign ports. Indian affairs (see *N. Y. col. mss,*
73:29).   71

Feb. 4   Letter from the duke of Newcastle about trade etc; order
thereon. Wheat forbidden to be exported. Draft of patent
to Stephen Bayard approved.   73

6   Petition of Jeremiah Lattouch and Joseph Hains for leave
to export wheat bought for Thos. Gunter and Thos.
Perkins of Boston granted. Col. John Moore and Col.
Joseph Robinson, allowed to export beer and candles
loaded on board a brigantine before the order of January
19th.   74

Mar. 12   Warrants for salaries signed. Petition of Corn's van Horne
(see *N. Y. col. mss,* 73:37, 40) rejected. Vincent Pearce
vs John Key and Michael Hubbard in error; same vs
George Cummins.   77

19   Records saved from the fire in the fort to be stored in the
city hall.   79

20   Arrangements to be made in the common council room of
the city hall for placing the records.   80

26   Archibald Kennedy vs Thomas Fowles.   81

28   Petition of Gulian Verplanck (see *N. Y. col. mss,* 73:42); not
granted. Petition of John Cruger (see *N. Y. col. mss,*
73:44); not granted. Council advise that the petitions of
Isaac and Abr'm de Peyster (see *N. Y. col. mss,* 73:45) and
of John Merrett (see *N. Y. col. mss,* 73:43) be granted.   87

Ap. 2   Royal order and proclamation concerning military stores
etc received; also letter from And'w Stone secretary of the
lords justices in relation to export of provisions; orders
thereon. Corn's van Horne's sloop Garrett to be sent
from Suffolk county to New York when found.   91

15   Request of the common council to offer by proclamation a
reward for the discovery of incendiaries (see *N. Y. col. mss,*
74:9); so ordered. Petition of Lauchlan Campbell et al
(see *L. P.* 13:73-74) referred. Comyns vs Pearce; Key and
Hubbard vs Pearce; Kennedy vs Fowles.   93

16   Information received concerning Langlazaree suspected of
being a French spy; to be arrested. Pearce vs Comyns;
same vs Key and Hubbard.   97

1741

23 Warrants: to Charles Kerr surgeon at Oswego; to Lieut.
Paschall Nelson for transporting soldiers; to Gov. Clarke
for same and for salaries signed. Petitions referred: of
Peter Winne and James Dillon (see *L. P.* 13:87) of Rev.
Henry Barclay (see *L. P.* 13:88).   123

25 Patents granted to the foregoing.   125

29 Petition of Jean Drouet (see *N. Y. col. mss,* 73:59-60) referred. Mayors etc of New York and Albany renominated.   126

Oct. 6 Petitions referred: of Leendert Gansevort, Henry Holland, Corns. ten Broeck, Jacob Wendell, Abr'm H. Wendell, Johannes H. Wendell, Johs. Hun, Abr'm Dow, Peter
Winne, Garrit Corns. van den Bergh, Dow Fonda, John
Lindesay, Anna widow of Johs. Everts Wendell and Edw'd
Holland (see *L. P.* 13:94); of John Schuyler (see *L. P.*
13:96); of Gerardus and John Groesbeck (see *L. P.* 13:97).
The last two granted; further information required on the
first.   Warrants signed to Wm Bradford for salary as
printer; to Andries Bratt for salary as commissary at
Oswego. Letters: from Gov. Wm Shirley of Boston;
from Jno. Minote about French intrigues among the
Indians: referred to the assembly. Report on petition of
Jean Drouet (p. 126).   128

29 Warrants: to contractors for victualling troops at Oswego;
to Henry van Rensselaer for same; to James Ramsay for
salary as surgeon there; to Gov. Clarke for military transportation.   132

Nov. 4 Warrant to Henry van Rensselaer for transporting powder
to Oswego signed. Patent granted to Leendert Gansevort
et al (p. 128; see *L. P.* 13:104).   132

16 Petition of Jean Drouet master of the ship Zephyr de
Bourdeaux for leave to sell some of his cargo to pay for
repairs to his ship granted.   134

26 License•to purchase Indian lands granted to Stephen Bayard,
Corn's van Schaick, John Baptist van Rensselaer, Johs. van
Duersen, Barent Vaasburgh and Jacobus van Rensselaer
(see *L. P.* 13:109); patent to Peter Schuyler et al (see *L. P.*
13:81). Petition of Robert Livingston, John Cannon, John
Cannon, jr, Jesse Montagnie, John Aspinwall and Gerard
Beekman for wharf right and land under water in Mont-
gomerie ward referred for further information.   135

Dec. 22 Order on complaint by inhabitants of Rye against Benj.
Brown justice of the Peace (see *N. Y. col. mss,* 73:65).
Warrants for salaries signed. License to purchase Indian
lands granted to Phil. Livingston jr, Henry Holland, Gerrit
Abramse Lansing, Jacob Lansing jr, Johs. Beeckman and

1741

Johs. Seger (see *L. P.* 13:110). Report on the petition of
Robert Livingston et al (p. 135); granted.   137

1742

Jan. 2   Conference with members of the assembly concerning military stores arrived from England. Petition of Altje Colden, Samuel Heath and Francis Sylvester (see *L. P.* 13:106) referred. Petition of Edw'd Collins, Arent Stephens, Cornelia widow of John Schuyler jr, and Henry Holland for the same tract of land granted.   139

Feb. 25   Answer of Benj. Brown to the complaint against him (p. 137; see *N. Y. col. mss*, 73:70). Order in regard to filing complaints.   142

Mar. 10   Protest and affidavit by the master and supercargo of the brigantine Sea Horse against Thos. Pickering governor of Tortola. Complaint against Benj. Brown (p. 137, 139) to be dismissed. Warrants for salaries signed. Negro Tom sentenced to be hanged for burning the house of Widow Bratt reprieved. Patent granted to Richard Bradley (see *L. P.* 13:115).   143

      12   Negro Tom to be executed. Bond given for the Sea Horse (p. 143) to be cancelled.   145

      18   Letter handed in by Col. Robinson, which directed to " Capt." Robinson was found under his door revealing some design against the city; opinion of council thereon.   146

Ap.   1   Smallpox reported raging at Curacao; vessels arrived from there to be inspected and quarantined if necessary.   147

       7   Quarantine measures. Indian affairs; southern Indians expected at Albany; Gov. Clarke to go there. License to purchase Indian lands granted to Hendrick Ramsen (see *L. P.* 13:116).   148

       9   Order on petition of Mary Burton (see *N. Y. col. mss*, 74:142-43). Warrant to Gov. Clarke for house rent.   149

      10   Fred'k Philipse and Dan'l Horsmanden certify that Mary Burton is entitled to the reward claimed. Minutes sent home.   151

      27   Indian affairs; meeting between six nations and southern Indians necessary; Georgia sends money for presents to six nations; Gov. Clarke advised to go to Albany.   152

May 12   Petition of Thomas, William, Richard, Nathaniel and Walter Hughson (see *N. Y. col. mss*, 73:72) rejected. License to purchase Indian lands granted to Adoniah Schuyler, Sam'l Bayard jr, J. B. van Rensselaer, Oliver de Lancey, Margaret Vetch, Claus van den Bergh, Marg't Guss, Abr'm Vaasburgh, John van Duerse, Hendrick Coster and Tobias ten Eyck (see *L. P.* 13:120). Petition of Joseph Sackett jr (see *L. P.* 13:117) not granted.   153

1742

22   Warrants to Gov. Clarke for Indian presents and for expenses of journey to Albany signed.   155

31   Difficulties to obtain the money on the above warrants from the treasurer.   156

June 24   Order on petition of James Alexander and John Moore (see L. P. 13:119). Warrants for salaries and Indian commissioners.   157

July 14   Report of the plague raging at Surinheim [Surinam]. Order on a petition of Stephen Bayard, Corns. van Schaick et al (p. 135; see L. P. 13:123), and caveat against it by the owners of Westenhook patent. License to purchase Indian land granted to Jeremiah Greslaer, Martinus Vrooman, Barent Vrooman and Jesaias Swart (see L. P. 13:124). Warrants to Gov. Clarke for firewood and candles to Fort George signed.   160

30   Letters from Capt. Wm Ellis, commanding the Gosport man-of-war, wanting men and announcing that he has orders to sail for S. Carolina; impress warrants issued; volunteers for the cruise called for.   163

Aug. 3   Letter received from Capt. Wm Ellis, asking that an embargo be laid on all ships, until he has completed the crew of the Gosport; council advise not to do it.   165

10   Edward Collins as agent of the Westenhook patentees withdraws the caveat against patent to Stephen Bayard et al (p. 160); it is granted.   166

Sep. 1   Patent granted to Richard Bradley (see L. P. 13:125). Petition of John and Eupham Alsop (see L. P. 13:127) not granted because the land asked for might lay in the Wawayanda or Minisinck patents. Letter received from Cadw. Colden concerning Luke Barrington arrested for seditious and treasonable words; Luke Barrington who has passed himself of for a schoolmaster and for a methodist preacher under the name of Singleton, to be kept in prison. Warrants for salaries signed.   167

3   George Jos. Moore deputy clerk of the council appointed upon her petition guardian of Mary Burton under age, for receiving a reward (p. 149).   170

29   Mayor, sheriff and coroner of New York renominated; Cornelius Cuyler nominated mayor, Henry Holland sheriff of Albany.   170

Oct. 13   Patents granted for land in Orange county: to John and Eupham Alsop (see L. P. 13:133); to Bartholomew Vrooman, Martinus Vrooman, Barent Vrooman, Jesaias Swart and Jeronimus Greslaer (see L. P. 13:131). Licenses to pur-

chase lands: to Johs. Lawyer jr, Nicholas York, John Eckerson and Peter Silly (see *L. P.* 13:130); to Wm Bauch and
Jacob Fred'k Lawyer (see *L. P.* 13:129). Warrants signed:
to Corns. ten Broeck for military transportation; to Chas.
Kerr for salary as surgeon at Oswego.   171

18   Letter from Thos. Corbett, secretary of the admiralty board
in regard to providing crews for men-of-war. Letter received from Capt. Peter Warren of the Launceston man-
of-war about desertions; proclamation to issue accord-
ihgly.   174

30   Warrants for the service at Oswego signed. Minutes sent
home.   176

1743

Ap. 27   Letter received from Lt. Gov. Wm Gooch of Virginia on
Indian troubles; Virginia and Maryland intend to send
commissioners for a treaty with the six nations. Indian
affairs; minutes of Indian commissioners Mar. 7, 20, 1743;
letter from Gov. Clarke to Indian commissioners.   177

28   Assembly votes received.   187

29   Warrants for salaries signed. Patents granted to Richard
Bradley and his daughters Anne and Catherine (see *L. P.*
13:138). License to purchase Indian lands to Moses
Northrup, Abigail his wife, and Moses Northrup jr (see
L. P. 13:140). Patent to Casparus Bronck, Gerrit van
Bergen, Martin van Bergen and Hendrick Ramsen (see
L. P. 13:137).   183

May 15   Letter received from Gen. Oglethorpe at Frederica on Indian
affairs, Spanish invasion and asking for guns and powder;
no guns can be sent on account of the threatening war
with France.   192

24   Order on a memorial by Patrick Houston (see *N. Y. col. mss,*
74:155) and a letter from Gen. Oglethorpe about the loan
of guns. Warrant of survey granted to John de Peyster
(see *L. P.* 13:145). Petition of Alex'r Colden (see *N. Y.
col. mss,* 74:157) granted.   193

27   Report on the memorial of Patrick Houston (p. 193); old
guns to be loaned. Order on petition of John Little (see
L. P. 13:147). Warrant of survey granted to Richard
Bradley (see *L. P.* 13:146).   198

June 16   Letter from Indian commissioners at Albany; minutes of
the same, May 2. Warrants for salaries etc signed. Patent
granted to Stephen Bayard (see *L. P.* 13:148).   201

21   License to purchase Indian lands granted to John Rutherford (see *L. P.* 13:152). Answer received from   Cadw.

1743

Colden to the petition of John Little (p. 198). Order on petition of John Cleves (see *N. Y. col. mss*, 74:151).   213

Sep. 22
House of
Geo. Clarke

Gov. George Clinton takes the oaths after the reading of his commission and swears in the members of the council present; Lt. Gov. Geo. Clarke delivers the seals. Proclamation to issue continuing all officers in their places. The governor's commission published at the city hall.   216

26   Dr Cadw. Colden takes the oaths. Assembly to be dissolved.   217

27   Writs to elect a new assembly to be made returnable on the 8th of November.   218

29   Mayors, sheriffs and coroner of New York and of Albany renominated.   218

Oct. 18   Philipp van Cortlandt and Dan'l Horsmanden sworn in. Letter from the lords justices about impending war with France. Council adjourns to the house of Geo. Clarke.   219

19   Lt. Gov. Clarke to be sworn in as councillor; refuses on account of infirmity; his opinion on what is necessary for the defense of the frontiers; orders given accordingly. Vessels to Albany to wait for letters.   220

Dec. 1   Warrants: to Indian commissioners for expenses; to Hyde Clarke for salary as commissary; for salaries to officials; to Johan Jost Herkeman etc.   224

7   Smallpox reported raging in Jamaica; quarantine measures. Warrant to Chas. Kerr surgeon at Oswego signed. License to purchase Indian land granted to Abr'm ₁ Lansing jr, Abr'm Dow, Peter Winne and Jacob Lansing (see *L. P.* 13:150).   225

22   Warrants for salaries signed (Goldsbrow Banyan and Christ'r Blondell doorkeepers of the council). Richard Warner and Amos Petit appointed pilots; captains Jasper Farmar, Rich'd Durham, Hugh Wentworth, Thos. Vater and John Lush to examine them.   229

1744

Jan. 12   Order of the king in council on an appeal of Vincent Pearce vs George Comyns in error.   230

Feb. 29   The brig Mary and Ann, James Jauncey master arrived from Jamaica with smallpox on board ordered to quarantine off Bedlar's island; certificate by Dr Roeloff Kiersted of health for said ship called in question; James Jauncey refuses to go into quarantine; prosecution against him for contempt ordered; Dr Kiersted examined and the Mary and Ann allowed to come to town. General quarantine measures.   237

1743

Mar. 27   Warrants for salaries signed. Letters received from Lieut.
Lindesay at Oswego and Indian commissioners complain-
ing of George Savan (see *N. Y. col. mss,* 74:167); order
thereon. Minutes sent home.   239

May 11   Warrants: to Gov. Clinton for Indian presents and ex-
penses of a journey to Albany; to Geo. Jos. Moore for
expenses in prosecuting counterfeiters. Patent granted to
Phil. Livingston jr, and Henry Holland (see *L. P.* 13:163).
License to purchase Indian lands to John Baptist van
Rensselaer, Jos. Yates et al (see *L. P.* 13:162).   240

16   Proclamation to issue forbidding the exportation of provisions and military stores (see *N. Y. col. mss,* 74:170);
merchants having made contracts to supply the French at
Cape Breton.   243

18   Troops to be sent to Oswego. Warrants: to Nicholas
Lazalere sheriff of Richmond county for expenses in arresting John Stephens; to the printer for salary. License to
purchase Indian lands granted to Stephen Bayard, Nicholas
Bayard, Samuel Bayard jr, Peter Kemble and David Provoost (see *L. P.* 13:164).   243

21   Letter received from Gov. Shirley with news of the declaration of war with France. Assembly dilatory in replying to
messages. Proclamation to issue forbidding export of
powder (see *N. Y. col. mss,* 74:169). Connecticut called
upon to help in case of an attack on New York city.   245

June 5   Gov. Clinton going to Albany. Militia to mount guard in
New York city.   248

13   Joseph Murray appointed to the council vice Henry Lane
Albany   deceased; sworn in he takes his seat. Military measures.   250

14   Order on letter from Lieut. Lindesay at Oswego to the
Indian commissioners. Connecticut will raise 200 men to
assist New York if attacked. Letters received from Gov.
Shirley on the subject of assistance and of carrying the
war into Canada from the duke of Newcastle with
declaration of war (see *N. Y. col. mss,* 74:171). Nathl.
Stanly and Roger Wolcott appointed by Gov. Low to
treat with the six nations. Propositions made by Gov.
Clinton to the six nations.   250

20   Answer of the six nations.   257

27   Warrants for salaries etc signed.   261
New York

29   Michael Houdon and wife escaped from Canada confined to
their lodgings; examined.   262

July 5   Letters received: from Lieut. Lindesay and Lieut. Butler
in relation to M. Houdon and French movements; from

1744

John Ashley to Col. John Stoddard of Massachusetts on Indian movements; from David Whitney to Roger Wolcott on the same. Gov. Clinton has written Col. Henry Beeckman justice of the peace for Dutchess county about Moravians; Col. Beeckman reports on the Moravians and Indians at Schacomico; Moravian priests summoned before the council (see *Doc. hist. N. Y.* 3:1012-13; Q 3:613).   262

17   Difficulties met in trying John Stevens for counterfeiting bills of credit; order thereon.   265

26   Advice of council concerning a private message from the assembly of dissatisfaction with Lieut. Lindesay at Oswego. Report received from Henry Filkin sheriff of Dutchess county in regard to the Moravians, Gudlop Bydner, Henrich Joachim Sinseman and Joseph Shaw living at Shacomico (see *Doc. hist. N. Y.* 3:1014; Q 3:614).   266

Aug. 1   Examinations of Joseph Shaw, of Hendick Joachim Sinseman and of Gudlop Buydner (see *Doc. hist. N. Y.* 3:1014-19; Q 3:614-17).   267

11   Gov. Clinton ill sends a message by his private secretary John Catherwood concerning George Swan (p. 239); also concerning Michel Houdon, and asks what should be done with the Moravians. Examination of George Swan concerning trade at Oswego; to be laid before the assembly. Michel Houdon allowed to live in town. Moravian priests dismissed.   273

20   Gov. Clinton present. Letter received from Indian commissioners relating to French designs upon Oswego; to be laid before the assembly (see *N. Y. col. mss*, 74:176).   276

22   Petition of John Stevens sentenced to death for counterfeiting and asking for pardon, rejected. French prisoners; how to be disposed of and provisioned.   276

25   French prisoners taken by the privateers Clinton, Hester, Polly, and Mary Ann disposed of. Letter received from Gouverneur Morris in regard to counterfeiters referred.   278

30   Another message to be sent to the assembly about provisions for the French prisoners. Peter v. B. Livingston and Abr'm van Horne will support some at their own charge.   279

Sep. 1   Assembly will make provisions for sending off the French prisoners.   280

4   Gov. Clinton ill sends by Mr Catherwood a letter received from Indian commissioners (see *N. Y. col. mss*, 74:177); to be referred to the assembly.   280

13   Gov. Clinton present. Warrants for salaries signed. Chief justice to have a commission "during good behavior."

1744

Dan'l Horsmanden moves the same for the other justices; referred. French prisoners to be sent to the French islands. 281

29 Stephen Bayard nominated mayor of New York, sheriff and coroner of New York, and mayor and sheriff of Albany renominated. Warrant to Surgeon Charles Kerr at Oswego for salary. French prisoners ordered out of town. Minutes sent home. 283

Oct. 15 Nicholas Bayard and Henry Cuyler willing to carry off French prisoners granted flags of truce. Letter received from Indian commissioners; Jean Coeur the French interpreter expected in the Seneca country; order thereon. License to purchase Indian lands granted to John Becker and Johs. Eckerson (see *L. P.* 13:167). 284

19 Warrants to Johan Joost Herkeemer, Henry van Rensselaer, Johs. H. Wendell and Garrit A. Lansingh for supplies to Oswego garrison signed. 286

Nov. 6 Warrants: to Andries Bradt commissary at Oswego for salary; to Stephen van Rensselaer for firewood and candles to Albany city and county garrisons. License to purchase Indian lands granted to Richard Nicholls et al (see *L. P.* 13:168). 287

27 Accounts of Adam Lawrence sheriff of Queens, and of Isaac Willett sheriff of Westchester counties, for subsisting French prisoners referred. Act of assembly for supporting the government read. Letters to be written to the sheriffs of Albany, Ulster and Dutchess counties concerning Moravians; justices of the peace also to be written to (see *Doc. hist. N. Y.* 3:1019-20; Q 3:617). 289

29 Permission given to export powder to the neighboring English colonies. 290

Dec. 13 Warrants for salaries signed. Report by Indian commissioners on the mission of Mr Bleecker to the Seneca country to counteract Jean Coeur's intrigues. 291

Vol. 20, 1741-46

Legislative minutes of council from Ap. 14, 1741 to May 3, 1746 printed in *Journal of the legislative council of the colony of New York*, 1:767-814, 2:819-926.

Vol. 21, 1745-51

1745

Jan. 14 Allowances made for transporting and subsisting French prisoners to Henry Cuyler jr, Nicholas Bayard, Wm Jamison, John Catherwood and Geo. Jos. Moore and warrants subsequently signed; Peter Warren, Joseph Murray and John Moore appointed to the council (see *N. Y. col. mss,* 74:164-66). Order on petition of Phil. Verplanck (see *L. P.* 14:2) and a caveat against it by James Lamb of Haverstraw (see *L. P.* 14:3). Petition of Phil. Verplanck (see *L. P.* 14:1) referred and subsequently granted. Gudlop Bydner, Christian Hendrick Rough and Johannis Martin Mock, Moravian preachers at Shacomico, summoned by Justices Francis Filkin, Lawrence van Kleek and Anth'y Yelverton of Dutchess upon the report of the sheriff.   1

31 Letter from the lords of trade relative to settlers on the island of Ratan (see *N. Y. col. mss,* 74:173); proclamation to issue accordingly (see *N. Y. col. mss,* 74:184-89).   5

Feb. 9 Letters received from Gov. Shirley about the intended expedition against Cape Breton and asking for men, money and artillery; guns can be sent but the assembly has to meet before any answer in regard to money can be given.   6

12 Letter received from Col. Phil. Schuyler about provisions for the militia stationed at Oswego; conference with members of the assembly in town about it and Gov. Shirley's letter. Moravians and a French deserter found by Capt. John Rutherford among the Moravians sent to New York for examination. Michael Houdon and wife to be confined to their lodgings.   7

p. m. Examination of the Moravians, David Seisberger [Zeisberger] and Christian Fred'k Post, and of the French deserter, Estien la Roche; the latter says, Michael Houdon was superior of the Recollects at Trois Rivières and his name is Father Potencien.   7

Mar. 5 Warrants for salaries signed.   10

29 Assembly wants the garrison at Oswego reduced by one half: letter received from Lieut. Butler at Oswego about French intentions against the place. Letter from Georgia on intrigues among the Chickasaws by Marquis de Bodderel, governor of New Orleans. Opinion of council is not to reduce the Oswego garrison. Petition of Joseph Sackett jr (see *L. P.* 14:6) rejected. Patent granted to Thos. Lamb (see *L. P.* 14:4); license to purchase Indian lands to Henry Lane and Hendrick Remsen (see *L. P.* 14:5). David Zeisberger and Christian Fred'k Post released on petition (see *N. Y. col. mss,* 74:191).   11

Ap. 4 Inquiry to be made of persons in Dutchess county suspected of forging bills of credit.   13

6 Examination of John Henry Lydius on Indian matters: copy of it to be sent to Indian commissioners.   14

11   Ordinance for changing time of holding the county court in
      Ulster county to be prepared. Assembly recommends
      Nichs. Schuyler and Jacobus Myndertse for resident agents
      among the Senecas; objections made against Nichs. Schuy-
      ler. Caveat entered by Barent van Benthuysen against
      patent to Thos. Lamb.   16

12   Report received from Commodore Knowles for Commodore
      Warren of a probable attack upon English settlements by
      troops and ships from Martinico. Nathaniel Marston be-
      fore the council with letters from Capt. Jeffery, command-
      ing the Greyhound privateer of New York and from Capt.
      Wentworth to Rich'd Durham on the same subject; affi-
      davit of Thomas Vardill on the same subject taken. Letters
      to Commodore Warren opened and copies sent to Gov.
      Shirley.   17

May 9   Mr Swartwout examined in relation to the counterfeiters
      living near the Oblong; John Scious and Joseph Boyce to
      be arrested and tried. John Brandt appointed branch
      pilot vice John Carten deceased (see *N. Y. col. mss*, 74:194).   19

10   Petition from Albany asking for relief against the Indians
      read and Martin van der Heyden examined about it; Gov.
      Clinton advised to go to Albany and lay the petition be-
      fore the assembly.   20

14   Assembly takes no notice of the above petition and neglects
      other things while assuming the control of military
      affairs; it is dissolved and writs issued.   21

16   Work on the battery at Copsey rock to go on. Capt.
      Rutherford at Albany reports that he has news from Lieut.
      Butler at Oswego of an intended escape from Niagara of
      the interpreter and two soldiers there.   22

21   Accounts of moneys appropriated for the Oswego service
      laid before the council. Accounts of commissioners for the
      Oswego duties called for. Accounts of building Fort
      George received and the commissioners, Roome and
      Roosevelt, ordered to continue. Order on a petition of
      John Francis, a free negro, for relief against Mr Huisman.
      French prisoners.   22

23   Messrs Bayard, van Horne, Lewis and Marsten offer to
      carry French prisoners to Petit Guave under flag of truce;
      commissions granted. Petition of John Francis (p. 22)
      dismissed upon the answer of Abr'm Huisman.   23

27   Letters received: from the duke of Newcastle approving of
      Gov. Clinton and ordering him to assist Commodore War-
      ren with men, provisions or shipping; from Commodore
      Warren on board the Superbe, Chapeaurouge bay, siege of

1745   **v. 21**

Louisburgh, wants assistance; from Gov. Shirley, calls for
assistance; money to be raised by subscription.   24

30   Letter received from Jacobus Swartwout with papers relating to counterfeiters (see *N. Y. col. mss*, 74:197-204).   27

June 6   Warrants for salaries signed. Order on a petition of Fernando Bernard and Antonio Agilar, Spanish negroes,
captured by the privateer Batchellors, Capt. Greenhill commanding.   27

10   Samuel Canfield of Connecticut examined in regard to an
account of Ephraim Seely about counterfeiters.   28

14   James Livingston, Stephen van Cortlandt, Brandt Schuyler
and Wm Bayard offer to carry French prisoners to the
French islands; commissions granted. Warrants to Gov.
Clinton for firewood, etc. to New York garrison and for
expenses of journey to Albany.   29

19   Smallpox reported at Curaçao; all vessels from there to be
quarantined.   29

29   Capt. Farmar offers to take Spanish prisoners to Santo
Domingo; commission granted.   30

July 6   Warrants signed: to Sheriff Adam Lawrence of Queens
county for quartering French prisoners; to Johan Joost
Herkemer and Gerrit A. Lansingh for victualling Oswego
troops; to residents among the Senecas.   30

16   Letters received: from Gov. Shirley giving an account of the
reduction of Louisburgh; from Gov. Laws on the same
and enclosing affidavits by Capt. Jonathan Smith and
David Umberville, taken prisoners by a French fleet and
discharged after examination. Minutes sent home.   31

29   Commission appointing John Catherwood secretary of the
province during the absence of George Clarke jr; he is
sworn in. Journal of Conrad Weiser the Pennsylvania interpreter of his sojourn among the six nations. Letters
received: from Indian commissioners, Mohawks going to
Canada, Orandax are near Fort Drummer, have killed two
men from New England; from Capt. Rutherford, same
topic; from Commodore Warren at Louisburgh, asking for
supplies of men and provisions; from Gov. Shirley, on the
murders by the Orandax Indians; from Gov. Laws, French
western Indians. Indian murders to be referred through
commissioners to the six nations. Meeting of Gov. Clin-
ton with the six nations deemed urgent.   32

Aug. 20   Letter received from Indian commissioners, Mohawks have
returned from Canada, Gov. Clinton must come. Petition of Abr'm Huisman and Gulian Verplanck in behalf
of John de Man and other subjects of the king of Den-

1745   v. 21

mark for leave to ship for St Thomas provisions on board
the sloop Hopewell, to rep'ace what was taken out of her
when taken by the privateers Castor and Pollox of New
York, not granted.   40

27   Letters received: from Lt. Gov. Phips asking for men, provisions and ammunition; from Commodore Warren, has
sent the Superbe and the Wager men of war to the south-
ward for the protection of trade, thinks the colonies ought
to protect their own trade; referred to the assembly.
Nath'l Marston, Henry Cuyler and Phil Phillips granted
commission to carry French prisoners to French places.   41

28   Assembly adjourned at their own request.   41

Sep. 3   Warrant to Gov. Clinton for Indian presents signed. Lt.
Gov. Phips reports he has declared war against the eastern
and Canada Indians. Copy of a letter from Col. Stoddard
to Indian commissioners received, Indian affairs. Report
from Indian commissioners; opinion of council thereon.   42

12   Quarantine business. Supreme court adjourned as two of
the judges, members of the council, have to accompany the
governor to Albany. Examination of Peter Mone concerning Boston Killet and John Ryan who have counterfeited
dollars at the house of Patrick Phagan [Fagan].   44

Nov. 1   Gov. Clinton reports proceedings of Indian conferences at
Albany on October 5, 10, 12, 14. Order of the lord
justices: to repeal certain acts of assembly; to give Peter
Warren and Joseph Murray the precedence of John Moore
in the council.   45

24   Settlement at Saraghtoga destroyed; Jacob Rutsen of
Livingston manor gives an account of it. All to be laid
before the assembly. Warrants for salaries signed.   65

27   Two men from the Fishkills 90 miles from Albany examined;
report that Woodstock has been taken by the enemy. Six
nations to be called out.   65

Dec. 4   Letters received from Col. Phil. Schuyler asking for 300
men, militia, from the lower counties for the defence of
Albany and Schenectady and recommending the building
of a fort at Saraghtoga. Council approves of building a
fort at Saratoga and at the carrying place; an independent
company having already been sent to Albany, militia is not
necessary. New York militia refuses to do guard duty; to
be fined according to law if they continue to refuse.   66

11   Letters received: from Gov. Laws, Stockbridge in danger;
from Indian commissioners, on security of the frontiers;
from Col. Schuyler, about Saratoga fort. Hosick has been
deserted by the inhabitants; from Jacobus Swartwout, the

French at Messasippi prepare great many snow-shoes to march against Albany, Esopus, Minisinck and the frontiers of Jersey and Pennsylvania; from Cadw. Colden, enclosing Swartwout's and giving information as to the enemies intentions. Governors of Connecticut, Jersey and Pennsylvania to be informed. Letters referred.   67

24   Letter received from Indian commissioners about the fort at Saraghtoga, militia and a message to the six nations. Governor has written that the message must be sent. Report on the letters received on the 11th.   68

1746

Jan. 15   Minutes of the Indian commissioners and letter from Col. Schuyler received, fortifications on the frontiers, militia. Letters received: from Arent Bratt, supplies for the security of Schenectady; from Cadw. Colden, blockhouses, petition from Kingston that the town be fortified; from John van der Heyden, fortifications at the carrying place. All except the last two referred to the assembly; the last two to a committee of council. [Remark in pencil, " Report never made tho' called upon by me several times."]   70

17   Account of what passed December 21 between Col. de Kay, Major Swartwout, Ensign Coleman, Adam W.sener, interpreter, Benj. Thompson and the Cashigton Indians who had withdrawn themselves from Orange county to their hunting houses; Col. Thos. de Kay examined in regard to it. Belt of wampum to be sent to the Cashigton Indians.   71

31   Letters received: from Gov. Shirley, military measures
Greenwich   recommended; from Indian commissioners, message to the six nations sent, fort at Saratoga; from Capt. Nichs. Schuyler, Saratoga fort; from John van der Heyden, fort at the carrying place; from the surgeon of the two companies sent to Albany, hospital conveniences; mayor of Albany to see to the latter. Proclamation to issue for a day of fasting and prayer (see *N. Y. col. mss*, 75:21). Guns loaned to Massachusetts to be recalled. Warrants for salaries signed.   73

Feb. 1   Capt. Scott, arrived with part of Gen. Fuller's regiment, allowed to land notwithstanding the smallpox " very rife " in the city.   74

10   Letter received from Dr Thos. Standard, accusing upon hearsay Dr Magraw of New York of being in French pay; referred for examination. List of strangers in the city called for. Three Frenchmen in the city to be confined.   74

11   Committee of council examines witnesses, Wm Brownejohn, Archibald Fisher, Mrs Garland, in regard to Dr Magraw;

Dr Standard's allegations not proved. Lewis Bernard a
French prisoner examined and committed to the care of
Capt. Hett and Mr Bemper. 75

Mar. 5 Letters received: from Indian commissioners (with minutes),
fort at the carrying place, six nations refuse to take up the
hatchet against the French; from Lt. Gov. Thomas of
Pennsylvania, meeting of commissioners from the colonies,
message from the assembly, desiring to adjourn on account of smallpox. Matters referred; council advised to
adjourn the assembly to Westchester. 76

13 Report on the preceding letters. Letters received: from
Admiral Warren and Sir Wm Pepperel at Louisburgh,
asking for men; from Gov. Wanton of Rhode Island,
promising assistance; referred to the assembly. Order on
a petition of sundry Germans for leave to maintain a
minister of the Lutheran church. Warrants for salaries
signed. 77

17 Assembly adjourned from Westchester to Brooklyn. 80

Ap. 2 Report on a message from the assembly about bills of credit.
Minutes of Indian commissioners received, Mohawks will
send men to Saratoga; Canajoharie Indians want their
town fortified. 80

11 Letter received from Gov. Laws, meeting of commissioners
from the colonies. Capt. Richard Collins, commodore of
the Gibralter transport convoy gives orders to Capt. Wm
Starkey, master of the Ruby transport, about sailing to
Louisburgh; opinion of council thereon. Letters received:
from lords of trade: M. Gorsdorff and Moravians; from
Marquis de Caylus, governor of Martinico about a prize
taken by Capt. Arthur Helme; from the governor of
Havannah about free negroes sold as slaves; referred. 81

20 Capt. Richard Collins, the Ruby transport and troops on
board of her under Capt. Scott: The Ruby may sail
under convoy of a privateer. Letters received: from Gov.
Thomas of Pennsylvania, meeting of commissioners from
the colonies; from Admiral Warren, wants support,
French militia and Indians are arming, to attack Louisburgh; the latter referred to the assembly. Royal order
to the master general of ordnance for sending an engineer
to New York. 82

25 John Ayscough appointed sheriff of New York, vice Wm
Jamison deceased. French prisoners. The case of the
prize taken by Arthur Helme referred to the governor of
Rhode Island who gave the commission. Letters received
from Indian commissioners, John Lydius has asked the

1746   **v. 21**

Cacknawaga Indians to settle in this province (see *N. Y.
col. mss,* 75:29); from Gov. Shirley to Lydius (see *N. Y.
col. mss,* 75:22); from Indian commissioners resigning
their office (see *N. Y. col. mss,* 75:31); from Lieut. Burrows at Ft William to Capt. Hubert Marshall of Albany,
French building a fort near Lydius house; from Indian
commissioners (with minutes) (see *N. Y. col. mss,* 75:32);
all referred.   85

May   3   Advice of council in regard to the governor signing an act
of Assembly creating bills of credit, contrary to his instructions. Report of committee on letters from lords of
trade, governor of Martinico and governor of Havannah.
Assembly adjourned.   86

8   Letters received: from Indian commissioners, doings of the
enemy, house of Simon Grocha burned, etc; from Arent
Stevens, Cacknawaga and Skeweandie Indians willing to
live among the six nations; opinion of council thereon.
Letters received: from Gov. Gooch of Virginia and Gov.
Wentworth of New Hampshire in regard to the meeting
of commissioners; from Gov. Shirley about the cannons
lent by New York. Abr'm Glen of Schenectady au-
thorized to raise a company of volunteers.   89

10   Petition from Kinderhook and Claverack for a garrison referred to the assembly. Circular letters to be written to
the members of the assembly to be prompt in meeting.
Military measures. Petition of John Lefever and Noah
Etting of Ulster county for land near Newpaltz (see *L. P.*
15:10) referred.   90

13   Letters received from Indian commissioners (see *N. Y. col.*
House of   *mss,* 75:40) (with minutes), frontiers, interview with
James de   Mohawks and Onondagas, murders by the enemy Indians;
Lancey   from Col. Schuyler, militia; referred.   91

14   John Lydius to be prohibited from intermeddling or treating
City hall   with the Indians. Quota of militia from Ulster, Orange,
Dutchess, Westchester, Queens and Suffolk counties to
be sent to Albany and Schenectady.   92

20   Letters received: from Jacob Ten Eyck, commanding at
Greenwich   Saratoga; from the same and Sybrant van Schaick to
Col. Schuyler, their men uneasy and want to be relieved;
from Col. Schuyler and Major Collins, blockhouses, rang-
ing the woods, insecure feeling at Albany; from Col.
Myndert Schuyler and Rutger Bleecker, frontiers; referred. Blank commissions for officers in Albany county
to be sent to Col. Phil. Schuyler. Exchange of prisoners.

1746   **v. 21**

Report of committee on letter from lords of trade relating to Moravians (see *N. Y. col. mss,* 75:38).   93

30   Dutchess county militia. Permission given to two French-
City hall   men captured by the Prince Charles privateer to return to
France by way of Holland. John Lodewick Hofgood forbidden upon complaint of Rev. Mr Knoll to officiate as
minister of the Lutheran church.   98

June 2   Goldsbrow Banyar appointed deputy secretary by John
Greenwich   Catherwood and sworn in. Letters received: from Mr
Warren and Mr Pepperel, levies required for the defence
of Louisburgh; from the duke of Newcastle on an expedition against Canada. Proclamations to issue: calling for
volunteers; embargoing all vessels for a month (see *N.
Y. col. mss,* 75:42). Letter received from Gov. Shirley.   99

3   Letter received from Indian commissioners (see *N. Y. col.
City hall   mss,* 75:41). French prisoners to be sent to Jamaica,
L. I.; vessels trying to leave port contrary to orders to
be fired upon.   102

5   Assembly wants to know how the troops raised and the
Indians will be stationed. Council advises to place 200 at
Saratoga with the 50 Indians, 30 at Kinderhook, 50 at
Connestigione, 170 between Albany and Schenectady; to
have 4 captains and 8 lieutenants. Necessaries for the
soldiers to be provided. Petitions for clearances tabled.
Absent members of council called to attend.   103

6   Orders to the sheriffs of Kings and Queens counties in re-
Brooklyn   gard to the French prisoners.   104

7   Draft of the proclamation calling for volunteers read and
New York   approved; to be printed.   105

9   Letter received from Gov. Thomas about embargoing vessels. Royal mandamus appointing Stephen Bayard to the
council vice Jeremiah van Rensselaer deceased; he is
sworn in and takes his place. Clearances given to the
sloop Sarah, Wm Williams master, and the brigantine
Abigail, Wm Carlile master, to Jamaica; sloop Jenny,
Thos. Hammond master, to New Providence; ship
William and Mary, Wm Walton master, to Louisburgh;
ship Arent, Wm Savary master, to Amsterdam; snow
York, Joseph Wilson master, to Hamburg; snow Sally,
Ferdinando Clark master, to London; sloop Don Carlos,
Abr'm Kip master, to Curaçao; ship Griffin, John Lum-
ley master, to Virginia. François D. Heurten, a French-
man from Hispaniola examined.   105

11   Governor's speech and the addresses of council and assem-
Greenwich   bly to be printed separately and in the New York post

boy. Clearances granted for the brigantine Anne, John
Stalberry master, to St Christophers; sloop Mary, John
Theobald master, to Surinam; ship William, James Sample
master, to Madeira. Bounty to be given to volunteers,
appropriation for provisions to the forces. Questions proposed by the governor relating to the intended expedition
referred.   107

13   Order on a complaint of Capt. Eleazer Hawkins of Suffolk
City hall   county militia against his major, John Merry. Report on
the above questions of the governor. Proclamation to
issue forbidding carpenters in the city to do other work
than on the bateaux. Order on a petition of Hermanus
Rutgers et al (see *N. Y. col. mss*, 75:48). Clearances
granted for the sloops Good Intent, Wm Cullin master,
to Boston, and Carolina, John Schermerhorn master, for
South Carolina.   109

16   Letter received from the Indian commissioners, difficult to
engage Mohawks for the Saratoga service; not advisable
to appoint Indian officers. Indian conference to be held
at Albany. Letter from Lieut. Ingoldsby at Saratoga on
the bad condition of the fort referred. Message to be sent
to the assembly concerning bateaux, etc for the expedition. Clearance granted for the sloop Huzza, Thos.
Barnes master, to Louisburgh.   112

17   Proclamation to issue to take off the embargo, ordered
Brooklyn   June 2, except for military stores. Report on the message
to the assembly amended. Jourdain, a French prisoner
in the service of Wm Smith of Ulster county to be employed as St Lawrence pilot. French prisoners allowed to
return to France via Madeira.   114

18   Report on the message to the assembly approved. Letter
City hall   of Lieut. Ingoldsby, after examination of Jacob ten Eyck,
referred to the assembly. Warrants signed for salaries,
public services, Indian presents, fortifications, transporting soldiers, etc., printing bills of credit.   115

23   Letter received from Pres. Hamilton of New Jersey, assembly of New Jersey has voted to raise 500 men and given
£20,000 for the expedition. Votes of the New York assembly concerning the expedition received.   118

30   Letters received: from Gen. Gooch, men for the expedition,
their clothing and equipments; from Gov. Laws, Connecticut assembly refuses to give money for paying the six
nations; from Gov. Thomas of Pennsylvania, assembly
refuses to send commissioners to treat with the Indians at
Albany. Warrants signed: to Indian commissioners for

1746   v. 21

pany; ordered accordingly. Spanish letters to Gov. Clinton translated (see *N. Y. col. mss*, 75:78, 79) and sent to him.
John Bryant, master of the ship Prince Charles, allowed
to take French prisoners to Leghorn.   133

p. m. Richard Langdon appointed captain, John Cuyler and George
Brewerton his lieutenants (see *N. Y. col. mss*, 75:59, 63). 134

25   Oliver de Lancey gives notice that the snow Catherine,
James Brown master, will be ready to sail for Louisburgh
with provisions in three weeks. Orders to the colonels
of militia in Westchester, Queens, Suffolk, Kings and
lower part of Orange counties in case of alarm. Letters
written: to Pres. John Hamilton of New Jersey asking for
establishing a beacon on the Highlands of Neversink and
to send the Bergen and Essex militia to New York in case
of alarm; to Thos. Cornell concerning a possible alarm.   134

28   Archibald Kennedy presides. Military necessaries to be provided; Arms. Letter from the duke of Newcastle to Gov.
Clinton cannot be opened, is to be sent to him at Albany.
Suffolk county militia men desert, to be arrested and returned to their regiment at Albany. James Fanning commissioned captain (see *N. Y. col. mss*, 75:68).   135

29   Letter received from Gov. Clinton to Arch'd Kennedy (see
N. Y. col. mss, 75:66); Companies which are complete to
be sent to Albany. Order on a petition of Joseph Espinosa, master of the sloop Migel y la Virgen de los
Dolores, Spanish flag of truce (see *N. Y. col. mss*, 75:68). 137

p. m. Chief Justice de Lancey presides. Not sufficient members
Brooklyn   present, the assembly is further adjourned.   139

30   Arch'd Kennedy presides. Members of the assembly to be
New York   admonished to be prompt in their attendance on the day
of adjournment. Peter Wraxall commissioned captain,
John Treadwell jr and Benj. Lewis his lieutenants (see
N. Y. col. mss, 75:71). Answer of Pres. John Hamilton re-
ceived (p. 134).   139

Aug. 4 Chief Justice de Lancey presides. Soldiers ordered to Albany want clothing; order thereon.   140

8   Robert Robinson and Timothy Hudson commissioned lieutenants in Capt. James Fannings company (see *N. Y. col.
mss*, 75:73). Order on a petition of Joseph Espinosa (see
N. Y. col. mss, 75:75).   141

12   Archibald Kennedy presides. Letter received from Gov.
Clinton (see *N. Y. col. mss*, 75:74); council's opinion
thereon (see *N. Y. col. mss*, 75:76).   141

12   The chief justice in the chair. Assembly adjourned, no
Brooklyn   quorum being present.   143

1746   v. 21

19   Order on a complaint of Joseph Espinosa that Thos. Barnes
New York   and Thos. Seymour intend to carry Spanish mulattoes out
         of the province as slaves.   143
p. m.   The chief justice in the chair. Assembly adjourned by order
Brooklyn   of Gov. Clinton.   144
20   Thos. Seymour and Thos. Barnes forbidden to carry the
New York   Spanish mulattoes, Antonio Joseph and Antonia Ferres,
         out of the province. Mr Kennedy presides.   145
28   Minute of council of New Jersey (see *N. Y. col. mss,* 75:77)
         and orders to the colonels of Monmouth, Bergen and
         Essex counties' militia. Letter of thanks to be written to
         Pres. John Hamilton. Orders in relation to deserters.   145
p. m.   The chief justice presides. Capts. Wraxall and Honeyman
         report that some deserters from their companies are
         probably concealed on board the Clinton privateer sloop,
         Thos. Beaven master; order thereon.   149
Sep. 2 Order in relation to deserters directed to the mayor, etc of
         New York.   149
p. m.   Assembly adjourned.   149
Brooklyn

16   Petition of Joseph Espinosa (see *N. Y. col. mss,* 75:84, 85)
New York   to be sent to Gov. Clinton.   150
p. m.   Assembly adjourned.   151
Brooklyn

20   Oliver de Lancey gives notice that the sloop Griffin, Wm
New York   Brown master, will be ready to sail with provisions for
         Louisburgh in three weeks. Order on an application of
         Mr Banker and other owners of the privateer brigantine
         William in regard to disposal of her French prisoners.
         Affidavit of Capt. René Het (see *N. Y. col. mss,* 75:87).
         Order in regard to Spanish mulattoes. French prisoners
         confined to Kings county to be arrested when found in
         New York.   151
25   Cl. Kennedy presiding. Charles Mort, a Frenchman fled
         from Acquin in the West Indies to Rhode Island, ordered
         to return to Rhode Island in the ship of Joshua Amy, in
         which he came thence. Capt. John Fred, royal coasting
         pilot, and the branch pilots to consider what part of the
         channel between the city and Sandy Hook could be most
         easily obstructed. Deserters caught to be held until the
         governor's return.   153
26   Report of Capt. Fred and other pilots on obstructing the
         channel received (see *N. Y. col. mss,* 75:87, 89, 90).   154
27   Order on a petition of Joseph Espinosa for a certificate of
         the number of prisoners delivered by him. Capt. Waldron

headgunner, Adam van den Berg, Jacobus Turck and John
Young examined in regard to cannons, etc carried out of
Fort George.   154

29   Letter received from Admiral Warren, appearance of a large
French fleet off the island of Sables. Armament for
Louries battery. Orders: to Capt. van Wyck and Waldron
in case of an alarm; to Capt. Isaac de Peyster, John Pro-
voost, Pierre de Peyster and Robert Livingston. John
Honeyman commissioned captain, Wm Proctor jr, and
Wm Hammersley jr his lieutenants (see *N. Y. col. mss,*
75:92, 94).   155

p. m.   Papers of French prisoners in the city to be examined to dis-
cover destination of the French fleet (see *N. Y. col. mss,*
75:95).   157

30   List of the French fleet under command of the Duke d'An-
ville found and to be sent to neighboring governors.   158

p. m.   Assembly adjourned.   158
Brooklyn

Oct. 1   Letter received from Col. Hamilton (see *N. Y. col. mss,*
New York   75:91). Orders: on a decree of the admiralty court (see
N. Y. col. mss, 75:93); on a letter from Wm Richards (see
N. Y. col. mss, 75:96). Ammunition ordered for Louries
battery and batteries at Burnets key, Rutgers wharf and
Red Hook.   159

4   Gov. Clinton returned. Letter received from Gov. Shirley,
wants men to be sent to Rhode Island in case of an attack
by the French fleet; to be considered. Virginia troops,
destined for Albany, in need of many necessaries.   160

7   Letter received from Gov. Shirley, French fleet. Leave
granted to Wm Richards to carry French prisoners in the
Caster, Sam'l Bourdet master, to Cape François (p. 159). 161

8   No troops from Albany to come down for the defence of
New York; Virginia and Maryland troops to remain in
the city for that purpose.   162

11   Maryland troops ordered to Albany. Letters received from
the governor of Havannah (see *N. Y. col. mss,* 75:78-80)
Thomas Barnes, arrived from Louisburgh, examined about
the French fleet. Order on a petition of Joseph Espinosa
concerning Indians and mulattoes in the possession of
Mr Leaycraft, Capt. Langdon, John Groesbeck, Francis
Johnson, and Mr Kilmasten.   162

14   Hearing on the above petition; deposition of Edward Light-
wood in support of it (see *N. Y. col. mss,* 75:98); order
thereon. Pilots for the Maryland transports ordered to
Albany to be impressed.   164

1746   **v. 21**

15   Order on a petition of Francis Lewis, Jasper Farmer and
      Thos. Barnes regarding their Spanish mulattoes slaves.
      Commission granted to Thos. Greenil (see *N. Y. col. mss,*
      75:100) for carrying French prisoners under flag of truce
      to the French West Indies. Examination of witnesses
      Hugh Wentworth and John Easom on the petition of
      Joseph Espinosa (p. 162).   166

16   Gov. Clinton ill, Cadw. Colden presides. Report on the
      petition of Joseph Espinosa (p. 162).   168

18   Message from Gov. Clinton about provisions to the troops at
      Albany. Letters received from Col. Roberts at Albany
      concerning a deficiency in the bounty money. Dominicus
      van der Veer appointed high sheriff of Kings county.   169

20   Message from Gov. Clinton about provisioning the troops;
      Gov. Bladen of Maryland writes that he ought to have
      nothing to do with it after the troops have left his province. 170

20   Gov. Clinton again in the chair. Rev. Henry Barclay to
      succeed Rev. Mr Vesey as rector of Trinity church. Re-
      ports on Gov. Bladen's letter and on Gov. Clinton's mes-
      sage of the 18th; the latter recommitted.   171

July 22   Indian conference.   172
Albany

23   Orders: to Indian commissioners; to Col. Schuyler and
      Major Collins. Letter received from Wm Johnson (see
      N. Y. col. mss, 75:67).   173

24   Minutes of Indian commissioners received. Warrant to im-
      press carpenters, etc. for building batteaux issued to
      Henry Holland.   175

27   Letter received from Lieut. Burrows about movements of the
      French. Troops sent to the Mohawk country for the pro-
      tection of Wm Johnson. Orders to the militia of Cana-
      joharie and Col. Schuyler's regiment.   175

29   Commission from Gov. Shirley appointing John Stoddard,
      Jacob Wendell, Samuel Wells and Oliver Partridge repre-
      sentatives of Massachusetts at the Indian treaty to be held.
      Letter from the same and Admiral P. Warren about the
      expedition against Canada.   176

Aug. 4   Scouts to be sent to the eastward for intelligence about the
      enemy. Esopus and Minissink Indians called to the meet-
      ing through Capt. Hornbeck. Gov. Shirley and Admiral
      Warren to be informed that Crownpoint must be taken.
      Minutes of Indian commissioners received. Instructions
      to Isaac States and Cornelius Vrooman as messengers to
      the Indians on the Susquehannah approved.   179

1747   **v. 21**

16   Order upon an application of Nathl. Marston, Nichs. Bay-
      ard, Edw'd Holland and Henry Cuyler, owners of the
      Greyhound, in regard to the La Fleur prize (see *N. Y. col.
      mss*, 75:121). Letter from Gov. Shirley with minutes of
      the council and assembly of Massachusetts, military opera-
      tions.   221

19   Report on the preceding letter from Gov. Shirley.   226

Feb. 2 Council's opinion asked about a winter campaign against
      Crownpoint. Lawrence Payne to command John Pintard's
      brigantine New Port, going as flag of truce (see *N. Y.
      col. mss*, 75:119).   226a

4   Report of council about a winter campaign against Fort St
      Frederick at Crownpoint. Objection raised by Mr Murray
      to the entries of the minutes of council held at Albany.   227

13   Letter received from Gov. Shirley about the march on
      Crownpoint; council advise against it. Warrants for
      salaries signed.   229

20   Goods taken from a French vessel by Thos. Willer and
      Abr'm Man considered free from infection. Proclama-
      tion to issue proroguing the assembly (see *N. Y. col. mss.
      75:120). Warrants signed; to Lieut. Walter Butler com-
      missary and Charles Kerr surgeon at Oswego for salaries. 230

Mar. 2 Petition of the owners of the Greyhound relating to goods
      on board their prize La Fleur denied. Gov. Shirley writes
      that he has given up the expedition against Crownpoint. 231

11   Order on a petition of the owners of the Greyhound (see
      N. Y. col. mss, 75:12). Letters from Capt. Livingston at
      Fort Clinton, Saratoga, to Col. Marshall received; attack
      by French Indians on a woodcutting party; Col. Schuyler
      and Major Collins complained of for not supplying fire-
      wood to Saratoga garrison. Kinderhook people want a
      garrison; order thereon.   232

16   Proclamation to issue proroguing the assembly (see *N. Y.
      col. mss*, 75:122).   233

Ap. 2 John Durfy master of the New Port brigantine granted a
      commission of flag of truce upon petition of John Pintard.
      Petition referred: of John Retou a French mulatto prisoner
      of war and sold to Capt. René Het for restoration to
      freedom; and of freemen of New York city against allow-
      ing tradesmen from New Jersey. Answer of Col. Schuyler
      and Major Collins to a complaint against them (p. 232)
      received (see *N. Y. col. mss*, 75:123-24). Petition of Corns.
      van Schaick et al of Kinderhook for a garrison referred to
      the assembly. Warrants for salaries signed.   234

9   Assembly wants to adjourn but council advises against it.
      Order on petition of Joseph Espinosa (see *N. Y. col. mss.
      75:127).   236

1747   v. 21

10 Report and order on petitions of John Retou (p. 234) and
of the freemen of New York.   238
14 Letters received from Capt. Trent and Livingston to Col.
Marshall, skirmishing with French and Indians near Fort
Clinton. Gov. Clinton asks who are to be appointed officers of the rangers.   239
18 Johannes Hough jr and Wm Hogan recommended and appointed captains, Andrew Lambert Hough and Johs. de
Wandelaer lieutenants of Albany county rangers.   240
29 Officers at Fort Clinton write to Col. Marshall that their
men are likely to desert in a body for want of pay; advice
of council thereon. Letter read from Col. Roberts to Col.
Wm Johnson about Indian troubles; order thereon. Order
on two copies of affidavits sworn to before Justice Johs.
Hardenbergh of Ulster county, charging Gysbert Crum
with rescuing a deserter. Proclamation to issue in regard
to apprehending deserters (see *N. Y. col. mss*, 75:130).   240
30 Letter from Col. Roberts at Saratoga to Col. Marshall at
Albany received, wholesale desertions; order thereon.
Officers appointed to command the rangers can not get
men to enlist; matter referred to the assembly. Peter de
Jon Court master of the brigantine Sarah granted a com-
mission of flag of truce over Wm Griffith (see *N. Y. col.
mss*, 75:134, 136). Warrant to John Joost Herkemer and
Gerrit A. Lansingh for provisioning Oswego garrison
signed.   242
May 2 Capt. Tiebouts' company and others refuse to march to
Saratoga; money to pay them to be raised in the city.
Agreement signed by David Clarkson, Paul Richards,
Joseph Haynes, John McEvers, John Livingston and
Robert Rob't Livingston to furnish £5500 sterling or
£9075 New York currency; accepted.   243
3 Col. Peter Schuyler writes that the Jersey troops are
mutinous for want of pay; deliberations thereon.   245
5 Difficulties about the money promised by the New York
merchants.   246
p. m. Time for drawing the bills of exchange, to be taken by the
merchants, extended to 90 days.   247
6 Difficulties with the troops at Saratoga; Massachusetts and
Connecticut troops called for. Hudson river counties
militia to be held in readiness for marching. Col. Schuyler to take part of his regiment to Saratoga. Provisions
for the rangers allowed by the assembly. Kinderhook
rangers to go to Saratoga. Col. Hambleton approves of
Gov. Clinton's action in regard to new levies.   248

1747   **v. 21**

14   Johs. de Wandelaer refuses the commission of lieutenant in
     the rangers. Blank commission sent to Major Collins to
     be filled by him with the advice of the mayor of Albany.
     Letters from Mr Hamilton to Peter Schuyler concerning
     New Jersey troops received; from Gov. Shirley with
     minutes of Massachusetts council, meeting among the new
     levies. Col. Phil Schuyler ordered to Albany.   249

20   Deposition of Bernard Eyrand (see *N. Y. col. mss*, 75:131)
     received from Gov. Thomas. Jean du Puy, mentioned in
     the same, to be examined.   250

30   Deposition of Jean du Puy, lieutenant (see *N. Y. col. mss*,
     75:133) of the ship Marguerite of Bordeaux, captured by
     three privateers, Triton, Capt. Mann commanding, Castor,
     Capt. Burges, and Pollux, captain unknown. The advo-
     cate general is ordered to prosecute the commanders of the
     privateers. Commissions of flag of truce granted: to Thos.
     Brown master of the Monmouth sloop, owned by Wm
     Griffith, and to Rob't Griffith jr, master of the Good Intent
     sloop, to carry French prisoners to Leogan and Guade-
     loupe; to Thos. Fish master of the Don Carlos sloop, Jacob
     and Wm Walton owners, to carry Spanish prisoners to St
     Augustine (see *N. Y. col. mss*, 75:132, 134, 135).   252

31   Representation to Col. Roberts at Albany from Captains
     of the new levies received. Letter from field officers J.
     Roberts, Hubert Marshall, Thos. Clarke and John Ruther-
     ford of the new levies. Minutes of a council of war held
     at Fort Frederick all in regard to the pay of the men re-
     ceived. Capt. John Honeyman examined about it; opinion
     of council.   255

June 6   Letter from Gov. Clinton to Col. Roberts (see *N. Y. col. mss*,
     75:137).   257

8   Alderman Johnson and Dr Baird examined in regard to
     Mr Wessells, arrived from Boston to be inoculated for the
     smallpox. Proclamation to issue forbidding inoculation
     for the smallpox (see *N. Y. col. mss*, 75:147).   259

19   Commission of flag of truce granted to Thomas Greenhil
     master of the Mary sloop. Warrants for salaries, etc.
     signed. Gov. Clinton intends to go to Albany.   260

July 28   Letters from Gov. Shirley, meeting of commissioners at
     New York; scouting parties to be sent from Saratoga to
     the Massachusetts fort; general court to meet for provid-
     ing means to prosecute the expedition against Crownpoint,
     orders of council thereon. Order on examinations of
     persons suspected of counterfeiting.   261

Aug. 1   Disposal of troops to be employed against Crownpoint and
     Niagara.   263

26   Warrant to Col. Roberts (see *N. Y. col. mss*, 75:161) and letter from the same (see *N. Y. col. mss*, 75:161) laid before the council; advice of council. Saratoga deserted by the levies (see *N. Y. col. mss*, 76:4); orders in relation to it.   272

29   Stephen Bayard suspended from the council. Henry Holland appointed mayor, John Ayscough sheriff, John van Cortlandt coroner of New York, John ten Broeck mayor and Jacob ten Eyck sheriff of Albany.   273

Oct. 1   Agreement made by the commissioners of the colonies referred to the assembly. Report of Mr Murray on his efforts to have forts ordered built by them at the great carrying place. Defense of the frontiers to be considered.   274

2   Defense of the frontiers and preserving the six nations in their allegiance submitted to the consideration of the council.   274

3   Mr Livingston lays a paper, " Proposals for the security of the frontiers" before the council; referred. Col. Johnson to be examined on Indian affairs.   275

6   Examination of Col. Johnson (see *N. Y. col. mss*, 76:8, 9).   275

14   Fort Clinton burnt, cannon and stores removed to Stillwater. Order on a deposition of Wm Johnson, charging Joseph, John and Lewis Clement with selling rum to the six nations. Lieut. Lindesay ordered to take command at Oswego upon petition of Oswego traders and Indians.   276

31   Commission of flag of truce granted upon petition of Edw'd Holland to Thos. Seymour master of the brigantine Good Friends (see *N. Y. col. mss*, 76:13). Exchange of prisoners in Canada.   277

Nov. 6   Letters received from Gov. Shirley and Knowles; pay of troops; discharge of troops. Opinion of council asked about measures for the defense of the frontiers.   277

7   Allowances of pay of troops by the assembly. Report on measures for the defense of the frontiers. Merchants to be asked to advance money for paying troops.   278

20   Troops stationed at the Mohawks and Canajoharie castles and at Wm Johnson's have deserted; new levies expected to enlist to be sent there.   279

25   Council advises the governor to sign acts creating new bills of credit notwithstanding objections thereto. Arent Stephens appointed Indian interpreter.   280

Dec. 31   Resolves of the general court of Massachusetts concerning the agreement between the commissioners of the colonies (p. 274) received with amendments. Petition of Jacob de Hart for rights of ferry, from Staten Island to New York and to Bergen county, N. J. tabled. New license to pur-

1747 v. 21

chase Indian lands south of Jeremiah van Rensselaer's land, west of Hudson river and near Johs. Hallenbeck, in Albany county, granted to Henry Lane and Hendrick Remsen. License to purchase Indian lands near the Kattskills granted to William and Abr'm Salisbury and Casparus Bronck. Report on Gov. Clinton's account (p. 269). Warrants to him to be prepared and warrant for his house rent signed. Mr Miln appointed surgeon to the forces. 280

1748

Jan. 2 Warrants to Gov. Clinton for contingent expenses signed. Writs for election of a new assembly to issue. 283

4 Gov. Shirley complains that Nicholas Schuyler has enlisted men in Hampshire county and asks them to be discharged; referred. Action on demand of president and council of Pennsylvania for loan of battering cannon deferred. 283

22 John Burnet appointed coroner of New York vice John van Cortlandt deceased. 284

26 Meeting of commissioners discussed. Order on a petition of mayor and aldermen of Albany for continuance of Capt. Nicholas Schuyler's company as garrison there. 284

Feb. 4 Letters received from Gov. Law about meeting of commissioners; from president of Pennsylvania about loan of cannons. No powder at Albany. Richard Smith appointed branch pilot, but must pass examination. 285

12 Governor's speech to be made to the council and assembly read (see *N. Y. col. mss*, 76:21 and *Jour.* 2:1004). 286

16 Commissioners to communicate letters to the general assembly, John Canon master of the brigantine William and Mary to be examined as to the cannon with which he sailed and did not bring back. 287

17 Letters received: from Phil. Ryley in the Seneca country to Col. Johnson, from Lieut. Lindesay at Oswego, and from Capt. Chew to Col. Marshall at Albany about movements of the French; from Col. Schuyler about orders he has given. 287

18 Arent Stevens sent to make inquiries among the Indians about the reported movements of the French. Advice of council in regard to the news in above letters. 288

24 Extract from a letter of the duke of Newcastle (see *N. Y. col. mss*, 76:10); referred. 289

29 Report of committee on the above letter 290

Mar. 15 Pennsylvania again asks for the loan of cannon; order thereon. Scouts from Albany taken or killed by the enemy. Petitions of Noah Elting and Nath'l Lefever (see *L. P.* 14:19), of Otto van Tuyl et al (see *L. P.* 14:14) with

1748   v. 21

caveat against patent to Jacob de Hart (see *L. P.* 14:23)
referred.   293

18 Cannons can be loaned to Pennsylvania. Patent granted to
Noah Elting and Nath'l Lefever.   294

28 Gov. Clinton ill, Mr Livingston presides. Gov. Shirley proposes a meeting with Gov. Clinton and an Indian conference; writes also about expedition against Crownpoint,
forts in the Indian country, Indian affairs. Council of
Massachusetts concur in the sentiments of the New York
council (p. 290). Letter received from Col. Johnson by
Mr Catherwood on killing of outscouts and garrisons
among the Indians.   295

29 Gov. Clinton present. Report on the letters laid before the
council yesterday.   296

Ap. 9 Council advises the governor to give his assent to several
acts notwithstanding objections thereto.   298

May 2 Letters received from Gov. Shirley with resolutions, etc. of
the Massachusetts representatives in regard to the Crownpoint expedition; advice of council thereon. Order on a
memorial of Advocate General Richard Bradley (see *N. Y.
col. mss*, 76:16). Petition of clergymen complaining that
justices of the peace perform the marriage ceremony re-
ferred.   299

23 Letters received: from Col. Johnson on Indian affairs; from
Col. John Stoddard to Mr Lydius with enclosure from J.
Williams, movements of the French; Col. Johnson's Jour-
nal of an Indian at Onondaga April 24, 25, 26. Exchange
of prisoners to be proposed to the governor of Quebec.
Copy of Col. Johnson's Journal to be sent to Gov. Shirley.
Letter received from Gov. Tincker, recommending Hugo
Grangent, a Frenchman. Warrant for salaries signed.   300

June 6 Assembly adjourned. Letter received from the governor of
Quebec to Gov. Shirley about exchange of prisoners.
Order of council in regard to three French prizes brought
to New York by the Royal Catherine privateer. Copy of
the report made by John Armstrong engineer on the fortifications of the city to be laid before the assembly. Report
of committee on letters and papers, received May 23, ap-
proved.   307

10 Royal proclamation prohibiting commerce with the French
received and to be reprinted (see *N. Y. col. mss*, 76:23).
French prisoners to be sent to the country.   308

20 Governor's message to the assembly read (see *N. Y. col. mss,.*
76:32). Message read from the general court of Massachusetts to Gov. Shirley about meeting of commissioners.

1748   v. 21

French privateers off the coast reported by Mr Wassel of the Pennsylvania council.   308

30   Resolutions of the general assembly relating to the exchange of prisoners received. Proposals for carrying 100 prisoners under flag of truce out of the province, made by Mr Richards, accepted. Order on a petition of Joseph Haviland, Gerard Smith et al (see *N. Y. col. mss*, 76:37). Warrants for salaries, etc. signed.   309

July 8   Governor Clinton is going to Albany.   311

11   Letters received from the duke of New Castle about giving
FortFrederick, presents to the Indians. Money to pay the troops ex-
Albany   pended, council advises to keep them in service, hoping the assembly will make appropriations. Letter from John Chandler to Gov. Shirley about counterfeiters living at Dover, N. Y.   311

23   Propositions made to the six nations and their allies, the Oghquages, Toataghreghroones and Scanehaderadeighroones.   311

26   Answer of the six nations.   314

27   Speech made to the river Indians and their answer.   316

Aug. 9   Letter received from the duke of Bedford with royal procla-
Ft George, mation announcing cessation of hostilities between Great
New York   Britain, France and the States General (see *N. Y. col. mss*, 76:25). Assembly adjourned.   317

17   Order on a petition of Lewis Bouvet master of the ship l'Amazone of Nantes (see *N. Y. col. mss*, 76:45)   317

25   Order on a petition of Joseph Blondi boatswain of the French polacca St Charles of Marseilles (see *N. Y. col. mss*, 76:43). Desertions reported by Col. Johnson from the companies on the frontiers.   318

26   Petition of Joseph Blondi (p. 318) dismissed for reasons given. Louis Bouvet allowed to sell cotton from his ship and purchase provisions. Thos. Carey and Teunis Rivett appointed branch pilots.   319

30   Assembly adjourned.   320

Sep. 1   Assembly adjourned by proclamation. Lottery tickets to raise funds for a college to continue on sale.   320

13   Masters and officers of the French ships Le Marechal de Saxe, Le Concord and Le Zephir, taken by the Brave Hawk privateer, Edw'd Menzie master, allowed to come ashore.   320

15   Order on a petition of Jean Larraldi, Joseph Ollier, Pierre le Prince, masters of the above vessels, and of Guillaume Chapelien, master of the brigantine L'Industrie (see *N. Y. col. mss*, 76:48).   321

1748   **v. 21**

17   Edward Menzie, commanding the Brave Hawk, heard in
     opposition to the foregoing petition with affidavits by
     Joseph Courts, James Biveau and Louis Flott (see *N. Y.
     col. mss,* 76:49, 51).   321

20   Assembly adjourned. The prizes of the Brave Hawk are re-
     stored to their masters, consenting to receive them under
     protest (see *N. Y. col. mss,* 76:52). Liberty granted to the
     flag of truce snow L'Hirondelle, S. Arnavielhe master, to
     refit and provision.   322

24   Dispatches from the governor of Canada delivered by M.
     Delignière. Difficulties in provisioning the troops.   323

29   Edward Holland appointed to the council vice Phil. van
     Cortlandt deceased; he is sworn in and takes his place.
     Edw'd Holland reappointed mayor, John Ayscough sheriff
     and John Burnet coroner of New York; Jacob Coenradt
     ten Eyck mayor, Thos. Williams jr, sheriff of Albany.
     Letters received from the governor of Canada about ex-
     change of prisoners and about cessation of hostilities.
     Stephen Arnavielhe allowed to allow his vessel for re-
     fitting.   324

Oct. 3. Letter received from the duke of Bedford announcing that
     Spain and Genoa have signed the preliminaries of the
     treaty of Aix la Chapelle. Proclamation to issue announc-
     ing cessation of hostilities with Spain. French prisoners
     among the Indians.   325

4   Above proclamation read, amended and ordered printed (see
     N. Y. col. mss, 76:54). Speech intended to be made to the
     Indians. Provisions to the troops.   326

6   Mr Richards explains why he has not sent provisions for
     the troops to Albany; Mr Catherwood contradicts him.
     Orders to ten Broeck and Cuyler, commissaries at Albany. 327

8   Monsieur de Lignière presents a memorial on the exchange
     of prisoners; referred. Minutes sent home.   328

13   Cadw. Colden presents a memorial of what passed in the
     council between him and Chief Justice de Lancey on the
     8th; copy to be sent to de Lancey. Charter of incorpora-
     tion granted to the parish church at Jamaica, Rev. Thos.
     Colgan rector.   328

21   Memorial of Cadwallader Colden (see *N. Y. col. mss,* 76:57);
     Chief Justice de Lancey's answer (see *N. Y. col. mss,* 76:58).
     Resolutions of the assembly received about pay and dis-
     charge of the troops on the frontiers; opinion of council
     thereon. Warrants for salaries, etc. signed.   329

Nov. 8   Reply of Cadw. Colden to Chief Justice de Lancey's answer
     (see *N. Y. col. mss,* 76:60).   335

1748   v. 21

14   Wm Beekman jr, son of Dr Wm Beekman, to be one of the
      managers of the public lottery vice Peter Vallett, resigned
      on account of ill health.   338

Dec. 7 Orders on petitions of Solomon Comes for ferry rights from
      Staten Island to New York (see *L. P.* 14:15, 16) and of
      John Dickinson (see *L. P.* 14:25). Patent granted to
      Thos. Smith (see *L. P.* 14:24).   338

15   Mayor and corporation of New York ask that exportation
      of flour, bread, corn and butter be prohibited; not granted. 340

1749

Jan. 12 Hearing on the petition of Solomon Comes and of Otto van
      Tuyl (see *L. P.* 14:29). Patents granted: to Sarah, Cath-
      erine, George, Elizabeth and Mary Bradley (see *L. P.*
      14:28); to Henry Lane and Hendrick Remsen (see *L. P.*
      14:54); to Abr'm and Wm Salisbury and Casparus Bronck
      (p. 280).   340

Feb. 23 Letter received from the governor of Canada about exchange
      of prisoners referred.   342

Mar. 6 Report on the preceding letter called for. Letter received
      from Capt. Rich'd Ferris commanding the Centaur man
      of war about a Spanish vessel carrying news of the peace
      to Porto Rico having been captured by one King of New
      York; referred to the judge of the admiralty.   342

9   Report on the letter of the governor of Canada relating to
      exchange of prisoners read and approved.   343

10   Hearing on the petition of Solomon Comes (p. 340); con-
      tinued.   343

14   Letter received from J. H. Lydius, Indian affairs. Petition
      of fishermen, badly treated by Jerseymen, referred to Gov.
      Belcher. Patents granted to Hendrick du Bois and Cor-
      nelius Schoonmaker jr (see *L. P.* 14:35) and to David
      Rees (see *L. P.* 14:33). Petition of Zacharias Hoffman
      and Abr'm Smeddies (see *L. P.* 14:30) tabled. Warrants
      for salaries signed.   344

16   Hearing on the petition of Solomon Comes (p. 343) post-
      poned.   346

17   License to purchase Indians lands granted to Thos. Lane
      and Joris Remsen, son of Hendrick Remsen (see *L. P.*
      14:36). Ferry rights granted to Solomon Comes; table of
      fees to be prepared.   346

22   Letter written to M. de Lignerie about his powers to treat
      for an exchange of prisoners and affirmative answer re-
      ceived; Chief Justice de Lancey and Mr Rutherford are
      appointed to treat with him.   347

27   Letter received from Wm Johnson about exchange of prisoners among the Indians; opinion of council. M. de Lignerie not to return to Canada by way of Oswego.   348

Ap. 4   Correspondence with M. de Lignerie about exchange of prisoners continued.   349

10   Orders on petition by Manuel Josepheé de la Mar (see *N. Y. col. mss*, 76:68); by David Seaman, Jacob Seaman, Thos. Seaman, John Jackson and Thos. Allen (see *L. P.* 14:38).   349

May 10   Letter received from the duke of Bedford with royal proclamation of peace; to be published.   350

18   Letter received from Wm Johnson, Indian affairs. Proclamation to issue for a day of thanksgiving. Proof laid before the council that David Seaman et al have complied with the order of April 10 and their petition is granted. Table of fees for Solomon Comes' Staten Island ferry approved.   351

June 7   Letter received from Wm Johnson about French prisoners among the Indians; order of council.   353

28   Letter received from French commander at Crownpoint to Capt. Marshall enclosed in a letter from the latter to the governor, Indian affairs; French movements toward the Belle Rivière; Gov. Hamilton and Shirley to be informed.   353

July 1   Depositions: of Thos. Cumming a quaker about disrespectful words spoken of the governor at the tavern of Andrew Ramsay; of John Woolaston; Oliver de Lancey to be prosecuted for them.   354

13   Speech of the governor in relation to the preceding; Phil. van Horne refuses to testify in regard to it.   358

14   Philipp van Horne, David Johnston and Wm Ricketts called before the council as witnesses in the above case.   359

17   Phil. van Horne and David Johnston examined, Nath'l Johnson dismissed not having heard anything (see *N. Y. col. mss*, 76:79, 80).   359

Aug. 8   Message from the assembly concerning redemption of prisoners among the Indians. Correspondence with the governor of Canada on exchange of prisoners approved. Warrants to Wm Johnson for supplying Oswego troops. Patents granted to Cornelius ten Broeck (see *L. P.* 14:44) and to Jane and Ellis Colden (see *L. P.* 14:45). Petition of Michael Christian Knoll, minister of the Lutheran church in New York (see *N. Y. col. mss*, 76:72) tabled. Minutes sent home.   360

Sep. 8   Order on a representation by Capt. Roddam, commanding the Greyhound man of war, about carpenters refusing to come to Turtle bay for repairing his ship. Letters received:

from Wm Johnson, Indian affairs, M. Beaubassin sent back from Albany, enclosing a letter from M. Louis a French engineer about latitude of Fort Niagara (45° 53′ 17″); from Marquis de la Jonquiere, governor of Canada, exchange of prisoners. Half of the garrison at Oswego may be withdrawn. Warrant to Thos. Butler administrator of Chas. Kerr for the latter's salary as surgeon at Oswego. **361**

29 Mayor, sheriff and coroner of New York reappointed, mayor of Albany also; Richard Miller appointed sheriff of Albany. Complaint of inhabitants of Dutchess county against their sheriff Wm Barnes rejected as frivolous. Otto van Tuyl to be prosecuted for speaking contemptuous words against the governor, as per affidavit of Solomon Comes. Constables in Dutchess and Orange counties, who have neglected to make census returns, to be prosecuted. **363**

Oct. 26 Letters received: from Robert Saunders sent to Canada for exchange of prisoners (see *N. Y. col. mss*, 76:90); from Gov. de la Jonquière about the exchange of Abenakis, prisoners near Boston, and of Amalacites, taken by Capt. Gorham, to be referred to Gov. Shirley. James Swan appointed branch pilot, if he can pass the examination (see *N. Y. col. mss*, 76:93). Petition of the Lutheran minister and congregation in New York (see *N. Y. col. mss*, 6:89) tabled. Order on a petition of Abr'm Kip for a ferry across the Hudson near Kingston (see *N. Y. col. mss*, 76:92). Patents granted: to George Murray and Jacobus Bruyn (see *L.P.* 14:50); to Peter van Brugh Livingston and John Provoost (see *L. P.* 14:51). Order on a petition for running the line between Ulster and Albany counties (see *N. Y. col. mss*, 76:91). **364**

28 Letter received from Col. Jacob Wendel, the Indians near Boston supposed to be prisoners are Pigwackit Indians who came of their own accord to escape the war. Mr Lannier, satisfied with this explanation, to return to Canada. **367**

Nov. 15 Letter received from the duke of Bedford in relation to an address by the house of commons on colonial bills of credit. Treasurer ordered to prepare an account of outstanding bills. Order on a letter from the governor of Leogan, concerning property belonging to Messrs Pazan and Gazan, taken away by the Polly sloop, Nath'l Beek master, John Willet & Co. of New York owners. **368**

Dec. 1 Account of outstanding bills of credit received from the treasurer; mistakes in it pointed out and the treasurer called, but he does not come. Orders to the treasurer to

1749   **v. 21**

give a correct account. Order in regard to Indian children, taken in pawn by Mr Bradt of Albany and Peter van Driesen of Schenectady. Negroes in Albany grown very insolent since the peace. Examinations of David Johnston and Phil. van Horne (p. 359) entered in the minutes.   369

14   Answer of the treasurer to the objections against his account of outstanding bills of credit.   371

21   Treasurer fails to come with a corrected account as ordered.   373

28   Excise matters. Proclamation to issue reviving an act of 12 Anne for laying an excise (see *N. Y. col. mss*, 76:104). Treasurer's account received. Patent granted to Douw Funda and Johs. H. Vrooman (see *L. P.* 14:56)   373

1750

Ap. 3   Letters received: from Gov. Benning Wentworth of New Hampshire (see *N. Y. col. mss*, 76:97, 98); from Col. Wm Johnson, Indian affairs, Mohawks want to go to war against the Catawbas, Oneidas want a smith; from mayor, etc of Albany; Indian children in pawn; from Thos. Hill, secretary of lords of trade with acts of parliament relating to the Unitas Fratrum [Moravians] and to whale fishery.   374

4   Advice of council regarding letters of Col. Johnson, from mayor, etc. of Albany received yesterday. New license to purchase Indian lands granted to Thos. Lane and Joris Remsen (see *L. P.* 14:61). Patents granted: to Anthony Tancret and Samuel Rogers (see *L. P.* 14:62); to George Harrison (see *L. P.* 14:60); to Thos. Ellison and Laurence Roome (see *L. P.* 14:58). Petition of Germans in New York (see *N. Y. col. mss*, 76:113) granted. Order on letter from the governor of Havannah claiming certain negroes as freemen.   376

12   Letter received from the duke of Bedford (see *N. Y. col. mss*, 76:102). Patents granted: to John Ayscough (see *L. P.* 14:65); to Hugh Wentworth (see *L. P.* 14:63); license to purchase Indian lands to Jacob Roseboom, John Jacobus Roseboom and John G. Roseboom (see *L. P.* 14:64). Order in regard to granting patents and licenses.   378

May 22   Account of the treasurer of outstanding bills of credit received. Letters received: from the duke of Bedford (see *N. Y. col. mss*, 76:108); from Capt. Stoddert at Quebec, exchange of prisoners; from Col. Johnson, French with western Indians intend to destroy the Indians on the Ohio in British interest and then the five nations. Assistance promised to the latter in case of attack. Gov. Hamilton writes about French designs against Ohio Indians.   380

1750   v. 21

June 5   Correspondence: with Gov. Wentworth (see *N. Y. col. mss,*
         76:114. 115); with Lt. Gov. Phips relating to a complaint by
         Gov. de la Jonquière about Indian prisoners (see *N. Y.
         col. mss,* 76:117).   381

25   Letters received: from Marquis de la Jonqvière, Abenaki
     prisoners; from Lt. Gov. Phips confirmi..g Col. Jacob
     Wendell's account of them; from Col. Wendell with affi-
     davits about the Pigwackit Indians; from mayor of Albany
     with affidavit of I. Switts master of the sloop on which
     M. Lanniere and the Abenaki sachem went to Albany;
     from Lieut. Lindesay to Col. Johnson, Indian affairs; all
     referred. Order on a petition of Robert Augustine Auvray,
     master of the brigantine St Michael (see *N. Y. col. mss,*
     76:120).   383

26   M. Beaubassin before the council reports on the Abenakis
     near Boston. Report on the letters received the 25th.
     Proclamation to issue forbidding Oswego traders to take
     Indian children in pawn (see *N. Y. col. mss,* 76:118). Lib-
     erty granted to R. A. Auvray for unloading his vessel and
     selling part of his cargo to pay for repairs.   385

July 2   M. Beaubassin again before the council receives dispatches
         for Canada. Patent granted to Wm Smith and James
         Brown (see *L. P.* 14:68). Order on petition of Hugh
         Wentworth (see *L. P.* 14 69). Petition of Hendrick Myer
         (see *L. P.* 14:73) tabled. License granted to Johan Joost
         Herkimer (see *L. P.* 14:72). Caveat entered by Abr'm
         Haasbrouck, Samuel Bevier, and Daniel Haasbrouck
         against Hugh Wentworth.   386

24   Writs for election of a new assembly to issue. Correspond-
     ence with the governor of Canada and Col. Johnson about
     exchange of prisoners. Letters received: from Gov. Went-
     worth (see *N. Y. col. mss,* 76:119); case to be laid before
     the king: from Gov. Glen of South Carolina, Indian affairs. 389

Aug. 6   Draft of an ordinance changing terms of the supreme court
         read and approved. Letters received from Thos. Lee,
         president of Virginia, Indian affairs.   391

9   Hearing on caveat against Hugh Wentworth's petition
    (p. 386).   391

Sep. 4   Royal mandamus appointing Edward Holland of the council
         vice Phil. van Courtlandt deceased; he is sworn in.   392

15   Order on an address from the assembly asking that the act
     for preventing importation of copper money be reprinted.
     Licenses to purchase Indian lands granted: to Teady
     McGin for 8000 acres between Stone Rabey and Canajo-
     harie patents on Canada's Kill: to John Becken and Johs.

1750   **v. 21**

Eckerson (see *L. P.* 14:80); patents for a ferry between
Staten Island and Bergen, N. J. to Jacob Corsen (see *L. P.*
14:82). Order on a petition of Staats Long Morris (see
L. P. 14:79). Order in regard to caveats entered against
granting patents.   392

19   Letter received from Gov. Wentworth (see *N. Y. col. mss,*
76:133). Order on a petition of Manachna and Aman
natives of Arabia (see *N. Y. col. mss,* 76:135).   395

24   Hearing on the caveat against Hugh Wentworth's petition
(p. 391); caveat dismissed. Papers received from Gov.
Hamilton; Twightwee Indians want to enter into an alliance with the six nations and Ohio Indians. Owendaets
on the Ohio want to be included in the peace with the
French; to be laid before the assembly. Letters received
from Lieut. Butler at Oswego and Col. Johnson, Indian
affairs. Patent granted to Hugh Wentworth. Petition
of Jacob, John Jacobus and John G. Roseboom (see *L. P.*
14:84) referred.   396

29   Edward Holland to be mayor, John Ayscough sheriff, Anthony Rutgers coroner of New York; Robert Saunders
mayor and Richard Miller sheriff of Albany. Representation of the attorney general on the eastern boundary (see
N. Y. col. mss, 76:135) referred. Patent granted to Jacob
Roseboom et al (p. 396).   398

Oct. 5   Letter received from Col. Johnson, Indian affairs and French
intentions; referred to the assembly. Petition of John
Joost Petrie (see *N. Y. col. mss,* 76:136) read.   399

8   Warrants granted to the above J. J. Petrie for supplying
Oswego troops; accounts for this service called for from
John de Peyster and Gerrit Corn's van den Bergh. Acts
of parliament relating to African trade, silk culture and exportation of iron from American colonies received from
Thos. Hill and to be fied for public inspection. Proclamation to issue in regard to the iron industry (see *N. Y.
col. mss,* 76:138).   400

15   Letter received from Gov. Hamilton, Indian affairs, the new
headman of the six nations a Roman catholic and greatly
attached to the French interest. Too late in the season for
an Indian conference at Albany.   401

Nov. 5   Journal kept by Conrad Weiser on his journey to Onondaga received with letter from Pres. Thos. Lee of Virginia
on Indian affairs, six nations will not go to Fredericks-
burgh, but meet Virginia delegates at Albany. Message
from Gov. Hamilton to Pennsylvania assembly and answer
on Indian affairs received and referred to the New York
assembly. Minutes sent home.   402

1750   **v. 21**

26   Mandamus of the lords justices restoring James Alexander
to his seat in the council; he is sworn in and takes his
place. Letters received from Pres. Lee of Virginia and
Gov. Glen of South Carolina, Indian affairs. Warrants for
salaries, etc signed.   403

Dec. 5   Letter received from the duke of Bedford with act of parliament relating to American iron; order thereon. Circular
letters to governors of English colonies to be written (see
N. Y. col. mss, 76:145).   405

14   Caveats entered: by the heirs of Dr Samuel Staats, deceased
(see *L. P.* 14:85); by Joseph Banks (see *L. P.* 14:85); by
Barent van Benthuysen and R. R. Livingston (see *L. P.*
14:85). Orders on the petitions: of Johannis Jansen (see
L. P. 14:88); of Staats Lang Morris (see *L. P.* 14:89, 87);
of Wm Bauch and Jacob Fred'k Lawyer (see *L. P.* 14:93);
of Johs. Becker and Johs. Eckerson (see *L. P.* 14:97).
Patent granted to Thos. Lane and Joris Remsen (see *L. P.*
14:95). Warrants for salaries signed.   406

1751

Jan. 3   Letter received from Col. Johnson, Cloron's leaden plate.
Johnson's conference with Scanaghradeya, a Cayuga
sachem who brought the plate; copies to be sent to Gov.
Hamilton. Patents granted: to Alex'r Phoenix, Abr'm
Bokee and John Exceen (see *L. P.* 14:99); to Richard
Durham (see *L. P.* 14:101). Alexander Colden to be
surveyor general with his father.   409

Mar. 12   Letters received: from Lt. Gov. Phips, Gov. Belcher and
Gov. Hamilton in answer to the circular letter (p. 405);
from Lieut. Lindesay at Oswego, about a Missisaga boy,
kept by Mr Bratt. Warrants for salaries signed. Assembly prorogued. Licenses to purchase Indian lands granted:
to Jacob Borst, Jerominus Greslaer, Mathias Bowman,
Barent Keiser, Hendrick Hens, Adam Zehe, Robert
Stuert, Barent ten Eyck and Jacob C. ten Eyck (see *L. P.*
14:102); to Benj. Nicol, John Rutse Bleecker, Valkert P.
Douw and Peter Laroway (see *L. P.* 14:104).   411

Ap. 12   Brigantine Sarah, Robert Leonard master, arrives from St
Christophers with smallpox; quarantine measures. Gov.
Wentworth writes that the assembly of New Hampshire
will not allow him to send a commissioner to the Indian
meeting at Albany and asks Gov. Clinton to appoint a New
York or Albany man as representative of New Hampshire,
can not be done without presents to the Indians. Gov.
Ogle of Maryland and Gov. Hamilton of Pennsylvania are
doubtful whether their assemblies will make the necessary
appropriations for the meeting; Gov. Phips will either

come himself or send commissioners. Time of meeting at Albany postponed until end of June and assembly to be prorogued from week to week. Warrants to Gov. Clinton for Indian presents and expenses to Albany signed.   413

May 16   Letters received from Mayor 'Saunders of Albany and Mr Bratt about the Indian boy; the latter refuses to give up the boy unless paid for; deferred until the governor 'is at Albany. Gov. Phips will have everything ready for the Indian conference. Ordinance for changing time of court of sessions in Westchester county approved. Assembly called to meet. Warrant to Martice van Dyck for taking care of cannons, etc. at Red Hook signed. Petitions of Richard Nicholls land waiter for sa'ary, of Wm Bauch and Jacob Fred'k Lawyer (see *L. P.* 14:107) tabled. Warrant of survey granted to Thos. Braine (see *L. P.* 14:108), patent to John Neilson (see *L. P.* 14:112), licenses to purchase Indian lands to Wm Johnson, Thos. Butler and John Butler'(see *L. P.* 14:114), to Hendrick Myer (see *L. P.* 14:115).   414

24   Death of the prince of Wales and change of prayer for the royal family to be announced by proclamation (see *N. Y. col. mss,* 76:158). Gov. Hamilton writes that the assembly of Pennsylvania will have nothing to do with the Indian meeting at Albany, but he intends to send Conrad Weiser with a present; approved. Letter received from Owen Rice and Rudolphus van Dyck in behalf of the Unitas Fratrum (see *N. Y. col. mss,* 76:157), intention approved.   417

30   Lieut. Lindesay at Oswego reports that the French are building forts at Oniagara and on the Ohio; referred to Gov. Hamilton and to the assembly.   418

31   Governor of Canada 'to be written to about the building of above forts. Mr Bull, commissioner for South Carolina, arrives with six sachems of the Catawbas. Indians displeased with act relating to Oswego duties; referred to the assembly.   419

June 6   Assembly prorogued. Letter received from Arent Stephens the Indian interpreter (see *N. Y. col. mss,* 76:160). Commission appointing Brig. Gen. William Bull as delegate to Albany.   420

12   Report at Albany that a great number of Catawbas are coming up spreads uneasiness among the New York Indians; to be contradicted. Letter received from the governor of St Augustine relating to Englishmen shipwrecked on the coast of Florida and by him sent to New York. Warrants for salaries signed: Licenses to purchase Indian lands granted: to Matthew Ferral (see *L. P.*

14:124, 125); to Luykas Johannes Wyngaard, John Garret Roseboom, Jacob Merkell and Nicholas Jacobus Lydius (see *L. P.* 14:109); to Theobalt, Adam, Frederick and Andries Yongh, Gerrit Staats, Henry Dow, Jacob ten Broeck, Corn's ten Broeck, Gerardus Groesbeck, Benj. Nicoll and Henry Holland (see *L. P.* 14:119); to Koenradt Kanterman (see *L. P.* 14:123); patents to Jacob Borst et al (see *L. P.* 14:116 and p. 411); to Johann Joost Herkemer and his son Hendrick (see *L. P.* 14:126).   421

19   Letters received: from Hendrick a Mohawk sachem to Rev. Mr Ogilvie asking that the sale of liquor to Indians be stopped; from Sec. Willard of Massachusetts, lieutenant governor is sick, commissioners are chosen by the general court. Speech of Gov. Clinton to the council (see *N. Y. col. mss*, 76:167); referred.   424

p. m.   Answer of the council to the governor's speech (see *N. Y. col. mss*, 76:168). Gov. Hamilton has sent Conrad Weiser to Albany with message of condolence on the death of Canasatego and presents to the six nations and asks permission for Weiser's son to remain a few years among them near Fort Hunter and learn the Indian language; granted.   425

July 15   Gov. Clinton lays minutes of proceedings at Albany June 28-July 8 before the council as follows.

June 28
Albany   Proclamation to issue forbidding the sale to or distribution among the Indians of rum.   428

July 1   Report of Lieut. Lindesay at Oswego: Onondaga sachems gone to Canada to forbid the building of forts in their country; Young Red Head has taken four squaws to Canada; Ninnack has carried six English traders to Niagara, confirmed by some of the five nations with Cocknawaga and Sienundie Indians; Micel Mackenock (Missilimackinak) Indians, arrived at Oswego, report war between the Twightwees and Ottawawas likely to break out; French interpreter and two Indians from Cadaraqui at Oswego, supposed with the intention of inviting all the five nations to Canada; recommends Chiquaquendi, an Onondaga sachem, of great influence. Letter to be sent to the governor of Canada remonstrating against the building of forts. Expenses of Rev. Mr Ogilvie in going to theMohawks about treaty with the Catawbas to be paid out of Indian treaty fund. Commission of Jacob Wendell, Joseph De Wight and Oliver Partridge, delegates of Massachusetts read. Gov. Clinton's speech to the Indians.   428

2   Cocknawaga Indians pay their respects to Gov. Clinton; speeches upon the occasion. Speech at a private conference with the six nations about Col. Johnson refusing to act longer as Indian agent.   430

1751   **v. 21**

3   Public condolence on ·the death of the prince of Wales by
     the Indians; Gov. Clinton condoles on the deaths of their
     sachems. His answer relating to Col. Johnson. Com-
     mission of Wm Pitkin and Johs. Chester as delegates from
     Connecticut and instructions to Conrad Weiser, as inter-
     preter for Pennsylvania read.   432

5   Col. Johnson gives his reasons for refusing to act any
     longer as Indian agent; he is asked to continue as such for
     the present, to which he consents but refuses to be sworn
     of the council.   434

6   Cocknawagas, 200 in number, to leave Albany as soon as
     possible.   436

8   Letter from Commissioner Bull, and his speech intended
     for the six nations read and approved, also Gov. Glen's
     letter to the nations. Expenses of the meeting heavy.   436

10   Speech of Massachusetts commissioners read. Order in re-
     gard to the Indian boy in possession of Johannes Bradt.   437

p. m. The Indian boy turned over to the sheriff; Johs. Bradt to
     be prosecuted by information. Col. Johnson given ·charge
     of the Indian boy to return him to his parents. Royal
     mandamus appointing Col. Wm Johnson of the council;
     he is sworn in and takes his seat. Letter from the com-
     missioners to Gov. Clinton (see *N. Y. col. mss*, 77:2); re-
     ferred. Speeches to and answers of the six nations, July **1**,
     6, 8, 10 and letter of Gov. Glen to them.   **438**

July 19   Report of committee on the above letter ·from the commis-
     sioners (see *N. Y. col. mss*, 77:4)   453

30   Lieut. Lindesay reports the arrival at ·Oswego of some
     Twightwees well disposed toward the English. Assem-
     bly prorogued. John Chambers appointed second justice
     of the supreme court vice Fred'k Philippse deceased.   455

31   John Chambers sworn in as justice.   455

Sep. 30   Mayors, sheriffs and coroner of New York and of Albany
     reappointed. Letters received: from Corns. Cuyler, sent
     with dispatches to Canada, no Indians of the six nations
     there on his arrival but Senecas came just before he left;
     from Marquis de la Joncquière, governor of Canada, to
     Gov. Clinton (see *N. Y. col. mss*, 77:7); from Col. John-
     son, 1200 French and 200 Orondacks have passed Oswego
     on an expedition against British western Indians and to
     prevent the Pennsylvanians from building a fort at or near
     the Ohio; ·from Lieut. Lindesay and Capt. Stoddard (see
     N. Y. col. mss, 77:5); same information; from Gov. Wool-
     cot, about sending missionaries to the six nations; from
     Gov. Hamilton, grant of ·land to Col. Johnson on the

1751   v. 21

Susquehannah objected to; referred. Warrants for salaries, etc signed.   455

Oct. 9   Report on the above letter of Gov. Hamilton. Petition of Jacob Borst et al for inserting the name of Anna Margrieta Greslaer in the patent, instead of her husband Jeronimus deceased (see *L. P.* 14:134) granted. Licenses to purchase Indian lands granted: to Johan Fred'k Bauch, Christian Zehe, Johs. Zehe, Michael Wanner and Johs. Knisker (see *L. P.* 14:135); to John Lawyer and Phil. Bergh (see *L. P.* 14:136); patent to S. Bayard, Nich's Bayard, Sam'l Bayard, Peter Kemble and David Provoost (see *L. P.* 14:137).   461

Vol. 22, 1746-52

Legislative minutes of council from June 3, 1746 to Nov. 11, 1752 printed in *Journal of the legislative council of the colony of New York*, 2:926-1107.

Vol. 23, 1751-64

1751

Oct. 18   Report of committee on the representation of the attorney general relating to boundary with New Hampshire (21: 398; and see *N. Y. col. mss*, 77:13). Col. Johnson's remarks on a petition of Abr'm van Eps and other Oswego traders for increase of duties; to be laid before the assembly. Answer of Gov. Clinton to letter of governor of Canada of Aug. 10 (21:455) referred to the assembly. Patent granted to John Leake (see *L. P.* 14:138).   1

25   Royal order received creating Prince George prince of Wales (see *N. Y. col. mss*, 76:153); proclamation to issue accordingly. Letter received from Lieut. Mills at Oswego, trading house in a ruinous condition; referred to the assembly.   11

28   Letter received from the same, expedition of M. Bellatre against the Twightwees failed because the Ottawawahs refused to join in it and of smallpox among the Indians; will be tried again in the spring with help of Orondacks, Abenakis and Micmack Indians; referred to Gov. Hamilton and the assembly. Message from the assembly that they will make provisions for sending smiths to Tierondequat, the Senecas and Onondagas and recommending Abr'm Wendell as resident agent among the Indians. Council will select an Indian agent if the assembly will make provisions.   11

30   Assembly has made provisions for three smiths by resolutions, copies to be sent to Albany for selecting proper persons.   12

1751   **v. 23**

Nov. 1   Correspondence with Gov. Glen of South Carolina and the
king of the Catawbas, six nations have killed some Catawbas; to be sent to the six nations. Treasurer to attend and
explain why he has not paid warrants issued to Col. John-
son.   13

4   Explanation of treasurer as called for. Petition of proprietors and inhabitants of the glebelands at Quassaick, formerly granted to the palatines, that the grant may be confirmed for the use of an English rector and schoolmaster;
granted.   14

7   Acts of parliament relating to naval stores, bills of credit and
pot ashes received from the lords of trade and to be published in the New York gazette. Order to prosecute the
commissioners for Oswego duties for neglect of duty.
Council's opinion on a private message from the assembly wanting to know who will be appointed commissioners
of Indian affairs.   17

19   Peter Vrooman, Corn's Vrooman and Hendrick Hagadorne
to be prosecuted on an affidavit of Jacob W. Vrooman, for
having helped Roger alias Ryer Baxter of Schoharie to
escape from jail. Reasons given by Col. Johnson for ob-
taining a deed for land on Onondaga lake from the Indians; to be laid before the lords of trade. Petition of
Wm Smith and James Brown (see *L. P.* 14:129) granted.   19

1752

Jan. 9   Letter received from Arent Stephens the Indian interpreter
with letter from the six nations to the Catawbas (see *N. Y.
col. mss*, 77:28). Assembly called to meet. Threatening
letter received by Robert Gilbert Livingston; reward for
discovery of writer offered by proclamation (see *N. Y. col.
mss*, 77:30).   21

Mar. 2   Letters received: from Arent Stephens, six nations unde-
cided about going to Canada; from earl of Holdernesse
(see *N. Y. col. mss*, 77:26). Warrants for salaries, etc.
signed. Order on a petition of lawyers practising in the
mayor's court for an ordinance on fees. Patent granted to
Goldsbrow Banyar, John Benson and Joseph Webb jr (see
L. P. 14:141).   23

May 4   Letter received from the governor of St Augustine, the New
York privateer Hester, Robert Troup commander, has
taken the Spanish sloop Carmen, Fernando Antonio
Laguna master, after cessation of hostilities; referred to
the judge of the admiralty court. Order on a petition of
Robert Livingston jr (see *N. Y. col. mss*, 77:39, 40; and,
Doc. hist. N. Y. 3:734-38; Q 438-41). Letter received from

Arent Stephens with messages from the Onondagas, Virginia and South Carolina endeavor to keep the five nations and the Catawbas peaceful; from the Cayugas and Senecas, French intrigues; and from the Mohawks, Twightwees have taken a French fort and want to destroy Niagara; Ohio Indians have taken Jean Coeur a prisoner. To be laid before the assembly.   25

8   Royal mandamus appointing John Chambers to the council vice Stephen Bayard; he is sworn in and takes his seat. Order directing John de Peyster one of the commissioners of duties on Indian goods to render an account of moneys received. Six nations send a belt of wampum asking them to come to Virginia, to be returned to the governor of Virginia; Albany being the place of treaty; advice of council thereon. Warrant to Lieut. Walter Butler for salary as commissary at Oswego signed. Licenses to purchase Indian lands granted: to Teady Magin et al (see *L. P.* 14:149); to Jacob Starnbergh (see *L. P.* 14:148); to Rudolph Staley and Johan Joost Herchheimer jr (see *L. P.* 14:144); to Jacob Timberman [Zimmerman] and John Joost Snell (see *L. P.* 14:147).   27

21   The sloop Maria, Fernando Laguna master, not to be restored. Order on a petition of Fernando Antonio Laguna for the discharge of Spanish negroes, freemen sold as slaves. Letter received from Lieut. Mills at Oswego. Twightwees on the warpath against the French; French intentions; to be communicated to governor of Pennsylvania and the assembly. Patents granted: to Henry Holland (see *L. P.* 14:150, 151, 153); to Abr'm Hasbrouck, Louis Bevier jr and Jacob Hasbrouck jr (see *L. P.* 14:128). Wampum belt received from the Senecas asking for a blockhouse to secure them against the French; recommended to the assembly.   29

25   Letter received from Don Melchior de Navarette governor of St Augustine, Spanish negroes sold as slaves; referred to the advocate general. Patent granted to Augustus van Cortlandt (see *L. P.* 14:154). Order in relation to the lands on Onondaga lake given by the Indians to Col. Johnson.   31

29   Letter received from Gov. Glen of South Carolina, Catawbas and six nations.   33

July 3 Letter received from Gov. Hamilton of Pennsylvania. Report on the petition of Rob't Livingston jr (p. 25) and petition of Westenhook patentees (see *N. Y. col. mss.* 77:44, 46, 47) referred. Warrants for salaries signed. Report of attorney general about Spanish negroes (p. 31) to be sent to the governor of St Augustine (see *N. Y. col. mss,* 77:50). Patents granted: to Coenradt Kanterman (see *L. P.* 14:157); to Johs Lawyer and Phil. Bergh (see *L. P.* 14:159); to John Leake (see *L. P.* 14:158); to Augustus van Cortlandt (see *L. P.* 14:154). Licenses to purchase Indian lands granted: to Arent Stevens et al (see *L. P.* 14:164); to David Schuyler, Peter D. Schuyler, Adolph Myer and John van Cortlandt (see *L. P.* 14:165). Ferry patent granted to Abr'm Kip and Moses Cantine (see *L. P.* 14:167).   33

14   Warrant to Johan Joost Petrie for supplies to Oswego garrison signed. Petitions of T. Young et al (see *L. P.* 14:161) with caveat against it by Nicholas Bayard, and of Stephen, Nicholas and Samuel Bayard, Peter Kemble and David Provoost (see *L. P.* 14:166) heard and decided in favor of the first. Patents granted: to Arch'd Kennedy (see *L. P.* 14:171); to John Chambers, Vincent Matthews, Evan Jones, Joseph Sacket, Samuel Bayard Mariner, James Tuthill, Eben'r Seeley, John Yelverton, Hezekiah Howell, Henry Brewster, Brandt Schuyler, Lodowick Bamper, Christ'n Hertell, John Sacket and Mathias Earnest (see *L. P.* 14:170).   37

Aug 14   Letter received from Arent Stevens Indian interpreter, six nations and Catawbas have made peace. John Dowgan, Michael Fin and John Colson to be arrested by the sheriff of Albany on depositions taken before the mayor charging them with mutiny at Oswego and desertion.   40

21   Col. Johnson writes that the six nations are in great want of provisions; peace with the Catawbas who return to South Carolina under escort of Iroquois warriors. Report received from Lieut. Mills and Oswego traders on the ruinous condition of buildings there; mayor of Albany to be asked to have it repaired and assembly to make necessary appropriation. Assembly prorogued. Letter and report received from Lewis Morris judge of the admiralty relating to Spanish negroes. Patents granted to Samuel Auchmuty, John Burges, Wm Ogilvie, Anne Avery, Morley Harrison, Josiah Crane, Wm Mitchell, Hendrick Cropsie and John Bickerton (see *L. P.* 15:6); to Thos. Ellison (see *L. P.* 15:5); to Abr'm Fonda (see *L. P.* 15:1). License to purchase Indian land granted to Teleman Cuyler, Joris Johnson and Henry Ramsen jr (see *L. P.* 14:174).   40

Sep. 29   Mayors, sheriffs and coroner of New York and Albany renominated. Assembly prorogued to meet at the house of Jacob Dyckman in Harlem. Warrants for salaries, etc.

signed. John Dowgan and Michael Fin, Oswego deserters,
to be brought to New York. Mayor of Albany writes it
is too late in the season to have repairs at Oswego made.   43

Nov. 16   Acts of parliament relating to correction of calendar, cultivation of coffee, attestation of wills received and ordered
published. Letter received from the lords of trade with
additional instructions. Commissioners of Indian affairs
appointed. Licenses to purchase Indian lands granted:
south of the Mohawk river and west of Schoharie to John
Christ'r Hardwick et al; on Otsego lake and Adaquicktinge creek to Fred'k Miller, Adam Scheffer, George Cuntz,
Adam Tippel, Luke van Ranst et al; between Schoharie
and Cobus kill to Lawrence Lawyer (see *L. P.* 15:21); to
Johs. Becker jr, Johs. Schafer jr, Hendrick Schafer jr and
Jacob Schafer (see *L. P.* 15:23); to Lambertus Starnbergh
(see *L. P.* 15:20); to Jacob Miller (see *L. P.* 15:22). Patent
granted to Arent Stevens, Barent Vrooman, Matthew Ferral, Rob't Adams, Cadw. Colden jr, John Young, John
Sewell, Ephraim Arnold, Dow Fonda and Jelius Fonda
(see *L. P.* 15:24). Lease of a house near Fort George
granted to Christ'r Blundell (see *L. P.* 15:25). Order on
petition of Wm Bauch, Jacob Fred'k Lawyer, Nich's York
and Thos. Eckerson (see *L. P.* 15:14). Minutes sent home.   45

21   Warrants signed: to John Wallace for salary as surgeon; to
Wm Livingston administrator of Lieut. John Lindesay,
for the latter's salary as commissary at Oswego. New
license to purchase Indian lands granted to Matthew Ferral (see *L. P.* 15:28).   50

Dec. 1   Patent granted to John Fred'k Bauch, Christian Zehe, Johannes Zehe, Michael Wanner and Johs. Knisker (see
L. P. 15:30). Caveat by Noah Elting and others against
a grant to Abr'm Hasbrouck et al (p. 29) dismissed and
patent confirmed. Warrants for salaries signed.   51

2   Letter received from Don Fulgencio Garcia de Solis governor
of St Augustine respecting the claim of the sloop Carmen,
Fernando Laguna master; referred to the attorney general.
Report made by the recorder and aldermen on the petition
of attorneys (p. 23) referred.   53

1753

Mar. 2   Report of the chief justice on petitions of Robert Livingston jr and Westenhook partners (p. 25, 33) to be sent to
the lieutenant governor of Massachusetts. Patent granted
to Nich's Colton and Edw'd Wilkins (see *L. P.* 15:42).
Warrants for salaries signed.   55

16   Report of the attorney general on the claim of the sloop
Carmen and Spanish mulattoes (see *N. Y. col. mss*, 77:70)
referred. Letter from Gov. Dinwiddie of Virginia about
treaties with the six nations (see *N. Y. col. mss*, 77:65) referred. Assembly prorogued.   61

1753   **v. 23**

Ap. 16   Letters received: from lieutenant governor of Boston,
           boundary affairs; from Col. Johnson on Gov. Dinwiddie's
           letter (see *N. Y. col. mss,* 77:76); from sachems of the six
           nations denying that they have been in Virginia to treat;
           all referred. Order on petition of Johs. Becker and Johs.
           Eckerson (see *L. P.* 15:43).   63

30   Royal mandamus appointing Wm Smith of the council vice
           Sir Peter Warren deceased; he is sworn in and takes his
           seat. Col. Johnson writes of a French army marching ap-
           parently to Ohio; sent to Gov. Hamilton. Massachusetts
           will appoint boundary commissioners; referred. Assem-
           bly prorogued to meet at the courthouse in Jamaica.
           Licenses to purchase Indian lands granted: to Johannes
           Samuel Pruyn and Dorick Bratt van Schoonhoven (see
           L. P. 15:44); to Rudolph Staley and Johan Joost Herch-
           heimer (see *L. P.* 15:46). Patent granted to Abr'm Duyon
           (see *L. P.* 15:48). Ordinance to issue regulating sessions of
           circuit courts.   65

May 1   Report on the appointment of commissioners to settle the
           boundaries with Massachusetts; to be sent to Boston.
           License to purchase Indian lands granted to Teady Magin
           (see *L. P.* 15:49).   67

30   Letters and papers received: from Robert Charles, colonial
           agent at London, concerning New Hampshire boundaries;
           referred to assembly; from Gov. Hamilton of Pennsylva-
           nia, robberies by French Indians in Kentucky; from Lieut.
           Holland at Oswego, Indian news, French army moving to
           the Ohio; all referred to assembly.   70

31   Letter from Capt. Stoddard to Col. Johnson, French move-
           ments (see *N. Y. col. mss,* 77:87); referred to assembly.   72

June 4   Memorial of Rob't Livingston jr (see *N. Y. col. mss,* 77:94)
           and petition of John van Rensselaer (see *N. Y. col. mss,*
           77:92) referred to assembly. Repairs of the Oswego build-
           ings. Six nations to be met at Albany.   72

12   Hendrick and other Mohawk sachems before the council;
           their speech.   73

13   Order on report of advocate general in relation to Spanish
           mulattoes (see *N. Y. col. mss,* 77:98-99). Corporation of
           Albany has provided transportation to the Mohawks.
           Letter received from Arent Stevens, he has tried to dissuade
           them from going to New York. Minutes of the conference
           with the Mohawks at New York (see *N. Y. col. mss,* 77:100-5.   75

15   Letter from the speaker of the assembly David Jones, allow-
           ance for Indian presents. Hendrick's speech referred. Pe-
           tition of corporation of Albany for an appropriation to
           fortify the city referred to assembly.   78

p. m.   Complaint by the Mohawks of encroachments upon their
           lands investigated.   79

1753   **v. 23**

16 Speech to be made in answer to the Mohawks, the reply of
    Hendrick, their speaker and concluding remarks.   80

18 Above speeches to be laid before assembly. Letters received:
    from Arent Stevens, wampum belt sent by the governor of
    Canada to the six nations forwarded to New York; from
    Lieut. Butler to Col. Johnson, same topic; referred to as-
    sembly and Gov. Hamilton. Indian affairs (see *N. Y. col.
    mss*, 77:88). Petition by inhabitants of Kinderhook for the
    building of two forts there referred to assembly.   84

July 3 Letters received: from Timothy Woodbridge to Col. John-
    son with belts of wampum, against sale of rum to five
    nations and Susquehanna Indians (see *N. Y. col. mss*,
    77:116), proclamation to issue accordingly (see *N. Y. col.
    mss*, 77:119); from Lt. Gov. Phips with report of committee
    on the boundary (see *N. Y. col. mss*, 77:109, 110), referred;
    from Gov. Hamilton, Indian affairs.   85

4 Time set for hearing on caveat by Thos. Ellison against grant
    of land under water to John Chambers et al (see *L. P.*
    15:45). Licenses to purchase Indian lands granted: to
    David Schuyler, Peter David Schuyler and Nicholas Picket
    (see *L. P.* 15:56); to John Schuyler and Abram Douw (see
    L. P. 15:57).   86

28 Report on Lt. Gov. Phips' letter (p. 85; and see *N. Y. col. mss*,
    77:144). Proclamation to issue ordering rioters in the
    manor of Livingston to be arrested (see *N. Y. col. mss*,
    77:146); copies of both to be sent to Gov. Phips (see
    N. Y. col. mss, 77:145). Message received from the sachems
    of the Canajoharie castle (see *N. Y. col. mss*, 77:115). Let-
    ters received: from Mayor Robert Saunders of Albany, he,
    Myndert Schuyler, Jacob C. ten Eyck, John Beeckman and
    the recorder have qualified as Indian commissioners (see
    N. Y. col. mss, 77:123); from the said commissioners with
    letters of Indian traders, prisoners of the French and In-
    dians (see *N. Y. col. mss*, 77:97, 140); Senecas, Shawanese
    and Cayugas will take up the hatchet against the French
    (see *N. Y. col. mss*, 77:143); all referred. Report of the
    advocate general on the cases of Josepho Antonio Fallo
    and Alexander Joseph de la Torre, Spanish negroes, re-
    ferred. Letter received from Gov. Belcher (see *N. Y. col.
    mss*, 77:141). Warrants for salaries, etc signed. Licenses
    to purchase Indian lands granted: to Jacob Starnberger,
    George Zimmer, Hendrick Weaver and Jacob Zeimer, all of
    Schoharie (see *L. P.* 15:55); to Jacob Timberman and John
    Joost Snell (see *L. P.* 15:61); to Johs. Lawyer jr, Jacob
    Borst jr, George Forster and Reinhart Heints (see *L. P.*
    15:63); to James Stewart et al (see *L. P.* 15:64). Petitions

1753   v. 23

referred: of Lambertus Starnbergh and Adam Starnbergh
(see *L. P.* 15:60); of Johs. Becker jr, Johs. Schafer jr, Hendrick Schafer jr and Jacob Schafer (see *L. P.* 15:59). Daniel Horsmanden appointed third justice of the supreme
court.   88

Aug. 8 Letters received: from Gov. Hamilton, Indian and Ohio
affairs, Conrad Weiser sent to Onondaga; from Lieut. Holland at Oswego, French troops going to the Ohio, troops
from the Mississippi to join them. Petition of Miguel
Joseph Fuentes a free Spanish negro referred.   94

10 Patents granted to Lambertus and Adam Starnbergh and to
Johs. Becker jr et al (p. 88). License to purchase Indian
lands granted to John McNiele, John McKillip, Charles
McKay, Alex'r Stewart and John Wilson (see *L. P.*
15:65). Order on a representation by the advocate general (see *N. Y. col. mss,* 77:150).   95

31 Letters received: from Col. Johnson, Indian affairs; from
Lieut. Holland, Indian movements (see *N. Y. col. mss,*
77:147); from Gov. Shirley, boundaries (see *N. Y. col. mss,*
77:152). Isaac Hubbard appointed collector of duties in
Suffolk county. License to purchase Indian lands granted
to Ury Rightmeyer and Hendrick Weaver (see *L. P.*
15:66). Patent granted to Augustine Moore and John
Myer cordwainer (see *L. P.* 15:67).   97

Sep. 1 Order on petition of Abel Hardenbrook (see *N. Y. col. mss,*
77:155). Warrants for salaries signed. Hearing on the
caveat of Thos. Ellison against grant to John Chambers (p.
86); patent granted.   99

20 Letters received: from Gov. Glen of South Carolina, Carolina
Indians, proclamation (see *N. Y. col. mss,* 77:113-14); from
Gov. Dinwiddie of Virginia, Catawbas and Cherokees har-
rassed by the Praying Indians (see *N. Y. col. mss,* 77:151);
from Col. Johnson, French Indian movements; opinion of
council thereon. Controversy between Wm Bauch & Co.
and Johs. Becker et al (p. 63) to be examined.   102

29 Edward Holland reappointed mayor, John Ayscough sheriff,
Anthony Rutgers coroner of New York; Robert Sanders
mayor, James Wilson sheriff of Albany. Letter and papers
received: from Gov. Shirley (see *N. Y. col. mss,* 77:157-60)
and referred; from the governor of St Augustine (see
N. Y. col. mss, 77:156) referred.   104

Oct. 10 Letter from duke of Newcastle granting leave of absence to
Gov. Clinton and enclosing lieutenant governor's commission for Chief Justice de Lancey.   106

10 Sir Danvers Osborn baronet has his commission as governor,
etc read and takes the oaths; Gov. Clinton delivers the

seals and proclamation to issue continuing all officers (see
N. Y. col. mss, 78:17). Sir Danvers publishes his commission at the city hall. 107

11 John Roberts appointed sheriff of New York vice John
Ayscough resigned to go to England. 109

12 James Alexander presides, Sir Danvers Osborn having
died. Thos. Pownall Sir Danvers' secretary delivers the seals
and commissions. James de Lancey sworn in as lieutenant
governor. Proclamation to issue continuing all officers
(see *N. Y. col. mss*, 78:18). Instructions to Sir Danvers
read, appointing Cadwallader Colden, James Alexander,
Arch'd Kennedy, James de Lancey, George Clarke jr,
Joseph Murray, John Rutherford, Edw'd Holland, Wm.
Johnson, John Chambers and Wm Smith of the council.
Lt. Gov. de Lancey advised to publish his commission without the usual solemnities at the gate of Fort George near
the Bowling Green. Committee of inquest on Sir Danvers'
death appointed. 110

p. m. Committee appointed to take an inventory of Sir Danvers'
estate and make arrangements for his funeral. 112

13 Cadwallader Colden sworn of the council, takes his seat. 112

18 Assembly prorogued (see *N. Y. col. mss*, 78:24). 113

25 Letter received from Lieut. Holland at Oswego, needed repairs; referred to assembly. Sir Danvers Osborn's papers
to be examined. 113

29 Letter received from Col. Johnson, French are making settlements on the Ohio and Mississippi, Swiss brought there;
his minutes of Indian conferences at Oswego with speeches,
July 26-27, Sep. 8, 10 (see *N. Y. col. mss*, 78:2-8). Letter
received from Lieut. Holland, Indian news. Instructions
to Sir Danvers Osborn to be laid before the council and
assembly. Oliver de Lancey, Thos. Pownall and Charles
Williams appointed administrators of Sir Danver's estate. 114

Nov. 7 Orders on petition of Hendrick, Abr'm Paulus, Johannes
and Nickas, Mohawk sachems (see *L. P.* 15:77). Inventory
of military stores in Fort George to be taken. Warrant to
John van Rensselaer for firewood and candles to Fort William and to Albany and Schenectady garrisons signed. 125

10 Letter from Lord Holdernesse to Sir Danvers Osborn, encroachments by foreign powers, mutual assistance of the
colonies; referred to assembly. 127

19 Report of committee on the eastern boundaries (see *N. Y.
col. mss*, 78:33) to be sent to Gov. Shirley. 128

21 Certificate granted on petition of the minister of the reformed church in New York (see *N. Y. col. mss*, 78:34, 35).
Isaac Honeywell justice of the peace and colonel of militia in Westchester county dismissed. 129

1753   **v. 23**

Dec. 6 Letter received from Lieut. Holland, French troops returned
from the Ohio will make another attempt next year; to be
sent to lords of trade and southern governors. Order on
message from assembly (see *N. Y. col. mss*, 78:37). Report
of committee on the death of Sir Danvers Osborn (see
N. Y. col. mss, 78:19-23) and representation of committee
on eastern boundaries (see *N. Y. col. mss*, 78:32) to be sent
to lords of trade.   130

10 Letter received from the lords of trade to Sir Danvers Osborn, Indian conference to be held; to be laid before assembly.   131

12 Council advise that the governor give his assent to fifteen
acts passed, Arch'd Kennedy dissenting. Assembly con-
sents to make appropriations for Indian presents. Indians
called to meet at Albany. Assembly prorogued.   133

1754

Jan. 11 Riot in New York city because the merchants refuse to take
copper money at standard rate. Proclamation to issue
for suppressing the disorders (see *N. Y. col. mss*, 78:50).
Wendal Ham and Mathias Sleght committed.   133

31 John Burnet appointed coroner of New York vice Anthony
Rutgers deceased. 26th and 27th articles of the instructions to Sir Danvers Osborn relating to appeals to governor and council from the supreme court; 56th and 59th of
same relating to grants of land (see *L. P.* 15:89), referred.
Petition of Ury Rightmeyer, Hendrick Weaver, John
Lansing, Abr'm Lott jr, Isaac Goelet and Edw'd Taylor
for land south of Schoharie referred. Letters received
from Gov. Belcher, the sheriff and justices of Orange
county about New Jersey boundary line and disturbances
there (see *N. Y. col. mss*, 78:53-62). Committee appointed
to establish a line of peace.   134

Feb. 4 Letters received: from Gov. Shirley, boundaries; from Mr
Smith to Gov. Shirley, French on the Ohio.   139

18 Col. Johnson takes the oaths as member of the council.
Letter received from Gov. Dinwiddie (see *N. Y. col. mss*,
78:63); advice of council thereon. Examination of Stephen
Coffin (see *N. Y. col. mss*, 78:49) received from Col. Johnson, French Forts at Presqu'ile and Rivière aux Boeufs.   140

Mar. 1 Report of committee on instructions relating to grants of
land. Assembly prorogued. Patent granted to Ury
Rightmeyer et al (p. 134) for 8000 acres of land in Albany
county. Petitions referred: of Matthew Ferral et al (see
L. P. 15:92); of John Christ'r Hardwick (see *L. P.* 15:95);
of Fred'k Miller, Adam Scheffer, George Cants, Adam Tippel and Luke van Raust (see *L. P.* 15:91). Order on report of committee on petitions of Spanish mulattoes.   142

1754   v. 23

4   Letter received from Gov. Shirley, wants Indian meeting
at Albany postponed; not consented. Report of committee on the disturbances along the New Jersey line (see
N. Y. col. mss, 78:74); copy to be sent to Gov. Belcher.   145

13   Dissent of James Alexander to the preceding report (see
N. Y. col. mss, 78:81); referred. Letter received from
Rob't Livingston jr (see *N. Y. col. mss*, 78:67); referred
to committee on eastern boundaries. A Frenchman arrived from Canada to be confined to his room.   151

p. m.   Report on petition of Matthew Ferral (p. 142); license
to purchase Indian lands granted. Report on the petitions of J. C. Hardwick and of Fred. Miller et al (see
N. Y. col. mss, 78:67); licenses granted. M. Paco the
above Frenchman examined and ordered to leave as soon
as possible. Order relating to people coming from Canada sent to Albany. Gov. de Lancey sworn in as chancellor.   158

14   Letter received from Gov. Dinwiddie, Virginia assembly has
granted £10,000 for operations against the French on the
Ohio, with proclamation (see *N. Y. col. mss*, 78:68). General plan of campaign to be concerted, Virginia proclamation sent to Connecticut. Petition of Wm Walton, Rob't
Crommelin, Thos. Barnes and James des Brosses (see
L. P. 15:98) referred.   164

18   Bills of credit of New York are reported counterfeited; governor of Connecticut to be asked to arrest Nath'l Key one
of the counterfeiters.   166

23   Assembly prorogued (see *L. P.* 15:80).   167

26   Letters received from Lord Holdernesse (see *L. P.* 15: 51),
referred to assembly; from Gov. Dinwiddie (see *L. P.*
15:75). Assembly called to meet promptly.   167

Ap. 4   Letters received: from Gov. Hamilton (see *L. P.* 15:86); from
Gov. Shirley (see *L. P.* 15:85); from Gov. Dinwiddie (see
(*L. P.* 15:76). Propositions to be made to assembly:
supplies for independent companies ordered to Virginia;
forts in the Indian country; double garrison at Oswego;
repairs at Oswego and Copsy battery. Independent companies to go by water in the station ship, Lieut. Kennedy
commanding. Letter received from Peter Bours (see *L. P.*
15:83). Communication from James Alexander (see *L. P.*
15:90) referred.   168

9   Proclamation to apprehend deserters (see *L. P.* 15:92)
signed. Speech to be made to the council and assembly
read (see *L. P.* 15:91).   171

p. m.   Letters left by M. Paco in the hands of Mr Stilwell to be
sent to the ministry.   172

1754   v. 23

15   Letters received: from the lords of trade, approving resolu-
      tion to assist other colonies when invaded, referred to the
      assembly; from John Pownal, secretary of the lords of
      trade, Indian conference approved. French deserters from
      Niagara examined, confirm news given in a letter of Dr
      Colhoun; to be further examined. Indian presents arrived
      from England to be inspected.   172

29   Letter and papers received from Gov. Shirley (see *N. Y. col.
      mss*, 78:98) referred to boundary commissioners. Vote of
      assembly in relation to gunpowder seized by Collector
      Kennedy referred (see *N. Y. col. mss*, 78:100). New char-
      ter granted to the corporation of Kingston (see *L. P.*
      15:99). Patent granted to Wm Walton et al (p. 164).   173

May 1 Assembly prorogued for one day. Recommendation to be
      made to provide means for securing the colony.   175

9   Letters received: from Gov. Dinwiddie, attack on the
      French at Kennebeque river may prevent their designs on
      the Ohio; from Gov. Hamilton with letter from Major
      G. Washington (see *N. Y. col. mss*, 78:111) and speech of
      the Half King (see *N. Y. col. mss*, 78:112); to be sent to
      Connecticut. Warrants to the governor, Indian commis-
      sioners, officer at Oswego for Indian expenses and to
      Indian interpreter for salary signed. Report of committee
      and eastern boundary commissioners (see *N. Y. col. mss*,
      78:110) read and ordered on file. Cadw. Colden, Joseph
      Murray, Wm Smith, Benj. Nicoll and Wm Livingston
      appointed commissioners to settle the boundaries with
      Massachusetts.   176

13   Letters received: from Gov. Belcher (see *N. Y. col. mss*,
      78:108-9); from Gov. Dinwiddie, Virginia and North
      Carolina troops have marched to the Ohio; from Gov.
      Wentworth, commissioners to the Indian meeting at Al-
      bany shall be fully instructed. Reasons of council why
      the station ship, Lieut. Kennedy commanding, should take
      the independent companies to Virginia, Capt. Diggs' or-
      ders notwithstanding.   178

17   Assembly decline to provide gunpowder on account of the
      seizures by the collector. Collector Kennedy releases
      some of the seized powder for transportation to Oswego.
      Warrant to Henry Brasier for going express to Virginia.   180

28   Assembly prorogued. Petition of the trustees of Kings col-
      lege (see *N. Y. col. mss*, 78:120); referred.   181

30   Report of committee on preceding petition approved. War-
      rant to issue to the attorney general to prepare letters
      patent for the college (see *N. Y. col. mss*, 78:121). Dissent
      of James Alexander and Wm Smith to the above report

1754   v. 23

11   Report and instructions continued.   208
25   Minutes of the proceedings at Albany laid before the coun-
Ft George   cil. Petition of Wawayanda and Minisink patentees (see
      N. Y. col. mss, 78:149) referred.   209
p. m.   Assembly prorogued.   210
27   Order on application made by Hendrick, Paulus and Nickus,
      Mohawks, that a patent for land be granted to Coenradt
      Mattys a poor man to whom they have given it.   210
Aug. 9   Plan for the union of the colonies referred. Petition of
      David Schuyler, Nich's Pickard, Peter D. Schuyler,
      Gerardus Stuyvesant, James Livingston, John Willet,
      Leonard Lispenard, Abr'm Lynsen, Gualtherus du Bois,
      Peter P. Schuyler, Nich's Bayard, Christ'r Bancker, Sam-
      uel Heath, John van Cortlandt, Phil. van Cortlandt, Wm
      Kelly, David van der Hyden, Robert Benson, John de
      Peyster jr, John Myer and Augustine Moore (see *L. P.*
      15:115) referred.   211
p. m.   Report of the Massachusetts boundary commissioners that
      no settlement has been made, referred. Representation
      of Cadw. and Alex'r Colden (see *N. Y. col. mss,* 79:1) re-
      ferred.   211
20   Order on information sent by the Indian commissioners that
      the six nations intend to go to Canada upon invitation of
      the governor.   212
28   Letters received: from Lieut. Holland, French Indians on
      the way to the Ohio; from Gov. Dinwiddie, Major Wash-
      ington defeated; to be laid before assembly.   213
31   Indian commissioners report with affidavit of Peter Hogg
      (see *N. Y. col. mss,* 79:17), that Hosick is burning (see
      N. Y. col. mss, 79:18).   213
Sep. 1   Orders on preceding report.   214
3   Letters received: from Indian commissioners (see *N. Y. col.
      mss,* 79:19); from Lieut. Holland (see *N. Y. col. mss,* 79:8).
      Fort to be built near Saratoga. Patents granted to James
      Stewart, Hamilton Stewart, John Vroman, John Wolf Bar-
      let, James Rogers, James Glen, John Thompson, Francis
      Burk, Dennis Maddin, James Dobbins, Wm Powell and
      Hendrick Philipps (see *L. P.* 15:119); to Hendrick ten
      Eyck (see *L. P.* 15:118). Order on petition of Samuel
      Rodman and John Wooley (see *L. P.* 15:116).   215
7   Letter received from Gov. Belcher with representation of
      council of proprietors (see *N. Y. col. mss,* 79:15-16); re-
      ferred.   218
16   Letters received: from Indian commissioners (see *N. Y. col.
      mss,* 79:23, 25, 30); from corporation of Albany, repairs of

fortifications; from Gov. Belcher (see *N. Y. col. mss*, 79:35);
from Messrs Schuyler and Cuyler (see *N. Y. col. mss*,
79:32). Patent granted to James Stewart et al (p. 215). 218

20 Letter received from Gov. Dinwiddie (see *N. Y. col. mss*,
79:29). Warrant signed to Lt. Gov. de Lancey for money
advanced to provision troops sent to Virginia. Message
from Gov. Dinwiddie to the six nations forwarded.
Orders: on petition of the magistrates of Schenectady for
cannons, etc; on the affidavit of Myndert Wemple (see
N. Y. col. mss, 79:36). Warrant to Henry Brasier for going express to Virginia signed. Letter received from
Indian commissioners (see *N. Y. col. mss*, 79:34). 220

29 Hans Hansen appointed mayor, Abr'm Yates jr sheriff of
Albany. 221

30 Mayor, sheriff and coroner of New York reappointed. Order
on a petition of Wm Bauch, Jacob Fred'k Lawyer and
Nich's York (see *L. P.* 15:121). Letter received from the
commissioners of Indian affairs (see *N. Y. col. mss*, 79:43).
Letter to be written to the governor of Canada complaining of hostilities by the French Indians. Patent granted
to David Schuyler et al (p. 211). 222

Oct. 31 Patent to the governors of the college of the province of
New York (Kings) approved, Mr Smith dissents. Warrant to John van Rensselaer for firewood and candles to
garrisons at Albany, Schenectady and Ft Hunter signed. 224

p. m. Letters received: from Indian commissioners (see *N. Y. col.
mss*, 79:25, 44-52, 59), from Gov. du Quesne of Canada
(see *N. Y. col. mss*, 79:38); from missionaries at the falls
of St Louis (see *N. Y. col. mss*, 79:37, 38). Petitions received from inhabitants of Schenectady (see *N. Y. col. mss*,
79:68) and from Canajoharie sachems (see *N. Y. col. mss*,
79:58). 225

Nov. 1 Hearing of Stephen Thorne and Abr'm Guyon against the
petition of Samuel Rodman and John Woolley (p. 215)
continued. 226

7 Warrants to Johan Joost Petrie for supplying the troops at
Oswego. 227

9 Bartholomew Crannel appointed coroner of New York vice
John Burnet absent. 228

14 Message from assembly (see *N. Y. col. mss*, 79:74) referred.
Letters received: from Sir Thos. Robinson secretary of
state, French on the Ohio must be expelled; from the same
to Gov. Shirley, plan for driving the French from the
Kennebeck approved; from lords of trade, general union
of the colonies, New Jersey boundaries; all referred to

1754   **v. 23**

assembly. Memorial of Capt. John Morke (see *N. Y. col.
mss,* 79:78, 79) referred to a joint committee of the council
and assembly. Charter for Kings college to be printed.   228

20   Letter received from the officers at Albany, their troops
need bedding; referred to assembly. Hearing in re Rodman and Woolley continued (p. 226); patent granted to
them for ferry between New Rochelle and Sands point,
L. I. Petition of Rudolph Staley, Johan Joost Herchheimer jr, Thos. Schoonmaker, Peter Bellingher jr, Fred'k
Arendorph, Hans Michael Itigh jr, Hendrick Spone, Aug.
Hess, Nich's Woolever, Christ'r Fox, Rud. Schoonmaker,
Sam'l Broughman, Jacob Itigh, Jacob and George Kesslaer, Nich's Herchheimer, Hans Dederic Staley (see *L. P.*
15:122) referred.   231

26   Letter received from Gov. Belcher with opinion of council
of New Jersey (see *N. Y. col. mss,* 79:83, 84) referred.
Order on a petition of James Flood to be appointed branch
pilot.   233

30   Petition of Col. Thos. de Kay (see *N. Y. col. mss,* 79:93) referred to assembly; James Alexander dissents. Order relating to the accounts of the Indian commissioners (see
N. Y. col. mss, 79:92). Order on complaint of the magistrates of Albany against Capt. Staats Morris for interfering
in civil jurisdiction.   234

Dec. 7   Council advises the governor to pass all the acts of assembly
except a bill for raising money by lottery for the church
at Oysterbay. Assembly to adjourn.   235

10   Patent granted to George Klock, Wm Nellis, Lendert Helmer, Johannis Klock, Hendrick Klock, Juria Wendecker,
Henry Klock jr, Fred'k Bellinger, Johannis Hess, Sig-
frenus Tygert, Coenradt Klock, Christ'n Nellis, Henry
Walrat and Godfred Helmer (see *L. P.* 15:127).   235

17   Letter received from Sir Thomas Robinson, secretary of
state: Sir Peter Halket's and Col. Dunbar's regiments to
go to Virginia; Gov. Shirley and Sir Wm Pepperel to
raise two regiments of 1000 men each. Council are of
opinion that as the forces are not in the province nothing
can be done. The ship Neptune arrived with palatines
from Rotterdam to be removed from Rotten Row to
Turtle bay for quarantine. French subjects to leave the
city. Report on the disturbances along the New Jersey
line (see *N. Y. col. mss,* 79:102).   237

18   Above report to be printed. Quarantine orders.   256

24   Cannons to be lent to Gov. Shirley on his demand (see
N. Y. col. mss, 79:101). John O'Bryant vs Wm Bryant in
error.   258

1754   **v. 23**

28   Letter received from Gov. Morris recommending two Indian
      chiefs with messages to the six nations; they explain their
      errand to the council and it is approved.   259

1755

Jan. 10   Indian affairs (see *N. Y. col. mss*, 79:105, 106). Assembly
          to be called to make provisions for driving the French
          from the Ohio; proclamation to that effect signed (see
          N. Y. col. mss, 80:1). Warrant to Peter Wraxall for cler-
          ical work.   260

31   Letters received: from Lieut. Holland at Oswego, French
      intrigues; from the Indian commissioners, Indian corn to
      be sent to Oswego for use of the six nations; from cor-
      poration of Albany, defenceless state of the city (see *N. Y.
      col. mss*, 80:5), referred to assembly; from Corn's Cuy-
      ler (see *N. Y. col. mss*, 80:3); from the governor of Can-
      ada, hostilities by French Indians prohibited; to be sent
      to Gov. Shirley. Mr Rutherford sworn of the council,
      takes his seat.   262

Feb. 5   Negroes insolent, proclamation to issue for enforcing the
          laws against them (see *N. Y. col. mss*, 80:13). Militia to
          do guard duty in the city. Patents granted to Rud. Staley
          et al (p. 231); to Jacob Timberman and Johan Joost Snell
          (see *L. P.* 15:135); to Johs. Samuel Pruyn and Dirck Bratt
          van Schoonhoven (see *L. P.* 15:134).   263

6   Application to be made to New Jersey for erection of a
      beacon near Sandy Hook.   266

19   The sheriff of Albany taken prisoner by people from Massa-
      chusetts and imprisoned at Springfield; letter to be written
      to Gov. Shirley about it. Council advise the governor to
      pass acts of assembly and adjourn the house.   266

21   Commissioners to purchase materials for fortifications are
      given instructions, Copsy battery to be repaired. Warrant
      to Indian commissioners for expenses in 1746 signed.   267

28   Minutes of a conference between Col. Johnson and the Mo-
      hawks on the 7th of February. Depositions of John and
      Henry van Rensselaer (see *N. Y. col. mss*, 80:31, 32) to be
      sent to Gov. Shirley with the affidavit of Abr'm Yates
      sheriff of Albany (see *N. Y. col. mss*, 80:24). Letter re-
      ceived from Gov. Shirley (see *N. Y. col. mss*, 80:18, 26).
      Regulations for the export of provisions (see *N. Y. col.
      mss*, 80:36, 38). A Frenchman, fled on account of a duel
      from Canada to Albany, ordered to New York. Patents
      granted: to Johs. Becker, Johs. Eckerson and Thos. Eck-
      erson (see *L. P.* 15:136); to Wm Bauch and Jacob Fred'k
      Lawyer (see *L. P.* 15:121). Order on a memorial of
      Josiah Martin (see *N. Y. col. mss*, 80:37).   267

1755   v. 23

Mar. 3 Order of council that entries of government affairs shall be
          kept separate from those concerning private persons.   272

      27 John O'Bryant vs. Wm Bryant.   272

Ap. 25 Petition of Jacob Foltz, Johan Joost Petrie, Johannes
          Petrie, George Klock, Johannes Schauman, Johannes
          Klock, Marcus Petrie, Hendrick Klock jr, George Wen-
          desker, Coenradt Klock, Casper Hannes, Jost and Adam
          Leyb, Hendrick, Devalt Hannes and Adam Merckell, Adam
          Gunterman, Dederick Horning, Adam Grey, Elias, Chris-
          tian and Lips Garlock, Daniel, Dederick and Christian
          Petrie, Ackus van Slyck, Michael Itigh, Henry Merckell
          jr, Hendrick and Peter Hauck, Adam Walrad, Jacob and
          Abr'm van de Wercken, Felix Meyer, Lodwick Kram,
          Wm Nellis, George Klock jr, Hendrick Windecker, John
          Jacob Ael, Hendrick Nellis, Adam Walrad jr, Fred'k
          Bellinger, Philipp Sternberger, Conradt Kels, Lips Bellin-
          ger, Abr'm Lansingh, Jacob Klock jr, Henry Walrad and
          Joost Petrie jr (see *L. P.* 15:138) referred.   272

      26 License to purchase Indian lands granted to the preceding.
          Patent granted to Richard Shuckburgh and Jacob van
          Dyck (see *L. P.* 15:124).   273

May 13 Patent granted to John Chris'r Hartwick, Theod. Frieling-
          hausen, Marcus Kuhl, Hendrick Keppele, George Kitner,
          Fred. Meyer, Thos. Tuermer, Carl Ewald, Hendrick
          Schleydorn, John Maurice, Goet Shius and David Seckel
          (see *L. P.* 15:137).   275

      19 Order on petition of the governors of Kings college for an
          additional charter enabling them to appoint a Dutch pro-
          fessor in divinity.   276

      30 Draft of the above additional charter read and approved.   277

June 5 The same is to be printed.   277

      30 Certificate granted upon a petition of Christ'r Bancker, John
          Morin Scott, John McEvers, John Alsop, Leonard Lispen-
          ard and Oliver de Lancey (see *N. Y. col. mss*, 80:43), Mr
          Jas. Alexander dissenting.   277

July 22 Patent granted to Gotfried Miller, Adam Scheffer, Adam
          Tippel, Luke van Ranst, Conradt Silbernagel, Johannes
          Silbernagel, Wm Williams, Wm Traffort, Neal McCarty,
          John Cock, Charles and Samuel Beeckman, George Peter-
          son, Erich Christian Hoyer and George Cantz (see *L. P.*
          15:140).   279

Dec.   1 Sir Charles Hardy, knight, governor. Order of the lords
          justices repealing the New York act for submitting the New
          Jersey line controversy to the king.   280

       6 Royal order approving the act enabling the Dutch church in
          New York to sell Fordham manor.   281

1755   v. 23

20   11th, 15th, 37th, 38th, 54th and 93d instructions to Sir Chas.
     Hardy. Petition of Gilbert Burnet eldest son of Gov. Wm
     Burnet (see *L. P.* 15:142) referred. Petition of Wm Brown
     for money due to the estate of Gov. Burnet referred.   283

30   Above petition of Gilbert Burnet granted. Petition of Wm
     Brown to be laid before assembly.   289

1757

Nov. 15 Lt. Gov. James de Lancey presides. Royal order approving
         the act disposing of part of Phil. van Cortlandt's estate.   290

1759

Feb. 8   Petition of John Albert Weygand minister, Charles Beek-
         man, John David Wolf, George Peterson and Jacobus van
         Boskerk, elders, and Charles Beeckman jr and Balthasar
         Dasch, deacons of the Lutheran church in New York for
         a charter referred.   291

15   Petitions referred: of Josiah Haywood, Wm Benson, Eben'r
     Moulton, Timothy Allen, James Lawrence, Freeborn Moul-
     ton, John and Samuel Moulton, Daniel Earle and Matthew
     du Bois (see *L. P.* 15:145, 146); of Samuel Robins, Asa
     Douglas, Jonas Marsh, Joseph Hanchet, Wm Warner,
     David Wright, Zebulon Robins, Solomon Bebee, David
     Russell, John Bebee, Ozias Curtis, Gamaliel Whiting, Eli-
     jah Russell, Elisha Hurlbutt, John Konickabaker, Abr'm
     Hallenbeck, Daniel Terris, James Bebee, Joseph Kellegg,
     Sam'l Wright, Benj. Willard, John Ensign, Solomon
     Demmon, Solomon Wright, Jon'n Chipman, Samuel Kelp,
     James Nicholls, Daniel Horsford jr, Wm Holmes, Andrew
     Stevens, David Wright jr, Chas. Belding, Elizur Wright,
     Nathan'l Dean, Asahel Bebee, Augustin Bryan jr, Jacob
     Bunce, Jeremiah Andruss, Jon'n Russel, Samuel Russel,
     John Dean, Stephen Russel, Gideon Ball and Timothy
     Hurlbutt (see *L. P.* 15:147).   292

Mar. 14 Charter granted to the Lutheran church of New York, pat-
         ent to be prepared.   293

30   Petition of the minister, elders and deacons of the Presby-
     terian church for a charter referred.   293

June 21 Patents granted: to Abr'm, Anne, Jacobus, Johannis, John
         Joseph, Sarah Montanie, Abr'm, Everardus jr, Jacob
         Jacob jr, John Brouwer, Anne and Benj. Payne, John and
         Mary Tompkins, Catherine and Stephen Callow, Elizabeth
         and George Giffing, Joseph and Sarah Devoe, John and
         Sarah Oliver (see *L. P.* 15:148); to John Tabor Kempe and
         Goldsbrow Banyar (see *L. P.* 15:147); petitions referred:
         Vincent and David Matthews (see *L. P.* 15:149); of Maurice
         Robinson, Christ'r Blundell, Garret Abeel and Henry
         White for land in Evans' patent; of Nicholas Colton and

Edw'd Wilkins for land in same and caveats entered by John Tabor Kempe (see *L. P.* 15:148) and Vincent Matthews (see *L. P.* 15:148).   294

1760

Jan. 3   Petition of John R. Bleecker, Isaac Sawyer, Edmond Wells, Abr'm J. Lansing et al (see *L. P.* 15:152) referred.   296

Feb. 1   Patent granted to James Bradshaw, Daniel and Nath'l Taylor, John Warner, Abel and Kent Wright, Benj. and Eben'r Silye, Preserved Porter, Partridge Thacher, Thos. Noble, Dan'l Bostwick, Samuel Carfield, John Prindle, Isaac and Jon'n Hitchcock, Benj. Wildman, Amos Northrup, Henry Burhorns, Peter Nicholls, Gaylord Hubbel, Israel Camp, Samuel Bronnson, John Hitchcock, Gideon Noble and Comfort Starr (see *L. P.* 15:153).   297

      9   Day fixed for a hearing between Nich's Colton and Edw. Wilkins of the one part and David and Vincent Matthews of the other.   299

     19   Order on petitions of Trueman Hinman et al (see *L. P.* 16:32); of Daniel Prindle et al (see *L. P.* 15:154); of Jehiel Hawley et al (see *L. P.* 16:156); of Ebenezer Lacey for land adjoining Daniel Prindle at South bay or Wood creek; of Benj. Hoyt et al (see *L. P.* 16:158). Patent granted to Daniel Prindle.   299

Mar. 20   Patent granted to Enos Ayres (see *L. P.* 16:162).   302

Ap.   5   License to purchase Indian land granted to Isaac Sawyer, John R. Bleecker, Edmund Wells and Abr'm Jacob Lansing (see *L. P.* 16:160); to John and Wm Winne, Johs. de Wandelaer, Hendrick Meyer, Hendrick van Beuren, Maes van Beuren jr, Harme Groesbeck and Harme Knickerbacker (see *L. P.* 16:172). Hearing in re Colton and Matthews (p. 299); continued.   304

May   5   Hearing in re Colton and Matthews (p. 304); continued.   307

      7   Same continued.   308

      9   Same; decided. Petition of Sarah widow of Teady Magin, Wm Fox, Peter Curtenius, Harme Gansevort, John Williams, Phil. Livingston, Edw. Smith, John Gansevort, James Moran, Isaac Goelet, Alida Hansen, John Ogilvie and John Keen (see *L. P.* 16:175) referred.   308

Aug. 28   Cadwallader Colden president of the council. Petitions referred: of Wm Smith and Edw'd Wilkins (see *L. P.* 16:183); of Wm Cockcroft, Beamsley Glazier, Barth'w le Roux, Mich'l Thedey, George Brewerton, George Brewerton jr, Rob't McGinnis, Peter Middleton and John Dies (see *L. P.* 16:178); of Arch'd McBride, James Crawford jr, James White and David Crawford (see *L. P.* 16:180); of Thos. Moore and Lewis Pintard (see *L. P.* 16:182).   311

1760   **v. 23**

Oct. 1   Patents granted: to Sarah Magin et al (p. 308); to Vincent
          and David Matthews (p. 294); to Thos. Moore and Lewis
          Pintard (p. 311); to Arch'd McBride et al (p. 311). Peti-
          tion of Wm Cockroft et al (p. 311) tabled.   314

Nov. 5   Patents granted: to Wm Smith and Edw'd Wilkins (p. 311);
          to Isaac Vrooman (see *L. P.* 16:11); to Hendrick ten Eyck
          (see *L. P.* 16:13). License to purchase Indian lands granted
          to George Klock (see *L. P.* 16:7). Petitions referred: of
          Oliver de Lancey, Peter du Bois, Philipp Schuyler, Garret
          Staats et al (see *L. P.* 15:187); of John, Philipp, Jacob and
          Valentine Benninckhoff, Moritz Gabel, George Weider
          Grundel,—Wise, George Heyner, John Lay, John Philipp
          Wiber, Lendert Islyng, Christophel Berrus, Lawrence
          Bamberger, Henry Peter Henry, Phil. Tick, Phil. Tick jr,
          Christian Smith, Benj. Lindner, Phil. Reis and Jacob
          Klock (see *L. P.* 16:16); of Jacob H. ten Eyck, George and
          Markes Rykert, Volgert Dason and John Roorback jr (see
          L. P. 16:4); of Phil. Livingston (see *L. P.* 16:8); of Fred'k
          Young and Corn's ten Broeck (see *L. P.* 16:9).   317

      26 Patent granted to Phil. Philippse, Beverley Robinson and
          Roger Morris for land between the Hudson river and the
          Connecticut line [Putnam county].   322

Dec. 31   Licenses to purchase Indian lands granted: to Oliver de
          Lancey et al (p. 317); to Jacob H. ten Eyck et al (p.
          317); to Phil. Livingston (p. 317); to Fred. Young et al
          (p. 317); patent granted to James Bradshaw et al for islands
          in the Hudson river opposite to their land. Return of sur-
          vey for Phil. Philippse et al (p. 322) approved and grant
          passed (see *L. P.* 16:23, 24). Patent granted to Cadw.
          Colden jr and David Colden (see *L. P.* 16:22).   325

1761

Jan. 14   Petitions referred: of Alex'r Colden, Wm Willet, Stephen de
          Lancey, and Christ'r Blundell (see *L. P.* 16:28); of Henry
          White et al (see *L. P.* 16:10); of Thos. Jones et al (see
          L. P. 16:19); of Jellis Fonda et al (see *L. P.* 16:27); of Wm
          Smith jr, Johs. Hendrickse Vrooman et al (see *L. P.* 16:26);
          of John Joost Petrie et al (see *L. P.* 16:5).   330

      28 Petitions referred: of Abr'm Dowe et al (see *L. P.* 16:30); of
          Wm Walton jr, Jacob Walton, Thos. Walton and Gerard
          Walton (see *L. P.* 16:20); of Arah Ward of Waterbury,
          Ct. et al (see *L. P.* 16:29); of Zachariah Hawkins of
          Derby, Ct. et al (see *L. P.* 16:29).   335

Feb. 4   Licenses to purchase Indian lands granted: to Peter van
          Bough Livingston, Hendrick Walraat, Thos. Smith et al
          (see *L. P.* 16:31); to Henry White et al (p. 330); to Thos.
          Jones et al (p. 330); to Jellis Fonda et al (p. 330); to Wm
          Smith jr et al (p. 330); to John Joost Petrie et al (p. 330);

to Abr'm Dowe et al (p. 335); to Wm Walton jr et al (p. 335); to Arah Ward (p. 335); to Zachariah Hawkins (p. 335).   337

May 19   Royal order approving the act of assembly empowering justices of the peace etc to try causes to the value of £5.   343

27   Patents granted: to Alex. Colden et al (p. 330); to Catherine Colden, Cath. Kennedy, Lawrence Reade, Aug. van Cortlandt, Rob't James Livingston, Wm Walton jr, Mary Magdalen Nicoll, Alex'r Colden, John Taber Kempe, Goldsbrow Banyar, Matthew du Bois, Josiah Martin jr and Wm Benson (see L. P. 16:51); to Major Robert Rogers, Joseph Dequipe, Esa Putnam, John Miller, Roger Prince, Francis Dayne, Jas. Osgood, Sam'l Osgood, Ephraim Dickison, Daniel Chase, James Miller, David Thompson, John Taggart, David Hughes, John Herring, Daniel Miller, Robert Miller, James Moores, Daniel Moores, John Evans, David Evans, John Shute, Benj. Osgood and Jon'n Chase (see L. P. 16:39). Licenses granted to purchase Indian lands: to Thos. Jones, surgeon et al (see L. P. 16:38); to John Jones et al (see L. P. 16:37); to Capt. James Rogers et al (see L. P. 16:34); to Moses Hazzens et al (see L. P. 16:40, 41). Charters granted to the parish church of Jamaica upon petition of Samuel Seabury jr minister, Robert Howell, Benj. Carpenter, John Hutchins, John Smith, Jacob Ogden, Joseph Oldfield, Joseph Oldfield jr, John Troup, John Comes, Gilbert Comes, Thos. Truxton, Thos. Braine, Benj. Whitehead, Samuel Smith, Wm Sherlock, John Innes, Rich'd Betts, Isaac van Hook, Thos. Hinchman and Adam Lawrence (see N. Y. col. mss, 89:128) and to the church at Flushing on petition of John Aspinwal, Thos. Grenel, Joseph Haviland, Daniel Thorn, Wm Thorn, Jacob Thorn, John Dyer, Christ'r Robert, John Morrel, Isaac Doughty, Jacomiah Mitchell, Francis Brown, Charles Cornell, Charles Wright, Joseph Bowne, Foster Lewis, Nath'l Tom, Benj. Thorn, John Marston, John Wilson and Benj. Fowler (see N. Y. col. mss, 89:129). Petition of Wm Hawkhurst (see N. Y. col. mss, 89:130) rejected (see Doc. hist. N. Y. 1:731; Q 1:496).   344

June 10   Petitions referred: of Isaac Sawyer, John R. Bleecker, Abr'm Jacob Lansingh, Edmond, Thomas and Joseph Wells, Samuel Gilbert, Daniel Ingham, Eliphalet House, Thomas Gilbert, Clement Sumner, Stephen Palmer, Edw'd Sawyer, Ebenezer Duevey jr, John and Thos. Sawyer, Azariah and Benj. Beach, Daniel Tillotson, Obadiah Horseford, Alex'r Phelps, Eleazer Pumroy, Jacob Abr'm and Johs. Jacob Lan-

singh, Jordan Post, Francis Lansingh, George Clinton,
Abr'm van den Bergh, Joel Jones, John Russ, Samuel Filer,
Joshua Phelps, Nath'l Phelps, Increase Porter, Elisha
Pratt, John and Gad Merrell, Jon'n Hutchinson, Jedediah,
John and Jazaniah Post, John Gilliot, Benj. Pumroy, Elijah
Lothrop, Ichabod Phelps, Benj. Trumble, Wm Sumner,
Samuel Gilbert jr, Derick and Jacob van der Heyden,
Levinus Winne, David Barber, Ephraim Wright, Stephen
Barber, Israel Post, Ezekiel Jones, Samuel Jones, Silas
Pipon, John Peters, Wm Winterton and Peter Marselius
(see *L. P.* 16:54, 65); of Capt. Walter Rutherford, Capt.
Quintin Kennedy, Lieut. John Duncan, Lieut. George
Coventry and 21 other officers and soldiers [not named]
(see *L. P.* 16:33); of Ryer Schermerhorn, Jacob Schermer-
horn, John Quackenbush et al (see *L. P.* 16:46). Order on
a petition of Vincent and David Matthews (see *L. P.* 16:56). 351

17 Patents granted: to John McNeile, Alex'r McKey, Alex'r
Stewart and Oliver Templeton (see *L. P.* 16:59); to Johs.
Lawyer jr, Jacob Borst, George Forster, Hendrick Heints,
Wm Bornheyer, Sam'l Denton and John Wessells (see
L. P. 16:58). Petition of Arent van Corlear, Nich's Lake
jr, Thos. Lake, James Lake and John Lake, all of New
Jersey (see *L. P.* 16:57) referred. Warrant of survey
granted to Johs. van der Pool and Robert van Duersen
(see *L. P.* 16:61). Charters for the churches at Jamaica
and Flushing approved.   355

22 Patents granted: to Isaac Sawyer et al (p. 351); to Arent
van Corlear et al (p. 355). License to purchase Indian
lands granted to Capt. Walter Rutherford et al (p. 351).
Warrant of survey to Ryer Schermerhorn et al (p. 351).
Clause to be inserted in all patents, Mr Watts dissenting. 363

24 Date fixed for hearing the land case between Matthews and
Smith; Charles Clinton to attend.   367

July 1 Matthews and Smith [incomplete].   367

8 Petitions referred: of Hendrick Schneyder, John Wetteck,
Hendrick Lake, John Johnson, Garret Williamson, Nath'l
Acherley, Benj. Abbot, Wm Taylor and Martinus Voor-
hies (see *L. P.* 16:69); of Sir Wm Johnson, Ferral Wade,
George F. Cheap, James Rogers, Dennis Maddin, John
Johnston, Wm Johnson, Peter Frax, Michael Russell, Wil-
helmus Russell, Paul Reiter, Peter H. Klyne, John Span-
genburgh, Lucas Veder, Lawrence Enan, Michael Sallen-
ger, Mathias Link, Hanthy Creitz, George Stam, George
Stam jr, John Johnson, Peter Servis, Christopher Servis,
Francis Rupert, Adam Rupert, Hannis Wert, Andreas Sny-

der, Conradt Creitzenbergher, Conradt Smith, Jon'n
French, Jacob Pickle, Hannis Wolfe Barlet, Aug. Eickler,
Jacob Sefer, Joh's Alt, Bastian Steenmyer, Stephen Kip,
George Kip and Peter Frederick (see *L. P.* 16:45); of Jacob
Hendrick ten Eyck, George Rykert, Volgert Dason and
John Roorback jr (see *L. P.* 16:71).   368

15 Petitions referred: of Abr'm Lott jr, Isaac Low, James
Duane, Samuel Staats Cojemans, Jacob Noorstradt, George
Hagewout, Adam Heyler, Thos. Strembeck, John Kleen,
Conradt Rossman, Isaac Post, Waldron Blauw, Nich's
Lake, Joseph Giffers, Derick and Hendrick Hogeland,
Daniel Huntington, John Baur, Henry Buel and Benj.
Southard (see *L. P.* 16:68); of Wm van Bergen, Martin
Garretse van Bergen and Jas. Humphrey jr (see *L. P.*
16:67).   370

Aug. 5 Patents granted: to Hendrick Schneyder et al (p. 368); to
J. H. ten Eyck et al (p. 368); to Abr'm Lott jr et al (p.
370); to Wm van Bergen et al (p. 370). Hearing on the
caveat of John van Rensselaer (see *L. P.* 16:77) against
a grant to Catherine Colden et al postponed.   373

19 Cadw. Colden, lieutenant governor. Petitions referred: of
Coenradt and Frederick Franck, George Herchheimer,
Michael Itigh and Peter Piper (see *L. P.* 16:53); of Wm
Cunningham (see *L. P.* 16:63, 64); of Phil. Livingston, Rud.
Keller, John Burk, Edw'd Earl, Samuel Bailey, Wm Den-
ning, Wm Livingston, Jeremiah van Rensselaer, Peter du
Bois, John Hansen, John James Beeckman, Peter Hansen,
Roger Townshend, Wm McCrackan, John Cuyler, Myn-
dert Burger, Michael Hugo Frazier, Wm Bailey, Gerardus
Lansingh and Phil. Lansingh (see *L. P.* 16:78); of Fred'k
Young, Corn's ten Broock, Adam Young, Hendrick
Mathias, Johannes Kesslaer, Andries Young, Nicholas
Oxiner, Francis Johnson, Christian Frolic, Robert Leon-
ard, Elias Bailey, Theobald Young, John Carman, John
Jas. Glen, John I. Cuyler, Garret Ab. Lansingh, Henry C.
Cuyler, Abr'm Yates jr, Simon Groot and Jonas Southerd
(see *L. P.* 16:95); of Wm Smith jr, Johs. Hend. Vroo-
man, John Read, John Glen, Abr'm Douw, Guysbert
Fonda, Peter Douw, Volkert Abr'm Douw, Johs. Hend.
ten Eyck, Barent C. ten Eyck, John C. ten Eyck, Francis
Welsh, Abr'm ten Broeck, Hendrick Young, Gisbert Marselis, Thos. Gordon, Wm Weyman, Rich'd Smith, Leonard
de Kleyn, and Sam'l Boyer (see *L. P.* 16:76).   376

Sep. 3 Order on petition of John van Rensselaer (see *L. P.* 16:77,
86). Charter of incorporation granted to the church at

Newtown, L. I. upon petition of James Hazard, Rich'd
Alsop, Wm Sacket, Sam'l Moore, Jacob Blackwell et al
(see *N. Y. col. mss*, 90:17). Patents granted: to Coenradt
Frank et al (p. 376); to Wm Cunningham (p. 376); to Phil.
Livingston et al (p. 376); to Fred'k Young et al (p. 376);
to Wm Smith jr et al (p. 376).   379

9   Petitions referred: of Dirck Schuyler, Samuel Pell, Jacob
Arding, Henry van Vleck, Jacob Kemper, Matthew Kem-
per, John Morton, Christ'r Miller, Ephraim Dickison,
Joseph Jukes, Abner Fowler, Nath'l Morton, Abr'm A.
Schuyler, Peter van Voorhuise, Jan van Voorhuise, Dirck
Schuyler jr, Abr'm D. Schuyler, Abr'm Wilson, Isaac Law-
rence, Anth'y van Dam, Thos. Kip, Abr'm Kip, Minnie
van Voorhuise, Jon'n Lawrence and Jarvis Roebuck (see
L. P. 16:81); of Michael Nestel (see *L. P.* 16:89). Minutes
sent home.   385

Cct 16   Order on petition of Arch'd Kennedy for directions to the
surveyor general to select a place for a wharf near Fort
George with right of ferriage to the Jersey shore. Warrant
of survey granted to John Borghart of Kinderhook (see
L. P. 16:100).   387

Dec. 2   Order on petition of John van Rensselaer (see *L. P.* 16:105). 388

4   Hearing on preceding petition postponed.   388

1762

Feb. 10   The 11th, 15th, 32d, 33d, 51st, 54th, 93d and extract from the
46th article of instructions to Gov. Robert Monckton.   388

17   Additional instructions restraining the grants of land; proclamation to issue accordingly (see *N. Y. col. mss*, 90:77).   394

Mar. 1   Petitions referred: of Ryer, Jacob, Freeman and Wm Scher-
merhorn, Johs. Nich's, Peter Quackenbosh, Thos. and John
Smith and Joseph Lynsen (see *L. P.* 16:112); of James
Bradshaw, Nath'l Taylor, Dan'l Taylor, John Warner,
Abel Wright, Benj. and Eben'r Silye, et al as above, p. 297
(see *L. P.* 16:113); of Daniel Prindle, Elihu Marsh, Thos.
Hungerford, Samuel Hungerford, John Buck, Daniel
Tryon, Amos Leach, Benj. Sea!ey, Anth'y Wanser, Jon'n
Weeks, John Page, Elihu Marsh jr, Abr'm Wanzer, Benj.
Elliot, John Seeley, Aaron Prindle, Thos. Northorp, Eze-
kiel Pain, Jedediah Graves, David Commins, Eben'r Pres-
ton, David Preston and Joshua Agard (see *L. P.* 16:114);
of Jacob Starnberger, George and Jacob Zimmer, Hendrick Weaver, John Joost Becker and John Schever (see
L. P. 16:98); of Wm van Bergen, Martin Gerritse van Bergen and James Umphrey jr (see *L. P.* 16:106).   396

1762   **v. 23**

Ap. 15 Opinion of council on the additional instruction relating to
        grants of land. Patents granted: to Ryer Schermerhorn
        et al (p. 396); to James Bradshaw et al (p. 396); to Dan'l
        Prindle et al (p. 396); to Jacob Starnberger et al (p. 396).   399

May 12 Charters granted: to the French church at New Rochelle
        upon petition of Rev. Michael Houdin, Jacobus Bleecker,
        James de Blez and David Lispenard, wardens (see *N. Y.
        col. mss*, 90:71); to church at Westchester village upon peti-
        tion of John Milner, John Bartow, Isaac Willet, Lewis
        Morris jr, Peter de Lancey, Nath'l Underhill, James Gra-
        ham and James van Cortlandt (see *N. Y. col. mss*, 90:105).   403

     13 Hearing on the caveat of John van Rensselaer against grants
        to Solomon Bebee and associates (p. 373, 379, 387, 388).   405

June 11 Royal order disapproving the act of assembly for the better
        government and regulation of seamen in the merchant ser-
        vice.   406

     25 Gov. Robert Monckton presides. Order on petition of Benj.
        Palmer, Joseph Palmer and Samuel le Rue (see *L. P.*
        16:115).   407

July 21 Hearing on the caveat of John van Rensselaer (p. 405) post-
        poned.   408

     28 Patent granted to Wm Ernst Spornheyer and Wm Heints
        (see *L. P.* 16:117).   408

Aug. 3 Hearing on the caveat of John van Rensselaer (p. 408); con-
        tinued.   410

     25 Patent granted to Benj. and Joseph Palmer and Samuel le
        Rue (see *L. P.* 16:120). Petition of Thos. Moore and Lewis
        Pintard (see *L. P.* 16:118) referred.   411

Sep. 29 Petition of Jacob Starnberger, George, Jacob, Petrus and
        Wm Zimmer, Hendrick Weaver, John, Joost Becker and
        John Schever (see *L. P.* 16:121) referred. Patent granted
        to Thos. Moore and Lewis Pintard (p. 411).   412

Oct. 7 Hearing on the caveat of John van Rensselaer (p. 410); con-
        tinued.   414

     20 Decision in preceding case.   415

Nov. 23 Petitions referred: of Samuel Deal sr, Samuel Deal jr, Wm
        Deal, John Dies, John Schureman, Matthew Dies, Evert
        Byvanck jr, Abr'm van Ranst, Jacob Boelen, Peter Praa,
        Provoost and David Provoost (see *L. P.* 16:129); of Hen-
        dricus and Solomon du Bois (see *L. P.* 16:125); of Matthew
        du Bois (see *L. P.* 16:131) referred.   415

Dec. 2 Charter for the church at Westchester village passed. Peti-
        tion of Frederick, Hendricus, John, Petrus and William
        Dederick (see *L. P.* 16:134) referred.   417

1762   **v. 23**

16   Copy of the petition of Sam'l Deal et al (p. 415) to be sent to
the lords of trade. Petitions of Fred. Dederick et al and
of Hendr. du Bois (p. 415) rejected. Petition of Abr'm
Haasbrouck and Isaac Haasbrouck jr (see *L. P.* 16:135)
tabled. Order on petition of Matthew du Bois (p. 415).
Petition of Wm Moore (see *L. P.* 16:133) rejected. Order
on petition of David Hunt (see *L. P.* 16:136).   417

22   Petition of Isaac de Forest, Wm Hunn, Johs. Hesse, Thos.
Conklin, and Jeremiah Wooll (see *L. R.* 16:137) tabled.   419

1763

Jan.   5   Petitions referred: of John Mason, Rich'd Cullin, Joseph
Wheten et al (see *L. P.* 16:126); of Garret Erickson, Her-
man Peters, Harman Vedder et al (see *L. P.* 16:127); of
Alex'r and James Turner, Thos. Johnston, Matthew Bol-
ton, John McCreles, John Crawford, John Lucore, Rob't
Hamilton, Chas. Kidd, Hugh Bolton, James Lukes, George
Thompson, Jon'n Marsh, Wm Crosset, Alex'r Turner jr,
Joseph Rugg, Thos. White, Benj. Southwick, Daniel Bal-
lard, Samuel Southwick, Daniel McCollem, Joshua Con-
key, Wm Edgar, Wm Conkey and Adams Clark Gray
(see *L. P.* 16:128); of Thos. Dick, David Southwick, Amos
Foster et al (see *L. P.* 16:130); of John Tabor Kempe, John
Morin Scott, John Bard et al (see *L. P.* 16:138); of Donald,
George and James Campbell et al (see *L. P.* 16:141).   420

6   Petition of Thos. Willet, Paul Miller et al (see *L. P.* 16:140)
referred.   423

12   Patent granted to David Hunt (p. 417).   424

26   Patent granted to John Anderson (see *L. P.* 16:87, 122). Pe-
titions referred: of Joseph Waiton, John Wilson, David
Standish, Thos. Davies, John Williamson, Walter Mitchel-
son, Thos. Dean Pearce, Wm Bruce, Wm Forman, David
Davies, Wm Grant, Henry Brown, Thos. Sibson, Joseph
Brome, Wm Godwin, John Kennedy, Thos. Sidwell, John
Godwin, Wm Wilson, Wm Ford, Arch'd Bruce, Samuel
Orem, Francis Lawson and Walter Marshall (see *L. P.*
16:146); of Robert Harper (see *L. P.* 16:145).   424

Feb.   9   Petition of Rev. Samuel Verbryck, John Corn's Haring, Roelof van Houten, Johs. Joseph Blauvelt, Johannes Haring,
elders, Corn's Blauvelt, Johs. Bell, Fredericus Haring and
Johs. Nagil, deacons (see *N. Y. col. mss*, 91:138) referred.
Counter petition of John Peterse Smith and Corn's Smith
(see *N. Y. col. mss*, 91:139); Petitions referred: of John
and Philipp Embury et al (see *L. P.* 16:148); of Wm. Cockcroft, Beamsly Glazier, Barth'w le Roux, Michael Thodey,
George Brewerton sr and jr, Robert McGinnis, Peter Middleton and John Dies (see *L. P.* 16:147).   426

1763   **v. 23**

16   Report on petitions for land of 5th, 6th, 29th of January and
      9th of February, pending in the council; all rejected (see
      L. P. 16:152). Memorial of Trueman Hinman, Eben'r
      Lacey and Jehiel Hawley with their respective partners (see
      L. P. 16:150) referred.   428

Mar. 2 Petition of Alex'r McNachten and other emigrants from
      Scotland (see *L. P.* 16:154) referred.   430

16   Memorial of Obadiah and Henry Wells, Daniel Goldsmith,
      Benj. Stout et al (see *L. P.* 16:161). Petition of Rev.
      Jean Carle, Peter Vallade, James des Brosses, elders,
      Daniel Bonnet and Charles Jandine, deacons of the French
      church at New York (see *N. Y. col. mss*, 91:146) referred.   431

Ap. 20 Royal order repealing the act of assembly for the payment of
      salaries, etc. Petition of Abr'm Thomas et al (see *L. P.*
      16:164) referred.   433

May 18 Clause to be added to the patent for Benj. Palmer et al (p.
      411). Report on petition of Alex. Turner et al (p. 420);
      granted. Petitions of John Wason, of Garret Erickson and
      of Thos. Dick with respective partners (p. 420) rejected.
      Reports on the petitions of Donald Campbell et al (p.
      420); of Isaac de Forest et al (p. 419) granted.   434

21   Reports on petitions granted: of Alex'r McNachten et al (p.
      430) (see *L. P.* 16:167) with schedule of names of grantees;
      of Joseph Walton et al (p. 424; see *L. P.* 17:2); of
      John, Phil., David and Peter Embury, James, George and
      Samuel Willson, Henry Power, Paul Heck, Phil. and John
      Cook, Jacob Dulmidge sr and jr, Edw'd Carscallen, Nich-
      olas and Peter Shoulds, Julius and Henry Shire, Peter Law-
      rence, Valentine Debtler, Wm Folk, Peter Poff, Valentine
      Shimmel, Peter Sparling and Elias Hoffman (p. 426); of
      Robert Harper (p. 425). Petitions of John Tabor Kempe
      et al (p. 420) and of Thos. Willet et al (p. 424) dismissed.
      Petition of John T., Elizabeth and Philadelphia Kempe,
      John Morin Scott, Whitehead Hicks, John Woods, Samuel
      Jones, Adrian Rutgers, Adrian Renaudet, James Emott,
      Rich'd Sharp, Benj. Kissam, John Bard, Wm Webb, Abr'm
      Cock, Bernard Lintott and Thos. Frost (see *L. P.* 17:3)
      referred.   438

June 8 Warrants of survey signed: for Alex'r Turner, for Donald
      Campbell, for Isaac de Forest, for Joseph Walton, for John
      Embury. Report on petitions of Wm Cockroft et al (p.
      426) and of John Tabor Kempe et al (p. 438) granted.
      Petition of Moses, Reuben and Jeremiah Clark, Benj.
      Tusteen, Henry Wisner sr and jr, Wm Smith, Nath'l and

1763   **v. 23**

Samuel Sacket, Daniel Sherwood, Wm Peet, John and
Samuel Arthur and Nath'l Hazard (see *L. P.* 17:5) referred. 445

Sep. 14   Lt. Gov. Cadw. Colden presides. Action on a memorial of
Duncan Reid, Neal Shaw, Arch'd Campbell, Alex'r
McNachten and Neal Gillespie (see *L. P.* 17:19) deferred. 448

29   Petition of Major Philip Skene (see *L. P.* 17:16, 26) tabled.
Order on petition of James Murray, husband of Lilly, the
daughter of Capt. Lauchlin Campbell, for a share in the
patent granted to Donald Campbell et al. Order on the
above memorial of Duncan Reid et al. Petition of Rev.
John Albert Weygand, Lawrence Eaman, George Peterson
and Charles Beeckman, elders, Henry Ricter, Henry Bear,
John van Orden and John Snous, deacons of the Lutheran
church in New York (see *N. Y. col. mss*, 92:33) to be sent
to the lords of trade.   450

Nov. 12   Petition of Major Phil. Skene (see *L. P.* 17:26) referred. 450

23   Report on preceding petition (see *L. P.* 17:26). Patent
granted to Phil., David and Andrew Skene, John Reid,
John Small, James Napier, Nath'l and John Marston,
Lawrence Reade, Thos. Scott, Robert Mercer, Magill Wal-
lace, Hugh Wallace, Samuel Willis, Wm Bailey, Joshua
Moore, John Hughes, Evert Bancker, Gerard Bancker,
James Deas, Joseph Allicocke, Rich'd Curson, Thos. Miller,
John Lamb and John Brooks. Warrant of survey granted
to Robert Harper of Kings college (see *L. P.* 17:27). 452

25   Patent granted to James de Lancey (see *L. P.* 17:24). 455

1764

Feb. 2   Patents granted: to Lieut. John Stoughton (see *L. P.* 17:31);
to Major Allan Campbell and Lieut John Kennedy (see
L. P. 17:32); to Captains Nicholas Sutherland, Robert Grant
and Alex'r McIntosh (see *L. P.* 17:36, 37, 38); to Lieut.
Donald Campbell (see *L. P.* 17:39); to Lieut. Roger Kellet
see *L. P.* 17:43); to Major John Wilkins, (see *L. P.* 17:53);
to Lieut. Alex'r Colquhoun, (see *L. P.* 17:33); to Capt.
Geo. Clarke (see *L. P.* 17:34); to Lieut. Hugh Wallace
(see *L. P.* 17:40); to Serg. James McBride (see *L. P.* 17:44);
to Capt. David Wooster (see *L. P.* 17:45); to Capt. Valentine Gardiner (see *L. P.* 17:47); to Capt. John Graham (see
L. P. 17:48); to Lieut. Allan Grant (see *L. P.* 17:54); to
Ensign Mervin Perry (see *L. P.* 17:46), to Qr. M'r Wm
Monro (see *L. P.* 17:57); to Captains John Small, Forbes
and Campbell, Lieut. Archibald Campbell, Arch'd Cameron, Charles McKenzie, ———— Gordon, ———— McGregor,
———— McCuloch and Adjutant Wm Gregor (see *L. P.*
17:51); to Lieutenants Alex'r Campbell and Wm Hagart

(see *L. P.* 17:50); to Lieutenants Donald Campbell, John McDonald, Alex'r Grant, James Campbell, James Rumsey, John Martin, Thos. Menzies and Alex'r Menzies (see *L. P.* 17:52); to Lt. Col. Sir John St Clair (see *L. P.* 17:42); to Lieut. James Dow (see *L. P.* 17:59); to Lieut. Henry Farrant (see *L. P.* 17:60); to Lieut. Thos. Polock (?), the last four not located.   456

8   Patents granted: to Chaplain Harry Munro (see *L. P.* 17:61); to Capt. James Robertson (see *L. P.* 17:65); to Sergeants John McKenzie, John Provoost, John McPherson, John Clarke, Joseph Ferguson, James Noble, James Campbell, John Chisholm, Robert Munro, Duncan Stewart, Wm Sutherland, Arch'd McVicar, James Shaw, Corporals Wm Ferguson, John McLean, George Murray, George Clark, John McDonald, Alex'r Wilson, John McIntire, John McIntosh, Duncan King, Joseph Hunt, John McNicol, Donald Fisher, Adam Davidson, John Grant, Robert McAullay, Donald Munro, David McConkey, Donald McDonald and John Reid and Privates Duncan McCarter, Hugh Sutherland, Alex'r Munro, Hugh McIntosh, Duncan Kenady, Alex'r McDermont and Angus McDonald; to Sergeants Moses Campbell, Alex'r McPherson and Alex'r Frazer and Corporal John McPherson (see *L. P.* 17:67); to Sergeants Wm Able, John Pearce and Corporal Wm Blaylock (see *L. P.* 17:70); to Private Cain Callannan (see *L. P.* 17:69).   460

22   Lands granted and to be surveyed: for Capt. John Campbell (see *L. P.* 17:72) for Lieut. Archibald Archibald Campbell (see *L. P.* 17:80); for Capt. Charles Forbes (see *L. P.* 17:73); for Lieut. Ann Gordon (see *L. P.* 17:75); for Lieut. Abr. Cuyler (see *L. P.* 17:79); for Serg. Abr'm Albey (see *L. P.* 17:78); for Lieut. Abr'm Low (see *L. P.* 17:55).   462

Mar. 7   Draft of letters patent to Duncan Read et al (see *L. P.* 17:91) amended.   463

21   Lands granted and to be surveyed: for Lieut. Peter Marquis de Conty (see *L. P.* 17:76); to Sergeants Allan Cameron, Alex'r·Fraser, James Ross and Alex'r Fraser and Privates John Anderson, Daniel McIntosh, Alex'r Frasier, John Fraser, John McIntosh, George Sutherland and Finlay McDonald (see *L. P.* 17:82); to Lieut. Barnaby Byrn (see *L. P.* 17:84); to Lieut. Erick Sutherland (see *L. P.* 17:85); to Capt. Robert Campbell and Lieut. Francis Hutchinson (see *L. P.* 17:88); to Lieut. Turbutt Francis, near Sabbath day point; to Corporals Henry Ertly, James Cherry, Andrew Frederick, of the 60th Reg't, Samuel Wade of the 48th, Privates Thos. Curton of the 48th, Wm

Callow of the 55th, Frederick Weelyart and Clements Pless of the 60th regiment (see *L. P.* 17:92); to Lieut. Phil. du Perron and Surgeon Alex'r Potts (see *L. P.* 17:90); to Lt. Col. Sir John St Clair (p. 456) located (see *L. P.* 17:93); to Lieut. James Dow (see *L. P.* 17:94); to Lieut. Arch'd Blane, (see *L. P.* 17:95); to Lieut. Arch'd Dow (see *L. P.* 17:96); to Lieut. Thos. Etherington, (see *L. P.* 17:97); to Lieut. Wm Leslie (see *L. P.* 17:98); to Lieut. Farquhar (see *L. P.* 17:101); to Capt. James Allaz, Lieutenants Edward Barron and David Borry (see *L. P.* 17:100); to Lieut. Abr'm Low (see *L. P.* 17:83); to 24 non-commissioned officers and 34 privates of the 42d regiment not named (see *L. P.* 17:103).   464

Ap. 4 Mary Lush administratrix of John Lush vs David Provoost.   467

18 Lanus located by the following petitioners to be surveyed: Lieut. David Mooney (see *L. P.* 17:107); Capt. Simon Ecuyer (see *L. P.* 17:106); Capt. Alex'r McDonald (see *L. P.* 17:108); Lieut. James Grant (see *L. P.* 17:110); Capt. Lieut. George Faesch (see *L. P.* 17:111); Surgeon's mate John Field (see *L. P.* 17:112); Lieut. Lancelot Hilton (see *L. P.* 17:114); Lieut. Arch'd Lamont (see *L. P.* 17:113); Lieut. Wm Brown (see *L. P.* 17:115); Lieut. Alex'r Fraser (see *L. P.* 17:116); James Ross, Apothecary's mate (see *L. P.* 17:35); John Connolly surgeon's mate, (see *L. P.* 17:117); Lieutenants Henry Farrant and George Phyn (see *L. P.* 17:120); 14 non-commissioned officers and 39 privates not named.   467

19 Petition of John Duncan, Daniel Campbell, John Visger and other inhabitants of Schenectady (see *N. Y. col. mss*, 92:104, 105) referred.   469

May 2 Lands granted and to be surveyed: for Lt. Col. Augustine Prevoost and his son Lieut. Augustine Prevoost (see *L. P.* 17:104); for Capt. John Dalrymple (see *L. P.* 17:118); for James Judd surgeon's mate (see *L. P.* 17:119); for Lieut. Wm McIntosh (see *L. P.* 17:121); for Surgeon David Hepburn (see *L. P.* 17:129); for Serg. Fred'k Hartell (see *L. P.* 17:122); Surgeon John Hicks (see *L. P.* 17:123); and for 9 non-commissioned officers and 19 privates not named. Order on petition of Valkert P. Douw mayor of Albany against granting the petition from Schenectady (p. 469). Bonds for settlement of lands within three years after date of grant by Michael Thodey, Wm Cockcroft, Isaac Corsa, George Brewerton jr, Peter du Bois and Peter Middleton—

1764   **v. 23**

and by John Tabor Kempe and John Morin Scott received
and filed.   470

June 9   Order on petition of Dr George Munro and Surgeon Wm
Barr (see *L. P.* 17:131). Lands granted and to be surveyed: for Lieut. Stair Campbell Carr (see *L. P.* 17:139);
for Lieutenants Arch'd Campbell sr and jr, Ach'd Cameron, John McIntosh, Charles Grant, Charles Menzies and
Nath'l McCullock (see *L. P.* 17:146); for Lieut. Edw'd
Jenkins (see *L. P.* 17:140); for Robert Bass senior apothecary (see *L. P.* 17:141); for Duncan Forbes surgeon's mate
(see *L. P.* 17:142).   473

July 10   Petitions of Captains John Graham, John Campbell, Lewis
Ourry, James Robertson, Alex'r McDonald, Lieuts. Arch'd
Lamont, Arch'd Cameron, Arch'd Campbell, James Grant,
Alex'r Frazier and soldiers of the 42d regiment (see *L. P.*
17:149); of Lieut. Thos. Etherington and Wm Lessley
(see *L. P.* 17:152), Lieutenants Wm Gaul (see *L. P.* 17:153),
Abr'm Low (see *L. P.* 17:154), James Henderson (see
L. P. 17:156), Wm Brown (see *L. P.* 17:156) and Henry
Watson (see *L. P.* 17:161) rejected on caveat by Wm
Smith jr and David Matthews, agents for John van Rens-
selaer and the Westenhook patentees. Lands granted and
to be surveyed for Capt. Jacob Mullen (see *L. P.* 17:162),
Lieut. Townsend Guy (see *L. P.* 17:147) and Sergeants
Joseph Franklin and Benj. Porter (see *L. P.* 17:158).
Mary Lush vs David Provoost. Hearing on petition of
George Munro and Wm Barr (p. 473) postponed.   474

11   Petition of George Munro and Wm Barr rejected.   476

Aug. 7   Royal order received to grant 20,000 acres of land to Major
Phil. Skene, with letter from the earl of Hillsborough.
The former grant of 25,000 acres to Major Skene sus-
pended. Patent to Joseph Walton and other officers of
the royal artillery to issue. Patents granted: to George
Munro and Wm Barr (see *L. P.* 17:164); to Christ'r Blun-
dell (see *L. P.* 18:14). Bond for settlement by Alex.
Turner et al filed by John van Cortlandt and Peter du
Bois. James Jackson ex dem Thos. Williams vs John van
Rensselaer.   477

Vol. 24, 1753-56

Legislative minutes of council from May 30, 1753 to Dec. 1, 1756, printed
in *Journal of the legislative council of the colony of New York*, 2:1111-1289.

Vol. 25, 1755-64

MINUTES OF PRIVATE AFFAIRS ARE IN VOL. 23.

1755

Mar. 3   Lt. Gov. James de Lancey presides. Minutes relating to government affairs to be entered separately from private affairs. Gov. Shirley writes that Mr Pownal and other commissioners will come to New York to meet the assembly; assembly not to be called until they have arrived. Mr Verplanck to view the ground and make plans for fortifications at Albany, Schenectady and Kinderhook.   1

10   Gunpowder already purchased by Mr Watts for Massachusetts to be shipped, but not more. Proposals from Gov. Shirley to join in an expedition against Crownpoint (see *N. Y. col. mss*, 80:39-40, 45).   2

11   Assembly adjourned (see *N. Y. col. mss*, 80:46).   4

12   Letter received from Gov. Morris about a meeting at Col. Johnson's house with the six nations for the purchase of land, and about complaints against John Lydius: Pennsylvania may attend the meeting but purchase no land; complaint against Lydius too vague. Gov. Dinwiddie of Virginia complains against the treaty of neutrality made by the Indian commissioners at Albany with the Cocknewagas; to be considered. Warrant to Wm Johnson for supplies to Oswego garrison signed.   4

14   Thomas Pownall commissioner from Massachusetts in council. Assembly to be called.   5

15   Scarroyady or the half-king of the Indians on the Ohio in council reports on his visit to the six nations; the governor replies.   6

21   The Oswego contractor refuses to furnish provisions being already greatly in advance; order thereupon.   9

25   Application of Lt. Col. Mercer from Sir Wm Pepperel's regiment for subsistance of soldiers referred to the assembly.   10

26   Treaty with the Cocknawagas to be observed until further orders. Letter received from Robt. Livingston jr. (see *N. Y. col. mss*, 80:44).   10

27   Gen. Braddock wishes Gov. de Lancey to come to Annapolis, Md. with Gov. Shirley. Gov. Morris renews his application for liberty to purchase land from the six nations; it must not be allowed.   11

29   Assembly adjourned. Proclamation signed inviting enlistments in Sir Wm Pepperel's regiment (see *N. Y. col. mss*, 80:63).   11

31   Corn to be sent to the Indians. Mr Paco a French merchant, not to leave the province without permission.   12

Ap. 1   Order on letter from the sheriff of Albany (see *N. Y. col. mss*, 80:61, 66). Order to proceed with the fortifications from

Flat Rock battery to Teunis Rivet's house which must be purchased. Beacons to be erected as directed in the act for regulating the militia. - 13

6 A French dancing master to be arrested as a spy, upon a letter from Col. Laurence, lieutenant governor of Halifax. Gov. de Lancey intends to go to Annapolis, Md. in obedience to orders from Sir Thos. Robinson (see *N. Y. col. mss*, 80:48). Orders sent to the colonels of militia in Richmond, Kings, Queens, Suffolk, Westchester and Orange counties, also to the colonel of the New York militia (see *N. Y. col. mss*, 80:67). Council authorized to open letters arriving for the lieutenant governor during his absence. Warrants to Christopher Bancker and John Dies for purchasing material for the fortifications signed. 14

7   Arch. Kennedy presiding. The Frenchman come from Al-
House of   bany (23:267) committed to the custody of the sheriff.
Joseph   Minutes of Indian commissioners (see *N. Y. col. mss*,
Murray   80:69-70) received. 16

9 Guns to be mounted on Copsy and Flat Rock batteries. Jacob Twick gunsmith to repair small arms. 16

11   John Dies to select places for beacons between Rockway and
Ft George   Staten Island. Branch pilots to be on the lookout. 16

23 Gov. de Lancey returned. Letter received from Lieut. Holland at Oswego to Col. Marshall (see *N. Y. col. mss*, 80:51). The council of war held at Alexandria desires the garrison of Oswego to be reinforced (see *Doc. hist. N. Y.* 3:471; Q3:305); order of council thereon. William Johnson appointed superintendent of Indian affairs by Gen. Braddock; his commission. Gov. Thos. Fitch of Connecticut writes that his colony will raise 500 men for the expedition against Crownpoint. 17

25 Rioters taken by the sheriff of Albany (p. 13) to be kept imprisoned by him; Wm Rees one of the rioters killed in the attempt to arrest him by Matthew Furlong; Furlong to be bailed. 19

26 The French dancing master sent to jail (p. 14). Council advise the governor to assent to a further emission of bills of credit. 500 men to be raised for the New York troops in Connecticut. Warrants to Oliver de Lancey for provisions to the troops ordered to Oswego, and to Edw. Holland for corn to the six nations signed. 20

May 2 Resolve of the assembly concerning artillery concurred in. Order concerning John Batist de Quanje, a Frenchman arrested at Albany. Warrant to John Dies for building bateaux signed. 21

3 Gov. Shirley wants cannon for the Niagara expedition. List of ordnance and stores called for. Letter received from Gov. Shirley (see *N. Y. col. mss*, 80:98). Assembly adjourned. Order on memorial of Lt. Col. Mercer concerning pay of the troops at Oswego. 22

6 Warrants issued to Col. Wm Johnson, Capt. John Bradstreet, Messrs John Dies, Bancker and ―――― Dies for impressing workmen on the fortifications. Proclamation to issue for enforcing quarantine measures (see *N. Y. col. mss*, 80: 139-40). Disposition of ordnance made. Bastions to be built between Copsy and Flat Rock batteries. Warrant to John de Peyster for provisions to the Oswego garrison signed. 24

8 Opinion of council on complaint of Robt. Livingston jr, that the Massachusetts people have taken the workmen from his ironworks at Ancram (see *N. Y. col. mss*, 80:143). 25

13 Lt. Gov. Phips of Massachusetts asks for the arrest of the man who killed Wm Race [Rees] (p. 19); Gov. de Lancey's answer. Order on a petition of Manuel du Cumana (see *N. Y. col. mss*, 80:148). Letter received from James Alexander (see *N. Y. col. mss*, 80:146) referred. Warrants signed: to John Cruger and John Watts for gunpowder; to Adam van der Bergh for entertainment of Scarroyady or the half-king and companions. 27

17 Act of parliament to punish mutiny and desertion received; also royal order to increase the regiments of Sir Peter Halket, Col. Dunbar and the Nova Scotia regiments to 1000 men each; assembly to provide means. Gov. Fitch agrees that New York may raise 500 men in Connecticut. Assembly adjourned. 29

19 Basseau a Frenchman to be arrested on an affidavit by Elizabeth Coen; also Alvertste another French subject. Samuel Stillwell to be examined concerning Basseau. Warrant to Oliver de Lancey for providing military stores etc signed. 30

20 Gov. Shirley wants more cannons; they are to be loaned. Basseau taken his papers to be examined. 31

26 French reinforcements sent to the Ohio (see *N. Y. col. mss*, 80:144). M. Jean Sylvestre and wife fled from Canada confined to their lodgings after having been examined (see *N. Y. col. mss*, 80:164). 32

29 John Pownall secretary of the board of trade writes that Charles Hardy has been appointed governor of New York. Medicines required at Oswego. John Adams accused by Gideon Hawley of having sold rum to the Oncoquagah Indians; Timothy McHarris, John McMullen and Mr Boyd

co be examined as witnesses at Albany. Warrant to Oliver de Lancey for provisioning Oswego garrison signed. Merlons of the batteries in New York to be made of white cedar wood; the north line and the line from Hunt's within the Half Moon battery to be finished.   33

30   Letters from Wm Smith, Robert R. Livingston and Robt. Livingston (see *N. Y. col. mss*, 80:166-67) referred to eastern boundary commissioners. Warrants signed: to John Dies and Christopher Bancker for building fortifications; to Ernest Spitzer for salary as surgeon at Oswego.   34

June 3 Opinion of council on application by Capt. Wm Eyre engineer of the Crownpoint expedition for more artillery. Proclamation to issue for arrest of deserters (see *N. Y. col. mss*, 81:9).   34

5   Proposal from Massachusetts for the appointment of arbitrators in the boundary cases referred (see *N. Y. col. mss*, 80:157). Order to discharge the rioters imprisoned at Albany. Cannons returned from Boston. Additional charter for Kings college to be printed.   35

6   Opinion of council on letter received from Gov. Shirley (see *N. Y. col. mss*, 80:163). Report of committee on the proposal from Massachusetts (p. 35). Account of charges for repairing the barracks in Fort George referred.   36

9   Connecticut refuses to accept the offer made by the New York assembly as to the money granted by Pennsylvania for the expedition; referred to the assembly. Proposal by Massachusetts to employ part of the forces raised for the Crownpoint expedition against Niagara, agreed to. Letter received from the recorder of Albany (see *N. Y. col. mss*, 80:171) referred to the assembly.   41

12   Letter received from Gov. Shirley, pay of Indians engaged for the Crownpoint expedition and their officers. Account for erecting beacons referred. Phil. Verplanck refuses to serve as commissary and paymaster of the New York troops; Phil. Schuyler and John de Peyster are appointed in his place.   42

14   Letter received from Capt. John Bradstreet at Oswego (see *N. Y. col. mss.* 80:170). Warrant to Bancker and Dies for the New York fortifications signed. Ordinance to issue regulating the sessions of the court of common pleas in Richmond county. Letter received from Gov. Shirley (see *N. Y. col. mss*, 81:16). Address from the Moravians (see *N. Y. col. mss*, 81:21) referred.   43

17   Plans of the forts to be erected at Albany, Schenectady and Kinderhook, and account of Phil. Verplanck for this ser-

vice referred to the assembly. Letter from Gov. Glen of
South Carolina, peace between the Catawbas and the six
nations disturbed; referred to Gen. Wm Johnson. John
Burnet appointed coroner of New York, vice ——— removed out of the county. Arms.   44

23   Letters received: from Gov. Shirley, export of provisions
from Massachusetts prohibited, and movement of French
troops, referred; from Gen. Johnson, Cocknawagas. Petition of Fred'k Wimpel smith among the Senecas for pay
referred to the assembly. Fortifications.   45

25   Letter received from Gen. Johnson (see *N. Y. col. mss*, 81:28).
Warrants signed: to Capt. Street Hall for pay of his com-
pany (see *N. Y. col. mss*, 81:35); to Jacobus Mynderse and
Peter Groenendyke for carrying corn to the six nations.   46

30   Letters received: from Gov. Wentworth (see *N. Y. col. mss*,
81:31); from Gov. Shirley, embargo for three months proposed; from the same, pay of engineer and artillery officers,
referred to the assembly; from Robert Livingston (see
N. Y. col. mss, 81:37), referred to Gov. Shirley.   47

July 5   Warrants signed: to Phil. Schuyler and John de Peyster for
pay of troops; to John Dies for expenses of erecting
beacons; to Christ'r Bancker and John Dies for expenses
of fortifications. Assembly adjourned. Frenchmen allowed to leave the city for Europe or the West Indies.
Pardon granted to Richard Aldridge sentenced for horse
stealing, on condition of his enlisting as soldier.   47

10   Warrants signed: to Gov. de Lancey for expenses on his
journey to Virginia; to Gen. Wm Johnson for military and
Indian disbursements; to Oliver de Lancey for arms etc;
to Phil. Verplanck for making plans of forts. Advice of
council on the application of Gov. Shirley for discharge of
people arrested in the boundary riots. Bateaux to be sold
for the artillery. Frenchmen may go to Philadelphia or
Boston.   48

19   Letter received from Sec. Richard Peters of Pennsylvania
(see *N. Y. col. mss*, 81:74, 84) to be sent to Gov. Shirley,
Gen. Johnson etc.   49

22   Another letter from the same (see *N. Y. col. mss*, 81:85) disposed of in the same way. Order on petition of Abeel and
wife on behalf of their son John to be tried for selling
rum to the Indians. Assembly adjourned.   49

25   Letter received from Capt. Rutherford (see *N. Y. col. mss*,
81:75). Assembly called. No provisions to be exported.
Warrant to Christ'r Bancker and John Dies for expenses
of building fortifications signed.   50

1755   v. 25

26 Vessels laden with provisions and bound for Halifax, Annapolis or Chicgnecto in Nova Scotia may be cleared.   51
28 Letter received from Robert Orme, aid to Gen. Braddock
announcing the general's death. Gov. Shirley's demand
for discharge of boundary rioters repeated and again referred to Rob't Livingston.   52
29 Letters received: from Admiral Boscawen, movements of his
fleet; from Sir Thos. Robinson, Admiral Boscawen or
Commodore Keppel to be called upon if necessary for
naval assistance. Application for leave to carry flour to
Rhode Island not granted.   52
Aug. 1 Gov. de Lancey suggests that the independent companies
sent to Virginia be recalled; advice of council thereon.
Opinion of council on Col. Dunbar's going into winter
quarters. Warrants signed: to Col. Wm Cockcrott for expenses of his table on the Crownpoint expedition; to James
Parker printer for paper for bills of credit.   53
4 Letters received: from Gen. Johnson, fears bad effect of
Braddock's defeat on the Indians; from Gov. Fitch, troops
for Crownpoint expedition; opinion of council on either.
Wall from the east line of the battery along the west side
of Whitehall slip to be continued.   54
6 Massachusetts proposes to raise 500 men more. Letters received: from Gov. Shirley to Sec. Willard (see *N. Y. col.
mss*, 81:89); from Gov. Lawrence to Lt. Gov. Phips (see
N. Y. col. mss, 81:92). Proclamation for a general fast to
issue (see *N. Y. col. mss*, 81:106); also proclamation for
discovery of the burglars who broke in to the consistory
room of the Dutch church (see *N. Y. col. mss*, 81:105).   55
11 Col. Dunbar's and the late Sir Peter Halket's regiments
ordered to Albany. New York independent companies
can not return.   56
12 The snow Irene, Nicholas Garrison jr master arrived from
London with smallpox on board quarantined at Bedloes
island. Gen. Shirley's letter read 11 August to be laid
before the assembly.   56
13 Quarantine measures.   57
14 Advice of council on application by Messrs Nicholls, Cranston, and Bours, Rhode Island committee of war for permission to export flour from New York. Assembly adjourned.   58
16 Opinion of council on application by Col. Joseph Blanchard
of the New Hampshire troops for their quota of the Pennsylvania provisions. Massachusetts will raise 800 men for
the Crownpoint expedition; referred to the assembly.   58

18 Col. Dunbar's orders changed; independent companies may perhaps return to New York. Assembly not to be called yet. 59

20 Order authorizing the sale of provisions belonging to the province. Quarantine measures. 60

23 Letters received: from Gen. Johnson with minutes of a council of war (see *N. Y. col. mss*, 81:118); from Gov. Phips, wants permission to carry provisions to Boston or Salem; from Gov. Fitch, orders for raising 500 men in Connecticut are issued, referred to the assembly. Assembly to be called. 60

25 Quarantine measures. Order on petition of John Miranda a Spanish negro servant to Sarah widow of Peter van Raust, and claiming to be a freeman. 61

28 Assembly adjourned for a few days no quorum being in town. Permission to ship provisions given to Capt. Matthew Cozzens on application by the governor of Rhode Island. Letter received from Rob't Livingston jr, will discharge Josiah Loomis one of the rioters, but must hold Pain a judgment debtor. Application to be made to Massachusetts for establishing a line of peace. 62

29 Letter received from Gen. Johnson (see *N. Y. col. mss*, 81:123); referred to the assembly. Proclamation for apprehending deserters (see *N. Y. col. mss*, 81:126) to issue. Lt. Gov. Jon'n Nicholls of Rhode Island desires permission for Capt. Richards to carry provisions from New York to Rhode Island; not granted. 63

Sep. 1 Connecticut will raise 1500 men more; referred to the assembly. Mrs van der Bilt nurse on Bedloes island granted permission to return to Staten Island. Quarantine of the Irene (p. 56) to be continued. Permission to export flour given to Capt. Richards (p. 63), and vessels bound to Honduras bay allowed to take small quantities. Order to search for and arrest two Frenchmen supposed to be spies seen in Mr de Visme's house. 63

3 Sir Charles Hardy knight has his commission read and takes the oaths. Instruction containing the names of the council [unchanged] read and members present sworn in. Seals delivered to the new governor; oath of chancellor administered to him. Proclamation to issue continuing all officers in their places (see *N. Y. col. mss*, 81:138). Governor's commission published at the city hall. 64

4 Messrs Horsmanden and Smith take the oaths as councillors. Draft of message to the assembly read and approved. 66

8 Vote of the assembly for raising £8000 for the 1500 men to be raised in Connecticut; letter from Gov. Fitch in regard to

it. Warrants signed: to Wm Johnson for charges of a fort at the upper Mohawk castle; to John Joost Petrie for provisioning Oswego troops. Order on petition by Wm Coventry and Andrew Barclay (see *N. Y. col. mss*, 81:146). Quarantine of the Irene continued (p. 63).   66

10   Letter received from Col. Cockcroft (see *N. Y. col. mss*, 81:124). New proclamation for the arrest of deserters (see *N. Y. col. mss*, 81:149) to issue. Warrant to Christ'r Bancker and John Dies for New York fortifications signed. Order on petition of Jacob le Roy (see *N. Y. col. mss*, 81:147).   67

13   News of a battle at Lake George received. The Irene (p. 66) permitted to come up to the city and unload on representation of Henry White army contractor and Capt. Nicholas Garrison. Invoice of Indian presents read.   68

p. m.   Gov. Hardy intends to go to Albany; gives instructions to the council, signs blank warrants for the £8000 (p. 66) and warrant to commissioners of New York fortifications.   68

14   Letters received: from Peter Wraxall, aid to Gen. Johnson, battle at Lake George, French defeated, Baron de Dieskau taken; from Gov. Wentworth, New Hampshire will raise 300 men; from Lt. Gov. Phips, Massachusetts has passed an act for raising 2000 additional troops. Provisions for the army to be purchased and sent to Albany. Instructions to the council during the governor's absence. Proclamation to issue for a day of thanksgiving on account of the victory at Lake George (see *N. Y. col. mss*, 81:153).   69

20   Committee of council sits in the secretary's office, James Alexander presiding. Letters received: from Gen. Johnson, returns of killed and wounded, copy to be sent to Sec. Pownal; from Lt. Gov. Phips; both forwarded to Gov. Hardy.   70

24   Order on letter from Gov. Hardy concerning pay of transportation of Col. Dunbar's regiment from Amboy to Albany.   70

26   French prisoners taken in the late battle placed in charge of the sheriff of New York and Dr John Bard.   71

27   The committee calls on the governor for directions as to the embargo of provisions; the act of assembly for it expiring shortly. Letter from the governor of St Domingo sent unopened to Gov. Hardy.   72

p. m.   Further orders for the care of French prisoners. Letters from Gov. Wentworth sent to Albany.   73

Oct. 7   Permission to export flour to Rhode Island given to Capt. Wm Richards on application from Gov. Stephen Hopkins.   74

1755   **v. 25**

Recorder van Schaick and Rev. Mr Ogilvie to the Mo-
hawks, Oneidas and Tuscaroras.   83

25   Moses Emerson commissary for the Massachusetts troops is
given permission to buy bread belonging to New York.
Colonels Dyer and Chauncey of Connecticut recommended
to join the army under Gen. Johnson. Major Hazelton of
Col. Willard's Massachusetts regiment gives his reasons
for staying behind.   85

27   Warrant to David Rowland for the use of the Connecticut
troops signed.   86

29   Edward Holland appointed mayor, John Roberts sheriff, John
Burnet coroner of New York; Hans Hansen mayor, Abr'm
Yates jr, sheriff of Albany.   86

30   Assembly prorogued. Letters received from Gen. Johnson
with plans of the fort building at the carrying place, of
fort on Lake George etc; referred.   86

Oct. 1   Report of committee on the preceding letters (see *N. Y.
col. mss*, 81:168). Report of Rev. John Ogilvie on the mission to the Mohawks with their speeches.   87

4   Impress warrants for bateaux and wagons issued to Lewis
Morris agent for supplying Oswego (see *N. Y. col. mss*,
81:169).   90

6   Assembly prorogued. Opinion of council concerning the
embargo of provisions (p. 72).   90

10   Carpenters to be sent to complete the work at Fort
Edward.   91

14   John Billings an officer of Gen. Shirley writes of delays in
transportation; new impress warrants issued. Conference
with 30 Mohawks from the lower castle on their way to the
army.   91

16   Opinions of council: on letter from Gen. Johnson concerning
the state of the army; on letter from Gen. Shirley about
barracks in Albany and Schenectady.   93

18   Warrant to Elihu Lyman for the use of the Connecticut
troops issued at the request of Gov. Fitch. Warrants to
issue for the arrest of persons who neglected to send their
wagons when ordered.   94

25   Warrant to Aaron Day for the use of the Connecticut troops
issued at the request of Gov. Fitch.   94

27   Opinion of council on letter from Gen. Johnson with minutes
of a council of war, who declare it inadvisable to go on
with the expedition. New Hampshire troops under Col.
Gilman to be discharged. Assembly prorogued.   95

Nov. 7   Letter received from Gen. Johnson suggesting an embargo
on boards. Warrant issued to Mr Montressor chief engi-

1755   **v. 25**

neer empowering him to impress boards and other materials for building barracks.   96

10   Funds for paying the troops exhausted; the treasurer to advance money (p. 81, 82).   96

12   Letter received from Gen. Johnson, French movements. Impress warrants for horses and wagons sent to the river
counties. Report of Sybrant G. van Schaick (see *N. Y.
col. mss*, 81:155).   97

17   Petition of Cornelius Sharp and Joseph Picksley (see *N. Y.
col. mss*, 82:3) referred.   98

20   Agreement for garrisoning Fort William Henry and Fort
Edward made between Gov. Hardy and the commissioners
from Massachusetts and Connecticut. Sybrant G. van
Schaick and Volkert P. Douw appointed New York commissioners under the agreement.   99

22   Orders: for paying the New York troops which are to be
discharged; as to clothing of the troops left in the forts.
Oliver de Lancey has contracted for a supply of cattle for
the forts; approved.   99

30   Gov. Hardy returned. Col. de Key of Orange county reports
Ft George   mischief done by the Minissink Indians; the six nations to
be asked to interfere.   100

Dec. 1   Gov. Hardy is instructed by the lords justices to ask for the
granting of a permanent revenue; governor's speech to be
made to the council and assembly read and approved.   100

6   Papers relating to disturbances on the Massachusetts line
(see *N. Y. col. mss*, 82:3, 6-8) referred. Warrants signed: to
Lieut. Hitchen Holland for pay as commissary at Oswego;
to John Dies for expenses in building bateaux; to John
Joost Petrie for provisions to Oswego garrison; to Ernest
Spitzen for salary as surgeon at Oswego.   101

16   Hostile Indians infest the northern parts of Pennsylvania and
New Jersey. Allowances to be made to the militia for
service on the frontiers. Bill for completing the quota of
the province to be recommended to the assembly.   101

20   Report on the papers relating to the Massachusetts boundary disturbances. Warrant signed to Goldsbrow Banyar for
carpenter work done in the secretary's office by Thos.
Brookman.   102

23   Council advise the governor to pass certain bills enacted by
council and assembly.   104

26   Cadw. Colden sworn of the council. Proclamation to issue
inviting the river Indians to remove with their families into
the towns of Ulster and Orange counties (see *N. Y. col.
mss*, 82:40).   104

1755   **v. 25**

30   Capt. Dudley Diggs commanding the Nightingale man-of-
        war to sail for England with Gen. Shirley's dispatches.   105

1756

Jan. 9   Gen. Wm Johnson sworn of the council. Gen. Shirley pro-
            poses a winter campaign against Ticonderoga, supported by
            reports from Capt. Rogers and Lieut. Poor.   106

p. m.   Council approves of Gen. Shirley's plan and advises to ask
            the assembly for the necessary means.   106

26   Letter received from Gov. Shirley, plan of operations and
        quota of colonies; assembly to be asked for an appropria-
        tion to raise 1000 men.   106

29   Votes of the assembly for subsisting 1000 men by new emis-
        sion of bills of credit received. Council advise the gover-
        nor to consent to the continuance of bills outstanding.   107

Feb. 3   The Belle Savage, John Lewis master, arrived from St
            Thomas to go into quarantine upon report of Dr John
            Bard.   108

5   James Wilks sentenced to death for the murder of John
        Christie to be reprieved (see *N. Y. col. mss*, 82:63). Im-
        press warrants for horses and wagons to carry carpenters
        to Oswego issued (see *N. Y. col. mss*, 82:70).   108

9   Warrant to impress Johannes Quackenboss appointed head-
        workman or director of the carpenters going to Schenec-
        tady to build boats (see *N. Y. col. mss*, 82:72).   109

19   Warrant to Bancker and Dies for expenses in building New
        York fortifications signed (see *N. Y. col. mss*, 82:74). The
        Belle Savage released from quarantine upon application of
        her owner Elias des Brosses (see *N. Y. col. mss*, 82:78).
        Barrack to be built near Whitehall slip.   109

21   Opinion of council on proposal made by inhabitants of
        Ulster and Orange counties for attacking the Indians at
        Shohawkin.   110

Mar. 1   Further mischief done by the Indians; papers laid before the
            assembly (see *N. Y. col. mss*, 82:83).   110

2   Massachusetts will raise 3000 men (see *N. Y. col. mss*, 82:81).
        Increase of men to be raised in New York to be recom-
        mended to the assembly. Gen. Shirley's proposal concern-
        ing the appointment of boundary commissioners not
        agreed to.   110

3   Connecticut agrees to raise 2500 men conditionally. Forces
        to be raised by New York for service against the Indians.
        Building and altering of barracks.   111

8   Letters received from Col. Ellison, Lt. Col. Clinton and
        Ebenezer Seely jr, Samuel Slaughter and party have
        wantonly killed some Indians at Wilemantown, Ulster

county; proclamation to issue for the arrest of Samuel
Slaughter (see *N. Y. col. mss*, 82:88).   111

14 River Indians brought to New York by Capt. Corn's Hornbeck complain about their treatment by the white people.   112

15 Gov. Hardy's answer to the river Indians. Rhode Island
has voted to raise 500 men. Massachusetts will increase
her contingent to 3500. Gen. Johnson complains of Col.
Bradstreet and Justice Visger intermeddling in Indian
affairs; Justice Visger ordered to desist.   112

18 New Jersey has voted to raise 200 men. New York assembly increases the quota to 1715. Proclamation to issue
calling for volunteers (see *N. Y. col. mss*, 82:95).   113

Ap. 1 Council advise the governor to sign the bills come from the
assembly, for paying debts due from the colony and for
raising 1715 men.   114

13 Gov. Morris of Pennsylvania writes that his government will
raise 400 men to build a fort at Shamokin and then march
against the Indians and that a reward for scalps has been
offered of which he does not approve; referred to Sir Wm
Johnson. Connecticut will supply 2500 men uncondition-
ally (p. 111). New Hampshire has voted to raise 500 men.
Warrants for payment of public debts issued. Independent
companies ordered to Albany; militia to do guard duty in
Fort George during their absence. Commissions of the
peace and pleas for Richmond issued.   115

18 Letters and papers received: from Albany, French intend to
attack Oswego; from Sir Wm Johnson, Indian meeting at
Onondaga. Indian presents to be sent to him for distribution. Lt. Col. Gage, commanding at Schenectady ordered
to send reinforcements wherever needed.   116

21 Oswego besieged by French and Indians; Sir Wm Johnson
intends to march for its relief and has ordered militia to
reinforce Forts Wm Henry and Edward (see *Doc. hist. N. Y.*
3:475-76; Q3:308); measures taken by the governor approved. Albany militia to be in pay. Lt. Gov. de Lancey
to go to Albany (see *N. Y. col. mss*, 82:125).   116

23 Accounts for making guncarriages at Albany audited. Warrants signed: to Oliver de Lancey, Beverley Robinson and
John Cruger, paymasters of the forces; to Christ'r Bancker
and John Dies for expenses in building New York fortifications; to Adam van den Bergh for boarding river Indians (see *N. Y. col. mss*, 82:129).   117

29 Warrant to Capt. Isaac Corsa for bounty and enlisting
money of his company signed.   118

1756   v. 25

30   People brought from Nova Scotia [Acadiens or French neutrals] by order of Gov. Lawrence; how to dispose of them. Warrants to be issued for bounty and enlisting money upon proof. Proclamation to issue for a day of fast (see *N. Y. col. mss,* 82:133-34). Commissions of the peace and pleas for Queens county to be issued.   118

May 4   Lt. Colonels Burton commanding at Albany, and van Rensselaer of the militia report on the ill situation of the garrison of Fort William Henry, Lt. Col. Glazier commanding; referred to the assembly.   119

6   Acadiens distributed as follows: Daniel Garsen wife and 11 children to Richmondtown, Staten Island; Joseph Malie, wife and 7 children to Flatbush, Long Island; Joseph Blanchard, wife and 3 children to Bushwick, Long Island; Glode Doucet, wife and 8 children to Jamaica; Seres Etben, wife and 8 children to New Town; Joseph Commo, wife and 7 children to Flushing; Zachary Richard, wife and 6 children to Hempstead; Chas. Matton, wife and 3 children, John Marten, wife and 2 children to Oysterbay; Lewis Geroid, wife and 6 children, Jerama Gouder, wife and 2 children to Huntington; Michael Richard, wife and 6 children to Southold; Francis Martin, wife and 5 children to Easthampton; Alex. Elbert, wife and 5 children to Southampton; Francis Commo, wife and 8 children to Brookhaven; Peter Loe, wife and 3 children to Smithtown; Charles Savoit, wife and 8 children, Ba Selena and wife, Charles Lamotten, wife and child to New Rochelle; Francis Quela, wife and 8 children, Jean Tournier, wife and 2 children to Rye. Letters from the governor of St Augustine and papers relating to Spanish negroes (see *N. Y. col. mss,* 82:121) referred. Warrant to James Parker for printing bills of credit signed. Fortifications (musket proof mantlets) and their armament.   119

15   Permission given to ship provisions for the fleet in Carolina in the brigantine Darling, Wm Lightfoot master on application of Henry White agent for Bowman & Yates of Charlestown, S. C. (see *N. Y. col. mss,* 82:139). Assembly adjourned (see *N. Y. col. mss,* 82:143). Order on petition of Hillario Antonio a Spanish free negro captured by the privateer Hester, Capt. Troop and sold to Capt. Hertell. Hearing of the case of John Miranda (p. 61) postponed.   121

20   Alex. Colden, John Livingston, Dirick Swart, Abrm Bonee and John Abeel examined concerning exportation of provisions; Peter Stoutenburgh cooper, and Gilbert Sherer tavernkeeper to be called for like examination.   122

22   Gilbert Sherer exmained (see *N. Y. col. mss,* 82:148); Stoutenburgh is out of town. Wm Kempe attorney general directed to prosecute Samuel Stillwell merchant of New York, and John Burroughs boatman of Middletown, N. J.   122

24   Sec. Richard Peters sends Pennsylvania acts forbidding the exportation of provisions. Gov. Belcher writes that no provisions will be exported from New Jersey. Collector of New York ordered not to clear vessels with provisions. Cannons belonging to private parties to be mounted on the river front. John Marschalk examined about illegal exportation of flour.   123

29   Warrant to Christ'r Bancker and John Dies for expenses in building fortifications signed. Peter Stoutenburgh examined (p. 122). Samuel Stillwell to give bonds for his appearance before the supreme court. Assembly adjourned.   124

31   Thos. Clark and Joseph Forman give security for Sam. Stillwell. Hearing in the case of John Miranda (p. 121).   124

June 10   Capt. Wm Richards allowed to carry flour to Rhode Island on application of Gov. Hopkins.   125

12   Proclamation to issue enforcing the act against selling rum to Indians (see *N. Y. col. mss,* 82:159). Assembly adjourned (see *N. Y. col. mss,* 82:158).   125

18   James Smith McBride convicted of having murdered Isaac Winter at Albany, and James Wilks (p. 108) pardoned by the king. Dumas a French officer staying at Mr Vallarde's ordered to leave.   126

24   Permission to export provisions: to Bermuda granted to the sloop Mary, John Sawyer master on application of Gov. Wm Popple of Bermuda; to Rhode Island granted to the sloop Sally, Joseph Shelding master on application of Gov. Hopkins. Camp equipage to be provided for the regiments of Lt. Gen. Otway and Lord John Murray. Letter from Henry Fox secretary of state, earl of Loudoun appointed commander-in-chief in America. Regiments to be recruited. Volunteers. Grant by parliament for the war to New York, New Jersey and New England. Indentured servants. Trade with the French.   127

July 5   Letter received from the lords of trade, Kayaderosseras, Canajohary and Oneida carrying place patents to be vacated. Proclamation to issue for the encouragement of volunteering (see *N. Y. col. mss,* 82:169). Account of postage and express referred (see *N. Y. col. mss,* 82:172). Warrant to Bancker and Dies for the fortifications signed. Battery to

1756   v. 25

be erected near Coenties dock. Sloop Industry, Isaac Law-
ton master allowed to carry provisions to Rhode Island.   129

7   Letters received: from Gen. Shirley wanting battering cannons for the Crownpoint expedition; from Maj. Gen. Abercrombie after consultation with Generals Shirley and Wins-
low and Col. Gridley affirms that more artillery is necessary. Warrants to Lt. Gov. de Lancey for postage etc
signed. Gov. Hardy intends to go to Albany.   131

9   Proof of notification concerning a private act in behalf of
Stephen and Pierre van Cortlandt filed by James Briggs;
certificate granted. Gilbert Drake, John Maha and one
Sylvester to be prosecuted on affidavit of James Kniffin
constable and Nehemiah Tomkins (see *N. Y. col. mss*,
83:11). Council advise the governor to pass the bills before him and to prorogue the assembly.   132

10   Order for continuing the embargo on provisions. Instructions to the council during the governor's absence. Repairs on Fort George to be completed. Great seal to be
repaired. Warrants to Christ'r Bancker and John Dies for
the fortifications.   133

19   Gov. Hardy presiding, Lt. Gov. de Lancey, Sir Wm John-
Albany   son and Mr Chambers present. Press warrants to issue to
keep ship carpenters at Oswego and to procure wagons for
transportation of provisions.   134

31   Press warrants for wagons to be used by Gen. Abercrombie's
regiment on the march to Oswego to be issued to the justices of Schenectady.   135

Aug. 6   Assembly prorogued.   135

11   Gov. Hardy to return to New York; issues general press
warrant to Sir John St Clair.   135

16   Gov. Morris of Pennsylvania writes that he will take off the
Fort George   embargo on provisions. Similar orders given in New York.
Sloop Proney, Thos. Mall master allowed to carry provisions to South Carolina on application of Samuel Bowman and J. O. Yates agents of the naval contractor (see
N. Y. col. mss, 83:5). Petition of merchants for taking off
the embargo received.   136

July 14   Archibald Kennedy presiding. Evert Byvanck and Christ'r
Fell examined concerning flour shipped by David Shadine
(see *N. Y. col. mss*, 83:17).   137

21   The sloop Retrieve of Bermuda, John Mackenny master allowed to carry out provisions on plication of Gov. Wm
Popple. David Shadine to be prosecuted on information.   137

31   Declaration of war against France received from England
through Gov. Hardy to be published by proclamation at

1756   **v. 25**

the city hall (see *N. Y. col. mss,* 83:36). Letter received
from Gov. Hardy, smallpox (see *N. Y. col. mss,* 81:35).   137

Aug. 3   Permission to carry provisions to Rhode Island given to

———————   138

19   Letters received: from Mr West secretary of the treasury,
quota of the money granted by parliament (p. 127); from
Messrs Tomlinson and Hanburg, transmitting the share of
New York; from Capt. Campbell of the Nightingale man-
of-war, French prisoners on board the prize ship Centaur,
they are placed in charge of the sheriff of New York. Warrant to Wm Kelly for the use of Sir Wm Johnson to pay
Cornelius Potman and James Elwood for building a fort
at the lower Mohawk castle signed (see *N. Y. col. mss,*
83:40).   138

21   The treasurer reports on the money received from England.
Permission to ship provisions to Maderia granted to the
sloops Success, Phil. Wilkinson master, Charming Nancy,
Balthazar Winthrop master, Elizabeth, John Anderson
master (see *N. Y. col. mss,* 83:54).   139

24   Order on report from Mayor Holland about French neutrals
sent back from Georgia (see *N. Y. col. mss,* 83:55).   140

25   French neutrals distributed as follows: Peter Dusaw, wife
and 5 children, Michael Basseaux, wife and 4 children,
Michael Borcea and 3 children, Peter Resha and 5 chil-
dren to Orange county; south of the Highlands, Jean
Devou, wife and 1 child, Paul Devou, wife and 2 children;
Jean Kase to Westchester; Jean Bastil Urian, wife and 2
children, Jean Baptist Urian, wife and 2 children to East-
chester; Peter Badrow, wife and 1 child, Paul Woodrow,
Francis Dusaw, Joseph Relivo, Jean Bornan, Joseph Juiah,
Joseph Guillan, Joseph Gilboa, Francis Sevoy, Peter
Reshaur to Bedford; Peter Sier, wife and 1 child, John
Devou, wife and 1 child, John Chosen, Peter Devou to
Northcastle; Jeremiah Juewah, Joseph Dusah, Jack Jeroir,
Loud Jeroir, Julian Rula, Peter Dusa, Peter Carries to
Northcastle; Jeremiah Juewah, Joseph Dusah, Jack Jeroir,
Richards, Joseph Sier, wife and 2 children, Francis Bodraw,
wife and 2 children, to Courtlandt manor. Abr'm Hanny
placed in charge of the Orange county contingent, Phil
Verplanck of those for Courtlandt manor.   141

27   East fort of Oswego taken by the French. Lord Loudoun
calls for assistance; must be more particular (see *Doc. hist.
N. Y.* 1:499; Q1:322).   142

Sep. 6   Lord Loudoun repeats his call for assistance. Militia ordered to join the other forces at German flats. Assembly

1756   V. 25

called. Report on foreigners and strangers in the city
called for.   143

24   Governor's speech to be made to the council and assembly
read and approved. Order on petition of Hillario Antonio
(see *N. Y. col. mss*, 83:112). Impress warrant issued to Col.
Stanwix for the sloop of Martin Garretsen van Bergen.
Juan Miranda vs Widow van Ranst (see *N. Y. col. mss*,
83:103-4). Committee to proceed on the Spanish free
negro cases.   144

29   Edw. Holland appointed mayor, John Roberts sheriff, John
Burnet coroner, of New York; Sybrant G. van Schaick
mayor, Abr'm Yates jr sheriff, of Albany. Proclamations
to issue for enforcing act about apprehension of deserters
(see *N. Y. col. mss*, 83:126-27) and for arresting French subjects.   144

Oct. 13   Smallpox case in New street; measures to prevent the disease from spreading. Burger's sloop arrived from St
Croix ordered into quarantine at Bedlows island.   145

18   Smallpox in Albany; orders to prevent its spreading.   146

29   Burger's sloop discharged from quarantine on certificate of
Dr John Bard.   146

Nov. 11   John Cruger appointed mayor of New York in place of Edw.
Holland deceased.   147

27   Embargo on provisions taken off. Council advise the governor to pass the bills before him.   147

Dec. 1   Bills before the governor to be passed and assembly prorogued.   147

3   Devices on the stamps. Proclamation to issue enforcing the
peddlars' act (see *N. Y. col. mss*, 83:159). Orders to the
land and tide waiters. Inoculation for smallpox may con-
tinue.   148

20   Proclamations to issue giving notice of the New York
stamp act (see *N. Y. col. mss*, 83:167) and for taking deserters (see *N. Y. col. mss*, 83:166). Letter received from
Rob't Livingston jr, riots in or near the manor; referred
to the earl of Loudoun. Warrants for salaries signed.
Governor's account of disbursements for express etc re-
ferred.   149

21   Guards ordered to protect Livingston manor. Warrants
signed: to Oliver de Lancey, John Cruger and Beverly
Robinson for pay of provincials; to Gov. Hardy for the
hire of expresses; to divers under act for clothing the
troops Proclamation to issue against straggling of sol-
diers (see *N. Y. col. mss*, 83:168).   151

29   Embargo laid on provisions except to the British colonies
by order from the lords of trade. Assembly prorogued.   152

1757   **v. 25**

Jan. 10   Philipp John Schuyler appointed manager of the excise on
          tea for Albany vice Herm. Wendell declined. Assembly to
          meet at Flatbush, L. I. on account of smallpox.   154

     13   Warrant to Oliver de Lancey, John Cruger and Beverly
          Robinson for paying the provincial troops (p. 151).   154

     31   Memorial of Wm Walton (see *N. Y. col. mss*, 84:24, 51) re-
          ferred. Warrant to Gov. Hardy for firewood and candles
          to Fort George signed.   154

Feb. 7   Assembly prorogued. Warrant to Oliver de Lancey etc for
          pay of troops signed (p. 154).   155

     14   Letters received: from Lord Loudoun calling for 1000 men as
          the New York contingent; from lords of trade and lieu-
          tenant governor of Massachusetts, boundaries. Speech to
          the council and assembly read and approved.   155

     21   Report on the memorial of Wm Walton (p. 154); permis-
          sion to ship provisions to St Augustine granted (see *N. Y.
          col. mss*, 84:30).   156

     26   Bills before the governor to be passed and the speaker di-
          rected to adjourn the assembly.   159

Mar. 2   A general embargo laid on all vessels at the request of Lord
          Loudoun. Impress warrants to issue when necessary.
          Master and wardens of the port nominated and commis-
          sions to issue to them. Warrants for salaries signed.   159

      8   Detachments from the militia to complete the provincial regi-
          ments. Warrants issued: for impressing watercasks, work-
          men to make more; and for taking Samuel Hart's ship into
          the service.   160

     16   The advocate general ordered to put in a claim for the
          Spanish ship Nostra Señora de Guadalupe, chartered by
          Philipp de la Pedra of Santona, Spain to Don Joseph
          Joachim de Oruna agent of the Royal company of Cuba
          and captured on her way to Santiago de Cuba by the
          privateer Charming Peggy, Richard Hadden commander,
          Manuel de Hoyo steward, Vizente de Herrera boatswain,
          and Manuel Rodriguez sailor of the captured ship to be ex-
          amined.   161

     17   Abr'm Sleeth master of the Charming Peggy, and ———
          Miller of the privateer Bermuda to be prosecuted.   163

     26   Assembly adjourned (see *N. Y. col. mss*, 84:45).   163

Ap.   6   Leave to ship provisions to St Augustine notwithstanding
          the general embargo granted to Wm Walton.   164

      9   Assembly adjourned (see *N. Y. col. mss*, 84:50). Account of
          Jacob Brewerton for boarding French neutrals and ferry-
          ing them across the East river referred.   164

     21   Warrant to Oliver de Lancey, John Cruger and Beverly
          Robinson for pay of troops signed.   165

25   Assembly adjourned. Order on memorial of Thos. Jones
      clerk of Queens county (see *N. Y. col. mss*, 84:54).   165
29   Vessels loaded before the general embargo was ordered may
      be cleared. Sir Wm Johnson writes that the Indians at
      Venango desire the release of two Indians confined in the
      jail at Albany.   166
30   Opinion of council on the request of the Venango Indians.
      Accounts referred: of Abr'm Peck (see *N. Y. col. mss*,
      84:53); of David van der Heyden for express service; of
      Isaac Willet high sheriff of Westchester county for French
      neutrals' charges. Judges and assistant justices for Queens
      county commissioned [no names given].   166
May 4 The Indians Johannes Vangelden and son accused of having
      killed Adam Rypenberger (p. 166) to be released upon ad-
      vice of Lord Loudoun. Letter received from Sir Wm John-
      son, Oswegatchie Indians come to trade at Oneida lake.
      Vessels cleared: sloops Charming Nancy, John Philipson
      master, Oswego, John River master, Crown Point, Thos.
      Lawrence master, Anne, Wm Emory master; snows Jevon,
      Wm Heysham master, Lord Russel, James Hathorne mas-
      ter, Prince of Wales, Ralph Wildridge master, Robert and
      Anne, John Legget master; brigantines Swan, le Chevalier
      Deane master, Achilles, Robert Brown master, Countess of
      Coventry, Wm Denny master; ship Dreadnought, James
      McLaughlin master.   167
9   Letters received from Sec. Wm Pitt and Lord Loudoun re-
      specting the operations of the campaign. Militia under
      standing orders to march when occasion requires. Assem-
      bly adjourned.   168
14   Riot in the manor of Livingston; Robert Livingston called
      upon for proofs to act thereon.   170
23   Assembly adjourned.   170
June 2 Warrants for salaries, contingencies etc signed. Gov. Hardy
      receives orders to join the fleet of Rear Admiral Holburne
      at Halifax. Embargo to be taken off in seven days. Ad-
      dress of council to the governor on his departure; gov-
      ernor's answer. Seals etc delivered to the lieutenant gov-
      ernor.   171
3   The oaths administered to Lt. Gov. de Lancey after the read-
      ing of his commission.   173
8   French prisoners to be distributed in the counties. Procla-
      mation to issue for arresting rioters in Livingston manor
      (see *N. Y. col. mss*, 84:87). Letter received from Gov.
      Belcher (see *N. Y. col. mss*, 84:85). Fortifications to be
      completed. Warrants signed: to the commissaries and pay-

masters of the forces for tents etc; to commissioners of fortifications for expenses. The sloop Ranger, John Cox master, and the schooner Nancy, John Taylor master, to clear for Halifax with provisions on application of Joshua Auger naval contractor to Butler and Franklin of New York. The Catharine private sloop of war, Isaac Sears commander to cruise off Block island and east end of Long Island to intercept illegal traders from Rhode Island to Hispaniola.   174

11   Roger Blameless of Shawungunck and part of his family killed by Indians (see *N. Y. col. mss*, 84:84). Scouts to patrol the woods.   176

20   Assembly adjourned. Schooner King Fisher not allowed to sail with provisions to Boston on application of Sir Wm Pepperel. Papers from Massachusetts about the boundary troubles referred. Proclamation to issue for a day of fasting (see *N. Y. col. mss*, 84:105).   177

21   Embargo taken off. Guncarriages for 18 and 32 pounders to be made.   178

25   Order on memorial of Wm Walton (see *N. Y. col. mss*, 84:109-10); petition granted.   178

30   Proclamation to issue for the arrest of deserters (see *N. Y. col. mss*, 84:119-21). Order concerning the pay of troops. Refreshments to be sent to troops suffering from smallpox at German flats. Assembly adjourned.   179

July 9   Order received from the earl of Holdernesse to take off the embargo for vessels bound to England or Ireland with provisions. John Pownall sends an act of parliament forbidding exportation of provisions from the colonies except to England and Ireland; the act to be published in the New York gazette.   180

11   Order to confine French neutrals who managed to escape and reached Fort Edward. Letter from John Osborne and remonstrance of Timothy Woodbridge relating to Massachusetts boundary troubles referred. Royal order received with instructions for commanders of privateers; to be communicated to the admiralty judge and commanders.   182

16   Letter received from the earl of Holdernesse with extract from a letter of Vice Admiral Townsend to Mr Cleveland relating to piratical behavior of the privateer Peggy of New York, Rich'd Hadden commander and of a Halifax privateer commanded by Snooke against the Spanish ship La Virgin del Rosario y el Santo Christo de buen Viage, Don Philipp dy Vanes master; Hadden to be arrested and tried. Proclamation to issue publishing the above instructions for privateers.   183

1757   **v. 25**

22   Warrant to commissaries and paymasters of the forces for
      pay signed. French prisoners not yet to be sent off under
      flag of truce but to be distributed in the country.   184

30   Report of committee on Massachusetts boundary troubles
      (p. 177, 182). Assembly adjourned.   185

Aug. 4   Col. Parker and his force of 300 men defeated by the French.
         Gen. Webb will march to Fort Wm Henry. News to be
         sent to Gov. Belcher.   190

5   Lt. Gov. de Lancey intends to go to Albany and gives in-
      structions to the council. Council's advice as to adjourn-
      ments of the legislature.   191

6   Archibald Kennedy presiding. Capt. Christie writes that
      Fort Wm Henry is invested by the French (see *N. Y. col.
      mss*, 84:139). Queens and Westchester county militia or-
      dered to Albany (see *N. Y. col. mss*, 84:141). Further
      correspondence from Col. Hoffman of Dutchess, from
      Capt. G. Bartman aid to Gen. Webb (see *N. Y. col. mss*,
      84:138) on the investment of Fort Wm Henry by 11,000
      French. News sent to New Jersey and Pennsylvania.
      Warrants issued to the mayor, to Wm Coventry, Henry
      Cuyler jr, and Anthony ten Eyck for impressing pro-
      visions. Embargo laid on all vessels.   192

13   Order on the military storekeeper Stevens for powder and
      ordnance to the detachments going to Albany. French
      'neutrals to be confined under military guard.   193

14   Fort William Henry surrendered to the French and capitula-
      tion broken by them. Gen. Webb needs reinforcements.   194

15   Order on letter from Col. Hicks of Queens county (see
      N. Y. col. mss, 84:159). Colonel and sheriff of Kings
      county called before the council.   194

16   French prisoners transferred from New York jail to the care
      of Col. Richard Stillwell and Sheriff Maurice Lott of
      Kings county. Mr Stevens kings storekeeper, and Christ'r
      Blundell storekeeper at Fort George ordered to deliver
      John Brant pilot material for the Neversink beacon fortifi-
      cations.   195

17   Letter received from Col. Richard Floyd of Suffolk county
      (see *N. Y. col. mss*, 84:162). Order concerning intercourse
      between French neutrals and negro slaves.   196

18   Report of Jacob Goelet on proper places to mount cannon
      for the defence of New York city; Dominies Hook on the
      North river, Des Brosses battery and Albany pier on the
      East river recommended and so ordered. Embargo re-
      moved. Letter received from Lt. Gov. de Lancey, troops
      from Fort Wm Henry returned in distressing condition.

Militia of Suffolk and Queens counties to return to their
homes. French prisoners to be sent to Suffolk county by
water.   197

19   Christ'r Blundell ordered to deliver the key of the magazine
under the northwest bastion of Fort George to Francis
Stevens kings storekeeper. Council advise the lieutenant
governor to call the assembly to meet either on Long
Island or in Westchester county. List of ordnance etc referred to the commissioners of fortifications with order.   199

22   Lt. Gov. de Lancey returned. Assembly to meet at Harlem
in the outward.   200

26   Warrant issued to Lieut. Duncan to impress vessels for transporting the earl of Loudoun and his troops from Halifax
to New York (see *N. Y. col. mss*, 85:8).   200

30   Pilots ordered to look out at Sandy Hook for Lord Loudoun's transports. Order concerning applications to engage French prisoners as workmen.   201

Sep. 16   Letters received: from Sec. John Pownall with resolutions
of the assembly of Jamaica, to be printed in the New York
gazette; from the lords of trade calling for an account of
iron made in the colonies. Additional instructions concerning privateers received. Warrant to commissaries and
paymasters for pay of troops signed.   201

29   John Cruger reappointed mayor, John Roberts sheriff, John
Burnet coroner, of New York; Sybrant G. van Schaick
mayor, Abr'm Yates jr sheriff, of Albany. Assembly adjourned. Order on memorial of Lorenzo Ghiglino (see
N. Y. col. mss, 85:16-17).   202

Oct. 14   Enemy Indians invade Ulster county. Regular troops ordered to Shawungunck, Rochester and Goshen; militia to
join them. Letter received from Sir Wm Johnson (see
N. Y. col. mss, 85:24).   203

17   Royal order allowing the exportation of provisions from
New York to St Augustine (see *N. Y. col. mss*, 85:25).
Order on petition of Juan Matheo (see *N. Y. col. mss*,
85:27).   204

22   Indians have burnt the house of one Sax at Rochester and
killed some people according to reports from Col. Hasbrouck (see *N. Y. col. mss*, 85:24) and Cadw. Colden. John
Cruger mayor, and Leonard Lispenard alderman, committee of the corporation want to borrow money from the
treasurer for building barracks; granted (see *N. Y. col. mss*,
85:32). Warrants to Christ'r Bancker and John Dies for
expenses of building fortifications.   207

Nov. 1   Well to be sunk near the new barracks. Assembly adjourned. Warrant to issue for impressing boats for military transportation. Commission of oyer and terminer for Dutchess county issued upon petition of Jacob ten Boss and Matthew du Bois (see *N. Y. col. mss*, 85:38).   209

4   Letter received from Cadw. Colden with map of the western frontier and recommending a line of block houses to be erected from near van Keuren's house or the Platkill to the outlet of the Drowned Lands or from Capt. Broadhead's along the road to Minisink; agreed to and so ordered. Two companies of rangers and Capt. Michael Thody's company to continue in service in Ulster and Orange counties. Warrant to Oliver de Lancey, John Cruger and Beverly Robinson for pay of provincials signed. 209

7   Letter received from Gov. Pownall of Massachusetts, boundaries; opinion of council thereon.   210

15 Report of Cadw. Colden concerning blockhouses places for which are to be selected by Lt. Col. Clinton and Lieut. Ray. Assembly adjourned.   212

19 French and Indians reported to be moving towards German flats.   213

22 Warrants to impress sloops for military transportation to Albany to be issued.   213

Dec. 7 The Nightingale man-of-war, Capt. Campbell arrived from Halifax reported by Surgeon Richard Ayscough to have contagious disease on board; order thereon. Papers referring to the appointment of Robert Cholmondeley as surveyor and auditor general of the revenues in America (see *N. Y. col. mss*, 85:26) received.   213

12 Tunis Rivet dismissed as branch pilot. Warrants for salaries signed.   214

19 Memorial of James Jauncey (see *N. Y. col. mss*, 85:54) tabled. James Warner, Thos. Crookshanks, Daniel Goff, James Ward and Joseph Price appointed branch pilots upon certificates (see *N. Y. col. mss*, 85:50). Accounts referred to assembly: of Sir Charles Hardy and John Dies for repairs of house in Fort George; of Major Matthews for pay of his company; of Margaret Stelles for boarding French prisoners; of Col. Hasbrouck 1st Ulster county regiment, for services on the frontiers; of John van Rensselaer for express services.   215

21 Accounts referred to the assembly: of John de Peyster for military services; of Volkert P. Douw for firewood and candles to garrisons at Schenectady and in the Mohawk country.   216

small vessels with firewood, provisions etc. Accounts of
Robert Hodge and John Martin for work done in the fortifications referred to Bancker and Dies.   226

18   The embargo extended to all vessels above 25 tons. Order
in case of Juan Miranda claiming his freedom (p. 61, 121).   227

22   Impress warrants for provisions to be issued at the request
of Gen. Abercrombie (see *N. Y. col. mss*, 85:102).   228

29   Opinion of council on letter from Gov. Thomas Fitch of
Connecticut proposing that commissioners be appointed to
agree upon a plan of campaign; not thought necessary.   229

Ap. 14   Letter received from Sir Charles Hardy at Halifax, vessels
carrying provisions there to be free from impress, desertion to be discountenanced; proclamation to issue accordingly (see *N. Y. col. mss*, 85:108), also proclamation for a
day of fasting (see *N. Y. col. mss*, 85:107).   230

17   The brigantine Prince of Orange, David Dickson commander, ordered to quarantine off Bedloe's island on report
of Dr John Bard. Printed copies of the act " to prevent
bringing in and spreading infectious distempers " to be distributed among the branch pilots.   231

19   The privateer Oliver Cromwell, John Nicoll commander arrived with yellow fever on board (see *N. Y. col. mss*, 85:118)
ordered into quarantine.   231

22   Warrants to the commissaries and paymasters of the forces
for pay of troops signed. Mayor Cruger and Aldermen
Coventry and Lispenard appointed appraisers of arms to
be purchased by Gen. Abercrombie. Quarantine regulations.   232

24   Inquiry into the circumstances of Capt. Jasper Farmer's
death and subsequent trial ordered.   234

May 1   Council advise that warrants on the treasurer be issued to
captains for bounty and enlisting money.   234

3   Opinion of council on complaint of Gov. Fitch that New
York officers have enlisted men in Connecticut. Order on
memorial of Christ'r Kilby contractor for victualling the
forces asking for surveyors of provisions.   235

5   The Oliver Cromwell discharged from quarantine.   236

8   The Prince of Orange likewise (see *N. Y. col. mss*, 86:10).   236

17   Embargo taken off on receipt of a letter from Gen. Abercrombie. Warrant to impress bateaux men issued to Lt.
Col. John Bradstreet (see *N. Y. col. mss*, 86:12) at request
of general.   236

20   Permission to ship necessary provisions granted to Morduck
Evers master of a vessel from St Eustatia. Assembly refuse to make further provisions for French prisoners.   237

1758 v. 25

25 Order on memorial of Advocate General Wm Kempe concerning the claim of Don Philipp y Banes (see *N. Y. col. mss*, 86:15). 238

27 Letter received from Gen. Abercrombie, a sentry who killed Burger Hassen to be tried by courtmartial. 238

June 3 Report of committee on the above memorial of Advocate General Wm Kempe (see *N. Y. col. mss*, 86:19, 21); Richard Haddon's securities to be prosecuted in consequence. Permission to ship necessary provisions granted to Pier Neynis master of the Dutch sloop Catharine who will take French prisoners to Curaçao. The governor is advised to pass bills before him. 239

10 Warrants for salaries signed. Royal mandamus to swear John Watts of the council vice James Alexander deceased (see *N. Y. col. mss*, 85:55); he is sworn in and takes his seat. Timber to be provided for the batteries at the Narrows according to the plans of Chief Engineer James Montressor. Master and wardens of the port appointed. Permission to ship necessary provisions granted to Lewis Parbon master of the Spanish sloop St Joseph captured by the privateer George, Peter Haley commander and released after condemnation of cargo (see *N. Y. col. mss*, 86:29). 241

17 Order on petition of Jan Jansen Myndertz master of the brigantine Hoop (see *N. Y. col. mss*, 85:33); granted. Commission of flag of truce granted to James Jauncey (see *N. Y. col. mss*, 86:36). 242

23 Assembly adjourned (see *N. Y. col. mss*, 86:38). Allowance made for the expenses of the port master and wardens. Fees for the surveyors of vessels or damaged goods fixed. New order relating to provisions for the Hoop (p. 242). Enemy Indians kill people on the western frontiers. 243

28 Militia to do guard duty in Fort George. Ordnance stores lost in the late fire to be replaced. Barracks in Fort George to be repaired. 244

July 4 Royal mandamus to swear Wm Walton of the council vice Edw'd Holland deceased. He is sworn in and takes his seat. Juan Cenea and Juan Garcia owners of the Spanish sloop Nuestra Señora de Guadalupe, taken by the privateer General Johnson, Samuel Little commander, granted a passport and leave to take on board French prisoners as mariners and the necessary provisions (see *N. Y. col. mss*, 86:42-43). 245

6 Conference with Cherokee Indians going to join Sir Wm Johnson. 246

8 Answer of Gov. de Lancey to the speech of the Cherokees; presents given to them (see *N. Y. col. mss*. 86:45). 247

1758   v. 25

12   Letters received: from Capt. Cunningham aid to Gen. Aber-
      crombie, death of Lord Howe, 140 French prisoners sent
      to New York; from Capt. de Lancey, army is repulsed and
      cannons are being reimbarked; from Brig. Gen. Stanwix
      at Albany, reinforcements from the militia needed. Gov.
      de Lancey intends to go to Albany by land and gives in-
      structions to the council. Embargo laid on all vessels; the
      packet boats to do guard duty in the harbor. Details
      made from the militia of New York, Queens, Suffolk,
      Kings and Richmond counties to march to Albany. As-
      sembly adjourned. Warrant to Oliver de Lancey, John
      Cruger and Beverly Robinson for pay of troops signed.   248

14   Archibald Kennedy presiding. French prisoners in the jail
      at New York have broken out; orders sent out for their
      rearrest.   251

15   Gen. Abercrombie has retreated with his army to the south
      end of Lake George; orders for forwarding the militia
      countermanded. Embargo taken off.   251

17   Capt. Jeremiah Richards of the Massachusetts forces brings
      125 French prisoners, among them 7 officers. A French
      captain recommended by Col. Schuyler to Mr Waters al-
      lowed to remain in town on parole, the rest sent by water
      to Brookhaven, Suffolk county, to be placed there in
      charge of Sheriff George Muirson.   252

27   Gov. de Lancey returned. The sheriff of Orange county
      reports the capture of two escaped French prisoners; to
      be returned to New York and put in irons. Permission
      granted to a flag of truce bound for Hispaniola to ship
      provisions. Mr Smith to act as assistant kings council in
      the trial of the parties who killed Capt. Jasper Farmer.
      Daniel O'Briant appointed branch pilot (see *N. Y. col. mss*,
      86:54).   252

Aug. 9 Proclamation to issue for arresting deserters (see *N. Y. col.
      mss*, 86:59). Application of the governor and council of
      Fayal for permission to export provisions to that island
      and to Pico not granted. George Shell appointed branch
      pilot (see *N. Y. col. mss*, 86:57).   253

16   Order on petitions: of Samuel Wells (see *N. Y. col. mss*,
      86:63); of Jacob le Roy (see *N. Y. col. mss*, 86:61-62). As-
      sembly adjourned (see *N. Y. col. mss*, 86:64).   253

25   Indians have killed Samuel Webb on the high road between
      Goshen and Wallkill, burned the house of Isaac Cooley
      near Goshen, killed a woman and carried off 3 children.
      Detachments of Orange and Ulster county militia ordered
      out.   254

Sep. 4 Letter received from Gov. Denny of Pennsylvania, report by
        Mr Ceoghan, Sir Wm Johnson's deputy at Easton on in-
        tended treaty by the upper nations; Gov. de Lanceys
        presence desired; not possible. Orders on petition: of
        Michael Welgedaan master of the Dutch sloop Elizabeth
        (see *N. Y. col. mss,* 86:70); of Nicholas Gouverneur (see
        N. Y. col. mss, 86:71). John Roberts sheriff of New York
        to hand in a list of all French prisoners-of-war in the city. 255

9   Permission to sell part of the cargoes of the Betsey, Four
        Friends, and Harlem (p. 253) granted. Warrants for
        salaries and to Jacob Brewerton for expenses of French
        neutrals signed. Assembly adjourned.   256

27   Warrant to Christ'r Bancker and John Dies for expenses
        of the fortifications signed. Letters received: from Sec.
        Wm Pitt, case of Lorenzo Ghiglino (p. 202); from the
        governor of St. Domingo, cases of Manuel Zamora and
        Don Joseph de Inchauraga referred to the judge of the
        admiralty.   257

29   Mayor etc of New York and of Albany reappointed. Pro-
        portion of provisions allowed to the flag of truce of which
        Wm Browne is commander fixed.   258

Oct. 4 Commission for trial of pirates from the lords of trade re-
        ceived through Robert Charles provincial agent at Lon-
        don. Warrant to impress bread and flour for the forces
        issued upon a letter from Mr Leake commissary of stores
        at Albany to Mr Kilby, contractor, and from the latter to
        John Watts agent of the contractors, Jacob Remsen and
        John Abeel; John Cruger, Wm Coventry, Leonard Lis-
        penard, Joseph Read, Nath'l Marston, Joseph Haines,
        Andrew Barclay, Henry Cuyler jr and David Clarkson
        to fix the prices of the provisions to be impressed (see
        N. Y. col. mss, 86:80).   259

6   Gov. de Lancey going to Albany gives instructions to the
        council. Assembly adjourned. Warrant signed to Oliver
        de Lancey, John Cruger and Beverly Robinson, commis-
        saries and paymasters of the forces for pay. David Jones
        appointed fourth justice of the supreme court on petition of
        Cornelius Brewer, baker (see *N. Y. col. mss,* 86:84). Order
        on memorial of Philipp y Banes (see *N. Y. col. mss,* 86:85). 259

13   Archibald Kennedy presiding. Order upon letter from Gov.
        de Lancey at Albany transmitting Gen. Abercrombie's re-
        quest for more ordnance (see *N. Y. col. mss,* 86:87-88).   261

19   Gov. de Lancey returned. List of ordnance which Christ'r
        Blundell storekeeper at Fort George is ordered to deliver
        to Mr Furnis comptroller of the ordnance.   261

1758   v. 25

26   More ordnance to be delivered to Mr Furnis upon a letter
     from Gen. Stanwix. Letter received from Gov. Stephens
     of Rhode Island, complaint made by the governor of St
     Domingo, that one Shearman had robbed the church at
     Porto Plata, and given the things to Capt. Gregg of New
     York. Order on memorial of Joseph Benito Buseta
     Paterio (see *N. Y. col. mss*, 86:93-94); Capt. Caldwell and
     the Spanish interpreter Garret Noel ordered before the
     council.   262

27   Joseph Benito Buseta Paterio and Capt. Caldwell examined,
     and order of council in the case. Order on affidavit of
     Philipp y Banes (see *N. Y. col. mss*, 86:95).   263

Nov. 1   Memorial of Manuel Semora and Joseph Inchauraga, Spanish
     subjects complaining of the capture of the sloop Il Santo
     Christo, Francisco del Valle master, by the privateer Gold
     Finch of New York referred to the judge of the
     admiralty.   264

3   John Watts and Wm Walton appointed of the commission
     to cancel bills of credit (see *N. Y. col. mss*, 86:99). Chris-
     topher Miller examined in re Phi'ipp y Banes vs Capt.
     Richard Haddon of the privateer Peggy (see *N. Y. col. mss*,
     86:96-97, 100-3). Money etc taken by Haddon to be
     restored. Proclamation to issue for the arrest of Richard
     Haddon. Christ'r Miller's commission as captain of a
     privateer to be suspended, but he can not be tried for
     piracy.   265

16   Christ'r Miller's commission is returned to him on affidavits
     by Vincent Pearce Ashfield chiefmate and Thomas Lane
     gunner of the Peggy (see *N. Y. col. mss*, 86:106, 108).   267

18   A sloop from Antigua —— Milbury master ordered to quar-
     antine off Bedloe's island.   267

24   Petition of the inhabitants of Kingston to have their town
     fortified referred to the assembly. Nath'l Robinson,
     Richard Treat and Jabez Hamlin, prisoners in the Albany
     jail for participating in the riots in the manor of Living-
     ston to be admitted to bail.   268

Dec. 1   Opinion of council on letter from Lewis Morris commissary
     and judge of the admiralty in re Phil. y Banes.   269

6   Accounts referred to the assembly: of field officers of 2d
     Ulster county regiment; of Lieut. Sutherland for military
     services on the frontiers; of Samuel Gale and Tappen for
     victualling the same. Capt. Caldwell (p. 263) to be tried
     for piracy. Warrant to Theodorus van Wyck and Jan
     Winne for presents to, boarding and transporting Chero-
     kees signed.   269

1759   **v. 25**

Mar. 6   James Warner's commission as branch pilot suspended (see
          N. Y. col. mss, 86:166). Proclamation to issue notifying the
          encouragement given to volunteers (see *N. Y. col. mss*,
          86:168).   277

      14 Proclamation to issue upon request of Admiral Durell at
          Halifax offering a reward to seamen enlisting in his squad-
          ron (see *N. Y. col. mss*, 86:169). Warrants for salaries
          signed to Lawrence Roome, John Long and John Hill,
          land and tide waiters. Commission of flag of truce granted
          to Richard Jeffery (see *N. Y. col. mss*, 87:1).   277

      23 Royal mandamus to swear Josiah Martin of the council; he
          is sworn in and takes his seat. Assembly adjourned. Let-
          ter received from Sec. Pitt, operations of the campaign.   278

      30 Rear Admiral Saunders appointed naval commander-in-chief
          in North America. Mourning for the princess royal of
          England, princess dowager of Orange. Order on com-
          plaint by Surgeon Jacobus van Dyck (see *N. Y. col. mss*,
          87:6-7).   279

Ap.   6   Assembly adjourned. Daniel Brand, Hugh Moet and James
          Wilkie appointed branch pilots. Gov. de Lancey intends
          to go to Philadelphia with the general after appointing
          John Johnston colonel of the provincial regiment.   280

      14 Mistake in printing bills of credit rectified. Admiral
          Saunders wants St Lawrence river pilots and seamen.   281

      26 Warrants to issue for payment of bounties and enlisting
          money. Warrants to Oliver de Lancey etc for clothing
          etc and pay of troops signed.   282

May   1   Assembly adjourned (see *N. Y. col. mss*, 87:63). Richard
          Maeslyes confined in Dutchess county jail on suspicion of
          counterfeiting bills of credit pardoned on condition that
          he enlist. Warrants to Oliver de Lancey etc delivered on
          having entered into the required bonds.   282

      7   Charles W. Apthorp financial agent for the army writes of
          difficulties in procuring money for the kings troops. Pay-
          masters de Lancey, Cruger and Robinson asked to lend
          from funds for the provincials, and warrant on the treas-
          urer issued accordingly. Warrant for impressing ships
          carpenters issued.   283

      25 Assembly adjourned. Gun carriages in the fortifications to
          be repaired.   284

June 2   Persons taken with fever etc to be removed out of the city.   285

      14 Letter received from Gen. Amherst at Fort Edward,financial;
          assembly to be called to act on the general's propositions.   285

      21 Warrants for salaries and for expenses of blockhouses at
          Kingston, Ulster county signed.   287

1759   **v. 25**

29   Mayors, sheriff and coroners of New York and Albany reappointed; Jacob van Schaick appointed sheriff of Albany.   296

Oct. 11   Money loaned to Gen. Amherst repaid by Mr Mortier deputy paymaster general. Warrants signed: for salaries; to Thos. Hill land and tide waiter; to commissioners of fortifications. Order for the arrest of New Jersey people who ejected Philipp Swartwout (see *N. Y. col. mss*, 87:126-27).   296

16   Assembly to meet at the house of Teunis Somerendyck in
Edw. Willet's   the Outward [Harlem].   299
house

18   Assembly has passed resolutions to continue the New York
Ft George   provincials in the service and is adjourned.   299

Nov. 1   Assembly further adjourned. Warrant to Oliver de Lancey etc paymasters for bounty money advanced by them signed. Proclamation to issue for a day of thanksgiving (see *N. Y. col. mss*, 87:137).   300

6   Waddel Cunningham, Wm Kelly, Thos. Linck and Phil. Branson to be arrested for rioting and assaulting George Spencer.   300

20   Benjamin Blagge appointed manager of the excise on tea in New York city vice Abr'm Lynsen deceased.   301

Dec. 6   Governor's speech to be made to the council and assembly (see *N. Y. col. mss*, 87:144-45) read and approved.   301

24   Council advise the governor to pass the bills before him and adjourn the assembly.   302

1760

Jan. 3   Warrants for salaries etc signed. James Warner reappointed branch pilot.   302

24   Assembly adjourned (see *N. Y. col. mss*, 88:1).   303

Feb. 9   Assembly adjourned (see *N. Y. col. mss*, 88:5).   303

16   Gen. Amherst requires the same number of men for the ensuing campaign as in 1759. Assembly called to proceed to business (see *N. Y. col. mss*, 88:7).   304

21   Letter from Sec. Pitt relative to military operations.   304

25   Cherokees and other Indians at war with South Carolina; warrant to impress vessels for transportation of troops there issued to Major Gabriel Christie, deputy quartermaster general.   306

Mar. 11   Speaker of the assembly not present; the house to be adjourned from day to day. Warrants for salaries signed.   306

22   Council advise the passing of bills before the governor. Proclamation to issue encouraging volunteering. Joseph Sherwood, justice of the peace of Westchester county removed from his office (see *N. Y. col. mss*, 88:12).   307

31   Gov. Pownall of Massachusetts writes that a fire has destroyed part of Boston (see *N. Y. col. mss*, 88:95); assembly

to be asked for a grant to the sufferers, and collections to
be made. Thos. Brown, Wm Hibben and Andrew Wallace
appointed branch pilots.   308

Ap. 3   Proclamation offering a reward for the discovery of incendiaries to issue (see *N. Y. col. mss*, 88:16). John Owen
appointed branch pilot.   309

22   Assembly adjourned. Complaint made by Nath'l Marston,
Lawrence Kortright and others (see *N. Y. col. mss*,
88:21-22). Gov. de Lancey advised to write thereon to the
governor of Curaçao.   310

May 7   Warrants to issue for bounty and enlisting money to captains of the three provincial regiments who prove that their
companies are complete. Warrants to John Cruger,
Beverly Robinson and Peter v B. Livingston, commissaries
and paymasters for pay and clothing etc of the provincials.   311

17   Proclamation to issue calling in bills of credit (see *N. Y.
col. mss*, 88:96).   311

29   Message to the assembly to provide for a deficiency until
money granted by parliament arrives, read and approved.   312

June 10   Council advise the passing of bills before the governor and to
adjourn the assembly.   312

13   Warrants for salaries etc signed: Josiah Smith appointed
land and tide waiter vice John Smith, absent beyond the
sea.   313

28   Assembly adjourned (see *N. Y. col. mss*, 88:123). Proclamation to issue for the arrest of deserters (see *N. Y. col. mss*,
88:122).   313

July 18   The snow Hercules a flag of truce taken by the man-of-war
Enterprise, Capt. Innis commanding, and put in charge of
master's mate Arthur Nevin, to secure her from being em-
bezzled; on affidavits of Felix Dewit and Robert Frazier
men of the Enterprise, the case is referred to the court of
admiralty. Warrant to the paymasters and commissaries
for pay of troops signed.   314

21   Royal commission to Witham Marsh to be town clerk, clerk
of the peace, and of the common pleas, at Albany, also
secretary or agent of Indian affairs read, and he is sworn
in.   315

29   Order to Archibald Kennedy receiver general for the payment of the salary to the secretary of Indian affairs (see
N. Y. col. mss, 88:128). Assembly adjourned (see *N. Y. col.
mss*, 88:133).   315

30   Lt. Gov. de Lancey dead. Express messenger sent to
Cadw. Colden with the news as upon him as oldest councillor devolves the administration of government.   316

Aug. 4   Cadw. Colden is sworn in as president of the council and commander-in-chief; the seals are delivered to him and he takes the chair.proclamation notifying the death of Gov. de Lancey and continuing all officers in their places (see *N. Y. col. mss*, 88:137-38) signed. Commission to Sir Danvers Osborn delivered by John Watts and ordered filed.   316

11   Opinion of council on letter from Gen. Amherst relating to Capt. Brown in charge of army teams, and arrested for trespass at the suit of Eyda Vroman (see *N. Y. col. mss*, 88:140). Order on complaint of Capt. Wm McCleverty commanding the man-of-war Norwich (see *N. Y. col. mss*, 88:139).   318

14   Cornelius Hoornbeck and Levi Pawling write that about 100 Delawares, Tuscaroraes and other Indians had come to the house of Andries de Witt at Neponagh, Ulster county and by Thos. Nottingham Indian trader sent word, that they wanted to renew the treaty of peace. The matter is referred to the assemblymen, justices of the peace, and prominent inhabitants of Ulster county.   319

20   John Frodsham, 3d lieutenant of the Winchester man-of-war Capt. Hale commanding deposes that some of his men were killed by the crew of the Sampson of Bristol, Osborn Greatrakes commander; his deposition is corroborated by those of Hugh Mode, Christ'r Horsefell, Thomas Cunningham and Thos. Willson. Proclamation to issue for the arrest of the Sampson's crew (see *N. Y. col. mss*, 88:142).   320

21   Militia ordered to assist in the above ordered arrest.   321

28   Assembly adjourned (see *N. Y. col. mss*, 88:147). Account of John Martin for work done in the fort to be paid by Bancker and Dies, commissioners of fortifications. Thos. Purtell, Thos. Moffit and Matthew Murphy convicted of felony pardoned.   322

Sep. 4   Gen. Amherst writes that Fort Levi has been taken; proclamation to issue publishing this success (see *N. Y. col. mss*, 88:149). Warrant to paymasters and commissaries for pay of troops signed. Report of Corn's Hoornbeck et al on their negotiations with the Delawares etc (p. 319; see *N. Y. col. mss*, 88:145) received.   323

11-25   Assembly adjourned (see *N. Y. col. mss*, 88:150, 155).   324

29   Mayors, sheriffs and coroners of New York and of Albany reappointed. Schooner from New Providence, John Lewis master ordered to quarantine off Bedloes island.   325

Oct. 1   Proclamation to issue for a day of thanksgiving on the reduction of Montreal (see *N. Y. col. mss*, 88:158). Warrant to Christ'r Bancker and John Dies for the fortifications signed. Order for quartering French prisoners on Long Island. Order on petition of Osborn Greatrakes master, and Josiah Moores mate of the Sampson (see *N. Y. col. mss*, 88:157); not granted. 326

8 Orders on petitions of John Roussel a mulatto French prisoner of war for freedom, and of Joseph de Casta (see *N. Y. col. mss*, 88:159). 327

10 Above petition of Joseph de Casta, on report of Justice Chambers and reading of affidavits (see *N. Y. col. mss*, 88:160-64) dismissed. 328

15 Letter from Sec. Pitt in regard to illicit trade with the French settlements; legal measures to be taken. Warrant to the paymaster etc for pay of troops signed. Capt. Skinner's answer to the petition of John Roussel (see *N. Y. col. mss*, 89:2). 328

24 Warrant to impress vessels for transporting Col. Foster's troops to Halifax issued to Hugh Wallace (see *N. Y. col. mss*, 89:9). 330

29 Cotton arrived from New Providence to be unloaded and aired on Bedloes island. 331

Nov. 4 Opinion of the attorney general on petition of Osborn Greatrakes and Josiah Moores (p. 326; see *N. Y. col. mss*, 89:16); commission to issue for their trial. 331

5 Lewis Morris judge of the admiralty, John Chambers, Daniel Horsmanden, David Jones, justices of the supreme court, John Cruger mayor, Simon Johnson recorder of New York, Wm Smith and Robert R. Livingston appointed commissioners for the trial of Greatrakes and Moores (p. 331; see *N. Y. col. mss*, 89:17-18). 332

8 Council advise the president to pass the bills before him. Warrant to Johannes Lott for beaconpoles in Kings county signed. 333

15 Order for a reprieve of Thos. Pearson convicted of having murdered Mary Allen granted on representation of Justice Chambers (see *N. Y. col. mss*, 89:29). 333

21 Warrant issued to David Price agent for transports to impress vessels for transportations of troops to Perth Amboy (see *N. Y. col. mss*, 89:29). Complaint of Cornelius Joyce surgeon, Wm Young boatswain, Wm James, James Aberdeen and Barney Callaghan, seamen, of the privateer Little Bob against their captain, ——— Hansen for protecting illicit traders, referred to the attorney general. Warrants for salaries signed. 334

Dec. 3 Wm Mackey, John Callahan and John Philipse, seamen of the Sampson committed as accessories in the killing of

John Jackson, Edw'd Thurston, Thos. Scudmore and Peter Lyal of the Winchester (p. 320) to be discharged from jail, the grand jury having found "ignoramus", and to be turned over to Capt. Percival, commanding the Dover man-of-war. Warrants for salaries signed. Order for the arrest of John Henry Lydius. 335

8 Gen. Amherst sends letters to him from George Spencer and Augustus Bradley (see *N. Y. col. mss*, 89:31, 33); the writers to appear before the council. 338

9 Augustus Bradley examined and the depositions of John Stevenson, John Meuls, of Alderman Philipp Livingston, of Allen Popham taken (see *N. Y. col. mss*, 89:34-37). Mate ——— McCuddy of the Hunter, John Jauncey, John Chris, Elias Davis, Wm Murray, Alderman Bogart, David van Horne, ——— Carmer, seaman of the sloop Good Intent, and ——— Widgery master of the schooner Little Esther summoned before the council. 339

11 Only Wm Murray, Alderman Bogart and David van Horne found by the doorkeeper of the council, Christ'r Blundel. They are examined, also Cornelius Livingston and Gilbert Ash jr (see *N. Y. col. mss*, 89:39-43) and deposition of Wm Coventry (see *N. Y. col. mss*, 89:38) received. George Spencer to be brought before the council. 340

12 George Spencer examined (see *N. Y. col. mss*, 89:44). John Cox and James Wendell in the custody of the sheriff to be brought before the council, and Balthazar Kipp summoned. 340

[12] Balthazar Kipp, John Cox and James Wendell examined (see *N. Y. col. mss*, 89:45-47). The case referred to the council for report. 341

24 Royal mandamus to swear Oliver de Lancey of the council, dated Dec. 30, 1758; he is sworn in and takes his seat. Report on the examinations before council concerning illegal trade (see *N. Y. col. mss*, 89:54). 341

31 Assembly adjourned (see *N. Y. col. mss*, 89:56). 347

1761

Jan. 1 Letter from Sec. John Pownall announcing the death of King George II. The new king not to be proclaimed until the necessary papers have been received from England. 348

3 Gen. Amherst writes that he has received news of the king's death through his aid de camp, Capt. Prescott; wants New York to furnish men for the campaign. Opinion of council that a new assembly cannot be called until orders arrive concerning the seal. 349

10 The king proclaimed at Boston, but council advise to wait a few days longer. 350

1761   **v. 25**

May 1   Lists of the commissions of the peace and pleas for Dutchess
          and Richmond counties approved.   374

    20   Warrants to paymasters and commissaries for pay etc of
          troops signed.   375

    27   Warrant to Bancker and Dies, commissioners of fortifica-
          tions for expenditures signed.   375

June 10 Assembly adjourned (see *N. Y. col. mss*, 89:141). Warrants
          for salaries signed.   376

    17   Harmanus Schuyler appointed sheriff of Albany vice Jacob
          van Schaick deceased.   376

    22   Gen. Amherst requests that 173 men of the New York pro-
          vincials be retained in the service (see *N. Y. col. mss*,
          89:142). Assembly not to be called to consider it until
          after the harvest. Warrant to paymasters and commissaries
          for pay of troops signed.   377

July 8 Assembly adjourned (see *N. Y. col. mss*, 90:2). Order on
          petition of Wm Smith jr, Whitehead Hicks, John Moriss
          Scott and Wm Wickham for a new ordinance relating to
          fees in the different courts.   378

    15   Action on memorial of three judges of the supreme court
          concerning renewal of their commissions deferred.   378

Aug. 5 Assembly adjourned. Capt. Thomas Lawrence of the pri-
          vateer Tartar summoned before the council in re Toussaint
          a creole negro of Martinico.   379

     6   Gen. Amherst writes that Rineau a Frenchman, and Mrs
          Willet of New York ship provisions to the Mississippi;
          Mrs Jerome the French milliner in New York being the
          informer. Petition of Richard Nicholls landwaiter (see
          N. Y. col. mss, 90:5) referred.   380

     8   Cadwallader Colden appointed lieutenant governor and
          sworn in. Letter from John Pownall secretary of the board
          of trade relative to the case of John de Noyelles. King's
          order in council of Jan. 18, 1699-1700 read (see *N. Y. col.
          mss*, 89:89-91). De Noyelles summoned before the council. 382

    10   John de Noyelles states the petition sent by Sec. Pownall
          is a copy of his petition; proof of his allegations wanted;
          de Noyelles insolent.   385

    19   Brief to collect money for building a parsonage at New
          Rochelle granted on petition of James de Blez and others
          (see *N. Y. col. mss*, 90:10). John de Noyelles refuses to
          produce proofs of his allegations (see *N. Y. col. mss*, 90:6).
          Case referred to Messrs Horsmanden, Chambers and Smith.
          Account of John Martin for salary as gunner to be paid
          by Bancker and Dies. Toussaint declared a freeman and
          prisoner of war.   386

26   Gov. Boone of New Jersey writes that the Delaware Indians living near Ulster and Orange counties appear dissatisfied and that he has given orders to the militia of Sussex, Morris and Hunterdon counties, N. J. to repel any attack; further information required. Warrant to the paymasters and commissaries for pay of troops signed.   388

Sep. 1   ·Ulster and Orange counties militia ordered to send out parties for the protection of the inhabitants against the Indians upon receipt of letters from Col. Hardenbergh, Messrs Hasbrouck and Bruyn. Assembly prorogued (see *N. Y. col. mss*, 90:14).   389

9   Message to be sent to the assembly recommending an appropriation for a treaty with the Delawares; also the letter from Corn's Hoornbeck, Levi Pawling and Jacob Hoornbeck (see *N. Y. col. mss*, 90:12). Brief to collect money for building a church at Connajoharie granted upon petition of John Casper Lappius minister of the German congregation there, Wm Seeber and Adam Young (see *N. Y. col. mss*, 90:19). Messrs Bleecker have given the land for it. Warrants for salaries signed.   390

11   Reasons of the governor for not passing the bills providing that the judges of the supreme court should hold their commissions during good behavior, and for preventing disputes etc arising by the demise of the crown. Assembly adjourned. Warrant to paymasters and commissaries for pay of troops signed.   391

16   Cornelius Hoornbeck, Levi Pawling and Jacob Hoornbeck appointed to hold a meeting with the Delaware Indians although the assembly has made no appropriation. Johannes Hardenbergh and Thomas Ellison, colonels of Ulster county militia joined to them on advise of council.   392

23   Letter received from Sec. Pitt, King George III intends to marry Princess Charlotte of Meklenburgh Strelitz.   393

29   Mayor, sheriff and coroner of New York reappointed. Volkert P. Douw appointed mayor, Harmanus Schuyler sheriff, of Albany.   394

Oct. 7   The treasurer to advance money for the pay of the troops. Gen. Amherst wants orders issued for drafting the 173 men to be employed during the winter; orders sent to Col. Thodey at Oswego accordingly. Warrant to the paymasters and commissaries for the pay of the 173 men signed. List of commissions of the peace and pleas for Kings county approved. Ordinance " declaring the commencement and duration of terms of the supreme court and circuit courts " (see *N. Y. col. mss*, 90:26) passed.   394

14 Memorial of judges (p. 378) considered; the lieutenant governor has no directions for continuing them during good behavior; Chambers and Horsmanden will continue during pleasure. Warrant to run the line between Albany and Ulster counties issued to the surveyor general on petition of Johannes Evertse Wynkoop and Johannes Trumbor (see *N. Y. col. mss*, 90:27). 396

16 Report of committee on the petition etc of John de Noyelles (see *N. Y. col. mss*, 90:22). 397

19 Permission to unload granted to Manuel Britto of La Vera Cruz for his brigantine Esperance (see *N. Y. col. mss*, 90:28). 400

26 Copy of an order in council repealing a New York act passed in 1700 " for restraining and punishing pirates ". Gov. Robert Monckton publishes his commission and takes the oaths. Proclamation continuing officers in their places signed. 401

31 Gov. Robert Monckton presides. Assembly prorogued. Warrant to impress ship carpenters for refitting military transports issued. 405

Nov. 6 Gov. J. Bosveld of Curaçao complains against Capt. Hansen commanding a New York privateer; Capt. Hansen summoned before the council. Leave to refit and passport granted to John Leate master of the sloop Adventure (see *N. Y. col. mss*, 90:30). 405

11 Wm Walton takes the oaths as councillor. Capt. Hansen answers to the complaint against him (p. 405). Royal order granting leave of absence to Gov. Monckton. Benj. Pratt appointed chief justice during pleasure vice James de Lancey deceased. 406

13 Gov. Monckton about to embark delivers the seals to Lt. Gov. Colden. 407

18 Lt. Gov. Colden presides and is sworn in. Warrants to the paymasters and commissaries for pay of troops signed. Order to arrest and bring John Henry Lydius before the council. Order to the corporation and clerk of Albany to show cause why they do not admit Witham Marsh to the offices of town clerk etc (see *N. Y. col. mss*, 90:32). 408

24 Council advise the governor to recommend to the assembly the passage of a law against dilatory proceedings in the courts. 410

Dec. 5 Letters received: from Sec. Pitt, king's marriage and coronation, prayer for the royal family to be altered accordingly; from Lord Egremont, Pitt has retired from office and he (Egremont) has been appointed secretary of state for the southern department. 411

1761   **v. 25**

15   Proceedings against John Henry Lydius for contempt and
intrusion on crown lands; Lydius produces copies of Indian
deeds and grants from Gov. Shirley of Massachusetts for
the land from the north bounds of Saratoga patent to the
northern limits of the province.   412

16   Proceedings continued; Lydius discharged on giving bail to
stand trial in the supreme court. John Peterson Smith,
justice of the peace in Orange county dismissed from office
on various complaints (see *N. Y. col. mss,* 90:33-35). Min-
utes sent to the board of trade.   413

23   Letter from Sir Wm Johnson complaining of George Klock
referred.   414

1762

Jan. 8   Complaint of Capt. Thos. Burnet commanding the Rochester
man-of-war (see *N. Y. col. mss,* 90:58) referred to the master
and wardens of the port. Peter Parker appointed branch
pilot (see *N. Y. col. mss,* 90:59).   415

27   Royal instructions to Gov. Monckton received and the members of the council present sworn in; absent members to
be called to qualify. Warrants for salaries signed. Order
touching the complaint of Capt. Burnet (see *N. Y. col. mss,*
90:61) upon a report of the master and wardens of the port.
Answer of the corporation and clerk of Albany to the com-
plaint of Witham Marsh (see *N. Y. col. mss,* 90:64).   416

Feb. 10   Order of the king for the ensuing campaign received from
Lord Egremont. Assembly prorogued (see *N. Y. col. mss,*
90:76). King's pardon for Thomas Pearson (p. 333) received (see *N. Y. col. mss,* 90:75). Permission to sell part
of his cargo granted to Manuel de Britto (p. 400). Reprieve granted to Abr'm van Ornem sentenced to death
for burglary (see *N. Y. col. mss,* 90:73). Alexander Colden
appointed surveyor general, his father the lieutenant gov-
ernor resigning.   418

17   List of commissions of the peace and pleas for Ulster county
approved. George Klock to appear before the council on
complaint made and papers sent by Sir Wm Johnson. Additional instructions relating to the granting of lands;
proclamation to issue accordingly (see *N. Y. col. mss,*
90:77). Royal order to give judicial commissions only
" during pleasure " received. Hearing ordered on the division line between Albany and Ulster counties upon petition of Johannes Snyder jr on behalf of the corporation of
Kingston (see *N. Y. col. mss,* 90:72).   421

Mar. 2   King's requisition for 479 men to fill up the regular regiments received. Letter received from Gen. Amherst

promising extra bounty to recruits enlisting in these regiments. Speech to be made by the governor to council and assembly (see *N. Y. col. mss,* 90:84) read and approved. Warrant to paymasters and commissaries for pay of troops signed.   426

6   Depositions of Francis Gondall and Peter Alvarez against their captain, Manuel de Britto referred.   428

8   Complaint against M. de Britto dismissed (see *N. Y. col. mss,* 90:90-91). Warrants for salaries signed. Pilots James Ward, John Owen and James Wilkie fined for neglect of duty (p. 415-16). Hearing on memorial of the attorney general in the case of John Henry Lydius (see *N. Y. col. mss,* 90:92) deferred. Thomas Griffiths imprisoned as accomplice of John Anderson and Abr'm van Ornem pardoned on condition of leaving the province.   429

17   The attorney general ordered to file a second information against John Henry Lydius. Gen. Amherst sends a list of deserters from the provincials in garrison at Fort Ontario, referred. List of commissions of the peace and pleas for Albany county received.   431

24   Judges of the supreme court called upon to decide whether they will accept commissions "during pleasure."   432

26   Daniel Horsmanden appointed second justice of the supreme court "during pleasure" vice Chambers resigned on account of age.   433

31   David Jones accepts commission of third judge "during pleasure". Proclamation to issue against riots in Livingston manor (see *N. Y. col. mss,* 90:83) on letter of Robert Livingston (see *N. Y. col. mss,* 90:100). Proceedings against George Klock.   433

Ap. 1   Letter from Lord Egremont with the declaration of war against Spain (see *N. Y. col. mss,* 90:55); order for publishing it.   434

2   Ceremonies of publishing the declaration of war against Spain. Order on petition of George Klock (see *N. Y. col. mss,* 90:106).   439

7   Col. Josiah Martin present takes the oaths as member of the council. The attorney general ordered to prosecute George Klock by information for procuring Indian deeds by fraud and to take proper measures for restoring the lands to the Indians.   440

13   Assembly adjourned (see *N. Y. col. mss,* 90:109). Proclamation to issue for a day of fasting and prayer (see *N. Y. col. mss,* 90:113, 115).   442

15   Provisions to be impressed for the army at the request of Gen. Amherst (see *N. Y. col. mss,* 90:111); John Cruger,

Joseph Read, Nath'l Marston, Gabriel Ludlow and Andrew Barclay to be appraisers. Proclamation to issue against carrying provisions to the enemy or to neutral ports (see *N. Y. col. mss*, 90:112, 114). Warrants to commissaries and paymasters for pay of troops and to commissioners of fortifications for repairs signed.   442

19   Thomas Shrieve appointed coroner of New York vice John Burnet deceased. Recommendation to the assembly to grant additional enlisting bounty. Warrants to issue for bounty and enlisting money upon production of vouchers.   443

May 4   Message to be sent by the governor to the assembly (see *N. Y. col. mss*, 90:131) read and approved. Peter Dannely, George Sears and Wm Thomas, sentenced for grand larceny to be burned in the hand, pardoned on condition of enlisting for the war (see *N. Y. col. mss*, 90:130); Archelaus Lewis (see *N. Y. col. mss*, 90:132) pardoned on giving bonds.   444

6   The assembly will not grant additional bounties and is adjourned. Chief Justice Pratt granted leave to Boston.   445

12   Order not to clear vessels with provisions except for the public service. Albany commissions of the peace and pleas approved with additions. Leave of absence to the West Indies granted to Col. Josiah Martin member of the council.   445

20   John Lickens and Mary White convicted of robbery pardoned on condition that he enlist and she leave the province (see *N. Y. col. mss*, 90:130). Brief to solicit charity granted to Joseph Lewis of Huntington for losses by fire. Warrant to commissaries and paymasters for pay of troops signed.   446

22   John Dislow and David Miller pardoned on condition of enlisting. Warrant to commissaries and paymasters for pay of troops signed. Assembly adjourned.   447

June 2   Warrants for salaries signed. Charter for the French church at New Rochelle ordered to be engrossed and to pass the seals.   448

11   Assembly adjourned (see *N. Y. col. mss*, 91:5). Garret Cowenhoven justice of the peace in Kings county to appear before the council on complaint of Justice Horsmanden.   449

14   Gov. Monckton returned; seals and papers are delivered to him.   449

25   Royal mandamus to swear Wm Alexander " claiming to be earl of Stirling " of the council; he is sworn in and takes his seat. Warrants to the commissaries and paymasters for pay of troops signed.   450

28   John Fox informs that illegal trade is being carried on by the
schooner Charming Polly; offenders ordered to be arrested.   451

July 7   Sir Wm Johnson present takes the oaths as member of the
council. Bounty appropriated for recruiting to fill up the
regular regiments. Assembly prorogued (see *N. Y. col.
mss*, 91:31). Joseph Buckland appointed branch pilot,
Nathaniel Freeman convicted of burglary pardoned (see
N. Y. col. mss, 91:30).   452

21   Assembly prorogued (see *N. Y. col. mss*, 91:37). Letter received from Gen. Amherst, the pasture at Albany claimed
by the Dutch church; referred to the attorney general.   453

28   Daniel Nimham an Indian claims lands in Dutchess county
in possession of Col. Hendrick Philippse's heirs and of Mr
Brett; attorney general ordered to examine the case.   454

Aug. 10   Assembly prorogued (see *N. Y. col. mss*, 91:47-48). Warrants to commissaries and paymasters for pay of troops
signed.   455

25   Petition of Matthew Ernest for pardon of his negro boy convicted of roberry (see *N. Y. col. mss*, 91:46) granted. Muster roll of Capt. Timothy Northam's company (see *N. Y.
col. mss*, 91:49) received. Opinion of council as to their
bounty.   456

Sep. 1   Assembly prorogued (see *N. Y. col. mss*, 91:60).   457

8   Gen. Amherst wants 173 men to be continued in pay during
the winter; ordered accordingly (see *N. Y. col. mss*,
91:62-63).   457

15   Assembly prorogued (see *N. Y. col. mss*, 91:64). Order on
petition of Johannes Evertse Wynkoop and Johs. Trumbor
(see *N. Y. col. mss*, 91:66). Report of the attorney general
concerning George Klock's land transactions (p. 440) received.   458

29   Mayors, sheriffs and coroners of New York and of Albany
reappointed. Assembly prorogued (see *N. Y. col. mss*,
91:71). Commissions of the peace and pleas for Suffolk
county issued. Attorney general's report concerning the
pasture at Albany (p. 453) received. Warrants for salaries
signed. Order for hearing on the complaint of the Connajoharie Indians against Geo. Klock (p. 440).   459

Oct. 13   Assembly prorogued (see *N. Y. col. mss*, 91:86). Order on
petition of Johannes Snyder jr on behalf of the corporation
of Kingston (see *N. Y. col. mss*, 91:85). Warrant to commissaries and paymasters for pay of troops signed.   461

Nov. 3   Indian testimony in re George Klock to be taken before Sir
Wm Johnson and justices of Albany county. Warrant to
Christ'r Bancker and John Dies for expenditures on the
fortifications signed.   462

1762   **v. 25**

9   Assembly prorogued (see *N. Y. col. mss*, 91:92).   462

23   Message to be sent to the assembly recommending provision
     for running the line between Albany and Ulster counties.
     Memorial of Abr'm de Peyster, Ann de Lancey, Lewis
     Johnson and Matthew Clarkson concerning riots in west,
     middle and east patents of Westchester county with de-
     position of Jonathan Browne, Elisha Budd and Charles
     Clinton referred to the attorney general, and he is ordered
     to file an information against Charles Green, John Rundle
     and George Dibble and all others concerned in the riots.   463

Dec. 2 Petition of John Morin Scott and other owners of land along
     the New York and New Jersey line for settlement of the
     boundaries referred to the assembly.   463

3   Message to be sent to the assembly recommending that the
     billeting and impressing laws be revived.   464

4   Instructions for altering the prayers for the royal family
     received; proclamation to issue accordingly (see *N. Y. col.
     mss*, 91:80).   464

11   Council advise the governor to pass the bills before him and
     adjourn the assembly.   465

15   Hearing on the complaint of the Connajoharie Indians
     (p. 440, 458, 462) postponed. Warrants for salaries, and to
     commissaries and paymasters for pay of troops signed.   465

22   Order on memorial and petition of Oliver de Lancey and
     Lambert Moore owners of Shenondehowah alias Clifton
     park, Albany county, supported by affidavits of Volkert P.
     Douw, Jacob H. ten Eyck and Abr'm ten Brook, charging
     Anthony van Schaick and Jacob C. ten Eyck with obstruct-
     ing the legal partition of said lands. Proclamation to issue
     enforcing the law relating to the partition of lands (see
     N. Y. col. mss, 91:127). Minutes sent to the board of trade. 467

1763

Jan. 5 Above proclamation signed. Petition of Captain Timothy
     Northam (see *N. Y. col. mss*, 91:128-29) referred to the pay-
     masters.   468

12   Order on the report of the paymasters relating to Capt.
     Northam's petition; warrants to Capt. Timothy Northam
     for bounty and enlisting money, and to commissaries and
     paymasters for pay of troops signed. Declarations of the
     Connajoharie sachems taken before Sir Wm Johnson etc
     (p. 465) received and day for hearing of the case fixed.   469

19   Hearing of the parties claiming under the Connajoharie
     patent and consequent order in the case.   470

22   Royal proclamation declaring a cessation of hostilities with
     France and Spain; ordered reprinted and published (see
     N. Y. col. mss, 91:105-7).   471

1763   **v. 25**

24   Ceremonies of publishing the above proclamation in the
parade and at the city hall.   474

26–Feb. 16   Assembly adjourned (see *N. Y. col. mss*, 91:137, 142).   474–75

Mar. 2   Assembly adjourned (see *N. Y. col. mss*, 91:143). Warrants
for salaries signed.   475

16   Assembly adjourned (see *N. Y. col. mss*, 91:147). Daniel
Horsmanden appointed chief justice of the supreme court
vice Benjamin Pratt deceased, David Jones second justice,
Wm Smith third, and Robert R. Livingston fourth.   476

22   Proceedings relative to the claims of the Connajoharie Indians. Ordinance for altering the time of holding the
court of common pleas in Orange county passed.   477

Ap. 6   Assembly adjourned (see *N. Y. col. mss*, 91:153-54). Warrant
to Bancker and Dies for the fortifications signed.   479

20   Letter received from Sec. John Pownall with a petition of
Charles Scott and Henry Holding (see *N. Y. col. mss*,
91:155); referred. Assembly adjourned.   479

May 18   Assembly adjourned (see *N. Y. col. mss*, 91:161).   480

June 8   Assembly adjourned (see *N. Y. col. mss*, 92:8). New Jersey
act for submitting the boundary controversy to the king
received (see *N. Y. col. mss*, 92:3). Warrants for salaries
signed. Brief to collect money for building a presbyterian
church at Wallkill, Ulster county (see *N. Y. col. mss*, 92:5)
granted. Petition of George Tabele, Samuel Falkingham,
Andreas Luckam, George Wachtel, Godfried Lydeback and
Michael Kayser on behalf of the high Dutch Lutheran
church in the Swamp at New York, to compel John Philipp
Leydig and Joseph Hawser to give an accounting of
moneys collected for the church in Europe, referred to the
attorney general. Memorial of Frederick Philippse (see
N. Y. col. mss, 92:9) referred.   481

15   Report on the above petition of Charles Scott and Henry
Holding (see *N. Y. col. mss*, 92:10).   483

18   Gen. Amherst writes that on learning that the Indians are
moving to the west he has ordered the New York troops
to continue in the service; approved and provision for their
pay to be recommended to the assembly.   486

22   Assembly adjourned (see *N. Y. col. mss*, 92:12).   487

25   Petition of Gabriel Dufau commander of the French ship
America, and of Jean Baptist Rince commander of the ship
La Ville des Cayes (see *N. Y. col. mss*, 92:14) granted.
Gov. Monckton intends to go to England and delivers the
seals to the lieutenant governor.   487

July 13   Lt. Gov. Colden presides. Assembly prorogued (see *N. Y.
col. mss*, 92:16). Treasurer directed to advance money to
the commissioners of fortifications.   488

1763   **v. 25**

19   Royal proclamation of peace with France and Spain (see
     N. Y. col. mss, 91:148); to be published and proclamation
     for a day of thanksgiving to issue. Ceremony of proclaim-
     ing the peace.   489

Aug. 10 Assembly prorogued (see *N. Y. col. mss*, 92:26). Account of
     charges for repairing the French ship America (see *N. Y.
     col. mss*, 92:15) filed.   491

Sep. 14 Assembly prorogued (see *N. Y. col. mss*, 92:30). Treasurer
     to advance money for paying troops on the frontiers (see
     N. Y. col. mss, 92:29).   491

29   Mayors, sheriffs and coroners of New York and of Albany
     reappointed. Court of general sessions in Dutchess county
     ordered to be held three times in the year. Wm van Drill
     and Wm Cassell appointed branch pilots (see *N. Y. col. mss*,
     92:32, 41-42). Warrants for salaries signed.   492

Oct. 17 Gen. Amherst writes that Indians (Senecas and Delawares)
     are gathering at Kaghraandote to attack settlements at
     Shamokin, Esopus, Cherry valley and on the Mohawk
     river above Schenectady; orders to the militia sent out (see
     N. Y. col. mss, 92:39).   494

26   John Smith sentenced to death for felony not a proper object
     of mercy.   494

Nov. 2 Gen. Amherst requires 1400 men to be used against the In-
     dians (see *N. Y. col. mss*, 92:43); to be recommended to the
     assembly. Order relating to the Spanish sloop Holy
     Christ, Francis Valle commander belonging to Don
     Manuel Zamora of St Domingo and taken by a New York
     privateer.   495

8   Speech to be made by the lieutenant governor to the council
     and assembly (see *N. Y. col. mss*, 92:45) read and approved. 497

12   Warrant to issue for enlisting 200 men for service on the
     frontiers.   497

16   Tom a negro slave of Mrs Jane Haynes sentenced to death
     for rape on Mary Ryen reprieved for a week.   497

23   Account of John Martin for pay as gunner of Copsey battery
     to be paid by John Dies surviving commissioner of fortifi-
     cations. Inquiry to be made, who cut down a tree on
     Bergen common which served as a landmark for the pilots. 498

25   Warrant to John Dies surviving commissioner of fortifica-
     tions for expenditures. Executors of Christopher Bancker
     called upon for the accounts of public moneys received by
     the deceased.   498

Dec. 1 Royal proclamation declaring the limits of the new govern-
     ments (see *N. Y. col. mss*, 92:37) received; to be published. 499

2   Warrants to issue for enlisting men. Memorial of Waddel
     Cunningham (see *N. Y. col. mss*, 92:54) referred to the at-
     torney general.   500

1763   **v. 25**

16   Warrant to the commissaries and paymasters for the pay of
      troops signed. Proclamation to issue asserting the right
      of New York to the boundary of Connecticut river (see
      N. Y. col. mss, 92:60-61).   500

21   Report of the attorney general on the memorial of Waddel
      Cunningham (see *N. Y. col. mss*, 92:56) received; also re-
      port of the admiralty judge concerning the Spanish sloop
      Holy Christ (p. 495). List of commissions of the peace
      and pleas for Westchester county (see *N. Y. col. mss*, 92:59,
      62) approved. Petition of Isaac Man, Garret van Horne
      and Peter R. Livingston (see *N. Y. col. mss*, 92:55) read.
      Warrants to issue for payment of bounty and enlisting
      money.   501

28   Warrants for salaries signed. Proclamation asserting the
      territorial right of New York (p. 500) signed.   502

1764

Jan. 9   Order to stop a large number of Indians coming from near
          Lancaster, Pa. and going to the head of the Susquehannah
          river (see *N. Y. col. mss*, 92:67). Royal requisition to raise
          troops against the Indians received from the earl of
          Halifax.   503

20   John Griffith appointed master of the port, vice Richard
          Jefferies resigned, James Jauncey, Thos. Vardill, Sidney
          Breese, Daniel Stiles, Anthony van Dam and John Smith
          wardens (see *N. Y. col. mss*, 92:75). Order to remove pilots
          complained of by the master and wardens of the port (see
          N. Y. col. mss, 92:73). Ordinance to issue extending the
          session of the supreme court.   505

Feb. 2   Assembly adjourned (see *N. Y. col. mss*, 92:81). Nolli
          prosequi to be entered in the case of John Glen of Schenec-
          tady (see *N. Y. col. mss*, 92:68-70, 79-80). Commission to
          issue for a special court of oyer and terminer in New York
          county.   505

8   All the suspended branch pilots except Wm Hibbins sus-
          pected of cutting down the tree on Bergen common re-
          stored to their duty. New ordinance establishing fees in
          the court of chancery to be prepared. Inquiry to be made,
          who broke open the jail in Dutchess county and released
          some prisoners. Search to be made by the sheriff of
          Queens county for Joseph Cornwell and Richardson Corn-
          well accused of having shot Timothy McCarty at the house
          of Henry Sands at Cowneck. Order on the sheriff of Al-
          bany county to produce proof of the assault upon him by
          an officer of the 55th regiment.   506

15   Action on petition of Johannes Evertse Wynkoop and
          Johannes Trumbor (see *N. Y. col. mss*, 92:84) deferred. 508

1764   **v. 25**

22   Adam Lawrence sheriff of Queens county and Justice Kissam of Cowneck examined concerning Joseph and Richardson Cornwell; Dr Samuel Latham, Richard Sands, Wm Doty boatman, Obadiah de Milt, Henry Sands and Mary Shoe, all of Cowneck summoned before the council in the same matter (p. 506).   508

27   They appear and are examined; Henry Sands committed. Justice Kissam, Thos. Thorne coroner of Queens county and Wm Baker to appear before the council.   509

Mar. 5   Letter received from Sir Wm Johnson recommending that the Indians from Pennsylvania be sent to Albany by water; council advise not to admit them into the province. Letter received from Gen. Gage with resolutions of Massachusetts, New Hampshire and Connecticut concerning the raising of troops against the Indians; they decline doing so, and council advise it is not necessary to call the assembly. Assembly prorogued (see *N. Y. col. mss*, 92:90). Proclamation to issue for the arrest of Joseph and Richardson Cornwell (see *N. Y. col. mss*, 92:91). Opinion of council on the petition of J. E. Wynkoop and J. Trumbor (p. 508).   509

7   Proclamation for the arrest of J. and R. Cornwell signed. Warrants for salaries signed.   511

8   Memorial of New York merchants on the sugar act sent to the lords of trade.   512

21   Assembly prorogued (see *N. Y. col. mss*, 92:95). Order for the prosecution of intruders upon crown lands pretending title under New Hampshire, to wit Samuel Robinson of Benningtown, John Fray of Sharpsberrytown and John Wallis of Allingtown.   512

Ap. 4   Assembly prorogued (see *N. Y. col. mss*, 92:96).   513

18   Letter received from Gen. Gage (see *N. Y. col. mss*, 92:97). Speech to be made by the governor to the council and assembly (see *N. Y. col. mss*, 92:106) read and approved. Copy of a mandamus to swear Charles Ward Apthorpe of the council vice Benj. Pratt, received and referred.   513

19   Warrant to commissaries and paymasters for pay of troops signed.   514

May 2   Assembly prorogued (see *N. Y. col. mss*, 92:107). Reasons for swearing Charles W. Apthorpe of the council given by the committee, and of Wm Smith against it (see *N. Y. col. mss*, 92:109-10).   514

9   Reasons of the lieutenant governor for not swearing in Charles Ward Apthorpe. Warrants for payment of bounty and enlisting money to issue.   517

June 9   Royal mandamus to swear Joseph Read of the council, vice Josiah Martin removed to Antigua; he is sworn in and takes his seat. Assembly prorogued. Warrants for salaries signed.   518

July 10   Account of bills of credit issued since 1749 called for by the lords of trade and so ordered. Acts of parliament relating to America received. Opinion of council on the application of the marquis de Fenelon governor of Martinique, to allow Sieur Nadeau de Belair to take 150 French Acadians to the West Indies (see *N. Y. col. mss*, 92:120).   519

Aug. 7   Assembly prorogued. Additional instructions relating to fees in public offices; proclamation to issue accordingly (see *N. Y. col. mss*, 92:24). Warrants to commissaries and paymasters for pay of troops. Brief to collect charity granted to —— Haynes of Dutchess county whose house etc were destroyed by fire. Order on complaint of Peter Reune against Matthew du Bois, justice of the peace of Dutchess county (see *N. Y. col. mss*, 92:128). Petition of the German congregation in New York (see *N. Y. col. mss*, 92:126) tabled. Sheriff Harm. Schuyler reports that in obedience to orders he has arrested Samuel Ashley, Samuel Robison, John Monfort and Isaac Charles who have ousted Peter Vass and Bastian Deal from their farms under pretence of New Hampshire jurisdiction.   521

Sep. 4   Speech to be made by the governor to the council and assembly (see *N. Y. col. mss*, 92:136) read and approved. Peace made by Sir Wm Johnson with the Hurons, Ottawaes, Chippiwaghs, Sakis, Puans, Reynards, Menominies and all the western nations, except 300 under Pondiac on the Miamis river and the Potawatomees; Shawanese and Delawares of the Ohio, now up on the Sioto did not attend. Cannajoharie Indians complain of Cobus Maybe; he is ordered away from the Indian country. Gov. Wentworth asks for the release of people from New Hampshire; can only be discharged on bail (see *Doc. hist. N. Y.* 4:576-77; Q 4:356-57).   523

5   Freeholders of Southold, L. I. to restore Indian lands to their owners. Indian prisoners in New York jail to be removed to Long Island.   525

17   Governor's answer to an address of the assembly.   526

19   Letter from the lords of trade, New Hampshire boundaries, and Lutheran congregation; New Jersey boundaries; complaints of violence on Spanish subjects made, but not proved. Moses Owen justice of the peace of Westchester on trial for perjury discharged from his office.   527

Vol. 26, 1765—83

The minutes on land grants from Sep. 5, 1764 to Nov. 13, 1776 will be found in vol. 29-31.

1765

Jan. 8   Assembly prorogued (see *N. Y. col. mss*, 93:20). Letter received from Gov. Bernard of Mássachusetts on the boundary question.   1

11   Hearing on the complaint against Abr'm Herring (25:535) postponed.   1

30   Dennis Hall and Mary Yates sentenced to death for stealing pardoned (see *N. Y. col. mss*, 93:30).   2

Feb. 6   Petition of Roger Morris, Beverly Robinson and Philip Philippse (see *N. Y. col. mss*, 93:32) referred: Form of license and bond for Indian traders approved (see *N. Y. col. mss*, 93:31, 33). Petition of John Anderson owner of three small islands in the sound for relief against Justus, David and Wm Bush and John Gregg, who claim the islands under Connecticut title read; proposed to refer it to the king.   2

Mar. 6   Order on petition of Shadrack Chatterton (see *N. Y. col. mss*, 93:38). Warrants for salaries signed. Hearing on the claim made by Daniel Nimham, Jacobus Nimham, One Pound Poctone, Stephen Cowenham and other Wappingen Indians to lands granted to Adolph Philippse; opinion of council thereon. Report on the petition of Roger Morris et al (p. 2); Samuel Munroe, Daniel Monroe, Stephen Wilcox and Joseph Craw named in the report to be prosecuted; Justices Jacobus ten Boss and John Akin to show cause why they should not be dismissed from office. Charles Lewis appointed branch pilot.   4

13   Assembly prorogued (see *N. Y. col. mss.* 93:44). Letter received from Gov. Bernard of Massachusetts (see *N. Y. col. mss*, 93:39-40) and filed because Lt. Gov. Colden had already written to the governor of Porto Rico about it. Order on the petition of Corn's Blauvelt et al against Abr'm Herring (p. 1).   9

15   Sir Wm Johnson writes of the dissatisfaction among the Indians in regard to land transactions [Kayaderosseras patent]; the attorney general is ordered to bring a scire facias at common law against claimants under patent of Nov. 2, 1708 to Nanning Harmense et al (see *L. P.* 4:161-62). Date for hearing the complaint against Abr'm Herring (p. 9) fixed.   10

27   Resolve of Massachusetts relating to the boundary question received. On representation of Surveyor General Alex.

Colden that the Minisinck patentees have taken possession of crown lands, the attorney general is ordered to file information against them.   Hearing on the petition of Shadrack Chatterton (p. 4).   Wm Hibbin reappointed branch pilot (see *N. Y. col. mss*, 93:49).   11

29   Case of Shadrack Chatterton against Justices John Coe, John Parcells and John van der Voort decided in their favor.   13

Ap.   3   Committee appointed for the case of Corn's Blauvelt et al (p. 10) against Abr'm Herring.   13

10   Hearing in re Minisinck patentees (p. 11).   13

30   Opinion of council concerning a letter from Abr'm Lott and Christ'r Smith, managers of the hemp lottery (see *N. Y. col. mss*, 93:66).   14

May   8   Assembly prorogued (see *N. Y. col. mss*, 93:70-71).   14

July   8   Order from the king received to prosecute the persons who burned the boat of the sloop-of-war Chaleur, Lieut. Langharne commanding (see *N. Y. col. mss*, 93:46); also resolution of the house of lords concerning two Mohawk Indians taken to London and exhibited in a public show by a Jew named Myers (see *N. Y. col. mss*, 93:41).   Letter from Gov. Fitch of Connecticut in regard to the islands claimed by John Anderson (p. 2; see *N. Y. col. mss*, 93:73). Assembly prorogued (see *N. Y. col. mss*, 93:75).   Warrants for salaries signed.   14

Sep.   4   Gen. Gage offers military assistance for support of the civil power.   Full council needed for an answer.   James McEvers scared by the occurrences at Boston resigns his office as distributor of stamps.   16

5   Warrants for salaries signed.   Warrant to the managers of the New York and New Jersey boundary controversy for expenses (see *N. Y. col. mss*, 93:91) signed.   Tom a negro slave of Wm Pontine under sentence of death for burglary pardoned to deportation to Honduras (see *N. Y. col. mss*, 93:92).   17

7   Opinion of council on the letter of Gen. Gage (p. 16); military assistance not needed.   18

9   Opinion of the corporation to the same effect.   Assembly prorogued (see *N. Y. col. mss*, 93:92).   19

25   Godfrey Swan sentenced to death for killing his own child pardoned to imprisonment for life (see *N. Y. col. mss*, 93:94).   Warrant to Lt. Gov. Colden for contingent expenses signed.   Case of the sufferers by fire at Montreal referred to the assembly (see *N. Y. col. mss*, 93:74).   20

30   Mayors, sheriffs and coroners of New York and of Albany reappointed.   Joshua Sands justice of the peace in Ulster

1765   **v. 26**

county superseded on complaint of inhabitants (see *N. Y.*
col. mss, 93:93).   21

Oct. 9   Sir Henry Moore newly appointed governor writes that he
will soon leave England. Assembly prorogued. Petition
of Thos. Chandler, Isaac Man, David Wooster, Daniel
Jones and Robert Harpur (see *N. Y. col. mss,* 93:99) referred.   21

15   Petition of Thos. Chandler et al withdrawing their former
petition and asking for the establishment of one county
within the stated bounds referred.   22

22   Petition of Thomas Chandler et al giving reasons for the
establishment of a new county referred (see *N. Y. col. mss,*
93:110-11).   23

23   James McEvers desired to take charge of the stamps just
arrived refuses. Report of committee on the petition for
establishing a new county (see *N. Y. col. mss,* 93:112) read.
Patrick McKay, justice of the peace in Ulster county superseded on complaint of inhabitants (see *N. Y. col. mss,*
93:95).   23

24   Order in relation to the unloading of the stamps brought
in Capt. Wm Davis' ship.   24

29   Assembly prorogued (see *N. Y. col. mss,* 93:117-18).   24

31   Oath of the lieutenant governor required to be taken under
the stamp act.   25

Nov. 2   Riot in the city. Threatening letter sent to the lieutenant
governor in connection with the stamps. Fort George
to be put into condition for defense.   25

p. m.   The lieutenant governor having no directions for the distribution of the stamps, council advise him to declare he
would do nothing with them but await the arrival of Sir
Henry Moore.   26

5   Minutes of the common council of New York, asking for
custody of the stamps (see *N. Y. col. mss,* 93:123-24); council advise that the stamps be delivered to them.   27

6   Letter from Lt. Gov. Colden to Gen. Thos. Gage (see *N. Y.*
col. mss, 93:122); Gen. Gage's reply advising that the
stamps be turned over to the corporation. Letter from
the lieutenant governor to the mayor etc of New York.
Mayor's receipt for the stamps.   28

12   Assembly to be adjourned from day to day by the speaker
until a quorum is in town. Minutes sent to the board of
trade.   31

13   Sir Henry Moore arrived takes the oaths, and the seals are
delivered to him by the lieutenant governor. The members of council present are sworn in. The new governor's

1765   **v. 26**

commission to be recorded and proclamation to issue for
continuing all officers in their places (see *N. Y. col. mss,*
93:126-27). The new governor publishes his commission
in the fort and at the city hall.   31

15   The governor declares himself ready to put the stamp act
in execution; council are of opinion it is impracticable at
present. Stamped paper arrived in the ship Minerva to
be delivered to the mayor. Assembly to meet, and council
advise that the governor make no allusion to the late disturbances. Fort George to be placed in the same condi-
tion as before the disturbances.   33

18   Action on letter from the collector and the controller of
customs (see *N. Y. col. mss,* 93:129) deferred.   35

20   Order on petition of Roger Morris, Philipp Philippse and
Beverly Robinson (see *N. Y. col. mss,* 93:130).   35

29   Opinion of council concerning an act of parliament for providing quarters for the royal troops in America.   36

Dec. 2   Letter of Gen. Thos. Gage (see *N. Y. col. mss,* 93:141) to be
laid before the assembly. Proclamation to issue offering
a reward as ordered by a resolution of the assembly (see
N. Y. col. mss, 93:138).   37

18   Order upon an application of the mayor and magistrates
for a military guard (see *N. Y. col. mss,* 93:148).   38

1766

Jan. 10   Address of the governor to the council on receipt of letter
from Sec. H. S. Conway relating to the late disturbances.
Proclamation to issue offering a reward for discovery of
the persons who destroyed the stamped paper (see *N. Y.
col. mss,* 93:157). Magistrates to declare whether the peace
can be maintained by civil authority.   39

11   The mayor and magistrates are of opinion they can for the
future preserve the peace of the city; the people in general
disapprove the destruction of the stamps.   42

14   Opinion of council on the above letter from Sec. Conway.   43

Feb. 12   Letter received from Gov. Bernard, designs of the "sons
of liberty." The governor proposes applying for military
assistance, council advise to defer it.   45

Mar. 1   Assembly prorogued (see *N. Y. col. mss,* 93:165).   46

22   Assembly prorogued (see *N. Y. col. mss,* 94:2).   47

31   Gen. Gage present. Order on an application of the general
to procure a vessel for securing the king's stores.   47

Ap. 2   The ship Minerva,—Tillet master taken into the public service with consent of her owners.   48

19   Assembly prorogued (see *N. Y. col. mss,* 94:5-6).   48

30   Assembly prorogued. Proclamation to issue offering a reward for the arrest of rioters in Westchester county (see

N. Y. col. mss, 94:7) on an affidavit of Benj. Randolph of
Cortland manor.   48

May 17   Assembly prorogued (see *N. Y. col. mss*, 94:9). Justices
Pawling and Hardenbergh to answer a complaint against
them made by Rev. Gerhard Daniel Cock (see *N. Y. col.
mss*, 94:10).   49

28   Stamp act repealed. Assembly prorogued (see *N. Y. col. mss*,
94:11). Opinion of council concerning Gen. Gage's requisition of quarters for the royal troops coming from the
outposts.   50

30   Magistrates in the province to be urged to exert themselves
in the suppression of riots and disorders.   51

June 7   Order on complaint of Wm Provoost as attorney against
Surveyor General Alex'r Colden for taking fees for surveying lands to be granted to disbanded soldiers. Warrants
of arrest to issue against Silas Washburn, Wm Pendergrast,
James Secord, Elisha Cole, Isaac Perry and Michael Veal
for traitorous conspiracy etc on affidavits of Samuel Peters
justice of the peace in Dutchess county and Simeon Bundy. 52

9   Draft of the speech to be made by the governor to council
and assembly (see *N. Y. col. mss*, 94:13) read.   53

10   James Livingston sheriff of Dutchess county reports that
John Way arrested at the suit of Petrus ten Broeck for
debt has been rescued by a mob giving as reason that the
debt was for rent which they do not approve of.   53

12   Warrants for salaries signed.   53

18   Answer of the surveyor general (see *N. Y. col. mss*, 94:18) to
the complaint of Wm Provoost (p. 52).   54

19   Council advise to apply for military assistance to suppress
disorders in Dutchess county. Merchants refusing to take
out "let pass" for vessels outward bound the governor proposes to apply to the men-of-war in the harbor to stop all
vessels going to sea without the paper; council needs time
to give advice. Order on petition of Joshua Sands (see
N. Y. col. mss, 94:20).   54

20   The 28th regiment on the way from Albany to land at
Pokeepsing. Proclamation to issue offering a reward for
the arrest of rioters (see *N. Y. col. mss*, 94:21).   56

23   Opinion of the judges and of council concerning the taking
out of "let pass."   57

July 2   Sheriff James Livingston of Dutchess reports the landing at
Pokeepsing of the 28th regiment and dispersion of the
rioters (see *N. Y. col. mss*, 94:26). Proclamation of 20
June to be sent to neighboring governments. Troops to
proceed to Albany to assist the civil authorities. Courts of
oyer and terminer to sit in Albany and Dutchess counties. 57

3   Council advise that the governor pass the bill for furnishing barracks with necessaries for the troops; the governor declares himself unable to pass the vendue and larceny bills unless a suspending clause be added. Assembly prorogued. Procamation to issue offering a reward for the arrest of Robert Noble of Claverack (see *N. Y. col. mss*, 94:29-30).   58

7   Reply to petition of inhabitants of Nobletown contradicting affidavits of Robert van Rensselaer and Sheriff Schuyler.   59

11   Ordinance for establishing a court of common pleas, and a court of general sessions in Cumberland county passed; commissions for the courts to issue. Nathan Stone the high sheriff of the new county to give bonds.   61

Sep. 3   Daniel Horsmanden presiding communicates a letter from the governor at Albany, that the mayor of New York wishes to resign; council defer recommending a new name.   61

4   Whitehead Hicks is recommended as new mayor of New York.   62

Oct. 4   Commission of Whitehead Hicks as mayor of New York, dated at Albany, Sep. 29, 1766.   62

13   Gov. Moore returned communicates a letter from Lord Shelburne, who has succeeded the duke of Richmond as secretary of state, about the act for providing necessaries to the troops. Assembly prorogued.   63

17   Warrants for salaries signed.   64

22   Complaint of Sir Wm Johnson against George Klock for purchasing lands from the Indians without license referred to the attorney general.   65

Nov. 6   Letter received from Lord Shelburne, violence and murders committed on Indians, settlements extended beyond limits prescribed. Speech to be made to council and assembly read (see *N. Y. col. mss*, 94:60). Assembly prorogued (see *N. Y. col. mss*, 94:58), the speaker not having arrived.   65

7   Lords of trade call for a report on manufactures set up and carried on since 1734 (see *Doc. hist. N. Y.* 1:732-33; Q 1:497).   66

19   Letter received from Gov. Carleton at Quebec, Justice Walker of Montreal assaulted on the street; referred to the commanding officer of the troops.   67

21   Papers relating to the assault on Justice Walker at Montreal to be sent to Gov. Franklin of New Jersey. Deborah wife of Wm Tongue, Elizabeth wife of John Dent, and Elizabeth Floyd capitally convicted are pardoned on representation of the chief justice and the other justices of the supreme court.   68

Dec. 17   Letter from Lord Shelburne, claim of Wappingen and Stockbridge Indians, referred.   69

1766   **v. 26**

18 Order on Jacobus ten Boss and John Akin (p. 4). Council
advise the passing of bills before the governor and prorogation of the assembly.   70

23 Report of committee on the letter of Lord Shelburne (p. 69).
Minutes sent to the board of trade.   71

1767

Jan. 3 Daniel Nimham sachem of the Wappingen Indians desires
a farther hearing on his claim against Ad. Philippse.   74

7 Hearing appointed on the claim of the Wappingen Indians
on a memorial of Daniel Nimham. Warrants for salaries
signed. Order for nolle prosequi granted on the petition
of Joseph Forman (see N. Y. col. mss, 94:78).   74

21 Order on petition of Ennis Graham for a nolle prosequi on
a provision bond. Brief to collect money for repairing
the church at Eastchester granted.   77

Feb. 4 John van Tassell, Elijah Tompkins, Samuel Field, John
Tompkins, David Paddock, Henry van Ambrugh, Johannes
Boyce, Peter Angevine, Richard Curry, Wm Hill, George
Curry, Jacobus ten Bush [Boss], James Dickinson, George
Hughson, James Phillips, Samuel Causten, Daniel Corn-
wall, Gilbert Bloomer, Joseph Merit, Nath'l Underhill,
John Depee, Wm. Ogden, Samuel Hozier, Nehemiah Hor-
ton and Joseph Travis called as witnesses for the Wappin-
gen Indians. Letter from the lords of trade, petition for
charter of the presbyterian church in New York; referred.   78

12 Memorial of Abr'm Lott, Isaac Low, Peter Remsen and
Nicholas Low for aid to recover debts from the French
referred to the attorney general. Justices ten Boss and
Akin given more time for their answer (p. 70).   79

17 Letter received from Lord Shelburne, New York and
Massachusetts boundary controversy; opinion of council
thereon. Order on petition of the ministers etc of the
presbyterian church in New York (see N. Y. col. mss,
94:84). Samuel Drake, Daniel Townsend, Capt. Crane
and Samuel Munroe summoned as witnesses for the Wappingen Indians.   80

Mar. 5 Hearing opened on the claim of the Wappingen Indians
represented by Mr Spaulding and Mr Marsh; Messers
Livingston, Scott and Duane, attorneys for Adolph
Philippse.   81

6-9 Case continued.   82-84

9 Assembly prorogued (see N. Y. col. mss, 94:91).   84

11 Judgment and opinion in the case.   85

20 Warrants for salaries signed. Proclamations to issue:
about Indian traders' passes and bonds; about prohibiting
purchases of Indian lands (see N. Y. col. mss, 94:92).   89

1767   **v. 26**

25   Gov. Bernard of Massachusetts writes that the general court
      has appointed Lt. Gov. Brattle and Capt. Sheafe bound-
      ary commissioners.   90

30   Gov. Bernard writes that the general court has prepared in-
      structions for the boundary commissioners.   91

Ap. 9 Assembly prorogued (see *N. Y. col. mss*, 94:98).   91

15   Report of committee on the petition of the minister and
      elders of the presbyterian church in New York (p. 80; see
      N. Y. col. mss, 94:93-94). Petition and remonstrance of
      river Indians [Mohkuhannuck tribe] (see *N. Y. col. mss*,
      94:100) referred to Sir Wm Johnson.   91

22   Order on letter from James Ross complaining that the sur-
      veyor general charges exorbitant fees for surveying land
      granted under royal proclamation of Oct. 7, 1763. Repre-
      sentation to be made to the home authorities for providing
      funds to defray charges of prosecution on the part of the
      crown.   94

May 5 Assembly prorogued (see *N. Y. col. mss*, 94:105).   95

13   Letter received from Lord Shelburne, pay of men under
      Col. Bradstreet in 1764; referred to the assembly.   95

27   Speech to be made by the governor to the council and as-
      sembly (see *N. Y. col. mss*, 94:108) read. John Anderson
      charged with murder and piracy on board the sloop
      Polly, Roeloff Durgue master to be examined and wit-
      nesses called.   96

28   Examination of John Anderson and witnesses [no details
      given].   96

June 3 Petition of Thos. Carrol, Richard Peters, Samuel Legget
      and John Haynes for the reward for apprehending Elisha
      Cole (p. 56) referred to the assembly.   97

6   Council advise the governor to pass the bills before him
      and to prorogue the assembly.   97

10   Opinion of council on the petitions to the king by the
      Society for propagation of the gospel, and by Samuel
      Robinson of Bennington and 1000 other grantees under
      New Hampshire.   97

22   Order to the mayor of New York for the quartering of
      troops expected to arrive. Warrants for salaries signed.   100

July 29 John Wentworth appointed governor of New Hampshire
      and surveyor general of the woods in America; proclama-
      tion to issue accordingly (see *N. Y. col. mss*, 94:114). Or-
      der for prosecuting George Klock by information etc.
      New York and Massachusetts boundary commissioners to
      meet at New Haven.   101

Aug. 6 Assembly prorogued (see *N. Y. col. mss*, 94:116).   102

1767   **v. 26**

14 William Johnson convicted of felony in stealing prayer books
out of St Pauls church, New York pardoned on condition
of leaving the province.   102

19 Order for hearing the complaint of Rev. Gerhard Daniel
Cock against Justices Levi Pawling and Johannes Hardenbergh (p. 49).   103

31 Assembly prorogued (see *N. Y. col. mss*, 94:118).   103

Sep. 16 Assembly prorogued (see *N. Y. col. mss*, 94:120). Warrants
for salaries signed.   104

Oct. 3 Acts of parliament received: 1, granting certain duties in the
British colonies etc; 2, prohibiting the governor from
passing acts until necessaries for the troops are provided
by the assembly. Assembly prorogued (see *N. Y. col. mss*,
94:123). Warrant for the use of a new great seal sent from
England.   104

7 Hearing of the case between Rev. G. D. Cock and Justices
Pawling and Hardenbergh; Mr Duane, counsel for Cock
produces Phil. Klum, Jacob Decker, Cornelius Muller,
Corn's Parser, Wm Elting, Johs. Kater, Edw'd Loonsbury
as witnesses, Rudolphus Ritzema interpreter; Mr Kempe
counsel for Pawling and Hardenbergh produces Abr'm
Haasbrouck, John Blanckjean, Benj. van Keuren and
Abr'm van Keuren as witnesses. Action on petition of
Rev. John Peter Tetard (see *N. Y. col. mss*, 94:125) de-
ferred.   106

8 Opinion of council in the case of Rev. G. D. Cock vs Justices Pawling and Harbenbergh.   107

Nov. 4 Royal mandamus to swear Wm Smith jr of the council vice
Wm Smith sr resigned; he is sworn in and takes his seat.
Frances Malone sentenced to death for stealing pardoned
on condition of leaving the province. Dutch consistory
of New York ordered to answer to the remonstrance of
Abel Hardenbrook et al (see *N. Y. col. mss*, 94:112, 117).   108

11 Royal mandamus to swear Henry Cruger sr of the council;
he is sworn in and takes his seat. Opinion of council on
the complaint of Abel Hardenbrook et al (p. 108).   109

16 Draft of the governor's speech to the council and assembly
(see *N. Y. col. mss*, 94:133-34) read. Catharine Crow
pardoned (see *N. Y. col. mss*, 94:129). Elizabeth Johnson
reprieved (see *N. Y. col. mss*, 94:135-36).   110

Dec. 21 Proclamation to issue for the discovery of the author of
certain seditious papers (see *N. Y. col. mss*, 95:5).   111

1768

Jan. 27 The king's order in council dismissing the petition of the
minister etc of the presbyterian church for a charter of
incorporation (see *Doc. hist. N. Y.* 3:306-7; Q 3:506-8).

1768   **v. 26**

The governor lays before the council his instruction on the
passing of private bills.   Warrants for salaries signed.   112

Feb. 6   Council advise the governor to pass the bill for vesting the
estate of the late treasurer, Abr'm de Peyster in trustees
to pay his debts as not a private act.   Warrant to John
de Peyster jr for military equipment signed.   Assembly
dissolved.   115

10   Commission of oyer and terminer for New York county to
issue 30 days before the commencement of the supreme
court terms.   Writs to issue for election of a new assembly.   Ordinance passed for erecting the county of Cumberland.   Order on petition of John Young and John
Storm (see *L. P.* 23:132).   Minutes sent to the board of
trade.   115

24   Warrant to Goldsbrow Banyar for express messenger's services signed.   117

Mar. 9   Warrants for salaries signed.   117

16   Assembly prorogued by " writ patent " under the great seal.   118

18   Letters patent for erecting the county of Cumberland read
and approved.   " Writ patent " for proroguing the assembly signed.   118

22   Elizabeth Clark, alias Elizabeth Johnson pardoned on condition of leaving the province (p. 110).   119

26   Warrant to John de Peyster jr for military equipments
signed.   List of judges, justices of the peace, sheriff,
clerk, and coroner for Cumberland county approved.   119

Ap.   7   Ordinance passed for establishing inferior courts in Cumberland county.   119

23   Ordinance of fees for the court of chancery and other courts
(see *N. Y. col. mss*, 95:38) passed.   120

May   2   Warrants signed: to Isaac Colton for services in apprehending counterfeiters; to Alex'r Colden for express messenger services.   121

18   The governor intends going to Albany to meet the Indians
and settle the boundary line with them.   Assembly
prorogued.   Warrant to John de Peyster jr for military
equipments signed.   Ordinance of fees for the court of
chancery signed (p. 120).   Ordinance for prolonging the
term of the circuit court at Albany signed.   Letter from
Lord Hillsborough with report of the solicitor and attorney
general on the acts of parliament 12 Anne and 4 George I
for preserving ships and goods cast ashore.   121

June 29   Letter received from Lord Hillsborough with report of the
lords of trade on Indian affairs.   Warrants for salaries
signed.   125

1768   **v. 26**

July 13   Warrant to Henry Holland, Frederick Philippse, John Morin
           Scott, Wm Bayard and Benj. Kissam for expenses in
           running New York and New Jersey partition line signed.   126

Aug. 3   Proclamation to issue for the arrest of the persons who
           robbed the New Jersey treasurer's office (see *N. Y. col. mss*,
           95:46-48). Warrant to John de Peyster for military equip-
           ments signed.   126

29   Letter received from Gov. Carleton of Quebec, Indian trade;
           advice of council thereon. Warrant to issue on the
           treasurer to order of Att'y Gen. John Tabor Kempe for ex-
           penses in a lawsuit against John van Rensselaer. Assem-
           bly prorogued.   127

Sep. 9   Sir Wm Johnson to prevent the purchase by Pennsylvania
           of Indian lands north of the 43d degree. Warrant for
           salaries signed.   128

28   Proclamation to issue offering a reward for the discovery
           of the author of certain seditious papers (see *N. Y. col.
           mss*, 95:57).   129

Oct. 21   Letter from Lord Hillsborough with papers relating to the
           New York and Quebec boundary line (see *Doc. hist. N. Y.*
           1:550-51; Q 1:354-55). Another letter received from the
           same with directions for inducing the New York assembly
           not to take any notice of a circular sent out by the speaker
           of the Massachusetts assembly.   130

Nov. 2   Order on a memorial of John Tabor Kempe (see *N. Y. col.
           mss*, 95:65).   135

19   Proclamation to issue offering a reward for the discovery
           of rioters in the city. Benjamin Peirson appointed branch
           pilot. Account of John Munroe (*N. Y. col. mss*, 95:68-69)
           referred to judges of the supreme court.   136

Dec. 2   Report on the above account of John Munroe, and warrant
           to him issued.   137

5   Proceedings of the Indian conference at Fort Stanwix for
           settling the boundary line received, with a letter from Sir
           Wm Johnson; to be laid before the assembly. Letter re-
           ceived from Sir Wm Johnson, Indian trade. Order on
           a petition of Dirck Swart (see *N. Y. col. mss*, 95:66). 137

15   Special commission of oyer and terminer to issue for Albany
           county. Trial of Joseph Andrews confined for piracy put
           off.   138

23   List of judges and justices for the counties of Albany,
           Dutchess, Orange and Westchester (see *N. Y. col. mss*,
           95:79-83) laid before the council.   139

31   Affidavit of John Cantine and John Keator (see *N. Y. col.
           mss*, 95:70) read.   139

1769 v. 26

Jan. 2 Resolution of the assembly in regard to taxation. Assembly
dissolved (see *N. Y. col. mss,* 95:87). 140

4 Writs to issue for the election of a new assembly. Isaac
Stonehouse convicted of burglary in store of Benj. Booth
pardoned. 142

18 Warrants for salaries etc. signed. Francis James appointed
branch pilot. Examination of ———— in regard to counterfeiters. 143

20 James de Lancey refuses the appointment to the council vice
Wm Alexander resigned. Royal mandamus to swear
Hugh Wallace of the council vice Wm Walton deceased;
he is sworn in and takes his seat. 144

31 Assembly prorogued by "writ patent." Warrant to David
Gould as reward for discovering counterfeiters signed.
Richard Hudnett and Owen McFarlane convicted of burglary at Albany, and John Hamilton Stewart convicted of
grand larceny, all sentenced to death, pardoned on condition of their leaving the province (see *N. Y. col. mss,*
95:88). 145

Feb. 22 John de Peyster jr, barrack master ordered to deliver his accounts. Warrant to Goldsbrow Banyar for money ad-
vanced for express messengers signed. 146

Mar. 1 Order on receiving John de Peyster's accounts. Assembly
to meet. 146

8 Royal mandamus to swear Henry White of the council; he
is sworn in and takes his seat. Warrants for salaries etc
signed. 147

15 Warrant on the receiver general for payment of expenses out
of the quitrents to Wm Cockburn surveyor and shower for
the crown in the suit against John van Rensselaer. 148

29 Letter received from Gen. Gage respecting the appointment
of officers to superintend the Indian trade; Pennsylvania
to appoint for Fort Pitt and the Illinois, New York for
Niagara and D'Etroit, Quebec at Misilimakinak; to be laid
before the assembly. Ordinance to be prepared amending
the ordinance for establishing fees of courts. 149

Ap. 5 Preceding ordinance read and passed. 150

May 20 The governor declares he can not sign the bill for a new emission of bills of credit and asks whether he shall pass the
bills: 1, for regulating elections; 2, for regulating auction
sales. Council advise him to sign the last two and to prorogue the assembly. Public notice that a private act will
be introduced for a division line between Kakiate and
Cheesecock patents, and affidavit relating thereto by David
Pye. 150

26   Commissions of the peace and of the pleas to issue for West-
     chester (see *N. Y. col. mss*, 95:115), Orange and Albany
     counties.   151

June 14   Warrants for salaries and to Gerard Bancker for necessaries
          to the troops signed.   152

July 5   Assembly prorogued (see *N. Y. col. mss*, 95:119).   153

12   Payment demanded for quarters of officers for whom there
     is no room in the barracks; referred to the assembly. John
     Smith appointed one of the justices of the quorum for
     Westchester county.   153

18   Letters received from the earl of Hillsborough, Indian
     lands ceded by the last treaty; proceedings in parliament
     concerning America.   153

Aug. 16   John Hennesy convicted of robbery and sacrilege pardoned
          and to be conveyed to Philadelphia as a lunatic. John
          Jubeart sentenced to death for counterfeiting reprieved. 155

22   Letter received from Sir Wm Johnson, necessity of appoint-
     ing officers for the Indian trade.   155

29   Assembly prorogued (see *N. Y. col. mss*, 95:126).   156

Sep. 12   Sir Henry Moore dead. The great seal delivered to Lt.
          Gov. Colden with Sir Henry's commission.   156

13   Lt. Gov. Colden takes the usual oaths. Proclamation an-
     nouncing the death of Gov. Moore and continuing all offi-
     cers in their posts (see *N. Y. col. mss*, 95:128) issued. Ad-
     ditional instruction read against lotteries. Gov. Moore's
     general instructions delivered to Lt. Gov. Colden by Mr
     Livingston, Gov. Moore's private secretary.   156

29   Municipal officers of New York and of Albany reappointed.
     Warrant issued on the petition of the manager of the New
     York and New Jersey boundary controversy (see *N. Y. col.
     mss*, 95:136). Warrants signed: for salaries; to John de
     Peyster jr and Gerard Bancker for necessaries to the troops
     (see *N. Y. col. mss*, 95:133). Assembly prorogued (see
     N. Y. col. mss, 95:135). Order on the petition of Thomas
     Lasalle, and Jacques Hermand (see *N. Y. col. mss*,
     95:129-32). A new recorder for New York to be appointed
     vice Simon Johnson who neglects his duties.   158

Oct. 17   Order on petition of Lewis Pintard (see *N. Y. col. mss*,
          95:140-43).   161

20   Assembly prorogued (see *N. Y. col. mss*, 95:146). Warrants
     signed: to Lt. Gov. Colden for postage; to Joseph Yates
     and Dirck Swart for expenses as elisors on the trial
     against John van Rensselaer for intrusion on crown lands;
     to Jeremiah Hogeboom and Jacob van Valkenbourgh for
     boarding Capt. Campbell and Wm Cockburn surveyors in

the same trial. King's order in council forbidding grants
of land claimed by New Hampshire; opinion of council
thereon (see *Doc. hist. N. Y.* 4:609-11; Q 4:375-76). 162

Nov. 17 Speech to be made by the lieutenant governor to council and
assembly read and approved (see *N. Y. col. mss*, 96:25).
Commissions of the peace etc for Ulster county (see *N. Y.
col. mss*, 96:10-11) to issue. Thomas Jones appointed recorder of New York. 165

22 Special commission of oyer and terminer to issue for New
York city and county. 165

29 Warrant issued for expenses of managers of the New York
and New Jersey boundary controversy. 166

Dec. 12 George Duncan Ludlow appointed justice of the supreme
court vice Smith deceased. Commission to the puisne
judges to issue distinguishing their rank by the date of
their appointment. Proclamation to issue for the arrest
of rioters in Wallumschack patent (see *N. Y. col. mss*,
96:28) on petition of Abr'm ten Broeck. 167

20 Proclamation to issue offering a reward for the discovery
of the authors of seditious papers (see *N. Y. col. mss*,
96:31) at request of the assembly. Campbell sentenced to
death for felony reprieved. 168

1770

Jan. 5 Council advise the lieutenant governor to pass the bill for
emitting new bills of credit (see *N. Y. col. mss*, 96:37). 169

12 Agreement to be made for articles to be furnished to the
troops. Daniel Lawrence justice of the peace for Orange
county superseded at his own request. 170

17 Agreement concerning articles for the troops made between
Gen. Gage and the lieutenant governor. Warrant to
Gerard Bancker for providing them signed. 170

18 Order on petition of John Graham (see *N. Y. col. mss*,
96:38); granted. 171

27 Council advise passing the bill declaring judges of the supreme court ineligible to the assembly. John Akin, Henry
Ellis and James Atwater appointed justices of the peace
for Dutchess county. 171

31 Military commissions for Claverack to be recalled, the same
having been issued in blank and distributed by Col. John
van Rensselaer with a view to countenancing his claims
against actual occupants. Warrants for salaries signed. 172

Feb. 7 James Parker, Michael Lane, Anthony Carr, John Carr and
Edward Fitzrandel examined about a seditious paper,
signed " Son of liberty ". 174

14 John Ryan and Hannah Hyatt sentenced to death pardoned
on recommendation of judges of the supreme court. 174

1770   **v. 26**

28   Ordinance to be prepared for erecting the county of Gloucester. Whitehead Hicks, James Duane and Thos. Jones to be
assistants to the attorney general in the trial against Alex'r
McDougal for libel. The managers of the New York and
New Jersey boundary controversy want more money; their
accounts are called for.   175

Mar. 7   Ordinance establishing Gloucester county passed. Warrants
for salaries signed. Assembly prorogued (see *N. Y. col.
mss*, 96:57). Order on petition of Henry Holland and
John van Cortlandt masters in chancery (see *N. Y. col.
mss*, 96:56).   176

9   Whitehead Hicks, David Clarkson, George Folliot, Wm Mc
Adam and David van Horne to audit accounts of the New
York and New Jersey boundary managers. Commissions
to issue to the judges, justices, clerk and sheriff of Gloucester county. Letter received from Gov. Penn with Pennsylvania act for forming regulations of the Indian trade.   178

14   Letter received from Gov. John Wentworth of New Hampshire complaining of Justice Samuel Wells with affidavits
of Benj. Whiting, Benj. Wait and Amos Tute (see *N. Y.
col. mss*, 96:49-50); Samuel Wells called upon for an
answer. Roper Dawson convicted and burned in the hand
for manslaughter granted restitution of his forfeited goods.
James Parker printer of the libel for which Alex'r Mc
Dougal is being prosecuted pardoned.   179

21   Samuel Wells delivers his answer and is found not innocent
of Gov. Wentworth's charges. Warrant signed to Gerard
Bancker for necessaries furnished to the troops. List of
judges and justices for Albany county referred.   180

28   Commission of the peace and pleas for Albany county to
issue.   181

Ap. 11   Time appointed for a meeting of commissioners to make
regulations for the Indian trade.   181

18   Names of Jeremiah Hogeboom, Phil. Emburg and Abr'm
Cuyler added to the list of Albany justices.   182

20   Further order concerning the French ship L'Esperance,
Jacques Hermand master (p. 158, 161) on petition of Lewis
Pintard (see *N. Y. col. mss*, 96:72, 77).   182

28   Assembly prorogued (see *N. Y. col. mss*, 96:76).   183

May 2   Lewis Pintard allowed to make further sales for the benefit
of the French ship L'Esperance (p. 182). Warrant to
Michael Cummings as reward for discovering the publisher
of the "Son of liberty" paper signed. Commissions of
the peace and pleas for Queens county (see *N. Y. col. mss*,
96:78) to issue.   183

1770   v. 26

9   Commissions of the peace and pleas for Kings county (see
     N. Y. col. mss, 96:88) to issue. Warrant to be prepared to
     John de Noyelles and Wm Wickham for surveying the
     New York and New Jersey boundary line with the New
     Jersey surveyors (see *N. Y. col. mss*, 96:86-87).   184
16   Jacob Osburn and Thos. Clay sentenced to death for bur-
     glary pardoned on condition of leaving the province (see
     N. Y. col. mss, 96:83). Draft of warrant to de Noyelles
     and Wickham read and approved, Mr Smith dissenting.   186
[13] Order on petition of John Sebron commanding the snow
     Chaste Marie of Bordeaux (see *N. Y. col. mss*, 96:88-90).
     Warrant to Gerard Bancker for necessaries to the troops
     signed.   187

June 6   John Sebron allowed to sell part of his cargo for refitting
          his ship (see *N. Y. col. mss*, 96:91, 92, 97). Assembly pro-
          rogued (see *N. Y. col. mss*, 96:93). Warrants for salaries
          signed. Minutes sent to the board of trade.   187

July 3   John Sebron allowed to ship the rest of his cargo to France
          in the brigantine King George, John Finglass master, or
          any other English bottom (see *N. Y. col. mss*, 96:101).   189
     25   Assembly prorogued (see *N. Y. col. mss*, 96:106). Warrant
          signed: to Goldsbrow Banyar for entertaining Okayo-
          weess, captain of the Tawan Indians and his interpreter
          on the way to Sir Wm Johnson. The commissioners for
          regulating the Indian trade appointed by Virginia and New
          York meet and adjourn, no commissioners from the other
          colonies having come (see *N. Y. col. mss*, 96:111). Letter
          from Capt. John Brown charging Mr van Evra, Indian
          trader from Albany with fraud (see *N. Y. col. mss*, 96:96);
          referred to the assembly. Opinion of council on the report
          of the auditors of the New York and New Jersey boundary
          managers' accounts; warrant to the managers for their ex-
          penses signed. Complaint by magistrates of Cumberland
          county of riotous proceedings of Justices Nathan Stone
          and Israel Curtis, and of Joseph Wait et al of Windsor re-
          ferred to the judges of the supreme court.   190

Aug. 14   Royal order received concerning meetings of the commis-
          sioners to settle the New York and New Jersey line; also
          five acts of parliament relating to the colonies. Letter and
          memorial of Gov. Wentworth (p. 179) referred.   192

Sep. 3   Assembly prorogued (see *N. Y. col. mss*, 96:119). Warrants
          for salaries signed.   194
     29   Mayor, sheriff and coroner of New York reappointed; Abr'm
          C. Cuyler appointed mayor, Henry ten Eyck jr sheriff of
          Albany. Assembly prorogued (see *N. Y. col. mss*, 96:122).

Report of committee on the charges against Samuel Wells (see *N. Y. col. mss*, 96:121). 195

Oct. 19   John, earl of Dunmore has his commission as governor etc read, takes the oaths and swears in the council present. Form of the oath of a privy councillor: Proclamation to issue confirming all officers in their places (see *N. Y. col. mss*, 96:127). The new governor publishes his commission at the city hall. 197

31   John Watts, Oliver de Lancey, Roger Morris and Hugh Wallace sworn. Assembly prorogued (see *N. Y. col. mss*, 96:129). Order on complaint of Abr'm ten Broeck and other Wallumschack patentees, accompanied by affidavits of John R. Bleecker et al (see *N. Y. col. mss*, 96:124). Proclamation to issue for the arrest of Simeon Hatheway, Moses Scott, Jonathan Phisk [Fisk] and Silas Robinson. 199

Nov. 17   Two negroes belonging respectively to Anthony Shackerly and Robert Gibbs pardoned, one to leave the province, the other to be taken to the West Indies. Order on petition of Frederick Philippse relative to royal mines on his manor (see *N. Y. col. mss*, 96:134). 201

19   The sloop Susannah, John Kain master arrived from Port au Prince ordered into quarantine off Bedlows island. 202

27   The sloop Susannah released from quarantine on petition of Peter Mesier jr (see *N. Y. col. mss*, 96:137-38). [202]

30   Lord Hillsborough writes that the governor of Buenos Ayres reports the Spaniards have taken Fort Egmont on the Falklands islands; war with Spain may be expected, measures to be taken accordingly. [202]

Dec. 10   Speech to be made by the governor to council and assembly read. John van Alen of Claverack, John Wattson, Robert Lewis and Benj. Spencer appointed justices of the peace for Albany county by writ of association. 203

18   Order on memorial of Robert R. Livingston justice of the supreme court asking that the king's veto of the New York act declaring the justices ineligible to the assembly, be laid before that body; not considered necessary as it has been published by proclamation. Order for the trial of Silas Robinson (see *Doc. hist. N. Y.* 4:671-72; Q4:411-12). Sheriff Henry ten Eyck jr of Albany to be commended for arresting Robinson. 203

1771

Jan. 17   Lord Hillsborough's letter received, Indian trade, referred to the assembly. Robert Gibbs arrived with his vessel from Hispaniola, and the pilot who brought him up to the city summoned before the council. 204

22 Order on memorial of John Morin Scott (see *N. Y. col. mss,* 96:150). Order on complaint by inhabitants of Ulster county against Justice Wm Elsworth and John Dumont attorney at law (see *N. Y. col. mss,* 96:151-52). Richard Smith pardoned. Richard [Robert] Gibbs and the pilot examined and order to the master and wardens of the port thereon. 205

Feb. 8 Hugh White appointed justice of the peace for Albany county vice Robert Lewis superseded because he is a tavernkeeper. Fine imposed on Patrick Walsh for misdemeanor remitted. Provision to be made for running the line between New York and Quebec. 207

9 Complainants against Wm Elsworth and John du Mont to give bonds for costs. 208

16 Notification and proof in the case of a private act relative to the estate of Philipp van Cortlandt. Former regulations for the Indian trade called for by the assembly. Gen. Gage needs money to pay for quarters of the troops; referred to the assembly. Assembly to be adjourned for ten days. 208

25 Governor's message to the assembly recommending provisions to be made for quartering troops read. Notification and proof in the case of a private act for partition of the common lands in Schenectady township subscribed by John B. van Epps, Jacobus van Epps, Harmin Vadder, Henry Glen, John Taller, John Shomaker, Aberhem Truex, Myndert van Gysling, Tunis Putman, Balmus Vadder, Tieman Schermerhorn, John S. Vroman, Daniel de Graft, Wm Taller, Jacobus Taller, Jacob Schermerhorn, Reyier Schermerhorn, John Glen, P. v. B. Benthuysen, Tunis van Vleek, Clous de Graft, Phil. van Patten, Handrick Brower jr, John Cuyler jr, John Schermerhorn, Abr'm Schermerhorn, Peter Calment, Arant Vadder, Peter Mabee and John Littel. 210

Mar. 4 Letter received from Lord Hillsborough with orders to encourage volunteering for the new light companies voted by parliament. Assembly prorogued (see *N. Y. col. mss,* 97:28). Warrant to Gerard Bancker for necessaries to the troops signed. 212

11 Assembly prorogued (see *N. Y. col. mss,* 97:33). Orders on petitions of inhabitants of Cumberland county to have the county court house moved from Chester to the river towns; on petition of Daniel Parish (see *N. Y. col. mss,* 97:22). 214

18-Ap. 1 Assembly prorogued (see *N. Y. col. mss,* 97:34-35). 215–16

3 Hearing and opinion of council on the complaint against Wm Elsworth and John du Mont (p. 205, 208). Johannes

1771   **v. 26**

Sleght, justice of the peace for Ulster county reprimanded for soliciting causes before other justices. Warrants for salaries signed.   216

10   Warrants to Lt. Gov. Colden for salary in 1770 signed. James Gray and Alex'r Grant appointed justices of the peace for Albany county. Assembly prorogued (see *N. Y. col. mss*, 97:44).   218

15   Isaac Sears inspector of pot and pearl ashes resigns, and a new one is to be appointed. Additional quarters for the troops needed. Assembly prorogued (see *N. Y. col. mss*, 97:47).   219

17   Abraham de la Montagne appointed inspector of pot and pearl ashes vice Isaac Sears resigned.   220

22-May 1   Assembly prorogued (see *N. Y. col. mss*, 97:48, 50).   220

William Smith of Huntington appointed judge of the common pleas for Suffolk county vice Rich'd Floyd, deceased. Warrant to Gerard Bancker for necessaries to the troops signed.   220

29   Assembly prorogued (see *N. Y. col. mss*, 97:54). Warrants signed: to Gerard Bancker for necessaries to the troops; to Samuel Verplanck on account of Adolphus Benzel for surveying the Quebec line (see *N. Y. col. mss*, 97:55).   221

31   Mayor and magistrates of Albany complain that they are not included in the commission of oyer and terminer; commission to issue as usual.   222

June 7   Time for meeting of commissioners to regulate the Indian trade fixed.   222

14   An Indian, Jan, sold as Pawnee by another Indian to Jacobus van Epps, Abr'm Fonda and Abd'm P. van Antwerp but claiming to be a free Shawanese, asks the protection of government against George Wray; referred to Sir Wm Johnson.   223

19   Warrants for salaries signed.   224

July 3   Assembly prorogued (see *N. Y. col. mss*, 97:66). Order on a letter from John Munroe (see *N. Y. col. mss*, 97:59).   225

9   William Tryon has his commission read, takes the oaths and swears in the council. Proclamation to issue confirming all officers in their posts (see *N. Y. col. mss*, 97:67). The new governor publishes his commission at the city hall.   225

24   Warrants signed: to Alex'r Colden for postage; to Lord Dunmore for firewood and candles for the garrison. Jan the Indian (p. 223) declared a free man. James Hamilton president of Pennsylvania, and Wm Nelson, lieutenant governor of Virginia write that commissioners from their government will attend for the Indian trade meeting. Assem-

bly prorogued (see *N. Y. col. mss*, 97:69). Order on complaint against John Chandler clerk of Cumberland county, for ill behavior. Instructions to Gov. Tryon, council, passing of laws, presents to the governor, lotteries, appeals from lower courts, appointment of judge and justices, salaries, land grants, Massachusetts boundary, French grants on Lake Champlain, Indian lands, forfeitures and escheats, powers of president of council. 227

31 Form of oath administered to Goldsbrow Banyar as deputy clerk of the council. Letter received from Lord Hillsborough, grant to Col. Bradstreet; referred. 238

Aug. 7 Royal mandamus to swear Wm Axtell of the council vice Joseph Reade deceased, he is sworn in and takes his seat. Assembly not to be dissolved. 239

14 Proclamation to issue calling on owners of French grants on Lake Champlain to file their claims in the secretary's office (see *N. Y. col. mss*, 97:75; and, *Doc. hist. N. Y.* 1:554; Q 1:357). Report of committee on Lord Hillsborough's letter (p. 238). 240

21 Letter written to the commander-in-chief at Quebec concerning French grants on Lake Champlain read and approved. Order on letter from Adolphus Benzel concerning the survey of the New York and Quebec line (see *N. Y. col. mss*, 97:81). Order on complaint of Donald McIntyre and six others against one Cockren and 14 others who had ejected them from their lands near Argyletown (see *N. Y. col. mss*, 97:80). 244

28 Lt. Gov. Colden sworn in. Assembly prorogued (see *N. Y. col. mss*, 97:82). Warrant to Gerard Bancker for necessaries to the troops signed. Brief granted to Alex'r Campbell of Schenectady for collecting charity (see *N. Y. col. mss*, 97:87). Petition of Daniel Frisby master of the sloop Hawke captured by a Spanish guarda costa commanded by Lawrence Canel, referred to the governor of St Domingo (see *N. Y. col. mss*, 97:98). 245

Sep. 18 Order on complaint of Lewis du Bois against Henry Rosekrans jr sheriff of Dutchess county. Warrants for salaries signed. 246

23 Order on deposition of Catherine Simpson (see *N. Y. col. mss*, 97:92-93) charging Han Joost Herckheimer, Peter ten Broeck, Coenradt Frank and Hendrick Fry justices of the peace with maladministration. 247

30 Mayors, sheriffs and coroners of New York and of Albany reappointed. Assembly prorogued (see *N. Y. col. mss*, 97:97). Letter to the governor of St Domingo (p. 245)

read and approved. Warrant to issue for the arrest of Seth
Warner, Elnathan Huble, and Amos Mateson on a deposition taken before Justice John Munroe of Albany county
(see *Doc. hist. N. Y.* 4:729-31; Q 4:444-45).

Samuel Wells
judge of the common pleas in Cumberland county writes
upon an affidavit of Nath'l Howe that Whiting and Grout
had made an erroneous survey of Connecticut river (see
N. Y. col. mss, 97:90-91); letter to be written about it to
Gov. Wentworth.   248

Oct. 9 Hearing of the complaint against Sheriff Henry Rosekrans jr
of Dutchess county (p. 246); Andrew Bostwick, John Childs,
Nich'l Hoffman, Lewis du Bois, Thomas Duncan, David
Bostwick, George Freligh, Edmond Terry, Noah Coleman,
Barent Lewis, Alex'r Barr, Nath'l du Bois, Wm Mercer
and Jacob van den Bergh witnesses for complainant, Darby
Doyle for defendant.   249

     10 Hearing continued; Henry Webb, Henry van Cleck, Nath'l
Bancker, Joshua Carman, Ichabod Rogers, Henry Luddington, Daniel ter Boss and Thos. Wooley sworn for the
complainant, Wooley not examined.   250

     11 Hearing closed after examination of Isaac Ryckman jr and
Derick Brinkerhoff for the defendant; opinion of council
on the case; Sheriff Rosekrans to be prosecuted for packing the jury in the trial of Peter Harris and Thos. Wooley,
Lewis du Bois on an indictment found in the last general
sessions; Peter Harris to be superseded as justice of the
peace.   250

     15 Lt. Gov. Nelson of Virginia writes that the commissioners
appointed by the last assembly for regulating the Indian
trade will not attend the meeting; notice to be sent thereof
to the New York commissioners.   251

Nov. 5 Petition of the corporation of Albany for an explanatory
charter received and action deferred. Affidavits of Robert
Yates and others summoned as a sheriff's posse to assist
him in serving a writ of possession on James Brakenridge
of Wallumschack patent, complaining of armed resistance;
tabled. Assembly prorogued (see *N. Y. col. mss,* 97:127).   252

     13 William Davison sentenced to death for pocket picking par-
doned. Letter received from Lt. Gov. Cramahé of Quebec,
French grants on Lake Champlain. Letter to Gov. Hutchinson of Massachusetts, boundary line troubles. Warrant to
Gerard Bancker for necessaries to the troops signed. Barrack master Gerard Bancker to repair the barracks. Letter
received from Gov. Benning Wentworth of New Hampshire in answer to letter (p. 248; see *Doc. hist. N. Y.*
4:748-49; Q4:455). Proclamation to issue accordingly.   254

1771 v. 26

27 Account of charges for surveying the New York and Quebec line settled and somebody to be appointed in Ad. Benzels place who will attend to his duties in person. Warrant to John Collins deputy surveyor general of Quebec for his charges. Letter received from Justice Alex'r McNaghten, of Albany county complaining of the riotous proceedings of Robert Cockran, Allen, Baker and Sevil, New Hampshire claimants in burning the houses of Charles Hutcheson and John Reid (see *N. Y. col. mss*, 97:133; and, *Doc. hist. N. Y.* 4:749-50; Q 4:456). Proclamation to issue for their arrest. 258

Dec. 2 Assembly prorogued (see *N. Y. col. mss*, 97:138). Letter received from Gov. Hutchinson of Massachusetts, boundary line (p. 254). 260

11 Gov. Penn of Pennsylvania writes that no commissioners from his province will attend the meeting to regulate the Indian trade. Proclamation as ordered (p. 258) signed (see *N. Y. col. mss*, 97:141). Justice John Munroe of Albany county writes that Robert Cockran and party have violently ejected John Todd and Robert Todd (see *N. Y. col. mss*, 97:129). 260

18 Letters and papers received from Lt. Gov. Cramahé of Quebec (see *N. Y. col. mss*, 97:119-22, 131-32; and, *Doc. hist. N. Y.* 1:554-56; Q 1:357-58). 262

31 List of papers referring to French claims on Lake Champlain (see *Doc. hist. N. Y.* 1:556-58; Q 1:358-59). Warrant to Gerard Bancker for necessaries to the troops signed. Petition of Dirck Brinckerhoff and Benj. Blagge (see *N. Y. col. mss*, 98:3) referred. List of fees charged in the governor's, secretary's, clerk of the councils and auditor's office for passing land grants called for. 263

1772

Jan. 6 Report of committee on the French claims to land on Lake Champlain; order of council thereon (see *Doc. hist. N. Y.* 1:567-72; Q 1:365-67). 266

22 Alexander Colden to run the New York and Quebec line either himself or by deputy. 271

29 Letter from Gov. J. Wentworth of New Hampshire with minute of New Hampshire council (see *N. Y. col. mss*, 98:39). Catherine Longworth 15 years old sentenced to death for felony pardoned. Messages to be sent to the assembly; 1, about necessaries for the troops; 2, Simon Metcalf's account against the province; 3, expenses for running New York and Quebec line. Instructions to the surveyor general concerning the New York and Quebec line read and approved. 271

1772   **v. 26**

Feb. 5   Table of fees on grants of land (see *N. Y. col. mss,* 98:44).
          Order on memorial of Andrew Elliot receiver general (see
          N. Y. col. mss, 98:53).   274

     19   Letter received from John Munroe (see *N. Y. col. mss,*
          98:42) tabled.   278

     26   Notification and proof in case of the private act allowing
          Zebulon and Robert Seaman to change their name to Will-
          iams.   278

     28   Warrant to Gerard Bancker for necessaries to the troops
          signed. Joseph Lord judge of the common pleas in Cum-
          berland county reports that a party of 70 to 80 men came
          across the river to the house of Jonas Moore at Putney and
          took property from it (see *N. Y. col. mss,* 98:25); he and
          Justices Thos. Chandler and Wm Willard are examining
          the case and are assisted by Justices Bellows and Olcott of
          New Hampshire (*N. Y. col. mss,* 98:60); order thereon.   279

Mar. 24   Council advise the governor to pass bills before him. Notifi-
          cations and proofs in cases of private acts: for ascertaining
          boundaries between New York city and Harlem (see *N. Y.
          col. mss,* 98:48); for selling undivided lands in Kakiate
          patent; for selling lands in Goshentown rights.   281

     26   Sheriff ten Eyck of Albany reports that Allen and Baker
          have escaped to New Hampshire (see *Doc. hist. N. Y.*
          4:770; Q 4:468). Gloucester county courts hitherto held in
          Kingsland to be held in Newsberry (see *N. Y. col. mss,*
          98:62, 83). Commissions of judges and justices in Glouces-
          ter county, in Cumberland county and in Albany county
          to issue (see *N. Y. col. mss,* 98:65-66).   284

Ap.   8   Report of committee on table of fees for land grants (see
          N. Y. col. mss, 98:82). Warrants for salaries signed: to
          Hugh Gaine public printer; to Gerard Bancker for neces-
          saries to the troops. Courts in Charlotte county to be held
          at the house of Patrick Smith near Fort Edward. New list
          of judges and justices for Cumberland read, approved and
          commissions to issue. Justices to be appointed for West-
          chester county including Duncan Campbell and Alex'r
          Grant.   285

     15   Princess dowager of Wales dead. Accounts received from
          Justice John Munroe of the temper of the rioters on the
          Hampshire grants.   288

     22   Prayer for the royal family to be altered by proclamation
          (see *N. Y. col. mss,* 98:89).   289

     29   Accounts of Gavin Lourie for repairing barracks and lodg-
          ing officers of the 26th regiment to be paid by Gerard
          Bancker the barrack master. Warrant to the same for

necessaries to the troops signed. Assembly prorogued (see *N. Y. col. mss*, 98:92). Proclamation to issue for the discovery of the thieves who stole wine out of the custom house (see *N. Y. col. mss*, 98:93). Commissions of judges and justices for Tryon county to issue when the courts there are established (see *N. Y. col. mss*, 98:94-95). Philipp Schuyler, Philipp Skene and Wm Duer to be judges of the common pleas in Charlotte county. Letter to be written to Justice John Munroe on the escape of Remember Baker. 290

May 2　Order on application for quarters and transportation for troops marching from Quebec to New York and vice versa. Warrant to Lt. Col. James Robinson for necessaries to the troops in 1770 signed. 292

9　Warrant to Jacob Walton and James Jauncey for repairing the fortifications signed. Opinion of the judges to be taken on the claim of Albany magistrates (p. 222, 252). Rensselaer Nicoll, Volkert P. Douw, Jacob C. ten Eyck, Daniel Campbell, John Duncan, Abr'm C. Cuyler, John K. ten Eyck, Peter Lansingh, Peter Sylvester, John van Rensselaer and Isaac Switts to be of the commission of oyer and terminer for Albany county. Hazard Wilcox of Bennington examined about the riots there; JamesBrakenridge, Jedediah Dewey and Stephen Faey leaders of the rioters called on for explanation. Ordinance to be prepared for establishing courts in Tryon county and appointing Johnstown as county town. 293

19　Letter received from Justice Munroe with letter from Eben'r Cole, the rioters have brought artillery from the fort at East Hoseck to Bennington; Remember Baker and party have maltreated Bliss Willoughby. Letter to the leaders care of Jed. Dewey read and approved. 294

26　Ebenezer Cole, Bliss Willoughby and Jonathan Wheate of Bennington to be examined. Assembly prorogued (see *N. Y. col. mss*, 98:107). Ordinance for establishing courts in Tryon county passed. 295

29　Opinion of council on letter from Thos. Sowers captain of engineers concerning the fortifications of New York city. Magistrates of Albany to appoint a barrackmaster. John Munroe, Eben'r Cole, Bliss Willoughby and Jonathan Wheate swear to their depositions. Dr Clarke of New Perth examined. All depositions with that of Lieut. Hugh Frazer referred. 296

June 3　Order on letter from Andrew Elliott and Lambert Moore (see *N. Y. col. mss*, 98:106). Letters received from Justice

Benj. Spencer of Albany county living at Durham with
deposition of Joseph Pringle that Bennington rioters
threaten to burn him out; from Major Philipp Skine that
Mr Fay and friends intend to wait upon the governor (see
Doc. hist. N. Y. 4:781-82; Q 4:475).   297

4   Commissions of judges and justices for Albany county to
issue. Account of John Faulkner for making council room
chairs to be paid out of the contingent fund.   299

9   Letters received: from sheriff of Albany with receipt of Mr
Dewey minister at Bennington for a letter (p. 294); from
Gov. Thomas Hutchinson of Massachusetts with act for appointing boundary commissioners: opinion of council on
the latter.   299

15   Opinion of judges on the Albany claim (p. 293) received
(see *N. Y. col. mss*, 98:108). Warrants for salaries etc
signed. Letter to Gov. Hutchinson in answer (see *N. Y.
col. mss*, 98:114) read and approved.   300

25   Proceedings of the supervisors of Cumberland county in re-
moving the county court house from Chester to Westminster after examination of Crean Brush county clerk approved. Assembly prorogued (see *N. Y. col. mss*, 98:119).
Major Phil. Skene writes that James Brakenridge and companions are afraid to go to New York. Action on memorial of Benj. Spencer, Jacob Marsh, Ebenezer Cole,
Bliss Willoughby and Jacob Pringle, asking for relief from
the Bennington rioters deferred (see *Doc. hist. N. Y.* 4:786;
Q 4:478). Order on information concerning a band of
counterfeiters at Pitsfield, Dutchess county.   302

27   Stephen Fay and his son Jonas delegates from the Bennington committee before the council.   305

29   Hearing of the preceding Fays, and of the above memorial-
ist [Spencer et al] continued. All papers referred.   306

July 1   Chief Justice Horsmanden authorized to bring James Bud
and Lemuel Gustine to trial for counterfeiting bills of
credit on a letter from Justice Metcalf Bowler of Rhode
Island. Draft of Thomas Valentine in favor of Robert
Jackson for New York and Quebec boundary line services
to be honored. Warrant to Gov. Tryon for same expenses. Report of committee on Bennington riots (see
Doc. hist. N. Y. 4:786-792; Q 4:478-81).   307

8   Frederick Tobias convicted of stealing a hog pardoned on
the report of Orange county judges that the verdict of the
jury was against the law (see *N. Y. col. mss*, 98:120-21).
Gov. Tryon intends to go to Albany. Assembly to be
prorogued.   312

29   Sir Wm Johnson, Messrs de Lancey and White present of
Johnson Hall   council. Sir Wm is sworn in. Speeches to be made by the
Tryon co.   governor to the upper and lower castles of the Mohawks
read and approved. Opinion of Sir Wm Johnson as to
lands referred to in the 51st article of Gov. Tryon's instructions. Letter from Thos. Valentine at Le Coles. The surveyors to complete the division line from Lake Champlain
to the St Lawrence river. Commission of oyer and terminer for Tryon county to issue to Chief Justice Horsmanden,
Sir Wm Johnson bart. David Jones, Robert R. Livingston,
George Duncan Ludlow, justices of the supreme court, to
Guy Johnson, Sir John Johnson knt. judges of the common
pleas and others [not named].   313

Aug. 21   Minutes of council held at Johnson hall read and approved.
Fort George   Minutes of the Indian conference to be filed. Capt. Hammond commanding the Arethusa man-of-war lays before
the council his instructions from Admiral Montagu. Order
concerning the proceedings and minutes of the New York
and New Jersey boundary commissioners. Peter Johnson
sentenced to death in Ulster county for felony pardoned
on condition of leaving the province within 48 hours.
Warrants signed: to Gerard Bancker for necessaries to the
troops; to Jacob Walton and James Jauncey for repairs of
the fortifications. John Terril appointed justice of the
peace for Dutchess county, John Griffiths for Charlotte
county. Letter received from Timothy Ruggles inspector
and surveyor of white pine trees, trees of the west side of
Connecticut river and map of the tract.   315

Sep. 8   Felix Meigs late of Connecticut and sentenced to death for
counterfeiting reprieved for 9 months on request of the
governor and lieutenant governor of Connecticut. Assembly prorogued (see N. Y. col. mss, 99:1). Warrants for
salaries signed. Letters received: from John Munroe,
Ebenezer Cole and Bliss Willoughby about Bennington
people; from inhabitants of Bennington explaining their
behavior; tabled (see Doc. hist. N. Y. 4:794-95; Q 4:483).   316

29   Opinion of council on the preceding letters and on the petition from Massachusetts and New Hampshire to the king
for an alteration in the jurisdiction of New York (see Doc.
hist. N. Y. 4:795-96; Q 4:483-84). Opinion on the Massachusetts report concerning the boundary line. Mayors,
sheriffs and coroners of New York and of Albany reappointed. Petition of Peter Dory master of the sloop
Sally imprisoned for altering his clearance papers and asking for release referred to the attorney general (see N. Y.
col. mss, 99:2).   318

1772   **v. 26**

Oct. 5 Assembly prorogued (see *N. Y. col. mss*, 99:7). Draft of a
         clause proposed to be inserted in the commissions of all
         colonial governors relating to insane persons (see *N. Y.
         col. mss*, 99:8); referred to Justice Horsmanden. Memorial
         of Lt. Col. Reid in answer to suggestions made by the
         Bennington people to be sent to England.   321

     12 Benjamin Blagge appointed coroner of New York vice
         Thomas Shrieve, deceased. Report of Chief Justice Hors-
         manden on the clause (see *N. Y. col. mss*, 99:10). Report
         of the attorney general on the petition of Peter Dory
         (p. 318) filed (see *N. Y. col. mss*, 99:9). List of judges and
         justices for Suffolk county (see *N. Y. col. mss*, 98:134-36)
         read.   322

     21 Warrant to issue for the arrest of Remember Baker, Ara
         Allen and five others [not named] for assault on Dep.
         Surveyor Benj. Stevens, John Brandon and John Dunbar
         at Onion river (see *Doc. hist. N. Y.* 4:799-800; Q 4:485-86).
         Firewood allowed to the Royal artillery camping on Nassau
         island. Sir Wm Johnson writes that New England people
         are passing counterfeit Spanish dollars among the Indians.
         Assembly prorogued (see *N. Y. col. mss*, 99:19).   323

Nov. 11 James Brown a soldier indicted for receiving stolen goods
         and witnessing against Jacob Moses convicted of the same
         crime pardoned. Commission of the peace and pleas for
         Suffolk county to issue including the names of John Sloss
         Hobart and Phineas Fanning as assistant judges. Time set
         for hearing the complaint of Stephen Case against Egbert
         du Mont sheriff of Ulster county (see *N. Y. col. mss*, 99:17).
         Letters received: from Capt. James Gray; from Donald
         McIntosh, sawmill on Col. Reid's land at Otter creek;
         tabled.   325

     17 Special commission of oyer and terminer to issue for Al-
         bany county.   326

     25 Major Philipp Skene writes that Jehiel Hawley and James
         Brakenridge are appointed to go to London and ask for a
         confirmation of their grants under New Hampshire (see
         Doc. hist. N. Y. 4:802-3; Q 4:487-88); opinion of council
         thereon. Writ to issue for electing two representatives for
         Tryon county. Assembly prorogued (see *N. Y. col. mss*,
         99:32). Accounts of barrack masters Evert and Gerard
         Bancker filed (see *N. Y. col. mss*, 99:14).   326

     27 Capt. Hammond commanding the Arethusa writes of a
         pirate being on the coast.   328

Dec. 16 Complaint of Stephen Case against Egbert du Mont (p. 325)
         heard and dismissed. Proposal for the appointment of two

1772   **v. 26**

lawyers as judges of the inferior courts in the northern and
southern districts rejected. Order on letter from Thos.
Valentine, Quebec boundary line. John Collins surveyor
of Quebec writes on the same topic. Justice John Munroe
of Albany county reports that John Searles and Comfort
Carpenter arrested for counterfeiting have escaped while
being taken to Albany; their utensils etc to be sent there.   329

23   Writs to issue for the election of two representatives for
Cumberland county. Warrant to Abr'm van Gelder and
Benj. Quereau constables for expenses in fetching two

1773   counterfeiters from Rhode Island signed.   331

Jan. 4   Speech to be made by the governor at the opening of the
legislative session (see *N. Y. col. mss*, 99:52) read and ap-
proved. Warrants signed: to the governor to pay John
Jones for boarding Kiah Sutta a Seneca chief while at New
York; to Gerard Bancker for necessaries to the troops.
Barrack utensils unfit for service to be sold at auction.
Henry Bleeker appointed judge of the common pleas for
Albany county vice ———— van der Heyden deceased.   332

6   Account of Thos. Valentine for expenses in surveying the
Quebec line referred to the assembly. List of persons indicted at Albany for counterfeiting (see *N. Y. col. mss*,
99:47) laid before the council and petition of John Smith
(see *N. Y. col. mss*, 99:49) rejected. Copper plates and
counterfeit bills delivered to Richard Morris clerk of the
assizes.   333

27   William Hulbert, Joseph Bill, John Wall Lovely, Gilbert
Belcher and John Smith convicted of counterfeiting at Albany. Wm Hulbert pardoned (see *N. Y. col. mss*, 99:53-56).
New commission of oyer and terminer for Albany county
to issue; Wm Hulbert to give bonds for his appearance as
witness.   334

Feb. 2   John Thorpe convicted of wife murder reprieved (see *N. Y.
col. mss*, 99:63-66). Ordinance to issue declaring Skenes-
borough as the county town of Charlotte county (see *N. Y.
col. mss*, 99:69-73).   335

5   Abr'm ten Broeck appointed judge of the common pleas,
Dirck ten Broeck assistant, justice and justice of the peace,
and John Knickerbacker jr, justice of the peace for Albany county.   336

10   The case of Felix Meigs (p. 316) laid before the king referred back to the governor of New York. Gerard
Bancker to pay the account of Peter Sharp barrackmaster
at Albany. Order on letters from Sheriff ten Eyck and
Justice Adgate of Albany county (see *N. Y. col. mss*,

99:76, 79); letter to be written to Gov. Hutchinson about
it.   336

15   Letter written to Gov. Hutchinson read and approved (see
     N. Y. col. mss, 99:82). Message to be sent to the assembly
     recommending the passage of a law for securing the Mo-
     hawks in the possession of their lands.   338

17   Draft of the above message read and approved. Henry van
     Schaack justice of the peace of Albany county writes (see
     N. Y. col. mss, 99:80) that Sheriff Williams and Justice
     Ashley of Massachusetts have been summoned before the
     Massachusetts assembly; Gov. Hutchinson to be thanked. 339

Mar. 1   The government of Massachusetts ask that the sentence
          against the counterfeiters be not carried out; council are
          of opinion the law must take its course. Message to be
          sent to the assembly for increasing the grant for the troops.
          Accounts of the governor for postage, of James and Alex-
          ander Stewart for gunpowder, and of Peter Vessels for
          making aprons to the battery guns to be paid out of the
          contingent fund.   339

      9   Council advise the passing of bills before the governor and
          a prorogation of the assembly. Report of committee on
          letting the law take its course in the case of the convicted
          counterfeiters.   340

     17   Warrants signed: to Alex'r Colden for postage; to Christ'r
          Blundel for gunpowder and gun aprons. Order on pe-
          tition of Wm Partridge (see *N. Y. col. mss*, 99:89). George
          Townsend, John Rodman, Joseph French, Dow Ditmars
          jr, Nath'l Coles and John Hewlit jr, appointed justices of
          the peace for Queens county by commission of association.
          Lands surrendered by Major Philipp Skene in Skenes-
          borough to be appropriated to the support of a minister
          and other public uses.   347

Ap.   5   Letters received: from Gov. Hutchinson, Justice Wood-
          bridge's action against Albany constables (p. 336),
          boundary commissioners to meet at Hartford; from Lt.
          Gov. Cramahé, boundary matters. Andrew Mitchel ap-
          pointed justice of the peace for Albany county. Warrants
          for salaries signed [Thos. Moore one of the gaugers]. 349

     12   Special commission of oyer and terminer for Westchester
          county to issue for the trial of Zephaniah Hubbs, Abr'm
          Miller jr and Thos. Smith charged with counterfeiting.
          Felix Meigs (p. 336) pardoned. Time set for hearing the
          petition of Silas Charles (see *N. Y. col. mss*, 99:100) against
          the town of Easthampton. Warrant to Gerard Bancker
          for expenses in repairing barracks signed.   350

21 Letter received from Sir Wm Johnson, Indians complain that no regulations for their trade have been made. Complaint of Wm Partridge against Justice Ephraim Paine (p. 347) not sustained. Assembly prorogued (see *N. Y. col. mss*, 99:114). Accounts of Thos. Valentine for expenses in surveying Quebec line and of Theophilus Hardenbrook for repairs in Fort George, in the mansion house and on the battery received, filed and warrants for them signed. 352

28 Charles Oliver Bruff reports a " malignant distemper " prevailing in Talbot, Dorset and Queen Annes counties, Md.; order to the pilots accordingly. Elizabeth Hubbs writes to Abraham Hatfield justice of the peace of Westchester county, that her imprisoned husband will make confessions; he is promised a pardon (see *N. Y. col. mss*, 99:110, 113). Bench warrant to issue for the arrest of Sylvanus Brown, Charles Quishman and ―――― Raws or Ross for pulling down the house of Nathan Nicholls of Socialborough and burning his fences. John Blagge appointed coroner of New York vice Benj. Blagge resigned. 353

May 7 The barrackmaster to provide new bedding and other articles for the barracks. Warrants signed: to Robert R. Livingston for expenses at the Tryon county court of oyer and terminer; to Gerard Bancker for necessaries to the troops. Gov. Tryon intends going to Hartford to be present at the meeting of the New York and Massachusetts boundary commissioners. 355

26 Agreement between the New York and Massachusetts boundary commissioners. Order upon letter from Lt. Gov. Cramahé of Quebec asking that one Ramsey an Indian trader arrested at Albany be sent to Quebec, where his brother is to be tried for killing some Indians. Sheriffs of New York and of Albany to send in the census returns. John Burn sentenced to death for burglary to be executed. Noah Elting, Matthew Rea, Johannes Jansen jr and Adnan Wynkoop appointed additional justices and assistant justices; Phil. Swartwout, Matthew Cantine, Wm Pick, Johannes G. Hardenbergh and Benj. de Pue additional justices of the peace in Ulster county (see *N. Y. col. mss*, 99:124-25). Order on memorial of inhabitants of Kings district, Albany county (see *N. Y. col. mss*, 99:126). Draft of Thos. Valentine in favor of Robert Jackson for Quebec boundary line expenses, and expenses of Wm Crossing jr in coming from Rhode Island as witness against John Burn to be paid. 355

June 9 John Thorpe (p. 335) pardoned by the king. Moulds for

1773

counterfeiting Spanish dollars delivered and placed in the secretary's office. Proclamation to issue for the arrest of Francis Personel charged with the murder of Robert White (see *N. Y. col. mss*, 99:131). Assembly prorogued. Warrants for salaries signed [John Griffiths one of the gaugers]. 358

26 Wm Banyar sworn in as deputy clerk of the council pro tem. Commissions of the peace and pleas to issue for Charlotte county. Warrant to Gerard Bancker for necessaries to the troops signed. Order on letter from Lt. Gov. Cramahé stating upon Lieut. Hope's certificate that Thos. Valentine is too ill to finish the survey of the New York and Quebec line. Minutes sent to the board of trade. 360

July 7 Zephaniah Hubbs offers to disclose the names of the persons who helped prisoners to escape from Westchester county jail on condition of pardon (see *N. Y. col. mss*, 99:120); accepted. Assembly prorogued. 361

12 Gov. Tryon intends going to Quebec to expedite the survey of the New York and Quebec line. John Herbert carpenter, Francis Beaujoe cook, and Charles Surisco mariner, of the snow York, John Marshall master, charge John Lovel chief mate with cruelty to slaves shipped on the coast of Africa; order thereon (see *N. Y. col. mss*, 99:141). Wm Dobbs appointed branch pilot vice Wm Hibbins deceased. 361

Aug. 26 Royal mandamus to swear John Harris Cruger of the council; he is sworn in and takes his seat. Proceedings of the Quebec council, Hector Theo. Cramahé, lieutenant governor, Wm Hey chief justice, Hugh Finlay, Thos. Dunn, Colin Drummond, Francis Levesque, John Collins, Edw'd Harrison members and correspondence between Gov. Tryon and Lt. Gov. Cramahé on boundary matters (see *Doc. hist. N. Y.* 1:580; Q 1:372). Two negroes belonging to Claas Viele and Ryer Schermerhorn sentenced to death at Albany for burglary pardoned (see *N. Y. col. mss*, 99:140). Letter and map of Thos. Ruggles (see *N. Y. col. mss*, 99:156) filed. Gov. Hutchinson writes that Major Hawley Massachusetts commissioner and Mr Miller will attend the running of the line on behalf of his colony. 362

31 Lt. Col. John Reid late of the 42d or Royal Highland regiment, Henry Ertley, Godfried Brookman and Johannes Snouse report new outrages by Seth Warner, Remember Baker, —— Allen and others (see *Doc. hist. N. Y.* 4:843-44; Q 4:511); military to be called to assist the civil authorities. 369

1773   v. 26

Sep. 3   Gen. Haldimand refuses to send regular troops against the
         New Hampshire grants rioters, thinking militia ought to
         be called out. Warrants for salaries signed.   370

     8   Opinion of council on Gen. Haldimand's refusal (see *Doc.
         hist. N. Y.* 4:845-46; Q 4:512). Ordinance to issue for es-
         tablishing courts of common pleas and general sessions for
         Charlotte county to sit at the house of Patrick Smith near
         Fort Edwards (see *N. Y. col. mss,* 100:5).   371

    10   New commission of oyer and terminer to issue for West-
         chester county.   372

    20   Wm Nicoll to be commissioner, Gerard Bancker surveyor
         on behalf of New York, for running the Massachusetts
         line (p. 362). Letter received from Justice Munro (see
         N. Y. col. mss, 99:159) to be sent to London. Warrants
         signed: to Abr'm van Gelder and John Falkanhier con-
         stables for expenses of bringing Francis B. Personel from
         Rhode Island; to Gerard Bancker for necessaries to the
         troops.   373

    29   Assembly prorogued (see *N. Y. col. mss,* 100:15). Deposition
         of John Cameron (see *N. Y. col. mss,* 100:12) filed. Draft
         of commissions for Wm Nicoll and Gerard Bancker. read
         and approved. Gen. Haldimand will send 200 men to
         Crownpoint and Ticonderoga for the suppression of the
         rioters; declined as too late in the season (see *Doc. hist.
         N. Y.* 4:855; Q 4:517). Thomas Jones appointed justice of
         the supreme court vice David Jones resigned. Whitehead
         Hicks reappointed mayor, John Roberts sheriff of New
         York; Abr'm C. Cuyler mayor, Henry ten Eyck sheriff of
         Albany, Edward Blagge appointed coroner of New York.
         Minutes sent home.   374

Oct. 15 Letter received from Adolphus Benzel, Sachlan McIntosh
         and Thos. Sparham, justices of the peace in Charlotte
         county with affidavits of Jonathan Eckert and John Beder
         (see *N. Y. col. mss,* 100:10-11) to be transmitted to the
         secretary of state in London. Warrant to Gov. Tryon for
         money advanced for running the Quebec line signed.   375

Nov. 17 Report of Wm Nicoll and Gerard Bancker on the running
         of the Massachusetts line received (see *N. Y. col. mss,*
         100:32); copies to be sent to England and to Gov. Hutchin-
         son. Elizabeth Donnohough and Neptune a negro sen-
         tenced to death for felony pardoned (see *N. Y. col. mss,*
         100:38). Thomas Valentine called upon for his accounts
         in surveying the Quebec line. Warrants to Robert R.
         Livingston and George D. Ludlow for expenses at the
         Tryon county court signed. Assembly prorogued (see
         N. Y. col. mss, 100:37).   376

1773   **v. 26**

Dec. 1   Proceedings of John Collins surveyor for Quebec, and
           Claude Joseph Sauthier surveyor for New York, for run-
           ning the New York and Quebec line laid before the coun-
           cil. Order on memorial of Henry White, Abr'm Lott and
           Benjamin Booth (see *N. Y. col. mss*, 100:39). Depositions
           of Angus McBean and James Henderson (see *N. Y. col.
           mss*, 100:14) to be sent to England. Joseph Robertson to
           be justice of the peace for Westchester county, Alex'r
           Webster jr for Charlotte county and Barnet Stillwell for
           Albany county.   378

     15   Further proceedings of council in regard to the tea consigned
           to Henry White et al (p. 378); the tea to be stored in the
           fort barracks. Warrant to Gerard Bancker for necessaries
           to the troops signed. Petition of Simon Jenny and Solo-
           mon Johns of Durham, Charlotte county, for relief from
           the Bennington mob to be sent to England. Mr Duane of
           council for the New York patentees granted access to the
           papers relating to the riots.   380

     17   Meeting of citizens to be held at the city hall; mayor and
           recorder directed to attend; they report the people are
           averse to the landing of the tea.   382

     29   Letters received from Adolphus Benzel (see *N. Y. col. mss*,
           100:13) and from Justice Nathan Stone with deposition of
           Charles Button relating an assault on Justice Benj. Spen-
           cer by the Bennington mob, to be sent to England. Letter
           received from Lord Dartmouth, grants of land, case of
           Rachel Smith's legatees.   382

1774

Jan. 5   Account of a fire in the governor's house. Speech to be
           made to the council and assembly read and approved.
           Minutes sent home.   383

     11   Depositions of Justice Benj. Spencer, Justice Jacob Marsh,
           Benj. Hough, Nathan Rice and Anna wife of Charles But-
           ton (see *N. Y. col. mss*, 100:43-47) to be sent to England
           with a letter to Benj. Spencer, Amos Marsh and the people
           of Clarendon by Jehiel Hawley, Abel Hawley, David Cas-
           tle, Ethan Allen, Gideon Hawley and Reuben Hawley.   384

     12   Letter received from Gov. Hutchinson of Massachusetts,
           boundary matters (see *N. Y. col. mss*, 100:51).   385

     26   Journal of the New York and Massachusetts boundary com-
           missioners received and filed in the secretary's office. Plan
           of Mr Dean, Connecticut member of assembly for shorten-
           ing the post road between New York and Hartford to be
           laid before the assembly.   385

Feb. 8   Resolution of the assembly asking the governor to offer by
           proclamation a reward for the arrest of Ethan Allen, Seth

1774   **v. 26**

Warner, Remember Baker, Robert Cochran, Peleg Sunderland, Sylvanus Brown, James Brakenridge and John Smith
(see *N. Y. col. mss,* 100:66); proclamation to issue accord-
ingly.   386

18   Estimate of expenses of additional necessaries for the troops
referred to the barrackmaster (see *N. Y. col. mss,* 100:70-71).
Grant of deodand to the widow of Daniel Brown of Rye.
Account of Evert Bancker jr and Gerard Bancker provincial barrackmasters (see *N. Y. col. mss,* 100:91) filed.   387

Mar. 2   Additional articles to be allowed to the troops. Nicholas de
la Vergne justice of the common pleas and of the peace
in Dutchess county superseded for maladministration.   388

9   James Jauncey jr appointed master of the rolls; commission
for him to be prepared by the attorney general. Benj.
Hough, Thos. Green and John McNeil to be justices of
the peace for Charlotte county, Bliss Willoughby and
Ebenezer Cole for Albany county. Jonas Williams justice
of the peace in Suffolk county complained of a petition of
freeholders (see *N. Y. col. mss,* 100:81).   389

16   Hearing of the complaint against Justice Jonas Williams
represented by his brother Nathaniel. Commissions for
additional justices of the peace and pleas in Albany and
Suffolk counties (see *N. Y. col. mss,* 100:84-85) to issue.
Walter Livingston to be judge of the common pleas in
Albany county, George Robinson, Jonathan Paulding
Horton and Gabriel Purdy justices of the peace in Westchester county. Warrant to the governor for losses by the
fire signed. Warrant to issue to John Watts for postage
of Gov. Monckton in 1763.   390

19   Council advise the governor to pass a bill of shorter duration
than two years and to prorogue the assembly.   391

23   Petition of the elders and deacons of the German reformed
church in New York (see *N. Y. col. mss,* 100:83-93)
granted. Draft of commission for James Jauncey jr as
master of the rolls approved. John Haring appointed
judge of the common pleas in Ulster county (see *N. Y.
col. mss,* 100:28, 86-87). Warrants signed: to John Watts
for Gov. Monckton's postage; to Gerard Bancker. Petition of Benj. Hough and others of Charlotte county for
protection against the Bennington mob to be sent to Eng-
land.   392

31   Warrants signed: to Gerard Bancker for necessaries to the
troops; to Alex'r Colden for postage. Map of the province
by Claude Joseph Sauthier laid before the council and declared the most complete work of the kind.   393

Ap.   6   Warrants signed: for salaries; to Gov. Tryon for various ser-
          vices; to Justice Ludlow for his burned up library; to
          Richard Morris for services as clerk of the circuits; to
          Hugh Gaine printer for services. Edmund Fanning pro-
          vincial surrogate granted leave of absence. Gov. Tryon
          intends to go to England and delivers papers to Lt. Gov.
          Colden. Minutes sent home.   393

      7   Lt. Gov. Colden presides after having taken the usual oaths.
          Proclamation to issue confirming all officers in their
          places (see *N. Y. col. mss*, 100:97).   395

     13   Additional instructions for granting crown lands; letter from
          Lord Dartmouth on the same subject. Ordinance to issue
          for changing the terms of Dutchess county courts. War-
          rant to Joshua and Abijah Rood signed (see *N. Y. col. mss*,
          100:97-98).   396

     16   Thomas Vardill warden of the post resigns and resignation
          is accepted (see *N. Y. col. mss*, 100:96). Power of attorney
          from Sec. George Clarke appointing Samuel Bayard his
          deputy; he is sworn in.   401

     22   The lieutenant governor asks the council's opinion on the
          above additional instructions and letter; council want time.
          Letter received from Wm Duer at Harriottville recom-
          mending Garret Keating of Skeensborough for the office
          of justice of the peace in Charlotte county and Jonathan
          Jones for the same office in Albany county. Commissions
          to issue to them.   403

May   2   Order on petition of inhabitants of New York city (see *N. Y.
          col. mss*, 100:109). Ordinance for fixing the time of hold-
          ing courts in Dutchess county (see *N. Y. col. mss*, 100:110)
          passed.   403

      5   Petition of Silas Cooke of Southampton (see *N. Y. col. mss*,
          100:35) granted. Lt. Gov. Colden intending to go to the
          country adjourns the council to Brookland ferry, L. I.   404

     16   Assembly prorogued (see *N. Y. col. mss*, 100:112). Isaac
Kings co. Smith appointed judge of the common pleas for Dutchess
ferry   county, and Peter Vrooman justice of the peace in Albany
           county. Act of parliament for closing the port of Boston
           received.   405

June 14   Assembly prorogued (see *N. Y. col. mss*, 100:117). Warrants
          for salaries signed [Jacob Roome land and tidewaiter].
          Thos. Welling appointed justice of the peace for Orange
          county, Nathan Smith for Ulster county, John Marlett (see
          N. Y. col. mss, 100:113) for Tryon county.   405

     29   Michael Myer convicted of felony in Ulster county pardoned
          on recommendation of Justice Jones of Kingston and in-

1774   **v. 26**

habitants. David Colden appointed surveyor general during the illness of Alex'r Colden.   406

Aug. 2   Assembly prorogued (see *N. Y. col. mss*, 100:130). John
Stanworth sentenced to death for burglary pardoned.
Commissions of judges, justices and additional justices for
Ulster county (see *N. Y. col. mss*, 100:131) to issue.   407

Sep. 1   Assembly prorogued (see *N. Y. col. mss*, 100:1). Opinion of
New York   council on letter received from Gov. Penn with a petition
of Thos. and John Penn to the king concerning the New
York and Pennsylvania boundary (see *N. Y. col. mss*,
100:147). Military aid to be called against the Bennington
mob on complaints of Benj. Hough, Benj. Spencer, Jacob
Marsh, Amos Chamberlain, Jeremiah Gardenier, Daniel
Walker, Phil. Nicolls, Thomas Brayton and Daniel Washburn (see *N. Y. col. mss*, 100:135-42). Letter received
from Col. Guy Johnson (see *N. Y. col. mss*, 100:132) filed.   407

2   Arthur Parks to be additional justice of the peace in Ulster
county.   408

29   David Colden resigns the office of surveyor general, Alexander being restored to health. Mayors, sheriffs · and
coroners of New York and of Albany reappointed. Assembly prorogued (see *N. Y. col. mss*, 101:12). Certificate
of Richard Morris clerk of the courts of oyer and terminer,
that Robert R. Livingston and Thos. Jones attended the
sessions of the court at Johnstown, Tryon county (see
N. Y. col. mss, 100:146). Gen. Gage refuses to send troops
against the New Hampshire rioters (see *N. Y. col. mss*,
101:9). Letter received from Col. Guy Johnson with
speech of the Conajohary Indians and memorial of inhabitants of Conajohary (see *N. Y. col. mss*, 101:6-8); to be laid
before the assembly. John Snyder sentenced to death for
burglary at Albany reprieved on petition of the mayor,
recorder and aldermen (see *N. Y. col. mss*, 101:10). Commissions of the peace and of the quorum for Dutchess
county (see *N. Y. col. mss*, 101:4-5) to issue. Peter Lansingh and Stephen Tuttle to be justices of the peace for
Albany county. John Peters to be judge of the common
pleas in Gloucester county (see *N. Y. col. mss*, 101:11).   410

Oct. 6   Warrants for salaries and for expenses of Judges Livingston
and Jones at Tryon county court signed. Ordinance to
issue for fixing the times of court sessions in Charlotte
county.   411

10   John McKesson notary public and deputy register of the
court of vice admiralty to bring to trial prisoners charged
with piracy.   412

28   Assembly prorogued (see *N. Y. col. mss*, 101:22). Special
      commission of oyer and terminer to issue for Dutchess
      county. Certificate of Richard Morris clerk of the courts
      of oyer and terminer that Judge Robert R. Livingston has
      attended the courts at Westminster, Cumberland county
      and at Newberry, Gloucester county; warrants for his ex-
      penses signed accordingly; warrants to Gerard Bancker for
      necessaries to the troops.   412

Nov. 8 Letter received from Gov. Penn of Pennsylvania, survey of
      boundary line; Capt. Holland to act on behalf of New
      York.   413

30   Assembly prorogued (see *N. Y. col. mss*, 101:34). Special
      commission of oyer and terminer to issue for New York,
      at the request of Mayor Hicks. Henry Bleecker appointed
      justice of the peace for Albany county.   414

Dec. 7 Order on letter from George Klock of Conajohary (see *N. Y.
      col. mss*, 101:26). New York and New Jersey boundary
      commissioners called on for a report of their proceedings
      and account of their expenses. Commissions of the
      quorum and of the peace to issue for Orange county (see
      N. Y. col. mss, 101:37).   414

20   David Colden appointed surveyor general vice Alex'r Colden
      deceased.   415

1775

Jan. 5 Draft of the lieutenant governor's speech for the opening of
      the general assembly read; council want time to consider it. 416

7   Speech approved after some amendments. John Snyder
      (p. 410) pardoned (see *N. Y. col. mss*, 101:40).   416

11   Speech to be made by the lieutenant governor again read
      and approved.   417

25   Report of the commissioners to fix the beginning of the 43d
      degree north latitude, Samuel Holland of New York and
      David Rittenhouse of Pennsylvania. Action on a petition
      from freeholders of Charlotte county for representation in
      the assembly postponed.   417

Feb. 2 Royal mandamus to swear James Jauncey of the council; he
      is sworn in and takes his seat.   419

8   Advice of council on the report that a vessel arrived from
      Glasgow had been cast off from the wharf by a mob.   419

9   Letter received from Capt. James Mountague commanding
      the man-of-war Kingfisher relating to the above Glasgow
      vessel; advice of council thereon.   420

28   Petition of James Done of Ulster county (see *N. Y. col. mss*,
      101:65) rejected.   421

Mar. 9 Account of barrackmasters Evert and Gerard Bancker (see
      N. Y. col. mss, 101:41) filed. Warrant to Gerard Bancker

for necessaries to the troops signed. Advice of council of complaints of Benj. Hough and others (see *N. Y. col. mss*, 101:69-75) against the Bennington mob. Commissions of additional justices of the peace and assistant judges of the common pleas to issue for Tryon, Albany, Westchester and Richmond counties. Ordinance to issue fixing the times of court sessions in Tryon county.   421

13   Letters received: from Gov. Tryon recommending moderate treatment of the people; from Lord Dartmouth, no delegates ought to be sent to the general congress at Philadelphia; council advise against issuing a proclamation to that effect.   423

20   Message to be sent to the assembly concerning the riots in Charlotte county. Order on complaint of James Duane, Col. Sternberger and Col. Lawyer of Schoharie, Albany county, against Justice Alexander Campbell. Phineas Fanning justice of the peace in Suffolk county superseded at his own request.   424

21   Col. Wells and Crean Brush, representatives of Cumberland county report a violent riot in their county during which Justice Butterfield was wounded (see *Doc. hist. N. Y.* 4:903-4; Q 4:544-45).   425

22   Oliver Church of Brattleborough and Joseph Hancock of Hopkinson, Middlessex county, Mass. examined concerning the riot in Cumberland county (see *N. Y. col. mss*, 101:74-76). Message to the assembly thereon read. Report of New York commissioners for running the New Jersey line. Warrant to Samuel Gale and Wm Wickham surviving commissioners, for expenses in marking the New Jersey line signed.   426

Ap. 1   Gilbert G. Marselis appointed justice of the peace and assistant judge of the common pleas, David McCarthy justice of the peace for Albany county; Lewis McDonald jr justice of the peace for Westchester county; Lawrence Lawrence, Thos. Baker, Corn's Humfrey, John Wilkinson, justices of the peace and quorum, Wm van Wyck, Peter I. Monfoort, Stephen Duryea, Corn's Dennis, John Wooley, James Germon, Eliab Yeomans and Daniel Ketcham justices of the peace for Dutchess county; Wm Shaw justice of the peace for Ulster county.   428

7   New list of judges and justices for Orange county to be made out. Order on petition of Benj. Hough and Daniel Walker (see *N. Y. col. mss*, 101:82).   428

11   Warrants for salaries signed. Wm Edminston to be justice of the peace and of the quorum, Wm Faulkner and Richarts Brooks, justices of the peace for Tryon county.   429

1775   **v. 26**

13   Gen. Robinson reports a riot in which two transports were cast off from the wharf, and threats of destroying the magazine at Turtle bay made; orders thereon.   430

24   A mob has seized arms lodged in the city hall and the public powder house. Rioters will hold a meeting. Judges of the supreme court, mayor and recorder, and field officers of the , militia called to join the council.   431

p. m.   Capt. Benj. C. Paine, 18th regiment, writes that the mob intend to attack Fort George. Present disorders said to be the consequence of what happened at Boston. Council cannot advise any further measures.   431

28   The attorney general to draw a charter for the protestant episcopal church at Schenectady.   432

May 1   Col. Lispenard granted leave to call out his regiment of militia for drill. Assembly prorogued (see *N. Y. col. mss*, 101:86). Reasons of council for advising a prorogation.   433

5   Petitions granted: of Samuel Wells, Wm Patterson sheriff, and Samuel Gale clerk of Cumberland county (see *N. Y. col. mss*, 101:91-92); of Jonathan Stearns (see *N. Y. col. mss*, 101:93) granted and warrants on the treasurer issued. Certificate of Richard Morris (see *N. Y. col. mss*, 101:89-90) filed and warrants issued. Lt. Gov. Colden intends to go to his country seat at Flushing, L. I.   435

June 3   Assembly prorogued (see *N. Y. col. mss*, 101:94). Warrants
Broockland   for salaries signed [Henry Law, land and tidewaiter]: No powder in the magazine for the usual salute on the king's birthday.   437

28   Gov. Tryon returned; the great seal is delivered to him. He
New York   requires the advice of the council on the present state of the colony.   438

30   Opinion of council on the state of the colony. Edmund Fanning sworn in as surveyor general of lands.   439

July 3   Assembly prorogued. Minutes sent to the board of trade.   440

11   Copies of an address by the mayor and corporation of New York (see *N. Y. col. mss*, 101:97) received and filed.   440

31   Assembly prorogued (see *N. Y. col. mss*, 101:98). Instruction received from Lord Dartmouth relating to the grant of charters to presbyterian churches; papers relating to it referred to the attorney general. Yerry Gillie convicted of felony, John Allen convicted of the same, and Nicholas Bassong charged with passing counterfeit money, pardoned.   441

Sep. 4   Letter received from Lord Darmouth, purchases of land from the Indians. Assembly prorogued (see *N. Y. col. mss*, 101:103). John Nesbit and Archibald Campbell appointed

1775   **v. 26**

judges of the common pleas for Charlotte county. Petition of Nathan Ker et al (see *N. Y. col. mss*, 101:102) referred to the attorney general.   442

29   Mayors, sheriffs and coroners of New York and of Albany
reappointed. Assembly prorogued (see *N. Y. col. mss*,
101:105). Special commission of oyer and terminer to issue
for Tryon county. Petitions for charters to Ulpianus van
Zinderen, and Johannes Casparus Rubel, ministers of the
reformed Dutch church at Flatbush (see *N. Y. col. mss*,
101:108); of the baptist church in Gold street, New York
(see *N. Y. col. mss*, 101:106, 109); of Mathias Burnet minister of the presbyterian church at Jamaica (see *N. Y. col.
mss*, 101:107), referred to the attorney general. Warrants
for salaries and to John Antill for postage (see *N. Y. col.
mss*, 101:96) signed.   443

Oct. 31   The governor's reasons for leaving the city and his corre-
On board the   spondence with the mayor about it. Assembly prorogued
Dutchess of   (see *N. Y. col. mss*, 101:118). Minutes sent to the board
Gordon   of trade.   445

Nov. 13   Royal proclamation for suppressing sedition and rebellion in
America received from John Pownall; to be published (see
N. Y. col. mss, 101:119). Advice of council on the application by persons in Westchester county for arms. Commission of oyer and terminer to issue for Dutchess county.   449

Dec. 1   Assembly prorogued (see *N. Y. col. mss*, 101:121). Gov.
Tryon obtains permission to return to England; his letter
to Samuel Bayard deputy secretary concerning safety of
the records.   450

4   Advice of council with respect to the records; part to be removed to the Dutchess of Gordon.   451

23   Assembly prorogued (see *N. Y. col. mss*, 101:124).   451

26   Assembly to be dissolved and writs for the election of a new
assembly to issue. Minutes sent to the board of trade.   452

1776

Jan. 29   John Bryan sentenced to death for felony, Wm Elkins and
Abr'm Stokes sentenced to be whipped for petit larceny,
pardoned. Commission of oyer and terminer to issue for
Westchester county. Warrant to Samuel Bayard for express messenger services signed. Adam Laucks appointed
assistant judge, John Thompson and Donald McGregor
additional justices of the peace for Tryon county. Jelles
Fonda judge, and John Marlett justice of the peace in the
same county removed. Assembly prorogued by writ
patent.   453

Feb. 14   Writ patent for proroguing the assembly signed. Whitehead
Hicks appointed justice of the supreme court vice Living-

1776   **v. 26**

ston deceased, David Matthews mayor of New York vice
Hicks. Royal artillery and ordnance removed from the
fort and lower battery. Records taken to the house of
Nicholas Bayard in the Outward, Samuel Bayard the
deputy secretary paroled. Letter from Robert Benson
secretary of the committee of safety on the subject.   455

Mar. 11   Assembly prorogued by writ patent. Letters received from
Lord Germain secretary of state with gazettes, communicated to the council.   457

1780

Mar. 23   Major Gen. James Robertson present produces his commis-
Government   sion as governor; Andrew Elliot his as lieutenant gov-
house   ernor. They take the usual oaths and the council and
deputy secretary are sworn in. Gov. Robertson publishes
his commission at the city hall.   458

Ap. 15   Proclamation publishing Gov. Robertson's appointment and
his majesty's gracious intentions signed and ordered
printed. Oath of secrecy taken.

1781

May 23   Lt. Gov. Elliott presiding informs the council that the governor had left the city for a short time and delivered the
seals to him; he takes the oaths.   463

Dec. 20   Gov. Robertson in the chair. Samuel Hake, in a letter to
Lt. Col. Oliver de Lancey adjutant general, transmitted
by Sir Henry Clinton, accuses Roger Morris of disloyalty;
order for hearing of the case.   463

22   Hearing on the accusation of Samuel Hake against Roger
Morris; Abr'm Teller, Hannah Watson sworn as witnesses
make their depositions; Roger Morris exonerated the
charge being scandalous and malicious.   464

1782

Mar. 21   Opinion of council on the expediency of reviving civil government; they advise against it, Chief Justice Smith dissenting.   467

May 4   Gov. Robertson appointed commander-in-chief of the forces
in America requires again the opinion of council as to civil
government. Letter received from Welbore Ellis secretary
of state on the same subject, with resolves of the house of
commons, laid before the council; council are against the
reestablishment of civil government, Mr Smith dissenting. 468

1783

Ap. 10   Address of the governor to the council; he is returning to
England; answer of council. Report of the deputy secretary on the records. The seals and papers to be left with
the lieutenant governor.   469

1783　　　　　　　　　　　　　　　　　　　　　　　　　　**v. 26**

17　Lt. Gov. Elliott in the chair. He reports that he has the
seals and instructions; he takes the oaths.　　　　　473

May 26　Letter from John Morin Scott dated Fishkill, records
claimed; opinion of council concerning it.

Vol. 27, 1757-62

Legislative minutes of council from Feb. 15, 1757 to Jan. 8, 1762 printed
in *Journal of the legislative council of the colony of New York*, 2:1291-1463.

Vol. 28, 1762-70

Legislative minutes of council from Mar. 2, 1762 to Jan. 27, 1770 printed
in *Journal of the legislative council of the colony of New York*, 2:1291-1463.

Vol. 29, 1767-72

1764

Sep. 5　Lt. Gov. Cadwallader Colden in the chair. Petitions referred:
of Francis Stephens storekeeper and paymaster of the
ordnance (see *L. P.* 18:18); of Wm Kempe, James Lamb
and John Crum (see *L. P.* 19:138); of Phil. Embury and
others (see *L. P.* 18:30); of Isaac Vrooman, John van Sice,
Isaac Marselis, Isaac Vredenbergh, Corn's van der Volgen,
Johannes Fort, Johannes van Etten, Abr'm Vredenbergh,
Thos. Murray, Reuben Horseford, Adam Smith, Arent Ans
Bratt, Wm Heemstrat, John Switman, Johannes Quacken-
boss, Herry Peak, Johan J. Bastianze, Hermanus Bratt,
Andrew Mitchel, Rynier Myndertse, Walter Vrooman,
John Duncan, Robert Callbeck, Richard Duncan, George
Smith and Alex'r Crukshank (see *L. P.* 18:143); of Ralph
Wilkinson, Philipp Steers, Jellys Fonda, Peter Conyn,
Hendrick Hanen, Jost Harnourf, Andries Schneyder, Fran-
cis Kysert, Wm Thompson, Joseph Cathcart, Thos.
Baarup, Philippus Sheaver, Peter Myer, Hendrick Buskerk,
John Butler, Barent Vrooman, David Mareness, James
Hare, John Smith, John Hicobs, Peter Mynderse, Johs.
Vrooman, Barent Wimple, Jacob Pikel and Adam Fonda
(see *L. P.* 18:31); of Edward Smith, Wm Jones, John
Felan and Charles Morse (see *L. P.* 18:26); of John Munro,
Henry Brower, John Rickey and Corn. Brewer (see *L. P.*
18:141).　　　　　　　　　　　　　　　　　　　　　　1

17　Petition of Francis Stephens (p. 1) granted.　　　　4

Oct. 11　Bond of Johannes Quackenboss (see *L. P.* 18:39) received
and filed.　　　　　　　　　　　　　　　　　　　　4

31　Instruction relating to appeals in civil causes from the
courts of common laws. Petition of Robert R. Waddel

bond in re Thos. Forsey vs Waddel Cunningham (see *N. Y. col. mss*, 92:154-56); writ of inhibition to issue to remove the case from the supreme court on appeal to the governor and council.   4

Nov. 7 Minister and members of Trinity church, New Rochelle vs Peter Flandreau, Sam'l Gillet and Elizabeth Rylander in error. Petition by the corporation of Albany against granting a township charter to Schenectady (23:469-70) dismissed. Bond of John Williamson, Wm Forman and Francis Stephens (see *L. P.* 18:45) filed.   8

14 Waddel Cunningham vs Thos. Forsey on appeal. Peter Flandreau et al vs Trinity church, New Rochelle in error.   9

16 Petition of Peter Jay, Elisha Budd, Christ'r Isinghart, Timothy Wetmore, Caleb Purdy, Joshua Purdy, John Guion, Joseph Purdy, Gilbert Willet, John Carhart, Thos. Sawyer, Gilbert Brundige, John Thomas, Wm Sutton, Anthony Miller and John Adee all of Rye for a charter of incorporation for their church (protestant episcopal) granted. W. Cunningham vs Thos. Forsey.   10

19 W. Cunningham vs Thos. Forsey; reasons offered by Chief Justice Horsmanden against making return on the writ for removal of the case from the supreme court; other judges asked for their reasons.   11

28 David Provoost vs Mary Lush administratrix of John Lush deceased, in error. John van Rensselaer vs James Jackson ex dem Thos. Williams et al in error. Peter Flandreau et al vs Peter Quiet ex dem minister etc of New Rochelle in error.   17

Dec. 5 Petition of John Duncan, Daniel Campbell, John Visger and others of Schenectady for a charter of incorporation granted.   17

6 David Provoost vs Mary Lush administratrix of John Lush deceased in error. Peter Quiet ex dem minister of New Rochelle vs Peter Flandreau et al in error. Petition of James Duane (see *L. P.* 18:100) referred. Minutes sent to the board of trade.   18

12 W. Cunningham vs Thos. Forsey; Justice Jones writes that he can give no reasons on the removal of the case from the supreme court because he does not know anything about it; Justices Smith and Livingston give their reasons. Peter Quiet ex dem minister of New Rochelle vs Peter Flandreau et al in error.   19

19 Peter Flandreau et al vs Peter Quiet ex dem minister of New Rochelle. Draft of the charter for the protestant episcopal church at Rye passed.   28

1764   **v. 29**

20   Order on memorial of Major Philipp Skene (see *L. P.*
        18:103).
                                                                        29
26   W. Cunningham vs Thos. Forsey; reasons of Justice David
1765   Jones against removal of the case from the supreme court.   30

Jan. 8   Order on memorial of Major Phil. Skene asking that the
        names of John Maunsel, Thos. Moncrief, Nath'l Marston,
        Lawrence Read, Hugh Wallace, Alex'r Wallace, Thomas
        White, John Marston, John Gill, Robert Stevens, Robert
        Alexander, John Moore, Joseph Alicock, Richard Curson,
        Evert Bancker, Gerard Bancker, James Deas, John Lamb,
        Boyle Roche, Acheson Thompson, John R. Myer, Peter
        Ketteltas, Levinus Clarkson and Abrm Brazier be inserted
        in the patent prayed for (see *L. P.* 18:109).   32

9   W. Cunningham vs Thos. Forsey.   32

11   W. Cunningham vs Thos. Forsey; reasons of council about
        removal of the case from the supreme court; additional
        reasons of Justice Livingston.   33

23   Petition of Robert R. Waddell of counsel for Waddel Cun-
        ningham vs Thos. Forsey (see *N. Y. col. mss*, 93:25) re-
        ferred.   58

Feb. 6   Opinion of council on the above petition, the lieutenant
        governor dissenting.   59

20   Petitions for land granted: Lieut. Guy Johnson (see *L. P.*
        17:105); John Allen private 40th regiment (see *L. P.*
        18:115); Capt. Daniel Disney 80th regiment (see *L. P.*
        18:110); John Young provoost marshal (see *L. P.* 18:116);
        Lieut. Daniel Wriesberg (see *L. P.* 39:129); Capt. John
        Wharton (see *L. P.* 39:132); Capt. John Small, Lieuts. Ann
        Gordon, John Gregor, Adjt. Wm Gregor, 42d regiment
        and Lieut. James Bain (see *L. P.* 17:130); Josias Harper
        surgeon's mate (see *L. P.* 18:107); Chaplain Michael
        Schlatter 60th regiment (see *L. P.* 17:165); Ralph Barrass,
        Skeen Douglass, Wm Sharp, John Smith and Thos. Saun-
        ders miners (see *L. P.* 18:150); Ensign John Watkins 60th
        regiment (see *L. P.* 18:104); Col. Ralph Burton (see *L. P.*
        18:46); Ralph Spooner, Samuel Richardson, Joseph Farly,
        Robert Robinson and Benj. Robinson miners (see *L. P.*
        18:54); Sergeant Alex'r McKenzie 48th regiment (see *L. P.*
        69); Corporal Isaac Reemar 48th regiment (see *L. P.*
        39:135); Sergeant Wm Beard (see *L. P.* 39:95); Capt.
        George le Hunte 80th regiment (see *L. P.* 39:144); John
        Friswell acting lieutenant in the navy (see *L. P.* 39:146);
        Peter Stewart master's mate (see *L. P.* 39:145); Lieut. Ed-
        mund Newland, 80th regiment, not located (see *L. P.*

18:119); Lieut. Richard Williams, 80th regiment, not located (see *L. P.* 18:120); Capt. John Carden 2d battalion Royal Americans, not located (see *L. P.* 18:48); Sergeant Patrick Stone Royal Americans (see *L. P.* 18:118); Quartermaster Duncan McVicar 55th regiment (see *L. P.* 18:111); Lieut. Nich's Ward 80th regiment (see *L. P.* 18:115) not located; Samuel Dick hospital mate, not located (see *L. P.* 18:113); Lieut. Gilbert King 80th regiment, not located (see *L. P.* 18:112); David Pryce, agent to transports with field officers rank (see *L. P.* 18:7); Lieut. George Demler 60th regiment, not located (see *L. P.* 17:144); Lieut. Samuel Steel 42d regiment, not located (see *L. P.* 17:38); James Boggs apothecary's mate, not located (see *L. P.* 18:102); Lieut. Alex'r Grant (see *L. P.* 18:80); Capt. Wm Sherriff 47th regiment, not located (see *L. P.* 18:47); Lieut. John des Bruyeres 56th regiment, not located (see *L. P.* 18:49); Lieut. Wm Potts (see *L. P.* 18:130); Lieut. Charles Menzies, 42d regiment (see *L. P.* 18:55); Surgeon John Hicks (see *L. P.* 39:131); Corporals Wm Blaylock Royal Americans, Thomas Denhard, John Viand (see *L. P.* 39:138-40); Sergeants John Betkie Royal Americans, John Smith Royal Americans, and John McCarthy 40th regiment (see *L. P.* 39:138-40); Joseph Handsforth, 35th regiment (see *L. P.* 39:138); Corporal Phil. Simon Royal Americans (see *L. P.* 39:140); Privates Francis Fay, Edward Blakeney, Dennis Hall, 17th regiment, Thos. Sidwell Royal artillery, and Corn's Hays 40th regiment (see *L. P.* 39:137); Peter Leckee (see *L. P.* 39:136); Wm Gillylan 35th regiment, Peter Sullivan 47th regiment, Michael Keough 44th regiment (see *L. P.* 39:142); Conrad Lefler Royal Americans (see *L. P.* 39:142); Surgeons George Monroe, Wm Barr and Jonathan Mallett (see *L. P.* 18:125). Order concerning grants of land to non-commissioned officers and soldiers. Petition of James Napier director general of hospitals (see *L. P.* 18:125) granted.   59

27 Favorable opinion of council on the following petitions for lands purchased from the Indians and surveyed before the receipt of the additional instruction of Dec. 9, 1761 (25:421), and patents granted: of Fred'k Young, Cornelius ten Broeck, Adam Young, Hendrick Mathias, Johannes Kesslaer, Andries Young, Nich's Oxinor, Francis Johnson, Christian Frolic, Robert Leonard, Elias Bailey, Theobald Young, John Carman, John Ja Glen, John Huyler, Garret Abr'm Lansingh, Henry C. Cuyler, Abr'm Yates jr, Simon Groot and Jonas Southerd for land on the Mohawk river

(23:376, 379); of Wm Smith jr, Johs. Hendrick Vrooman,
John Reade, John Glen, Abr'm Dowe, Guysbert Fonda,
Peter Douw. Valkert Abr'm Domo, Johs. Hendrick ten
Eyck, Barent C. ten Eyck, John C. ten Broeck, Francis
Welsh, Abr'm ten Broeck, Hendrick Young, Guysbert
Marselis, Thos. Gordon, Wm Weyman, Rich'd Smith,
Leonard de Kleyn and Samuel Boyer for land on the Mo-
hawk river (23:379); of Coenradt Franck, Fred'k Franck,
George Herchheimer, Michael Itigh and Peter Piper
(23:379); of Wm Cunningham (23:379; see *L. P.* 19:49); of
Jacob Starnberger, George Zimmer, Hendrick Weaver,
Jacob Zimmer, John Joost Becker, Wm Zimmer, John
Schever and Petrus Zimmer for land adjoining Schoharie
patent. Report on a petition of James Duane to erect
certain lands into a township (see *L. P.* 8:100); favorable. 64

Mar. 13   Reports on petitions: of Isaac Vrooman et al (p. 1); of Ralph
Wilkinson et al (p. 1), granted. Draft of patent to Major
Phil. Skene (p. 32) and for the town of Duanesburgh
(p. 64) passed. Reports on petitions: of Phil. Embury et al;
of John Munroe et al (p. 1). Petitions granted: of Evert
Bancker jr, Gerard Bancker, John Bancker, Abr'm Heyer,
John West, John Hughes, Thomas Burgie, George Cooke,
James Lynas, Edward Anderson, Edward Prior, Edward
Prior jr, Elizabeth Bancker, Robert Barland, Mary
Bancker, John Harris and James Deas (see *L. P.* 18:40); of
Surgeon John Storm 60th regiment, not located (see *L. P.*
18:124); of Lieuts Nich's Ward and Edw'd Newland (see
L. P. 18:139); of Lieut. George McDougal Royal Ameri-
cans (see *L. P.* 18:140); of Lieut. Benj. Wickham, not
located (see *L. P.* 18:146).   66

15   Bond for settlement of lands signed by Major Phil. Skene
(see *L. P.* 18:147) filed.   70

27   Lieutenant governor's reasons against taking cognizance of
causes in error. Order concerning the location of lands to
be granted to Evert Bancker jr et al (p. 66).   70

Ap. 10   Royal order fixing the boundaries between New York and
New Hampshire. Petition of John Montresor, Francis
Mee and Robert Wallace (see *L. P.* 17:99) referred. Peter
Quiet ex dem minister of New Rochelle vs Peter Flandreau
et al in error.   72

May 8   Petitions granted: of Peter de Lancey (see *L. P.* 18:175); of
David Johnson and Oliver de Lancey (see *L. P.* 18:177);
of David Jamison, son of Wm Jamison (see *L. P.* 19:6);
of John Montresor et al (p. 72). Petition of Lewis
Powell Williams surgeon's mate (see *L. P.* 18:163) tabled.

Petition of John Cook, Phil. Cook, Edw'd Carscallen, George Long, Julius Shire, Paul Sparling, Peter Sparling, Paul Heck, Jacob Heck and Elias Huffman (see *L. P.* 18:151) referred. Petitions granted: reduced officers, Lieut. John Crukshank 47th regiment (see *L. P.* 18:157), John Waterhouse surgeon's mate (see *L. P.* 18:179), Kennedy Farrel wagon master general (see *L. P.* 18:161), Lieut. John Bowen, 45th regiment (see *L. P.* 18:166), John Carter, surgeon's mate (see *L. P.* 18:167), all not located; Lieut. Thos. Roskruge Royal artillery (see *L. P.* 18:173); Sergeant Alex'r Dingwall 55th regiment (see *L. P.* 18:176); Sergeants Porter, —— McKenzie barrack master at Crownpoint, Corporals Henry Jeffery and John O'Neil, 60th regiment (see *L. P.* 18:159); Conrad Ball, Simon Bennis, Edmond Bowman, John Williamson, Thos. Stafford, Henry Moore and Daniel Morarty, non-commissioned officers (see *L. P.* 39:148); Daniel Buxton, Phil. Richards, Donald Cuthbert, Rich'd Aspinwall, George Tingle, John Smith, Daniel Kells and James Smith privates, Robert Alexander and Christ'r Dugan, non-commissioned officers (see *L. P.* 39:147). 74

15   Petitions granted: of reduced officers Capt. James Rogers independent company of rangers (see *L. P.* 18:181), Lieut. James Gorrell, 60th regiment (see *L. P.* 18:180); of Rev. John Ogilvie (see *L. P.* 19:21); of Robert Harpur of Kings college (see *L. P.* 19:4). Petitions referred: of Peter Hasenclever, Daniel Vriesbergh, James Richie, Nich's Hoffman and Gabriel H. Ludlow (see *L. P.* 19:20). 78

22   Petitions of Joseph Randall gunner Royal artillery, Evan Cameron, Allan Cameron and Roderick Fraser corporals 78th regiment, Timothy Leonard and Jon'n Davis privates 80th regiment, for land not located granted. Petition of Benj. Whiting et al, township of Newberry, (see *L. P.* 19:24) granted. Lands actually possessed by claimants under New Hampshire grants to be reserved to such actual settlers (see *Doc. hist. N. Y.* 4:577-78; Q 4:357). Council being interested in the land prayed for decline giving an opinion on the memorial of Lieut. James McDonald 60th regiment (see *L. P.* 18:158). 81

July 8   Petitons of reduced officers and soldiers for land granted: Major Henry Gladwin 80th regiment (see *L. P.* 18:41); Surgeons Mate Jas. Edwards (see *L. P.* 18:150); Lieut. James Grant 45th regiment (see *L. P.* 19:52); Capt. John Treby 80th regiment (see *L. P.* 19:58); Lieut. Peter Brown Royal artillery (see *L. P.* 19:87); Capt. Nathan Whiting (see *L. P.* 19:60); Capt. Norman McLeod 80th regiment

(see *L. P.* 19:62); Surgeon Donald McLean 77th regiment
(see *L. P.* 19:63); Lieut. Hugh Frazer 78th regiment (see
L. P. 19:67); Lieut. James Eddington, 42d regiment (see
L. P. 19:82); Surgeons Mate Peter Brown (see *L. P.* 19:86);
Sergeants Leeks de Keyser, John Colly, John Able, Garret
Kating, Wm Patterson, Corporals John Underhill, Thos.
McGuire, Thos. West, Thos. Goldsmith, John Cotten,
Privates John Durgan, John Williams, Edw'd Fitspatrick,
Samuel Taylor, Peter Kerns, Joseph Badley and Daniel
Bayard, for land north of Otter creek; of Sergeants Wm
Moore and John Andrew 80th regiment, Corporals David
Taylor, 55th regiment, Rob't Monroe 47th, Alex'r Young
77th, Drummers David Davidson 77th regiment, David
Mustard 55th, Privates Francis Mee, Rich'd Benson, Fred'k
Hardburger, Arch'd Montgomery 80th, and Samuel Skinner
Royal Americans, not located. Oliver de Lancey protests
against granting patents for lands set apart for paying ex-
penses of the partition of Minisink patent (see *L. P.* 19:85).
Petitions granted: of Wm Smith (see *L. P.* 19:17); of Gual-
terus du Bois and other heirs of Henry van Bael and John
Nicoll, and heirs of Dr John Nicoll (see *L. P.* 19:26).
Patent to Wm Cunningham (p. 64) passed.   83

Sep. 4   Certificates of Sir Wm Johnson concerning the lands prayed
for by Coenrad Frank et al (p. 64) and by Wm Smith et al
(p. 64) filed, and patents to be granted.   86

25   Petition for land by 13 non-commissioned officers and 29
privates [not named] granted. Hearing appointed on a
caveat by Thos. Jonas in behalf of Oysterbay, L. I. against
granting lands there to Gilbert Lester surgeon's mate (see
L. P. 17:155). Petitions granted: of Peter Goelet (see *L. P.*
19:88); of Benj. Doughty (see *L. P.* 19:136); of George
McNish, Thos. Gale, Abrm Gale and David Curwin (see
L. P. 19:161).   87

Oct. 9   Petitions for land granted: by quarter master John Clark
60th regiment (see *L. P.* 20:10); Charles Clinton apothecary's mate (see *L. P.* 19:129); Lieut. Allan Grant 60th
regiment (see *L. P.* 19:133); Lieut. James McDonald 60th
regiment (see *L. P.* 19:161); Lieut. John Hall 80th regiment (see *L. P.* 20:9). Royal order for allowing an appeal
in re Waddel Cunningham vs Thos. Forsey. Action on the
petition of Robert Ross Waddel (see *N. Y. col. mss*, 93:98)
deferred.   90

15   W. Cunningham vs Thos. Forsey admitted on appeal.   93

22   Petitions for land granted: Lieut. Jehu Hay Royal Americans (see *L. P.* 19:128); Capt. Wm Williams, 52d regiment
(see *L. P.* 20:33); Capt. Cortland Schuyler and Commis-

1765   **v. 29**

sary Henry Cuyler (see *L. P.* 20:47). Patents to Capt.
John Small and hospital director James Napier (p. 59) to
pass, notwithstanding the caveat of Jacob Marsh (see *L. P.*
20:18).   94

23   Hearing on the caveat of Oysterbay (p. 87) postponed.
Charter for erecting the " free borough town " of
Schenectady to pass the seals.   95

29   Petition granted: of Thomas Chandler et al for a confirma-
tion of the township of New Hamstead (see *L. P.* 19:162);
of Zedekiah Stone, Nathan Stone and David Stone 2d (see
L. P. 19:155) for confirmation of Winsor; of Oliver Partridge et al for confirmation of Halifax (see *L. P.* 20:5).
Patent granted to Wm Kempe, James Lamb and John
Crum (p. 1). Petition of John Reid, George Etherington,
Phil. Livingston jr, James Gray, Hugh Parker, George
Souter and Angus McKay (see *L. P.* 20:71) referred. Petition for land by 18 non-commissioned officers and 19
privates [not named and not located] granted.   96

31   Petitions for land granted: Capt. Wm Sherriff on behalf of
his brother Lieut. Charles Sherriff 45th regiment (see
L. P. 20:96); Lieut. Alex'r Graydon Royal Americans (see
L. P. 19:102).   100

Nov. 12   W. Cunningham vs Thos. Forsey on appeal. Chief Justice
Horsmanden says that his court cannot comply with the
king's order (p. 90).   101

29   Surveyor general called upon for a map of the lands west
of Connecticut river and north of the Massachusetts line.   102

Dec. 20   Petition of Lt. Col. John Vaughan (see *L. P.* 20:102) referred.   102

1766

Jan. 8   The king vs Theophilact Bache; the king vs Ennis Graham;
the king vs Joseph Forman: in error, all on provision
bonds.   103

Mar. 22   Opinion of the lords of trade, the attorney and solicitor
general on the appeal in re W. Cunningham vs Thos.
Forsey. Royal instructions confirming Daniel Horsmanden, George Clarke, Sir Wm Johnson, Wm Smith, John
Watts, Wm Walters, Oliver de Lancey, Wm Alexander
claiming to be earl of Sterling, Chas. Ward Apthorpe, John
Reade and Roger Morris as members of the council and
concerning land grants.   103

Ap. 2-23   Hearing on the caveat of Oysterbay (p. 87, 95).   113-14

30   Petition of Martin Garretson van Bergen, Thos. Lynot, John
French, Wm Cain, Hugh Dennison, John Morin Scott,
Daniel Denison and Joseph Blanchard (see *L. P.* 20:152)
granted.   115

1766   **v. 29**

May 7   Opinion of council on the petition of Captains John and
David Brewer and Lieutenants John Butler and Joshua
Lock for land (see *L. P.* 20:164).   117

28   Order concerning claimants to patents under former licenses
to purchase Indian lands. Petitions of Capt. Jonathan
Brewer (see *L. P.* 20:170) and Lieut. John Butler (see
L. P. 20:171) granted. Petition of Adolphus Benzel, Rebecca Benzel, Anna Ulrica Benzell (see *L. P.* 20:178) read. 117

June 2   Petitions granted: Samuel Wells et al (see *L. P.* 20:185);
Oliver Willard et al (see *L. P.* 20:184); James Rogers et al
(see *L. P.* 20:18).   119

3   Petitons granted: Col. James Robertson on behalf of hospital director John Adair (see *L. P.* 21:1); Samuel Adams
(see *L. P.* 17:148).   123

6   Order on petitions: of Lt. Col. Richard Maitland and Captain Sir Henry Seton (see *L. P.* 20:167); of Lieut. Walter
Stewart Welch volunteers (see *L. P.* 21:6). Order to notify
claimant under New Hampshire grants to support their
claims.   124

9   Petition of Samuel Stevens (see *L. P.* 20:94) granted; the
names of Samuel Stevens, Samuel Hunt, Abr'm Downer,
John Chamberlain, Joseph Hubbard, Joseph Billing, Elea-
zer Porter, Benj. Baldwin, Eben'r Green, Zebede Howard,
Elisha Hunt, Nehemia Wright, Simeon Strang, Richard
Chancy, Elisha Hubbard, Bread Batchalder, Solomon Bott-
woort, David Persons, Josiah Chancy, Arad Hunt, Josiah
Chancy jr, Samuel Hunt jr, Dan'l Shattuck and Daniel
Jones to be inserted in the patent [town of Fairlie]. Re-
port on the petition of John Reid et al (p. 96); granted.
Petition of Surgeon's Mate James Murdock, 42d regiment
(see *L. P.* 19:118) granted.   126

10   Order on petition of Sergeant Hugh Munroe (see *L. P.*
20:163). Surveyor's returns with maps to be laid before the
council before patents are granted. Petition of Josiah Willard and Medad Pomroy (see *L. P.* 19:56) for Putney
granted; the names of Josiah Willard, Joshua Hide, Daniel
Hubbard, Josiah Willard jr, Lois Butler, Thos. Frink,
Jeremiah Hall, Joseph Hammond, Thos. Hill, Eunice Willard, Elijah Alexander, Sampson Willard, John Ellis, Henry
Foster, Thos. Lee, Micah Lawrence, John Gould, James
Scott and Nehemiah Houghton to be inserted in the patent. 128

12   Petitions granted: Gabriel H. Ludlow, Samuel Gale, Thos.
Ludlow jr, Wm Wickham, Richard Morris, Miles Sherbrook, John Morris and associates (see *L. P.* 21:29); Adolphus, Rebecca and Anna Ulrica Benzel (see *L. P.* 21:28). 130

13   Petition of Capt. Archibald Hamilton, 108th regiment (see
      L. P. 21:14) granted.   132
19   Petition of Lewis P. Williams, surgeon's mate (see *L. P.*
      21:27) granted.   133
23   Petition of Major Thomas James (see *L. P.* 21:37) granted. 134
27   Order concerning the lands to be granted to Capt. Arch'd
      Hamilton (p. 132). Patent for land granted to Sir John
      St Clair (see *L. P.* 21:32, 34); order concerning these lands.
      Petition of Lt. Col. Vaughan (see *L. P.* 21:46) granted.
      Hearing on the caveat by the owners of Coeymans patent
      against a grant to Richard Maitland and Sir Henry Seton
      (p. 124). Thomas Chandler, John Chandler, Thos. Chand-
      ler jr, Elizabeth Chandler, Timothy Olcott, Joseph Lord,
      Joseph Lord jr, Stephen Lord, Jotham Lord, Nathan Earl,
      Joshua Farwell, Jabez Sargent, Edw'd Johnson, Isaiah
      Johnson, Cyrus Whitcomb, Joshua Church, Ebenezer Hol-
      ton, Jonathan Holton, David Hutchinson, Gersham Hobart,
      Wm Hoar, Hezekiah Hoar, David Young, Matthew Pat-
      terson, John Thorp, John Myer, Nath'l McKinley, Alex'r
      Lamb, Wm Swan, John Crosby, Christ'r Kennedy and
      John Osborn to be patentees in the township of Chester. 135
30   Petitions of Lieut. John Nordbergh 60th regiment (see *L. P.*
      20:142) and of Sergeant Hugh Munroe (p. 128) granted;
      of Peter Hasenclever, David Green, Andrew Seton et al
      (see *L. P.* 21:51) referred. Certificate of Sir Wm Johnson
      that Jacob Starnberger et al (p. 64) have purchased the
      lands prayed for, from the Indians; patent granted accord-
      ingly. Order concerning the laying out the township of
      Kent (see *L. P.* 21:52). Petition of Aaron Brown, Daniel
      Pond, Jonathan Hammond, Jonathan Houghton, Abner
      Ousgood, Robert Powers, Glasher Wheeler, Peter
      Wheeler, Abijah Powers, James Maxwell, Luke Brown,
      Jacob Waters, Abiatha Houghton, Mat'w Powers, Stephen
      Shadduck, David Taylor, John Taylor, Nathaniel Rament,
      Peter Wright, Whitcom Powers, Dan'l Amason, Daniel
      Prest, Silas Brown, Josiah Powers, David Fales, Joseph
      Hucher, Edw'd Fuller, Wm Kennedy, Peter Buckle, Joseph
      Fuller, Stephen Powers, Benj. Abbot, Robert Powers jr,
      Joseph French, Oliver Sawyer, Oliver Corey, Ebenezer
      Griffin, Jonathan Pekham, Ezra Genet, Ephraim Brown,
      David Spafford, Nahum Powers, Abel Powers, Robert Cut-
      ler, Josiah Horing, John Cuming, Jeremiah Powers and
      Joseph Storie of the township of Leicester (see *L. P.* 21:33)
      granted.   138

July 7 Petitions granted: Elkana Deane, Elkana Deane jr, Richard Deane, Nesbit Deane, Wm Deane, John Deane and Samuel Deane, lately arrived from Ireland (see *L. P.* 20:109; 21:31); Peter Hasenclever et al (p. 138). 142

9 The king vs Theophilact Bache; the king vs Ennis Graham; the king vs Joseph Forman; all in error. The names of Zedekiah Stone, Nathan Stone, David Stone, Samuel Stone, Israel Curtis, Jacob Hossington, Steel Smith, Willard Stevens, Enos Stevens, Joel Stone, Thos. Cooper, David Young, Wm Pearson, Robert McGinnis, John Armstrong, John Fitzpatrick, George Wilson, Peter Prim, Wm Swan, Martha Stone, Alexander Dalles, John Paisley, Mary Stone and Samuel Hunt to be inserted as grantees in the Windsor patent. 143

11 Hearing on the caveat by the owners of the Coeymans patent (p. 124, 135). 144

14 Map of the Minisink angle called for. Petition of David Embury, David Embury jr, Wm Dunlap, John Winters, Wm Green, John Embury, Peter Lawrence, George Embury, John Lewis, Andrew Embury, Michael Steep, Phil. Embury jr, John Wilson and Abr'm Harris (see *L. P.* 20:126) referred. 144

18 Petitions for land granted: officers of the rangers, Lieut. Samuel Stevens, Ensign Wm Haldane, Lieut. Wm Jones, Ensign Edmund Munroe, Lieut. Willard Stevens, Capt. David Brewer, Capt. Joseph Waite, Ensign Benj. Waite, Lieutenants Joshua Lock, Noah Porter, David Stone and Wm Barron (see *L. P.* 21:15-26); Sergeant James Ross 78th regiment (see *L. P.* 20:107); Corporals Rich'd Colliet, James Read, 44th, Peter McGrowder 46th, John Garrison 47th, John Dunnavon 45th, Henry West, John Almann and Richard Ford 40th, John McCann independent company, near Argyle; Sergeant James Rose 55th regiment near Crownpoint (see *L. P.* 21:17-19); of Samuel Ward, Jonas Cutler, Clark Chandler, Daniel Ward, Daniel Ward jr, Henry Ward, Wm Ward, Zacheus Cutler, Eben'r Cutter, Levi Willard, Abel Willard, James Putnam, Benj. Whiting, Phineas Ward, Benj. Stout jr, Hugh Cosgriff, Thos. Carmer, Peter Taylor, Peter Wright, John Webster, Viner Mitchell, Rich'd Edwards, Adolph Delpove and Daniel Thorpe of the township of Corinth (see *L. P.* 20:72); of Alex'r Phelps, Wm Buel, John Phelps, John Phelps jr, Israel Post, Obadiah Horseford, Samuel Filer, Ebenezer Green, Daniel Horseford, Asahel Phelps, Nehemiah Huntington, Charles Hinkley, Abiel Stark, Amos Phelps, Joshua

Phelps, Benj. Buel, Enos Horseford, Aaron Phelps, Roger
Phelps, Gamaliel Little and Aaron Stiles of the township
of Thetford (see *L. P.* 20:125); of Hannah Horsey (see *L. P.*
20:115); of Andrew Gautier, Benj. Blagge, Robert Boyd,
Jonathan Hampton sr and jr, of the township of Orwell
(see *L.P.* 20:106); of Adam Gilchrist, Jas. Boggs, Abr'm ten
Eyck, Wm Newton, Robert Hull, Elizabeth Barnard, Jane
Harle, Samuel Jobs, Thos. Pringle, John Thompson,
Samuel Selby and Wm Hume (see *L. P.* 20:157); of Oliver
Corey, Jonathan Whitney, Wm Holt, Nath'l Harris, Phil.
Goodridge, Benoni Boynton jr, Peter Reid, Jonathan
Wood, Ephraim Whitney, Benj. Wheatherbee, Jacob Gould
jr, Oliver Gould, Jacob Gould, Thos. Gould jr, Joseph
Goodridge, Rogers King, John Buttrick, Zachariah Whit-
ney, Stephen Stickney, Joshua Stickney, Oliver Stickney,
Nehemiah Bowers, Samuel Larrabee, Isaac Holden,
Eleazer Lawrence jr, Samuel Preston, James Preston,
Jonathan Whitcombe, Joseph Baker jr, Eleazer Davis, John
Baker, James Allen, Nathan Chase, Simon Tuttle, Joseph
Wooster, Simon Tuttle jr, Thomas Warren, Jonas Warren,
Oliver Warren, James King, John Fox jr, Peter Fox,
Daniel Fox, Jacob Fox, Stephen Shattuck, Stephen Chase,
Joshua Chase, Ezekiel Chase, Benj. Shattuck and Thos. Bell
of the township of Thomlinson (see *L. P.* 20:97).   144

22   Petition of Lieut. George Demler 60th regiment (see *L. P.*
21:93) granted. Petition of Gerrit Slover, Samuel Loudon,
Robert Ewing, Rudolphus Ritzema, Samuel Kissam, John
Valleau, John Winn, John Kelly, John Woodward, John
Shipboy, Daniel McCormick, Daniel Neil, John de Bow
and James A. Stewart (see *L. P.* 20:122) referred.   156

Oct. 17   Gov. Bernard desires that his interest in lands granted by
New Hampshire may be secured to him; opinion of coun-
cil thereon; Gov. Wentworth expresses the same wish.
Petition of Phineas Lyman, Daniel Lyman, Daniel Lyman
jr, Joseph Little, Medad Lyman, Samuel Miles, Samuel
Miles jr, Enos Allen, James Rice, Joseph Trobridge, Ross-
well Woodward, Thos. Trobridge, Abr'm Thompson jr,
Abr'm Thompson, Jacob Thompson, Stephen Allen,
Gideon Lyman jr, James Storer, Sylvanus Bishop, Samuel
Bishop jr, John Mix, John Peirpoint, John Bradley jr,
Phineas Bradley, Elijah Lyman, .John Cornall, Lemuel
Hotchkins, Jonah Bradley, Hezekiah Parmerly jr, John
Osten, Israel Monson, Joel Gilbert, Joseph Thompson,
Caleb Gilbert, Joseph Dorman, Joseph Worder, Timothy
Potter, Ebenezer Johnson, Selah Wright, Naomi Lyman,

John Lyman jr, Gad Lyman, Benj'n Sheldon, Reuben
Wright, Phineas Lyman Hodley, Eleazer Burt, Elnathan
Wright, Ephraim Wright jr, Bildad Wright, Elias Lyman
and Nath'l Phelps of the township of Wheathersfield (see
L. P. 22:4-6), granted. Gov. Moore reports on purchases
of Indian lands made by him at the late conference in Sir
Wm Johnson's house.   156

22   Time appointed for a hearing on the caveat of Wm O'Brien
against a patent to the earl of Ilchester, Lord Holland et
al of lands located by Walter Paterson (see *L. P.* 19:160;
21:110). Agents of transports not entitled to military
bounty lands (see *L. P.* 18:7).   159

24   Hearing on the caveat of owners of Coeymans patent post-
poned (p. 144). Petitions referred: of Gen. Thomas Gage,
Peter Hasenclever, Phil. Schuyler, John French and Peter
Lewis (see *L. P.* 22:16); of Wm Bayard, John French,
Thomas Shipboy, Wm Kane, Wm Proctor, Thos. Browne,
Wm Hogan, Kennedy Ferral, Marte Gerretse van Bergen,
Daniel Steel, David Edgar, Gerard Chesnut, Wm Benson,
Daniel Denniston, Hugh Denniston, Abr'm Lyle, John
Constable, Thos. Lotteridge, Patrick Smith, Robert Adams,
Dunlap Adems, Aaron Bradt, John Bradt, Walter Butler
and Robert Henry (see *L. P.* 22:14); of Lt. Col. Vaughan
60th regiment (see *L. P.* 22:10); of Michael Byrne, Frans
Ruport and Lucas Vedder (see *L. P.* 22:11); of Nich's Mat-
thias and Lawrence Lawyer (see *L. P.* 22:17); of Hendrick
Heeger, Jacob Myer, Adam Zee and Nicholas Becker (see
L. P. 22:12); of David Prym (see *L. P.* 22:13); of Johannes
Lawyer, Jacob Zimmer, Moses Ibbet and Jacob Enters
(see *L. P.* 22:15) with caveat against it by James Duane. 159

29   Opinion of council on the caveat of Wm O'Brien (p. 159).
Order concerning the lands granted to Ralph Wilkinson
(p. 66). Hearing on the caveat of James Duane (p. 159).
Petition of John Kathan for the township of Fulham referred.   163

Nov. 3   Petitions granted: of Lt. Col. Vaughan; of Mich'l Byrne et
al; of Nich's Mathias et al; of Hendrick Heeger et al; of
David Pryn; of Johannes Lawyer et al (p. 159); of Garret
Slover et al (p. 156); of John Kathan, Alex'r Kathan,
Daniel Kathan, John Kathan jr, Charles Kathan jr,
Daniel Serjeant, Rufus Serjeant, Moses Watkins, Alex'r
Bulson, Samuel Smith, Thos. Broaderick, Lemuel Bowers,
Benj. Smith, Eben'r Howard, Stephen Tuttle, John Tuttle,
Joseph Tuttle, Charles Boyle and Robert Mountain of the
township of Fulham (see *L. P.* 20:120); of Ebenezer Jessup,

Wm Johnson, David Hunter, Dederick Miller, Jonathan Jones, Isaac Matson, Timothy Knap, Samuel Bishop, Edward Jessup, Rutger Bleecker, Johannes Beeckman, Jacob Hat, Joseph Jessup jr, Jonas Meyer, and James Murray (see *L. P.* 21:172); of Ebenezer Cole, Jacob Marsh, Samuel Waters, James Draper, Edward Fitsimmons, Abiather Waldow, Simeon Cowell, John Trumble, Ichabod West, James Draper jr, Ebenezer Wright and heirs of Elihu Marsh (see *L. P.* 22:24); of Lieut. Thos. Etherington (see *L. P.* 22:38); of Lieut. Thos. Gamble (see *L. P.* 21:56); of Lieut. Dennis Carleton (see *L. P.* 22:29). Petitions referred: of Joseph Reade jr, and Wilhelmus van Antwerp (see *L. P.* 22:32); of Wm Livingston, Wm Smith jr, Whitehead Hicks, John Brevoort, Elias Brevoort, Thos. Hicks, John Woods, Gilbert Hicks, Elizabeth Livingston, Thos. Jackson, Garret Noel, John Brown, Joseph Royal, Peter Yates, Gerard Bancker, John Robinson, Gilbert Ash, Wm Sorral, John Dutton Cramshire, Frances Brown, John Smith, Moses Nicolls, Garret Roorbach, John Powers, John McKenney, Isaac Heron, James Mathers, Elias Nixon, Francis Child and Wm Feris of the township of Royalton (see *L. P.* 22:35); of Wm Kelly, Isaac Ogden, David Rogers, Benj'n Johnson, Isaac Ball, Joseph Rogers, John Nisbit, Gabriel Ogden, Nath'l Firran, John Cockeran, Ebenezer Ward, Isaac Longworth, Thos. Richards, Nath'l Richards, Elias Crane, James Banks, Solomon Davis, James Johnson, David Johnson, Thos. Longworth, David Person, Daniel Crane, Eleazer Brewer and John Brewer of the township of Gageborough (see *L. P.* 22:30); of Pierre G. de Peyster, Thos. Smith, Winter Fargie, Nicholas C. Bogart, David Shaw, Peter Bard jr, Benj'n Tusten, John Bogart jr, Adrian Bancker, Samuel Hobbs, Wm Weaver, Isaac Ryckman jr, John Lewis, Henry Ritter, Thos. Nutman, Thomas Johnston, John Doe, John Dawize, John Shine, Stephen Elmes, Andrew Cunningham, Jacob Shaver, John Elliot, Samuel Bard, Faucenier Valleau, John Bassenett, John Turner, Edw'd McDermot, Wm Ruttlidge, Miles Keen, Henry Dougherty, John Cree, James McCartney, Wm McDermot and Joseph Frazer (see *L. P.* 21:159).   165

6   Petition of Francis Legge (see *L. P.* 22:40) granted. Petition of Robert R. Livingston, Robert R. Livingston jr, John Will, Henry Will, Phil. Will, Wm Will, Chris'n Will, Isaac Stoutenburgh, Wm Scott, John Whiteman, Henry Wells, Rich'd Wootton, Wm de Peyster, Adolph de Grave, Robert Griffith, Henry Beeckman, James Wessel, Henry

Brevoort, John Stout, Thos. Broockman, John Vernor,
John McDovall, John McCurdy, Andrew Cusack, George
Shaw, John Crum, John Wool, Joseph Mountford, Edward
Lawrence, James Barron, Wm Meeks, John Ran, John
Evans, Wm Christie and Samuel Moore of the township of
Camden (see *L. P.* 22:45) referred. Order concerning Gov.
Benning Wentworth's allotment in the township of Putney. 173

7   Petition of Peter Hasenclever (see *L. P.* 22:46) granted.
Lands granted to: Lt. Col. James Robertson (see *L. P.*
21:127); Lieut. John Nordbergh (see *L. P.* 22:38); Lieut.
John Walker of Major Joseph Goreham's company of
Rangers (see *L. P.* 21:148); Capt. David Skene 108th regiment (see *L. P.* 22:27); Corporal James Duncan 55th regiment, Sergeant John St Leger 80th, and Sergeant Thos.
McCarty 60th (see *L. P.* 21:122); Privates John Duggin
43d, George Clayton, James Philipps and Noah Flood 44th
(see *L. P.* 21:121); Drummer Johan Christ'r Long 48th
regiment (see *L. P.* 21:126): John French and 23 others not
named (see *L. P.* 22:39). Petitions granted: of Joseph
Reade jr et al; of Wm Livingston et al; of Wm Kelly et
al; of Pierre G. de Peyster et al (p. 165); of Robert R.
Livingston et al (p. 173). Grant to Henry Cuyler commissary of stores and provisions (p. 94) enlarged.   174

12 Petitions granted: of Stephen Dannall armorer (see *L. P.*
22:58); of Elkanah Deane, Elkana Deane jr, Richard
Deane, Nisbet Deane, Wm Deane, John Deane and Samuel
Deane (see *L. P.* 21:147); of Oliver Willard in behalf of
Prince Tracey, Benj. Wright, Benj. Burck, Joseph Marsh,
Benajah Strong, Elisha Marsh, John Baldwin, John Ben-
nett, Nath'l Holbrook jr, Noah Dewey jr, Solomon Strong,
Jonathan Marsh, Amos Robinson, Rufus Baldwin, Daniel
Pinneo, Elijah Strong, Ebenezer Gillet jr, Giles Alexander,
Abel Marsh, and Zadock Wright of the township of Ware
[Hartford], excepting lots of Daniel Warner, Joseph New-
march, Thos. Bell and Samuel Wentworth (see *L. P.* 20:98). 179

19 The name of the township of Fulham changed to Galway.
Township of Cavendish granted to David Sternes, Amos
Kimball, Phineas Stewart, David Goodridge, Benj'n
Stewart, Ephraim Kimball, Josiah Bayley, Simon Butler,
Samuel Read jr, James Descomb, Abijah Sternes, Nathaniel
Hastings, Rich'd Taylor, John Buss, John Buss jr, George
Kimball, Peter Page, Jonathan Wetherbee, Oliver Capree,
Giles Alexander, James Scott, and Simeon Alvard, reserv-
ing the lot of Benning Wentworth (see *L. P.* 21:77). Peti-
tion of Lieut. Alex'r Dowe, son of Lieut. James Dowe 60th

regiment deceased (see *L. P.* 21:91) granted. Petitions referred: of John de Witt, Matthew Hopper, Peter Williams and Anthony Bulson (see *L. P.* 20:19); of Elijah Alexander, Eben'r Alexander and Ephraim Dorman (see *L. P.* 20:103); of Samuel Asly, Hilkiah Grout and Wm Smeed (see *L. P.* 20:91); of Jeremiah Hall, Jonathan Hammon, John French and John Hunt (see *L. P.* 20:92).   181

28   Wessel van Dyck and Gerrit van Dyck, grandchildren of Jacob Lockerman to show cause why they should not be prosecuted for intrusion on crown lands, on the petition of Francis McDermott (see *L. P.* 22:87). Petition of George Williams, Paul Swift, Wm Reed and Evan Jones sergeants, Simon Solomon, John Little, Daniel Campbell, John White and John McGee privates 28th regiment (see *L. P.* 22:18) granted. Petition of Israel Putnam (see *L. P.* 21:3) referred. The names of Willard Stevens, Thos. Williams, Wm Griggs, Benj. Stout, John Armstrong and Caleb Hyatt to be inserted in the patent for the township of Fairlie instead of Benj. Baldwin, Bread Bachelor, Daniel Shattuck, Daniel Jones, Nehemiah Wright and Josiah Chancey jr (p 126).   186

Dec. 3 Report of committee on the petition of Israel Putnam (p. 186); Putnam to be prosecuted for forgery. Petition of John de Witt et al (p. 181) granted. Township of Falkland granted to the Hon. Lucius Ferdinand Carey, Anne Maria Carey, James Vanegan, George McIntosh, Francis Schlosser, Christ'r Pauli, Thomas de la Main, John Peter Rochet, John Burent, Wm Prescot, Perkins Margea, Andrew Nelson, James Deas, John Larey, Thos. Doughty, Adam Gilchrist, George Lenach, Edw'd Farrel, Rich'd Kent, Isaac Goelet, Thos. Freeman, Wm Ferris, John Dutton Cramshire, Francis Child, James Brown, John Smith, Moses Nicholls, Benj. Garrison, Isaac Noble and Joseph Whipple (see *L. P.* 22:19). Petitions granted: of Aug. van Cortlandt, Henry White, Isaac Low, Fred'k van Cortlandt, Aug. van Horne, Benj'n Helmes, Dirck de la Metter, Abr'm Lent, Phil. Kissick, Joseph Young, Wm Miller, John Waldron, Michael van der Cook jr, Richard Mandevil, John Cotgrave, Alex'r Cocken, James Oliver, Daniel Sullivan, George Crookshanks, Michael Power, Ephraim Bennet, John Clark, Wm Lightburne, Francis Cowenhoven, John Kanon, David Brooks, Nath'l Earle, Jacob Lent, Hendrick Quackenboss, Joseph Jadwin, Thos. Hayet, Moses Nicholls, James Brown, Michael van der Cook sr, and Benj. Garrison (see *L. P.* 22:52); of John Jackson,

Thos. Allen and Samuel Seaman (see *L. P.* 22:74). License
to purchase Indian lands granted to Phil. van Petten,
Simon Schermerhorn and John Glen jr (see *L. P.* 21:175). 189

5　Township of Springfield granted to Gideon Lyman, Joseph
Little, Elijah Lyman, Phineas Lyman, Selah Wright, Elias
Lyman, John Phelps, Medad Alverd, John Burt jr, Oliver
Lyman, Simeon Parsons, Nath'l Day, Elias Lyman jr,
Samuel Parsons, Eleazer Root, Ephraim Wright, Benj'n
Parsons, James Lyman, Reuben Coates, John Lyman,
Caleb Lyman, Josiah Pearce, Israel Lyman, Stephen Root
and Thos. Quiner; the shares of Benning Wentworth,
James Apthorpe, John Gould, Henry Hilson to remain
vested in the crown (see *L. P.* 22:97). 193

10　Hearing on the caveat of the owners of Coeymans patent
(p. 159). 195

12　Opinion of council sustaining the caveat as the owners of
Coeymans patent are entitled to all the lands comprehended
in the patent of confirmation given in 1714. The king vs
Joseph Forman; the king vs E. Graham. 195

20　Township of Westminster granted to Bildad Andross,
Michael Metcalf et al not named (see *L. P.* 21:40). Town-
ship of Clarendon granted to Elijah Alexander et al
(p. 181), names of Ephraim Dorman, Samuel Whitmore,
Jeremiah Whitmore, Benj'n Melven, Benj'n Melven jr,
Ebenezer Alexander, Hilkiah Grout, Oliver Ashley, Wm
Smead jr, Elijah Grout, Thos. Bridgman, Zadock Hawks,
Eliphalet Carpenter, Seth Heaton, Seth Heaton jr, Thos.
Baker, Thos. Riggs, Jeremiah Thayer, Henry Bond, Abr'm
Scott, Elijah Dodgejim, Elisha Marsh and Joshua Tucker
to be inserted in the patent. Township of Shrewsbury
granted to Samuel Asley et al (p. 181), names of Samuel
Ashley, Orlando Bridgeman, Wm Smead, Jonathan
Houghton, Clement Sumner, Joseph Whitcomb, Nath'l
Heaton, Gideon Ellis, Joseph Ellis, Phinehas Stevens,
Simeon Alvard, John Wheeler, Elijah Dodge, Wm Heaton,
Moses Wright, Abijah Tucker, Moses Tucker, Samuel
Hills, Joseph Whitcombe, Joseph Stone, Wm Frink,
Gideon Ashley, Joseph Ashley and Wm Warner to be in-
serted in the patent; Benning Wentworth's lot to remain
vested in the crown. Township of Saltash granted to
Jeremiah Hall et al (p. 181), names of Ichabod Fisher,
David Nims jr, Michael Metcalf jr, Moses Field, Nathan
Blake, Paul Field, Wm Wright, Thos. Christen, James
Grimes, Samuel Hall, John Hunt, Eleazer Burt, John
French, Wm Grimes, Joseph Ashley jr, Jeremiah Hall,

1766

Samuel Field, Reuben Alexander, Jesse Hall, Ebenezer
Nims, Wm Carr, Phinehas Stevens and Samuel Hills to
be inserted in the patent; Benning Wentworth's lot to remain vested in the crown. Minutes sent to the board of
trade.   196

1767

Jan. 7 The king vs Ennis Graham. The name of Caleb Hyatt to
be inserted in the patent of New Windsor vice Alex'r
Dallas. Order on petitions of Surgeon Donald McLean,
Surgeon's Mate Malachi Treat and Lieut. Neal McLean,
and of Surgeon Wm Young (see *L. P.* 22:129, 138).   201

13 Hearing on the preceding petitions of Surgeon Donald Mc-
Lean et al.   202

19 Opinion of council thereon; grants of land to be made to:
Lt. Col. Augustine Prevoost and his son; Lt. Col. Richard
Maitland; Lieut. Hugh Frazer; Lieut. Walter Stewart;
Martin Garretsen van Bergen; Surgeon Donald McLean;
Malachi Treat; Lieut. Neal McLean; Surgeon Wm Young;
Abr'm Lott.   202

21 The king vs Ennis Graham.   204

28 Township of Woodstock granted to Levi Willard, Jonathan
Grout, Israel Curtice, John Church, Wm Powers, Jonathan
Hunt, Aaron Burt, Nathan Willard, Joseph Stibbins, James
Call, Ebenezer Dike, Wm Syms, Aaron Smith, Elijah
Grout, Joel Grout, Moses Belding, Daniel Warner, James
Powers and Andrew Powers (see *L. P.* 20:155); the lots of
Richard Wiberd, James Nevin, Jonathan Tuck, Zebulon
Giddings and Abner Morrell to remain vested in the crown.
Township of Bridgewater granted to Seth Field, Rufus
Field, Elisha Hunt, Stephen Pomroy, James Harwood,
Thos. Sergent, Oliver Field, Oliver Warner, Wm Syms,
Zur Evans, Shammah Pomroy, John Sarjeant, Ezra Pom-
roy, Jonathan Hildreth, Hilkiah Grout, Smith Ingram, Joel
Smith, Abel Emans and Daniel Shattuck (see *L. P.* 20:154),
excepting the shares formerly allotted to Benning Went-
worth, John Downing, Sampson Sheafe, Thos. Wiggins,
Wm Richardson, Abel Morse, Samuel Wentworth, Rev.
Mr McClintosh, Rev. Mr Chace, Rev. Mr Bayley and
Meshek Ware, which are to remain crown lands. Town-
ship of Somerset granted to Thos. Denny, James Taylor,
Daniel Serjeant, John Moffet, John Beaman, John Holton,
Nehemiah Wright, Daniel Jones, Elijah Williams jr,
Samuel Denny, Wilder Willard, Daniel Field, Samuel
Field, Samson Willard, Obadiah Dickenson, Lucius Doo-
little, Amasa Wright, Lemuel Hastings, Joseph Willard
and Abel Walker; reserving the lots of Sampson Sheafe,

John Downing and Benning Wentworth as crown lands
(see *L. P.* 21:86). Township of New Fane granted to Luke
Brown, Jacob Hallett, Charles Morse, Samuel Brown,
Magnus Garrett, Samuel Bailey, John Brizell, James
Bryan, Thos. Arden, Giles Alexander, George Shaw,
James Armstrong, Matthew Hopkins, Crosfield Rushton,
Christ'r Hannon, Nich's Parsell, John Lent, John Arm-
strong, John Corselius, Thos. Stooley, Alexander Wilson,
Samuel Hopson, James Smith, Abr'm Ingraham and
Gregory Ives (see *L. P.* 22:169); excepting the lots of
Daniel Warner, Mark Hunking Wentworth and Theo. At-
kinson. Petitions granted: of Col. Nathan Whiting,
Samuel Fitch, Col. Eleazer Fitch, Col. James Smedley,
David Baldwin, And'w Myers, Samuel Whiting, Robert
Aiton, Amos Hitchcock and Nathan Haynes Whiting (see
L. P. 22:65); of John Springer, Elizabeth Springer and Ann
Catherine Parlin (see *L. P.* 22:54). Lands to be granted
as prayed for by: Captains John Skinner and Norman Mc-
Leod, Lieutenants Wm Irvin, Walter Patterson, Samuel
Steel, James Henderson, Wm Brown, Thos. Hopson and
Alexander Fraser (see *L. P.* 22:174); Surgeon Wm Young
(see *L. P.* 22:129); Capt. Wm Sherriff for Capt. Wm Hand-
field and Lieut. Charles Sherriff (see *L. P.* 22:171-72);
Lieut. John Hamilton (see *L. P.* 22:42); Lieut. Adolphus
Benzel 50th regiment (see *L. P.* 22:50); Lt. Col. John
Maunsell (see *L. P.* 22:175); Private Andrew Rusk (see
L. P. 22:49).   204

Feb. 4   Order on memorials of Robert Leake commissary general
and his deputies (see *L. P.* 21:124; 22:100) and on caveats
against them by Henry Beeckman and Robert Livingston,
by Andrew Morehouse and Samuel Waldo (see *L. P.*
22:84), by John Morin Scott (see *L. P.* 22:84), by David
Johnston (see *L. P.* 22:86) and by Jonathan Dennis
and John Ryder. Petition of the governors of Kings college (see *L. P.* 23:11) referred.   212

12   Report on the petition of the governors of Kings college;
township of Mooretown granted to them. Township of
Socialborough granted to John Harris Cruger, Wm Walton jr, Thos. Jones, Jacob Walton, Thos. Hicks, Theophilact Bache, John Jones, Isaac Low, Peter du Bois,
John de Lancey, Fred'k van Cortlandt, Fred'k de Peyster,
Gerard Walton, Henry White, Petrus Stuyvesant, Robert
Cam Livingston, James Emot, Christ'r Smith, Anthony
van Dam, John van Dam, Teleman Cuyler, Derick Schuyler, Thos. Lawrence, Thos. Bayeux, John Elliot, Wynant

van Zandt, John Vernor, James Seagrove, Wm Kennedy, Wm Hutton, John Riker, John Thompson, Samuel Shelby, John Taylor, Lewis Relay, Wm Cockburne, Arch'd Campbell, John Woodward, John Smith, James Long, Hamilton Young, Fleming Colgan, Robert Robinson, Samuel Bayer, John Keen, Charles Ramage, John Wilson and Moses Nicoll (p. 437; see *L. P.* 22:115). Town of Barnet granted to Simon Stevens, Willard Stevens, Joel Stone, James Blanchard, Nathan Stone, John Smilly, Rob't McMenomy, John Manbrut, Samuel Stevens, Jonathan Grout, Jacob Hallett, Charles Morse, Giles Alexander, Shem Kentfield, Enos Stevens, Benj. Allen, Simeon Alvard, Phineas Stevens, Jonathan Weatherby, Silas Whitcomb, Nath'l Powers, Lemuel Hastings and Benj. Whiting (see *L. P.* 21:104); excepting the lots of Theodore Atkinson, Wm Temple, John Odiorne, John Lard and Meshek Bell which remain vested in the crown. Township of Sharon granted to David Rowland and associates not named (see *L. P.* 23:33). Petition of Whitehead Leonard of Kingston, N. J. (see *L. P.* 22:34) granted. Boundary lines of Newberry altered according to petition of Benjamin Whiting (p. 81). Order that the principal owners in townships under New Hampshire grants attend the council before action is taken on their petitions.   214

Mar. 4   Order on petition of Johs. van der Pool, Robert van Deursen, Peter Vosburgh and Hendrick Remsen (see *L. P.* 21:61).   220

11   Hearing on the caveats against granting patents to Robert Leake (p. 212) postponed.   221

20   Warrant of survey granted to Rob't Leake (see *L. P.* 22:148). Petitions for land granted: Surgeon Samuel Dick (see *L. P.* 22:128); Capt. John Wilson 59th regiment (see *L. P.* 23:81); Capt. Joseph Williams 59th regiment (see *L. P.* 19:146); Abr'm Lott, Nich's C. Bogert, Engelbert Lott, Johs. Lott, John Abeel, James Abeel, John Nielson, Thos. Cral, Abr'm P. Lott, Peter T. Curtenius, Isaac Roosevelt, Jacobus Roosevelt jr, Dirck Brinckerhoff, Dirck Brinckerhoff jr, Theodorus van Wyck, John Oothout, Anth'y ten Eyck, Coenradt A. ten Eyck, Wm Lupton, Jacobus van Zandt, Wynant van Zandt, Wm Horsefield and Phineas McIntosh of the township of Monckton (see *L. P.* 23:26).   222

25   Petitions granted: Mary Graham (see *L. P.* 23:63); John Munro, Henry Brower, John Richey, Corn's Brower, Moses Nicholls and John Smith (see *L. P.* 23:25). Hearing on the petition of Francis McDermot (p. 186).   224

30   Petition of Francis McDermot (p. 224) dismissed. Orders
on petitions: of Lieut. Thos. Swords (see *L. P.* 22:168);
of Henry Smith sr, Samuel Fowler and Isaac Fowler of
Newburgh (see *L. P.* 23:28, 35). Township of St Catharine
granted to Adam Gilchrist and associates not named (see
L. P. 23:22, 28). Petition of Corporal Wm Gravis Royal
Americans (see *L. P.* 23:90).   225

Ap.   1   Patents granted to: John Monier and John N. Bleeker (see
L. P. 22:135); Samuel Chandler, Gardiner Chandler, Joshua
Chandler sr and jr, John Chandler sr and jr, Moses Chand-
ler, Charles Church Chandler, Theophilus Chandler, Win-
throp Chandler, John Chandler 2d, Joseph Chandler, David
Chandler, Josiah Chandler, Seth Chandler, Timothy Paine,
James Putnum, John Murray, Levi Willard, Samuel Mc-
Clallen, John Green, John Green 2d, Benj. Green sr and jr,
Nath'l Green, Daniel Hubbard, Russell Hubbard, David
Holmes and Daniel Paine (see *L. P.* 22:137); Lieut. Josias
Banks, independent company (see *L. P.* 21:125); Philipp
Castles, John Smart, John Mason, Wm Sheels, Thos.
Fisher, John Thorley, John McVey, Brien McKinley, Thos.
Skinner, Robert Mercer, Stephen Row, Henry Plank, An-
drew Knowles, John Douglas, John Neal, Wm Andrews,
Corn's Brown, Robert Gray, Patrick Quin, Jacob Bates,
Thos. Sutton, Samuel Lewis, Henry McDougal, Rob't
Wheary, late Privates Daniel Corbin, Ebenezer Hodgkins
and Rich'd Beatley sergeants, Edward Yarrow corporal
(see *L. P.* 23:12); Privates Charles Hughes, John Simpson,
John Cammock, Corporals Henry Biram, Peter St Clair,
Charles Halbert, John Miller, James Downs, Richard
Tenor, Arthur Rogers, Alex'r Marshall, James Wilson,
Sergeants James Rogers, Zopher Haaden, Musician Wm
Harbourn (see *L. P.* 23:141): the same with lots formerly
granted to Lieutenants John Cruckshanks, John Bowen,
Ensign Alex'r Fraser, Surgeons James Boggs and Peter
Brown and vacant lands north of Princetown to be erected
into the township of Chatham. Patent granted to Philipp
Daulton, Alex'r Blackwood, Patrick Kelly, Francis Taylor,
John Donnelly, John Bevan, James Webster, Edmund
Carney, Wm Pearce, John Vaughan, Richard Frederick,
Rich'd Kellet, Peter Maturin, Thos. Dunning, Wm Mc-
Donald, John Callaghan, Wm Smith, Thos. Fisher, Francis
Sumpter, John Dobbs, James West, Timothy Johnson,
John Nash, Barney Mailey, William Burns late privates,
Sergeants Robert Calhoon, John Felding, Wm Christie,
James Moffat, Corporals Wm Gibson, Edward Lawrence,

Joseph Hudson, John McVae, John Baker, Wm Thompson, Evan West, Patrick Fitzsimmons, Wm Little, James Heavy and Robert Haisty (see *L. P.* 23:19).   227

9   License to purchase land from the Onoughquage Indians at the head of Delaware river granted to John Harper sr and jr, Wm Harper, Joseph Harper and Alex'r Harper (see *L. P.* 23:92). Petitions granted: Major Paul Rycaut 17th regiment (see *L. P.* 24:21); Capt. Lewis van Fuser 60th regiment for 3000 acres east of Otter creek; Ensign John Clarke (see *L. P.* 23:40); Corporal Alex'r Frazer 78th regiment (see *L. P.* 23:48); Sergeant Hugh Patrick 44th regiment (see *L. P.* 23:403); Wm Halyburton, D. D. (see *L. P.* 23:37); Wm Sherriff, Rich'd Maitland, Gabriel Maturin, John Small, Stephen Kemble, Samuel Kemble, Rich'd Kemble, Wm Kemble, Henry Munro, John McNeal, Francis Panton, Buckridge Webb, Henry Hornefer, John Sackerby, Thomas Wallis, James Glassford, Samuel Verplanck, Thos. Wm Moore, Edw'd Gold, Medad Pomroy, Ebenezer Harvey, Jos. Burt and Shem Kentfield of the township of Halesborough (see *L. P.* 23:49).   229

15   Hearing on the petition of John van der Pool et al (p. 220) postponed. Warrant of survey granted to Henry van Vleck et al (see *L. P.* 23:24). Petitions granted: Abr'm van Vleck, John van Vleck, Benj. Booth, Abr'm Brasher and Thos. Bartow jr (see *L. P.* 23:23); Hugh Wallace and Alex'r Wallace (see *L. P.* 22:111); Jacobus Montanye, Jacobus van Zandt, Wm Waddel, Wm Newman, Jacobus Montanye jr, John Levine, Phil. Doughty, Thos. Gordon, Samuel Wharton, Edmund Millne, Smith Ramadge, Christian Demure, Samuel Plume, Benj'n Plume, Abr'm Plume, Robert Plume, James Carter, John Lewis, John Keen, James Armstrong, Moses Nicholls, John Smith, Dudley Davis, John Dutton Cremshier, Isaac Wilkins, Abr'm Montanye and Andrew Cunningham (see *L. P.* 23:142); of Sergeant Wm Freind 1st regiment (see *L. P.* 21:149); Private James Scott 44th regiment for land near Rogers Rock; Private Hugh Gackson [Jackson] (see *L. P.* 21:152); Private George Robertson 22d regiment (see *L. P.* 21:151). Order for correcting a mistake in the Indian purchase made by Wm Bayard and partners (see *L. P.* 23:88).   231

16   Township of Reading granted to Simon Stevens, Joel Stone, Willard Stevens, George Wilson, Cornelius van den Burgh, George Shaw, John Armstrong, Matthew Hopkins, James Armstrong, Evert Kip, Wm Bailey, Joseph Blanchard, Garret van den Bergh, Rynier Hopper, Richard

Varian, Thomas Arden, Daniel Goldsmith, Daniel Gold-
smith jr, Caleb Hyatt, John Stout and James Wessells (see
L. P. 23:56); excepting the lots of Benning Wentworth,
Wiseman Clagget, Daniel Warner and Samuel Wentworth
which remain crown lands. Petitions granted: of **Arch'd**
Campbell, Wm Stewart, Thos. Buchanan, Arch'd Currie,
Wm Pagen and John Murray (see *L. P.* 23:118); of Henry
Erklev, John Enny, John Snouse, Godfrey Snouse, George
Workhout, Michael Nestle, Wm Sobke, **Peter Pyster,**
Theodorus Anthony, Nich's Anthony, Thos. Sloker, Edw'd
Carrol, John Lockhart, John Watson, James O'Brien,
Charles Berrow, Joseph Ogden, Isaac Peirsen, John Bowlls,
Moses Nicholls, Benj. Garrison, Rich'd Curson, Isaac
Wilson, Samuel Plume and Thos. Stewart (see *L. P.* 23:51);
of James Gilliland, James Anderson, James Campbell and
Richard Wootton (see *L. P.* 23:52); of John Brackan (see
L. P. 23:82); of Wm Cockburn, Alex'r Ellice, Robert El-
lice, John Portius, George Phyn, Wm Duncan, Alex'r
Campbell, John Smyth, George Lewis, John Lewis, Fran-
cis Child, John Ramsey, Walter Buchannan, John Thomp-
son, James Phyn, John Bowles and Crean Brush (see *L. P.*
23:61); of Major Gen. Ralph Burton (see *L. P.* 23:87); of
Rev. John Ogilvie, chaplain Royal Americans (see *L. P.*
23:86); of Lieut. Francis Turbut 44th regiment (see *L. P.*
23:100); of Sergeants Peter Deacon 46th, John Kane 44th,
Corporals John Baus, Samuel Whitehouse, John Rotstone
80th, John Smith 17th, James Connor 55th and Privates
Joseph Halbrouk, John Neal, Wm Adley, John Waller,
George Smith, Walter Middon 46th, Donald McDonald
highland regiment, Michael Ralf 55th, John Dunn, Wm
Watson, Benj. Grosman, James Blair 66th (see *L. P.* 23:39);
of Sergeants John Inwood, George Lenach, John Maccay,
Royal Americans, John Stewart 28th regiment, Corporals
Rich'd Moss, John Moon, Joseph Lambert, James McLean
60th, Wm Pitts, Richard Irwin 28th, Drummers David
English 28th, John Fellows 44th, Privates Robert Gray,
Rich'd Livingston 28th, John Cross, Joseph Coppney, John
Thomas, Angus Fletcher, Simon Burley, John Marshall,
Wm Wheeler, John Hulsey, Lazarus Marchan, John
Bogan, Manuel Cats 60th, John Brown 45th (see *L. P.*
23:74); of Corporal James Brown 80th regiment (see *L. P.*
23:99); of Corporals John Norman 28th, Daniel Taylor 80th,
and Privates Alex'r McKenzie, John Robertson 42d, John
Fotheringham 40th, John Kerens 28th (see *L. P.* 23:108);
of Private John Woodman 27th regiment for 50 acres on

Lake Champlain; of John Morin Scott, John French and
Joseph Blanchard (see *L. P.* 23:73).   233

29   Townships of Bernard and Stockbridge granted to Wm
Story agent (see *L. P.* 23:44-45). Petitions referred: of
Phineas Bradley, Samuel Bishop, Benj. Dodgester and
Eliakim Hall (see *L. P.* 21:180); of Eliakim Hall (see *L. P.*
19:169).   238

May 5   Warrant of survey to issue for the whole of the Indian pur-
chase made by Johannes Lawyer et al (p. 159, 163, 165).
Petition of Henry Smith sr, Samuel Fowler and Isaac
Fowler (p. 225) granted. Hearing appointed between
Thos. Swords and the corporation of Kingston (p. 225).
The king vs Ennis Graham; the king vs Joseph Forman.   240

13   Order on petition of Abr'm Lott, John Bratt, Richard Yates,
Isaac Lefferts, Thos. Wells, Simon Lott, Richard Mercer,
Jonathan Lawrence, Wm Heyer and Henry Remsen jr
(see *L. P.* 22:177). The king vs Ennis Graham; the king
vs Joseph Forman. Petition of Nath'l Marston, Gabriel
Ludlow, Charles Williams, Robert Crommelin, Edw'd
Man, David Clarkson, Andrew Barclay, Elias des Brosses,
Nicholas Wm Stuyvesant, Theophilact Bache, Adrian
Renaudet, Alex'r Colden, Thos. Hill, Edward Laight,
Anthony van Dam, Robert R. Livingston, John Charlton,
Humphrey Jones, Matthew Clarkson, Benj. Kissam, John
Provoost, James Duane, Lambert Moore and Wm Bedlow
(see *L. P.* 23:137) granted. Township of Windfall granted
to Phineas Bradley, Abr'm Thompson sr and jr, Isaac
Thompson, Benj'n Dorchester, Erastus Bradley, Phineas
Bradley jr, John Bradley, Samuel Bishop jr, Eliakim Hall
sr and jr, Isaac Hall jr, Hezekiah Hall, Caleb Hall and
Stephen Hall (p. 238); excepting the lot of Benning Went-
worth which remains crown land. Township of Walling-
ford granted to Eliakim Hall sr and jr, Isaac Hall jr, Hezekiah Hall, Stephen Hall, Caleb Hall, Samuel Hall, Elisha
Hall, Samuel Bishop jr, Phineas Bradley, John Mix, Enos
Tuttle, David Austin, Isaac Doolittle, Daniel Lyman,
James Rea, John Sacket, Jeremiah Townsend, Isaac Townsend and Medad Lyman (p. 238); excepting the lots of
Benning Wentworth, Daniel Warner, Joseph Newmarch
and Samuel Willis which remain crown lands. Petition of
John Kerr, James McMillan, John Cook and John Trotter
(see *L. P.* 23:134) rejected because deputy commissaries of
stores are not entitled to bounty lands under the proclamation of October 1763.   241

June 3   Order concerning the lands to be granted to Lt. Col. Aug.
Prevoost and his son, Lieut. Aug. Prevoost. Petition of
Lieut. Pierce Pensonby Butler (see *L. P.* 23:145) referred. 244

10   Petition of Lady Susannah widow of Sir Peter Warren, Wm
      Bayard and Jellis Mandeville (see *L. P.* 23:146) referred.   244

July 6   Warrant of survey to issue for Lieut. Pierce Pensonby
      Butler. Order for hearing on caveat of Isaac Fort vs
      Joseph Reade jr (see *L. P.* 23:135). Warrant of survey
      granted to Quarter Master George Butrick (see *L. P.*
      23:148). Licenses to purchase Indian lands granted: to
      George Croghan and associates not named (see *L. P.*
      23:159); to Valkert P. Douw, Lambert Moore and others
      not named (see *L. P.* 23:162).   245

Aug. 6   Hearing between Thos. Swords and corporation of Kings-
      ton (p. 240) postponed. New charter to be granted to the
      borough of Schenectady (see *N. Y. col. mss,* 94:115).   246

14   Corporation of Kingston to show cause why the above order
      for a hearing should not be revoked. Proprietors of Min-
      isink patent called upon for a statement of their claims.   247

19   New date for the hearing between Thos. Swords and cor-
      poration of Kingston fixed. Hearing on the petitions of
      Abr'm Lott et al (p. 241), and of Johannes van der Pool
      et al (p. 231) postponed without day.   247

31   Order on representation of Abel Hardenbrook and others
      (see *N. Y. col. mss,* 94:112, 117).   248

Sep. 16   Hearing between Thos. Swords and corporation of Kings-
      ton (p. 247); decided in favor of Thomas Swords, Surgeon
      Josiah Harper 80th regiment, and Wm Spaight master
      royal navy.   248

Oct. 8   Royal orders disallowing the New York acts for furnishing
      the barracks with firewood and for establishing the county
      of Cumberland; to be published by proclamation.   249

Nov. 16   Petition of Lieut. John Hallum R. N. (see *L. P.* 24:34) re-
      ferred.   250

19   Hearing on the petition of Robert Leake (p. 221); adjourned.
      Hearing on caveat of Isaac Fort (p. 245).   251

23   Petition of Ebenezer Jessup, Wm Johnson, David Hunter,
      Dederick Miller, Jonathan Jones, James Dole, Timothy
      Knap, Cornelius van Santvoort, Edward Jessup, Rutger
      Bleecker, Johs. Beekman, Jacob Hatt, Joseph Jessup jr,
      Jonas Meyer and James Murray (see *L. P.* 24:17) granted. 251

1768

Jan. 27   Petitions for land: of Quartermaster Thos. Fricket for 2000
      acres between Crownpoint and Ticonderoga; of Lieut.
      Edw'd Tudor (see *L. P.* 23:135); of Surgeon Donald Mc-
      Lean 77th regiment, Surgeon's Mate Malachi Treat and
      Lieut. Neal McLean 47th regiment (see *L. P.* 24:8); of
      Corporals Neal McKinnon 77th, Arch'd McIntire 40th and

Private Dugal McDugal 40th regiment (see *L. P.* 22:31);
of Charles Friedenberg, Gottlieb Friedenberg, Wm Bis-
chausen, Ernest Friedenberg, Hans Friedenberg, Samuel
Williams, Thos. French, Henry Pace, Henry Seton, Wm
Price, Charles Hand, John Meyer, John Inlos, James Pace,
Christ'r Pauly, Wm Samuel, Daniel Vels, Miguel Vels,
Thos. Dibden and John Jones (see *L. P.* 24:15); of David
Matthews and Jacob Shafer for 2000 acres south of Ticon-
deroga; of Simon and George Metcalfe (see *L. P.* 23:147);
of Lieut. John Carden (see *L. P.* 24:71); of Michael Sals-
bergh (see *L. P.* 23:107); of Capt. Harry Gordon (see
L. P. 24:14) granted.   252

Feb. 10   Lieut. John de Berniere 44th regiment, John Taylor and
associates, Lieut. P. P. Butler, Lieut. Abernethy Cargil,
Simon Remsen and three others, John Muller and Nicholas
Killman, Simon Metcalf attorney (see *L. P.* 24:29, 78;
23:105, 109, 145) to support their petitions for land in the
Minisink patent; Johannes Trumper et al, John Monk (see
L. P 24:45), Henry Freligh jr, Petrus Schart (see *L. P.*
24:46), Capt. Thos. Farrel to support their petitions for
land along the Albany and Ulster county line. The king
vs Ennis Graham. Warrant of survey granted to George
Croghan (see *L. P.* 24:73).   254

17   Time for hearing on the above and on a petition of Robert
Leake (p. 251) extended. Orders on petitions: of Kennedy
Farrel and Christ'r Horsefall (see *L. P.* 20:175-76); of
Roger Smyth (see *L. P.* 22:161). Hearing on the caveat of
Isaac Fort (p. 251) further postponed.   255

24   Order on petition of Sergeant Joseph Smeeton 47th regi-
ment (see *L. P.* 24:37). Lands granted to: Corporal
David McClay 73d regiment (see *L. P.* 24:84); Sergeants
Daniel McIntosh, Wm Patterson, Thos. Scott, Drummers
James Smith, Wm Thursting, John Roulson, Privates
James Winterbottom, Aaron Lyllie, Stephen Gale, John
Grant, Giles Power, Patrick Reed 80th regiment, Benj.
Crumpton, John Barlow, Tobias Tyre and John Johnson
60th regiment (see *L. P.* 23:95); Sergeants James Coleman
60th, Henry Greenshields 46th, Corporal John Black,
Drummers James Scott and Thos. Cowans, 55th, Corporal
James Barker Royal Americans, Privates Jacob Johnson
60th, Gabriel Woods 46th, James Smith 44th (see *L. P.*
24:81). James Jackson vs John van Rensselaer in error.
Names of Moses Ibbit, Edward Roach, John Mitchum,
John Brachan, Gilbert Tice, And'w Hanlon, Achilles Preston, Joseph Irwin, Jonathan Runnion, Wm Philipps, John

Fraser, Wm Fraser, Wm McIntire and Dan'l Campbell to be added to the patent issued to Michael Byrne, Francis Rupert and Lucas Vedder (p. 165). Licenses to purchase Indian lands granted to: Henry White, James A. Stewart et al (see *L. P.* 24:27); Guy Johnson, Marcus Prevoost et al (see *L. P.* 24:25); Gabriel Maturin, Abr'm Benn, et al (see *L. P.* 24:24); Daniel Claus, John Powell et al (see *L. P.* 24:26); John Leake, Ann Leake et al (see *L. P.* 24:22). 255

Mar. 2 Lands granted to: Sergeant Samuel Moore, Privates Anthony Williams, Wm Tappar 80th, Abr'm Fairbanks, Stephen Gaffen 28th, Henry Towell 17th, John Elmor 48th, Dennis Connell, James Terpley 44th, Philipp McCullogh 55th, Christ'r Syfard 60th regiment (see *L.P.* 22:71); Private Thos. Frazer 17th regiment, not located. Patents granted to: Peter Hasenclever, David Greem, James Crawford, Arthur Forrest, John Elves et al (see *L. P.* 24:82); Peter Lewis sr and jr, Moses Ibbit, Samuel Runnion, Peter Miller, Lucas Veder, Peter Friederick, Stephen Hipp, Michael Russell, Peter Fiax, Coenradt Crutzenburger, Michael Gallenger, Andreas Snyder, Nicholas Shafer, George Hipp, Johannes West, Adam Rupert, Francis Beard, George Keep, George Stam, Lawrence Ceman, Mathias Link, Thos. Morgan, Joseph Mordaunt and John Timms (see *L. P.* 24:77). 259

16 Hearing on petitions ordered Feb. 17 postponed. Petition of Wm Walton jr, Jacob Walton, Thomas Walton, Gerard Walton et al (see (*L. P.* 24:88) referred. 260

18 Hearing on the petition of Robert Leake (p. 251); adjourned. 261

21 Hearing continued. Hearing on the caveat of Isaac Fort against Joseph Reade jr, and Wilh. van Antwerp (p. 251). 262

22 Opinion of council in re Fort vs Reade and van Antwerp and in re Leake. 263

24 Hearing in re petitioners (p. 254) for lands in Minisink patent. 264

26 Opinion of council that there is no vacant tract between the Philippse and Rumbout patents as prayed for by Robert Leake. Opinion concerning Poghkeepsingh patent; lands east of the 20 mile line, Minisink. Patent granted to Wm Walton jr (p. 260). 264

29 Opinion of council on the petitions of John Taylor, Judah Harlow, George Stewart, Joseph Allicock, and Robert Harding (see *L. P.* 24:29), and of Lieut. Pierce Ponsonby Butler (p. 245) granted. Action on the petition of Johannes Trumper et al (p. 254) deferred. 266

1768   **v. 29**

Ap. 7 Petitions granted: of Sergeant Joseph Smeeton (p. 255); of
Sergeant David Reid 42d, Privates Thos. Frazer 17th,
Daniel McQuin 17th, Alex'r Reid 42d, Roderick McKenzie
55th regiment (see *L. P.* 24:44); of Sergeants Robert Allen,
Wm Herring, Corporal Wm Trost, Privates Wm Darling,
John Wiseman, Olirick Esick, John Dinsley, Robert Mid-
dleton, Tobias Pouder 60th, Peter Reid 28th, John Do-
mini 48th regiment (see *L. P.* 24:89); of Wm Butler in
behalf of Sergeant Archibald Brecken 28th, Corporal Wm
Arison Ogden's rangers, Privates Thomas Dougel 28th,
Jesse Waddle, Wm Trigger, Wm Saunders and Fred'k
Smith Royal Americans (see *L. P.* 24:22).   267

22 Patent for land purchased by Johannes Samuel Pruyn and
Derick Bradt van Schoonhoven granted to Thomas and
Cornelius Eckerson (see *L. P.* 24:111).   269

May 2 Order on deposition of Martin Garretsen van Bergen, Wm
Kane, Thos. Lynot of Albany county and Peter Short (see
N. Y. col. mss, 95:29, 33). Order on petition of Stephen
van Rensselaer (see *L. P.* 24:122). Order for laying out
the lands granted to Sergeant Samuel Moore et al (p. 259;
see *L. P.* 24:113). Petitions for land granted: of Corporals
Solomon Davenport, John Morgan 60th, Terence Kill-
patrick 28th, John Hubbert, Andrew Bowen, Edward Holt
80th, Privates Richard Baker 28th, Wm Haddock 47th, and
John Parker 17th regiment (see *L. P.* 22:176); of Drummer
John Tilsey 77th, and Private Michael Law 60th regiment
(see *L. P.* 23:115); of Sergeant Fred'k John for 200 acres
north of Kingsbury; of Corporals Thos. Ford, John Killing, Edw'd Oates, Henry Browall, Wm Totton, Peter
Hughs, Jeremiah Dogherty, Drummer Hugh Baines,
Privates George Robinson, James Russet, Joseph Richard-
son, Thos. Carr, John Prusk, John Aggaton, Thos.
Mitting, Wm Penny, John Howard, James Bears, John
Hooper 60th, Robert Brodie, Thomas Frazier, Joseph
Barnes 55th, Hamilton Elliot 44th regiment (see *L. P.*
24:41); of Private James Osburn 60th (see *L. P.* 24:53); of
Wm Watcock, Wm Ruston, Thos. Mount, Wm Risdell
60th, Jasper Martin 80th, Nicholas Woobrick, Robert Gil-
more 44th regiment (see *L. P.* 24:64); of Privates Edward
Quin, Hugh Speers, Thos. Webster, Phil. Anterbush 60th,
Richard Evans, John Shine 80th, Thomas Grindle 46th
regiment (see *L. P.* 24:65); of Sergeant John Mountfort,
Corporal John Murray 60th, Drummer Peter Buzzard 80th
regiment (see *L. P.* 24:66); of Sergeant Wm Christie 80th
(see *L. P.* 24:67); of Sergeant Wm Douglass, Corporals

John McGinnis and John Harrison 60th, Corporals John Newland 55th, James Richardson 46th, (see *L. P.* 24:96); of Corporals Thos. Cearnes, Joseph Aunets 55th, John Bunteel, Gabriel Smith 28th, Thos. Reilly 60th regiment (see *L. P.* 24:97); of Sergeants John McKinsey, James Bellany, Drummers John Burk, John Anderson, Valentine Metcalf 55th regiment (see *L. P.* 24:98); of Sergeant James Rossbottom, Corporals John Johnson, Wm Bourke, Drummers John Luson and Moses Patterson 55th regiment (see *L. P.* 24:102); of Sergeant Wm Price, Corporal James Woodworth and Drummer Isaac Taylor 60th, Sergeant Edward Downe, Corporal Hugh Gurnal 28th regiment (see *L. P.* 24:100); of Sergeant Edw'd Leader, Corporal Thomas Hasborn, Privates Hugh Scott, John McCaber, John Tool 46th regiment, Wm Barron, Wm Manson, Phil. White 44th, James Dougherty, Wm Meachen 17th, John Bridgeman 60th, John Hodge 80th, John Miller 55th, John Buckley 28th, Wm Mitchel 45th, Solomon Bickerton 47th (see *L. P.* 24:99); of Edward Jessup and Ebenezer Jessup (see *L. P.* 23:88); of Samuel Deal (see *L. P.* 24:83); of John Morin Scott, Henry Andrew Franckin, Martin Garretse van Bergen et al (see *L. P.* 24:86, 90); of Peter Dejo sr and jr (see *L. P.* 24:113); of Privates Thos. Moore, Abr'm Gallaugher, Donald Millson, Isaac Cotteril, Richard Shaw, Thos. Thallay, Wm Bennet, Matthew Holland, Robert Gray, Alex'r Simpson, James Jack, John Downie, James Snowden, Wm Carrol 55th regiment (see *L. P.* 24:103); of Corporal Phil. Lambert 46th regiment for land on the Katskill. 270

18 Petition of minister of St Peter's church at Albany (see *N. Y. col. mss*, 95:42) referred. 276

July 13 Report on the preceding petition; charter of incorporation granted. Petitions granted: Theophylact Bache, James Barclay, Wm Lucas, John Roome, John Hardenbrook, John Singleton, John Lambert, John Wm Vredenbergh, Peter Goelet, David Morld, Wm McDermot, Wm Kennedy, Rich'd Lewis, James Seagrove, Wm Cockburne, John Vernor, Dennis McCready, and Alex'r McCullough (see *L. P.* 24:119); of Wm Kelly in behalf of Sir George Yonge, David Banks, Joseph Ball, John Dobbs, Stephen Johnson, Samuel Huntington, James Bankes, Jeremiah Breuen, Jonas Peirson, Solomon Davis, James Johnson, Daniel Buen, Theophilus Langworth, John Robinson, James Nuttman, James Nuttman jr, Nath'l Richards, Isaac Langworth, John Bruen and Daniel Baldwin (see *L. P.* 24:118); of Wm

Beekman sr and jr, Richard Bancker, Abr'm Beekman,
James Beekman, Robert Rutgers, Mary Beekman, Abr'm
de la Noy sr and jr. Francis Child, Wm Ferris, Rudolphus
van Dyck, Garret Keteltas, John Sydel, Elias Jones,
Francis Marschalck, Andrew Marschalck, John Vreden-
burgh, James Cobham, Hendrick Suydam, Corn's van der
Veer, Jacobus van der Veer, Adrian Voorhis, Johannes
Ditmars, Jacob Suydam, Thos. Hammersley, John I. Kip,
Peter Goelet, Eleazer Miller jr, and Benj'n Jones (see *L. P.*
24:126); of Ennis Graham, John Keily, Thos. Royce and
Thos. Griggs (see *L. P.* 24:128); of Drummer Wm Smith
6oth regiment (see *L. P.* 24:120); of Jeremiah van Rens-
selaer, Philipp van Rensselaer, Henry K. van Rensselaer,
Jacob Bleecker jr, Rutger Bleecker et al (see *L. P.* 24:129).
Orders on petitions: of Minne Fisher (see *L. P.* 24:140);
of Abr'm Haasbrouck, Louis Bevier, Abr'm van Keuren,
Levi Pawling, Jacob Hoornbeck, Jacobus Bruyne and John
Cantyne (see *L. P.* 24:107).   277

Aug. 3 Petitions granted: of John McNeile, Alex'r Stewart, John
Talbert, Alex'r Stewart jr, James Stewart, Daniel Mc-
Cormick and John Shaw (see *L. P.* 24:18); of Samuel
Stringer hospital steward (see *L. P.* 22:122); of Samuel
and Isaac Fowler (see *L. P.* 24:104).   281

29 Petitions granted: of John Harper et al (p. 229; see *L. P.*
25:12); of Henry White, James A. Stewart, Thomas
Stewart, John Besant, Charles Dickinson, John Singleton,
Richard Stevens, Oliver Templeton, Samuel Breese, Hugh
Wallace, Thomas Pettit, Samuel Bayer, Hugh Gaine, Thos.
Lowrie, John Allen, Thos. Newland, Jacob Wilkins, James
Deas, Moses Nicholls, John Moore, Thos. Freeman, Rich'd
Wenman, Marinus Willet, John Lasher, Rob't McMennomy,
John Bowles, Isaac Rykman jr, Crean Brush, Joseph Beck
and Jacob van Voorheis (see *L. P.* 25:13); of Gabriel
Maturin, Abr'm Benn, Joseph Ogden, Charles McCafferty,
James Martin, Michael Savage, Andrew Hunter, Rob't
Ridley, George Jackson, Robert Johnson, Wm Page,
Buckridge Webb, John McNeil, Francis Panton, Daniel
Philipps, James Spears, Samuel Deal, Joshua Mullock,
Samuel Bayard jr, Robert McWilliams, John Seekly, John
Lambert, George Ball, Miles Sherbrooke, John Dumond,
John Berea, Dennis Hagerman, Fred'k Jay, Nichs.
Quackenboss, and Peter Goelet (see *L. P.* 25:15); of Guy
Johnson, Marcus Prevost, Fred'k Prevost, Ann de Visme,
Peter de Visme, Samuel de Visme, Phil. de Visme, Coen-
radt Rapp, Henry Andrees, Benj. Oldes, David Acker-

man, Augustine Prevost jr, John Chambers, Benj'n Jackson, Josiah Halsted, Jacob Dennis, John Tucker, Joseph Leonard, John West, Stephen West, Samuel Hutchins, Robert Adams, John Adems, James Rogers, Catherine Adems, James Ralph, John Roberts, Thomas Wilson, John Wilson and Samuel Powells (see *L. P.* 25:10); of Daniel Claus, John Powel, John Stevenson, James Sharpe, John Owens, George Brown, Wm Brown, David Williams, And'w Williams, William Jackson, John Jackson, James Rutherford, John Rutherford, John Sisnay, Wm Sisnay, John Burnay, James Doyle, John Moore, Wm Rogers, John Williamson, James Livingston, James Glassford, Gamaliel Wallace, Thomas Wallace, George Burns, David Brown, John Robinson, Wm Sills and John Taylor (see *L. P.* 25:11); of John Leake, Ann Leake sr and jr, Rob't Wm Leake, John George Leake, Robert Leake, Wm Fenwick, Ann Fenwick, Thos. Strafford, Ann Strafford, Richard Galley, Thos. Dougal, John Leake Burrege, Robert Burrege, Ann Burrege, Martha Burrege, Roger Richards, Susannah Richards, Richard Ball, Roger Gifford, Augustine Prevost, George Prevost, Garret Hopper, John Hopper, Catherine Smith, Jonathan Holmes, Wm Holmes, Catherine de Visme, John Zabrisky sr and jr (see *L. P.* 25:14). 283

Sep. 9 Petitions for licenses to purchase Indian lands granted: to Philipp Schuyler, Rutger Bleecker, Nanning Vischer and Cortlandt Schuyler (see *L. P.* 25:9); of John Bradstreet, Thos. Carpenter, Wm Goddard (see *L. P.* 25:7); of Thos. Woods, Volkert P. Douw, Thos. Ferguson, Jonathan Plummer et al (see *L. P.* 25:17); of Jellis Fonda et al (see *L. P.* 25:19); of Thos. Wharton sr, Reese Meredith, Joseph Wharton and Samuel Morris jr (see *L. P.* 25:18). 288

Nov. 21 Order on petition of Johan Nicholas Mathias sr and jr, and Volkert P. Douw (see *L. P.* 24:132). 291

Dec. 5 Names of John Archer, Aaron Jefferys, Gilbert Tice, David Jecocks, Matthew Hind, Alex'r Clarke, Peter Miller, Peter Young, Praise Wadman, Joseph Irwin, Joseph Fitchet, Arent van Sickler, Matthew Sapwith, Lawrence Lawyer, Harman Sidnigh, Thos. Bowden, Chris'r Markel, John Bowers, Christ'r Redigh, Michael Markel, Johannes, Banck jr, Jacob Borst, David Hosack, Abr'm Starnberger, Hendrick Weber, James Wilkinson, Johannes Becker, Peter Zimmer, Gerviss Hawksford, George Zimmer, Peter Zeely, Josias Swart and Peter Snyder to be added to the patent

1768   **v. 29**

to Johannes Lawyer, Jacob Zimmer, Moses Ibbit and
Jacob Enters (p. 240).   292

23 Royal order granting to Gen. Thos. Gage a patent for Indian
lands purchased by him (p. 159; see *L. P.* 24:162). Petition
of Peter Hasenclever, David Greeme, Mary Crofts, James
Crawford, George Jackson, John Elves, Arthur Forrest,
Richard Willis, Thos. Dampier, John Dewal, Wm Robertson, Wm Berry, Neal Ward, Mary Lucy Sleech, Hutchinson Mure, Catherine Hasenclever, Mary Elizabeth Hasen-
clever and Charles Crofts (see *L. P.* 25:44) granted.   293

1769

Jan. 18 Names of Gabriel Sprong and Samuel Waldron to be inserted
in the patent to Elkanah Deane et al (p. 179) instead of John
and Samuel Deane, minors (see *L. P.* 25:6).   295

20 Petitions of Wm Kelly in behalf of Sir George Yonge and
19 others not named (see *L. P.* 25:38), and of John Mouatt
secretary to Admiral Durell (see *L. P.* 24:74) granted.
Minutes sent to the board of trade.   295

31 Lands granted: to Lord Henry Holland by royal mandamus
(see *L. P.* 25:64); to Francis Legge (see *L. P.* 25:104); to
John Small (see *L. P.* 25:103).   297

Feb. 22 Draft of charter for St Peters church Albany read and ap-
proved. James Jackson ex dem Thos. Williams et al vs
John van Rensselaer. Warrant of survey granted to John
Glen jr, Simon Schermerhorn, Phil. van Petten, Henry
Glen, Abr'm C. Cuyler and Cornelius Glen (see *L.P.* 25:63). 298

Mar. 1 Petitions granted: of Corporal James Glassford 27th regiment (see *L. P.* 25:50); of Drummer John McCarty 80th
regiment (see *L. P.* 25:27); of Sergeants Godlieb Sweitzer
and Aeneas Mackay Royal Americans (see *L. P.* 24:155).
Order on petition of Corporal Simon Bennis 1st regiment
against which a caveat has been entered by Thos. Smith
for John Naugel et al (see *L. P.* 24:20). Township of
Beekman erected (see *L. P.* 24:70). Petitions granted: of
Oliver de Lancey and John Morin Scott (see *L. P.* 24:59);
of John Bard, Henry Wisner jr, and John Morin Scott
(see *L. P.* 24:62); of Evert Bancker, Adrian Renaudet and
Benj. Kissam (see *L. P.* 24:66); of John Miller and
Nicholas Kilman (see *L. P.* 24:148). Warrants of survey
granted to Capt. Wm Edmeston and Lieut. Robert Edmeston (see *L. P.* 25:53); to Major John Wrightson (see
L. P. 22:96, 113).   299

8 Petition of James Livingston, Clear Evert Beaudevine Lacount and other inhabitants of Poughkeepsie (see *L. P.*
25:58) referred.   303

15 James Jackson vs John Rensselaer. Petitions granted: of
Surgeon General Peter Middleton (see *L. P.* 25:76); of Ser-
geant Augustine Stine 60th regiment and Corporal James
Richardson (see *L. P.* 25:1); of John Watts (see *L. P.*
25:67); of George Croghan, Volckert P. Douw and Lam-
bert Moore (see *L. P.* 25:73); of John Morin Scott, Martin
Garretse van Bergen and associates (see *L. P.* 25:83); of
Francis Child, Crean Brush, John Bowles, Alex'r Mac-
Cullagh, John Thompson and John Lewis (see *L. P.*
25:75); of Achilles Preston, Francis Beard, George Rowe,
Peter Grove, Samuel Runnion, Peter Frazer, John Frazer,
Peter Weaver, Ury Kreitz, Michael Gallinger, James Davis,
Mathias Link, John McIntire, Arent van Sicler, Wm
Philipps, Lucas Veeder, Peter Miller, Wm Farlington,
Mark Reeve, Moses Ibbit, George Kass, Johs. Wert, An-
dreas Snyder, John Koughnot, Peter Servis sr and jr,
Valentine Dorn, James Rogers, John Brachan, Daniel
Campbell, Jelles Funda, Michael Byrn, Douw Funda, Adam
Funda, John Funda, Stephen Schuyler, Christ'r Yeates,
Francis Phister, Benj. Roberts, Wm Smith, Thos Barton,
George Shape and Norman McLeod (see *L. P.* 25:57, 72). 304

22 Petitions granted: of John Butler and 39 others not named
(see *L. P.* 25:88); of John Wetherhead, John Tabor Kempe,
Elizabeth Kempe, Philadelphia Kempe, Catherine Kempe,
Jane Kempe, James Downes, Robert Watts, Catharine
Morris, Wm Proctor, Cardan Proctor, John van Allen,
John R. Bleecker, Allen McDougal, Henry Remsen, Thos.
Fisher, Anthony Rutgers, Harmanus Rutgers, Joseph Alli-
cocke, John Lamb, Grove Bend, John Lambert, Charles
Nicoll, Jonathan Lawrence, Thos. Jones, Alex'r Rob-
ertson, Paul Miller, Nicholas Bogert, Jacobus van Ant-
werp, Wm Campbell, Wm Benson, Alex'r McDougal,
Phil. John Livingston, Samuel Bayard, Robert Harper,
Joseph Haviland, Patrick McDavit, Robert Adams and
James Phyn (see *L. P.* 25:91); of Stephen Skinner and 39
others not named (see *L. P.* 25:89); of Alex'r McKee and
39 others not named (see *L. P.* 25:92); of John Bowen,
Bartholomew Pickle, Jacob Snook, John Davis, Hugh Craw-
ford, Jelles Fonda, Michael Byrn, Robert Adams and Gil-
bert Tice (see *L. P.* 25:94); of Staats Long Morris, Wm
Wickham, Lewis Morris, Benj. Kissam, Vincent Pearce,
Ashfield, Anthony Rutgers, Thos Walton, Gerard Walton,
Samuel Schuyler, Rich'd Morris, Rud. Ritzema, Lewis Graham, John McKesson, Joseph Sutherland, Nath'l Reid,
Charles Hughes, Samuel Kissam, Gabriel H. Ludlow,

Jonathan Landan, Gilbert Burger, John Anderson, George Brewerton jr, Thos. Ludlow jr, Augustine Graham, Egbert Benson, Anth'y Glean, Stephen Steel, Jacob Parcell, John Kilman and Jasper Marinot (see *L. P.* 25:74, 85); of Thomas Webb, Charles Arding, Wm Lupton, James Jarvis, George Robinson, Wm Forman, Rich'd Sause, Charles White, Paul Heck and Henry Newton (see *L. P.* 25:86). Land granted to Clotworthy Upton in obedience to a royal order (see *L. P.* 25:39). Warrant of survey granted to Sampson Fleming in obedience to a royal mandamus (see *L. P.* 20:129). Order on petition of the clergy of the church of England in the province asking for a charter of incorporation to enable them to raise funds for the support of clergymen's widows and orphans. Petition of Robert Leake (see *L. P.* 25:79) received.   308

29   Petitions granted: of Wm Trent, Charles Reade, Thos. Wharton sr and 97 others not named (see *L. P.* 25:97); of Isaac Low and associates (see *L. P.* 25:82); of Thos. Moore and John Osburne for land in Orange county; of John Rapalje and 29 others not named (see *L. P.* 25:84); of Wm Walton, Thos. Walton, Gerard Walton, John Harris Cruger, Teleman Cruger and Nicholas Cruger (see *L. P.* 25:96).   313

Ap. 5   Warrants of survey granted: to Peter Lansingh and associates for land near Fort Stanwix; to Alex'r Wallace, Hans Wallace sr and jr, John Shaw and John Kennedy (see *L. P.* 25:99).   315

19   Petitions granted: Wm Bayard, Robert Bayard, Joshua Mullock, Thos. Shipboy, Peter Sylvester, Henry van Schaack, Robert Adams, Richard Cartwright, James Phyn, Wm Kane, Allan McDougal, George Lindsey, Wm Nixon, Kennedy Farrell, Robert Leake, John George Leake, Daniel Steel, Robert Wm Leake, Ann Leake jr, Thos. Lotteridge, Thos. O'Brien, Gerard Chessnut, Henry Thomas, Jacob Broeuver, John van Dalsem, Ruloph Sickels, Wm Benson, James A. Stewart, Alex'r Stewart jr, Robert Henry, Robert McLallan, John Vernon, Wm Proctor, Cardan Proctor, Adrian Renaudet, John Edwards, Richard Nassau Stevens, Thos. Edwards, John Constable, Alex'r Ellice, John Duncan, Dunlap Adams, Wm Adams, James Adams, David Edgar, Wm Edgar, James Rankin, Jane Lyle, John van Allen, Barent van Allen, Abr'm Schenck, Henry Remsen sr and jr, John Tayor and Joseph Griswold (see *L. P.* 25:111); of Lieut. Richard Robert Crowe (see *L. P.* 25:114).   316

26   Petitions granted: of Jacob Hendrick ten Eyck, Alex'r Colden, John R. Bleecker and Goldsbrow Banyar (see

L. P. 25:117); of Adam Vrooman (see L. P. 25:112); of
Sergeant Thos. Mason and Private Peter Crean of the
Iniskilling regiment (see L. P. 25:119); of James Living-
ston, Clear Everit, Beaudevine Lacount, Evert Pels, Barent
Kip, Abr'm Palmatier, Jacobus van Kleeck, Leonard van
Kleeck, Hendrick Hendrickse, Wm Forman, Johs. Steen-
berg, John Seabury, Hugh van Kleeck, Christoffel Ostran-
der, Barent Lewis, Daumond Palmatier, Robert Kidney,
Michael Pells, Jacobus Palmatier, Henry Pells, Gale Yel-
verton, Daniel Roberts, Peter Palmatier, Abr'm Freer,
Alex'r Griggs, Isaac Fitchet, Michael Palmatier, Myndert
van den Bogert, Peter van den Bogert, Johs. Swartwout,
Cornelius Viele, Hendrick Blercom, Jacobus van den
Bogert, Myndert van den Bogert, John Beardsley and
Myndert van Kleeck (p 303). 318

May 3 James Jackson ex dem Thos. Williams vs John van Rensselaer. 323

24 Warrant of survey granted to Charles de Freudenbergh (see
L. P. 25:127). Petition of Wm Sherriff, Margaret Sherriff
and Peter du Bois and other heirs of Blandina Bayard
(see L. P. 25:124) to be considered with the petition of
Capt. Samuel Bayard, Sir James Jay and Henry Flower
when the New York and New Jersey line is settled. 323

June 14 Lands granted to Gen. Thos. Gage erected into the township of Firle (see L. P. 25:131). Petitions of Private
David Reid 21st regiment (see L. P. 25:60) and of Rev.
Thos. Brown, deputy chaplain 60th regiment (see L. P.
18:122) granted. 324

21 Petitions of Lt. Col. Dudley Ackland (see L. P. 25:132), and
of Phil. Livingston, Henry Holland, Garret Abr'm Lansingh and Joseph Lansingh (see L. P. 25:133) granted. 325

Aug. 22 Warrants of survey granted: to Corporals Joseph Mountfort
46th regiment and Thos. Donally 28th regiment (see L. P.
25:116); to Lieut. Adolphus Benzel 50th regiment (see L. P.
25:45); to Lieut. Andrew Phil. Skene 72d (see L. P. 25:115);
to Sergeants John Jones 44th, John Bruce 55th and Private
Wolf Camp 60th regiment (see L. P. 25:125); to Ensign
James Savage 76th (see L. P. 25:138); to Sergeant James
McCrindle 60th for land on the south side of the Mohawk
river; to Lieut. Wm. Houghton of the artillery (see L. P.
26:2); to Thos. Ford et al (p. 271). Order on petition of
Private James Osburn 60th regiment (see L. P. 25:135).
Petitions granted: of Matthew Dies and Roger Smith (see
L. P. 25:142); of Wm Ogilvie, Caleb Hyatt, Richard Wen-
man, Monson Ward, Jacob Wilkins, Wm Lowry and Wm

Kennedy (see *L. P.* 25:140); of John Rightmyre (see *L. P.* 25:144); of Isaac Levy and 12 others not named (see *L. P.* 25:146); of Dr John Bard, James Bennett, Monson Ward, Patrick Smith, Alex'r Havie, Isaac Ryckman jr, and Daniel Crowther (see *L. P.* 25:147); of John Wattson sr and jr (see *L. P.* 25:45); of John Andrews (see *L. P.* 25:83); of Henry Glen, Alex'r Campbell, John Visger jr, Phil. Garlock, Harmanus H. Wendle and Alex'r Ellice (see *L. P.* 26:1); of Leonard Lispenard sr and jr, Anthony Lispenard, David Johnston, Stephen de Lancey, John Fitzpatrick, Jordan Cock, Peter Stuyvesink, Teunis Somerindyck, Martin Shier, George Stanton, Henry Stanton, Rose Graham and Mary Graham (see *L. P.* 25:144). Warrant of survey granted to Daniel Coxe and associates of New Jersey (see *L. P.* 25:148). 327

Sep. 29 Draft of charter of incorporation for the relief of clergymen's widows and orphans read and approved. Petition of Thomas Jones attorney at law and associates (see *L. P.* 26:7) referred. 334

Oct. 20 Names of Augustus van Cortlandt, Frederick van Cortlandt, Isaac Low, Augustus van Horne, John Jay, Egbert Benson, Arent Schuyler, Abr'm Lent, John Waldron, George Crookshanks, Jacob Lent, Hendrick Quackenboss, Joseph Jadwin, Thos. Hyatt, Michael van der Cook sr and jr, John Cotgrave, Peter van Brugh Livingston, Gerardus Bancker, Wm McDermott, Joseph Griswold, Thos. Griswold, Joseph Hildreth, Phil. Kissick, John Cosine jr, Francis Cowenhoven, Dirck de la Mater, John Crum, Wm Kennedy, Thos. Grigg, Wm Gillilen, James Seagrove, John Outhout, Jacob Keen and Stewart Wilson to be inserted in the patent to Aug. van Cortlandt (p. 189; see *L. P.* 26:14) and the lands granted to be erected into the township of Middlessex. Names of Robert R. Livingston sr and jr, John Will, Henry Will, Phil. Will, Christ'n Will, John Skeffington, Isaac Stoutenburgh, Wm Scott, Peter Montanye, Rich'd Nassau Stevens, Benj'n Jones, James Yeoman, John Vernor, John Collins, John Wilson, George Shaw, John Bowles, Catherine Bowles, John Lewis, Andrew Myer, Isaac Ryckman jr, Henry Brevoort, John McDoval, John Keen, Alex'r MacCullagh, James Bennett, Thos. Ryan, Henry Wills, John Stout, Wm de Peyster, Adolph de Grove, Robert Griffith, Henry Beeckman and Thos. Broockman (see *L. P.* 26:12) to be inserted in the patent to Robert R. Livingston et al (p. 174). Names of Wm Livingston, Wm Smith jr, Whitehead Hicks, John

Kelly, Susannah Livingston, Elizabeth Livingston, John Brevoort, Elias Brevoort, Thos. Hicks, John Woods, Gilbert Hicks, John W. Smith, Samuel Smith, Garret Noel, John Brown, Gerard Bancker, John Robinson, Gilbert Ash, Wm Sorrall, John Dutton Crimshier, Garret Roorback, John McKenney, Isaac Heron, Elias Nixon, Robert Hyslop, Francis Child, James Moran, Isaac Myer, John Lewis and Samuel Boyer to be inserted in the patent granted to Wm Livingston et al (p. 174).   334

Nov. 7   Petitions of Pierre G. de Peyster and associates (see *L. P.* 26:11), and of John Reade and associates (see *L. P.* 26:19) granted.   336

17   Lands granted to John Wetherhead and associates (p. 308) to be erected into the township of Blenheim and the names of Stephen de Lancey, Jacob le Roy, Rich'd Francis and James Lamb to be substituted in the patent for those of Harmanus Rutgers, John van Allen, John R. Bleecker and John Lamb (see *L. P.* 26:36).   338

29   Township of Harpersfield granted to John Harper sr and jr, Wm Harper, Joseph Harper, Alex'r Harper, Andries Rebar, Wm Gott, Thos. Henry, John Wells jr, Joseph Harper jr, John Thompson sr and jr, Robert Thompson, James Moore, Robert Wells, James Harper, Timothy McIlwain, John Rebar and Johs. Walrad (p. 229; see *L. P.* 26:41).   339

Dec. 12   Petition of minister of the society's mission at Newburgh for a charter of incorporation (see *N. Y. col. mss,* 96:27) granted. Petition of John Butler et al (see *L. P.* 26:42) referred. Names of Stephen Skinner, Matthew Cushing, Patrick McDavit, Smith Ramage, Isaac Heron, Rich'd Graham, Thos. Stewart, John Stewart, Charles Ramage, John Turner, Eleazer Miller jr, Francis Lewis jr, James Seagrove, Alex'r McAllester, John Dunlap, George Traile, Wm Campbell, James Bennet, John Morton, James Dunscomb, Alex'r Forbes, John Shaw, James Sacket, Samuel Stevens, Rich'd Nassau Stephens, Edmond Carrol, Wm Barker, Thos. Lupton, John Lamb, Fred'k Carrol, Edw'd Smith, John Marshall, Francis Koffler, John Lambert, George Brewerton jr, Robert McMennomy, Marinus Willet, Thos. Ryan, Alex'r McGinnis and Joseph Beck to be inserted in the patent granted to Stephen Skinner et al (p. 308).   339

20   Letter from Lord Hilsborough; the lands agreed to be sold by the Indians before the treaty of Fort Stanwix not to be considered as part of the land ceded to the crown by that treaty. Patent granted to John Butler et al (p. 339).   341

Jan. 5   Names of Alex'r McKee, Daniel Dunscomb, And'w Cunningham, Francis Koffler, Rich'd Nassau Stephens, James Nixon, James Dabell, James Howard, John Eccles, John Sands, Robert Harpur, Matthew Cushing, James Sacket, John Shaw, Alex'r Forbes, James Dunscomb, John Morton, Wm Campbell, James Bennet, John Kelly, Thos. Lupton, Wm McDermott, Chas. Ramage, Smith Ramage, Wm Manoe, Joseph Beck, James Stevens, Edw'd Smith, Crean Brush, John Bowles, Joseph Blanchard, John Shipboy, James Cobham, John Vredenburgh, Edw'd Carrol, Wm Barker, Fred'k Carrol, John Dunlap, John Lamb and Roger Richards to be inserted in the patent granted to Alex'r McKee et al (p. 308).   342

25   Names of Charles Reade, Thos. Wharton sr and jr, Joseph Galloway, Reese Meredith, Isaac Wharton, Samuel Preston Moore, Charles Moore, Thos. Moore, Henry Hill, Samuel Burge, George Roberts, Thos. Fisher, Samuel Fisher, Sam'l Morris jr, Phil. Kinsey, Samuel Sansum jr, Joshua Howell, John Drinker, Henry Drinker, Joseph Coleman, Peter Reeve, Charles Wharton, Carpenter Wharton, Thos. Carpenter, Stephen Collins, Isaac Parish, Josiah Franklin Davenport, Cadwallader Evans, Jonathan Odell, Wm Lovett Smith, Wm Dilwyn, Rich'd Smith, Samuel Allinson, John Hopkins, Richard Wells, Daniel Smith, Robert Smith sr and jr, James Kinsey, George Price, James Sterling, Daniel Ellis, John Neal, Thompson Neal, Joseph Smith, Abigail Smith, Ann Decow, James Veree, John Smith, Samuel Smith, Peter Worrell, Charles Pettit, Thos. Pryor jr, Thos. Rodman, John Shaw, Isaac Hewlings, Wm Hewlings, Thos. Palgreen, John Lawrence, Edw'd Cathrall, Samuel How, Thos. Powell, Thos. Scattergood, Dan'l Bacon jr, David Clayton, John Carty, James Craft and Thos. Parke to be inserted in the patent granted to Wm Trent et al (p. 313); Trent being in England.   343

31   Memorial of Thos. Webb (see *L. P.* 26:50) granted. Lands granted: to Capt. James Grant 80th and Lieut. Allan Grant 60th regiment (see *L. P.* 26:67); to Corporal John Wifreld 80th, and Private John Clifford 60th regiment (see *L. P.* 26:77). Lands surveyed for Daniel Coxe et al (p. 327) to be erected into the townships of Carolana and Coxeborough (see *L. P.* 26:86). Petitions granted: Col. Nathan Whiting (see *L. P.* 26:84); of Lawrence Kortright, Peter van Schaack, John Woods, Hubert van Wagenen of the township of Bessborough (see *L. P.* 26:20); of John Woods et al (see *L. P.* 26:33); of Wm Swan, Harman Rutgers et

al (see *L. P.* 26:32); of John Morin Scott, Thos. Smith et al of the township of Kingsborough (see *L. P.* 26:34, 38); of James Abeel of the township of Halton (see *L. P.* 26:27); of Jacobus van Zandt of the township of New Brook (see *L. P.* 26:30); of Wm Shirreff and Sam'l Bayard (see *L. P.* 26:31); of Phil. John Livingston et al (see *L. P.* 26:37); of John Jay, Jacob Townsend et al for land between the towns of New Stamford, Woodford, Draper and Cumberland; of Sergeant Thos. Oliver 46th, Corporal Edward Lawrence, Drummers John Rockenfoos and John Widsell 60th, Corporal James Barron 80th, Privates Jeremiah Thomson, Fred'k Dawson, John Fergee, Peter Michael, Henry Hassels, Conradt Meissenger, Joseph Anthony, Thos. Price, Miles Cunningham, Andrew Kainnard 60th, Ludwig Simon, John McNeal, Charles Dougherty, Wm Dutton, Philipp Waller, Thos. Tumblin 44th, Samuel Cunningham, John Smedley, Walter Bond, Daniel Campbell, Henry Furniss, John Fosson 46th, Evan Grant 48th, Murdock Kennedy 42d, Richard Gamblin 35th, Robert Broadie 55th, Robert Mathews, John Oswell, John Garrow independents, James Swift, John Mason, Thos. Kempeton, John Fielding, Peter Cummings, Samuel Knight, Robert Gill, Abr'm Rooker, Phil. Lafell, Joseph Stringer 28th, Wm Meeks, John Ran, John Daweze, John Evans, John Doe, Phil. Harry, John Donolly, Wm Bowen and Phil. Penicuff 80th regiment (see *L. P.* 26:35); of John Tabor Kempe and Goldsbrow Banyar (see *L. P.* 26:3, 8).　　344

Feb. 7　Township of Kortright granted to Lawrence Kortright, John Harper et al (see *L. P.* 26:68); township of Franklin to Thos. Wharton, Reese Meredith, John Harper et al (see *L. P.* 26:89); township of Kingsland to the governors of Kings college (see *L. P.* 26:95); township of Charlotte to Nath'l Marston, Gabriel Ludlow, Charles Williams, Robert Crommelin, Edward Man, David Clarkson, Andrew Barclay, Elias des Brosses, Nich's Wm Stuyvesant, Theophilact Bache, Adrian Renaudet, Alex'r Colden, Thos. Hill, Edward Laight, Anthony van Dam, Robert R. Livingston, John Charlton, Humphrey Jones, Matthew Clarkson, Benj'n Kissam, Rich'd Nicholls, John Livingston, James Duane, Lambert Moore, and Lewis Pintard (see *L. P.* 26:94).　　352

14　Township of Whiteborough granted to Henry White et al (see *L. P.* 26:102). Petitions granted: of Walter Franklin et al (see *L. P.* 26:54); of Richard Loudon, John Yates jr, John Thompson, Wm Steuart, James Downes, Wm Kennedy, Walter Thomas, Henry Thomas, Richard Kip, Richard Wenman, Thos. Ryan, Richard Nassau Stephens and Thomas Lupton (see *L. P.* 26:49). Township of Belvidere granted to George Croghan. Petitions granted: of the governors of Kings college for additional powers (see *N. Y. col. mss*, 96:53); of Robert Leake, inspector general of provisions, Lieuts. James Clarke, John de Bernière and Charles Babbington (see *L. P.* 26:85); of Lieut. Hezekiah Somner, rangers (see *L. P.* 26:90); of Lieut. Wm Snow Steel 55th regiment (see *L. P.* 26:100); of Lieut. Abernethy Cargill, rangers, Corporals John Creag, Henry Freaker, Benjamin Robeson, Drummers John Russell and Thos. Lang 55th regiment (see *L. P.* 26:105); of Corporal Donald McKay 42d regiment (see *L. P.* 26:103); of Hugh Wallace, Alex'r Wallace and John Kennedy of Sadachqueda patent (see *L. P.* 26:93).   355

28 Charter granted to the corporation of the chamber of commerce in the city of New York, John Cruger president. Petitions granted: of John Leake et al of the township of Bedlington (see *L. P.* 26:114); of Wm Walton, John Harper et al of the township of Walton (see *L. P.* 26:112); of James Jauncey et al of the township of Jaunceyborough between Ryegate, Topsham and Peachum; of Thos. Lawrence, Francis Dominick, Alex'r Stewart jr et al of the township of Chatham (see *L. P.* 26:111); of Alex'r McKee, Wm Thompson, John Little, Hugh Crawford, Thos. Smallman and Henry Montour (see *L. P.* 26:116). Order for hearing between Dan'l Coxe et al, and the owners of Oriskene patent.   361

Mar. 7 Lands granted: to Sergeant David Smith, Corporal Alex'r Ogilvie, Sergeant Hugh Henry, Gunner Joseph Randill, Private John Cawley et al (see *L. P.* 26:65); to Sergeant Thos. Porter (see *L. P.* 27:149); to Sergeant Neal McDonald et al (see *L. P.* 26:110); to Corporal John Laulb, Private George Sutherland 78th, Sergeant Wm Baker 28th and Private John Havill 44th regiment (see *L. P.* 26:81); to Private Ross McKabe et al (see *L. P.* 27:46); to Hans Springsteel et al (see *L. P.* 26:128); to Gilbert Wilson et al (see *L. P.* 26:115); to Henry Halstead et al (see *L. P.* 26:113); to Dietrich Echardse et al (see *L. P.* 26:104); to Edw'd Wm Kiers et al, north east of Argyle. Township of Kelso granted to Wm Cockburn and Arch'd Campbell (see *L. P.* 26:76). Order on petition of Leonard Lispenard, Samuel Verplanck, Linus King, Wm Walton, John Harris Cruger, James Jauncey et al for a charter to the Marine

1770 v. 29

society (see *N. Y. col. mss*, 96:55). Draft of charter for the chamber of commerce read and approved. Order on memorial of Wm Butler attorney for Arch'd Brachen et al (see *L. P.* 26:69). 365

9 Lands granted to John Watts as per royal mandamus (see *L. P.* 26:117). Charter of incorporation for a public hospital granted to Drs Peter Middleton, John Jones and Samuel Bard. 370

14 Hearing between Daniel Coxe and Oriskene patentees (p. 361). Draft of letters patent to the governors of Kings college (p. 355) read and approved. 371

21 Names of Cornelius Cuyler, Abr'm Cuyler, Henry Cuyler, Catherine Cuyler, Andrew Myer, Adam Borger and James Stevenson to be inserted in the patent to Lt. Col. John Vaughan (see *L. P.* 26:152). Petition of Sir Wm Johnson et al for land (see *L. P.* 26:127) granted. Charter of incorporation granted for the episcopal church at Peekskill to Beverley Robinson, Charles Moore, Jeremiah Drake, Caleb Ward, John Johnson, Joshua Nelson, Thomas Davenport and Henry Purdy. Land in the Minissink angle granted to Jonathan Smith, George Smith, heir-at-law of Joshua Smith, Isaiah Veal, Nath'l Owen, Henry Smith and Wait Carpenter (see *L. P.* 26:155). Hearing on the memorial of Wm Butler (p. 365). 372

28 Charter granted to the Marine society (p. 365). Township of Moore granted to Wm Smith et al (see *L. P.* 27:3). Final order on the memorial of Wm Butler (p. 372). 375

Ap. 11 Lands granted: to Wm Wood clerk of ordnance, David Buffington and Robert Morrison conductors Royal artillery (see *L. P.* 26:101; 27:13); to Lieut. Trevor Newland on the south side of the Mohawk and west side of the Schoharie river; to Lieut. Thos. Moncriefe and Ensign James Stevenson 50th regiment (see *L. P.* 22:51); to John Whitehead et al (see *L. P.* 27:18); to Wm Annin, John Campbell, Grear Brown, Jacob Starnbergh, Richard Cartwright and James Wilson (see *L. P.* 27:2); to Charles McEvers, Theophilact Bache, Hamilton Young et al (see *L. P.* 27:12). Draft of charter for the Marine society read and approved. Order upon letter from Abr'm Lott (see *L. P.* 27:10). 377

18 Order on petition of Teunis van Veghten (see *L. P.* 25:4). Petition of Teunis van Veghten (see *L. P.* 25:5) granted. 380

20 Royal order vetoing the New York act for emitting £120,000 in bills of credit. 382

May 2 Charters of incorporation granted: to St George's church, Newburgh (see *N. Y. col. mss*, 96:70); to St Andrew's church, Wallkill precinct (see *L. P.* 27:26); to St David's church, Cornwall precinct (see *N. Y. col. mss*, 96:71). Petition of John Morin Scott and Thos. Smith (see *L. P.* 27:35) granted.   383

9   Order concerning the grant to Jonathan Smith et al (p. 372; see *L. P.* 27:36). Petitions of Lieut. Trevor Newland (see *L. P.* 27:41), and of Sergeants Daniel Crean, Francis Elliot, Corporals Wm Whitefield, James Realy and Drummer Felix Daugherty (see *L. P.* 27:25) granted. Time for hearing on the petition of Teunis van Veghten (p. 380) fixed.   384

16   Petitions granted: of Archilles Preston et al for 37,000 acres adjoining Vrooman's and Leonard Gansevoort's patent and Northampton patent; of John Butler (see *L. P.* 26:5, 9); of Lieut. Wm Houghton Royal artillery (see *L. P.* 27:40); of Sergeant John Stinson, Corporal Paul Sarson, Privates Nich's Deverick and George Underwood 80th, Corporal Price Roach 77th, Corporal Thos. Hasborne, Private James McGowen 46th, and Private Thos. Lowrey 35th regiment (see *L. P.* 27:43). Hearing on caveat by John Andrews against granting a patent to Thos. Moore and John Osbon (see *L. P.* 27:66, 78). Petition of Stephen de Lancey, John de Lancey, Daniel Harris, James Babcock, Samuel Gardner, Wm Haight, James Meade and Daniel Harris jr (see *L. P.* 27:27) granted.   385

30   Petitions granted: of Lieut. Alex'r Colhoun independents (see *L. P.* 27:54); of John Goodridge in behalf of Lieut. Samuel Stevens, Ensign Wm Haldane, Sergeant Peter Muerenbelt, Corporal Benj. Dickson 60th, Corporal James Stevenson 1st, Corporal George Rogers 27th, Privates Hugh McBride 45th and Robert Bresier 60th regiment (see *L. P.* 27:50). Township of Leyden granted to Peter Keteltas et al (see *L. P.* 27:34). Draft of patent to Daniel Coxe, Wm Coxe, Rebecca Coxe, John Tabor Kempe and his wife Grace Kempe for Carolana and Coxeborough read and approved. Caveat of John Andrews (p. 385) dismissed (see *L. P.* 27:52). Order on petition of Col. John Bradstreet (see *L. P.* 27:53).   389

June 6 Petitions granted: of Hugh Wallace, Magill Wallace and Alex'r Wallace (see *L. P.* 27:55); of Gerard W. Beekman, Wm Beekman, Abr'm Beekman et al of the township of Mecklenburgh (see *L. P.* 27:42); of John Woods, Charles Nicoll, Evert Bancker, James Sacket, Isaac Heron et al (see *L. P.* 26:121); of John Glen jr, Simon Schermerhorn, Phil. van Petten, Henry Glen, Abr'm C. Cuyler and Cornelius Glen (see *L. P.* 27:64). Township of Goldsborough

granted to Lieut. Edward Tudor 85th, Ass't Engineer
Barnard Ratzer and Quartermaster John Clarke 60th regi-
ment (see *L. P.* 27:58). Land granted to Lieut. Duncan
Campbell 42d regiment (see *L. P.* 27:57). Order for hearing on the petitions of John Glen and Henry Glen (see
L. P. 26:48), and of Simon and John Remsen (see *L. P.*
27:47). Hearing on the petition of Col. John Bradstreet
(p. 389) postponed. Lands granted to Sergeant Alex'r
Kennedy 78th, Corporal Peter Kelly 46th, Privates James
Axtence 60th, Anthony Harper 35th, Hoseah McFalls 28th,
Wm Bolton 60th, Isaac Freeborn 46th, James Philipps 44th,
and Sergeant Henry Welt 60th regiment. Minutes sent to
the board of trade.   391

July 25   Petitions granted: of James Abeel (see *L. P.* 27:29); of Elias
Brookland   Bland et al (see *L. P.* 26:145); of Benj. Stout et al of the
Kings co.   township of Virgin Hall (see *L. P.* 27:77); of Wm Far-
quhar, James Farquhar, John Amiel jr, Thos. Farmer and
James Farmer (see *L. P.* 27:68); of John Lawrence, Henry
Boel and Stephen Tuttle (see *L. P.* 27:66); of James
Downes et al (see *L. P.* 27:79); of John Woods and Wm
Swan (see *L. P.* 27:74); of Privates Wm Gill 28th, Peter
Chapman 60th and Sergeant Alex'r Kennedy's party
(p. 391; see *L. P.* 27:67); of Robert Saunders, miner Royal
artillery (see *L. P.* 27:65). Drafts of charters for the
churches of St George, St Andrew, and St David (p. 383)
read and approved. Royal order vetoing the New York
act explaining the duties of loan officers.   395

Aug. 14   Royal order repealing the New York act declaring certain
Ft George   persons ineligible for the general assembly; to be published
by proclamation. Hearing on the petition of Teunis van
Veghten (p. 380); land prayed for granted. Drafts of charters for St Peter's church at Peekskill (p. 372), and for the
public hospital (p. 370) read and approved.   401

Sep. 3   Petitions granted: of Archibald Hamilton, Alice Hamilton,
Anthony and Elizabeth Farrington, John and Margaret
Antill, Richard Nicolls Colden, Jane Colden, John Colden,
Elkanah Deane, George Traile, Rich'd Deane, Wm Forman, George Wray, Samuel and John Tudor, Lewis Antill,
Lambert Cadwallader, Archibald Mercer and Samuel Burling of the township of Kersborough (see *L. P.* 27:83); of
Claus 60th, Norman McLeod 80th, and Lieut. Benj. Roberts
46th regiment (see *L. P.* 27:86). List of names to be inserted in the patent to John Bowen (see *L. P.* 25:95) received and filed.   404

1770   v. 29

29   Hearing on the petitions of Glen and Remsen (p. 391);
decided in favor of John and Henry Glen. Order on petition of Private Henry Stilson 80th regiment (see *L. P.*
27:84).   406

Oct. 31   Lord Dunmore governor. Petitions granted: of Wm Mc-
Adam et al (see *L. P.* 27:104, 118); of Francis Stephens et al
of the township of Truro (see *L. P.* 27:110); of Thos.
Barnett et al of the township of Penryn (see *L. P.* 27:109);
of Samuel Stitt and John Zabrisky (see *L. P.* 27:113); of
Waldron Blaau, Francis Groome, Nich's Roach et al (see
L. P. 27:114); of Samuel Jones et al (see *L. P.* 27:75, 103,
115); of Jacob Brewerton, Hubert van Waggenen, Samuel
Wells, Thos. Valentine et al of the township of Fincastle
(see *L. P.* 27:119); of Wm Thorne, Walter Thomas, Henry
Thomas, Jacob Wilkins and John Lewis (see *L. P.* 27:120);
of Samuel Bayard sr and jr, Thos. Grant et al for land
north of Ebenezer Jessup between Hudsons river and Lake
George; of Jotham Bemus, Thos. Hunt, John Taylor,
Asa Woodruff, John Moore, Henry Ertley, Asa Flint and
Barent de Klyn for land adjoining the preceding; of John
Bergen et al (see *L. P.* 27:117); of Robert Leake for license
to purchase Indian lands on the south west branch of Hudsons river; of Peter Remsen for same; of Dirck Lefferts
for same; of Isaac Low for same; of Thos. Palmer for
same; of Sergeant Peter Tobin 48th regiment (see *L. P.*
27:116) and Sergeant Wm Adams (see *L. P.* 27:112).   417

Nov. 27   Petitioners for land neglecting the necessary steps for obtain-
ing their grants for three months to lose the benefit of
their applications. Hearing appointed in re Col. John
Bradstreet and Hardenbergh patentees (p. 391; see *L. P.*
27:128).   418

Dec. 10   Hearing in re Bradstreet vs Hardenbergh patentees (p. 418).
Order on petition of Thomas Tobias, son of Christ'r
Tobias of Oysterbay, L. I. (see *L. P.* 27:129).   420

1771

Jan. 17   An office to be found for the lands petitioned for by Thos.
Tobias. Petition of Adolphus and Anna Ulrica Bentzel
(see *L. P.* 28:10) granted.   421

Feb. 5   Further hearing between Bradstreet and Hardenbergh
patentees (p. 420). Regulations for causes to be heard before the council.   423

8   Hearing between Bradstreet etc continued. Petition of
Alex'r McClure and 50 others (see *L. P.* 28:44) referred.
Hearing between Ebenezer Jessup, attorney for Henry Stil-
son (p. 406), John Tabor Kempe council, and Kayaderos-

seras patentees, Isaac Low attorney; decided in favor of
Stilson.   424

16   Report on the above petition of Alexander McLure et al;
granted.   426

25   Petitions granted: of Thos. Ludlow jr, John Schuyler jr et
al (see *L. P.* 27:101); of Lawrence L. van Boskerk, John
van Boskerk, Jacobus van Boskerk jr et al of the town-
ship of Leighton (see *L. P.* 27:145); of James Sacket, Mat-
thew Cushing, Gerardus Bancker, Wm Swan and Benj.
Jones (see *L. P.* 27:7); of Caleb Spencer sr and jr, Abr'm
Sedgwick et al (see *L. P.* 26:143); of Phineas Mun, Seth
Cuttin et al (see *L. P.* 27:85); of Nanning Vischer, Simon
M. Veeder, Abr'm Veeder, Abr'm Wemple, Gerrit S.
Veeder, Abr'm Yates jr, Stephen de Lancey and Hendrick
B. ten Eyck; of John Watts innholder in behalf of Ser-
geant Daniel Campbell, Corporals Charles Gordon and
John Laviston and Private Rich'd Livingston, all of the
28th regiment for land on the west side of Hudsons river
north of Batavia; of David Abeel jr, John Dederick,
Jacobus Abeel and James Abeel (see *L. P.* 27:111). Order
granting the petition of Wm Bayard (see *L. P.* 28:48).   426

Mar. 7 Land granted to Corporals Thos. Murphy and Edward Ford
80th regiment (see *L. P.* 27:126). License to purchase Indian land granted to Edward and Ebenezer Jessup (see
L. P. 27:134). Names of Edward and John McDonald to
be inserted vice those of John Rickey and Cornelius
Brower deceased, in the patent to John Munro et al (p.
224) upon petition of John Munro, Henry Brower, Edward and John McDonald (see *L. P.* 28:61). Royal order
repealing four New York acts of 1767, 1768 and 1769; to be
published by proclamation (see *N. Y. col. mss,* 96:144;
97:27). Order on petition of Petrus ten Brook (see *L. P.*
28:83). Patent for land granted to Lt. Col. John Reid,
Phil. Livingston jr, Arch'd Clark, Evert Bancker jr, Adam
Berger, Alex'r Wylly and Fred'k Guion (see *L. P.* 28:63).
Order on petition of Cornelius Low, Cornelius Teabout
and Dirck Lefferts (see *L. P.* 28:81).   432

11   Further hearing between Bradstreet and the Hardenbergh
patentees (p. 424).   436

12   Opinion of council in the preceding case between Bradstreet etc.   436

13   Petition of John Bradstreet (see *L. P.* 28:98) referred. Order
concerning grants to Abr'm Lott, Capt. John Wilson et
al (p. 222) and to Capt. Lewis van Fuser (p. 229). Hearing on petition of Benj. Spencer et al (see *L. P.* 27:132)

and the caveat of Crean Brush against granting it, postponed. Names of James Duane, John Jay, Cornelius
Duane, Thos. Stewart, James Yeomans, Robert Ross Wad-
del, Egbert Benson, John Devan and James Sacket to be
inserted in the patent to John Harris Cruger et al (p. 214)
vice Fleming Colgan, James Long, Teleman Cuyler, James
Seagrove, Wm Hutton, John Smith, Robert Robinson,
Moses Nicoll and John Verner (see *L. P.* 27:99). Town-
ship of Chesterfield granted to Edw'd Wm Kiers, Peter
Barberie, John Lewis, Joshua Mullock, Lawrence Kilburn,
Manuel Josephson, Alex'r Stewart jr, Thos. Lawrance,
John Long, Peter Stoutenburgh, Garret Waldron, Lewis
Relay, John Elliot, John Wilson, Rich'd Graham, John
Stewart, Samuel Stevens, Benj. Jones, George Bell and
John Woods (see *L. P.* 27:97).   437

18   Action on the above petition of John Bradstreet deferred.
Petition of Henry Stilson (see *L. P.* 27:102) granted.   440

20   Lands prayed for by John Bradstreet (p. 437) granted. Peti-
tions of Michael and Ann Long of Philadelphia (see *L. P.*
27:9), and of Thos. Duncan et al (see *L. P.* 26:87) granted.
Petitions dismissed: of Ass't Surgeon John Carter (see
L. P. 28:114); of John de Bernier, Thos. Swords, John An-
thony Kerns, Charles de Bernier, Niel McLean, Edward
Smyth, James McMillan and Draper Simon Wood (see
L. P. 28:116); of Lt. Col. Rich'd Maitland in behalf of
Capt. David Skene (see *L. P.* 28:113); of Robert Leake,
Fred'k Wm Hecht, Robert Ross, Wm Butler, Allen Mc-
Lean, Dugald Campbell and John Trotter (see *L. P.*
28:115); of Col. John Montresor (see *L. P.* 28:111); of
Lieut. John Montresor 48th regiment (see *L. P.* 28:112);
the lands prayed for being in the Hardenbergh patent.   441

Ap. 1 Names of John Hay, Robert Dixon, Joseph Black, Benj.
Ried, Daniel Frazier, John Wilson, Wm Swan, Samuel
Stevens, Samuel Wells and Anthony van Dam to be in-
serted in the patent to Wm Shirreff et al (p. 229) vice John
McNiel, Wm Kemble, Buckridge Webb, John Sackerly,
Henry Hornefer, Medad Pomroy, Ebenezer Harvey,
Joseph Burt, Shem Kentfield and James Glassford (see
L. P. 28:108). Order on petition of John Bradstreet (see
L. P. 28:124). Order on caveat by Joseph Greswold (see
L. P. 28:99).   444

3   Name of Samuel Boyer to be inserted in the patent to Abr'm
Lott et al (p. 222) vice Wm Horsefield (see *L. P.* 28:128). 446

10   Final order concerning the grant to Henry Stilson (p. 440)
and a caveat against it by Thos. Clarke. Caveat by

1771 v. 29

Joseph Griswold dismissed (p. 444) and patent granted to
Wm Bayard et al (p. 426). 446

15 Hearing between Benj. Spencer et al and Crean Brush
(p. 437) postponed. 447

22 Hearing of the preceding case. Township of Durham
granted to Benj. Spencer et al. 447

May 1 Hearing appointed on the petition of the Dutch reformed
church at Schenectady (see *L. P.* 28:69). Petitions
granted: of Lieut. Adolphus Benzell 60th regiment (see
L. P. 28:86); of Ensign Kenneth McCullock 78th regiment
(see *L. P.* 28:89); of Corporal James Brown 80th regiment
(see *L. P.* 28:91); of John Springer, Elizabeth Springer and
Ann Catherine Parlin (see *L. P.* 28:85); of John Wilson,
Richard Graham and Robert Hyslop for addition to Fincastle township (see *L. P.* 28:82); of Richard Maitland and
Andrew Elliot as guardians to John the infant son of Sir
John St Clair (see *L. P.* 29:2); of Stephen de Lancey, John
de Lancey, Daniel Harris, James Babcock, Wm Haight,
James Meade, Samuel Gardiner and Daniel Harris jr (see
L. P. 28:104); of Gerardus W. Beekman et al (see *L. P.*
28:129); of Richard Morris et al of the township of Mor-
risfield, substituting the name of Henry Ludlow jr for John
Morris removed to New Jersey (see *L. P.* 29:7). 448

29 Charter granted to the Society of the hospital in the city of
New York. Township of Newry granted to Charles Mc-
Evers, Theophylact Bache and Hamilton Young (see *L. P.*
28:123). Petition of Robert Leake, Fred'k Wm Hecht and
Robert Ross (see *L. P.* 28:95) granted. 454

31 Petitions granted: of Colin Drummond, John Livingston and
Jacob Jordan of Quebec (see *L. P.* 27:121); of Phineas
Lyman, John Hinsdale, Samuel Field et al (see *L. P.*
28:13); of Richard Slack et al of the township of Holywood
(see *L. P.* 28:30); of James Christy et al (see *L. P.* 28:32);
of John Earl et al (see *L. P.* 28:31); of Edward Smith et al
(see *L. P.* 28:28); of Samuel Wells et al (see *L. P.* 28:96);
of Jacob and George Brewerton (see *L. P.* 28:110); of
Jacob Walton et al (see *L. P.* 28:143); of Dr Thomas Clark
of New Perth, Albany county, for islands in the Battenkill;
of Hugh White (see *L. P.* 28:65); of Simon McTavish on
behalf of his father Lieut. John McTavish 78th regiment
(see *L. P.* 28:45); of Sergeant Donald McIntosh 42d regiment for land on Otter creek; of Lieut. Josiah Banks independents, Surgeon's Mate Albert Meinert Lubcken, 32
non-commissioned officers and 35 privates (see *L. P.*
28:107). 455

June 7 Order on petition of Lt. Col. Reid and Capt. James Gray
         (see *L. P.* 29:40). Hearing on petition of Pierre Guillaume
         de Peyster (see *L. P.* 29:6) appointed. Order on petition
         of Sergeant Kenneth Morrison 55th regiment (see *L. P.*
         28:19-22). Petitions granted: of Joseph Griswold et al (see
         L. P. 28:103); of Gerrit van Sante (see *L. P.* 28:37); of
         Jeston Homfray, Miles Sherbrook and 28 others of the
         township of Prattsburgh (see *L. P.* 28:121); of Wm Will-
         iams et al of the township of Summerhill (see *L. P.*
         28:150); of Benj. Hugget et al (see *L. P.* 28:125); of George
         Brewerton jr (see *L. P.* 28:126); of Edward Thatcher et al
         (see *L. P.* 28:135); of John Davan et al of the township of
         Richmond (see *L. P.* 29:7); of Wm Smith and Wm Liv-
         ingston of the township of Newport Pagnel (see *L. P.*
         29:27); of Thos. McCrae, Andrew Lytle, John McCrae and
         Dr Thos. Clarke all of New Perth (see *L. P.* 29:33); of
         Thos. Hicks, Whitehead Hicks, Gilbert Hicks, John Bre-
         voort, Elias Brevoort et al (see *L. P.* 29:61); of Evert
         Bancker jr and Mary Bancker (see *L. P.* 29:42); of Simon
         and Catherine Metcalf (see *L. P.* 29:52); of Joseph Totten
         and Stephen Crossfield (see *L. P.* 28:141); of Lt. Col.
         Robinson in behalf of Sir Jeffrey Amherst (see *L. P.*
         99:12); of Sergeants Wm Crawford, James Thompson,
         Corporals James Ross, Thos. Birtch, Privates Wm Legus,
         George Pringle, Peter Stalker, James Currant 55th, Cor-
         poral Anthony Williams 80th, Private Joseph Anderson
         17th regiment (see *L. P.* 29:46; 28:119); of Sergeants Thos.
         Millet 46th, Robert Davidson, Thos. Whiten 55th, Cor-
         porals Phil. Lambert 46th, Benj. Niblet and Wm Forbes
         55th regiment (see *L. P.* 28:118); of Sergeant John Watts
         and Private Michael Wells (see *L. P.* 29:13); of Capt. Gil-
         bert McAdam (see *L. P.* 29:35); of Capt. John Ross 95th
         regiment (see *L. P.* 29:38). Order on memorial of Lt. Col.
         John Reid (see *L. P.* 28:53). List of names to be inserted
         in the patent to Samuel Wells (p. 455; see *L. P.* 29:51)
         filed.   461

      12 Hearing between Lt. Col. Reid and Capt. James Gray of the
         one part, and G. W. Beekman et al of the other (p. 461);
         decided in favor of Beekman. The surveyor general or-
         dered to attend the council.   474

      14 The surveyor general produces a list of persons who have
         failed to take the necessary steps for obtaining patents
         petitioned for by them, and their names are struck out.
         Petitions granted: of Moses Clements (see *L. P.* 27:51); of
         John Bruster and Thos. Moffat for land in Orange county;

of James Leadbetter and Charles Giles (see *L. P.* 28-66); of
Joseph Stringham, Wm Smith et al (see *L. P.* 28:140); of
Donald Stewart, 16 other privates and Corporal Roderick
McLoed Royal highlanders (see *L. P.* 28:59); of David
Matthews et al (see *L. P.* 28:59); of Joseph Smith and 29
others (see *L. P.* 28:83); of Wm Stepple [Staples] and 29
others (see *L. P.* 28:88); of Alex'r McLure and 29 others
(see *L. P.* 28:92); of Andrew Elliot and 29 others (see *L. P.*
28:90); of Peter Sylvester et al of the township of Spring-
hill (see *L. P.* 27:139); of Abr'm P. Yates et al of the township of Bloomingdale (see *L. P.* 27:146); of Samuel Bayard
jr et al of the township of Jamaica (see *L. P.* 27:147); of
Lambert Moore et al of the township of Barbadoes (see
L. P. 27:138); of James Smith et al of the township of
Tyrone (see *L. P.* 27:137). Warrant of survey granted to
Philipp Skene (see *L. P.* 29:82).   475

19   Petitions granted: of Privates Donald Frazer, Henry Frazer,
Duncan Bayne, John Cameron, Robert Stewart 42d, John
Higinson, Michael Lyon 46th, Richard Pricket Inniskill-
ings, Sergeants Robert Bell 43d, John McDougal 6oth regiment, for land west of the Green mountains; of Sergeant
John Campbell, 28 other non-commissioned officers and
four privates for land east of Lake Champlain; of Lieut.
Alex'r Donaldson (see *L. P.* 28:109); of Charles Robinson
et al (see *L. P.* 28:133); of Oliver Willard and 27 others
(see *L. P.* 29:64); of Francis and Samuel Mackay (see *L. P.*
29:65); of John Tuder (see *L. P.* 29:66); of John Shaw,
John Kennedy and 23 others (see *L. P.* 29:84); of
Broughton Reynolds et al (see *L. P.* 29:85); of Wm
Nicholls, Wm Swan, Simon Stevens, Wm Malcom,
Gamaliel Wallace, Richard Wenman et al (see *L. P.* 29:87);
of Charles Nicoll, Joseph Allicock, Evert Bancker and
Isaac Heron (see *L. P.* 29:86); of John Tabor Kempe (see
L. P. 29:68); of Lieut. Richard Price, R. N. (see *L. P.*
29:73); of Philipp Skene (see *L. P.* 29:70); of Capt. Beamsley Glasier (see *L. P.* 29:31); of Hugh Gaine (see *L. P.*
29:45); of Jelles Fonda (see *L. P.* 29:88). Order on petition of Abr'm Jacob Lansingh (see 29:72, 76).   484

July 3   Orders on petitions: of Henry van Vleck and four others
(see *L. P.* 29:97); of Henry Erkly and eight others (see
L. P. 29:90); of Mary widow of Lewis Foy conductor of
ordnance stores for land not located.   492

Aug. 7   Gov. Wm Tryon in the chair. Time appointed for hearings
on the petitions: of James Leadbetter and Joseph Stringham (see *L. P.* 29:122), caveat of John Terwilliger (see

1771   **v. 29**

L. P. 29:128); of Eneas McKay and Godlieb Switzer (see
L. P. 29:123); of John Miller and Nicholas Killman (see
L. P. 29:127); of Surgeon Lewis P. Williams (see L. P.
29:51); of Peter van Ness, Peter Vosburgh, Hendrick
Remsen, and Robert van Duersen (see L. P. 29:54); of
the Dutch church at Schenectady and George Smith (see
L. P. 29:47). Petitions granted: of John Montanye (see
L. P. 29:115); of Richard Morris and Wm Wickham (see
L. P. 28:76); of George Brewerton et al (see L. P. 29:116);
of Alexander McLure et al (see L. P. 29:117); of Sergeant
Daniel McIntosh 42d and Private John Alder 60th regiment
(see L. P. 29:99); of James Davis collar maker Royal art'y
(see L. P. 29:80); of Sergeant Wm Guise 27th, Corporals
Lodowick Stewart, James Duncan, Thos. McWilliams 55th,
Privates Fred. Shonnard 60th, Edward Barber, Samuel
Robinson, James Putman 27th regiment (see L. P. 29:104);
of Kenneth Morison in behalf of John Kennedy private
55th regiment (see L. P. 29:118); of James Kay petty
officer and linguist on board the Fame man-of-war (see
L. P. 29:114).   494

14   Additional instructions concerning gold and silver mines on
Philippsburgh manor. Petition of Fred'k Philippse (see
L. P. 29:129-30) granted.   499

21   Petition of Oliver de Lancy and Peter du Bois for land near
New Perth or Turner's patent (see L. P. 29:132) granted.   501

28   Draft of patent to Fred'k Philippse (p. 499) amended. Petition of John Butler et al of the township of Strasburgh (see
L. P. 29:142) granted.   503

Sep. 5   Draft of patent to Fred'k Philippse (p. 503) further
amended. Royal orders confirming the New York act
enabling aliens to hold real estate and vetoing three others;
to be published by proclamation (see N. Y. col. mss, 97:63-
64, 85-86). The surveyor general to prepare a map of the
land between Hudsons and Connecticut rivers.   504

18   Patent to Fred'k Philippse passed (p. 504).   507

Oct. 2   Caveat of John Terwilliger (p. 494) dismissed. Order on
caveat entered by Simon Remsen, John de la Meter, Dirck
Lefferts et al (see L. P. 29:128); lands to be granted James
Leadbetter, Charles Giles et al and to James Creassy (see
L. P. 29:113). Petitions granted: of Simon Remsen, John
de la Meter, George Lindner and Henry Thomas (see
L. P. 30:64); of Abr'm Lefferts (see L. P. 27:123); of Cor-
poral Wm Sutherland 77th regiment (see L. P. 29:91).   507

3   Hearings: between Lewis P. Williams and Peter van Ness
et al (p. 494); between P. G. de Peyster of the one part,
Phil. Schuyler and Jeremiah van Rensselaer of the other

(p. 461); between Schenectady church and George Smith
(p. 494).   510

15   Petitions granted: of Sergeant Kenneth Morrison, Corporal
Wm Stephison and Private Daniel Lucas 55th regiment
(see *L. P.* 31:136); of Private Philipp Grindlemeyer 60th
regiment (see *L. P.* 30:11). Orders on petitions: of Dirck
Lefferts (see *L. P.* 30:22); of Crean Brush, John Grumley
and Joseph Beck (see *L. P.* 30:20).   511

23   Petitions granted: of David Abeel jr (see *L. P.* 30:24); of
John Taylor, Judah Harlowe, George Stewart, Joseph Allicocke and Robert Harding (see *L. P.* 30:23). Report on
the above petition of Crean Brush et al; granted.   513

Nov. 13   Petitions granted: of Drummer Donald McIntosh jr,
Corporal Robert McConnachy 78th, Privates Anthony
Fox 46th, Donald McIntosh sr 70th, John Black 63d, John
McKenzie, John Stewart and Donald Henderson (see
L. P. 29:148); of Privates Thos. Biddeford 27th, John
McIntosh 77th and Corporal John McGilliray 78th regi-
ment (see *L. P.* 29:147); of Corporal Alex'r Graey 78th
regiment (see *L. P.* 28:148); of Lieut. Archibald Campbell
42d regiment (see *L. P.* 30:28); of Samuel Deal in behalf
Corporal Thos. Tomlin, Private Stephen Blundel 44th and
James Stewart 46th regiment (see *L. P.* 30:31); of Ensign
Wm Bard 80th regiment (see *L. P.* 30:38); of Joseph Gres-
wold and John Watts (see *L. P.* 29:141); of Hugh Monro,
Walter Thomas and Henry Thomas (see *L. P.* 30:29); of
John Glen and Abr'm C. Cuyler (see *L. P.* 30:21); of Dr
Thos. Clark (see *L. P.* 29:143). Grant of land issued to
Lt. Col. Thomas Howard in accordance with royal man-
damus. Charter of incorporation granted to Trinity
church at Fishkill upon petition of Rev. John Beardsley
(see *N. Y. col. mss*, 97:99).   514

27   James Abeel, Jacobus Abeel and John Dederick release to
David Abeel jr their respective shares in the patent
granted on October 23. Opinion of council as to lands
granted to Lewis P. Williams et al (p. 510). Hearing between Schenectady church and George Smith (p. 510)
postponed.   518

Dec. 2   Order on petition of Michel Chartier de la Biniere of Quebec
for confirmation of French grants on Lakes Champlain
and George.   519

11   Map of lands east of the Hudson river laid before the council
by the surveyor general. Map of patented lands on the
Mohawk river called for. Order on petition of Johannes
Freud asking that the land improved by him and associates

be not included in the grant to Lewis P. Williams (see *L. P.* 30:53). Township of Win Hall granted to Abr'm Thompson, Benj. Dorchester, Phineas Bradley, Samuel Bishop jr, Samuel Stevens, Simon Stevens, John Kennedy, John Shaw, Jacob Wilkins, Waldron Blaau, James Cabham, James Abeel, John de la Mater, Alex'r Blackburn, Joseph Blanchard, Giles Alexander, James Smith, Hugh Rider, Isaac Roosevelt, John Alsop, Richard Yates, John R. Myer, Peter Keteltas, Wynant Keteltas and Benj. Stout jr (see *L. P.* 30:50).   520

31   Orders on petitions: of inhabitants of Poughkeepsie (see *L. P.* 29:150); of Rev. John Beardsley (see *L. P.* 30:15); of Robert Leake et al (see *L. P.* 29:146).   522

1772

Jan. 22   Names in the patent for the township of Wallingford (p. 241) to be changed to Eliakim Hall sr and jr, Isaac Hall jr, and wife Hester, Hezekiah Hall and wife Elizabeth, Stephen Hall, Caleb Hall, Samuel Hall, Elisha Hall jr, Isaac Doolittle, John Hotchkiss, Caleb Johnston, Miles Johnston and Ruth Johnston jr his wife, Sarah Johnston widow of Israel Johnston, Rachel Johnston, Roger Sherman, Rev. Nathan Williams, Mary Williams, Jesse Cook and Elizabeth Hall; all the reserved lots except that of Benning Wentworth to be added (see *L. P.* 30:88).   523

29   Names in the patent for the township of Windsor (p. 96) to be changed to Nathan Stone, Wm Swan, Waldron Blaau, John Abeel, Wm Puntine, Michael Nan, John McGinniss, Richard McGinniss, Robert McGinniss, Patrick Walsh, James Abeel, Edward McCollom, Marinus Low, Edward Patten, Andries Reiglar, George Klein, Thos. Lupton, Duncan Robertson, Samuel Stevens, John Peisinger, George Lucam, Francis Groome and James Cobham (see *L. P.* 30:100). Patent for the township of New Fane (p. 204) to issue in the names of Walter Franklin, Giles Alexander, John Thompson, John Franklin, Jacob Watson, Joseph Bull, Peter Bard, Isaac Corsa, Samuel Franklin, Robert Brown, Lawrence Kortright, Teddeman Hull, James Bown, Anth'y Byvanck, Robert Benson, Lindley Murray and Wm Backhouse; all the lots formerly reserved except that of Benning Wentworth to be added (see *L. P.* 30:98). License to purchase Indian lands granted to James Creasey et al (see *L. P.* 30:48, 55).   525

Feb. 5   Order on petition of the owners of the great nine partners patent (see *L. P.* 30:28). Patent for the township of Weathersfield (p. 156) to issue to Daniel Lyman, Medad

Lyman, Enos Allen, James Rice, Roswell Woodward,
Abr'm Thompson sr and jr, Samuel Birch jr, John Mix,
John Pierpoint, John Bradley jr, Phineas Bradley, John
Cornell, Lemuel Hotchkiss, Jonah Bradley, Hezekiah
Parmell jr, John Austin, Israel Monson, Joel Gilbert,
Joseph Thompson, Caleb Gilbert and Joseph Dorman; in-
cluding the lots formerly reserved, except that of Benning
Wentworth (see *L. P.* 30:103). Patent for the township of
Reading (p. 233) to issue to Simon Stevens, George Wil-
son, Cornelius van der Bergh, George Shaw, Wm Bailey,
Garret van der Bergh, Rinier Hopper, Richard Varian,
Thos. Arden, Daniel Goldsmith, Caleb Hyatt, John Stout,
James Wessels, Waldron Blaau, Obadiah Wells, Henry
Gulick, John Brook, Samuel Stevens, Isaac Corsa, Marinus
Willett, James Cobham and Wm Kennedy; including the
shares formerly allotted to Wiseman Clagget, Daniel War-
ner and Samuel Wentworth (see *L. P.* 30:106). Patent for
the township of Newberry (p. 81, 214) to issue to Jacob
Bayley, John Taplin, Stephen Little, Samuel Stevens,
Joseph Blanchard, Nathan Stone, Waldron Blaau, James
Cobham, Joseph Beck, Samuel Bayard, John Wetherhead,
Wm Williams, James Creasey, John Bowles, John Grumly,
Marinus Willett, Richard Wenman, John Kelly, John Shat-
ford Jones, James Downes, Samuel Boyer, John Keen,
John Lewis, Crean Brush, and John Taylor; including the
lots formerly reserved except that of Benning Wentworth
(see *L. P.* 30:111). Patent for the township of Wood-
stock (p. 204) to issue to Oliver Willard, Isaac Corsa,
Joseph Bull, John Blagge, Wm A. Forbes, Benj. Stout sr
and jr, Corn's van der Bergh, Peter van der Voort, Wm
Talman, George Birks, Henry Gulick, Wm Clarke, John
B. Stout, Henry Beekman, John Fowler, Caleb Hyatt,
Daniel Goldsmith, Daniel Green, Samuel Stevens, Charles
McEvers, James Seagrove, Christ'r Blundel and Adam
Gilchrist, including all the lots formerly reserved (see
L. P. 30:107). Petition of Sergeant Daniel McIntosh 42d,
Corporal Thos. Brown 60th, Drummer Alex'r Leslie 1st,
Privates Christ'n Aloon, Edward Kingsley, John Flint-
larm, Wm Douglass and John Alder 60th, Andrew Flint
77th regiment (*L. P.* 30:112) granted.   529

11   Hearing between the owners of great nine partners patent
     and the inhabitants of Poughkeepsie (p. 529).   535
12   Hearing continued and caveat of the great nine partners
     people dismissed. Patent for the township of Corinth
     (p. 145) to issue to Samuel Holland, John Taplin, Henry

Moore, Wm Wickham, Cornelius van der Burgh, Adam
van der Burgh, Gilbert Burger, Thos. Duncan, John Shatford Jones, John L. C. Roome, Garret Abeel, John Fowler,
Joseph Charter, Wm Crossley, John Blacklock, Samuel
Roberts, Oliver Willard, John Someryndyck, Henry Broad-
well, Peter Webbers, John Carpenter jr, and Obadiah
Wells, including the lots formerly reserved (see *L. P.*
30:120). Order on petition of Wilder Willard of Brattleborough, Cumberland county, by Wm Shepherd his attorney (see *L. P.* 30:122).   536

19   Patent for the township of Bridgewater (p. 204) to issue
to John Church et al and to include the lots formerly re-
served except that of Benning Wentworth (see *L. P.*
30:128). Patent for the township of Westminster (p. 196)
to issue to Bildad Andross, Michael Metcalfe, Benj.
James, Samuel Boyer, Daniel Mesnard, Lawrence Kilburn,
John Lewis, Wm Williams, Alex'r White, Oliver Willard,
Giles Alexander, Benj. Stout, John B. Stout, Samuel Wells,
Samuel Stevens, John Church, John Kelly, Wm Malcom,
Benj. Garrison, Gamaliel Wallace, Francis Elsworth,
Joseph Beck, Wm Thompson, Egbert Benson and Wm
Willard; including lots formerly reserved except that of
Benning Wentworth (see *L. P.* 30:130). Patent for the
township of Fulham (p. 165) to issue to John Kathan,
Peter Sim, Daniel McFee, Thos. Lupton, Jacob Albright,
Samuel Wells, Thos. Barnet, John Shatford Jones, Abr'm
Spier, Edw'd Perine, John Peters, Josiah Willard, Daniel
Whipple, John Fowler, Oliver Willard, John Church,
Nathan Stone, Wm Deane and Wm Williams; excepting
500 acres in the northwest corner and the lot of Benning
Wentworth (see *L. P.* 30:138). Petition of Lieut. Peter
Pinniere (see *L. P.* 30:134) granted. Order on petition of
Aaron Paine, Ebenezer Judd and Martin Preston (see
L. P. 30:127). Patent for land prayed for by Lieut. John
Thompson (see *L. P.* 30:124) to issue in obedience to royal
mandamus.   539

28   Order concerning the grant to Wm Nicoll et al (p. 484).
Township of Windham granted to Joseph Beck et al.
Order that no land grants pass unless all the names of the
parties are given. Order on petition of Thos. Hendrickson, John Whitson and Daniel Hendrickson (see *L. P.*
31:5).   544

Mar. 26 Patent for the township of Springfield (p. 193) to issue in
the names of Charles Shaw, Wm Sidney, Gabriel H. Ludlow, Richard Hatfield, Richard Morris, Wm Wickham,

Thos. White, Stephen Steel, Samuel Jones, Benj. Kissam, John Barret, Jasper Drake, Cornelius van Alen, James Armitage, Jacob Parcel, Anthony Gleen, Gilbert Taylor, John McKesson, Lewis Graham, Miles Sherbrook and Thos. Ludlow jr; including lots formerly reserved except that of Benning Wentworth since granted to Lieut. Thos. Etherington (see *L. P.* 31:23). Patent for the township of Fairlie (p. 126) to issue to Samuel Stevens, Isaac Corsa, John Blagge, John Vredenbergh, Joseph Bull, Waldron Blaau, James Cobham, John Abeel, John de la Mater, Gercord Bancker, James Abeel, Ennis Graham, Matthew Lane, Alex'r McLean, Wm. Wilcocks, John Warner, Alex'r Bradburn, Caleb Hyatt, John Grumly, Abr'm Wilson, Andrew Myer, Lewis Relay, Henry Relay and Simon Stevens (see *L. P.* 31:25). Patent for the township of Barnet (p. 214) to issue to Simon Stevens, Benj. Allen, Joseph Bull, Jonathan Grout, Simeon Alvard, Phil. Brasher, Henry Beekman, Wm Nicoll, Jonathan Weatherbee, Wm Swan, Samuel Stevens, Nathan Stone, John Manbout, Enos Stevens, Robert Andrews, Peter Thompson, Cornelius van der Burgh, Adam van der Burgh, Willard Stevens, Caleb Hyatt, James Abeel and Phineas Stevens; including lots formerly reserved except that of Benning Wentworth (see *L. P.* 31:49). Township of West Camden granted to John Monier and John Nicholas Bleecker (see *L. P.* 31:52, 54). Township of Norbury granted to Samuel Chandler, Edmund Fanning, Charles Preston, Wm. Bayard, James Duane, Arch'd Kennedy, Jonathan Mallet, Andrew Elliot, Isaac Willet jr, Thos. Moncrief, Goldsbrow Banyar, Andrew Gordon, Charles Williams, Samuel Wells, John Reid, Johnston Fairholme, James Moran, John Kelly, Samuel Stevens, Benj. John Johnston, Christ'r Blundell, John Grumley, Joshua Littlewood, Francis Panton, Malcolm McIsaac, John Hodges and Moses Marden (see *L. P.* 31:43). Patent for the township of Grafton (p. 385) to issue in the names of Stephen de Lancey, John de Lancey, John Harris Cruger, James de Lancey jr, John de Noyelles, Peter du Bois, John Kelly, Samuel Wells, Crean Brush, John Bowles, Nathan Stone, John Wetherhead, John Church, James Rogers, Samuel Stevens, Charles Nicoll, Isaac Heron, Joseph Allicocke, John Woods, James Moran, George Janway, James Yeaman, John Davan, Francis Panton, Joseph Beck, Adam Gilchrist, Wm Smith, Samuel Boyer, John Keen, John Lewis and James Cobham. (see *L. P.* 31:65). Minutes sent to the board of trade.   546

Vol. 30, 1770-75

Legislative minutes of council from Dec. 11, 1770 to Ap. 3, 1775 printed in *Journal of the legislative conncil of the colony of New York*, 2:1744-1998.

Vol. 31, 1772-76

Ap. 8   Patent for the township of Cavendish (29:181) to issue to John Church, Waldron Blaau, John de la Mater, Jacob Shafer, John Machett jr, John Gardineer, James Cobham, Jacobus Verveelen, John van Order, Wm Day, Christian de Marrees, John Lee, John de Groot, James Abeel, Nathan Stone, Simon Stevens, Joseph Beck, Wm Kennedy, Cornelius van der Burgh, James Christy, Samuel Steetens, and John Abeel (see *L. P.* 31:26). Patent for the township of Hartford (29:179) to issue to Jonathan Burtch, Hugh Gaine, John Kaine, James Lanckashire, Wm Ross, Wm Smith, Valentine Nutter, Isaac Heron, Robert Neille, Daniel Neille, Robert Neille jr, Wm Young, Wm Todd, Christian Will, Johannes Will, Peter Montagnie, John Schevington, Wm Scott, James Thompson, James Roles, Matthew Gleves, George Ball, Christ'r Dudley and John Kelly; including lots formerly reserved except that of B. Wentworth (see *L. P.* 31:73). Names of Carey Ludlow, Patrick Dennis, Thos. Smith, Peter Goelet, Thos. Duncan and Rudolphus Ritzema to be added to the patent for the township of Springfield (29:546; see *L. P.* 31:76). Order on petition of John Grout in behalf of Hannah widow of John Spafford, Nath'l Powers, James Call, Ebenezer Dike, Oliver Farnsworth, and Noah Porter (see *L. P.* 31:61). Township of Townsend granted to Lord George Townsend, John Osburn, Wm Longhead, Robert Hoakesly, Jacob Wilkins, Robert Hall, Alex'r Lessley, Stephen Thompson, Simon Metcalf, Wm Kennedy, Joseph Beck, Joseph Allicock, Charles Nicoll, Wm Swan, John Grumly, Samuel Wells, James Leadbetter, Thomas Lupton, John Shatford Jones, Samuel Stevens, James Abeel, John de la Mater, John Abeel, Lewis Relay, Henry Relay, Garret Abeel, Evert Byvanck, Simon Stevens, Phil. Lott and Henry Kelly (see *L. P.* 30:113). Lands granted: to Corporal Dougal McAshlin 42d regiment (see *L. P.* 30:89); to Lieut. Neal McLean 42d regiment (see *L. P.* 30:87).

15   Patent for the town of Saltash (29:196) to issue to Eleazer Oswald, Benj. Stout, John Stout, John Fowler, Caleb Hyatt, John L. C. Roome, Corn's van der Burgh, James Cobham, Alex'r Bradburne, John Stout 3d, Benj. Stout jr,

John Church, Simon Stevens, Joseph Beck, Wm Boyer,
Henry Beekman, Wm Swan, John Lewis, Samuel Stevens,
Benj. Garrison, John Keen, Waldron Blaau, James Thompson, Wm Kennedy and Benj. James; including lots formerly reserved except that of Benning Wentworth (see *L. P.* 30:91). New survey of the township of Wallingford ordered (see *L. P.* 30:133).   4

22   Petition granted: of Ebenezer Clark and Thos. Watson (see *L. P.* 30:47); of Elihu Spencer, Peter Schenck, Peter Nefius, Joseph Philipps, Jonathan Philipps, Edmond Bambridge, Wm Philipps, Joseph Laboyteux, John Laboyteux and Benj. Stevens (see *L. P.* 30:66); of Alex'r Grant, Duncan Campbell and Benj. Spencer (see *L. P.* 30:82); of Dougal Campbell, Thomas Burnet and John Godfrey (see *L. P.* 30:85); of Colin Campbell (see *L. P.* 30:83); of John McEwen, Benj. Prime and John Taylor (see *L. P.* 30:84); of Dugal Campbell (see *L. P.* 30:70); of John Lawrence (see *L. P.* 30:91); of Sergeants Peter Sharpe 55th and Donald Munroe 60th regiment (see *L. P.* 30:86); of Corporal John Gillaspie 27th regiment (see *L. P.* 30:80); of Robert Leake commissary general, his deputies, and Garret van Sante (see *L. P.* 30:73). Warrant of survey granted to Lieut. Donald Campbell, his brothers George and James, and his sisters Rose Graham, Margaret Eustace and Lilly Murray (see *L. P.* 31:106). Patent granted to Henry van Vleck et al (29:492).   5

May 2 Order on royal mandamus in favor of Lt. Col. Josiah Martin 68th regiment (see *L. P.* 27:69). Land granted to Sergeants Charles Mair 42d Wm Anderson 77th and Corporal Alex'r Gray 78th regiment (see *L. P.* 31:115). Hearing appointed between Robert Leake et al, inhabitants of Poughkeepsie, and Rev. John Beardsley.   9

8   Petitions granted: of Lieut. Joseph Conway, Royal marines, (see *L. P.* 31:122); of John Holland master of the Deal Castle man-of-war (see *L. P.* 31:125). Township of Minto granted to Andrew Elliott et al (see *L. P.* 31:120). Order on petition of Elizabeth Mathews (see *L. P.* 31:107). Hearing between Leake and Beardsley (p. 9); decided.   10

19   Charter of incorporation for the episcopal church at Poughkeepsie granted to Rev. John Beardsley, Wardens Barth'w Crannel, Samuel Smith, Vestrymen Richard Davis, John Child, John Davis, John Ferdon jr, John Medlar, Zachariah Ferdon, Isaac Baldwin jr, and Dr David Brooks (see *L. P.* 31:134). Royal order confirming New York act vesting in Phil. van Cortlandt an estate in fee simple passed in February 1771.   12

June 3   Petitions granted: of Daniel Horsmanden, Miles Sherbrook,
Samuel Camfield and Wm Sidney (see *L. P.* 31:144); of
Samuel Avory, Garret Rapalje, Wm Butler, Jacob Town-
send, Abr'm Schenck, Davis Hunt, Samuel Bunce, John
Adams, John Cline, Joseph Hunt, John Hunt, John Felt-
hausen, Henry Edwards, Edward Blagge, John Myers,
Gerardus Myers, Jacobus Turk, John van Sice, Ludwick
Hinsbee, John Anderson, John Stout, Henry Riker, An-
dreas Riker and Peter Riker (see *L. P.* 30:142); of Hum-
phrey Avory, Jonathan Trumbell, Hezekiah Huntington,
Ebenezer Avory, Joseph Morgan, Solomon Morgan,
Ebenezer Avory jr, Latham Avory, John Perret, Joseph
Carpenter, Gardiner Carpenter, Ebenezer Whiting, Ebene-
zer Bacchus, Isaac Tracy, Zebdiel Rogers, Theophilus
Rogers, Benj. Butler, Joseph Gale, Wm Morgan, Joseph
Rose, Daniel Lathrop, Joshua Lathrop, Job Taylor, Gers-
ham Budd, Peter Lanman, Samuel Coit, Isaac Coit and
Benj. Coit (see *L. P.* 30:143); of Sergeant David Reid 42d
regiment (see *L. P.* 31:158).   13

15   Confirmatory patents granted: to Samuel Wells and John
Kelly for the township of Guilford and Wilmington; to
Wm Williams for Marlborough; to Samuel Stevens and
Timothy Bradley for Ludlow; to James Rogers for Rock-
ingham; to Jacob Bayley and John Peters for Strafford; to
John Church for Ryegate; to Phineas Lyman for Peacham;
to John Peters for Topsham; to Samuel Stevens for Tun-
bridge; to Jacob Bayley for Maidstone; to Joseph Smalley
for Norwich; to Jonathan Grout for Lunenburgh; to Amos
Babcock for Andover; to Israel Putnam for Pomfret (see
L. P. 30:123; 31:48). Confirmatory patents granted: to inhabitants of Maidstone, Minhead, Limington and Averill
(see *L. P.* 31:121); to Isaac Searles et al for Stratton (see
L. P. 30:37); all former New Hampshire grants. Lands
ungranted in Shrewsbury granted to Samuel Ashley, Ephraim Dorman et al (see *L. P.* 30:132). Order on petition
of Benj. Edwards, James Weyman, Giles Alexander et al
for part of the township of Draper alias Wilmington (see
L. P. 30:39). Petitions granted: of John de la Mater and
39 others (see *L. P.* 31:109); of Peter Schenck et al (see
L. P. 31:156); of Wm Wickoff and 26 others (see *L. P.*
31:160); of Josiah Willard et al (see *L. P.* 31:73); of Abel
Walker et al (see *L. P.* 31:108); of Nathan Stone and 34 others
of the township of New Rutland (see *L. P.* 31:16); of
Samuel Ashley and 25 others (see *L. P.* 31:118); of Thomas
Pettit and 29 others (see *L. P.* 31:114); of James Canneff,

Hans Springstale, Jonathan Hobbs and Samuel Knight (see *L. P.* 31:128); of Robert Bound and 30 others (see *L.P.* 31:105); of John Woods et al of the township of Meath (see *L. P.* 31:138); of David Mathews and 19 others of the township of Thirming (see *L. P.* 31:139); of Garsham Lott and Gersham Mott (see *L. P.* 31:143); of Hugh Duncan, Mathew Lane, John Wallis, Gamaliel Wallis and Alexander Wallace (see *L. P.* 30:140); of John Blagge, John Grumley, Benj. I. Johnson, Edmond Fanning, John Kelly and Wm Kennedy (see *L. P.* 31:137); of John Peters and 23 others of the township of Peterstown (see *L. P.* 31:53); of Daniel McKeuen and Lawrence L. van Alen (see *L. P.* 31:82); of Joseph Philipps et al (see *L. P.* 30:34); of Jelles Fonda (see *L. P.* 31:90); of Robert and Thos. Clark (see *L. P.* 32:1); of John Jones deputy barrack master at Fort George (see *L. P.* 31:15). Licenses to purchase Indian lands granted: to Dirck and Rikert van Vranken (see *L. P.* 30:94); to John Williams et al (see *L. P.* 31:31); to John Graham et al (see *L. P.* 31:36); to Jesse Fairchild et al (see *L. P.* 31:35); to John Jones et al (see *L. P.* 31:40); to James Eldridge et al (see *L. P.* 31:39); to Neal Nicholson et al (see *L. P.* 31:38). Lands granted: to Ensign Kenneth McCullock 78th regiment (see *L. P.* 31:6); to Privates Walter Graham, John Urhard, Andrew Hutton 42d regiment (see *L. P.* 31:157); to Privates Allan Grant, Duncan McCall, Wm McLean 42d, John Black 55th regiment (see *L. P.* 31:159); to Sergeant Richard Gregory 60th, Privates Robert Masdam 60th, and George Kennimine 44th regiment (see *L. P.* 31:79); to Capt. Beamsley Glasier (see *L. P.* 31:126); to Private James Black 42d, Corporal John Craney 3d regiment, and Matross John Grigg Royal artillery (see *L. P.* 31:68); to Sergeant Edward Morrison 35th regiment (see *L. P.* 31:135); to Sergeant Charles Mair 42d, Wm Anderson 77th, and Corporal Alexander Gray 78th regiment (see *L. P.* 31:155). Petitions granted: of John Ogilvie in behalf of the heirs of Major General Ralph Burton (see *L. P.* 31:129); of Jeremiah French in behalf of himself and other inhabitants of Dover, Dutchess county (see *L. P.* 31:50; 32:28); of Timothy Bush, Robert Barnet, John Mann sr and jr, James Chalkins, Henry Moore, Joseph Phelps, Thos. Chamberlain, David Sutton, John Taplin sr and jr, Nehemiah Sovwell, Daniel Horsford sr and jr and Daniel Miller (see *L. P.* 31:115). Minutes sent to the board of trade.

| 1772 | | | v. 31 |

July 1   Hearing appointed on the petitions of Abr'm J. Lansing (29:492) and of the inhabitants of Half Moon (see *L. P.* 31:56).   28

8   Lands granted to Corporal Gregor Drummond 55th, Privates Hugh Morrison, James Stuart, Malcom Stuart, Andrew Yates, John Fisher; George Gun, John Hickie, George Monro, Robert McPherson, Duncan Fraser, Alex'r Baxter 42d regiment (see *L. P.* 32:26); to John Robinson boatswain of the Onondaga, snow-of-war, Capt. Joshua Loring (see *L. P.* 32:11). Order concerning petitions for land under the proclamation of 1763.   28

Aug. 21   Royal order vetoing three New York acts of 1770 and 1771. Patent granted to Henry Thomas, John de la Mater et al (29:507) to issue in the names of Thomas de la Mater, Robert Harding and Wm Butler (see *L. P.* 31:1). List of Indian lands purchased before Gov. Tryon at Johnson hall; by Joseph Totten, Stephen Crossfield et al; by Ebenezer Jessup, Edward Jessup et al; by Thomas Palmer, Isaac Low, Dirck Lefferts, Peter Remsen, Robert Leake et al; by John Glen and Christopher Yates; by John Bergen et al; by Jeremiah van Rensselaer et al; by Jelles Fonda et al (see *L. P.* 32:40-45).   29

Sep. 8   Petitions granted: of Joseph Ingell, David McWithey, James van Duser, Wm Fairfield, Abr'm van Duser, Gidion Esquire, Isaac McWithey, Charles Miller, John Monroe, Reuben McWithey, Samuel Colver, Jonathan Ingell, Benj. McIntier and Aron Cormstock (see *L. P.* 32:20); of Andrew Little, James Little and 32 others for 32,000 acres between Skeensborough and Kelso. Charter of incorporation for a public library granted to Wm Smith, John Watts, Robert R. Livingston, Whitehead Hicks, Wm Livingston, Goldsbrow Banyar, Samuel Jones, Peter van Brugh Livingston, Peter Keteltas, Walter Rutherford, David Clarkson and Samuel Bard.   32

Oct. 12   Draft of charter for the Society library read and approved.   34

21   Committee to hear parties on the petition of Abr'm J. Lansing (29:484).   34

Nov. 11   Opinion and advice of council on the preceding petition [Lansingburgh]. Warrant of survey for the township of Thetford granted (see *L. P.* 32:105). Petitions granted: of Stephen Greenleaf, Benj. Butterfield, John Grout and Samuel Knight (see *L. P.* 32:10); of David van Rensselaer, Jacob J. Lansingh and Samuel Stringer (see *L. P.* 31:51); of Wm Graham, John Graham, Benj. Egbertse, Jacob G. Lansingh, George Tuttle, Abr'm ten Eyck, Walter V.

Wemple and Stephen McCrea (see *L. P.* 31:50); of Thos.
Swords, Christ'r Francis, Robert Hatton, John Vernon,
Robert Ross, Fred'k Wm Hecht, John Donoldson, Thos.
Hunt, Wm McDougal, John Stanhouse and John Riviere
(see *L. P.* 31:83); of John Bell et al (see *L. P.* 31:85); of
Stephen Moore and 30 others (see *L. P.* 31:25); of Wm
Wentworth and 35 others (see *L. P.* 31:125); of Thos.
Scott, John Bracken, Wm Lucky, James Seymour and
Thos. Adems (see *L. P.* 31:78); of Sir Wm Johnson, James
Bennet, Samuel Sutton, Nathaniel Hyllyard, Moses Ibbit,
Joseph Erwin, Edward Donnellan, James Darby, James
Cotter, Wm Fraser jr, John Friel and John Looney (see
L. P. 31:77); of Samuel Holland, John Holland, Henry Hol-
land et al of the township of Goodwood (see *L. P.* 31:47);
of Mary Fisher widow of Sergeant Wm Fisher 17th regi-
ment (see *L. P.* 31:4). Orders on petitions: of Andrew
Elliot et al (see *L. P.* 31:80); of Donald Campbell et al
(see *L. P.* 31:92). License to purchase Indian lands
granted to James de Lancey jr et al (see *L. P.* 32:30, 128).
Lands granted: to Corporals Robert Russel 55th, and John
Holmes 1st regiment (see *L. P.* 31:88); to Sergeant John
McKenzie 55th regiment (see *L. P.* 32:7); to Bombardier
Joseph Sexton, Sergeants Archibald Weir, Thomas Bow-
den Royal artillery, Samuel Stevenson 56th, Cooper Un-
derwey 60th, Wm Baven 46th, Gawen Lowries 1st, Peter
Forster 9th, John McGarrah, Wm McGee, John McGarry
28th, Henry Grant 44th, John Deane 49th, Henry Lawson
61st, Corporals Daniel Tomlinson 9th, John Hunter 45th,
Robert Anderson 1st, Drummers John Dunn 38th, John
Philipps 76th, Privates Manasses Bradley, Godlyr Beart-
man 60th, Richard Dorrington 40th, Elijah Wedy of Major
Gorham's rangers, Thos. Harman 1st, Richard Kitchen,
George Showler 45th, Jacob Monroe 46th regiment (see
L. P. 32:64); to Lieut. Donald Campbell (see *L. P.* 32:93);
to Lloyd Danbarry and his wife Mary for William Coventry Calder infant son of Mary by her first husband, Capt.
James Calder Independents (see *L. P.* 32:98). Orders on
petitions: of John David of Albany, vintner (see *L. P.*
32:9); of Cornelius Burhans, Johannes Planck, Leonard
Planck, Petrus Planck and Johannes Row (see *L. P.*
32:61); of Henry Fonda (see *L. P.* 32:59); of Frederick
Johannes Cluet (see *L. P.* 32:33).   34

25   Petitions granted: of Catharine Lodge, Catharine Morris,
Augustus van Cortlandt, Robert Crommerline, Rich'd
Francis and Samuel Bayard jr for 3000 acres on Little

1772.   **v. 31**

Schohary kill; of John Glen, Henry Glen, Simon Schermerhorn, Adam M. Veeder, John Butler, Christ'r Yates,
Gerrit S. Veeder, Yellis Yates and Abr'm Wimple (see
L. P. 32:65); of Edward and Ebenezer Jessup cum al of the
township of Hyde (see *L. P.* 32:108); of Corporal John
Miller 28th, and Private Stephen Blundell 44th regiment
(see *L. P.* 32:112).   42

Dec. 23   Order on the petitions of John van Rensselaer (see *L. P.*
32:138) and Peter van Schaack (see *L. P.* 32:136). Petitions granted: of Wm Anstruther, Archibald Campbell,
Finley Miller et al (see *L. P.* 32:121); of Waldron Blaau
et al (see *L. P.* 32:119); of Luke Knoulton and John Taylor
et al (see *L. P.* 32:120); of John Bergen et al (see *L. P.*
32:130); of Jeremiah van Rensselaer, James Abeel et al
(see *L. P.* 32:137); of Leonard McGlashan (see *L. P.*
32:135); of Lieut. Edward Newland and Nicholas Ward
80th regiment (see *L. P.* 32:89). Order on the petitions of
Jellis Fonda and others (see *L. P.* 32:131) and of James
Creassij et al (see *L. P.* 32:139); the former granted, the
latter dismissed.

Minutes sent to the board of trade.   44
1773

Jan. 4   Order on a royal mandamus, granting lands to William,
bishop of Chester, George Markham and Major Enoch
Markham (see *L. P.* 32:5).   52

15   Proceedings relative to the intended grant and confirmation
to John van Rensselaer (p. 44; see *L. P.* 32:2, 157); including orders on petitions of John Borghert et al (see *L. P.*
32:4) and of Capt. Lieut. Alex'r McDonald (see *L. P.*
32:154).   54

Feb. 2   Petition of Capt. Lieut. Alex'r McDonald (see *L. P.* 33:10)
referred.   58

5   John van Rensselaer surrenders certain lots of the Claverack
lands claimed by him, and the surrender is accepted.   58

17   Order on petition of James Savage in behalf of the people
of New Concord, Spencertown and New Britton (see *L. P.*
33:34). Opinion of council on the letter and caveat of
Capt. Lieut. Alex'r McDonald, the report of the attorney
general and the draft of a confirmatory patent to John van
Rensselaer (see *L. P.* 33:18-19, 21, 29, 32). Charter of incorporation for the episcopal church at Poughkeepsie
passed.   59

Mar. 1   Petitions of Peter Garnsey (see *L. P.* 33:38) and John Garnsey (see *L. P.* 33:39) referred to the ministers in England.   68

3   Petition of inhabitants of New Britain, Kings district, Albany
county (see *L. P.* 33:36) referred to the ministers in Eng-
land.   68

5   Answer of Justice David Jones to the attorney general's
      reasons for not proceeding to the reversal of the judgment
      obtained by John van Rensselaer (p. 59). Minutes sent
      home.   69

Ap. 21 Petitions of Capt. Solomon Uhhaunnaunaunmut (see *L. P.*
      33:49-50) rejected, Indians not being entitled to grants of
      land under the proclamation of 1763. Order on petition of
      the inhabitants of Spencertown (see *L. P.* 33:51).   71

May 7 Petition of Samuel Deal for ferry rights over Lake George
      and the carrying place to Lake Champlain granted. Peti-
      tion of Johannes Montanye, John Montanye, Joseph Mon-
      tanye and Everardus Brouwer, in behalf of the legatees of
      Rachel Smith (see *L. P.* 29:115) referred.   73

June 9 Royal order prohibiting all grants of land until further
      orders.   74

26   Unlocated land granted to Capt. Benoni Banks as a reduced
      officer. Minutes sent home.   75

Aug. 26 Order upon royal mandamus for granting land to Major
      Wm Markham 47th regiment (see *L. P.* 29:29). Order on
      petition of Mary Lavoyne widow of Lieut. Louis Demetral
      60th regiment (see *L. P.* 33:60). Lands granted to Lieut.
      Archibald Campbell 42d regiment (see *L. P.* 33:59); to
      Daniel Coxe of New Jersey in Charlotte county.   76

31   Petition of Major Gen. John Bradstreet (see *L. P.* 33:62)
      granted.   77

Sep. 20 Order on the petitions for land by Capt. Daniel McAlpine
      60th regiment (see *L. P.* 33:63), and Capt. Samuel Pintard
      50th regiment.   78

Oct. 5 Petition of Sergeant John Donnaldson 55th regiment (see
      33:69) granted.   78

Nov. 1 Petitions of Capt. Daniel McAlpine (see *L. P.* 33:70) and
      Lieut. John Thompson 95th regiment (see *L. P.* 33:70)
      granted.   79

17   Lands in Charlotte county on the southwest side of Lake
      George granted to Sergeant Hector McKenzie 60th, Cor-
      poral Morris Dodd 35th, Corporal John Armstrong 80th,
      Private Richard Kelly 60th regiment; an island in Lake
      George to Private John Cameron 60th regiment. Order
      on petition of John Baptist van Eps (see *L. P.* 33:73).   80

Dec. 1 Royal orders confirming two New York acts of 1771 and
      1772. Royal orders repealing two acts of 1772; to be pub-
      lished by proclamation. Lands granted near New Perth
      to Gregor Drummond et al (p. 28); to Daniel Jaquire
      clerk of stores, Royal artillery (see *L. P.* 33:79).   83

1773   **v. 31**

15   Petition of Lt. Col. Thos. Ord Royal artillery (see *L. P.*
33:81) granted. Order on petition of Charles Mair and
Wm Anderson (see *L. P.* 33:74). Land granted to Private
Dougal McVicar 55th regiment (see *L. P.* 33:87). Minutes
sent home.   84

1774

Jan. 26   Order on petition of the corporation of the Dutch church at
Schenectady for an enlargement of their powers. List of
persons to whom royal mandamus for land grants had been
issued: Lord Stephen Ilchester, 20,000 acres (see *L. P.*
18:1); Lieut. Donald Campbell, George Campbell, James
Campbell, Rose Graham, Margaret Eustace and Lilly Murray, 30,000; Lt. Col. Charles Lee, 20,000 (see *L. P.* 18:106);
Capt. Walter Patterson, 20,000 (see *L. P.* 18:105); Sir Wm
Mayne, 5000; Robert Mayne, 5000; Edw'd Mayne, 5000
(see *L. P.* 19:144-45); Capt. John Small, 5000 (see *L. P.*
19:143); Capt. Joseph Williams (see *L. P.* 19:146); John
de Berniere, Thos. Swords, John Anthony Kernes and
Charles de Berniere, 10,000 (see *L. P.* 19:141); Robert
Leake, 5000 (see *L. P.* 20:139); Fred'k Wm Hecht, 3000 (see
L. P. 20:140); Robert Ross, 3000 (see *L. P.* 20:141); Wm
Butler, 3000 (see *L. P.* 20:136); Draper Simon Wood, 3000
(see *L. P.* 20:131); Allan [Neil] McLean, 3000 (see *L. P.*
20:130); John Read, 3000 (see *L. P.* 20:127); Dugald
Campbell, 3000 (see *L. P.* 20:130); John Trotter, 3000 (see
L. P. 20:133); Edward Smyth, 3000 (see *L. P.* 20:135);
James McMillan, 3000 (see *L. P.* 20:132); Joshua Moore,
3000 (see *L. P.* 20:137); Robert Moore, 3000 (see *L. P.*
20:138); Capt. David Price, 5000. Petitions granted: of
Fred'k Wm Hecht for the residue of 2620 acres due him
agreeably to royal mandamus; of Daniel Jaquiere (see
L. P. 33:102).   85

Mar. 2   Petition of Private Cornelius Malone 60th regiment (see *L. P.*
33:112). Order on petition of Thos. Stone non-commissioned officer 48th regiment (see *L. P.* 33:108). Charter of
incorporation granted to the episcopal church at Schenectady, Rev. John Doty rector, John Brown, Robert Clench
wardens, John Croushorn, Michael Grass, Charles Miller,
John Wood, Joseph Kingsley and Thos. Jay vestrymen
(see *N. Y. col. mss,* 100:73). Order on petition of the inhabitants of Spencertown and Nobletown (see *L. P.*
33:109).   88

9   Lands granted: to reduced officers Wm Barron, David Stone,
Noah Porter and Joshua Lock (see *L. P.* 33:111); to Susannah Reilly widow of Commissary John Watts (see *L. P.*

33:110). Order on petition of Richard Harrison in behalf
of Andrew Faneuil Philipps of Boston (see *L. P.* 33:116).
Lands granted: to Corporal Gregor Drummond 55th regiment (see *L. P.* 33:115); to Privates Peter Quin and Richard Mease 60th regiment, not located.   90

16 Cadwallader Colden lieutenant governor. Order concerning
two royal mandamus granting to Thos. Graeve and to
James Porteous each 3000 acres. Lands granted: to Capt.
Mark Prevost (see *L. P.* 33:107); to Mary widow of Lieut.
———— Airey, Independents (see *L. P.* 33:121); to Private
Hercules Brown 47th regiment (see *L. P.* 33:117); to Cor-
porals Abr'm Frazier 42d, and Wm Campbell 55th regi-
ment.   92

23 Petition of Lt. Col. Samuel Cleaveland, Royal artillery (see
L. P. 33:130) granted. Order concerning two houses in
New York city, one in Wall street, the other in Cortlandt
street, escheated to the crown and petitioned for by John
Montanye et al legatees of Rachel Smith, and by widow
Elizabeth Brown.   94

31 Petitions granted: of Quartermaster Duncan Campbell 42d
regiment (see *L. P.* 33:9, 106); of Sergeants Samuel Willis
15th regiment and Wm King Lovell, Royal artillery (see
L. P. 34:86). Tract no. 3, Totten and Crossfield purchase,
to be erected into a township. Lands granted to the
bishop of Chester, Enoch, George and Wm Markham to
be erected into the township of Markham. Order on petition of Dirck Lefferts, Isaac Low, Henry Remsen, Thos.
Palmer, John Bergen and Robert W. Leake for patents
to lands purchased from the Indians in 1772 (p. 30).   96

Ap. 16 Hearing appointed on petition of Edward Hallock et al
against granting a patent to Charles Mair and Wm Anderson (p. 84). Petition of Hugh Morrison 42d regiment
(see *L. P.* 33:124) granted.   97

22 Petition of Hugh McNabb 80th regiment (see *L. P.* 33:145)
referred to the surveyor general. Petition of Gasper Un-
derweg 60th regiment for land not located granted.   98

May 2 James Jackson ex dem trustees of Kingston vs Wm Dederick in error.   98

5 Hearing in re Edward Hallock vs Charles Mair and Wm
Anderson (p. 97); petition of Mair and Anderson dis-
missed. Petitions granted: of Corporal Patrick McGregor
78th regiment (see *L. P.* 34:2, 6); of Privates Manasses
Bradley 60th, Richard Dorrington 40th regiment, Elijah
Weedy of Gorham's rangers (see *L. P.* 34:5); of Lieut.
Alex'r Grant (see *L. P.* 34:3). James Jackson ex dem trus-
tees of Kingston vs Wm Dederick in error.   99

16   Petitions granted: of Sergeant John Jones 44th regiment
Ferry in   (see *L. P.* 34:7); of Lt. Col. Samuel Cleaveland (see *L. P.*
Kings co.   34:8). James Jackson ex dem, Thos. Williams et al vs
John van Rensselaer in error; royal order in the suit.
Further time allowed for selling the estate of Patrick Smith
for the benefit of Rachel Smith's legatees (p. 94). Peti-
tions granted: of Sergeant Peter Deacon 46th, Corporals
John Breese, Samuel Whitehouse, John Robinson 80th,
John Smith 17th, James Conner 44th, Privates Joseph Hal-
brook, John Neal, Wm Adley, John Walter, George Smith,
Walter Midden 46th, Donald McDonald 42d, Michael
Ralph 55th, John Dunn, Wm Weston, Benj. Grosmer, John
Blare 16th regiment (see *L. P.* 33:126); of Charles Tate and
George Smart, non-commissioned officers, Royal artillery
(see *L. P.* 33:62; 34:52); of Capt. James Neil, rangers (see
L. P. 33:146); of Humphrey and Samuel Avery (see *L. P.*
34:21); of Samuel Ashley et al for a confirmatory patent
of lands granted by New Hampshire; of Luke Knoulton,
John Taylor et al (see *L. P.* 34:15); of Josiah Willard et al
(see *L. P.* 33:151).   100

June 14   Petitions granted: of Lieut. Wm Brown (see *L. P.* 34:22);
of Elias Bland and other proprietors of Hillsborough (see
L. P. 34:17); of Humphrey and Samuel Avery et al (see
L. P. 34:21); of Nathan Stone et al (see *L. P.* 34:24).   105

29   Water lot at Claverack granted to Peter van Ness, and Law-
rence Fonda (see *L. P.* 34:26). Petitions granted: of Josiah
Willard et al (see *L. P.* 34:32); of Samuel Ashley et al
(see *L. P.* 34:31); of Luke Knoulton et al, names of Daniel
Whipple, David Joy, Joseph Charters, Jonathan Hunt,
Simeon Alcott, Elijah Williams, and Wm Wentworth to
be substituted for John Grout, Josiah Armes, Malachi
Church, John Sergent, John Wilson, Elisha Harding and
Wm Ellice (see *L. P.* 34:33); of Phineas Lyman, John
Hinsdale, Samuel Field et al (see *L. P.* 34:37); of John Felt-
hausen et al (see *L. P.* 34:28); of John Woods, Charles
Nicoll et al (see *L. P.* 34:34).   107

Aug. 2   Royal order confirming New York act for the partition of
Goshentown rights in the Wawayanda patent; to be published by proclamation (see *N. Y. col. mss,* 100:133). Petitions granted: Jacob Walton et al of the township of
Colden (see *L. P.* 34:72); of Edward Foy and 29 others (see
L. P. 34:80); of Edward Thatcher and 11 others (see *L. P.*
34:71); of James Jauncey et al of the township of Jauncey-
burgh (see *L. P.* 34:27); of James Stevenson (see *L. P.*
34:77); of Ass't Surgeon Robert Kennedy (see *L. P.* 34:76);

1774   **v. 31**

of Elizabeth widow of Lieut. James Henderson (see *L. P.*
33:143; 34:35). Order on petitions of Benj. Evans and his
wife Joan, sister of Lewis P. Williams deceased (see *L. P.*
34:56), and of Johannes Friend et al (see *L. P.* 34:81).   111

Sep. 1   Draft of letters patent to Stephen de Lancey jr in trust for
New York   the devisees of Rachel Smith (p. 100) read and approved.
Corporal Joseph Robinson 55th and Private John Michael
60th regiment, allowed to locate lands due to them under
the proclamation of 1763 (see *L. P.* 34:[100], 103). Petitions of John Blagge, Edmund Fanning et al (see *L. P.*
34:100), and of Rev. John Ogilvie and other devisees of
Lancaster Symes (see *L. P.* 34:102) granted. Order on
petition of Stephen Hogeboom, Wm H. Ludlow, Robert
van Rensselaer et al (see *L. P.* 34:[100]).   115

2   Hearing appointed on the petitions of Benj. Evans and of
Johs. Friend (p. 111). Land granted to Lieut. John Montresor 48th regiment (see *L. P.* 34:105). Private Adam
Vandil 60th regiment allowed to locate land under the
proclamation of 1763. Petitions granted: of Daniel Whipple et al of the township of Whippleborough (see *L. P.*
34:61); of Oliver de Lancey and John Morin Scott (see
L. P. 34:107); of John Bard, Henry Wisner and John Morin
Scott (see *L. P.* 34:104). Order on petition of Wm Bayard,
Cornelius van Schaack, John Schuyler et al (see *L. P.*
34:82).   117

29   Royal order vetoing a New York act of 1773; to be published by proclamation (see *N. Y. col. mss,* 101:13). Widow
of Capt. John Rudolph Fesch 60th regiment allowed to
locate lands under royal proclamation of 1763 (see *L. P.*
34:112). Mayor etc of New York vs executors of Hendrick Remsen deceased, in error. Hearing appointed on
petition of Peter van Ness and Lawrence Fonda (see *L. P.*
34:116). Order on petitions: of Hezekiah Baldwin, Martin
Beebe, David Pratt and other inhabitants of New Canaan,
New Concord, Spencertown, New Britain etc (see *L. P.*
32:94, 116); of Henry Remsen, Peter Vosburgh, Robert
van Deusen and Johannes van der Poel (see *L. P.* 34:110);
and of a caveat entered by Alex'r McDonald and other
officers (see *L. P.* 34:109).   120

Oct. 6   Petition of Wm Smith et al (see *L. P.* 23:379; 34:113, 117)
granted. Sergeant Nicolas Harrison and Private John
Garrison 47th regiment allowed to locate lands under the
proclamation of 1763. Hearing between the proprietors of
Wawieghnunk patent and the proprietors of Westenhook
patent; the petition of the former, Wm Bayard et al
(p. 117) rejected.   124

Nov. 8   Draft of letters patent to Harry Gordon brother and heir to Peter Gordon (see *L. P.* 33:132; 34:30, 63) read and approved. Hearing on the petitions of Peter van Ness and Lawrence Fonda (p. 107, 120) and of Stephen Hogeboom et al (p. 115); the former rejected. Hearing appointed on petition of the proprietors of Westenhook patent and the caveats against it (see *L. P.* 34:75, 110, 121). Petitions granted: of John van Alen (see *L. P.* 34:130); of Samuel Holland et al asking that the names of James Abeel, John Abeel, Robert Snell, Jacob Albright, James Cobham and Alex'r Bradburn be substituted in the patent for John and Henry Holland, Matthew Hallenbeck, John Rogers, Wm Hume and John Elliot jr, dead or removed out of the province (see *L. P.* 34:66).   125

12   Petitions granted: of Thos. Clark et al (see *L. P.* 34:119, 134); of Walter Rutherford and Henry Balfour (see *L. P.* 34:122); of Surgeon's Mate John Cochran (see *L. P.* 34:120, 131). Orders on the petitions: of Jacobus Perse (see *N. Y. col. mss,* 101:28); of John Peters et al (see *L. P.* 34:138); of James Downs, Christ'r Duyckinck and Wm Kennedy (see *L. P.* 34:111). Petitions granted: of John Blagge, Edmund Fanning et al (see *L. P.* 34:137); of Samuel Jones and 19 others of the township of Jonestown (see *L. P.* 34:125); of Richard Slack et al (see *L. P.* 34:126); of John Earle and 27 others (see *L. P.* 34:127); of Robert Bowne et al (see *L. P.* 34:99); of Abel Walker et al (see *L. P.* 34:74); of John Zabriski jr et al (see *L. P.* 34:98).   127

Dec. 7   Hearing on the petition of Westenhook patentees (p. 125) postponed. Hearing on the petition of John Peters et al (p. 127); granted.   134

20   Hearing on the petition of the Westenhook patentees (p. 134); continued.   134

1775

Jan. 5   Hearing on the petition of Westenhook patentees (p. 134) postponed on a petition of inhabitants of Kings district (see *L. P.* 35:10).   136

15   Petitions of Josiah Willard, John Stout et al (see *L. P.* 35:16), and of Lawrence Kortright, John Harpur et al (see *L. P.* 34:40) granted. Names of Stephen Lush, Richard Varick, John L. C. Roome, John Lawrence, David Wells and Wm Todd to be inserted in the patent to Edward Wm Kiers in place of his former associates (29:437; see *L. P.* 34:148). 136

25   Hearing on the petition of Westenhook patentees (p. 136); continued.   137

Feb. 8   Petition of Edmund Fanning and Moses Mardin (see *L. P.* 35:17) to have the names of Samuel Avery, John Peters,

1775   **v. 31**

James Cobham, Wm Kennedy and Samuel Boyer inserted into their patent in place of Benj. J. Johnston, John Hodges, Joshua Littlewood, Malcom McIsaac and John Grumley granted.   138

22   Hearing on the petition of Westenhook patentees (p. 137); continued.   138

Mar. 9   Order on caveat entered by inhabitants of Canistegione against granting the petition of Jacobus Perse (p. 127).   139

Ap. 7   Petitions granted: of Samuel Avery and the associates of Daniel Whipple deceased (see *L. P.* 35:58); of Henry Cuyler, Robert Adems et al of the township of Edinburgh (see *L. P.* 35:49). Order on petition of Corn's Tymonse and 89 others (see *L. P.* 35:59).   140

11   Hearing on the caveats against the petition of Jacobus Perse postponed. Minutes sent to the board of trade.   141

13   Petition of John Wetherhead and Rachel, his wife (see *L. P.* 34:153) granted.   142

June 3   Petitions granted: of John and Garret Rapalje, to have the names of Wm Thom, Walter Thomas, Joseph Smith, Rem Remsen, Jacob Remsen jr, John Remsen jr, John Lewis and John Hansen inserted into their patent vice Aaron Simonson jr, Francis Koffler, Edward Joice, Alex'r McAlester, John Wilson, Richard McGuire, Andrew Myer and Patrick Smith, deceased or removed out of the province (see *L. P.* 35:70); of John Church et al of the township of Ryegate (see *L. P.* 35:68). Minutes sent to the board of trade.   142

July 11   Gov. Wm Tryon returned. Petition of James Stevenson (see *L. P.* 35:78) granted.   144

31   Col. John Leland late major in Col. Grey's corps, Lieut. John Bruyers 56th, and Private George Murray 42d regiment allowed to locate lands under the proclamation of 1763. Petition of Edmund Fanning et al of the township of Stratton (see *L. P.* 35:79) granted. Capt. David Pryce allowed to locate lands as above.   145

Sep. 4   Petitions granted: of Christ'r Duykinck, James Downs, Wm Butler and Wm Kennedy (see *L. P.* 35:84); of Gertrude Pinhorn, widow of Lieut. John Pinhorn 45th regiment (see *L. P.* 35:87); of Sergeant John Pounset and Corporal Gilbert Wier 55th regiment (see *L. P.* 35:76). Order on letter from Agatha Butlar and Martha Bradstreet daughters of Gen. Bradstreet deceased (see *L. P.* 35:65).   146

29   Petitions granted: of Corporal Gilbert Wier (see *L. P.* 35:90); of Francis Panton (see *L. P.* 35:92); of Amos Babcock et al of the township of Andover (see *L. P.* 35:88). Minutes sent to the board of trade.   148

1775   v. 31

Nov. 13   Petitions granted: of Fred'k Rhinelander et al of the town-
           ship of Rhineland called Underhill (see *L. P.* 35:107); of
           Henry Franklin et al of the township of Milton (see *L. P.*
           35:106); of Wm Rhinelander jr et al of the township of
           Westford (see *L. P.* 34:140; 35:112).   149
    Minutes, lacking in both vol. 26 and 31, to be found among rough drafts
accompanying vol. 31.

1774
Dec. 4   Petitions granted: of Samuel Holland and others for town-
Ship   ship of Topsham, Gloucester county, according to orders
Dutchess of   of June 15, 1772, reserving share of Benning Wentworth
Gordon,   to the crown; of Luke Knoulton, John Taylor and others
N. Y. harbor   for two strips of land surveyed for, but not included in the
               New Hampshire grant of the township of New Fane.
1775
Jan. 23   Petitions granted: of Chas. W. Apthorp and others for the
           township of Lunenberg, Gloucester county, according to
           orders of June 15, 1772, reserving to the crown the share
           of B. Wentworth; of Wm Baylis late staff officer for 2000
           acres owned by Edward and Ebenezer Jessup north of the
           township of Hyde.

Dec. 26   Petitions granted: of Alex'r Grant for 5000 acres south of
           Crownpoint and north west of Ticonderoga near a grant
           to Capt. James Stevenson; of Frederick Rhinelander, James
           Downes, Wm Butler, Wm Kennedy that the name of
           Rhinelander be inserted vice that of Christopher Duyc-
           kinck in letters patent granted to said Downes and others
           as associates of James Leadbetter.
1776
Jan. 29   Petitions granted: of Edmund Fanning and others for the
           township of Tunbridge, Gloucester county, according to
           orders of June 15, 1772, reserving the share of B. Went-
           worth to the crown; of Chas. Moore a late officer for 2000
           acres in Charlotte county, adjoining 7550 acres granted
           Ebenezer Jessup; of Mark Noble, Thomas Reade, Henry
           and Wm Philips for 2000 acres each in one parcel in Al-
           bany county between Massachusetts and Stephentown.

Feb. 14   Petitions granted: of Samuel Wells and John Kelly agents
           of the proprietors of Guilford for confirmatory patent, re-
           serving the allotment of B. Wentworth to the crown; of
           Robert Rodgers and others for land on Lake Momphra
           Magog to be erected into the township of Rogersborough,
           in compensation for the township of Dunbar granted to
           Rodgers in 176[2] by New Hampshire but already oc-
           cupied; of Lt. Col. Thomas Howard, Chas. Howard and
           others for letters patent to lands west of Crownpoint peti-
           tioned for in 1772.

CORRECTIONS

Errors have not been noted where the correct form of word or right meaning of phrase is obvious.

p. 12, Jan. 11, l. 5, add page reference 42 at end
p. 12, Feb. 24, l. 7, for Vigue read Vigne
p. 33, Oct. 4, l. 1, for schems read sachems
p. 34, Dec. 15, l. 4, for Madmans read Madnans
p. 36, Mar. 20, l. 1, for Harmaus read Harmans
p. 42, Ap. 3, l. 4, for Murtens read Martens
p. 51, Nov. 18, for l. 7 substitute: hampton to be arrested for publishing a seditious libel (see
p. 67, Aug. 3, for l. 2 substitute: from the sloop Planter, Cornelius Jacobs master
p. 76, Sep. 15, l. 1, for Heath read Heathcote
p. 76, Sep. 15, l. 11, for Demgre read Demyre
p. 78, Nov. 24, l. 3, for Missepatt read Nissepatt
p. 92, Oct. 23, l. 1, for Brashen read Brasher
p. 95, Feb. 3, l. 2, for county read country
p. 96, Mar. 28, l. 1, for Abany read Albany
p. 97, May 14, l. 3, for Caus read Claus
p. 97, May 16, l. 7, for Crexier read Crevier
p. 97, July 2, for l. 2 substitute: Treat that it is rumored Gov. Fletcher intends to make
p. 100, Sep. 9, l. 3, for Cadaraequi read Cadaracqui
p. 109, Sep. 5, l. 4, for whals read wheels
p. 110, Nov. 14, l. 2, for Madera read Madeira
p. 120, May 6, l. 3, for Matinconk read Matiniconk
p. 124, June 5, l. 2, for Swieter read Swieten
p. 132, July 4, l. 5, for Codeberand; read Codeber and [no semicolon]
p. 142, Aug. 18, l. 5, for 42: read 43:
p. 142, Aug. 23, l. 2, for 44: read 43:
p. 147, July 31, l. 3, for Waudell read Wandell
p. 149, Oct. 8, l. 2, for Manritz read Mauritz
p. 151, Nov. 27, l. 14, for 186 read 184
p. 163, Feb. 9, l. 7, for Scriben read Scrifen
p. 164, Mar. 12, l. 9, insert 3: before 39-41
p. 170, June 10, l. 3, for 33: read 3:
p. 176, Nov. 24, l. 7, for Slaten read Slater
p. 177, Dec. 1, l. 5, for Handon read Hawdon
p. 182, Ap. 13, l. 1, for Carten read Carter
p. 198, June 15, l. 2, for Peviett read Peirett
p. 199, Aug. 24, l. 7, read: revenue.   Petition by
p. 202, Nov. 6, l. 3, for Carten read Carter
p. 209, Ap. 11, l. 2, for Foy read Toy
p. 209, Ap. 25, l. 4, for kayaderosseras read Kayaderosseras
p. 211, July 18, l. 3, for 5: read 51:
p. 223, Nov. 16, l. 4, for 4: read 53:
p. 234, Feb. 27, l. 3, for Crombine read Cromline

p. 234, Mar. 4, l. 1, for Maneuil read Mareuil
p. 238, June 8, l. 6, for conselos read Conselos
p. 247, June 5, l. 3, for 55: read 5:
p. 253, Oct. 1, l. 1, for Fatham read Tatham
p. 259, July 15, insert after l. 2: of C. Van Brunt (see *L. P.* 6:128) referred.   327
p. 262, Nov. 1, l. 5, insert Hanson after Hendrick
p. 269, Ap. 9, l. 7, insert 7: before 24-26
p. 270, June 20, l. 2, for 6: read 61:
p. 272^1-73^2, for Melchoir read Melchior
p. 281, July 8, l. 2, for 52: read 54:
p. 281, Aug. 24, l. 4, insert 8: before 61-62
p. 282, Oct. 3, l. 4, for 184 read 181
p. 289, Jan. 17, for l. 2 substitute: 9:22) referred and warrant of survey granted.   81
p. 295, Aug. 6, l. 12, for Bobn read Bobin
p. 295, for Aug. 3 read Sep. 3
p. 296, l. 5, for renominates read nominates
p. 297, Jan. 28, l. 5, for 66: read 67:
p. 300, Nov. 8, l. 1, insert 1: before 522
p. 300, Nov. 9-10, l. 1, insert 1: before 523
p. 305, Dec. 19, l. 4, for 168: read 68:
p. 305, Dec. 19, l. 5, for 16: read 10:
p. 305, Mar. 2, l. 2, for Lowet read Low
p. 308, June 13, l. 3, for 110 read 113
p. 313, July 27, l. 1 and Aug. 21, l. 6, for Soumans read Sonmans
p. 313, for Aug. 21 read Aug. 2
p. 314, Sep. 22, l. 3, for Set read Sex
p. 319, Sep. 29, l. 2, for Horsmander read Horsmanden
p. 319, Sep. 29, transpose l. 7 and 8
p. 322, Aug. 23, l. 2, for Horsmander read Horsmanden
p. 325, Mar. 10, l. 5, insert comma after seal
p. 325, Mar. 25, l. 3, for 37 read 7
p. 327, Aug. 5, l. 2, for of read to
p. 331, May 8, l. 5, for Pemiston read Penniston
p. 343, Dec. 22, l. 1, for Banyan read Banyar
p. 344, Mar. 27, l. 3, for Savan read Swan
p. 344, June 14, l. 7, for Low read Law
p. 352, Ap. 20, l. 6, cancel comma after arming
p. 360, for second Oct. 20 read Oct. 22
p. 367, Sep. 29, l. 1, for Henry read Edward
p. 374, Oct. 26, l. 9, for 6: read 76:
p. 376, Sep. 15, l. 5, for Becken read Becker
p. 383, May 4, l. 7, insert 3: before 438-41
p. 392, Mar. 23-Ap. 9, for *L. P.* 15: read *N. Y. col. mss,* 78:
p. 399, Ap. 25, l. 5, insert comma after Devalt
p. 401, Feb. 19, l. 3-Aug. 28, for *L. P.* 16: read *L. P.* 15:
p. 407, Nov. 23, l. 3, cancel comma after Praa
p. 408, Jan. 5, l. 1, for Mason read Wason
p. 424, Dec. 6, l. 6, for Spitzen read Spitzer

p. 428, May 22, l. 1, for exmained read examined
p. 430, l. 2, for 81: read 83:
p. 430, Aug. 25, l. 9, for Dusaw read Dusau
p. 430, Aug. 25, for l. 15 substitute: Philippsburgh manor; Charles and Michael Gooda, Jean
p. 440, June 17, l. 2, for 85: read 86:
p. 453, July 8, l. 2, for Moriss read Morin
p. 465, Aug. 7, l. 7, for Reune read Renne
p. 481, Ap. 18, l. 1, for Emburg read Embury
p. 485, June 14, l. 2, for Abd'm read Abr'm
p. 498, Oct. 15, l. 1, for Sachlan read Lachlan
p. 500, Mar. 9, l. 6, read: complained of by a petition
p. 502, Sep. 1, l. 1, for 100: read 101:
p. 512, l. 3, for Domo read Douw
p. 515, Oct. 29, l. 2, for Hamstead read Flamstead
p. 520, Nov. 3, l. 3, for Pryn read Prym
p. 524, Dec. 20, l. 10, for Dodgejim read Dodge jr
p. 538, Dec. 5, l. 6, cancel comma after Johannes
p. 539, Mar. 8, l. 1, for Evert read Everet,
p. 541, Ap. 19, l. 16, for Tayor read Taylor
p. 550, Sep. 3, after l. 7 insert: Matthew Gleeves (see *L. P.* 27:78); of Captains Daniel
p. 555, June 7, l. 23, for 99 read 29
p. 562, l. 10-11, for Gercord read Gerard
p. 562, l. 19, for Manbout read Manbrut
p. 569, Dec. 23, l. 12, for Creassij read Creassy

INDEX

It has been impossible in many cases to identify persons because of inconsistencies in spelling, irregularity in use of 'van,' 'sr' and 'jr' and omission of other designations. If there are few references to the same form of name they are grouped together, though referring to more than one person, unless the text furnishes some means of distinction. The same method is followed for names under which there is a large number of entries when many can not be certainly identified. In cases of different spellings of what might be the same name, if the identity seemed certain, entries have been made under one form with references from other forms; if uncertain, entries are made under the different forms, with cross references. As it is quite unlikely that all such cases have been recognized, it will be well to have at hand all possible variants of a name one wishes to find. Where surname alone or with a distinguishing title is given the person may be identical with one entered later under full name.

The superior figures tell the exact place on the page in ninths; e. g. 558^3 means page 558 beginning in the third ninth of the page, i. e. about one third of the way down.

Abbot, Benjamin, 404^8, 405^4, 517^8.
Abeel, Mr, 418^3.
Abeel, Mrs, 241^6.
Abeel, Christopher, 275^7.
Abeel, David, 301^2, 301^7.
Abeel, David, jr, 552^4, 558^3, 558^7.
Abeel, Garret, 400^9, 561^2, 563^8.
Abeel, Jacobus, 552^5, 558^7.
Abeel, James, land grants, 527^7, 546^1, 550^4, 552^5, 552^9, 559^2, 559^6, 562^5, 562^5, 563^3, 563^8, 569^4, 575^3; releases share in patent, 558^7.
Abeel, John, commissioner, 76^6, 236^6; warrants, 96^2, 100^4, 103^8, 106^1, 106^8, 107^7, 110^2, 170^3, 175^7, 176^8, 181^4, 183^1, 184^5, 190^5, 193^2, 193^7, 194^9, 197^4, 198^9, 198^5, 201^5, 202^3, 204^9, 205^2, 210^3, 214^1, 217^6, 221^9; accounts, 105^8, 200^9, 204^4, 221^8, 223^4; member of court of oyer and terminer, 172^9; petitions, 182^8, 190^4, 197^3, 197^8, 210^2, 210^8, 211^3, 213^9, 217^3, 225^5, 237^6; land grants, 210^5, 211^8, 221^4; quitrent, 210^6, 211^5; licenses to buy land, 214^3, 214^4; time for settling land extended, 219^7. See also Albany, mayors.
Abeel. John (2d), before council, 361^4, tried for selling rum to Indians, 418^9; examined, 427^9; warrant, 442^6; land grants, 527^7, 552^9, 559^6, 562^3, 563^4, 563^8, 575^3.
Abercrombie, James, 429^9, 438^8, 441^1; letters from, 429^2, 439^8, 440^2; commander in chief, 438^8; requests, 438^9, 439^2, 442^9; arms purchased by, 439^6; retreats, 441^4.
Aberdeen, James, 450^8.
Abigail (brigantine), 354^7.
Able, John, 514^2.

Able, William, 411^5.
Abrahamse, Ryck, 39^7, 86^7, 90^1.
Abrams, see Abrahamse.
Abramse, Joras, 95^7.
Acadians, 427^1. See also French neutrals.
Acherley, Nathaniel, 404^8, 405^4.
Achilles (brigantine), 433^5.
Ackerman, David, 537^9-38^1.
Ackland, Dudley, 542^6.
Acquin, 358^5.
Adair, John, 516^3.
Adams, Catherine, 538^2.
Adams, Dunlap, 520^6, 541^8.
Adams, James, 541^8.
Adams, John, 416^9, 538^2, 565^2.
Adams, Robert, land grants, 386^4, 538^2, 540^7, 540^8, 541^6, 544^3; petitions, 520^5, 576^2.
Adams, Samuel, 516^3.
Adams, Thomas, 568^2.
Adams, William, 541^8, 551^6.
Adaquicktinge creek, 386^8.
Addison, Joseph, 265^5, 266^5.
Adee, John, 509^4.
Adems, see Adams.
Adgate, Matthew, 494^9.
Adley, William, 530^6, 573^3.
Admiralty court, 63^8, 270^2; fees, 131^8, 202^8, 202^9, 203^5, 203^6, 217^7, 217^8, 285^8, 286^3, 286^6, 335^4; officers' salaries, 203^5, 212^4; petition of officers, 216^2.
Adriaensen, Joost, 16^6.
Adrianse, Goosen, 223^8.
Adriansen, Cornelius, 45^2.
Adriansen, Lambert, 45^2.
Adventure (ship), 43^2, 51^9, 52^2, 52^6, 116^6, 138^6, 139^6, 144^2, 145^2, 147^7, 455^8.

Advice (man-of-war), 155^1, 155^4, 155^7, 161^2.
Ael, John Jacob, 399^4.
Aertsen, Garret, 61^2, 173^7.
Aertsen, Jacob, 104^8, 184^4, 185^2.
Aertsen, John, 101^8, 121^8.
Aertsen, Simon, 112^2, 116^2, 119^5.
Aertsen, William, 235^5.
Affidavits, proclamation against taking in clandestine manner, 43^9.
African trade, 377^7.
Agard, Joshua, 406^8, 407^2.
Aggaton, John, 535^7, 542^9.
Agilar, Antonio, 349^2.
Airey, Mary, 572^8.
Aiton, Robert, 526^4.
Aix la Chapelle, treaty announced, 371^1.
Aker, Charles, 294^2.
Aker, Nicholas, 294^8.
Akin, John, 467^6, 473^1, 473^6, 480^7.
Albany, 14^2, 26^8, 30^7, 232^4, 244^4; Canadians to attack, 100^7, 111^6, 117^7, 207^7; caveat against patents, 310^4, 312^4, 328^1, 328^2, 330^4; changes made in, 26^7; churches, see Churches; clerk of peace and common pleas, 148^6; collector of excise, 148^6; commissaries, 22^8, 31^8; commissioners to meet at, 335^2; complaint against, 455^7, 456^5; complaints from, 258^2; court of oyer and terminer at, 185^1; expeditions, 99^7, 193^5; express from, 81^5; fortifications, 13^6, 54^6, 87^4, 94^1, 147^2, 236^2, 243^8, 248^6, 278^9, 387^9, 395^9, 398^8, 414^2; flour, 37^4, 38^9; French designs on, 94^4, 351^1; French officers sent from, 242^4; French on way to, 246^9; grain exportation, 114^8, 120^2, 127^8; hospital, 114^1; huts on hill, 17^5; inhabitants enumerated, 12^2; journals kept at, 256^8; land patent, 56^2; laws against riots, 259^8; magistrates, 19^8, 24^2; messengers to, 71^9; murders, 18^1, 263^8; petitions, 16^7, 40^8, 88^2, 132^2, 135^8, 190^8, 216^8, 313^8, 330^1, 387^9, 487^7, 490^4, 491^8, 509^7; pier, 435^9; post route, 229^8; public stores, 237^2; quitrents, 180^9; remonstrance from officers, 246^8; representatives, 135^6; rioters discharged, 417^4; salaries of officials, 13^6; schout, 11^9, 19^9; scouts killed, 368^9; sexton, 16^7; shoemaker, 24^1; no strange sloops to go to, 13^8; smallpox in, 333^7, 431^4; subcollector, 100^8; taxes, 13^6, 19^9, 24^1, 25^4, 26^6, 27^1, 28^2, 28^9, 120^2, 121^8, 125^2, 126^2, 131^2, 133^2, 149^6, 151^5, 152^6, 160^9, 173^2, 209^6; timber, 28^4; Sybrant van Schaick, recorder, 388^6, 417^6; war rumors, 313^8; writs sent to, 32^6; fort: 12^1, 89^8, 90^6; condition, 81^9, 274^2; inspection, 100^8; plan, 417^9; repairs, 17^6, 42^9, 44^6, 59^3, 73^6, 80^7, 87^4, 98^4, 110^2, 189^9, 205^2, 206^6, 238^6, 260^8, 263^9, 265^7, 273^4, 298^7; Indians: 24^4, 24^6, 35^2; approach of, 81^4; attack by, 97^6; cause alarm, 70^8, 73^8, 129^5; from Canada, 87^3; conferences, 72^4, 98^4, 109^5, 169^8, 188^6, 239^2, 277^8, 277^7, 281^9, 302^2, 336^2, 355^6, 377^8, 378^6, 379^1, 387^7, 391^4; Indian post, 57^4; negotiations with, 28^8; peace between Maquaes and Mahicanders, 15^8; powder sold to, 24^5, 24^6; Indian presents, 226^8; provides transportation to Mohawks, 387^8; relief against, 348^6; trade, 54^6, 293^7; treaty, 190^6; Waganhaes Indians asked to come to, 170^8;

[1]mayors: Abeel, John, 105^5, 232^8; Bancker, Evert, 117^5, 217^2, 217^5; Bleecker, Rutger, 302^1, 304^2, 305^9, 306^2, 306^4, 306^7; Cuyler, Abraham C. 482^2, 485^5, 486^9, 492^9, 498^6, 502^5, 506^7; Cuyler, Cornelius, 341^8, 343^8, 346^2, 351^7; De Peyster, John, 308^8, 310^8, 311^2, 318^8; Douw, Volkert P. 454^7, 459^7, 462^8, 466^2, 468^9, 479^6; Holland, Edward, 319^8, 324^8, 327^4, 330^8, 332^7, 334^2; Livingston, Robert, jr, 240^5, 249^8, 265^5, 268^2; Saunders, Robert, 377^5, 381^7, 385^7, 385^9, 386^1, 389^8; Schuyler, John, jr, 336^7, 339^2; Schuyler, Peter, 55^2, 55^7, 56^1, 73^9, 74^6, 76^1, 87^3, 87^4, 88^2; Ten Broeck, Dirck, 361^8, 368^4; Ten Eyck, Jacob Coenradt, 371^4, 374^8, 375^4, 375^5, 376^2; Van Brugh, Peter, 143^6, 282^2, 288^2, 293^1, 296^2; Van Schaick, Sybrant G. 431^8, 436^6, 442^4, 447^1, 449^8; Wessells, Dirck, 128^2, 133^8;
soldiers: barracks, 120^4, 271^5; deserters, 78^8, 114^8; fusileer companies, 83^8; guard, 230^8; militia, 97^7, 230^9, 242^4; musterrolls of companies, 92^8; officers' quarters, 114^8, 115^8, 115^4, 115^9, 116^8, 121^6, 150^9; pay, 71^8, 85^7, 96^9, 120^6, 333^2; subsistence, 69^8, 74^4, 74^6, 76^8, 92^4, 93^7, 96^6, 97^2, 101^2, 107^7, 238^8; troops sent to, 65^8, 67^9, 69^4, 72^6, 77^5, 77^6, 80^1, 81^8, 84^8, 91^7, 92^9, 95^4, 232^9, 354^5, 359^7;
trade, 28^8, 31^1; with Canada, 32^7, 279^1, 303^9; Indian, 31^4, 54^6, 293^1;

[1]Names of persons under Albany city and county include only references pertaining to the office under which they are entered; for other references see individual names in main alphabet.

Alstine, see Van Alstyne.
Alsup, see Alsop.
Alt, Johannes, 405[1].
Alvard, Simeon, 522[9], 524[7], 527[3], 562[4].
Alvarez, Peter, 457[2].
Alverd, Medad, 524[2].
Alvertste, ——, 416[7].
Aman (Arabian), 377[2].
Amason, Daniel, 517[7].
Amboy, see Perth Amboy.
Ambusco (sachem), 24[3].
America (ship), 461[8], 462[2].
Amherst, Jeffery, letters from, 444[8], 445[9], 446[2], 452[7], 459[3]; occupies Crownpoint, 446[3]; application for cannons, 446[6]; suggestion by, 446[8]; requests continuing New York provincials, 446[9]; repays money, 447[1]; number of men required by, 447[7]; writes that Fort Levi has been taken, 449[7]; sends letters, 451[2]; receives news of king's death, 451[8]; requests that provincials be retained in service, 453[3]; writes about provisions, 453[8]; wants men employed during winter, 454[8], 459[5]; promises extra bounty to recruits, 456[9]; sends list of deserters, 457[4]; requests provisions for army, 457[9]; orders New York troops to continue in service, 461[7]; writes about Indians, 462[4]; requires 1400 men, 462[5]; land grant, 555[5].
Amiel, John, jr, 550[4].
Amity (sloop), 102[3].
Amsterdam (Holland), 336[5], 336[6], 354[8], 446[6].
Amy, Joshua, 358[8], 422[2].
Anchorage, fees, 30[6].
Ancram, ironworks at, 416[4].
Anderson, ——, 222[8], 224[6].
Anderson, Edward, 512[5], 512[8].
Anderson, George, 144[7], 147[1].
Anderson, Isaac, 276[5].
Anderson, James, 274[8], 278[7], 530[4].
Anderson, John, 430[4], 457[4]; petition, 316[8], 317[5]; land grants, 408[6], 536[2], 541[1], 565[2]; land survey for, 411[8]; islands claimed by, 467[4], 468[5]; charged with murder, 474[5].
Anderson, John, of Barbadoes, 73[2].
Anderson, Joseph, 555[6].
Anderson, Robert, 132[6].
Anderson, Robert, corporal, 568[4].
Anderson, William, 214[8], 236[5]; warrants, 186[8], 309[6]; petitions, 216[8], 223[8], 233[7], 235[5], 237[4]; security as sheriff, 225[1], 236[4]; suspended, 239[8]. See also N. Y. (county), sheriffs.
Anderson, William, sergeant, 564[6], 566[7], 571[2], 572[7] 572[8].
Andover, 565[6], 576[9].

Andrees, Henry, 537[9].
Andrews, John, 514[8], 543[2], 549[6], 549[8].
Andrews, Joseph, 477[8].
Andrews, Mary, 44[4].
Andrews, Robert, 562[5].
Andrews, William, 528[5].
Andrews, William, missionary to Mohawks, 258[1].
Andros, Edmund, 130[4]; meeting in fort, 20[8], 20[5], 21[7]; goes to Connecticut, 22[9], 23[1]; goes to Albany, 25[2], 26[1], 28[6], 28[8]; conferences with Mohawks, 25[3]; meeting with New York ministers, 27[8]; goes to Nantucket, 28[8]; goes to England, 30[6]; goes to Pemaquid, 31[3]; receives seals of province, 61[2]; letters from, 115[8]; vs Richard Pattishall, 122[6]. See also N. Y. (colony), governors.
Andross, Bildad, 524[5], 561[4].
Andruss, Jeremiah, 400[6].
Angevine, Peter, 473[4].
Annapolis (Md.), 415[2], 419[1].
Annapolis (Nova Scotia), 242[2].
Anne, queen, proclaimed, 172[3], 172[4]; approves act, 187[2]; fixes governor's salary, 188[8]; birthday, 190[6]; approves appointments to council, 207[8]; order in council, 218[4]; approves acts of assembly, 218[4], 225[4], 238[8]; order on attendance of council, 219[8]; addresses to, 222[2], 229[5], 230[4], 232[4], 244[7], 245[6]; appoints William Peartree and David Provoost to council, 224[2]; letter about palatines, 225[4]; instructions about land grants, 225[4], 235[8], 235[9], 241[6]; instructions to Col. Vetch, 227[7]; letter about Canada expedition, 227[7]; memorial to, 229[7]; order about coin, 230[8]; recommendation signed by, 231[8]; revokes Ingoldsby's commission, 236[3]; reinstates Dr Staats, 238[8]; letter about new seal, 239[1]; reinstates Thomas Walters, 239[8]; order concerning Thomas Byerly, 243[5]; letter about trial of cases concerning church, 253[8]; death, 256[7].
Anne (brigantine), 355[1].
Anne (sloop), 433[4].
Anne Hook's neck, 25[9].
Annett, Robert, 33[4], 122[4].
Annin, William, 548[7].
Anstruther, William, 569[3].
Anterbush, Philip, 535[8].
Anthony, Allard, 16[6], 21[6].
Anthony, Engeltie, 114[2].
Anthony, Hendrick, petitions, 255[2], 255[9], 259[6], 263[7], 265[8]; vs Stephen Gasherie, 264[6], 267[5].
Anthony, Joseph, 546[2].

Blanck, Annetie, 18[8].
Blanck, Nicholas, 107[7], 107[9], 151[5].
Blanckjean, John, 475[5].
Bland, Elias, 550[4], 573[3].
Blane, Archibald, 412[2].
Blankistein, William, 67[7].
Blare, John, 573[3].
Blathwayt, William, 58[2], 69[5], 80[7], 106[2].
  See also N. Y. (colony), auditors general.
Blauvelt, Cornelius, 408[8], 466[7], 467[7], 468[2].
Blauvelt, Gerrit, 307[2].
Blauvelt, Johannes Joseph, 408[8].
Blauw, see Blaau.
Blaylock, William, 411[5], 511[4].
Bleecker, Mr, 346[7].
Bleecker, Messrs, 454[5].
Bleecker, Henry, 494[4], 503[4].
Bleecker, Jacob, jr, 537[3].
Bleecker, Jacobus, 407[2].
Bleecker, Jacobus Rutger, 336[3].
Bleecker, Jan Jansen, magistrate, 45[7]; justice of peace, 65[6]; commissioner, 76[6]; manager of building of new barracks, 120[4]; commissioner of oyer and terminer issued to, 148[2]; mayor, 149[7]; warrants, 155[4], 168[9], 169[2]; recorder, 159[7]; petition, 301[2], 301[7].
Bleecker, John, sr, warrants, 125[8], 144[5], 149[5], 160[5]; pass for trade with Indians, 136[7]; mayor, 148[8]; goes to Onondaga, 157[4]; journal of visit at Onondaga, 158[6], 159[5]; accounts, 160[1]; instructions to, 160[4]; Oneidas want him to go to Canada, 231[4]; Indian commissioner, 279[6].
Bleecker, John, jr, 159[7], 172[9].
Bleecker, John Nicholas, 528[2], 562[6].
Bleecker, John Rutger, land grants, 336[8], 404[6], 540[8], 541[9], 544[3]; sheriff, 361[8]; licenses to buy Indian lands, 378[7], 401[6]; petitions, 401[2], 403[8]; affidavit, 483[3].
Bleecker, Nicholas, 148[3], 306[8], 307[7], 308[7].
Bleecker, Rutger, licenses to buy Indian land, 306[8], 538[6]; land grants, 307[7], 521[1], 532[8], 537[8]; petitions, 308[7], 321[4]; letter from, 353[9]. See also Albany, mayors.
Bleeke, Ariantie, 17[3].
Bleeker, Bleker, see Bleecker.
Blenheim, 544[4].
Blercom, Hendrick, 539[9], 542[8].
Blin, Francis, 63[4].
Block, Hans, widow of, 26[8], 28[9], 29[7].
Block island, 117[8], 434[2].
Blockhouses, 101[7], 110[8], 111[7].
Blom, Aaron, 144[6], 151[6].
Blom, Jacob, 167[8].
Blomer, see Bloomer.

Blondell, Christopher, 343[9].
Blondi, Joseph, 370[6], 370[7].
Blood, Edmund, 314[8].
Blood, Edward, 296[8].
Bloom, see Blom.
Bloomer, Gilbert, 473[5].
Bloomer, Robert, sr, 33[8], 67[5], 67[6], 70[5].
Bloomer, Robert, jr, 67[5], 67[6].
Bloomingdale, 556[8].
Blossom (pink), 126[8].
Blovelt, see Blauvelt.
Blue Cock (sloop), 29[6].
Blue hills, 248[6].
Blundell, Christopher, house leased to, 386[4]; petitions, 400[9], 402[7]; land grants, 403[2], 413[7], 560[7], 562[7]; to deliver material for fortifications, 435[7]; to deliver key of magazine, 436[2]; to deliver ordnance, 442[8], 446[7]; doorkeeper of council, 451[4]; warrant, 495[6].
Blundell, Stephen, 558[8], 569[2].
Blycker, see Bleecker.
Blydenburgh, Joshua, 78[5].
Bobin [Bobn], Isaac, deputy secretary, 274[2]; petitions, 274[3], 291[7], 292[2], 309[8], 309[9]; warrants, 274[8], 295[8]; land grant, 274[4]; denies treaty right, 282[2].
Bobin, James, 136[2].
Bodderel, marquis de, 347[7].
Bodein, Guy, 99[8].
Bodine, John, 220[9], 221[2].
Bodraw, Francis, 430[8].
Boeckhoult, Peter Johnson, 44[7].
Boel, Henry, 550[4].
Boelen, Jacob, 98[5], 99[4], 169[4], 407[8], 408[1].
Bogan, John, 530[8].
Bogard, Henryck Cornelius, 96[4], 96[7], 118[9].
Bogard, Jacob Uyten, 41[7].
Bogardus, Mr, 214[9].
Bogardus, Anna [Anneke Jans], 12[5].
Bogardus, Cornelius, 62[6], 62[8], 79[1].
Bogardus, Evert, 91[7], 93[1].
Bogardus, Peter, 60[6], 105[8], 106[1], 123[7], 126[8].
Bogart, Coenrat, 279[4].
Bogart, John, jr, 444[7], 451[3], 521[7], 522[5].
Bogart, Nicholas C. 521[7], 522[3], 527[7], 540[7], 544[8], 552[9].
Boggs, James, 511[8], 519[2], 528[7].
Boisbellau, John, 44[2].
Bokee, Abraham, 378[3].
Bolland, John, 230[2].
Bolting act, 132[4].
Bolton, Hugh, 408[4], 409[4].
Bolton, Matthew, 408[4], 409[4].
Bolton, William, 550[3], 550[5].
Bombay hook, 13[7].
Bonan, Amon, 83[7].
Bond, Henry, 524[4].

Burcham, Samuel, 291⁵, 300², 300⁴, 300⁶.
Burchild, see Burcham.
Burck, see Burk.
Burent, John, 523⁶.
Burge, Samuel, 545⁴.
Burgen, see Burgers.
Burger, Elias, 77³.
Burger, George, 37³.
Burger, Gilbert, 541¹, 561¹.
Burger, Harmanus, 37³, 271⁹.
Burger, Johannes, 215⁸, 327⁶.
Burger, Myndert, 405⁶, 406².
Burger, Sarah, 80⁹, 83⁹.
Burgers, Mrs Engeltie, 47³, 47⁶, 101⁵, 101⁸.
Burges, captain, 365⁴.
Burges, John, 385⁸.
Burgesse, Samuel, 90⁶.
Burgett, David, 151⁹, 152².
Burgh, Johannes de, see Van Brugh.
Burgie, Thomas, 512⁵, 512⁸.
Burhans, Cornelius, 568³.
Burhans, [Burhorns], Henry, 401⁸, 402⁶, 406⁷, 407¹.
Burhorns, see Burhans.
Burk, Benjamin, 522⁶.
Burk, Francis, 395⁸.
Burk, John, 405⁵, 406², 536².
Burley, Simon, 530⁸.
Burling, Samuel, 550⁸.
Burlington (N. J.), 150⁸.
Burn [Burns], Charles, 288⁵, 293⁵, 293⁷.
Burn, John, 496⁷, 496⁹.
Burn, Samuel, 333⁸.
Burnay, John, 538⁸.
Burnet, George, 284⁸, 301³, 320³.
Burnet, Gilbert, 400¹, 400².
Burnet, John, 396⁸, 458². See also N. Y. (county), coroners.
Burnet, Mary, 305⁸, 307⁷, 309⁸, 314⁹.
Burnet, Mary, jr, 300⁸.
Burnet, Mathias, 506⁸.
Burnet, Thomas, 456³, 456⁵, 564³.
Burnet, William, takes oath as governor, 278⁶; goes to New Jersey, 280⁸, 285³, 291², 293², 294³, 298³, 301⁷; reports on Indian conference, 281⁹; conference with five nations, 287³, 287⁴, 287⁸; instructions to, 287⁹, 293³, 297⁷, 303³; takes oath as chancellor, 290⁸; goes to Albany, 296², 301⁹; propositions to six nations, 296⁴; letters from, 299³, 307⁶; delivers seals to Gov. Montgomerie, 306²; warrant, 306⁴; petition of son, 400¹; money due estate of, 400¹. See also N. Y. (colony), governors.
Burnet, William, jr, petitions, 288⁸, 296⁵, 298⁴; licenses to buy Indian lands, 289¹, 293⁷, 294⁵; land grant, 298⁶.

Burnets key, battery, 359⁵.
Burns, George, 538².
Burns, William, 528⁹.
Burns, see also Burn.
Burre, Daniel, 25⁵.
Burrege, Ann, 538⁴.
Burrege, John Leake, 538⁴.
Burrege, Martha, 538⁴.
Burrege, Robert, 538⁴.
Burroughs, Eden, 165⁸, 166⁴, 169⁵.
Burroughs, Edward, 167⁴, 167⁷, 195³.
Burroughs, John, 20⁷, 21¹, 251⁸, 428².
Burroughs, Joseph, 80⁴.
Burroughs, Mary, 169⁵.
Burrows, lieutenant, 353², 360⁶.
Burrows, Edward, 329⁸, 329⁹.
Burst, Jacob, 305⁸, 310⁸.
Burt, Aaron, 525⁵.
Burt, Benjamin, 269⁵, 310⁴.
Burt, Eleazer, 520¹, 524⁹.
Burt, John, jr, 524².
Burt, Joseph, 529⁴, 553³.
Burt, Richard, 56⁴, 56⁶, 88².
Burt, Samuel, 56⁴, 56⁵, 56⁷, 88², 88³.
Burtch, Jonathan, 563⁴.
Burton, Cassibelam, 20⁶.
Burton, Mary, 340⁶, 340⁷, 341⁸.
Burton, Ralph, 510⁸, 530⁵, 566⁸.
Burton, Robert, 427².
Bush, David, 467⁴.
Bush, Johannes, 167⁸.
Bush, Justus, 467⁴.
Bush, Timothy, 566⁸.
Bush, William, 467⁴.
Bushwick [Boswyck], Acadians settle at, 427⁴; boundaries, 15⁶, 16², 38³, 47¹, 80⁶; land patents, 37⁵, 38³, 38⁷, 47²; vs Newtown, 10⁶, 17³, 79⁷, 209⁷, 209⁸, 212³, 212⁵, 214², 215¹, 215², 217⁸; patent, 218⁵; petitions, 48¹, 79⁵, 217⁸; quitrent fixed, 218⁶.
Buskerk, Hendrick, 508⁷, 512⁴.
Buss, John, 522⁹.
Buss, John, jr, 522⁹.
Butchers, regulations concerning, 26⁵.
Butlar, Agatha, 576⁸.
Butler, Mr, 120⁴, 434².
Butler, captain, 319¹, 394⁸.
Butler, Benjamin, 565⁴.
Butler, Charles, 310², 310⁸.
Butler, Elizabeth, 119⁶.
Butler, John, letters from, 344⁹, 347⁷, 377⁴, 388²; news from, 348⁶; license to buy Indian lands, 379⁴; land grants, 508⁷, 512⁴, 516¹, 516², 540⁵, 544⁸, 544⁹, 549⁴, 557⁸, 569¹.
Butler, Lois, 516⁸.
Butler, Pierce Pensonby, 531⁹, 532², 533³, 534⁷, 534⁹.
Butler, Simon, 522⁸.
Butler, Thomas, 374², 379⁴.
Butler, Walter, petitions, 319⁶, 319⁹, 320⁸, 322⁹, 326⁸, 520⁵; licenses to buy

Campbell, Duncan, 139⁴, 148⁸, 212⁹.
Campbell, Duncan (2d), 489³, 550², 564³, 572⁵.
Campbell, George, 408⁵, 409⁵, 564⁵, 571³.
Campbell, James, petition, 408⁵, 409⁵; land grants, 411¹, 411³, 530⁴, 571³; warrant, 564⁵.
Campbell, John, 411⁶, 413³, 548⁷, 556⁵.
Campbell, Lauchlan, 337³, 338², 410².
Campbell, Moses, 911⁵.
Campbell, Robert, 411⁹.
Campbell, Ronald, 332⁸.
Campbell, William, 540⁷, 544³, 544⁷, 545², 572³.
Campeachy, 15⁹, 55⁹.
Campell, ——, 52⁵.
Canada, articles of peace with, 208¹; attack on Albany planned, 86⁵, 207⁹; claims the five nations, 132⁵, 133¹; commissioners to be sent to, 130⁸; Frenchmen and Indians from, 163⁴; export of horses to forbidden, 145³, 145⁵, 145⁶; Indians, 350⁴; co-operation with Indians against, 65⁸; Indians on warpath against, 75⁹; maps, 110⁷; messenger sent to, 133³; order relating to people coming from, 392³; exchange of prisoners, 367⁹; Peter Schuyler's expedition to, 67², 67⁵, 67⁶, 67⁹; smuggling to, 215⁵; trade with, 32⁷, 279¹, 281⁶, 281⁷, 285⁸, 293¹, 296³, 303⁹; expedition: 227⁹, 228⁴, 228⁵, 229², 229⁴, 229⁵, 229⁶, 230³, 230⁶, 233², 240³, 241⁸; arms repaired for, 228⁷; command of, 228²; commissioners, 231², 231³, 257⁵; meeting of joint committees, 229³; expenditures for, 230⁴, 230⁷, 242⁵; failure, 243⁷; flag of truce, 234⁸; iron and steel for, 231⁸; land expedition to return to Albany, 243⁸; letter from Queen Anne, 227⁷; letter from duke of Newcastle, 354⁸; letter from Gov. Shirley, 356³, 360⁸; letter from Admiral Warren, 356³, 360⁸; Long Island Indians called to serve, 229⁸; pay of managers, 244⁸; necessaries called for, 230⁹; order concerning, 241⁹; provisions for, 242⁵, 242⁹; provisions remaining from, 244⁸; volunteers called for, 243²;
governors: Beauharnois, Charles, 303⁵; Denonville, marquis de, letter, 54³; Du Quesne, marquis de, 388², 396⁵, 398⁴; Frontenac, count, 26⁸, 104¹; La Galisonnière, comte de, 366³, 369⁶, 369⁷, 371³, 371⁴, 372⁴, 372⁵; La Jonquière, marquis de, 373⁷, 376⁷, 379⁷, 380⁸, 382⁵; Vaudreuil, marquis de, 246⁹, 280⁴, 281⁹.
Canada creek, 290⁷.

Canada Indians, see Indian tribes.
Canada's kill, 376⁹.
Canadagaia (Mohawk chief), 394⁴.
Canajoharie [Cannajoharie, Conajohary, Connajoharie], 376⁹, 503⁴; memorial of inhabitants, 502⁹; money for building church, 454⁴; orders to militia, 360⁷; patent to be vacated, 428⁸; petition for assistance against Indians, 438⁵.
Canajoharie Indians, see Indian tribes.
Canary merchant (ship), 30³, 335¹.
Canasatego (Onondaga sachem), 380⁴.
Canastagione [Canestagione, Canistegione, Cannestigaioenna, Kanestigione], 73⁶, 202⁸, 240³, 267¹, 272², 272³, 576², 576⁴.
Candles, exported, 337⁴.
Canel, Lawrence, 486⁷.
Canfield, Samuel, 349³.
Caniacka (Mohawk sachem), 26⁹.
Canneff, James, 565⁹.
Cannestigaioenna, see Canastagione.
Cannon, Andrew, 64³, 130².
Cannon, John, 339³, 340¹.
Cannon, John, jr, 339³, 340¹.
Canoes, 12².
Canon, John, 368⁶.
Cantine, John, 477⁹.
Cantine, Matthew, 496⁶.
Cantine, Moses, 385³.
Cants [Cantz], George, 391⁶, 399⁸.
Cantwell, Edmund, 18⁴, 20¹, 26⁸, 26⁹, 27³, 29⁸.
Cantyne, John, 537⁴.
Cape Breton, 320⁴, 344⁴, 347⁴.
Cape François, 359⁷.
Cape May, 140⁶.
Capela, Bernard, 273², 273⁹.
Capitaine, John, 63⁷.
Capre, Jan de, 14².
Capree, Oliver, 522⁹.
Cardale, Thomas, 180⁶, 180⁷, 181³, 181⁸, 188⁷, 192⁹.
Cardall, Ralph, 34⁸, 37⁹, 38⁴, 41⁵.
Carden, John, 511¹, 533³.
Carell, Thomas, 182⁹.
Carey, Anne Maria, 523⁸.
Carey, Lucius Ferdinand, 523⁶.
Carey, Thomas, 370⁷.
Carfield, Samuel, 401³, 402⁸, 406⁷, 407¹.
Cargil, Abernethy, 533³, 534⁵, 547³.
Carhart, John, 509⁴.
Carhart, Thomas, 64², 64⁹, 65².
Caribbean islands, 22⁷.
Carle, Jean, 409³.
Carle, Thomas, 13⁸.
Carleton, Dennis, 521³.
Carleton, Guy, 472⁸, 477².
Carlile, William, 354¹.
Carman, Caleb, 40⁴.

Cobey [Cobet], Ludovicus, 23[9], 31[5].

Cobham, Jacob, 575[3].

Cobham, James, land grants, 537[2], 545[3], 559[2], 559[7], 560[4], 560[5], 562[3], 562[9], 563[3], 563[9], 576[1].

Cobrun [Cobrim], John, 104[6], 115[5], 118[2], 123[7].

Cobus kill, 386[3].

Cochart, John, 35[3].

Cochran, John, 575[4].

Cochran. See also Cockran.

Cock, Abraham, 409[8].

Cock, George, 239[5], 239[9].

Cock, Gerhard Daniel, 471[2], 475[2], 475[4], 475[6].

Cock, John, 399[8].

Cock, Jordan, 543[8].

Cock, Peter, 213[6].

Cock, Thomas, 284[3].

Cockburn, John, 108[3], 111[3].

Cockburn, William, 478[6], 479[9], 527[1], 530[4], 536[3], 547[9].

Cockcroft, William, petitions, 401[8], 402[2], 408[9], 409[9]; bonds for settlement of lands, 412[9]; warrant, 419[4]; letter from, 421[2].

Cocken, Alexander, 523[8].

Cockeran, John, 521[5], 522[5].

Cockerill [Cockrill], Thomas, 226[8]; called on to deliver seals, 227[5]; before council, 229[1]; report on estate of, 234[3]; Dr Johnstone executor, 238[6].

Cockerill, Thomas (2d), 318[3], 318[9], 320[8].

Cockerthal, Joshua, see Kocherthal, Joshua.

Cockram, John, 12[8], 13[3], 13[4].

Cockram, Robert, 33[3].

Cockran [Cochran, Cockren], Robert, 486[5], 488[2], 488[4], 500[1].

Cockshaky, see Coxsackie.

Cocksingh, see Coxsinck.

Coddington, William, 25[2]. See also Rhode Island.

Codeber, Jacob, 127[3], 132[5].

Coden, James, 312[3], 317[3].

Codman, Thomas, 273[1].

Codner, Richard, 43[2].

Codrington, Margaret, 299[4].

Codrington, Thomas, 37[6], 68[7], 77[4], 121[9], 299[5].

Codweis, John Conrad, 231[7], 231[8], 255[7], 255[8].

Codwise, Christopher, 334[3], 334[4].

Cody, Robert, 49[5].

Coe, Mr, 13[2].

Coe, John, 179[1]; petition, 75[3]; vs Thomas Hicks, 76[2]; prisoner, 62[4]; before council, 143[7]; petitions referred to, 154[3], 158[5]; examined, 203[3]; security, 237[6]; vs Shadrack Chatterton, 468[2].

Coe, Robert, 10[6], 203[2].

Coen, Elizabeth, 416[7].

Coenties dock, 428[9].

Coeur, Jean, 311[6], 346[3], 346[7], 384[2].

Coeyman, Abraham, 256[4], 295[9].

Coeyman, Andries, petitions, 133[2], 255[9], 283[7], 295[7], 297[8], 300[3], 300[5]; before council, 194[6]; warrant, 253[3]; license to buy land, 300[4]; caveat against patent, 324[8].

Coeymans, Barent Pieterse, 135[6], 141[3], 193[7], 196[7], 203[9]; land grant, 193[9]; vs Kilian van Rensselaer, 194[5], 195[9], 196[3].

Coeymans patent, 517[8], 518[4], 520[3], 524[4].

Coffee, Donald, 54[7].

Coffee, cultivation, 386[2].

Coffin, Stephen, 391[8].

Coffin, Tristram, 14[5], 20[2], 22[4], 78[1].

Coins, address to queen about, 222[2]; foreign, 202[7], 224[3]; letters about, 207[8]; order concerning, 230[8]; valuation, 32[8], 82[7], 336[9]. See also Money.

Coit, Benjamin, 565[4].

Coit, Isaac, 565[4].

Coit, Samuel, 565[4].

Coker, Thomas, collector of excise, 33[9]; testifies, 50[7]; recommended for custom house officer, 50[9]; member of council, 63[1]; accounts examined, 64[9]; payments to, 71[1], 73[2]; warrants, 93[3], 98[3]; petition, 105[8].

Cojemans, Samuel Staats, 405[2], 405[4].

Colbache, Thomas, 51[1].

Colden, Alexander, land grants, 326[7], 403[1], 403[3], 531[5], 541[9], 546[8]; petitions, 334[4], 342[7], 402[7]; surveyor general, 378[3], 456[7]; representation of, 395[5]; examined concerning exportation of provisions, 427[9]; claim concerning Minisinck patentees, 468[1]; warrants, 476[7], 485[8], 495[5], 500[9]; complaint against, 471[8]; to run Quebec line, 488[8]; illness, 502[1]; death, 503[5]. See also N. Y. (colony), surveyors general.

Colden, Altje, 340[2].

Colden, Cadwallader, 285[8], 298[2], 307[3], 448[9]; petitions, 268[3], 282[9], 288[3], 307[3]; warrants, 268[4], 288[6], 289[3], 293[3], 468[3], 479[8], 485[2]; patent granted, 269[4]; surveyor general, 275[5], 456[7]; caveat against Joseph Budd, 277[7]; to examine quadrant used in boundary survey, 279[9]; master in chancery, 280[7]; appointed to council, 280[9], 390[3]; memorials, 288[4], 298[6], 328[3], 328[6], 371[4], 371[8], 371[9]; report, 296[9]; commissioner to run Connecticut line, 298[7], 310[5]; takes oaths, 304[4], 343[3], 501[2]; answer to petition of Jeremiah Dunbar, 333[9]; letters from, 341[7], 343[1], 351[2], 351[4], 437[2], 469[7];

Ellswordt, Elswordt, *see* Elseworth.
Elmes, Stephen, 521[7], 522[5].
Elmor, John, 534[3], 535[5].
Elseworth [Ellswordt, Elswordt], Clement, 111[4], 120[5], 144[5], 148[4].
Elseworth [Elswordt], George, 151[7], 239[4], 239[6].
Elsworth, Francis, 561[5].
Elsworth, William, 484[1], 484[3], 484[9].
Elting, Joachimintie, 91[2].
Elting, Noah, 353[6], 368[9], 369[2], 386[6], 496[7].
Elting, William, 475[4].
Elton, John, 61[2].
Elves, John, 534[4], 539[2].
Elwood, James, 430[3].
Emans, Abel, 525[7].
Emanuel, Claus, 45[2].
Embargo, *see* Provisions; Vessels.
Embree, John, 186[2], 186[7], 187[5], 188[3].
Embury, Andrew, 518[5].
Embury, David, 408[9], 409[5], 518[4].
Embury, David, jr, 518[4].
Embury, George, 518[5].
Embury, John, 408[9], 409[5], 409[9], 518[4].
Embury, Peter, 408[9], 409[5].
Embury, Philip, 408[9], 409[5], 481[7], 508[5], 512[2].
Embury, Philip, jr, 518[5].
Emerson, Moses, 423[1].
Emett, ——, 146[2].
Emmett, James, 63[5].
Emory, William, 433[4].
Emott, James, land grants, 102[8], 121[9]; sits on Dutch church charter, 112[9]; attorney for Miles Forster vs Lockermans, 113[1]; attorney in case Bennet vs Aertsen, 116[2]; Indian purchase produced by, 163[6]; appears for Brooklyn, 181[5]; Bickley, 208[8].
Emott, James (2d), 409[7], 526[9].
Emott. *See also* Emett; Emmett.
Empie, John, 325[6].
Enan, Lawrence, 404[9].
Endeavour (sloop), 88[9], 217[9], 230[2].
England, acts of assembly sent to, 71[4], 168[2]; church of, 113[4]; communications concerning Indian presents, 224[2]; council minutes sent to, 71[4]; peace with France, 252[9], 253[8]; war with France, 249[7], 429[9]; guns transported from, 99[6]; proclamation concerning agreement with Holland, 198[8]; letters from, 257[6]; prisoners sent to for trial, 253[7]; soldiers sent to, 149[8]; troops, 98[3], 100[5]; victories, celebration of, 109[7]; war with Spain declared, 173[2].
English, David, 530[8].
English, Nicholas, 309[3].
English, William, 333[4].
Enlisting money, 427[1], 448[3], 452[9], 458[3], 463[3], 464[9].

Enny, John, 530[2].
Ensign, John, 400[5].
Enterprize (man-of-war), 287[1], 448[6].
Enters, Jacob, 520[6], 520[8], 531[3], 539[1].
Episcopal churches, *see* Churches.
Erickson, Garret, 408[8], 409[4].
Erkley, Henry, 530[2], 556[8].
Ernest, Matthew, 459[4].
Ertley, Henry, 411[9], 497[8], 551[4].
Erwin, Joseph, 568[3].
Esick, Olirick, 535[2].
Esopus, affairs, 10[9], 14[1]; petition, 36[2]; approach of Indians, 81[4]; English laws, 19[5]; express from, 81[5]; French prisoners escape to, 67[8]; French to march against, 351[1]; garrison, 10[8]; Indian affairs, 24[4], 24[5]; Indians to attack, 462[4]; justice of peace of, 13[9]; land matters, 28[3], 37[2]; land patent, 55[8]; magistrates, 19[8], 26[7]; schout, 18[3], 20[1]; powers of sheriff, 27[6]; taxes, 27[1]; writs sent to, 32[6].
Esopus Indians, *see* Indian tribes.
Esperance (brigantine), 455[3].
Espinosa, Joseph, petitions, 357[6], 357[8], 358[5], 358[9], 359[8], 360[2], 360[3], 362[4], 363[9]; complaint, 358[1]; examination, 362[4]; captured, 362[3].
Espy, William, 309[2].
Esquire, Gidion, 567[6].
Essex county, militia, 357[4], 358[3].
Estates, administration, 28[5]; valuation, 77[6].
Etben, Seres, 427[4].
Etherington, George, 515[4], 516[6].
Etherington, Thomas, 412[2], 413[4], 521[3], 562[2].
Eustace, Margaret, 564[5], 571[3].
Evans, Benjamin, 574[1], 574[4].
Evans, Cadwallader, 545[5].
Evans, David, 403[4].
Evans, Joan, 574[1], 574[4].
Evans, John, 91[9], 92[3], 92[7], 96[3]; land patents, 95[7], 97[5]; allowed to impress sailors, 97[4]; wants a sloop, 117[4]; petition against, 126[7]; defends his proceedings, 126[8]; under bail, 131[1]; warrant, 160[1]; order concerning lands, 235[4]; land surveyed, 268[5]; boundaries of patent, 284[6], 284[7], 285[3], 285[6], 286[5], 286[7], 286[8], 287[1]. *See also* Evans' patent.
Evans, John (2d), 403[4], 522[2], 522[5], 546[5].
Evans, Katherine, 275[1].
Evans, Randolph, 58[5].
Evans, Richard, 535[8].
Evans, Zur, 525[7].
Evans' patent, 362[2], 400[9].
Everet [Everit], Clear, 539[9], 542[2].
Everet, John, 203[3], 237[5], 237[6].
Everett, Richard, 299[2].
Everit, *see* Everet.

with, 189[1], 258[3], 369[9], 428[8], 450[3];
war, 53[6].
French Indians, see Indian tribes.
French neutrals, 427[1], 430[3], 434[7], 435[8].
French prisoners, 59[5], 126[9], 127[7], 135[3],
352[9]; assembly refuses to make
further provisions for, 439[9]; on
board Centaur, 430[3]; letters of denization granted, 127[4]; escaped, 67[5],
67[8], 74[5], 441[8]; exchanged, 116[9], 234[2];
among Indians, 371[6], 373[4]; in New
York, list, 438[3], 442[2]; of Kings
county, 358[7]; quartered on Long
Island, 450[1]; taken from New York
jail, 435[7]; ordered out of town, 346[2];
papers of, 359[3]; pass signed, 235[3];
proclamation about, 446[5]; engaged
as workmen, 436[4]; taken as sailors,
440[8], 444[3]; subsisting, 121[2], 346[9];
warrant to, 86[2];
  disposal of: 345[7], 345[8]; sent to
country, 369[9], 435[1]; taken to
Curaçao, 440[8]; sent to England,
119[1]; sent to Flatbush and Hempstead, 230[4]; to return fo France,
355[6]; sent to Cape François, 359[7];
sent to French islands, 346[1]; carried to French West Indies, 249[5],
360[2]; sent to Jamaica, 354[4]; carried
to Leghorn, 357[2]; carried to
Leogan, 365[5]; sent to New York,
441[1], 441[5]; sent to Petit Guave, 348[8];
sent to Suffolk county, 436[1], 446[6].
French privateers, 107[8], 199[4], 199[7],
200[5], 204[5], 204[6], 204[9], 217[8], 225[9], 243[1],
244[4].
French protestants, 109[6], 112[5], 132[5].
French West Indies, 249[9], 360[2].
Frere, Hugo, jr, 247[7], 247[9], 259[3], 259[5].
Frere, Isaac, 247[7], 247[9].
Frere, Simon, 247[7], 247[9].
Fresneau, Andrew, 213[5], 237[1], 237[4],
285[4], 285[5], 285[6], 293[9].
Freud, Johannes, 558[9].
Freudenbergh, Charles de, 542[4].
Frew, ——, 241[6].
Fricket, Thomas, 532[8].
Friedenberg, Charles, 533[1].
Friedenberg, Ernest, 533[1].
Friedenberg, Gottlieb, 533[1].
Friedenberg, Hans, 533[1].
Friel, John, 568[3].
Frielinghausen, Theodore, 399[5].
Friend, Johannes, 574[2], 574[4].
Friend, William, 529[7].
Friendly galley (ship), 238[3].
Friendship (sloop), 230[3].
Frink, Thomas, 516[8].
Frink, William, 524[8].
Frisby, Daniel, 486[7].
Friswell, John, 510[9].
Frodsham, John, 449[5].
Froeman, Thomas, 321[7].

Frolic, Christian, 405[7], 406[2], 511[9].
Fromanteel, Ahasverus, 84[8].
Frontenac, count, 93[8], 100[7], 117[7]. See
  also Canada, governors.
Frost, ——, 241[8].
Frost, Abraham, 11[3].
Frost, Thomas, 409[8].
Fry, Hendrick, 486[8].
Fuentes, Miguel Joseph, 389[3].
Fulham, 520[7], 520[9], 522[8], 561[6].
Fuller, general, 351[8].
Fuller, Edward, 517[8].
Fuller, Henry, 298[9].
Fuller, Joseph, 517[8].
Fullerton, ——, 241[8], 245[6].
Fullerton, James, 146[2].
Fullerton, Robert, 80[5].
Fullerton, Thomas, 80[4], 80[5].
Funda, see Fonda.
Furlong, Francis, 272[2].
Furlong, Matthew, 415[7].
Furnis, ——, 442[9], 443[1].
Furniss, Henry, 546[4].
Fusileer companies, 83[2], 83[6], 99[8].

Gabel, Moritz, 402[3].
Gabry, Mr, 19[8].
Gabry, Charles, 15[6].
Gackson, see Jackson.
Gaffen, Stephen, 534[3], 535[5].
Gage, Thomas, agreement about
  articles for troops, 480[6]; com-
  mander at Schenectady, 426[6]; land
  grants, 539[2], 542[5]; letter to, 469[7];
  letters from, 464[3], 464[7], 468[7], 470[4],
  478[7]; money for troops, 484[4]; offers
  military assistance, 468[9]; petition,
  520[4]; refuses to send troops against
  New Hampshire rioters, 502[6];
  requisition of quarters for royal
  troops, 471[2].
Gageborough, 521[6].
Gaigneau [Gaineau], Etienne
  [Stephen], 12[9], 34[3].
Gaine, Hugh, 489[7], 501[2], 537[6], 556[8],
  563[4].
Gaineau, Stephen, see Gaigneau.
Galatian, David, 269[5], 269[8], 270[3].
Gale, Abraham, 514[7].
Gale, Joseph, 565[4].
Gale, Samuel, 443[9], 504[6], 505[4], 516[9].
Gale, Stephen, 533[7].
Gale, Thomas, 514[7].
Gallaugher, Abraham, 536[5].
Gallenger, Michael, 534[5], 540[3].
Galley, Richard, 538[4].
Galliott, Jacob, 213[8], 214[2].
Gallop, Jacques, 45[4].
Gallop, Thomas, 266[9].
Galloway, Joseph, 545[4].
Galway, 522[8].
Gambier, James, 422[8], 422[5].
Gamble, Thomas, 521[3].

Hopkins, Matthew, 526², 529⁹.
Hopkins, Stephen, 421⁹, 422², 422⁷, 428⁵, 428⁷.
Hopkinson (Mass.), 504⁵.
Hopper, Garret, 538⁵.
Hopper, John, 538⁶.
Hopper, Joseph, 123³.
Hopper, Matthew, 523¹, 523⁵.
Hopper, Rynier, 529⁹, 560³.
Hopson, Richard, 189⁷, 192⁷, 193², 214⁶, 215⁵.
Hopson, Samuel, 526³.
Hopson, Thomas, 526⁵.
Horing, Josiah, 517⁹.
Hornbeck, captain, 360⁹.
Hornbeck, Cornelius, see Hoornbeck.
Horne, Abraham, 282⁹.
Horne (frigate), 68⁴.
Hornebeck, ensign, 248⁶.
Hornebeck, Johannes, 303⁹, 305³.
Hornefer, Henry, 529⁴, 553⁸.
Horner, Isaac, 40⁷, 40³, 44⁴.
Hornet, Edward, 40⁷.
Hornet, Mrs Mary, 40⁷.
Hornigold, Benjamin, 264⁸.
Horning, Dederick, 399³.
Horsefell, Christopher, 449⁵, 533⁶.
Horsefield, William, 527⁵, 552⁹, 553⁹.
Horseford, Daniel, 400⁶, 518⁸, 566⁹.
Horseford, Enos, 519¹.
Horseford, Obadiah, 403⁹, 404⁶, 518⁹.
Horseford, Reuben, 508⁵, 512⁴.
Horses, exportation to Canada forbidden, 145⁶, 145⁸; disease, 281⁹.
Horsey, Hannah, 519¹.
Horsmanden, Daniel, member of council, 319⁷, 366⁶, 420⁹, 515⁸; license to buy Indian lands, 322¹; judge of court of vice-admiralty, 326⁹, 327¹; certifies concerning Mary Burton, 340⁷; sworn in council, 343⁴; motion in council, 346¹; justice of supreme court, 389², 457⁵, 461²; commissioner for trial of Greatrakes and Moores, 450⁶; case of De Noyelles referred to, 453⁹; judge of supreme court, 455¹; complaint, 458⁸; communicates letter from governor, 472³; to bring counterfeiters to trial, 491⁷; member commission of oyer and terminer, 492³; clause relating to insane persons referred to, 493²; opinion in case Cunningham vs Forsey, 509⁵, 515⁵; land grant, 565¹. See also N. Y. (city), recorders.
Horton, Mr, 41⁵.
Horton, David, 283⁶.
Horton, John, 67⁶, 163⁸, 283⁶.
Horton, Jonathan, 180⁶, 180⁷.
Horton, Jonathan Paulding, 500⁶.
Horton, Joseph, 78⁸, 112⁶, 283⁶.

Horton, Nehemiah, 473⁵.
Horton, Nicholas, 444⁵.
Hosack, David, 538⁹.
Hosick, see Hoosick.
Hosman, captain, 263², 263⁵.
Hossington, Jacob, 518².
Hotchkiss, John, 559⁴.
Hotchkins, Lemuel, 519⁹, 560².
Houdon, Michael, 344⁹, 345⁵, 347⁵, 347⁶, 407².
Hough, Andrew Lambert, 364³.
Hough, Benjamin, 499⁷, 500⁴, 500⁸, 502³, 504¹, 504⁹.
Hough, George [Jurch], 314⁶, 314⁷, 316¹, 316⁶.
Hough, Johannes, jr, 364².
Houghton, Abiatha, 517⁷.
Houghton, Jonathan, 517⁷, 524⁷.
Houghton, Nehemiah, 516⁹.
Houghton, William, 542⁸, 549⁴.
Houmbs, John, 39⁸.
House, Eliphalet, 403⁹, 404⁶.
House of representatives, 226⁷.
Houston, Patrick, 342⁷, 342⁸.
How, James, 143⁸.
How, Samuel, 545⁷.
Howard, Charles, 577⁹.
Howard, Ebenezer, 520⁹.
Howard, James, 545².
Howard, John, 535⁷, 542⁹.
Howard, Thomas, 59², 558⁷, 577⁹.
Howard, Zebede, 516⁶.
Howdon, Michael, see Hawdon.
Howe, lord, death of, 441¹.
Howe, Nathaniel, 487².
Howel, Mathew, 153⁹.
Howell, captain, 17⁸.
Howell, Hezekiah, 385⁵.
Howell, John, 20⁶, 55⁴, 55⁵; petition referred to, 34⁵; to command militia, 55¹; assessor, 87⁷; order to, 87⁸; military accounts, 108⁸.
Howell, Joshua, 545⁵.
Howell, Robert, 403⁵.
Howell, Theodore, 266⁶.
Hoyer, Erich Christian, 399⁸.
Hoyt, Benjamen, 401⁵.
Hoyt, see also Hoit.
Hozier, Samuel, 473⁵.
Hubbard, Daniel, 516⁸, 528⁴.
Hubbard, Elisha, 516⁶.
Hubbard, Isaac, 389⁴, 438⁷.
Hubbard, James, 22³, 24⁷.
Hubbard, John, 186⁶.
Hubbard, Joseph, 516⁵.
Hubbard, Michael, 337⁵, 337⁹, 338¹, 338², 338³.
Hubbard, Russell, 528⁴.
Hubbard, William, 438⁶.
Hubbard, see also Hobart.
Hubbard's plantation, 98⁷.
Hubbart, Mr, 51³.
Hubbart, Daniel, 122³.

Marselis, Gilbert G. 504^7.
Marselis, Gisbert, 405^8, 406^2, 512^2, 514^5.
Marselis, Isaac, 508^5, 512^4.
Marselius, Peter, 404^8, 404^9.
Marsh, Mr, 473^3.
Marsh, Abel, 522^7.
Marsh, Amos, 499^7.
Marsh, Elihu, 406^7, 407^2, 521^2.
Marsh, Elihu, jr, 406^8, 407^2.
Marsh, Elisha, 522^6, 524^6.
Marsh, Jacob, 491^5, 499^7, 502^3, 504^1, 515^1, 521^2.
Marsh, John, 138^6, 152^9, 248^7.
Marsh, Jonas, 400^4.
Marsh, Jonathan, 85^3, 408^4, 409^4, 522^7.
Marsh, Joseph, 522^6.
Marsh, Thomas, 301^6.
Marsh, Witham, 448^8, 455^8, 456^5.
Marshall, Gervase, 41^1, 41^6, 41^6, 41^8; salary, 65^3, 70^1; order of council, 70^5, 89^3; warrants, 81^2, 85^7, 89^7, 89^9, 93^1, 97^5, 98^5, 208^8; land patents, 98^8, 101^3, 121^8; vs Robert Hamond, 122^7.
Marshall, Hubert, letters to, 353^2, 363^6, 364^2, 364^3, 364^4, 368^7, 415^5; letters from, 365^6, 373^3.
Marshall, John, 497^5, 530^3, 544^8.
Marshall, Walter, 123^1, 123^2, 408^7, 409^5.
Marshall's land, 103^9.
Marston, John, 403^7, 410^4, 510^3.
Marston, Nathaniel, before council, 348^2; transports French prisoners, 348^8, 350^3; application, 363^1; land grants, 410^4, 510^2, 531^4, 546^7; to fix prices of provisions, 442^6; complaint, 448^2; appraiser of army provisions, 458^1.
Marten, John, 427^4.
Martensen [Martins], Roeloff, 42^2, 45^6, 73^6.
Martha's Vineyard, 20^2, 24^2, 74^6, 82^4; court of oyer and terminer, 43^6; depredations, 107^8; disorders, 67^8; Massachusetts threatens to take, 78^1, 80^4, 81^5; news from, 25^9; proposals concerning, 14^6, 14^8; protection against Indians, 23^7; relations to New York, 11^5; representative, 32^7; illegal trading at, 47^4.
Martin, Francis, 427^5.
Martin, James, 537^7.
Martin, Jasper, 535^8.
Martin, John, 142^3, 411^1, 439^1, 446^7, 449^6, 453^9, 462^7.
Martin, Josiah, 398^9, 445^3, 457^8, 458^8, 465^1, 564^6.
Martin, Josiah, jr, 403^3.
Martineau [Martino], François, 43^8, 43^4, 94^6, 166^1.
Martinico, 85^2, 348^8, 453^5; French prisoners to go to, 250^3, 250^8; let-

ters from governor, 246^8, 352^6, 353^3; rebellion, 265^5, 265^8; no vessels to be cleared for, 265^5.
Martinique, 465^2.
Martino, see Martineau.
Martins, see Martensen.
Martin's Vineyard, see Martha's Vineyard.
Martinstock, Dederick, 290^8, 290^9.
Martlie, Archill, 35^3.
Mary, queen, 82^8, 105^7, 105^9.
Mary (sloop), 161^6, 162^1, 164^8, 164^9, 174^8, 175^4, 175^5, 176^4, 176^6, 184^1, 191^5, 193^3, 355^1, 365^8, 428^7.
Mary and Ann (brig), 343^8, 343^9.
Mary Ann (ship), 264^4, 264^7, 345^7.
Maryland, assistance from, 76^7, 83^7, 85^9, 90^3, 103^2, 108^5, 111^7, 116^6, 184^7; bills of exchange, 76^8, 83^7, 94^1, 95^5, 97^8, 100^6, 108^8, 109^4; claims on Whorekill, 16^4; commissioners at Albany conference of 1754, 394^8; commissioners for treaty with Iroquois, 342^4; disputes pecuniary liabilities, 116^8; letter to Gov. Nicholson, 103^4; letters from, 85^4; mission to about pirates, 145^7; plague reported, 496^3.
Masdam, Robert, 566^8.
Mase, Jacob, 336^8.
Mase, Peter, 77^6.
Mashloe, Joshua, 77^6.
Mashpeage [Masepeag], 23^2, 33^6, 63^7. See also Maspethkills.
Maskake, 161^2, 184^3.
Mason, Alexander, 149^3.
Mason, John, 528^4, 546^5.
Mason, Thomas, 542^1.
Maspethkills, 16^2, 20^8, 37^3, 37^5. See also Mashpeage.
Massachusetts, annexation of New York, 121^6; application for surrender of Indians, 27^2; application for line of peace, 420^5; boundaries, see Boundaries; charter, 274^6; circular of speaker of assembly, 477^5; commissioners at Albany conference of 1754, 394^4; concurs with New York council, 369^3; petition for counterfeiters, 495^8; delegates to Indian conference, 360^8, 366^4, 380^8, 380^9, 381^4, 381^6; export of provisions prohibited, 418^2; five nations spread terror in, 252^3; fort, 365^9; message from general court, 369^9; resolves of general court, 367^9; guns loaned to, 351^7; Indian commissioners, 282^7, 366^5; Indian presents, 99^9, 100^2; letter to, 153^5; letters from, 302^8, 303^2; report sent to Lieut. Gov. Phips, 386^8; memorials from, 226^6, 226^7; men for

---

¹Names of persons under N. Y. city, colony and county include only references pertaining to the office under which they are entered; for other references see individual names in main alphabet.

---

[1]See footnote, p. 669.

Paulsen, Pauls, 26².
Paulus, Abraham (Mohawk sachem), 390⁷, 394⁷, 395².
Paulus, Hendrick, 122⁷.
Pauly, see Pauli.
Pauw, Jan, 444⁹.
Pavia, Francisco, 256³.
Pawling, Henry, 10³, 18³, 19⁴, 35², 95⁷.
Pawling, Levi, negotiations with Indians, 449³, 454⁶; letter from, 454³; vs G. D. Cock, 471², 475², 475⁴, 475⁶; petition, 537⁴.
Pawling, widow, 101⁹, 104⁶, 104⁷, 114⁷.
Paxton, captain, 107³.
Payne, Mr, 14⁴.
Payne, Anne, 400⁸.
Payne, Benjamin, 400⁸.
Payne, Lawrence, 363².
Payton, Samuel, 290⁴, 297².
Pazan, ——, 374⁸.
Peache, John, 63⁸.
Peachum, 547⁵, 565⁶.
Peacock, Elizabeth, 119⁵.
Peagrum, John, 324⁴.
Peak, Henry, 508⁶, 512⁴.
Pearce, captain, 266⁷, 267³.
Pearce, John, 411⁵.
Pearce, Josiah, 524³.
Pearce, Thomas Dean, 408⁷, 409⁵.
Pearce, Vincent, 266¹, 334⁶; letter from, 266⁵; petition, 276⁶, 277²; patent granted, 281¹; vs George Comyns, 337⁵, 337⁹, 338¹, 338², 338³, 343⁶; vs John Key and Michael Hubbard, 337⁵, 337⁹, 338¹, 338², 338³.
Pearce, William, 528⁸.
Pearle (man-of-war), 267⁵.
Pearsall [Piersall], Nathaniel, 27⁸, 46⁵, 152⁸, 153¹.
Pearson, Thomas, 450⁷, 456⁶.
Pearson, William, 518³.
Peartree, ——, 241⁴.
Peartree, Anne, 275⁹, 276², 277⁷, 281⁶.
Peartree, William, takes oath of abjuration, 190³; license to buy land, 191⁹; petitions, 195⁶, 214⁴, 232⁷; letter from, 204⁹; loan refunded, 218⁶, 225⁸; land grants, 220⁴, 222⁷, 234³; warrant, 223⁸; appointed to council, 224²; dismissed from council, 238⁸. See also N. Y. (city), mayors.
Peartree (sloop), 204⁶, 204⁹.
Peck, Abraham, 433².
Peck, Benjamin, 266⁸.
Peck, Michael, 56⁴.
Pedlars, 41⁹, 431⁶.
Pedra, Philipp de la, 432⁷.
Peecks creek, 217³.
Peekskill, 548⁴, 550⁷.
Peet, William, 410¹.
Peggy (privateer), 434⁸, 443³, 443⁶.
Peirce, Nehemiah, 24⁴.
Peiret, Margaret, 203⁴.

Peiret, Peter, 127⁴, 131⁷, 140⁸, 177⁵, 189⁴, 198².
Peirpont, John, 519⁸.
Peirsall, Henry, 51³.
Peirsen, Isaac, 530³.
Peirson, Benjamin, 477⁶.
Peirson, John, 189⁷.
Peirson, Jonas, 536⁹.
Peisinger, John, 559⁷.
Pekham, Jonathan, 517⁸.
Pelham, Francis, 313⁵.
Pelham manor, 56².
Pell, John, 24⁷, 26², 48⁸; land dispute, 15⁹; to buy land, 51⁹; land patent, 56²; before council, 59⁸, 73⁷, 89¹; boundary commissioner, 61⁸; commissioner, 76⁶; assessor, 87⁷; vs Bathstina Wessells, 110⁴, 110⁶.
Pell, Samuel, 406².
Pell, William, 120⁵.
Pelletreaux, Elias, petitions, 177⁷, 194¹, 221⁶, 224⁸, 239⁷; warrants, 178⁹, 181⁸, 187⁶; account, 180⁹.
Pelletreaux, John, warrants, 69⁸, 78⁵, 80³, 89⁹, 90⁵, 93⁴, 96⁶, 102², 104⁷, 107⁸, 110⁹, 112⁸, 118³, 121¹, 127⁸, 129⁸, 178⁹, 181⁸; petitions, 177⁷, 194¹; account, 180⁹.
Pelletreaux, Magdalena, 152⁸.
Pellinger, Frederick, 208³, 308¹.
Pells, Henry, 539⁹, 542⁸.
Pells, Michael, 539⁹, 542³.
Pels, Evert, 539⁹, 542².
Peltry, order concerning, 22¹.
Pemaquid, 29⁸, 30⁴, 31³; court of sessions at, 38⁷; fort, 117⁶; government of, 30⁸, 34⁴; Indian war, 27²; petition of inhabitants, 40⁴; quitrents, 48⁹; sheriff, 32⁶; taken possession of for duke, 29³.
Pemberton, Judith, 163⁴, 170⁹, 187⁸.
Penalosa, Diego de, 361².
Pendergrast, William, 471⁴.
Penford, John, 30².
Penicuff, Philip, 546⁶.
Penn, John, 502⁸.
Penn, Thomas, 502³.
Penn, William, 38⁵, 156², 481⁴, 488⁴, 502², 503³.
Penniston, Thomas, 199⁵, 331⁹.
Pennoyer, Robert, 13².
Pennsylvania, 83⁶, 414¹; accounts referred, 111⁸; boundaries, see Boundaries; commissioners at Albany conference of 1754, 394⁴; Col. Fletcher made governor, 83²; hostile Indians in, 424⁷; letter from Pres. Palmer, 368⁵; letter to Gov. Gookin, 227¹; letters to, 60⁸, 156⁸; men to build fort, 426⁴; mission to about pirates, 145⁷; money for Crownpoint expedition, 417⁶; money for Indians, 119⁸; Pres. Pal-

collected, 128[4]; order about, 47[5]; to be paid in money, 83[4]; proposals about, 322[7]; sheriffs to collect, 119[1]; statement called for, 158[9]. *See also names of towns and counties.*

Race, *see* Rees.
Rainer, captain, 243[1]. *See also* Rayner.
Ralph, James, 538[2].
Ralph [Ralf], Michael, 530[6], 573[3].
Ramage, Charles, 527[2], 544[7], 545[2].
Ramage, Smith, 529[9], 544[7], 545[2].
Rambo, Peter, 13[1].
Rament, Nathaniel, 517[7].
Ramepogh, 126[7].
Ramon, Peter, 200[6].
Ramsay, Andrew, 373[6].
Ramsay, James, 339[5]. *See also* Rumsey.
Ramsen, Hendrick, 338[7], 340[6], 342[6].
Ramsen, Henry, jr, 385[9].
Ramsey, ——, 496[6].
Ramsey, Alexander, 329[5].
Ramsey, John, 530[5].
Ran, John, 522[2], 522[5], 546[5].
Randall, Joseph, 513[6], 547[7].
Randall, Rebecca, 144[1].
Randolph, Benjamin, 471[1].
Randolph, Edward, 130[9], 131[6].
Ranger (sloop), 434[1].
Rankin, James, 541[8].
Ranking, William, 272[6], 272[7].
Ranslear, *see* Van Rensselaer.
Rapalie [Rapale, Rapallese, Rappalle], Jeronimus, 37[2], 45[3], 58[5], 196[6], 196[8], 197[3], 223[7].
Rapalje, Garret, 565[1], 576[4].
Rapalje, John, 541[4], 576[4].
Rapp, Coenradt, 537[9].
Rascarrick, George, 121[4].
Ratan, island of, 347[3].
Ratzer, Barnard, 550[1].
Raws, *see* Ross.
Ray, lieutenant, 437[4].
Rayner, Elizabeth, 28[9].
Rayner, John, 290[5]. *See also* N. Y. (colony), attorneys general.
Rayner, Samuel, 246[5].
Raynes, John, 274[5].
Rea, James, 531[8].
Rea, Matthew, 496[7].
Reade, Charles, 541[4], 545[4].
Reade, Edward, 33[3], 122[4].
Read, James, 518[7].
Read, John, petitions, 283[9], 290[4], 304[9], 405[8]; land grants, 406[2], 512[1], 514[5], 544[3], 571[5]; member of council, 515[8].
Read, Joseph, 442[6], 458[1], 465[1], 486[3].
Reade, Joseph, jr, 521[4], 522[5], 532[2], 532[7], 533[6], 534[7].
Read, Lawrence, 76[4], 118[2], 403[2], 410[5], 510[2].

Read, Robert, 235[5].
Read, Samuel, jr, 522[8].
Reade, Thomas, 577[7].
Read, *see also* Reed, Reid.
Reader, Kilian, 304[7].
Reading (township), 529[9], 560[3].
Realy, James, 549[2].
Reaux, John, 91[8], 92[2], 92[3], 93[2], 96[3], 101[3], 102[8], 103[1].
Rebar, Andries, 544[5].
Rebar, John, 544[5].
Rebecca (ship), 34[7], 35[3], 444[6].
Recollects, 347[6].
Red Head (Onondaga sachem), 380[3].
Red Hook, 140[8], 359[5], 379[3].
Redigh, Christopher, 538[3].
Redknap, John, 227[3].
Rednap, Mr, 237[7].
Reeckford, lieutenant, 116[3].
Reed, Lawrence, 210[2].
Reed, Patrick, 533[7].
Reed, William, 523[3].
Reed, *see also* Read, Reid.
Reemar, Isaac, 510[3].
Rees, David, 372[7].
Rees, William, 415[7], 416[4].
Reeve, Mark, 540[4].
Reeve, Peter, 545[5].
Reformed Dutch churches, *see* Churches.
Regnier, Elizabeth, 258[6].
Regnier, Jacob, petitions, 193[8], 197[5], 197[6], 198[1], 203[1]; vs Susannah Vaughton, 198[2], 198[3], 200[2]; appears for Capt. Claver, 200[5]; new patent, 201[1]; vs Philip Headman, 237[9], 238[3]; answer to petition, 255[8].
Reid, Alexander, 535[1].
Reid, David, 535[1], 542[6], 565[4].
Reid [Read], Duncan, 410[2], 410[3], 411[7].
Reid, John, land grants, 410[4], 411[4], 552[7], 562[7]; house burned, 488[8]; memorial, 493[2], 555[7]; sawmill on land of, 493[6]; reports new outrages, 497[8]; petitions, 515[4], 516[6], 555[1], 555[3].
Reid, Nathaniel, 540[9].
Reid, Peter, 519[9], 535[2].
Reid, *see also* Read, Reed.
Reiglar, Andries, 559[7].
Reilly, Susannah, 571[9].
Reilly, Thomas, 536[2].
Reis, Philip, 402[4].
Reiter, Paul, 404[9].
Relay, Henry, 562[4], 563[8].
Relay, Lewis, 527[1], 553[3], 562[4], 563[3].
Relivo, Joseph, 430[7].
Remsen, Daniel, 237[2].
Remsen, Hendrick, license to buy Indian lands, 347[3], 368[1]; land grants, 372[4], 540[6], 544[3], 541[8]; son of, 372[8]; petitions, 527[6], 529[9], 532[5], 557[2], 557[9], 572[8], 574[7], 574[8].

NOTES

NOTES

NOTES

NOTES

NOTES

NOTES

NOTES

NOTES

NOTES